MEASUREMENT FOR MANAGEMENT DECISION

MEASUREMENT FOR MANAGEMENT DECISION

Richard O. Mason
School of Business
University of Southern California

E. Burton Swanson
Graduate School of Management
University of California, Los Angeles

ADDISON-WESLEY PUBLISHING COMPANY
Reading, Massachusetts ● Menlo Park, California
London ● Amsterdam ● Don Mills, Ontario ● Sydney

ADDISON-WESLEY SERIES ON DECISION SUPPORT

Consulting Editors
Peter G. W. Keen
Charles B. Stabell

Decision Support Systems: An Organizational Perspective
Peter G. W. Keen and Michael S. Scott Morton

Decision Support Systems: Current Practice
and Continuing Challenges
Steven L. Alter

Electronic Meetings: Technical Alternatives and Social Choices
Robert Johansen, Jacques Valee, and Kathleen Spangler

Computers and Profits: Quantifying Financial
Benefits of Information
Jack P. C. Kleijnen

Measurement for Management Decision
Richard O. Mason and E. Burton Swanson

Library of Congress Cataloging in Publication Data

Main entry under title:

Measurement for management decision.

(Addison-Wesley series on decision support)
Bibliography: p.

1. Management—Decision making—Addresses,
essays, lectures. 2. Statistical decision—Addresses, essays, lectures. 3. Management information systems—Addresses, essays, lectures. I. Mason,
Richard O. II. Swanson, E. Burton. III. Series.
HD30.23.M4   658.4′033   80-14946
ISBN 0-201-04646-6

ISBN 0-201-04646-6
ABCDEFGHIJ-MA-8987654321

FOR WEST

Once a little girl and her mother were walking through the woods near Mount Tamalpais. The mother spied a waterfall and walked ahead to enjoy its beauty. Alone, the little girl wandered over to talk to a man seated on a bench nearby. She sat down beside him. The man asked, "How old are you?" She replied, "Five years old." "How old will you be next year?" he asked. The little girl hesitated, then, showing him one hand with fingers spread, she counted to five, thrust up the thumb on the second hand and shouted "six!" "And the next year?" He pointed to her index finger. She added, "seven." A twinkle came to her eyes and she began to count enthusiastically "eight, nine, ten. I'm going to be ten years old," she said with glee.

"How old will you be after that?" the man inquired. Suddenly, saddened, the little girl replied, "I don't know." The man smiled, "Take off your shoes." She did and he showed her how to count on her toes. "Eleven, twelve, ..." By now the mother was returning. "Mommy, Mommy," the little girl cried, overjoyed, "I'm going to be twenty years old!"

There is a human side to measurement. Our hopes and our fears are often embodied in our numbers. Some numbers can expand our horizons and bring us joy, others can restrict our vision and bring us misery. This is especially true of the numbers used to guide the allocation of social resources. West helped us understand this.

SERIES FOREWORD

Decision Support is concerned with improving the effectiveness of managerial decision making through the selective application of computer-based technologies to tasks that require some balance between judgement and analysis.

A key dilemma for research and practice in the Decision Support field is that the qualitative and multidimensional nature of "effectiveness" and of the decision process in such "semi-structured" tasks limit systematic observation and evaluation. Evaluating improvements in the quality of decision making requires measurement. The broader the scope of the decision process and the definition of effectiveness, the more general must be the concept and methodology of measurement.

There is also room for a variety of approaches to increasing decision making effectiveness. Most of these focus on improving either the decision process or the inputs to that process. In general, research in the decision support field, emphasizes process, rather than inputs. The first two titles in the Decision Support series reflect this focus. Keen and Scott Morton build in the "decision-centered" methodologies of, among others, Gerrity and explicitly define improved effectiveness in terms of a change in the manager's problem-solving behavior. Johansen, Vallee and Spangler similarly discuss the process of group meetings and the use of teleconferencing to support and improve it. "Measurement for Management Decision", the fifth book in the series, provides a complement to these earlier studies and addresses the links between input and process more directly.

We may improve the quality of the inputs to the decision process through more timely information, a clearer identification of relevant variables, or better estimation of parameters. We may improve how the inputs are used, by increasing the number of alternatives examined, building models that are better representations of the phenomena of interest, or identifying more meaningful criteria for assessing solutions.

Whatever strategy—technology—we choose to facilitate these improvements, we need to distinguish between the subject and object of decision making. The object is the "real-world" entity or entities that are the focus for action. The subject is the actor (or actors) who must make a choice. In a business planning situation, the object may be a target market, a set of competitors and financial allocations, and the subject a division manager.

Operations Research and Management Science (OR/MS) focus on the object of decision making. A planning model may generate a normative—"optimal"—recommendation independent of the perceptions and activities of the subject. Improving decision making here involves improving the model. Behavioral scientists tend by contrast to focus on improving subjects' decision process: their understanding of the situation, use of information, avoidance of bias and errors, etc. To an extent, the distinction between subject and object is also one between procedural and substantive rationality.

In trying to improve decision making, we may choose, as researchers or practitioners, to use our resources to change the behavior of the subject or to learn more about the object and to define better techniques for assessing it. The traditional applications of analytic methods to decision making choose one of the two extremes. Accounting and OR/MS have made their major contributions by improving our ability to manage objects: this is implicit in the concepts of a "model" "optimization" or "profit". Statistical decision theory, by contrast, and the newer field of Multicriteria Decision making (MCDM) try to balance subject and object. Decision theory provides both a way of organizing information about the object and a formal procedure for deciding. MCDM involves both models and ways of using models.

Decision Support *explicitly* aims at balancing subject and object, although it has tended to emphasize the subject, partly because it began as a challenge to OR/MS and MIS, whose normative concepts of decision making largely ignored the decision *process* and the individual characteristics of the decision *maker*. The concepts of "iterative" problem-solving and of meshing human judgment and procedural analysis are at the core of Decision Support.

The Decision Support field can claim some distinctive contributions to improving decision making, in relation to other efforts to apply computer technology and analytic techniques. It has helped shift the emphasis from problem-solving, which focuses on object, to problem-finding, which emphasis subject. It supports a divergent as well as convergent decision process, and has provided ways of addressing unstructured as well as structured problem domains.

The emphasis on problem-finding highlights both the issue of subject and of inputs to the decision process. A key question then becomes how do we improve problem-finding?" Some general answers are to change the kind of variables one looks at, to change where one looks, and to change one's assumption of what a given variable "means". We then need general procedures for scanning and a broader conception of measurement than traditional accounting and OR/MS provide in their focus on problem-solving and object.

Measurement for Management Decision is concerned with such a conception. Unlike the other books, it is not directly concerned with technology, but with the criteria for selecting the inputs that technology processes. As such, it provides a more balanced concept of Decision Support. To an extent, the earlier books take inputs as given and focus on Decision Support *Systems,* the means for which Decision Support is the end. Mason and Swanson stress the end. Their position is that "the impact of (these) data for decision making rests on the adequacy of the measurement methods on which they are based". The book provides some formalized approaches to considering the "attention-directing", "problem-solving" and "score-card keeping" aspects of data. These categories correspond to 1) problem-finding, 2) problem-solving, and 3) decision implementation, evaluation and control. As stated earlier, we may address our efforts to improving decision making to any or all of these stages of the decision process. Mason and Swanson thus help us link inputs to outputs, and data to procedures.

The book also introduces to the series a useful contrast and perhaps counterbalance to the Carnegie School's concept of decision making and which, through the work of Simon, Cyert and March have strongly shaped the Decision Support field. The readings in Mason and Swanson and the authors' use of them reflect what may be called the Berkeley approach, most associated with Brunswick and Churchman. *Key* words throughout the book are "knowledge", "inquiring" and "observation". Wherever the Carnegie School emphasizes the use of information, this approach stresses its generation. This book thus enlarges our general understanding of decision making as well as our ability to harness computer technology to improve it in specific contexts.

November 1980   Peter G. W. Keen
                                                                         Charles B. Stabell

PREFACE

This book is the result of ten years of inquiry into the role of measurement in management, and into methods for teaching this subject. It is predicated on the authors' belief that the concept of measurement is a centrally important theoretical basis for the design of information systems for the support of managerial decisions. This importance stems in part from the pervasiveness of measurement in modern management. Both accounting and statistics are constructed on measurement foundations. Most other quantitative methods, from formal model building to techniques of financial analysis, require measurement data. Methods for assessing individuals and organizations and their performance depend increasingly on measurement data. Finally, our ability to understand the complex social system in which we live depends on measurements such as gross national product, unemployment, and other social indicators. All of these measures are a part of the manager's information base.

We arrived at the text and readings in the book after a series of trials with different approaches at the Graduate School of Management at the University of California, Los Angeles. In the spring of 1969 Mason taught the first course on measurement in management as part of the new information systems curriculum. The pedogogy involved studying classical decision-making models, usually as reported in applications articles, and analyzing them for data and measurement requirements. The simple inventory model was studied first, followed by the transportation model, and finally, a large scale social simulation. The course proved useful, but suffered from several deficiencies. It was difficult to select a set of models rich enough in measurement implications. Many of the same measurement issues were repeated in each model, while a number of important issues were not covered. It was also difficult to bring out adequately the relationship between accounting and statistical concepts and the variables and parameters in each model. More importantly, however, the management orientation was never fully established.

The following year Professor Theodore Mock, currently at the University of Southern California, taught the course. The subject matter focused on readings in the mathematics of measurement, information theory, and decision theory. Again the course was comparatively successful, especially for Ph.D. students with a deep interest in the topic. Once more the management orientation proved somewhat elusive.

Mock taught the course for several years until the spring of 1974. Then Mason again taught the course, this time using a selection of readings and a series of exercises and cases from the management control area. Using this approach he achieved the management orientation, but at the cost of some depth of understanding of measurement theory.

Mason then went to the National Science Foundation for a two-year period where, among other things, he directed a research funding program in productivity and social measurement. Swanson came to UCLA and began teaching the measurement course. Beginning with the articles used by Mason, Swanson sought to deepen and extend the readings, retaining the management orientation, but broadening the scope of management and measurement problems covered. This approach appeared to strike an appropriate balance. Swanson has continued to teach the course since that time, and both authors have worked closely together to improve the framework and selection of readings. This book is essentially a progress report on that undertaking.

In the Spring of 1979, Mason taught the course once again, in a final test of the material presented here.

We have intended that the book be suitable for reading in a variety of contexts:

1. as the text for a graduate level seminar in measurement within a school of management, business, or public policy and administration

2. as a supplementary text and source of readings for a wide variety of related courses in such schools, e.g., courses in information systems, accounting, management planning and control, personnel management, and public policy

3. as a book which may be read and studied independently by managers, administrators, planners, and others in positions associated with managerial decision making in organizations.

To these ends, we have attempted to organize the readings into carefully selected subtopics, with introductory essays and commentary interspersed for guidance.

A further feature of the book is the use of "Questions for Study and Discussion" following each reading. Many of these questions serve as possible focuses for class discussion of the articles. Often the questions have an integrative purpose, e.g., to link the reading to one studied earlier in the book. Other questions function as points of departure for further readings referenced but not included in the book. In each case, an attempt is made to stretch the thinking of the reader beyond the obvious points of the article read.

In selecting the articles for the book, we have attempted to adhere to certain criteria:

1. *readability*—the articles are for the most part in essay form, and maintain a high overall level of exposition, in our judgment.

2. *enduring quality*—the articles have something to say beyond the measurement concerns of the moment; their respective messages should be as timely ten years hence as they are now.

3. *unique perspective*—the articles offer a set of unique perspectives on measurement for management to the thoughtful student.

4. *complementarity with other readings*—the articles have ties to one another; in some cases these ties are explicit, one article being based on another; in other cases, we have sought to indicate the ties by means of text, commentary, or study questions.

We hope that our adherence to these criteria has resulted in a book that offers substantial enjoyment to the reader.

Los Angeles, California   R. O. M.
January 1981   E. B. S.

CONTENTS

DETAILED CONTENTS

INTRODUCTION

PART ONE

THE ROLE OF MEASUREMENT IN MANAGEMENT

CHAPTER **ONE**

MEASUREMENT AND DECISION

Measurements, like decisions, are ubiquitous. Wherever people are found making decisions, one is also likely to find people measuring things. Since the beginning of recorded history measurement schemes have been developed to guide important economic and social decisions. So compelling is the need for measurement that some of history's most important documents—the Code of Hammurabi, the Magna Charta and the Constitution of the United States—contain specific provisions for conducting measurements in the public interest.

Organizational life is no less affected by the central role of measurement. In every type of organization—private and public; for-profit and not-for-profit; small, medium and large—measurements are collected, processed, and distributed. Virtually all organizational decisions are informed in some way by measurement data. And so close is the link between measurement and decision, the quality of a decision often rests on the quality of the measurements made to inform it.

Our book is intended for those who receive measurements and base decisions on them. Management decisions are seldom made in a measurement vacuum. More typically there are substantial data available, many of them quantified. If additional data are needed they may frequently be obtained through research and analysis. Consequently decision makers seldom suffer from the lack of measurement data. Their problem is more likely to be (1) to secure the data that are most relevant to the current decision, (2) to grasp more fully the meaning of the data at hand, and (3) to derive the proper implications from the available data in order to relate them to alternative courses of action.

Most management information systems fail to solve this problem for managers. Emphasis is typically placed on automating structured data processing procedures, and little attention is given to the interpretation of output data by managers. However, the recent development of a new design philosophy, called Decision Support Systems (DSS), promises to give new emphasis to the role of managerial judgment. The design of a DSS is based on (1) decisions where there is sufficient structure for computer based aids to be of value, but where managers' judgment is essential; (2) the improvement of management effectiveness, as distinct from management efficiency; (3) the creation of supportive tools which do not automate the decision process, predefine objectives, or impose solutions (Keen and Scott Morton, 1978).

In our view, the essence of any decision support system should be the relationship established between managers and the data they receive. This leads us to propose two basic principles for the design of a DSS:

1. The reports presented by a DSS should be based on those measures which promote the most effective management decisions.

2. The managers who receive reports from a DSS should possess a critical faculty with respect to the measurement data presented. They must be skilled at uncovering the underlying assumptions of the data, and at developing the range of permissible inferences that may be drawn from the data.

Our book is dedicated to these principles. Adhering to these principles requires that the theory and technique of measurement be expanded to include the decision context as well as the manager's "disposition to respond" to measurements in various ways. These organizational, social, and psychological dimensions become an integral part of measurement and reporting procedures. In this way concepts of effective communication are also incorporated into the measurement process. Each of the book's essays and articles contains some valuable lessons or insights which serve to guide the design of better measurement systems for DSS. As a result DSS designers should benefit by studying this material.

Our primary concern, however, is for the manager. The book's lessons and insights serve to develop a manager's skill in the critical examination of data and the systems that produce that data. The readings and exercises deal with the kinds of questions one should always ask of one's data before basing action on them. Consequently the book develops a point of view about measurement data that should help managers to relate better to their decision support systems and ultimately to make better decisions.

KEY CONCEPTS

It will be useful here to identify our key concepts and to define our terms. *Decisions* are choices made among alternatives. A decision is required whenever there is doubt about which of two or more courses of action to follow. The choice is made in part on the basis of information supplied for that purpose.

Management, for us, is the social role responsible for making decisions on the allocation of social resources. It includes the voting public, labor leaders, and political leaders as well as corporate executives. Its skill is decision making. Its purpose is effective and equitable resource allocation. Management's guidance comes from information derived, in large part, from measurement.

Technically, *measurement* is the process of obtaining symbols to represent the properties of objects, events, or states. These symbols should have the same relevant relationship to each other as do the things they represent. Hence it is proper to refer to measurement as a mapping from the world of real objects, events, or states into the abstract world of symbology. The symbols, in turn, are numbers or have quantitative implications.

The entire book is devoted to adding substance to these skeletal concepts. As we shall see there are many things to take into account when one is considering management, measurement, and decisions. Before delving more deeply into the specifics, however, let us first illustrate the problem area by means of a few practical examples.

Television Ratings

A friend of ours was infuriated when the management of the Columbia Broadcasting System (CBS) decided to drop his favorite television program. Why was the program dropped? It had not fared well by a measurement system which is used to allocate air time and to guide advertisers' media decisions. The system was the famed A. C. Nielsen ratings. What kind of measurement for management decision is the Nielsen rating?

Contrary to some popular belief, the Nielsen rating does not measure how "good" or "bad" a show is. It merely estimates the number of households watching the show. The ratings are basically a reflection of audience preference for one telecast over others on the air at the same time. Hit shows are, in part, the product of advantageous scheduling against weaker shows. The stakes are quite high. For a top-rated show, a sponsor will pay approximately $75,000 to $200,000 per minute for commercial time. Shows with low ratings, like our friend's show, are canceled.

A rating of 30 is supposed to indicated that 30 percent of the television homes were watching. Does it? Not really. The Nielsen Audimeter, which is installed on the television set in the home, records only whether or not the set was turned on and which channel it was tuned to. It records no data about who was watching. Indeed, stories are told about the distortion of a household record because someone left the television on for twenty-four hours just to keep the family dog "company."

The Nielsen ratings are also not "counts" of exposure as are the circulation statistics for newspapers. Nielsen samples about 1200 sets out of the approximately ninety-five million in the United States. Although statistical theory attests to the adequacy of the sample, many people question whether the cross section is representative of the television audience at large. Nielsen has responded by attempting to keep the composition of his sample panel more in tune with United States census trends. He also monitors the relative market penetration of products sold within the sample, such as automobiles, as compared with national market penetration averages.

Yet according to a March 11, 1967, issue of *TV Guide*, many people still don't believe in this sampling procedure as a basis for measurement. For the skeptics, A. C. Nielsen, Jr., president of the firm founded by his father, has an answer: "If you don't believe in sampling, be sure—the next time you have a blood test—to get yourself pumped dry . . . make them take it all!" Our friend believes in sampling but he is still not so sure that the Nielsen rating is the best measurement to use for making this particular management decision. What do you think?

Measurement in MIS

A large United States equipment manufacturer has implemented a nationwide management information system in order to support decisions made by its marketing management. The purpose of the system is to provide various levels of marketing management with information relative to the effectiveness of the company's sales coverage and sales supervision. The company has sought to improve its decision making in six areas: (1) supervision and direction, (2) sales support, (3) changes in territory assignment, (4) marketing planning, (5) provision of training programs, and (6) personnel development and promotion. To accomplish this the company felt that it needed to measure individual and group performance in attaining marketing objectives. It wanted to use these measurements to evaluate the effectiveness of the marketing effort in districts, branch offices, and sales territories.

The method the company used divided the United States into about 60,000 geographical units called sales blocks. Each sales block had accounted for approximately the same average sales volume during the last three years. Thus building in New York City constituted a sales block, as did an entire county in northern Nevada. In the organizational structure of the company a collection of one or more sales blocks made a sales territory, a collection of territories made a branch office, and a collection of branches made a district. Consequently aggregations of sales block data yielded summary sales data for territories, branches, districts, and the corporation as a whole.

The following were among the data provided for each sales block each month:

1. Actual sales, by product line
   (a) This month
   (b) Year to date
   (c) Unbilled sales outstanding

2. Inventory of current installation of equipment

3. Number of sales calls and sales hours, this month and year to date, by the following purposes:
   (a) Sales promotion
   (b) Proposal development
   (c) Sales presentation or demonstration
   (d) Installation
   (e) Sales service to customer
   (f) Maintenance problems
   (g) Other

These data were summarized monthly and reported to salesmen, branch managers, district managers, and corporate marketing executives. The data were analyzed quarterly by a cost accounting planning and control model which estimated the profitability of each sales block and other sales units. Periodically the data were used as input into a territory alignment model which produced new territory assignments designed to equalize the sales potential of each territory.

On the whole the company's management believes that the new measurement system has aided them in the six areas of decision it was installed to support. However, the system is not without measurement problems. An underlying assumption of the system is that sales are a function of geographical distribution. Yet increasingly, sales are being made to organizations that have multiple locations but purchase centrally or provide guidelines for equipment purchases from a central location. Thus a salesman's effort in one sales block may affect the sales in another.

Consequently the sales block measurement system does *not* adequately measure the sales performance of the salesman. Nor does it measure the true sales potential of the block, or any aggregate of blocks. To counter this deficiency management supplements the system with a "large account" (significant multiple location customers) system and personal knowledge of the areas.

The sales block system and the television rating system are illustrations of measurement of organizational performance. Measurements also influence decisions at the individual and societal levels, as indicated by the next two illustrations.

Student-Faculty Contact

In 1977 the legislative analyst of the state of California recommended that twenty-two faculty positions for the University of California be deleted from the governor's budget. The factual basis for this recommendation came from a measurement system which indicated that the average number of hours a professor spent in contact with students each week dropped from 6.5 in 1972–73 to 6.3 in 1975–76. These data led the legislative analyst to conclude that the faculty was not working as hard as it had in the past and, therefore, the twenty-two positions were not warranted. Was this really the case?

A detailed study of the measurement system undertaken by the university administration revealed several misinterpretations and flaws. For example, faculty/student contact hours, as measured, included only the time instructors spent in class teaching, but not office hours, individual consultation, or time spent preparing for class. A university teacher normally spends less time in the classroom than in preparation, consultations, grading, and supervision of remedial or advanced student work. Yet none of these factors was measured by the system being used. Furthermore, significant questions arose about who should be included as faculty, and how a faculty full-time equivalent should be calculated. For example, in 1972 the campuses counted teaching assistant and upper-division student time spent in leading discussion sessions and seminars as faculty contact hours. The following school year this practice was discontinued, causing an automatic drop in contact hours. On one campus this resulted in a 26% drop in faculty contact hours!

Because of the flaws and uncertainties in the measurement system the legislative analyst ultimately rescinded his recommendation. Meanwhile, the university administration went to work to design a better measurement system.

Plant Operating Rate

An article in the March 11, 1977, *Wall Street Journal* by Alfred Malabre, Jr., opened with the following observation: "A highly unreliable set of statistics is getting even more unreliable—just as federal policy makers are relying on the figures more heavily than ever." The measurement in question was the plant operating rate—the percentage of overall factory capacity actually in use.

The plant operating rate is a critical factor in setting national policy with respect to inflation. If the plant operating rate is high, policies intended to spur business activity might raise demand above capacity and thereby accelerate inflation. If the rate is low there is little risk that such efforts would overburden the economy. At the time of the article the Carter administration was using a currently reported rate of 80% of capacity to support its proposed business stimulation policy, and to claim that it was unlikely to add to inflation.

Many other government and private sources were not convinced, however. They claimed that error in the estimate could range as high as ±10%, meaning that the true plant operating rate may be as high as 88% or as low as 72% (one estimate was 67%). The 88% rate was considered dangerously high. The fact that an 86% rate was reported just prior to the 1974–75 leap to double-digit inflation was cited as evidence of peril.

Critics of the measure had several important reservations in addition to the question raised above about the sampling error. The plant operating rate is calculated as an *average* over all industries. Some industries may be operating very near to their capacities while others are well below theirs. Consequently a key industry could exceed capacity and create substantial inflationary pressure while other industries were operating far below the inflationary level and keeping the average operating rate down. Another reservation relates to the way the data are collected. A one-page questionnaire is sent out to companies asking them, "At what percentage of manufacturing capacity did your company operate?" The questionnaire does not distinguish between product lines—a difficult problem with conglomerates and multi-product, multi-plant companies—nor does it provide a standard definition of capacity. Is capacity based on one eight-hour shift? Two eight-hour shifts? Longer? Shorter? Does it include overtime and weekends? These labor-oriented aspects of capacity are not standardized. Assumptions made about other factors of production also influence capacity estimates. For example, the steel industry reduced its plant operating rate because of fuel shortages although no real change in plant size and facilities occurred. Adding to the confusion is the fact that many current expenditures for capital improvements—a frequently used indicator of changes in capacity—are devoted to pollution control and OSHA related job safety improvements and do not affect the production capacity of a plant at all. For these and other reasons the measurement of plant operating rate has become so unreliable and misleading that one economist refers to it as a "jelly-like concept."

In response to these criticisms the various federal agencies involved in estimating the plant operating rate—the Bureau of Census, the Bureau of Economic Analysis, and the Federal Reserve Board—as well as several private organizations have undertaken studies to improve the measure and to educate those who use it for policy-making purposes.

OVERVIEW OF THE BOOK

Each of these four cases illustrates some important points about measurement for management decision. In each case decisions were being made which affected the lives of many people and the conduct of their organizations. Measurements were made to inform those decisions. Consequently concerns about who would use the measure, in what context and for what purpose, became as integral a part of the measurement process as did concerns for the data collection procedure and its precision and reliability. Each case demonstrates that the underlying distinctions and concepts used to measure are the result of critical judgments made in the measurement process. A useful measure must be based on the distinctions and concepts which are applicable to the decision purpose at hand. For this reason it is necessary for the managers and policy makers who use the measures to examine them carefully and critically. These general themes are repeated and illustrated throughout the book.

The cases also illustrate that measurements for management decision may be made at three levels—the organizational, the individual, and the societal. The rationale for these three levels is developed in the introductory reading—"Measurement For Management Decision: A Perspective"—which proposes a general theory of measurement from this point of view. The article concludes Part One of the book.

Part Two deals with foundations. It begins with an explication of the basic logic and technique used in the measurement process. This is a necessary grounding for understanding some of the technical issues involved. A series of articles that cover issues such as the purpose of measurement and the relationships between measurement and statistics, information systems, economics, and decision theory completes Part Two.

Building on the foundations set in Part Two, Parts Three, Four, and Five treat measurement at three levels. Part Three deals with the measurement of organizational performance. It begins with discussions of accounting systems—the basis for much organizational measurement—and goes on to cover such concepts as profitability, productivity, efficiency, effectiveness, equity, total performance systems and the behavioral aspects of these measures. The public sector is treated as well as the private sector.

Part Four is devoted to measurement at the individual level. Work measurement, criteria for individual performance, rating systems, psychological measurement, and consumer measurement are covered in text and articles.

Part Five is about social measurement and relates to the environment of the organization. It contains text and articles on the measurement of economic activity, social problems, social indicators, social information systems, and the measurement of social value. Part Five concludes with a summing up in the form of three articles which pose some enduring questions about measurement as it relates to society and to social decisions.

In our first reading we present the conceptual framework which determines the subsequent design of the book. The ideas contained in the essay have dictated the structure of the book, the selection of articles and the content of the study questions following each article.

MEASUREMENT FOR MANAGEMENT DECISION: A PERSPECTIVE

Richard O. Mason • E. Burton Swanson

READING 1

. . . [A] basic element in the work of the manager is measurement. The manager establishes yardsticks—and few factors are as important to the performance of the organization and of every man in it. He sees to it that each man has measurements available to him which are focused on the performance of the whole organization and which, at the same time, focus on the work of the individual and help him do it. He analyzes, appraises and interprets performance. As in all other areas of his work, he communicates the meaning of the measurements and their findings to his subordinates, to his superiors, and to colleagues. (Peter Drucker, *Management*)[1]

Most managers would agree with Drucker's observations on measurement. Much organizational decisionmaking is based on subtle distinctions between workloads, costs, performance, capabilities, and the like—distinctions that often can be made only on the basis of some quantitative judgment. Yet, despite the pervasiveness of measurement and its centrality to management decision making, relatively little attention has been given in the management literature to the development of a general theory of measurement in the managerial context.

Why do we measure? What do we measure? How do we measure? What happens when we measure? How does measurement affect management decisions? In our judgment, these fundamental questions deserve more thoughtful examination by students of management than they have thus far received. In most cases in which these questions have been addressed, it has been generally assumed that managerial measurement is a form of scientific measurement and, hence, as an ideal managerial measurement should seek to satisfy the principles of scientific measurement. We disagree. We have no quarrel with drawing on the vast history of scientific measurement in order to improve measurement for management decision. But, as we will argue, the principles of scientific measurement largely ignore a factor that is crucial in measurement for management decision, namely the *user*.

As the opening quotation from Peter Drucker emphasizes, in organizations measurement is information that guides the behavior of the manager and of others. Thus, any managerial measurement system must be designed with primary attention

Reprinted from the *California Management Review*, Vol. 21, No. 3 (Spring 1979), pp. 70–81.

given to the purposes of organizations and their individual members and to the processes by which participants assimilate and act on measurement data.

In our view, measurement may be likened to a lens through which a manager sees organizational reality. As with any lens, measurement can magnify, reduce, contort, or distort the manager's images of reality. Thus, the design problem is to fit the manager with that measurement lens which best assists him or her in the achievement of organizational purposes. Unfortunately, at present there is little in the way of a perspective on measurement for management decision to guide the designer of the managerial lens.

In this article we attempt to establish a perspective for measurement for management decision. The nature of this perspective, to be developed fully in the sections to follow, may be summarized briefly by a threefold set of assertions.

1. Scientific measurement is a necessary, but not sufficient basis for measurement for management decision. The former tends to emphasize the semantic aspects of measurements in communications; the latter requires emphasis on pragmatics. From the pragmatic perspective, the concerns relate to the three managerial functions of information: attention directing; problem solving; and scorecard keeping.

2. A systems approach to organizations permits the identification of a three-level domain of measurement for management decision: the organizational level; the individual level; and the societal level. An understanding of this domain is necessary for a full appreciation of measurement for management decision.

3. Measurement for management decision is the *sine qua non* of foundations for the design of management information systems. Each basic function of an information system is built upon measurement foundations.

The perspective represented by these assertions is developed here through a series of arguments. An attempt is made to step the reader through these arguments in a straightforward manner, and references are held to only those necessary. The relevance and importance of the suggested perspective to management practice and theory are underscored in a concluding section.

MEASUREMENTS AS SIGNS

A measurement may be considered to be a quantitative sign. It consists of numerals used for the representation of some property associated with an object or event of interest. Thus, measurement may be considered from the viewpoint of semiotics, the theory of signs.

Charles Peirce and C. W. Morris[2] classified the theory of signs into three major subdivisions: *syntactics*—signs and their relations to other signs: *semantics*—signs and their relations to the "outside world"; and *pragmatics*—signs and their relations to users.

Pragmatics is the most general level of the three and includes "all personal, psychological factors which distinguish one communication event from another, all questions of purpose, practical results and value to sign users. It is the 'real-life' level."[3] Semantics is an abstraction from the real life of pragmatics and deals with the rules which relate signs with the things they designate. It is also a necessary component of pragmatics. Syntactics is, in turn, a further abstraction from semantics and, at the same time, a necessary component of semantics. Each more general level of semiotics extends but also depends upon the previous level.

In our view, traditional scientific measurement is focused primarily at the semantic level. It deals with the question, "How well does the numerical sign reflect the 'real' nature of the object or event referred to?" On the other hand, measurement for management decision addresses the pragmatic level. It deals with the question, "How well does the numerical sign relate to the users and their purposes?" Thus, measurement for management decision extends but also depends upon the concepts of scientific measurement.

SCIENTIFIC MEASUREMENT

The principal objective of a science is to explain, account for, or predict empirical phenomena by means of laws and theories. Measurement in this context is frequently defined as "the process of assigning numerals to objects or events according to rule."[4] Thus, measurement represents the link between the empirical world and the theoretical world. It enables the use of mathematics in scientific reasoning and facilitates the making of predictions and explanations.

The scientific measurement process begins with the identification of the object or event to be measured. The scientist then develops a *construct* pertaining to the thing to be measured. A construct is an idea or concept that defines and describes a particular thing in terms of its properties. Constructs also include some notions about what gives properties magnitude. As such, constructs are artifacts of the mind. The 38th parallel or profitability are examples—you cannot trip over either.

Constructs are important, however. They describe such things as people, behavior, machinery, and money—that is, the referent items about which the scientist hopes to learn. Following Suppes and Zinnes,[5] we term this system of referent items the *empirical relational system*.

Properties are the observable aspects of characteristics of objects within the empirical relational system. They include attributes or characteristic qualities such as length, weight, monetary value, output, and so forth. It is properties which may be measured. Measures are thus a form of observation of an object's properties.

Objects or events can possess different *magnitudes* of a property. Some may have more, some less. The basic operation of measurement is to compare the magnitudes of a common property possessed by two or more items. A comparison may result in a "same/different" judgment or "less than/greater than" judgment. The result permits the classifying and ordering of items according to their properties.

Often it is useful to compare the magnitudes of a property of one or more items with the magnitude of a *standard unit* of the property. These standard units may be such things as inches, pounds, dollars, or watts. As Churchman[6] points out, the use of standard units permits a wide range of comparisons to be made over an extended period of time.

The use of standard units also permits a wider range of statistical and mathematical tools to be brought to bear in the scientific tasks of describing, explaining, and predicting phenomena. With the proper choice of a "zero" or anchor point and the consistent use of a standard unit, the scientist may employ extremely powerful quantitative techniques for relating empirical observations to theory.

This scientific concept of measurement, however, concerns itself primarily with measures as semantic entities. It is concerned with the way a measure reflects the nature of the real world. When a scientist measures the attributes of objects or events he is primarily concerned with associating numbers with these objects or events in such a way that the properties of the attributes are faithfully represented as numerical properties in what Suppes and Zinnes[7] call a *numerical relational system*.

The scientist wants to describe, explain, or predict nature, so his test of a measure is the semantic one: "How well does this measure reflect the aspects of nature I wish to describe, explain, or predict?" At the semantic level, this broad question generally breaks down into three specific questions about a measure.[8,9]

- Referent or designative: "Does the measure properly signify an observable property of the object or event?"

- Prescriptive or decisive: "Does the measure properly signify how the object or event is to be reacted to so as to satisfy purposes or objectives?"

- Appraisive or evaluative: "Does the measure signify the values inherent in the properties of the object or event?"

These three questions have the common property of seeking a "semantic rule" which links the measure to the real-world object or event it is intended to signify. In speaking fundamentally to the issues of *signification*, emphasis is placed on the semantic import of the sign per se, rather than on the uses to which the sign will ultimately be put. From the semantic perspective, a good measure is an *accurate* measure.

Accurate measurement is indeed important in management; however, it is not the overriding issue. From a management point of view, the *user* of measures must be more closely considered. A good measure must be an *influential* one, as we argue in the next section.

MANAGERIAL MEASUREMENT

It was the great insight of C. W. Morris that the fundamental relationship between a sign and its user or interpreter involved the habits or "disposition to respond" of the user. "A disposition to respond to something in a certain way is a state of an organism at a given time which is such that under certain additional conditions the response in question takes place."[10]

Thus, at the pragmatic level different questions are used about a measure. They concern the user's disposition to respond to the measure in a certain way.[11,12]

- Referent or designative: "What is the user's disposition to react to the measured object or event as if it had certain observable properties?"

- Prescriptive or decisive: "What is the user's disposition to act in a certain kind of way to the measured object or event?"

- Appraisive or evaluative: "What is the user's disposition to act toward a measured object or event as if it would be satisfying or unsatisfying?"

Note that each of these questions shifts the emphasis from the thing measured to the user and his response to the measure.

These three pragmatic questions concerning the user's disposition to respond to a measure in a prescribed way relate directly to the three managerial functions of information developed by March and Simon.[13]

- Attention directing: "What problems shall I look into?"

- Problem solving: "What course of action is better?"

- Scorecard keeping: "How well am I doing?"

These three questions also relate directly to the principal objective of management, namely, to achieve the purposes of a social system. Measurement in this pragmatic context is now redefined. It becomes the assignment of numerals to objects or events in such a way that it aids the manager in pursuing the social system's purpose. Measurement for management decision is both pragmatic and teleological. It becomes the assignment of numerals to objects or events in such a way that it aids the manager in pursuing the social system's purpose. Measurement for management decision is both pragmatic and teleological. It requires an understanding of purpose as well as the social, psychological, and technical aspects of measurement as they relate to achieving that purpose.

Of all the purposeful entities, the ones which are most important for management are those we call *organizations*. Consequently, we shall focus on measurement for management decision in the context of organizations.

Following Ackoff and Emery,[14] we conceive of an organization as:

1. A purposeful system that contains at least two purposeful elements (such as people) which share a *common purpose*. The system has

2. A *functional division of labor*, and

3. The functionally distinct subsets can respond to each other's behavior through *observation* and *communication* (such as by measurement), and

4. At least one subset of the system, called *management*, has the system *control* function.

Generally speaking, management is the function in organizations which allocates the organization's resources to its components according to the functional division of labor. Its intention is achievement of the organization's purpose. Its responsibility is decision making. In order to discharge its responsibility, management requires measurement data of the attention directing, problem solving, and scorecard variety. In the section to follow, we develop a specification of what we term the *domain* of measurement data required in management. This development is based upon viewing an organization as a system.

SYSTEMS, ORGANIZATIONS, AND MEASUREMENT

In *The Design of Inquiring Systems*,[15] Churchman identifies nine necessary conditions that must be met in order to conceive of something, S, as a system. Here we review these conditions and draw our own interpretation of their implications for organizations, and for measurement for management decision.

1. "S is teleological." This means that a system has a purpose. Thus, in studying organizations as systems, we must identify the underlying value system of the organization and determine how it directs the formation of the organization's goals and objectives. The statement of purpose becomes the primary criterion for the relevance of a measure and it serves as the basis for constructing a measure of performance.

2. "S has a measure of performance." That any organization, as a system, must have a measure of performance implies that the principal task in measurement for management decision is measurement at the *organizational level*. The organizational level is the central level of measurement within the management domain.

A measure of performance is a quantitative answer to the organizational scorecard question, "How well are we doing?" A firm may measure performance in terms of profitability or productivity, for example. A health program may measure performance in terms of the number of incidences of people diagnosed with a disease.

A measure of performance should reveal how much of a desired end was achieved, how much of an objective was attained, or how well an important job was done. It is obtained by being explicit about what the organization is trying to accomplish and by devising methods for measuring the degree or magnitude of that accomplishment. In this regard, it is useful to distinguish among four aspects of organizational activity: expenditure, input effort, outcome, and performance.

Expenditure, E, refers to the monetary outlays associated with the activities of an organization, for example, a budget or statement of expenses. *Input Effort*, I, refers to actual level of physical effort put into the activities; man-hours, equipment-hours, and counts of materials are examples. *Outcome*, O, refers to the physical results of an organization's activity, such as number of products produced, square feet of floor cleaned, or number of patients served. *Performance*, P, refers to the overall value placed on outcomes in terms of the accomplishment of the organization's purpose.

There are two major concepts which guide organizational performance measurement—efficiency and effectiveness. An *effectiveness* measure of performance reveals how many units of the purpose were accomplished. It is a response to the question, "Are we doing the right things?" On the other hand, an *efficiency* measure of performance reveals how many units of the purpose were accomplished per unit of resources consumed. It is a response to the question, "Are we doing things the right way?"

An illustration, based on the work of Ridley and Simon,[16] will help clarify these notions on measures of performance. Let us suppose that the system under review is the street cleaning function in a city's public works department. The purpose is to maintain the street in a refuse-free condition. A possible measure of performance, let us call it M, is the number of pounds of refuse in place per square foot of pavement. The smaller M is, the more effective the street cleaning function is.

Under conditions of limited resources, however, the manager is also concerned with how efficiently resources are being used in order to achieve this performance. Thus, he or she may be interested in several efficiency measures of performance which may be formulated: (1) M/E (pounds of refuse per square foot per unit of dollar expenditure); (2) M/I (pounds of refuse per square foot per man-hour, equipment-hour, or total factor input hour); (3) M/O (pounds of refuse per square foot per number of curb-miles swept); (4) O/E (curb-miles swept per dollar of expenditure; (5) O/I (curb-miles swept per man-hour; equipment-hour, or total factor input hour); and (6) I/E (man-hours, equipment-hours, or total factor input hours per dollar of expenditure).

There is one fundamental technical requirement of any measure of performance. The measure value (or its inverse) should increase monotonically as the organization's purpose is increasingly achieved (that is, purpose or goal accomplishment is the "property" whose magnitude is to be measured). The measure value should decrease in the event of failure to achieve purpose. This correspondence requirement is often violated in actual performance measurement systems. Frequently a specific measure of performance has only a limited range of applicability. Improvements reflected by the measure are consistent with actual achievement of purpose up to a point. Then as the measure value is maximized (or minimized) dysfunctional consequences begin to dominate, and improvements reflected by the measure no longer correlate with actual accomplishment of purpose. Performance measures for profitability, absenteeism, turnover, crime solution and library circulation have all suffered this problem.

Returning to our discussion of the Churchman conditions, we consider next the third condition:

3. "There exists a client whose interests (values) are served by S in such a manner that the higher the measure of performance, the better the interests are served, and more generally, the client is the standard of the measure of performance."

An important question for any manager to ask is whose purposes should be served by the organization. Is it stockholders, employees, the "public", suppliers, customers, managers themselves or some combination of these? The answer identifies the client of the organization. The value structure inherent in the organization's measure of performance should be the client's value system. If the client prefers to be paid dividends that implies one measure of performance; if he wants clean streets, that implies another. The client has preferences as to the current and future performance of the organization. Alternative states of performance can be related by means of a trade-off principle which indicates how much of one objective the client is willing to relinquish in order to acquire more of another objective. A well conceived measure of performance should assign numerals to current and future performance levels so that the client's trade-off preferences are maintained.

The next of Churchman's conditions is:

4. "S has teleological components which co-produce the measure of performance of S." Part of the difficulty in performance measurement is that organizations are complex entities comprised themselves of purposeful subsystems or components. Each of these subunits pursues its own purposes and responds to the actions taken by other subunits. Consequently, the global measure of performance, M, for the organization must be related to the performance measures for each subunit, m_i. Finding this relationship is sometimes referred to as the "criterion problem." Churchman spells out three possible types of relationships between the subunits' measure of performance and the total system measure.

- *Weakest* (necessary condition): M is maximized (the whole system performs perfectly) if and only if every subunit measure, m_i, is maximized. This condition essentially assumes that the subunits are independent of each other. Many performance measurements systems used in organizations assume this condition. For example, many organizations are divided into responsibility centers each of which is measured in terms of profit (profit center), or expense (expense center), or revenue (revenue center), or return on investment (investment centers), where it is assumed that an improvement on the measure of performance, m_i for any center, i, will result in an improvement in the total organization measure, M.

- *Moderate:* A positive change in the value of m_i is a producer of a positive change in M for at least some range of value of m_i. This is probably the most realistic assumption to make with a *well-designed* management control system in a company or governmental entity. The critical problem is to determine what the relevant ranges are.

- *Strongest:* There exists a mathematical formula which expresses M as a function of the m_i's only; and, the "global" maximum of this function exists. This condition essentially says that a weighting scheme can be constructed which will express M as a function of the individual subunit's m_i's. Ridgeway[17] refers to such measures as "composites" and points out the difficulty of designing effective measures of this sort.

As systems theory tells us, any subsystem of a system may in turn be further subdivided. Ultimately, organizations are comprised of the activities of individual persons. For this reason, measurement at the *individual level* is a critical part of measurement for management decision. Measures of job performance and of individual attributes, such as skills, health, and motivation which relate to the individual's value to the organization are important building blocks in any overall measurement system. That is, the organization should measure the individual's contribution toward the achievement of organizational purpose. However, individuals are themselves purposeful and pursue personal goals and objectives not necessarily the same as those of the organization. These personal goals and objectives possess the same legitimacy as organizational goals. In our society it is thus incumbent upon organizations to measure their contribution to the individuals who serve them in terms of increasing the individuals' ability to achieve their personal goals. Personal development and growth, regardless of its relation to organizational goals, is an important consideration for performance measurement.

Returning again to the Churchman conditions, we encounter:

5. "S has an environment (defined either teleologically or ateleologically) which also co-produces the measure of performance of S."

The environment of a system consists of those things outside the system which nevertheless influence the ultimate performance of the system. It contains the "fixed" or "given" aspects for an organization which cannot be changed by the organization's own activities. These aspects must be understood by an organization and its management. The implication is that an organization should also measure beyond its own boundaries. It should measure at the *societal level*. Indices of important environmental variables such as economic expansion, inflation, consumer attitudes, community health, and social mobility are required to aid the organization in achieving its purpose. Such measurements reveal opportunities, threats and the changing nature of the forces which affect the organization and its performance.

Just as at the individual level there is a social obligation to measure contributions to individuals qua human beings so too is there an obligation to measure the organization's contribution to social purpose. Environmental impact statements, pollution controls, and OSHA standards require in effect that the organization demonstrate its contributions to social goals. Thus, environmental measurement involves not only the measurement of constraints but also the measurement of accomplishment with respect to socially imposed goals and objectives. The societal level constitutes the third of the three levels of measurement within the managerial domain. We continue with our review of the Churchman conditions:

6. "There exists a decision maker who—via his resources—can produce changes in the measures of performance of S's components and hence changes in the measure of performance of S."

In organizations, the decision-making function is the responsibility of *management*. In order to execute its responsibility, an organization's management requires information about the resources available to it and their relative effectiveness for achieving the organization's purpose. Resources are acquired, allocated, motivated and manipulated under the manager's control. They include people, materials, plant and equipment, money, and information.

There are several important questions the manager has about the organization's resources which appropriate measures can help answer. These are:

- What and how many resources are available?

- Where are they located (both geographically and organizationally)?

- What are their performance characteristics and capabilities?

- How is a resource consumed as it produces, that is, what are its cost characteristics?

- How does the performance of each resource (its "m_i") relate to the overall measure of performance of the organization (M).

Managerial accounting systems offer partial answers to these questions. Balance sheets say something about what resources are available and where they are located. Operating statements and supporting documents reveal something about costs and the relationships between resources and performance. However, there is still a great deal of additional measurement work to do in this area. For example, there is a significant need for better measures of human resources.

The measurement of resources may take place at any of the three levels within the managerial domain: the organizational, the individual, and the societal. At the organizational level, the manager needs to know the collective value of human resources, for example, to assess organizational policies in the acquisition, development, allocation, conservation, utilization, evaluation, and rewarding of these resources.[18] At the individual level, the manager needs that information necessary for the making of decisions relative to individual resources, such as in hiring and promoting. At the societal level, the manager acquires information relative to potential resources, such as by obtaining information on community employment levels and skills, in deciding whether to build a plant in a new location.

Finally, we note that management is itself an organizational resource, subject to measurement in the same fashion as are other resources of the organization.

The next Churchman condition for conceiving something to be a system is:

7. "There exists a designer, who conceptualizes the nature of S in such a manner that the designer's concepts potentially produce actions in the decision maker, and hence changes in the measures of performance of S's components, and hence changes in the measure of performance of S."

Viewing the organization as a system, the designer is that individual who specifies the components for the functional division of labor and who links them together by means of lines of work flow, communication, authority, and responsibility. This specification of the components and their linkages must be based on a concept of the organization as a whole, in particular, on the purposes of the organization and on the overall measurement of its performance. The design of a measurement system for an organization is thus seen to be a central task in organizational design.

Churchman's eighth condition is:

8. "The designer's intention is to change S so as to maximize S's value to the client." With respect to measurement for management decision, this condition amounts to an "oath of office" for the designer of the measurement system. The system should be designed by someone whose interests are fundamentally allied with those of the client.

A final condition is:

9. "S is 'stable' with respect to the designer, in the sense that there is a built-in guarantee that the designer's intention is ultimately realizable."

This condition is especially relevant to the design of measurement systems. For example, there is a continual need for a guarantor of the standard units used for measurement and for their consistent application in the measurement system. Social institutions are thus devised to serve the guarantor function. To illustrate, in financial accounting, the Financial Accounting Standards Board (FASB) acts as a guarantor of accounting measurements.

In order to achieve its goals of legitimacy, credibility and trustworthiness a measurement system also requires *auditors*. Auditors maintain the standards by overseeing the processes by which measurements are obtained. They play the vital social role of attestation, standing ready to certify to the internal reliability of the measurements. In the event of a dispute, auditors are prepared to resolve disagreements concerning the adequacy of a measurement. Auditors thus are also important as guarantors of a measurement system.

In summary, then, measurement for management decision proceeds from the assumptions that the organization pursues goals and objectives and has measures of performance; the organization serves a client; it is comprised of subunits which themselves pursue goals and objectives and have measures of performance; it operates in the context of a series of constraints and demands which constitute its environment; it has a managerial function which makes decisions on the allocation of resources; it has a designer who conceptualizes the organization and its measurement system; the designer's intent is to maximize the value rendered to the client; and, there is a guarantor for the organization, its performance and its measurement system. As has been seen, this perspective requires that performance be measured not only at the organizational level but also at the individual and societal levels.

The implementation of a measurement system for management takes the form of a *management information system*. In the section to follow, we examine the fundamental role of measurement from the information systems point of view.

MEASUREMENT AND INFORMATION SYSTEMS

Almost all information systems contain substantial amounts of quantitative data. The impact of these data for decision making rests on the adequacy of the measurement methods upon which they are based.

Overall, the purpose of a management information system is to help guide managerial action with respect to some real-world system (the empirical relational system discussed earlier). This real-world system involves some organizational situation or context. The real-world organization consists of various objects (production equipment, employees, inventories) and events (sales, purchases, job completions) and their associated properties to be measured (capacities of equipment, skills of personnel, on-order quantities of inventories, units and dollars of sales or purchases, units of input consumed, units of output produced). The manager seeks to inform himself or herself about certain aspects of the system in order to choose a course of action which will increase the flow of value from the system to the client.

While the manager may observe and act upon the real-world system directly, his capacity for informing himself is greatly enhanced by a well-designed management information system. Such a system constitutes an indirect form of managerial observation, and supplements that which may be learned by the manager firsthand.

The basic structure of an information system may be portrayed as in Figure 1. Three subsystems are seen to comprise the information system: (1) a data gathering subsystem; (2) a data processing subsystem; and (3) an inquiring and deciding subsystem. An understanding of the nature of each subsystem is necessary for a full appreciation of the role of the information system.

The *data gathering* function in an information system converts primary sensations of the real world into data. Data consist of fundamental observations or "facts" about the real world, taken to be true. Much of these data will be measurement data. Measurement data are data the truth or falsity of which depends on the aspects of *quantity* imbedded in the data. Data gathering includes such processes as sensing, observation, and recording. Instrumentation and calibration of instruments for data gathering are also important.

The *data processing* function maintains and updates a *data base*, from which it generates reports for management decision making. It performs various computation, editing, and formatting functions, as well as those of data organization, storage and retrieval. The data base consists of current and past observations and measurements, representing current and past states of the real-world system. The data processing function processes data according to the rules of the numerical relational system

FIGURE 1   *Measurement and Information Systems*

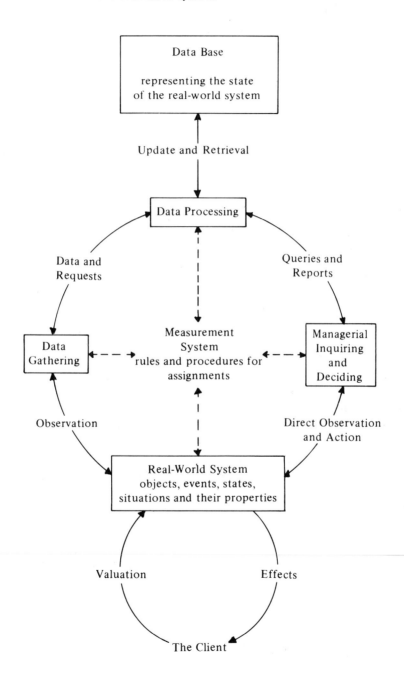

mentioned earlier. In doing this processing, it should employ only those quantitative operations permitted by the units and scales defined by the underlying measurement systems.

The *inquiring and deciding* function submits queries to the data processing system. It also converts the reports it receives into information upon which decisions may be based. As we have already seen, inquiring and deciding is basically the managerial role. Its queries are based generally on issues of the attention directing, problem solving, and scorecard keeping variety. Reports respond to these queries in terms of (a) the current state of the real-world system; (b) its trends; and (c) on the basis of prediction models, its possible or likely future states. In some cases, such as with the use of optimization models, the data processing function may report specific recommended courses of action to be undertaken.

The inquiring and deciding function is a central element in measurement for management decision. It is the manager's queries and the range of alternative actions available to the organization which establish the criteria for the relevance and adequate precision of a measure. Precision here refers to the ability of a measure to make more refined distinction among magnitudes. Precision is a cherished value in scientific measurement. A measurement for management decision, however, need only be precise enough to discriminate between critical magnitudes and to inform the decision-maker relative to appropriate courses of action.

Ashby[19] refers to this necessary level of precision as "requisite variety." His concept derives from the observation that for an organism to survive it must possess as many responses or different actions in its repertoire as there are distinctive states in its environment. It follows that information about the organism's real world must be precise enough to enable the organism to choose properly from among the different responses, but that further precision may be useless, irrelevant or uneconomical.

Marschak[20,21] takes a similar approach. He defines information in terms of a partition defined on the possible states of the real-world system. If the partitioning provides enough distinctiveness to choose the appropriate or maximum pay-off action, the information set is called "payoff adequate." The coarsest partition from among the set of payoff adequate partitions is called "payoff relevant." In Marschak's terms, managerial measures need only be precise enough to yield a payoff relevant partition.

There is much elaboration which can be added to the simple model of an information system illustrated in Figure 1. For example, Marschak distinguishes processes of message encoding, transmission, and decoding. However, for present purposes, the simple model of Figure 1 should suffice.

We are arguing here for the necessity of measurement as a management information system foundation. In Figure 1, we show the measurement process as impacting upon each of the three subsystems of an information system, as well as upon the real-world system itself. The full nature of this impact may be clarified and emphasized by means of a rather straightforward illustration.

Consider the processing of job applications by an organization seeking new employees. Data on applicants would typically be gathered by means of an application form. Certain of these data would be measurement data. For example, level of education completed and scholastic rank might be requested, as well as types and amounts of previous work experience. Measurement is thus a basis for the gathering of data in this context.

An aptitude test might also be administered to those applicants passing an initial screening. The automatic scoring of the test would be an example of measurements generated in data processing. Such measures are *derived* measurements; that is, they are produced by performing operations on data already gathered. The elementary units of initial measurement are often called *fundamental* measures. Most management reports contain derived measures computed on the basis of other measurement data. In the present example, the item responses to questions on the aptitude test are fundamental measures; the resulting scores calculated are derived measures. As is seen, measurement is thus a foundation of data processing, as well as data gathering.

Finally, given the results of the aptitude test, and on the basis of selected interviews as well, the job candidates might be ranked, and final choices made. Note that such a ranking constitutes an example of measurement in the inquiring and deciding phase of job application processing.

The preceding illustration reveals an important characteristic of measurement, in the context of management information systems. The measurement process is not restricted to the original observations of objects and events; rather, it pervades all of the functions of the information system, including the managerial inquiring and deciding function. For this reason, we regard measurement as the *sine qua non* of foundations for the design of management information systems.

SUMMARY AND CONCLUSIONS

In summary, we see measurement as a fundamental process of management. Measurement for management decision focuses on the manager as a user of measures and must therefore take into account the manager's disposition to act in certain ways. This explicit incorporation of the manager's disposition and intention distinguishes measurement for management decision from traditional scientific measurement, although the techniques of scientific measurement are a necessary and integral part of managerial measurement.

By relating the pragmatic theory of signs to communication in organizations, three specific kinds of managerial dispositions have been identified: "What problems shall I look into?" (attention directing), "What course of action is better?" (problem solving), and "How well am I doing?" (scorecard keeping). We have seen that the appraisive function of scorecard measures is particularly central to measurement for management decision.

We view the organizations which management attempts to guide as purposeful systems. Purposeful systems have goals and objectives and, thus, require measures of performance which answer the question of how well the organization is doing in achieving its goals and objectives. These goals and objectives serve the interests of a client, for it is the client's value system which underlies the purposes of the organization.

From systems theory we also know that purposeful systems are comprised of purposeful subsystems which also require measures of performance. Some of these subsystems are themselves organizations, but, ultimately, an important primary component of any organization is its people. Thus, the measurement of human capabilities and activities is fundamental to measurement for management decision. Similarly, organizations as systems are part of a larger suprasystem called the environment. An organization's environment is the source of its constraints or uncontrolled influences on its behavior. Consequently, environmental measures, i.e., measures at the societal level, are equally fundamental to measurement for management decision. The result is that three levels of measurement—organizational, individual, and societal—constitute the domain of measurement for management decision.

Management, we have seen, executes its decision-making responsibility via the allocation of resources. Thus, the measurement of resources and their capabilities is also central to managerial measurement. The measurement of resources is necessary at each of the three levels within the managerial domain.

Measurement systems are created by a designer who must understand the disposition of management and the alternatives available to the organization so that management responds to the measures in an appropriate way. This places at least two requirements on the designer. The designer's intentions must be consistent with the client's values, and the designer must design a system that guarantees that the intention of the measurement system is realized.

The actual implementation of a measurement system takes the form of a management information system. The primary functions of a management information system are data gathering, data processing, and managerial inquiring and deciding. Measurement for management decision underlies all three of these functions.

In conclusion, this article suggests a new perspective on measurement for management decision. Such a perspective is needed, we feel, to orient the student of management to the study of measurement as a *management subject*. Measurement in management is a ubiquitous phenomenon. The impulse to measure in support of management is a strong one, and the need for good measurement systems is recognized by many managers. Yet the roots of measurement in science continue to dominate prevailing perspectives on measurement. The result is the common view of measurement as a component of scientific methodology. Obscured is the role of measurements as *influential* information, as opposed to merely accurate information, in management. We are arguing here that a fresh perspective is needed for the study of measurement from a managerial point of view. The purpose of this paper has been to lay some essential groundwork for the full development of this perspective.

REFERENCES

1. Peter F. Drucker, *Management: Tasks, Responsibilities, Practices* (New York: Harper & Row, 1973), p. 400.

2. Charles W. Morris, *Writings on the General Theory of Signs* (The Hague, Netherlands: Mouton & Co. N.V., 1971).

3. Colin Cherry, *On Human Communication* (Cambridge, Mass.: M.I.T. Press, 1957), p. 223.

4. S. S. Stevens, "Measurement, Psychophysics and Utility," in C. West Churchman and Philburn Ratoosh (eds.), *Measurement: Definition and Theories* (Englewood Cliffs, N.J.: Prentice-Hall, 1967), pp. 18–63.

5. P. Suppes and J. L. Zinnes, "Basic Measurement Theory," in R. D. Luce, R. R. Bush and E. Galanter (eds.), *Measurement: Definition and Theories* (New York: Wiley, 1959), pp. 18–63.

6. C. West Churchman, "Why Measure?" in Churchman and Ratoosh, op. cit., pp. 83–94.

7. Suppes and Zinnes, op. cit.

8. Russell L. Ackoff and Fred E. Emery, *On Purposeful Systems* (Chicago: Aldine-Atherton, 1972), p. 171.

9. Morris, op. cit., pp. 79–109.

10. Morris, op. cit., p. 86.

11. Ackoff and Emery, op. cit.

12. Morris, op. cit., pp. 79–109.

13. James G. March and Herbert A. Simon, *Organizations* (New York: Wiley, 1958), pp. 161–162.

14. Ackoff and Emery, op. cit.

15. C. West Churchman, *The Design of Inquiring Systems* (New York: Basic Books, 1971), pp. 42–78.

16. Clarence E. Ridley and Herbert A. Simon, *Measuring Municipal Activities* (Chicago: The International City Managers' Association, 1938).

17. W. F. Ridgeway, "Dysfunctional Consequences of Performance Measurement," *Administrative Sciences Quarterly* (September 1956), pp. 240–247.

18. Eric Flamholtz, *Human Resource Accounting* (Encino, Ca.: Dickenson Publishing Company, 1974), p. 11.

19. W. Ross Ashby, *Design for a Brain* (New York: Wiley, 1952).

20. Jacob Marschak, "Economics of Inquiring, Communicating, Deciding," *American Economic Review*, Proceedings (May 1968), pp. 1–18.

21. Jacob Marschak, "Information Economics Reconsidered," Working Paper No. 149, Western Management Science Institute, University of California, Los Angeles, June 1969.

Questions for Study and Discussion

1. Consider the four examples of measurement for management decision discussed in the introduction to this reading:
   (i)   the Nielsen ratings
   (ii)   profitability of sales units
   (iii) faculty/student contact hours
   (iv)   plant operating rate
What questions might be raised in the evaluation of these measures, from the scientific point of view? What questions might be raised from the managerial point of view?

2. In an article entitled, "Decision Suport Systems: An Application to Corporate Planning" (Sloan Management Review, Winter 1974), Charles Meador and Davis Ness describe a DSS named PROJECTOR, a "Long range financial planning model for new enterprise, acquisition, and project analysis." Review the authors' description of the PROJECTOR system. What are the measurement underpinnings of this system? (See also Keen and Scott Morton, 1979, pp. 126–130.)

3. How may measurement assist the manager of a firm in the following situations:
   (i)   In analyzing a history of monthly sales data
   (ii)   In determining optimal reorder quantities in an inventory control system
   (iii) In developing a forecast of customer orders
   (iv)   In deciding on the acquisition of new plant capacity
   (v)   In evaluating the net worth of the enterprise as a whole
   (vi)   In deciding among alternative risky ventures of capital
   (vii) In assessing customer satisfaction with products and services

In Part Two, we establish the foundations necessary in order to fully address questions such as these.

FOUNDATIONS

PART TWO

An appreciation of the application of measurement to management decision making requires a familiarity with a variety of fundamental concepts. Part Two is intended to provide the reader with this familiarity.

We begin with a brief review of measurement as it is understood in science, in terms of its essential logic, and as a technique for quantitative observation. The first reading provides a special perspective in this regard. In a brief but classic essay, "Why Measure?," C. West Churchman places the traditional notion of scientific measurement in a broad and revealing light.

The second section deals with measurement and statistics. Two readings are provided. The first, by Frederic M. Lord, utilizes a humorous story to draw an important distinction between the respective realms of measurement and statistics. The second, by S. S. Stevens, one of the most prominent figures in the history of measurement theory, provides a thoughtful examination of the complementary roles of measurement and statistics in general scientific inquiry.

The third section departs from the traditional scientific perspective, and offers a view of measurement within the context of providing information for the support of management decision making. In the first of two pivotal articles, Churchman develops a typology of measurements from a managerial perspective. Mason builds from this in the second article, clarifying the implications for the design of management information systems.

The fourth section is concerned with the measurement of two fundamental management concerns: value and uncertainty. Three readings are included, all offering unique insights based upon distinct theoretical approaches. In the first Kenneth Boulding provides a broad examination of valuation from the economic point of view. In the second George Miller examines "information theory," and it is seen to consist essentially of a theory of uncertainty and its measurement. In the third Jacob Marschak illuminates the scaling of utilities and probabilities from the point of view of decision theory.

THE LOGIC AND TECHNIQUE
OF MEASUREMENT

CHAPTER **TWO**

In this section we undertake to describe the basic concept of measurement, and to present its underlying logic and structure, and its technique in application.

By necessity our description will be somewhat concentrated, and lacking in full breadth and depth of coverage. The aim is to introduce and familiarize the management student with certain basic terminology and technical material. No attempt will be made to teach formal measurement theory per se.

A comprehensive treatment of measurement theory from the scientific viewpoint is to be found in a variety of sources, in particular, Churchman and Ratoosh (1959). The mathematical foundations of measurement in behavioral science are examined in Krantz, *et al.* (1971).

THE BASIC CONCEPT

Measurement, narrowly conceived, involves the assignment of numbers to objects (or events or situations) in accord with some rule (Kaplan, 1964). The *properties* of the objects are represented by the numbers assigned, and the numbers themselves are termed *measures*. Properties of objects may be related one to another, constituting what has been called an *empirical relational system* (Suppes and Zinnes, 1963). Measures of these properties may be correspondingly related one to another, constituting a *numerical relational system*. The basic overall concept is portrayed in Fig. 2.1.

A simple example should assist in clarifying the concept. Suppose I consider two sacks of oranges for purchase at the local market. The oranges are priced at $.25 per pound, and I wish to know how much I will be charged for each of the two sacks. I weigh the sacks on a produce scale in turn, finding that their weights are 10 lbs. and 8 lbs. An act of weighing, one of the most common measurement tasks, has thus been undertaken.

In this simple example the measured objects are "sacks of oranges," and their measured property is "weight." The numbers assigned are 10 and 8. The rule of assignment involves the employment of a produce weighing scale in this case, and the taking of "readings" from this scale.

Note that the oranges themselves are not the objects of direct measurement consideration. The property of weight is attributed to a sack of oranges, and no statement about the weight of an individual orange can be made in the absence of further observation and reasoning.

The weights of the sacks may be related to each other physically, within an empirical relational system. Should I purchase both sacks, and carry them home one in

FIGURE 2.1   *The Basic Measurement Concept*

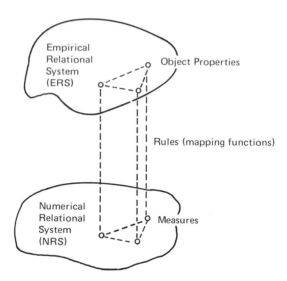

each arm, the sack of the greater weight should become the greater burden as I walk. (Of course, this greater burden may be lightened somewhat by the thought that it implies more orange juice as compensatory refreshment.)

The numbers 10 and 8, representing the respective weights, may themselves be related within a numerical relational system. For example, 10 is "not equal" ($\neq$) to 8. Further, it is "greater than" ($>$) 8, as well as "greater than or equal" ($\geq$) to 8. Each of these statements relates the numbers to one another.

Now if any measurement process is to be successful, the numerical relational system must represent the corresponding empirical relational system in such a way that inferences drawn from the former correspond to inferences that are valid in the latter. From the fact that $10 > 8$, I infer that the sack associated with 10 is heavier than the sack associated with 8. But suppose it is also the case that the sack associated with 8 is *lighter* than a sack associated with the measure 6 (a perverse produce scale indeed!). Now it is true numerically that $10 > 6$, but one is hard pressed to infer which of these two sacks is the heavier.

The correspondence of the numerical relational system to the empirical relational system is termed the *representation problem* of measurement.

Relational systems are an important aspect of measurement. In the two sections that follow, we explore the nature of these systems in more depth.

THE LOGIC OF RELATIONS

In this section, we follow closely the discussion by Ackoff (1962) and take a more formal approach than in the previous section.

Consider a set, S, of objects, and let x, y, and z represent variables ranging over S. Let R denote a relationship, and interpret xRy to mean that x bears the relation R to y. Define R' to be the complement of R, where xR'y is true if and only if (termed "iff") xRy is false. (For example, if R is the relation "equal," denoted "=", then R' would be the complement "not equal," denoted "≠".)

Several properties of relations are of particular interest from the point of view of measurement. These are:

reflexivity

symmetry

transitivity

connectivity

In general terms, a relationship is reflexive if it holds between an object and itself. A relationship is symmetric if, when it holds between a first object and a second, it also holds between the second object and the first. A relationship is transitive if, when it holds between a first object and a second, and between the second object and a third, it also holds between the first object and the third. Lastly, a relationship is connected over a set of objects if it holds for every pair of these objects taken in one order or the other.

Examples may be used to illustrate. Where S is the set of positive integers, the relation = is reflexive and symmetric, the relation > is transitive and connected.

Expanding from the four basic properties, a total of thirteen properties may be formally defined. These are shown in Table 2.1.

The examples in Table 2.1 are based upon S, the set of positive integers, and the relations established are those of a numerical relational system. However, it is also possible to illustrate the properties of relations within an empirical relational system. Suppose that S is instead a set of human beings. The reader is invited to consider the properties illustrated by the following relations:

"resembles"

"is married to"

"employs"

"is parent of"

"is brother of"

"is ancestor of"

"is father of"

"is blood relative of"

Are there any of the thirteen properties which are *not* illustrated by the above? Can you construct your own illustration, in the context of an empirical relational system?

ORDERING RELATIONS

Certain relations are notable in that they provide an ordering within a set of objects.

An ordering requires a relationship that is *not* symmetric. A relation which is symmetric and transitive— e.g., =—permits the grouping of chains of similar ob-

TABLE 2.1. Types of Relations

Property	Definition (Relative to a Set of Elements, S)	Examples (S = The Set of Positive Integers)
1a. Reflexive	x:xRx	=
1b. Irreflexive	x:xR′x	>
1c. Nonreflexive	[∃x:xRx] and [∃x:xR′x]	Equals the square of
2a. Symmetric	x,y:xRy⊃yRx	=
2b. Asymmetric	x,y:xRy⊃yR′x	>
2c. Nonsymmetric	[∃x,y:xRy and yRx] and [∃x,y:xRy and yR′x]	Is less than twice as large as
2d. Antisymmetric	x,y:[xRy and yRx]⊃xIy	≥
3a. Transitive	x,y,z:[xRy and yRz]⊃xRz	>
3b. Intransitive	x,y,z:[xRy and yRz]⊃xR′z	Immediately succeeds
3c. Nontransitive	∃x,y,z:[xRy,yRz, and xRz], and ∃x,y,z:[xRy,yRz, and xR′z]	Is less than twice as large as
3d. Quasi-transitive	x,y,z:[xRy,yRz, and xI′z]⊃ xRz	Is different from
4a. Connected	x,y:xI′y⊃[xRy and/or yRz]	>
4b. Nonconnected	∃x,y(xI′y):[xRy and/or yRx], and ∃x,y(xI′y):[xR′y and yR′x]	Immediately succeeds

Read "x:" as "for every x," "∃x:" as "there exists an x such that," and "⊃" as "implies."
From Ackoff (1962)

jects, but not their ordering. For an ordering, the relation must be either asymmetric or antisymmetric.

Three types of order are of interest in measurement:

partial order

weak order

complete order

A partial ordering is formed by a relation which is reflexive, antisymmetric, transitive, and nonconnected. An example would be any numerical relation—e.g., ≥—as applied to the typical "character set" defined for a computer (the alphabetic characters A,B, ...,Z; the digits 0,1,2,...,9; and various special characters, e.g., $,/,...). Only the digits are comparable by the numerical relation, ≥; hence the relation is nonconnected over the character set.

A weak ordering is formed by a relation which is reflexive, antisymmetric, transitive, and connected. An example would be the numerical relation ≥, as applied to a set of managers' salaries. Managers with identical salaries would not be ordered among themselves, hence the term, "weak ordering." Note in passing that whether a relation generates a partial or weak ordering depends on the set of objects to which it is applied. The numerical relation ≥ has been used in both our examples.

A complete ordering is formed by a relation which is irreflexive, asymmetric, transitive, and connected. An example is the numerical relation $>$, as applied to the set of all positive integers. A single "chain," containing each member of the set of objects, is generated by a complete ordering. Note that with respect to the earlier example of the character set associated with a computer, a "collating sequence" relation is typically defined to generate a complete ordering of the characters for sorting purposes.

A summary of the properties of the basic types of orders is shown in Table 2.2.

The reader is invited to illustrate the properties of partial, weak, and complete orderings by means of several examples. Some suggestions for consideration are:

the relation "is older than" applied to a set of siblings

the relation "is of higher military rank than" applied to employees of the Department of Defense

the relation "had a better student record than" applied to graduates of an MBA program in a university

Note that you may have to make some assumptions in each case, and that the illustrations constructed will vary accordingly.

The above examples are in terms of empirical relational systems. Can you develop a rule of assignment for the establishment of a numerical relational system to solve the representation problem in each case?

An important characteristic of measurement, from a technical point of view, is that the rules of assignment, such as those just suggested, tend to be of certain fundamental types. In the two sections that follow, we turn our attention to these types. We begin by means of an illustrative measurement problem, which is elaborated in several steps.

The Furniture Problem

The question of interest is: what types of rules exist for the assignment of numbers to objects for measurement purposes, and what are the implications of these rules with respect to the information conveyed by the numbers assigned?

TABLE 2.2.   *Properties of Types of Ordering*

Property	Types of Orders		
	Partial	**Weak**	**Complete**
Reflexive	X	X	
Irreflexive			X
Asymmetric			X
Antisymmetric	X	X	
Transitive	X	X	X
Connected		X	X
Nonconnected	X		

From Ackoff (1962)

Suppose, for purposes of illustration, that I am faced with a rather simple "furniture problem." Having decided to purchase a new bookcase for my office, I am now in a store, and have identified five bookcases as likely candidates. At this point I am concerned primarily about that property of the bookcases we term "length." There is only one section of free wall space in my office, and I need a bookcase that will fit in this section.

Proceeding in the usual fashion I extract a tape measure, and measuring each bookcase in turn, arrive at the following measures of length:

72 inches

48 inches

36 inches

36 inches

24 inches

Now an important question is: what can I say about the comparative lengths of the bookcases, given these measures? Among other things, I can say, "This bookcase is twice as long as that one," and this statement will be true of three pairs of bookcases. Note also that the truth of this statement is independent of the choice of a particular unit of measurement, in this case inches.

Having applied the tape measure earlier to the section of free wall space and determined its length to be 36 inches, I establish by this measurement procedure that two bookcases of the five are an exact fit.

But suppose that when I was in my office I had no tape measure in my possession. Finding a roll of a string at my disposal, I cut a length of string to match the length of the free wall section. I then took this string with me to the store.

At the store, I stretch the length of string against the lengths of the bookcases, one at a time. The clerk, anxious to be of help, produces a tape measure and measures the difference between the length of the string and that of each bookcase, producing the following numbers:

36 inches

12 inches

0 inches

0 inches

–12 inches

Do these numbers measure the lengths of the bookcases in any way? Of course they do! As I could with the first measurement procedure, I can make statements about the comparative lengths of the bookcases. In particular I can say, "This bookcase is twelve inches longer than that bookcase," and this statement will be true for four pairs of bookcases. Should the unit of measurement be changed, to meters say, then the statement, reformulated to read, "This bookcase is .305 meters longer than that bookcase," would remain true of the same four pairs of bookcases.

Of course, with the original set of measures 72, 48, 36, 36 and 24 inches, I could make exactly the same type of statement. But note that on the basis of the new set of measures, 36, 12, 0, 0, and –12 inches, I can no longer make a statement of the form, "This bookcase is twice as long as that one." The revised measurement procedure is less powerful in enabling me to make empirical statements, in this sense.

An important difference between the two measurement procedures is that the measure value "0" (zero) is "natural" in the first case, with respect to the length of the bookcases. That is, the value 0 corresponds to "no extent" of length. In the second case the numbers are not "anchored" to the attribute "no extent," with respect to bookcase length.

Note finally that my basic measurement problem, determining which bookcases will fit in the section of free wall space equivalent to my length of string, is easily resolved. The measure 0 (zero), in this case, indicates a perfect fit.

To continue our illustrative variations, let us suppose that I find myself in the store with my length of string as before, but without a clerk in possession of a tape measure. Ignoring my length of string for the moment, I line the bookcases up, one against the other, and arrange them in an order associated with their respective observed relative lengths, assigning the numbers 3, 2, 1, 1, and 0 to the individual bookcases according to their place within the order.

Can these newly assigned numbers be said to be measures of the bookcase lengths? Again, the answer is yes. Relying on these numbers, I may now make statements of the form, "This bookcase is longer than that bookcase." Note that this will be true for nine pairs of bookcases.

Of course, it is also the case that I no longer have a *unit* of measurement, and hence statements of the form, "This bookcase is twelve inches longer than that bookcase," may not be made on the basis of this measurement procedure. Once again, our capacity for empirical statement has been narrowed.

Nevertheless I may still resolve my basic measurement problem. Pulling the string from my pocket, I stretch its length against the respective lenghts of the bookcases, and assign it the number 1, representing its position within the order of lengths established. In doing so, I determine that two bookcases are of a length identical to that of the extended string, and hence, identical to the length of the section of free wall space.

Consider one final variation on our illustration. I am in the store as before, carrying my length of string representing the section of free wall space for which I seek a bookcase. I am interested only in those bookcases which fit exactly into the wall space. Once again, I line up the bookcases, one against the other, seeking this time only to discover those bookcases which are the same length. I arrange the five bookcases into four groups of identical length, with two bookcases in one group and a single bookcase in each of the other three. I number the groups arbitrarily, but uniquely: 1, 2, 3, and 4. Can these numbers be said to be measures of the lengths of the bookcases?

One may be tempted to answer, "Surely not!" at this point, for the numbers appear to convey none of the information we seek with respect to bookcase length. With arbitrary number assignment, we cannot infer, for example, that a bookcase in Group 2 is longer than a bookcase in Group 1, let alone determine how *much* longer.

But it is nevertheless possible, with this latest scheme, to make statements of the form, "This bookcase is equal in length to that bookcase," and such statements will be true for every pair of bookcases in the same group, and false for all pairs not in the same group. While the numbers associated with the groups serve only as identification labels, they permit me to make limited statements about the lengths in question. Thus this grouping and labeling process constitutes a form of measurement.

It remains only to resolve my basic measurement problem with this limited scheme. Extracting the string from my pocket, I compare its extended length to that of a single bookcase from each of the four groups. I find the string length identical to that of one of the bookcases, and assign the group number of this bookcase to the string. If I possess a say Group 2 string then my wall space constitutes an exact fit for a Group 2 bookcase, of which this store possesses two. The problem is thus resolved.

SCALES OF MEASUREMENT

The furniture problem of the previous section was designed to illustrate the existence of four basic types of *scales* associated with the application of rules of measurement. These scale types are said to represent ratio, interval, ordinal, and nominal levels of measurement.

A ratio scale was defined by the first measurement procedure applied to the furniture problem. Its essential characteristics are a specific unit of measurement (e.g., inches) and a zero point corresponding to "no extent" with regard to the attribute being measured. The interval scale, the second to be introduced in the furniture problem, retains the unit of measurement, but possesses no natural zero point. The ordinal scale, the third to be introduced, possesses no unit of measurement, but orders the objects measured (e.g., bookcases) according to whether they possess "more" or "less" extent of the attribute in question (e.g., length). The nominal scale, the last to be introduced, simply classifies the objects measured according to whether they possess identical extents of the attribute measured. (The notion of "extent" may also fade from the nominal level of measurement, for example, in classifying objects according to their color.)

The four fundamental scale types were first defined by Stevens (1959), and in Table 2.3, reproduced from his original classic article, the properties of these types are stated precisely, with corresponding examples of application.

Note in particular in Table 2.3, that within any scale type, certain forms of mathematical transformations on the measures leave the scale form invariant. For example, any one-to-one substitution of measures is permitted for a nominal scale. Any increasing monotonic function may be employed for an ordinal scale, any linear function for an interval scale, and any multiplication by a constant is allowed for measures on a ratio scale.

An illustration may be helpful with regard to scale transformation possibilities. Suppose one is given the measures 5, 4, 3, 2, and 1, applied respectively to the properties of five objects. What is an example of a transformation which would be permitted at the nominal level of measurement, but not at the other three levels? What is a corresponding example at the ordinal level? the interval level? the ratio level?

The problem of determining the type of scale induced by a rule of assignment is termed by Suppes and Zinnes (1963) the *uniqueness problem* of measurement. Earlier we discussed the representation problem, as you recall. Closely related is a third problem: the *meaningfulness problem*. The meaningfulness problem is rather narrowly interpreted: it is to show that the truth or falsity of a "numerical statement" is con-

TABLE 2.3.   A Classification of Scales of Measurement*

Scale	Basic Empirical Operations	Mathematical Group Structure	Typical Examples
NOMINAL	Determination of equality	Permutation group $x' = f(x)$, where f(x) means any one-to-one substitution	"Numbering" of football players Assignment of type of model numbers to classes
ORDINAL	Determination of greater or less	Isotonic group $x' = f(x)$, where f(x) means any increasing monotonic function	Hardness of minerals Street numbers Grades of leather lumber, wool, etc. Intelligence-test raw scores
INTERVAL	Determination of the equality of intervals or of differences	Linear or affine group $x' = ax + b$, $a > 0$	Temperature (Fahrenheit or Celsius) Position Time (calendar) Energy (potential) Intelligence-test "standard scores"(?)
RATIO	Determination of the equality of the ratios	Similarity group $x' = cx$, $c > 0$	Numerosity Length, density, work, time intervals, etc. Temperature (Rankine or Kelvin) Loudness (sones) Brightness (brils)

*From Stevens (1959, p. 25) . . . The basic operations needed to create a given scale are all those listed in the second column, down to and including the operation listed opposite the scale. The third column gives the mathematical transformations that leave the scale form invariant. Any numeral x on a scale can be replaced by another numeral x', where x' is the function of x listed in column 3.

stant under admissable scale transformations of any of its numerical assignments. Examples of numerical statements are:

1. "The ratio of the maximum temperature today to the maximum temperature yesterday is 1.10."

2. "The ratio of the difference between today's and yesterday's maximum temperature to the difference between today's and tomorrow's maximum temperature will be 0.95."

The first example is said to have no clear empirical meaning, i.e., if it is true for one temperature scale, it is false for another. The truth or falsity of the second holds, however, regardless of the scale implicit. The reader is invited to construct several similar illustrative examples.

TECHNIQUE OF APPLICATION

Several other important aspects of measurement emerge when its application is considered.

Three properties of applied measures are especially significant: validity, sensitivity, and reliability. Generally speaking, a measure is understood to be *valid* if it measures "what it is supposed to measure." A measure is *sensitive* to the extent that it discriminates along the dimension of concern. And a measure is *reliable* to the extent that it remains constant under repeated measurements taken under conditions held or taken to be constant. The design of any measurement technique or system is based fundamentally upon the consideration of these three properties.

Determining the validity of a measure is a particularly difficult matter. In part this is because validity is more than a technical problem. What a measure is supposed to measure depends first of all on the purposes at hand. Reflecting on this, Kaplan offers a broader definition: "The validity of a measurement consists in what it is able to accomplish, or more accurately, in what *we* are able to do with it." (Kaplan, 1964, p. 198).

In a sense, the greater portion of this book is directed toward an understanding of the validity of measures. In looking forward to the material to come, the reader might ask the following questions: what is a valid measure of the profitability of a firm? the productivity of a service-providing government agency? the performance of an executive? the value of the human resources of an organization? the quality of working life of an office worker? the level of unemployment in a society? the amount of crime in a city?

In the physical sciences the sensitivity and reliability of a measure are typically largely dependent on the *instrumentation* associated with the measurement process. In the social sciences and in management, however, these properties often depend more on the *human observer*. To the extent that the instrumentation dominates a measurement process, the measures are often held to be *objective*. To the extent that the human observer dominates, the measures are frequently said to be *subjective*. Unfortunately, the term "subjective" is often used pejoratively, as if instrumentation were inherently superior as a means of measurement.

Again, issues of measure subjectivity and objectivity dominate many of the readings in this book. A variety of interpretations is offered, and the reader is encouraged to form an independent judgment as to the appropriate respective roles of instrumentation and human observers in measurement for managerial decision making.

Lastly, a distinction is sometimes also made between the use of *fundamental measures* and the use of *derived measures*. A fundamental measurement is conceived to be "one which presupposes no others, save those which consist in establishing an order or making a count" (Kaplan, 1964, p. 187). A derived measurement, on the other hand, is based on fundamental measurements. Weight is commonly cited as an example of fundamental measurement; density as an example of derived measurement, based on the measurement of both mass and volume. The distinction is due to the work of Campbell (1957). It has been much criticized as not holding up under close examination. See, for example Ackoff (1962), who concludes that "measures always presuppose and hence involve other measures" (p. 198).

PREFACE TO THE READING

It is time to emerge from our rather narrow, technical look at measurement, and to perceive the basic issues in a broader, more integrative light. In Reading 2, C. West Churchman does this through the identification of four fundamental measurement problems:

1. language

2. specification

3. standardization

4. accuracy and control

Note that these are "existential problems" of measurement, that is, intrinsic to measurement as a pursuit. No general solutions exist; the problems must be dealt with within the context of the larger inquiry problems at hand.

The Churchman article is a classic in the measurement literature and a necessary foundation for the study of measurement from both scientific and managerial perspectives.

WHY MEASURE?

C. West Churchman

INTRODUCTION

"Measurement" is one of those terms which has attained a social prestige. Apparently—all other things being equal—it is better to measure than not to measure. Some people think that the social sciences do not—or cannot—measure; and one implication of the thought is "less power to them!"

Why should measuring have this preferential status? What is it that measuring accomplishes that nonmeasuring does not? These are the questions to be dealt with in this paper.

At the outset one can suggest a rather obvious answer to this question, namely, that measurement assigns numbers to objects. But this suggestion can scarcely be adequate to explain why measurement is to be preferred to nonmeasurement in some contexts. Why is number assignment a good idea? Whatever it is that number assignment accomplishes may give us a clue to the meaning of measurement. The contrast between quantitative and nonquantitative information seems to imply a contrast between "precise" and "vague" information. Precise information is information that enables one to distinguish objects and their properties to some arbitrarily assigned degree of refinement.

We are thus driven to a first formulation of the function of measurement which will suffice to define the problem area of this paper. There is no reason to be precise for precision's sake, of course. But the reason that precision is useful is that precise information can be used in a wide variety of problems. We know that we can measure the lengths of some objects very precisely. This means that, in the various situations where we want information about length, we can obtain the information we want. Sometimes we do not need to make a fine distinction between objects, and sometimes we do. But whatever our needs, length measurements can be found to satisfy them—within bounds, of course. Beyond the bounds there are still problems of length measurement which have not been solved—the very fine and the very far.

Suppose, then, we propose that the function of measurement is to develop a method for generating a class of information that will be useful in a wide variety of problems and situations. This proposal is very tentative. It needs defending in terms of the historical usage of the term "measurement" and the practice of measurement.

From C. West Churchman and Philburn Ratoosh, eds., *Measurement: Definition and Theories* (Wiley, 1967) pp. 83–94; reprinted by permission.

It needs clarification, since "wide variety" may include time, place, persons, problem type, and many other properties of breadth and depth.

Instead of considering these important questions, I want to continue the theme with which I started. Suppose we acted as though we knew what the proposal meant to a sufficient extent to enable us to develop the problems entailed in such a functional definition.

We can begin by noting one rather striking consequence of the proposal. The objective of measurement can be accomplished in a number of ways, as this volume of papers clearly shows. The qualitative assignment of objects to classes and the assignment of numbers to objects are two means at the disposal of the measurer for generating broadly applicable information. But which means is better? The striking consequence of the proposal is that measurement is a decision making activity, and, as such, is to be evaluated by decision making criteria.

In this sense, i.e., measurement taken as a decision making activity designed to accomplish an objective, we have as yet no theory of measurement. We do not know why we do what we do. We do not even know why we measure at all. It is costly to obtain measurements. Is the effort worth the cost?

I have no intention of developing a functional theory of measurement here. Instead, I want to reconsider some of the well-known aspects of measurement in the light of the tentative proposal given above. In each case, I want to ask what alternative decisions the measurer has, and to what extent he has guides which enable him to select the best alternative. The topics selected for discussion do not necessarily represent the best way of organizing measurement activities; I have selected them because they have each received considerable attention in the literature on measurement. In each case, it will be found that the measurer is caught between at least two desirable aims, and the more he attempts to emphasize one aim, the more he must sacrifice another—which is the typical problem setting of the decision maker.

The topics to be considered are: (1) the selection of a *language*; (2) *specification* of the items and their properties; (3) *standardization* of the information to permit adjustment to various times and places; and (4) *accuracy* and *control* of the measurement process.

Any "scheme" of measurement does violence both to reality and to the functional meaning since there are many methods of accomplishing a goal. I do not intend to imply, therefore, that these topics must occupy the attention of the measurer in this order. But it is safe to assume that every measurer must decide:

1. In what language he will express his results (*language*).

2. To what objects and in what environments his results will apply (*specification*).

3. How his results can be used (*standardization*).

4. How one can evaluate the use of the results (*accuracy* and *control*).

There is a distortion which I will have to introduce in order to discuss these topics. The method of deciding how to handle any one of the problems does eventually involve consideration of all the rest. But the main point here is to show that a true decision problem does occur in the case of each of the four topics, rather than to suggest how the decision problem is to be solved.

LANGUAGE

The measurer must develop a language which adequately communicates to another person what the user must do to utilize the information contained in the measurement. The emphasis here is on the language of communication.

One aim of the language of measurement is to communicate to as many potential users as possible since this will increase the scope of utilization. Another aim is to enable the user to employ the information when there is need for fine distinctions since this also will increase the scope of utilization. These two aims are apparently in conflict—the more common the language the more difficult it is to use the language for portraying fine distinctions.

One way out of a dilemma is to escape through the horns. This I think has been the solution proposed by advocates of "fundamental" measurements. Suppose there are some operations which can be described in unequivocal language so that virtually every intelligent person will understand what is meant, or can be trained to understand. Suppose, too, we can find a process by which other operations can be understood in terms of these more elementary ones, and that these operations permit greater and greater refinement. If this were so, then we could accomplish *both* a wide scope of communication and a in which the process of going from the "simple" language and "simple" operation might be the comparison of straight rods: by successive steps we go from the "simple" language of comparison to the more complicated language of measuring the distances between the planets. Another example of a "simple" operation is the preference comparison of commodities: we may try to go from the "simple" language of preferences to the more complicated language of utilities.

In recent years there has been considerable study of the various ways in which the process of going from the "simple" language and "simple" operations can take place. These studies have resulted in formalizations of measurement language which are undoubtedly important in the development of the theory of measurement. For example, the symbol "$<$" can be made to denote an operation of comparison of two objects (e.g., "shorter than," or "is preferred to"). Sometimes the comparisons obey some simple rules like transitivity ($a < b$ and $b < c$ implies $a < c$), which enables us to introduce into the language the concept of ordering. But we can only introduce the concept if the comparisons obey the rules; i.e., we cannot enrich the language unless certain rules are upheld. The measurer is faced with a decision making problem when the rules fail. He may look about for another comparison operation with which he is satisfied and for which the rules hold, or he may abandon the rule itself and look for other rules to enrich the language. In any case, it seems to be confusing to say, for example, that "transitivity" fails over the class of preference comparisons. Such statements hide the fact that the measurer may always select another meaning for "preference" (there are clearly very many possible meanings) rather than let the rule fail *if* this seems economically advisable.

The language of measurement may be enriched in many ways. In each case the measurer has to decide whether the formalization is advisable. An enrichment of the language often makes the measurements more useful as items of information. But additional rules must be satisfied, often at the expense of a great deal of research time. For examples of some of the kinds of measurement languages one may construct, see Stevens' paper, p. 25. Stevens is not concerned, of course, with comparisons of the values of the language schemes he discusses.

The process of developing a measurement language which I have been discussing has the following character. A formal system is constructed which includes terms, and relations between the terms. Some of the terms and at least one of the relations are taken to be "primitive" in the formal sense: the terms and relations are not explicitly defined. These terms and relations are also taken to be semantically primitive: the things and the comparisons which they denote are supposed to be simple to understand or to perform. This method of constructing the language of measurement is neither the only one nor necessarily the best one available to the measurer. A language without semantic primitives has many obvious advantages, besides more realistically reflecting the actual operations of measurement (where nothing is simple to understand or to perform). But the techniques of developing such a language have not yet been explored. Further discussion of this point would take the present discussion too far from its central purpose.

Finally, the amount of complexity that one should permit in a measurement language is also a problem of considerable importance. The more complicated a language, no matter how it is developed, the fewer the number of people who will understand it. In some cases, this restriction on communications seems clearly desirable. In other cases, e.g., in inspection work, one tries to develop a language that will be widely understood although it may not be very precise.

In sum, the language of measurement does entail a decision problem. The more precise a language the less broadly is it understood. To put it otherwise—if one wanted to be cute about it—the clearer a language the more confusing it is to most people. Precise languages narrow the class of users but increase the degree of refinement that any user can attain. The proper balance between breadth and depth is the linguistic decision problem of measurement.

SPECIFICATION

The problem of the specification of measurement is the problem of deciding what objects are being described and under what circumstances. This is simply the problem of deciding on the scope of application of the measurements in terms of time, place, and individuated items. This is not a decision about how the application is to be made, which will be considered under another head.

A conflict of aims is clear in this instance as well. It would be very fine if we could develop information that could be used in connection with all our problems, i.e., on all things at all times and places. But the more general information becomes the more expensive it becomes to acquire, or, else, the more useless it becomes in any specific context.

Perhaps one illustration will suffice to clarify the issues. In the theory of detonation, we would like to measure the sensitivity of various compounds. It would be a nice thing if we could measure how sensitive a piece of mercury fulminate is wherever the piece may be, no matter what its size, and no matter what is happening to it. But we do not do this at all. The term "sensitive" applies only to compounds which have a specific kind of shape and which exist in a specific class of environments. We restrict the term to these items and environments because we feel it would be entirely too costly to try to extend the scope beyond them, relative to the gains made from the more extensive information. Generalizing: each measurer is involved in the economic problems of balancing the "costs" of extending the application of measurement and the "returns."

STANDARDIZATION

We turn now to the aspect of measurement that enables us to utilize information in a wide variety of contexts. In searching for a suitable title under which this topic could be discussed, I could find no better one than "standards." Standards of measurement are designed to provide a basis for adjusting experience in widely different contexts. Although the term is usually used in a narrower sense than the one adopted here, the purpose of standards so exactly corresponds to the notion of "wide applicability" that the extension of meaning seems legitimate.

It is strange that in philosophical discussions of measurement, the problem of standards is often neglected. This may be because it is often assumed that the problem is trivial, or not nearly as important as setting up an adequate language. Yet even a casual inspection of the process of measurement shows how very intricate and delicate is the operation of standardizing measurement readings.

The necessity for standards of measurement is based, in part, on an almost obvious observation that not all human experience takes place at the same time or in the same circumstance. Even if there were but one mind in all the world, such a castaway would need to compare the experience of one moment and place with that of another moment and place. He would have to communicate with his own past. The devices that men have used to make these comparisons are many indeed. One of the most direct methods consists of reconstructing each experience into an experience of a given moment and a given time, i.e., the present experience is "adjusted" into the experience that would have taken place under some standard set of conditions. This is not the only way in which experiences of various moments can be communicated, but it is a very powerful device for communication. Robinson Crusoe cannot bring along his hut as he searches for a flagstone for his hearth. But he does need to compare an experience on the beach with a past experience in his hut. He does this (say) by the use of a piece of string. He argues that if the string length fits the flagstone, the flagstone will fit the hearth. What he is really saying is that each experience—of the hearth and the flagstone—can be adjusted to a comparison with the string under "standard" conditions.

The general purpose of standards can now be made clear. One wants to be able to assert that x has property y under conditions z at time t in such a manner that the information contained in the assertion can be used in a wide number of other conditions and times to enable many different kinds of people to make decisions. The assertion that company x had a net income of y dollars in the U.S.A. during 1919 means nothing at all unless there is some way in which this property can be compared with a net income in 1956, say, or in England. Hence, the need for a "standard" dollar. Even the standard dollar does not accomplish the desired result of transmitting meaningful information if the circumstances in which the company operated (e.g., postwar economy) were different from the circumstances of today (cold-war economy). We require richer standardization to enable us to make meaningful comparisons of such a company's activities.

The decision problem of standards arises because of two rather obvious needs. First of all, one wants to find a method of measurement such that a minimum amount of adjustment is required when times, places, and people change. This desire for simplification is so strong that many thinkers have believed that certain simple sensations have this very desirable property: reports about such sensations can be understood intelligibly by a wide number of people in a wide variety of circumstances. A witness of an accident can report which car was going faster, a laboratory technician can report the color of litmus paper, a stock clerk can report the number of items in a bin; in each case the report is supposed to be reliable, no matter how the surrounding conditions vary.

The other need that standards are supposed to supply is precision. This is the need to differentiate aspects of the world we live in. The planning of a large meeting only demands a rough notion of the size of the crowd, say, between 2000 and 3000, in order to select a meeting hall economically; but the planning of a dinner meeting requires much greater precision. The decisions about instrument readings, highly refined products, bridges, and the like, all demand extreme precision.

It requires little reflection to see that the aim of minimizing the effort to adjust data usually conflicts with the aim of precision. In effect, the "cost" of adjusting data rises as more precision is attained, just as the cost of the absence of precision goes up as we attempt to find "simpler" data. Experience has shown that it is possible to be naive with respect to precision in an attempt to be simple in procedures. All of the supposedly "simple" instances mentioned above—a report of a witness, of a laboratory technician, of a stock clerk—are not simple at all if the decision on which they are based has any importance. There are countless instances in which such reports have been shown to be faulty, and these instances have pointed to the need for "checking" the accuracy of the data. Such checks amount to setting up standards to which the data can be adjusted. For example, what is meant by saying that one car was seen to be speeding more rapidly than another? As a first approximation: the witness who saw this was "reliable." What does "reliable" mean? As a second approximation: had any other normal person been at the scene, he would have made the same report. What does "normal person" mean? As a third approximation: a person with an intelligence quotient in a certain range, with emotional factors below a certain level of intensity, with vision in a certain range, etc.

This "normal" is the standard of measurement for a "witness" report. It may be noted that defense attorneys often argue that the witness's report is *not* adjustable to this standard, e.g., that the witness is excitable, or known to exaggerate, etc. Usually, when the witness is shown to have a property significantly different from the standard, his report is rejected. In this case, we can say that the "adjustment" has been a rejection. This terminology will enable us to emphasize the economic gains that occur when "unreliable" reports can be adjusted to reliable ones, rather than rejected. If we knew, for example, that a witness was normal on all counts except an emotional instability of a certain type, then we might be able to adjust his report to the report that would have occurred if a completely normal person had been at the scene of the accident. We could do this if we could establish a law relating visual reports in various circumstances to the degree of a specific emotional disturbance. This kind of thing Bessel accomplished in his study of observer reaction times. It is not necessary to discard the readings of a "slow" observer if we can find a method of adjusting his readings, e.g., by adding a constant to each one.

Thus, we see three "levels" of standardization of data. The first tries to restrict itself to data reports that are virtually certain to remain invariant with time and place so that zero adjustment is required. This level minimizes the cost of adjustment, but the data themselves have little precision and, consequently, little value where refined distinctions are needed. The second level consists of rejecting data not collected under standard conditions. The method of adjustment is simple, but the waste of information may be considerable. The third level consists of adjusting data to standards by means of "laws" that enable one to say: *if* report R_1 was made at time t_1 in circumstance z_1 by a person having properties w_{11}, w_{12}, etc., then report R_0 would have been made at time t_0 in circumstance z_0 by a person having properties w_{01}, w_{02}, etc. The "standards" are specified in terms of circumstance, observer, and observer actions.

It seems natural enough to ask why reports should be adjusted to a standard report. If laws exist that enable one to adjust in the manner stated above, why not adjust directly from one circumstance to the problem context without going through the medium of a standard?

The reason for standardized data is easy enough to give. Without standards, one would have to report all the relevant information about the time, place, persons, etc., in addition to the data report itself. Otherwise, no one would know what values to assign to the variables in the laws that enable one to use the report in other circumstances. But once a standard has been given, then all data reports can be adjusted to the standard, and all that is needed is the data report itself. Thus, the standard conditions constitute a data-processing device that simplifies the amount of reporting required. But the construction of an optimal standard is a very complicated problem, as anyone knows who has followed the literature on the selection of a standard of length. Indeed, the whole problem of standards has received a great deal of attention by various professional societies. But as far as I know, the philosophers of measurement, i.e., those interested in tying together the whole structure and function of measurement, have tended to ignore this work.

ACCURACY AND CONTROL

There are two other aspects of measurement—each fully as important as those just discussed. These are concerned with the accuracy of the measurements and with the control of the measuring process.

Accuracy is itself a measurement—the measurement of the degree to which a given measurement may deviate from the truth. No procedure can claim the name of measurement unless it includes methods of estimating accuracy.

"Deviation from the truth" must be defined in terms of the uses to which the measurement is put. This remark has the awkward consequence that accuracy is a highly relative term, the meaning of which depends on the individual decision maker. But measurements are pieces of information applicable in a wide variety of contexts and problems. This means that it must be possible to find accuracy measurements which are applicable in a wide variety of contexts and problems. It must be admitted that, at present, we tend to adopt a rather naive solution to the problem of measuring accuracy by using one overall figure such as the probable error or standard deviation of the mean. For example, in statistical literature, accuracy is sometimes defined in terms of a "confidence interval." In so far as this computed interval has any meaning, it tells us that a certain range of numbers constructed out of observations has a specific probability of including the "true" measurement. Each set of observations is the basis for forming a net to "catch" the truth, and the confidence interval tells us the probability of a successful catch. But it is almost always difficult to determine how the information supposedly contained in a confidence interval can be used; i.e., what difference would it make if the confidence interval were twice as large, or half as large? Most statisticians seem to prefer to negotiate this tricky question by urging the decision maker to set his own size of confidence interval. Since most decision makers honestly do not see the purpose of the interval in the first place, the interval is set "arbitrarily," i.e., pointlessly.

Now the problem of accuracy is to develop measures that enable the measurement user to evaluate the information contained in the measurements. It seems clear that to date we have overemphasized one aim and underemphasized another. We have tried to develop general measures of accuracy at the cost of their meaningfulness in specific contexts. The decision problem of accuracy, therefore, has not been adequately solved, except possibly for some industrial processes where there is repetition of data and cost functions can be obtained.

Control is the long-run aspect of accuracy. It provides the guarantee that measurements can be used in a wide variety of contexts. In other words, a control system for measurement provides optimal information about the legitimate use of measurements under varying circumstances. The economics of control are extremely difficult to work out. It is certainly not economical to check measurements at every feasible instant, nor is it economical to use measurements without any check. What the proper amount of control should be and what its structure should be are in general unsolved problems.

It may be noted that control is, in effect, the test of a good standard. If adjustments can satisfactorily be made to a standard in accordance with the criteria of control, then the standards have been sufficiently specified. If not, then either the laws of adjustment must be changed or, else, additional specifications must be added to the standard.

SCIENCE AND DECISION MAKING

Enough has been said to establish the point that measurement involves highly complicated—and as yet unsolved—decision problems. It is important, I think, to point out that I realize that many people feel that decision making models cannot be applied to scientific work. They arrive at the feeling in various ways. Some feel that formal decision models applied to scientific decisions would stifle the creative powers of the scientist. Others feel that the "costs" and "returns" of the scientific input and output are intangibles. These feelings may be right, but at least we owe it to ourselves as scientists to determine whether they are right, and this means a frank statement of our decision problems, which is what I have started to do in this paper. My argument is not with people who feel this way.

But others may feel that science is immortal, and what is not solved today will be solved sometime. Existing decision making models implicitly or explicitly assume a penalty for delays. Perhaps to an immortal mind no such penalty is relevant. Thus, we can investigate some aspects of our measurements now, and let the next generation solve some more. People with this attitude are serious opponents of the endeavor of this paper. However, they cannot be right. Science may be immortal—and I hope it is—but this does not imply a zero penalty for delay. It is ridiculous (I feel) to think that science is a gradual accretion of bits of knowledge. Instead, we ought to think that, as time goes on, scientists will feel that the distance between what they know and what they could know is greater and greater. Hence, the penalties for wrong steps become magnified, not diminished, the longer the life of the institution. Therefore, the decision making problems of science are terribly important ones, and decision making models that penalize for delay, i.e., for overemphasis or underemphasis of some kind of activity, can be appropriately applied to science today.

SUMMARY

The decision making problems of any of the aspects of measurement are enormously difficult, and even an approximation to their solution still escapes us. Everything that has been said here about measurements is applicable to a broader class called "information" and "data." A rather significant portion of our resources is devoted to generating and processing data. However, it is apparent that no one knows how the data should be expressed (the decision problem of data *language* is unsolved), what data are needed (the decision problem of data *specification* is unsolved), how the data are to be used in various contexts (the decision problem of *standardization* is unsolved), and how the data are to be evaluated (the decision problem of *accuracy* and *control* is unsolved).

Questions for Study and Discussion

1. Consider the data which might be included in a personnel record in an organization. Develop examples of measures which might be included in this data, illustrating each of the four basic types of scales:

nominal

ordinal

interval

ratio

Using your examples, demonstrate the basic properties of each scale type. (That is, show how certain mathematical transformations leave the scale form invariant, in each case.)

2. Apart from the four basic scales types identified by Stevens, other types also exist. An example is the *ordered metric*, identified by Coombs (1950). In an ordered metric, intervals are not equal, but may be ordered in magnitude. An example taken from Coombs (1953) is the measurement of the amount of "authority" possessed by individuals of military rank, e.g., private, corporal, buck sergeant, and master sergeant. If the data about "who bosses whom" is available, a rational construction of the authority scale is possible at the ordered metric level. Can you see how?

3. Imagine that a systems planning department is attempting to choose among five alternative data base management software packages offered by competing suppliers. The five packages are equally priced, more or less. It is decided to rank each package from "1" ("best") to "5" ("worst") on each of several "effectiveness" criteria, including:

data manipulation capability

data & file definition capability

security provisions

report generation capability

operating system compatibility

storage requirements

file maintenance capability

vendor service and support

inquiry capability

The package with the lowest total points will then be selected. What do you think about this method of selection?

4. Consider the four measurement problems identified by Churchman. How do these problems manifest themselves in financial reporting by business firms? What are the implications for the determination of accounting standards and principles?

5. For an extended treatment of the issues raised in "Why Measure?" see Churchman (1961), Chapter 5, *The Teleology of Measurement.* There, Churchman writes:

"A 'variance' in a standard cost-accounting system is supposedly a measure of the deviation of a given cost from a 'standard' cost. That is, a variance is a measure of a cost difference. But to date there is no generally accepted method of comparing different variances." (p. 114)

In terms of measurement, how does this pose a problem?

CHAPTER **THREE**

The use of statistical methods is an important aspect of the support of management decisions. This is no doubt appreciated by the modern student of management. But it is less appreciated that the use of statistical methods rests upon measurement foundations. In this section the relationship of measurement to statistics is reviewed briefly.

The design of a computer-based decision support system (DSS) may be used to illustrate the measurement bases of statistics. The Portfolio Management System developed by Gerrity (1971) and reviewed by Keen and Scott Morton (1978) is based in part on the use of a graphic display system to analyze various data. One such standard display is a scattergram whose points represent two data items associated with the securities held by an account, e.g., the current price/earnings ratio and a 10-year average price/earnings ratio. A least-squares line is fitted to the data. (See Fig. 3.1.) A correlation coefficient might also be computed and displayed.

The use of a least-squares line and computation of a correlation coefficient presume that certain measurement criteria have been satisfied by the data items employed. Specifically it is presumed that both items are measured at the interval level or higher. The reader should verify that this is, in fact, the case. What units of measurement are involved?

Most modern texts on statistics now include a discussion of the measurement criteria which must be met by the various computations and tests described. See for example, Blalock (1960), and Nie, et al. (1975). The reader should review several of these discussions for the more popularly employed computations and tests.

Subtle problems in the interpretation of a data analysis within a DSS may arise, because of the underlying interplay between measurement and statistics. For example, consider the "10-year average price/earnings ratio" which is a datum in the Portfolio Management System. What alternative interpretations of the datum exist, and under what circumstances might this influence the conclusions drawn from the subsequent data analysis?

Any statistic is *itself* a measurement, as well as being based on measurements. Thus a mean, or standard deviation, or correlation coefficient, may be examined in terms of the basic measurement concept presented in Figure 2.1. What is the nature of the empirical relational system described by such statistical measures? Is it "real" or abstract?

Recognition of the measurement bases of statistics has led occasionally to the establishment of certain rules to be followed by practitioners so as not to "violate" the

FIGURE 3.1   SCATTER. This function allows the managers to examine the relationship between two data items associated with securities held by an account. (Letters shown on the screen are the identification codes for particular securities, for example, MGI might be Magneto Industries.) Source: Keen and Scott Morton (1978), p. 117.

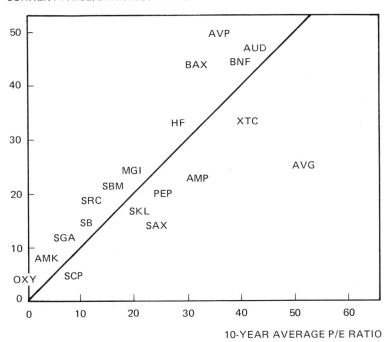

CURRENT PRICE/EARNINGS RATIO

10-YEAR AVERAGE P/E RATIO

underlying measurement assumptions. For example, it is often said that "ordinal numbers may not be added." By extension, the computation of the mean of a distribution of ordinal numbers would also be wrong. Is the reader inclined to agree? In the first reading Frederic Lord takes a humorous look at this old issue.

In the second reading, the measurement theorist S. S. Stevens looks forward to the demise of "the age of statistical indifference to the demands of measurement." In Stevens' words, "the relation between statistics and measurements is not a settled issue."

ON THE STATISTICAL TREATMENT
OF FOOTBALL NUMBERS

Frederic M. Lord

Professor X sold "football numbers." The television audience had to have some way to tell which player it was who caught the forward pass. So each player had to wear a number on his football uniform. It didn't matter what number, just so long as it wasn't more than a two-digit number.

Professor X loved numbers. Before retiring from teaching, Professor X had been chairman of the Department of Psychometrics. He would administer tests to all his students at every possible opportunity. He could hardly wait until the tests were scored. He would quickly stuff the scores in his pockets and hurry back to his office where he would lock the door, take the scores out again, add them up, and then calculate means and standard deviations for hours on end.

Professor X locked his door so that none of his students would catch him in his folly. He taught his students very carefully: "Test scores are ordinal numbers, not cardinal numbers. Ordinal numbers cannot be added. *A fortiori*, test scores cannot be multiplied or squared." The professor required his students to read the most up-to-date references on the theory of measurement (e.g., 1, 2, 3). Even the poorest student would quickly explain that it was wrong to compute means or standard deviations of test scores.

When the continual reproaches of conscience finally brought about a nervous breakdown, Professor X retired. In appreciation of his careful teaching, the university gave him the "football numbers" concession, together with a large supply of cloth numbers and a vending machine to sell them.

The first thing the professor did was to make a list of all the numbers given to him. The University had been generous and he found that he had exactly 100,000,000,000,000,000 two-digit cloth numbers to start out with. When he had listed them all on sheets of tabulating paper, he shuffled the pieces of cloth for two whole weeks. Then he put them in the vending machine.

If the numbers had been ordinal numbers, the Professor would have been sorely tempted to add them up, to square them, and to compute means and standard deviations. But these were not even serial numbers; they were only "football numbers"—they might as well have been letters of the alphabet. For instance, there were

2,681,793,401,686,191 pieces of cloth bearing the number "69," but there were only six pieces of cloth bearing the number "68," etc., etc. The numbers were for designation purposes only; there was no sense to them.

The first week, while the sophomore team bought its numbers, everything went fine. The second week the freshman team bought its numbers. By the end of the week there was trouble. Information secretly reached the professor that the numbers in the machine had been tampered with in some unspecified fashion.

The professor had barely had time to decide to investigate when the freshman team appeared in a body to complain. They said they had bought 1,600 numbers from the machine, and they complained the numbers were too low. The sophomore team was laughing at them because they had such low numbers. The freshmen were all for routing the sophomores out of their beds one by one and throwing them in the river.

Alarmed at this possibility, the professor temporized and persuaded the freshmen to wait while he consulted the statistician who lived across the street. Perhaps, after all, the freshmen had gotten low numbers just by chance. Hastily he put on his bowler hat, took his tabulating sheets, and knocked on the door of the statistician.

Now the statistician knew the story of the poor professor's resignation from his teaching. So, when the problem had been explained to him, the statistician chose not to use the elegant nonparametric methods of modern statistical analysis. Instead he took the professor's list of the 100 quadrillion "football numbers" that had been put into the machine. He added them all together and divided by 100 quadrillion.

"The population mean," he said, "is 54.3."

"But these numbers are not cardinal numbers," the professor expostulated. "You can't add them."

"Oh, can't I?" said the statistician. "I just did. Furthermore, after squaring each number, adding the squares, and proceeding in the usual fashion, I find the population standard deviation to be exactly 16.0."

"But you can't multiply 'football numbers,' " the professor wailed. "Why, they aren't even ordinal numbers, like test scores."

"The numbers don't know that," said the statistician. "Since the numbers don't remember where they came from, they always behave just the same way, regardless."

The professor gasped.

"Now the 1,600 'football numbers' the freshmen bought have a mean of 50.3," the statistician continued. "When I divide the difference between population and sample means by the population standard deviation. . . ."

"Divide!" moaned the professor.

". . . And then multiply by $\sqrt{1,600}$, I find a critical ratio of 10," the statistician went on, ignoring the interruption. "Now, if your population of 'football numbers' had happened to have a normal frequency distribution, I would be able rigorously to assure you that the sample of 1,600 obtained by the freshmen could have arisen from random sampling only once in 65,618,050,000,000,000,000,000 times; for in this case these numbers obviously would obey all the rules that apply to sampling from any normal population."

"You cannot . . ." began the professor.

"Since the population is obviously not normal, it will in this case suffice to use

Tchebycheff's inequality,"[1] the statistician continued calmly. "The probability of obtaining a value of 10 for such a critical ratio in random sampling from any population whatsoever is always less than .01. It is therefore highly implausible that the numbers obtained by the freshmen were actually a random sample of all numbers put into the machine."

"You cannot add and multiply any numbers except cardinal numbers," said the professor.

"If you doubt my conclusions," the statistician said coldly as he showed the professor to the door, "I suggest you try and see how often you can get a sample of 1,600 numbers from your machine with a mean below 50.3 or above 58.3. Good night."

To date, after reshuffling the numbers, the professor has drawn (with replacement) a little over 1,000,000,000 samples of 1,600 from his machine. Of these, only two samples have had means below 50.3 or above 58.3. He is continuing his sampling, since he enjoys the computations. But he has put a lock on his machine so that the sophomores cannot tamper with the numbers again. He is happy because, when he has added together a sample of 1,600 "football numbers," he finds that the resulting sum obeys the same laws of sampling as they would if they were real honest-to-God cardinal numbers.

Next year, he thinks, he will arrange things so that the population distribution of his "football numbers" is approximately normal. Then the means and standard deviations that he calculates from these numbers will obey the usual mathematical relations that have been proven to be applicable to random samples from any normal population.

The following year, recovering from his nervous breakdown, Professor X will give up the "football numbers" concession and resume his teaching. He will no longer lock his door when he computes the means and standard deviations of test scores.

ENDNOTES

1. Tchebycheff's inequality, in a convenient variant, states that in random sampling the probability that a critical ratio of the type calculated here will exceed any chosen constant, c, is always less than $1/c^2$, irrespective of the shape of the population distribution. It is impossible to devise a set of numbers for which this inequality will not hold.

REFERENCES

1. Coombs, C. H. Mathematical models in psychological scaling. *J. Amer. stat. Ass.*, 1951, **46**, 480–489.

2. Stevens, S. S. Mathematics, measurement, and psychophysics. In S. S. Stevens (Ed.), *Handbook of experimental psychology*. New York: Wiley, 1951. Pp. 1–49.

3. Weitzenhoffer, A. M. Mathematical structures and psychological measurements. *Psychometrika*, 1951, **16**, 387–406.

Questions for Study and Discussion

1. In the light of Lord's story, what is meant by the statistician's admonition not to perform arithmetic on ordinally scaled numbers?

2. A popular control procedure for the design of computer-based information systems involves the computation of what is termed a *hash total*. An example is the arithmetic sum of employee identification numbers in the processing of a batch of payroll transactions. Does such a computation violate underlying measurement assumptions? Should it be forbidden?

MEASUREMENT, STATISTICS, AND
THE SCHEMAPIRIC VIEW

S. S. Stevens

A curious antagonism has sometimes infected the relations between measurement and statistics. What ought to proceed as a pact of mutual assistance has seemed to some authors to justify a feud that centers on the degree of independence of the two domains. Thus Humphreys (1) dispenses praise to a textbook because its authors "do not follow the Stevens dictum concerning the precise relationships between scales of measurement and permissible statistical operations." Since that dictum, so-called, lurks as the *bête noire* behind many recurrent complaints, there is need to reexamine its burden and to ask how measurement and statistics shape up in the scientific process—the schemapiric endeavor in which we invent schematic models to map empirical domains.

In those disciplines where measurement is noisy, uncertain, and difficult, it is only natural that statistics should flourish. Of course, if there were no measurement at all, there would be no statistics. At the other extreme, if accurate measurement were achieved in every inquiry, many of the needs for statistics would vanish. Somewhere between the two extremes of no measurement and perfect measurement, perhaps near the psychosocial-behavioral center of gravity, the ratio of statisticizing to measuring reaches its maximum. And that is where we find an acute sensitivity to the suggestion that the type of measurement achieved in an experiment may set bounds on the kinds of statistics that will prove appropriate.

After reviewing the issues Anderson (2) concluded that "the statistical test can hardly be cognizant of the empirical meaning of the numbers with which it deals. Consequently," he continued, "the validity of the statistical inference cannot depend on the type of measuring scale used." This sequitur, if we may call it that, demands scrutiny, for it compresses large issues into a few phrases. Here let me observe merely that, however much we may agree that the statistical test cannot be cognizant of the empirical meaning of the numbers, the same privilege of ignorance can scarcely be extended to experimenters.

Speaking as a statistician, Savage (3) said, "I know of no reason to limit statistical procedures to those involving arithmetic operations consistent with the scale properties of the observed quantities." A statistician, like a computer, may perhaps feign

Reprinted from *Science*, 30 August 1968, Vol. 161, No. 3844, pp. 849–856. Copyright 1968 by the American Association for the Advancement of Science.

indifference to the origin of the numbers that enter into a statistical computation, but that indifference is not likely to be shared by the scientist. The man in the laboratory may rather suspect that, if something empirically useful is to emerge in the printout, something empirically meaningful must be programmed for the input.

Baker, Hardyck, and Petrinovich (4) summed up the distress: "If Stevens' position is correct, it should be emphasized more intensively; if it is incorrect, something should be done to alleviate the lingering feelings of guilt that plague research workers who deliberately use statistics such as *t* on weak measurements." If it is true that guilt must come before repentance, perhaps the age of statistical indifference to the demands of measurement may be drawing to a close. Whatever the outcome, the foregoing samples of opinion suggest that the relation between statistics and measurement is not a settled issue. Nor is it a simple issue, for it exhibits both theoretical and practical aspects. Moreover, peace is not likely to be restored until both principles and the pragmatics have been resolved.

THE SCHEMAPIRIC PRINCIPLE

Although measurement began in the empirical mode, with the accent on the counting of moons and paces and warriors, it was destined in modern times to find itself debated in the formal, schematic, syntactical mode, where models can be made to bristle with symbols. Mathematics, which like logic constitutes a formal endeavor, was not always regarded as an arbitrary construction devoid of substantive content, an adventure of postulate and theorem. In early ages mathematics and empirical measurement were as warp and woof, interpenetrating each other so closely that our ancestors thought it proper to prove arithmetic theorems by resort to counting or to some other act of measurement. The divorce took place only in recent times. And mathematics now enjoys full freedom to "play upon symbols," as Gauss phrased it, with no constraints imposed by the demands of empirical measurement.

So also with other formal or schematic systems. The propositions of a formal logic express tautologies that say nothing about the world of tangible stuff. They are analytic statements, so-called, and they stand apart from the synthetic statements that express facts and relations among empirical objects. There is a useful distinction to be made between the analytic, formal, syntactical propositions of logic and the synthetic, empirical statements of substantive discourse.

Sometimes the line may be hard to draw. Quine (5) the logician denies, in fact, that any sharp demarcation can be certified, and debate on the issue between him and Carnap has reached classic if unresolved proportions. For the scientist, meanwhile, the usefulness of the formal-empirical distinction need not be imperiled by the difficulty of making rigorous decisions in borderline cases. It is useful to distinguish between day and night despite the penumbral passage through twilight. So also is it useful to tune ourselves to distinguish between the formally schematic and the empirically substantive.

Probability exhibits the same double aspect, the same schemapiric nature. Mathematical theories of probability inhabit the formal realm as analytic, tautologous, schematic systems, and they say nothing at all about dice, roulette, or lotteries. On the empirical level, however, we count and tabulate events at the gaming table or in the laboratory and note their relative frequencies. Sometimes the relative frequencies stand in isomorphic relation to some property of a mathematical model of probability; at other times the observed frequencies exhibit scant accord with "expectations."

Those features of statistics that invoke a probabilistic schema provide a further instance of a formal-empirical dichotomy: the distinction between the probability model and the statistical data. E. B. Wilson (6), mathematician and statistician, made the point "that one must distinguish critically between probability as a purely mathematical subject of one sort or another, and statistics which cannot be so regarded." Statistics, of course, is a young discipline—one whose voice changes depending on who speaks for it. Many spokesmen would want to broaden the meaning of statistics to include a formal, mathematical segment.

In another context N. R. Hanson (7) pressed a similar distinction when he said, "Mathematics and physics on this account seem *logically* different disciplines, such that the former can only occasionally solve the latter's problems." Indeed, as Hanson later exclaimed, "Physicists have in unison pronounced, 'Let no man join what nature hath sundered, namely, the *formal creation* of spaces and the physical *description* of bodies.' " Yet it is precisely by way of the proper and judicious joining of the schematic with the empirical that we achieve our beneficial and effective mappings of the universe—the schemapiric mappings known as science. The chronic danger lies in our failure to note the distinction between the map and the terrain, between the simulation and the simulated. The map is an analogue, a schema, a model, a theory. Each of those words has a separate flavor, but they all share a common core of meaning. "Contrary to general belief," wrote Simon and Newell (8), "there is no fundamental, 'in principle,' difference between theories and analogies. All theories are analogies, and all analogies are theories." Indeed, the same can be said for all the other terms that designate the associative binding of schematics to empirics— what I have called the schemapiric bond.

SCALES AND INVARIANCE

Although it could be otherwise if our choice dictated, most measurement involves the assignment of numbers to aspects of objects or events according to one or another rule or convention. The variety of rules invented thus far for the assignment of numbers has already grown enormous, and novel means of measuring continue to emerge. It has proved possible, however, to formulate an invariance criterion for the classification of scales of measurement (9). The resulting systematization of scale types has found uses in contexts ranging from physics (10) to the social sciences (11), but the conception has not enjoyed immunity from criticism (12).

Let me sketch the theory. It can be done very briefly, because details are given in other places (13). The theory proposes that a scale type is defined by the group of transformations under which the scale form remains invariant, as follows.

A *nominal scale* admits any one-to-one substitution of the assigned numbers. Example of a nominal scale: the number of football players.

An *ordinal scale* can be transformed by any increasing monotonic function. Example of an ordinal scale: the hardness scale determined by the ability of one mineral to scratch another.

An *interval scale* can be subjected to a linear transformation. Examples of interval scales: temperature Fahrenheit and Celsius, calendar time, potential energy.

A *ratio scale* admits only multiplication by a constant. Examples of ratio scales: length, weight, density, temperature Kelvin, time intervals, loudness in sones.

The foregoing scales represent the four types in common use. Other types are possible. The permissible transformations defining a scale type are those that keep intact the empirical information depicted by the scale. If the empirical information has been preserved, the scale form is said to remain invariant. The critical isomorphism is maintained. That indeed is the principle of invariance that lies at the heart of the conception. More formal presentations of the foregoing theory have been undertaken by other authors, a recent one, for example, by Lea (*14*).

Unfortunately, those who demand an abstract tidiness that is completely aseptic may demur at the thought that the decision whether a particular scale enjoys the privilege of a particular transformation group depends on something so ill defined as the preservation of empirical information. For one thing, an empirical operation is always attended by error. Thus Lebesgue (*15*), who strove so well to perfect the concept of mathematical measure, took explicit note that, in the assignment of number to a physical magnitude, precision can be pushed, as he said, "in actuality only up to a certain error. It never enables us," he continued, "to discriminate between one number and all the numbers that are extremely close to it."

A second disconcerting feature of the invariance criterion lies in the difficulty of specifying the empirical information that is to be preserved. What can it be other than the information that we think we have captured by creating the scale in the first place? We may, for example, perform operations that allow us simply to identify or discriminate a particular property of an object. Sometimes we want to preserve nothing more than that simple outcome, the identification or nominal classification of the items of interest. Or we may go further, provided our empirical operations permit, and determine rank orders, equal intervals, or equal ratios. If we want our number assignments to reflect one or another accrual in information, we are free to transform the scale numbers only in a way that does not lose or distort the desired information. The choice remains ours.

Although some writers have found it possible to read an element of prescription—even proscription—into the invariance principle, as a systematizing device the principle contains no normative force. It can be read more as a description of the obvious than as a directive. It says that, once an isomorphism has been mapped out between aspects of objects or events, on the one hand, and some one or more features of the number system, on the other hand, the isomorphism can be upset by whatever transformations fail to preserve it. Precisely what is preserved or not preserved in a particular circumstance depends upon the empirical operations. Since actual day-to-day measurements range from muddled to meticulous, our ability to classify them in terms of scale type must range from hopelessly uncertain to relatively secure.

The group invariance that defines a scale type serves in turn to delimit the statistical procedures that can be said to be appropriate to a given measurement scale (*16*). Examples of appropriate statistics are tabulated in Table 1. Under the permissible transformations of a measurement scale, some appropriate statistics remain invariant in value (example: the correlation coefficient r keeps its value under linear transformations). Other statistics change value but refer to the same item or location (example: the median changes its value but continues to refer to mid-distribution under ordinal transformations).

TABLE 1. *Examples of statistical measures appropriate to measurements made on various types of scales. The scale type is defined by the manner in which scale numbers can be transformed without the loss of empirical information. The statistical measures listed are those that remain invariant, as regards either value or reference, under the transformations allowed by the scale type.*

Scale Type	Measures of Location	Dispersion	Association or Correlation	Significance Tests
Nominal	Mode	Information *H*	Information transmitted *T*	Chi square Fisher's exact test
Ordinal	Median	Percentiles	Rank correlation	Sign test Run test
Interval	Arithmetic mean	Standard deviation Average deviation	Product- moment correlation Correlation ratio	*t* test *F* test
Ratio	Geometric mean Harmonic mean	Percent variation Decilog dispersion		

RECONCILIATION AND NEW PROBLEMS

Two developments may serve to ease the apprehension among those who may have felt threatened by a theory of measurement that seems to place bounds on our freedom to calculate. One is a clearer understanding of the bipartite, schemapiric nature of the scientific enterprise. When the issue concerns only the schema—when, for example, critical ratios are calculated for an assumed binomial distribution—then indeed it is purely a matter of relations within a mathematical model. Natural facts stand silent. Empirical considerations impose no constraints. When, however, the text asserts a relation among such things as measured differences or variabilities, we have a right and an obligation to inquire about the operations that underlie the measurements. Those operations determine, in turn, the type of scale achieved.

The two-part schemapiric view was expressed by Hays (*17*) in a much-praised book: "If the statistical method involves the procedures of arithmetic used on numerical scores, then the numerical answer is formally correct. . . . The difficulty comes with the interpretation of these numbers back into statements about the real world. If nonsense is put into the mathematical system, nonsense is sure to come out."

At the level of the formal model, then, statistical computations may proceed as freely as in any other syntactical exercise, unimpeded by any material outcome of empirical measurement. Nor does measurement have a presumptive voice in the creation of the statistical models themselves. As Hogben (*18*) said in his forthright dissection of statistical theory, "It is entirely defensible to formulate an axiomatic approach to the theory of probability as an internally consistent set of propositions, if one is content to leave to those in closer contact with reality the last word on the usefulness of the outcome." Both Hays and Hogben insist that the user of statistics, the man in the laboratory, the maker of measurements, must decide the meaning of the numbers and their capacity to advance empirical inquiry.

The second road to reconciliation winds through a region only partly explored, a region wherein lies the pragmatic problem of appraising the wages of transgression. What is the degree of risk entailed when use is made of statistics that may be inappropriate in the strict sense that they fail the test of invariance under permissible scale transformations? Specifically, let us assume that a set of items can be set in rank order, but, by the operations thus far invented, distances between the items cannot be determined. We have an ordinal but not an interval scale. What happens then if interval-scale statistics are applied to the ordinally scaled items? Therein lies a question of first-rate substance and one that should be amenable to unemotional investigation. It promises well that a few answers have already been forthcoming.

First there is the oft-heeded counsel of common sense. In the averaging of test scores, says Mosteller (*19*), "It seems sensible to use the statistics appropriate to the type of scale I think I am near. In taking such action we may find the justification vague and fuzzy. One reason for this vagueness is that we have not yet studied enough about classes of scales, classes appropriate to real life measurement, with perhaps real life bias and error variance."

How some of the vagueness of which Mosteller spoke can perhaps be removed is illustrated by the study of Abelson and Tukey (*20*) who showed how bounds may be determined for the risk involved when an interval-scale statistic is used with an ordinal scale. Specifically, they explored the effect on r^2 of a game against nature in which nature does its best (or worst!) to minimize the value of r^2. In this game of regression analysis, many interesting cases were explored, but, as the authors said, their methods need extension to other cases. They noted that we often know more about ordinal data than mere rank order. We may have reason to believe, they said, "that the scale is no worse than mildly curvilinear, that Nature behaves smoothly in some sense." Indeed the continued use of parametric statistics with ordinal data rests on that belief, a belief sustained in large measure by the pragmatic usefulness of the results achieved.

In a more synthetic study than the foregoing analysis, Baker *et al.* (*4*) imposed sets of monotonic transformations on an assumed set of data, and calculated the effect on the *t* distribution. The purpose was to compare distributions of *t* for data drawn from an equal-interval scale with distributions of *t* for several types of assumed distortions of the equal intervals. By and large, the effects on the computed *t* distributions were not large, and the authors concluded "that strong statistics such as the *t* test are more adequate to cope with weak [ordinal] measurements. . . ." It should be noted, however, that the values of *t* were affected by the nonlinear transformations. As the authors said, "The correspondence between values of *t* based on the criterion unit interval scores and values of *t* based on [nonlinear] transformations decreases regularly and dramatically . . . as the departure from linear transformations becomes more extreme."

Whatever the substantive outcome of such investigations may prove to be, they point the way to reconciliation through orderly inquiry. Debate gives way to calculation. The question is thereby made to turn, not on whether the measurement scale determines the choice of a statistical procedure, but on how and to what degree an inappropriate statistic may lead to a deviant conclusion. The solution of such problems may help to refurbish the complexion of measurement theory, which has been accused of proscribing those statistics that do not remain invariant under the transformations appropriate to a given scale. By spelling out the costs, we may convert the issue from a seeming proscription to a calculated risk.

The type of measurement achieved is not, of course, the only consideration affecting the applicability of parametric statistics. Bradley is one of many scholars who have sifted the consequences of violating the assumptions that underlie some of the common parametric tests (21). As one outcome of his studies, Bradley concluded, "The contention that, when its assumptions are violated, a parametric test is still to be preferred to a distribution-free test because it is 'more efficient' is therefore a monumental *non sequitur.* The point is not at all academic . . . violations in a test's assumptions may be attended by profound changes in its power." That conclusion is not without relevance to scales of measurement, for when ordinal data are forced into the equal-interval mold, parametric assumptions are apt to be violated. It is then that a so-called distribution-free statistic may prove more efficient than its parametric counterpart.

Although better accommodation among certain of the contending statistical usages may be brought about by computer-aided studies, there remain many statistics that find their use only with specific kinds of scales. A single example may suffice. In a classic textbook, written with a captivating clarity, Peters and Van Voorhis (22) got hung up on a minor point concerning the procedure to be used in comparing variabilities. They noted that Karl Pearson had proposed a measure called the coefficient of variation, which expresses the standard deviation as a percentage of the mean. The authors expressed doubts about its value, however, because it tells "more about the extent to which the scores are padded by a dislocation of the zero point than it does about comparable variablities." The examples and arguments given by the authors make it plain that the coefficient of variation has little business being used with what I have called interval scales. But since their book antedated my publication in 1946 of the defining invariances for interval and ratio scales, Peters and Van Voorhis did not have a convenient way to state the relationship made explicit in Table 1, namely, that the coefficient of variation, being itself a ratio, calls for a ratio scale.

COMPLEXITIES AND PITFALLS

Concepts like relative variability have the virtue of being uncomplicated and easy for the scientist to grasp. They fit his idiom. But in the current statistics explosion, which showers the investigator with a dense fallout of new statistical models, the scientist is likely to lose the thread on many issues. It is then that the theory of measurement, with an anchor hooked fast in empirical reality, may serve as a sanctuary against the turbulence of specialized abstraction.

"As a mathematical discipline travels far from its empirical source," said von Neumann (23), "there is grave danger that the subject will develop along the line of least resistance, that the stream, so far from its source, will separate into a multitude of insignificant branches, and that the discipline will become a disorganized mass of details and complexities." He went on to say that, "After much 'abstract' inbreeding, a mathematical subject is in danger of degeneration. At the inception the style is usually classical; when it shows signs of becoming baroque, then the danger signal is up."

There is a sense, one suspects, in which statistics needs measurement more than measurement needs statistics. R. A. Fisher alluded to that need in his discourse on the nature of probability (24) "I am quite sure," he said, "it is only personal contact with the business of the improvement of natural knowledge in the natural sciences that is capable to keep straight the thought of mathematically-minded people who have to grope their way through the complex entanglements of error. . . ."

And lest the physical sciences should seem immune to what Schwartz (25) called "the pernicious influence of mathematics," consider his diagnosis: "Thus, in its relations with science, mathematics depends on an intellectual effort outside of mathematics for the crucial specification of the approximation which mathematics is to take literally. Give a mathematician a situation which is the least bit ill-defined—he will first of all make it well defined. Perhaps appropriately, but perhaps also inappropriately. . . . That form of wisdom which is the opposite of single-mindedness, the ability to keep many threads in hand, to draw for an argument from many disparate sources, is quite foreign to mathematics. . . . Quite typically, science leaps ahead and mathematics plods behind."

Progress in statistics often follows a similar road from practice to prescription—from field trials to the formalization of principles. As Kruskal (26) said, "Theoretical study of a statistical procedure often comes after its intuitive proposal and use." Unfortunately for the empirical concerns of the practitioners, however, there is, as Kruskal added, "almost no end to the possible theoretical study of even the simplest procedure." So the discipline wanders far from its empirical source, and form loses sight of substance.

Not only do the forward thrusts of science often precede the mopping-up campaigns of the mathematical schema builders, but measurement itself may often find implementation only after some basic conception has been voiced. Textbooks, those distilled artifices of science, like to picture scientific conceptions as built on measurement, but the working scientist is more apt to devise his measurements to suit his conceptions. As Kuhn (27) said, "The route from theory or law to measurement can almost never be travelled backwards. Numbers gathered without some knowledge of the regularity to be expected almost never speak for themselves. Almost certainly they remain just numbers." Yet who would deny that some ears, more tuned to numbers, may hear them speak in fresh and revealing ways?

The intent here is not, of course, to affront the qualities of a discipline as useful as mathematics. Its virtues and power are too great to need extolling, but in power lies a certain danger. For mathematics, like a computer, obeys commands and asks no questions. It will process any input, however devoid of scientific sense, and it will bedeck in formulas both the meaningful and the absurd. In the behavioral sciences, where the discernment for nonsense is perhaps less sharply honed than in the physical sciences, the vigil must remain especially alert against the intrusion of a defective theory merely because it carries a mathematical visa. An absurdity in full formularized attire may be more seductive than an absurdity undressed.

DISTRIBUTIONS AND DECISIONS

The scientist often scales items, counts them, and plots their frequency distributions. He is sometimes interested in the form of such distributions. If his data have been obtained from measurements made on interval or ratio scales, the shape of the distribution stays put (up to a scale factor) under those transformations that are permissible, namely, those that preserve the empirical information contained in the measurements. The principle seems straightforward. But what happens when the state of the art can produce no more than a rank ordering, and hence nothing better than an ordinal scale? The abscissa of the frequency distribution then loses its metric meaning and becomes like a rubber band, capable of all sorts of monotonic stretchings. With each nonlinear transformation of the scale, the form of the distribution changes. Thereupon the distribution loses structure, and we find it futile to ask whether the shape approximates a particular form, whether normal, rectangular, or whatever.

Working on the formal level, the statistician may contrive a schematic model by first assuming a frequency function, or a distribution function, of one kind or another. At the abstract level of mathematical creation, there can, of course, be no quarrel with the statistician's approach to his task. The caution light turns on, however, as soon as the model is asked to mirror an empirical domain. We must then invoke a set of semantic rules—coordinating definitions—in order to identify correspondences between model and reality. What shall we say about the frequency function $f(x)$ when the problem before us allows only an ordinal scale? Shall x be subject to a nonlinear transformation after $f(x)$ has been specified? If so, what does the transformation do to the model and the predictions it forecasts?

The scientist has reason to feel that a statistical model that specifies the form of a canonical distribution becomes uninterpretable when the empirical domain concerns only ordinal data. Yet many consumers of statistics seem to disregard what to others is a rather obvious and critical problem. Thus Burke (*28*) proposed to draw "two random samples from populations known to be normal" and then "to test the hypothesis that the two populations have the same mean . . . under the assumption that the scale is ordinal at best." How, we must ask, can normality be known when only order can be certified?

The assumption of normality is repeated so blithely and so often that it becomes a kind of incantation. If enough of us sin, perhaps transgression becomes a virtue. But in the instance before us, where the numbers to be fed into the statistical mill result from operations that allow only a rank ordering, maybe we have gone too far. Consider a permissible transformation. Let us cube all the numbers. The rank order would stand as before. But what do we then say about normality? If we can know nothing about the intervals on the scale of a variable, the postulation that a distribution has a particular form would appear to proclaim a hope, not a circumstance.

The assertion that a variable is normally distributed when the variable is amenable only to ordinal measurement may loom as an acute contradiction, but it qualifies as neither the worst nor the most frequent infraction by some of the practitioners of hypothesis testing. Scientific decision by statistical calculation has become the common mode in many behavioral disciplines. In six psychological journals (*29*), for example, the proportion of articles that employed one or another kind of inferential statistic rose steadily from 56 percent in 1948 to 91 percent in 1962. In the *Journal of Educational Psychology* the proportion rose from 36 to 100 percent.

What does it mean? Can no one recognize a decisive result without a significance test? How much can the burgeoning of computation be blamed on fad? How often does inferential computation serve as a premature excuse for going to press? Whether the scholar has discovered something or not, he can sometimes subject his data to an analysis of variance, a *t* test, or some other device that will produce a so-called objective measure of "significance." The illusion of objectivity seems to preserve itself despite the admitted necessity for the investigator to make improbable assumptions, and to pluck off the top of his head a figure for the level of probability that he will consider significant. His argument that convention has already chosen the level that he will use does not quite absolve him.

Lubin (30) has a name for those who censure the computational and applaud the experimental in the search for scientific certainty. He calls them stochastophobes. An apt title, if applied to those whose eagerness to lay hold on the natural fact may generate impatience at the gratuitous processing of data. The extreme stochastophobe is likely to ask: What scientific discoveries owe their existence to the techniques of statistical analysis or inference? If exercises in statistical inference have occasioned few instances of a scientific breakthrough, the stochastophobe may want to ask by what magical view the stochastophile perceives glamour in statistics. The charm may stem in part from the prestige that mathematics, however inapposite, confers on those who display the dexterity of calculation. For some stochastophiles the appeal may have no deeper roots than a preference for the prudent posture at a desk as opposed to the harsher, more venturesome stance in the field or the laboratory.

The aspersions voiced by stochastophobes fall mainly on those scientists who seem, by the surfeit of their statistical chants, to turn data treatment into hierurgy. These are not the statisticians themselves, for they see statistics for what it is, a straightforward discipline designed to amplify the power of common sense in the discernment of order amid complexity. By showing how to amend the mismatch in the impedance between question and evidence, the statistician improves the probability that our experiments will speak with greater clarity. And by weighing the entailments of relevant assumptions, he shows us how to milk the most from some of those fortuitous experiments that nature performs once and may never perform again. The stochastophobe should find no quarrel here. Rather he should turn his despair into a hope that the problem of the relevance of this or that statistical model may lead the research man toward thoughtful inquiry, not to a reflex decision based on a burst of computation.

MEASUREMENT

If the vehemence of the debate that centers on the nature and conditions of statistical inference has hinted at the vulnerability of the conception, what can be said about the other partner in the enterprise? Is the theory of measurement a settled matter? Apparently not, for it remains a topic of trenchant inquiry, not yet ready to rest its case. And debate continues.

The typical scientist pays little attention to the theory of measurement, and with good reason, for the laboratory procedures for most measurements have been well worked out, and the scientist knows how to read his dials. Most of his variables are measured on well-defined, well-instrumented ratio scales.

Among those whose interests center on variables that are not reducible to meter readings, however, the concern with measurement stays acute. How, for example, shall we measure subjective value (what the economist calls utility), or perceived brightness or the seriousness of crimes? Those are some of the substantive problems that have forced a revision in our approach to measurement. They have entailed a loosening of the restricted view bequeathed us by the tradition of Helmholtz and Campbell—the view that the axioms of additivity must govern what we call measurement (31). As a related development, new axiomatic systems have appeared, including axioms by Luce and Tukey (32) for a novel "conjoint" approach to the fundamental measurement. But the purpose here is not to survey the formal, schematic models that have flowered in the various sciences, for the practice and conception of measurement has as yet been little influenced by them.

As with many syntactical developments, measurement models sometimes drift off into the vacuum of abstraction and become decoupled from their concrete reference. Even those authors who freely admit the empirical features as partners in the formulation of measurement may find themselves seeming to downgrade the empirical in favor of the formal. Thus we find Suppes and Zinnes (33) saying, "Some writers . . . appear to define scales in terms of the existence of certain empirical operations. . . . In the present formulation of scale type, no mention is made of the kinds of 'direct' observations or empirical relations that exist. . . . Precisely what empirical operations are involved in the empirical system is of no consequence."

How then do we distinguish different types of scales? How, in particular, do we know whether a given scale belongs among the interval scales? Suppes and Zinnes gave what I think is a proper answer: "We ask if all the admissible numerical assignments are related by a linear transformation." That, however, is not a complete answer. There remains a further question: What is it that makes a class of numerical assignments admissible? A full theory of measurement cannot detach itself from the empirical substrate that gives it meaning. But the theorist grows impatient with the empirical lumps that ruffle the fine laminar flow within his models just as the laboratory fellow may disdain the arid swirls of hieroglyphics that pose as paradigms of his measurements.

Although a congenial conciliation between those two polar temperaments, the modeler and the measurer, may lie beyond reasonable expectations, a tempering détente may prove viable. The two components of schemapirics must both be accredited, each in its own imperative role. To the understanding of the world about us, neither the formal model nor the concrete measure is dispensable.

MATCHING AND MAPPING

Instead of starting with origins, many accounts of measurement begin with one or another advanced state of the measuring process, a state in which units and metrics can be taken for granted. At that level, the topic already has the crust of convention upon it, obscuring the deeper problems related to its nature.

If we try to push the problem of measurement back closer to its primordial operations, we find, I think, that the basic operation is always a process of matching.

That statement may sound innocent enough, but it contains a useful prescription. It suggests, for example, that if you would understand the essence of a given measuring procedure, you should ask what was matched to what. If the query leads to a pointer reading, do not stop there; ask the same question about the calibration procedure that was applied to the instruments anterior to the pointer: What was matched to what? Diligent pursuit of that question along the chain of measuring operations leads to some of the elemental operations of science.

Or we may start nearer the primordium. The sketchiness of the record forces us to conjecture the earliest history, but quite probably our forefather kept score on the numerosity of his possessions with the aid of piles of pebbles [Latin: *calculi*] or by means of some other tallying device. He paired off items against pebbles by means of a primitive matching operation, and he thereby measured his hoard.

Let us pause at this point to consider the preceding clause. Can the ancestor in question be said to have measured his possessions if he had no number system? Not if we insist on taking literally the definition often given, namely, that measurement is the assignment of numbers to objects or events according to rule. This definition serves a good purpose in many contexts, but it presumes a stage of development beyond the one that we are now seeking to probe. In an elemental sense, the matching or assigning of numbers is a sufficient but not a necessary condition for measurement, for other kinds of matching may give measures.

Numbers presumably arose after our ancestor invented names for the collection of pebbles, or perhaps for the more convenient collections, the fingers. He could then match name to collection, and collection to possessions. That gave him a method of counting, for, by pairing off each item against a finger name in an order decided upon, the name of the collection of items, and hence the numerosity of the items, was specified.

The matching principle leads to the concept of cardinality. Two sets have the same cardinal number if they can be paired off in one-to-one relation by each other. By itself, this cardinal pairing off says nothing about order. (Dictionaries often disagree with the mathematicians on the definition of cardinality, but the mathematical usage recommends itself here.) We find the cardinal principle embodied in the symbols used for the numerals in many forms of writing. Thus the Roman numeral VI pictures a hand V and a finger I.

Let us return again to our central question. In the early cardinal procedure of matching item to item, fingers to items, or names to items, at what point shall we say that measurement began? Perhaps we had best not seek a line of demarcation between measurement and matching. It may be better to go all the way and propose an unstinted definition as follows: Measurement is the matching of an aspect of one domain to an aspect of another.

The operation of matching eventuates, of course, in one domain's being mapped into another, as regards one or more attributes of the two domains. In the larger sense, then, whenever a feature of one domain is mapped isomorphically in some relation with a feature of another domain, measurement is achieved. The relation is potentially symmetrical. Our hypothetical forefather could measure his collection of fish by means of his pile of pebbles, or his pile of pebbles by means of his collection of fish.

Our contemporary concern lies not, of course, with pebbles and fish, but with a principle. We need to break the hull that confines the custom of our thought about these matters. The concern is more than merely academic, however, especially in the field of psychophysics. One justification for the enlarged view of measurement lies in a development in sensory measurement known as cross-modality matching (34). In a suitable laboratory setup, the subject is asked, for example, to adjust the loudness of a sound applied to his ears in order to make it seem equal to the perceived strength of a vibration applied to his finger. The amplitude of the vibration is then changed and the matching process is repeated. An equal sensation function is thereby mapped out, as illustrated in Fig. 1. Loudness has been matched in that manner to ranges of values on some ten other perceptual continua, always with the result that the matching function approximates a power function (35). In other words, in order to produce equal apparent intensity, the amplitude of the sound p must be a power function of the amplitude of the vibration a, or $p = a^b$, where b is the exponent. Or, more simply, the logarithms of the stimuli are linearly related, which means that ratios of stimuli are proportional.

Experiments suggest that the power function obtains between all pairs of intensive perceptual continua, and that the matchings exhibit a strong degree of transitivity in the sense that the exponents form an interconnected net. If two matching func-

FIGURE 1. Equal-sensation function for cross-modality matching between loudness and vibration. The squares indicate that the observers adjusted the intensity of vibration on the fingertip to match the loudness of a noise delivered by earphones. The circles indicate that the observers adjusted the loudness to match the vibration. Each point is the decibel average of 20 matches, two by each of ten observers. Since the coordinates are logarithmic, the straight line indicates a power function.

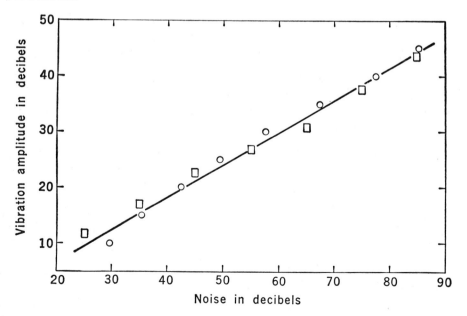

tions have one continuum in common, we can predict fairly well the exponent of the matching function between the other two continua.

Now, once we have mapped out the matching function between loudness and vibration, we can, if we choose, measure the subjective strength of the vibration in terms of its equivalent loudness. Or, more generally, if all pairs of continua have been matched, we can select any one continuum to serve as the reference continuum in terms of which we then measure the subjective magnitude on each of the other continua.

In the description of a measurement system that rests on cross-modality matching, no mention has been made of numbers. If we are willing to start from scratch in a measurement of this kind, numbers can in principle be dispensed with. They would, to be sure, have practical uses in the conduct of the experiments, but by using other signs or tokens to identify the stimuli we could presumably eliminate numbers completely. It would be a tour de force, no doubt, but an instructive one.

Instead of dispensing with numbers, the practice in many psychophysical studies has been to treat numbers as one of the perceptual continua in the cross-modality matching experiment. Thus in what has come to be known as the method of magnitude estimation, numbers are matched to loudness, say. In the reverse procedure, called magnitude production, the subject adjusts the loudness to match a series of numbers given by the experimenter (36). And as might be expected, despite all the other kinds of cross-modality matches that have been made, it is the number continuum that most authors select as the reference continuum (exponent = 1.0) in terms of which the exponent values for the other perceptual continua are stated. But the point deserves to be stressed: the choice of number as the reference continuum is wholly arbitrary, albeit eminently convenient.

SUMMARY

Back in the days when measurement meant mainly counting, and statistics meant mainly the inventory of the state, the simple descriptive procedures of enumeration and averaging occasioned minimum conflict between measurement and statistics. But as measurement pushed on into novel behavioral domains, and statistics turned to the formalizing of stochastic models, the one-time intimate relation between the two activities dissolved into occasional misunderstanding. Measurement and statistics must live in peace, however, for both must participate in the schemapiric enterprise by which the schematic model is made to map the empirical observation.

Science presents itself as a two-faced, bipartite endeavor looking at once toward the formal, analytic, schematic features of model-building, and toward the concrete, empirical, experiential observations by which we test the usefulness of a particular representation. Schematics and empirics are both essential to science, and full understanding demands that we know which is which.

Measurement provides the numbers that enter the statistical table. But the numbers that issue from measurements have strings attached, for they carry the imprint of the operations by which they were obtained. Some transformations on the numbers will leave intact the information gained by the measurements; other transformations will destroy the desired isomorphism between the measurement scale and the property assessed. Scales of measurement therefore find a useful classification on the basis of a principle of invariance: each of the common scale types (nominal, ordinal, interval, and ratio) is defined by a group of transformations that leaves a particular isomorphism unimpaired.

Since the transformations allowed by a given scale type will alter the numbers that enter into a statistical procedure, the procedure ought properly to be one that can withstand that particular kind of number alteration. Therein lies the primacy of measurement: it sets bounds on the appropriateness of statistical operations. The widespread use on ordinal scales of statistics appropriate only to interval or ratio scales can be said to violate a technical canon, but in many instances the outcome has demonstrable utility. A few workers have begun to assess the degree of risk entailed by the use of statistics that do not remain invariant under the permissible scale transformations.

The view is proposed that measurement can be most liberally construed as the process of matching elements of one domain to those of another domain. In most kinds of measurement we match numbers to objects or events, but other matchings have been found to serve a useful purpose. The cross-modality matching of one sensory continuum to another has shown that sensory intensity increases as the stimulus intensity raised to a power. The generality of that finding supports a psychophysical law expressible as a simple invariance: equal stimulus ratios produce equal sensation ratios.

REFERENCES AND NOTES

1. L. Humphreys, *Contemp. Psychol.* **9,** 76 (1964).
2. N. H. Anderson, *Psychol. Bull.* **58,** 305 (1961).
3. I. R. Savage, *J. Amer. Statist. Ass.* **52,** 331 (1957).
4. B. O. Baker, C. D. Hardyck, L. F. Petrinovich, *Educ. Psychol. Meas.* **26,** 291 (1966).
5. W. V. O. Quine, *The Ways of Paradox and Other Essays* (Random House, New York, 1966), pp. 126–134.
6. E. B. Wilson, *Proc. Natl. Acad. Sci, U.S.* **51,** 539 (1964).
7. N. R. Hanson, *Philos. Sci.* **30,** 107 (1963).
8. H. A. Simon and A. Newell, in *The State of the Social Sciences,* L. D. White, Ed. (Univ. of Chicago Press, Chicago, 1956), pp. 66–83.
9. S. S. Stevens, *Science* **103,** 677 (1946).
10. F. B. Silsbee, *J. Wash. Acad. Sci.* **41,** 213 (1951).
11. B. F. Green, in *Handbook of Social Psychology,* G. Lindzey, Ed. (Addison-Wesley, Reading, Mass., 1954), pp. 335–369.
12. Among those who have commented are B. Ellis, *Basic Concepts of Measurement* (University Press, Cambridge, England, 1966); B. Grunstra, "On Distinguishing Types of Measurement," *Boston Studies Phil. Sci.,* vol. 4 (Humanities Press, in press); S. Ross, *Logical Foundations of Psychological Measurement* (Scandinavian University Books, Munksgaard, Copenhagen, 1964); W. W. Rozeboom, *Synthese* **16,** 170–233 (1966); W. S. Torgerson, *Theory and Methods of Scaling* (Wiley, New York, 1958).
13. S. S. Stevens, in *Handbook of Experimental Psychology,* S. S. Stevens, Ed. (Wiley, New York, 1951), pp. 1–49; _____, in *Measurement: Definitions and Theories,* C. W. Churchman and P. Ratoosh, Eds. (Wiley, New York, 1959), pp. 18–64.

14. W. A. Lea, "A Formalization of Measurement Scale Forms" (Technical Memo. KC-T-024, Computer Research Lab., NASA Electronics Res. Ctr., Cambridge, Mass., June 1967).

15. H. Lebesgue, *Measure and the Integral*, K. O. May, Ed. (Holden-Day, San Francisco, 1966).

16. Other summarizing tables are presented by V. Senders, *Measurement and Statistics* (Oxford Univ. Press, New York, 1958). A further analysis of appropriate statistics has been presented by E. W. Adams, R. F. Fagot, R. E. Robinson, *Psychometrika* **30**, 99 (1965).

17. W. L. Hays, *Statistics for Psychologists* (Holt, Rinehart & Winston, New York, 1963).

18. L. Hogben, *Statistical Theory* (Norton, New York, 1958).

19. F. Mosteller, *Psychometrika* **23**, 279 (1958).

20. R. P. Abelson and J. W. Tukey, *Efficient Conversion of Non-Metric Information into Metric Information* (Amer. Statist. Ass., Social Statist. Sec., December 1959), pp. 226–230; see also _____, *Ann. Math. Stat.* **34**, 1347 (1963).

21. J. V. Bradley, "Studies in Research Methodology: II. Consequences of Violating Parametric Assumptions—Facts and Fallacy" (WADC Tech. Rep. 58-574 [II], Aerospace Med. Lab., Wright-Patterson AFB, Ohio, September 1959).

22. C. C. Peters and W. R. Van Voorhis, *Statistical Procedures and Their Mathematical Bases* (McGraw-Hill, New York, 1940).

23. J. von Neumann, in *The Works of the Mind*, R. B. Heywood, Ed. (Univ. of Chicago Press, Chicago, 1947), pp. 180–196.

24. R. A. Fisher, *Smoking, the Cancer Controversy* (Oliver and Boyd, Edinburgh, 1959).

25. J. Schwartz, in *Logic, Methodology and Philosophy of Science*, E. Nagel *et al.*, Eds., (Stanford Univ. Press, Stanford, Calif., 1962), pp. 356–360.

26. W. R. Kruskal, in *International Encyclopedia of the Social Sciences* (Macmillan and Free Press, New York, 1968), vol. 15, pp. 206–224.

27. T. S. Kuhn, in *Quantification*, H. Woolf, Ed. (Bobbs-Merrill, Indianapolis, Ind., 1961), pp. 31–63.

28. C. J. Burke, in *Theories in Contemporary Psychology*, M. H. Marx, Ed. (Macmillan, New York, 1963), pp. 147–159.

29. The journals were tabulated by E. S. Edgington, *Amer. Psychologist* **19**, 202 (1964); also personal communication.

30. A. Lubin, in *Annual Review of Psychology* (Annual Reviews, Palo Alto, Calif., 1962), vol. 13, pp. 345–370.

31. H. v. Helmholtz, "Zählen und Messen," in *Philosophische Aufsätze* (Fues's Verlag, Leipzig, 1887), pp. 17–52; N. R. Campbell, *Physics: the Elements* [1920] (reissued as *The Philosophy of Theory and Experiment* by Dover, New York, 1957); _____, *Symposium: Measurement and Its Importance for Philosophy*. Aristotelian Soc., suppl., vol. 17 (Harrison and Sons, London, 1938).

32. R. D. Luce and J. W. Tukey, *J. Math. Psychol.* **1**, 1 (1964).

33. P. Suppes and J. L. Zinnes, in *Handbook of Mathematical Psychology*, R. D. Luce *et al.*, Eds. (Wiley, New York, 1963), pp. 1–76.

34. S. S. Stevens, *J. Exp. Psychol.* **57**, 201 (1959); *Amer. Sci.* **54**, 385 (1966).

35. _____, *Percept. Psychophys.* **1**, 5 (1966).

36. _____ and H. B. Greenbaum, *ibid.*, p. 439.

37. This article (Laboratory of Psychophysics Rept. PPR-336-118) was prepared with support from NIH grant NB-02974 and NSF grant GB-3211.

Questions for Study and Discussion

1. Stevens argues that, "if you would understand the essence of a given measuring procedure, you should ask what was matched to what." How does this apply to the "furniture problem" discussed earlier? (see p. 33) How might this apply to a system for measuring managerial performance in a firm?

2. According to one author quoted by Stevens, "the validity of the statistical inference cannot depend on the type of measuring scale used." Stevens responds: " . . . let me observe merely that, however much we may agree that the statistical test cannot be cognizant of the empirical meaning of the numbers, the same privilege or ignorance can scarcely be extended to experimenters." In your view, what is at stake in this disagreement? How does this pertain to the statistical treatment of football numbers discussed by Lord? (For further views on the issue, see Behan and Behan, 1954, and Stevens, 1959.)

CHAPTER **FOUR**

A recent article in the *Wall Street Journal* (February 23, 1977) reports a dispute involving the Motor Vehicle Department of the state of California. According to the department, a clerk needs ten minutes to process a driver's license application. Not so, according to the state's auditor general staff, which figures that only six minutes are required. "Who cares?" one might ask. What is at stake in this measurement dispute?

At stake is the department budget. According to the auditor general staff, the four-minute difference translates into 158 more workers at an annual cost of $1.9 million.

The choice of a budget level represents a decision, in this case a political, more than a managerial decision. The measurements of the time required to process a driver's license application are examples of *work measurement,* which will be discussed in more detail in a forthcoming section. They are made not for scientific but for practical reasons, in support of the decision-making process. In the present subsection, the foundations of measuring in support of decision making are examined.

The first reading, by C. West Churchman, presents a typology of measurements which is fundamental to decision support. The article by Mason develops the implications of this typology for the design of management information systems. In their departure from the traditional measurement concerns of the scientist, the two articles serve as the central linking pin to the readings in the rest of the book.

SUGGESTIVE, PREDICTIVE, DECISIVE AND SYSTEMIC MEASUREMENTS

C. West Churchman

This is an essay on the subject of measurement, with "safety" as a central illustration. The interest is not so much in the technical characteristics of measurements as in their use. The thesis is that measurement is a special type of information which is applicable in many different contexts ("broad") and permits a high degree of differentiation ("deep"). The thesis has been explored in general in an earlier essay[1]; this paper attempts to take the basic idea further by classifying information into four categories, *suggestive*, *predictive*, *decisive*, and *systemic*. To get the flavor of these categories before exploring their meaning in depth, consider the following pieces of information:

1. *suggestive:* the fatality rate per man year in this factory has been .01%.

2. *predictive:* 20% of all serious accidents in this plant were caused by failure of the workers to wear safety equipment.

3. *decisive:* masks of this type when used in this plant would cost $20,000 per year, and the benefit per year in accident reduction would be $100,000.

4. *systemic:* reduction in accidents in this factory is the third most important project of the system.

In considering these categories, it will be worthwhile placing this effort within the general setting of the literature on measurement. One large section of this literature is logical, and attempts to classify various types of measurement scales.[2] A second part of the literature is technical, and concerns itself with specific calibration techniques.[3] In neither branch of the literature is there a specific interest in the way in which measurement is used, except to say that it is "quantitative," and imply that this is a good thing.

Now merely to assign numbers to events or objects in the world is not necessarily a good thing at all; it may, in fact, be as dreary a process as one can imagine, as any non-baseballer can attest after listening to two fans discussing some history. A better idea of what is involved in measurement can be obtained by recalling the "Maine mile"; if you ask a Maine farmer how far it is to Grand Lake, he might well reply "about a mile." What he means is "some distance" or "not around the next

Paper presented at the 2nd Symposium on Industrial Safety Performance Measurement, National Safety Council, Chicago, December, 1968.

bend." A more literal minded measurer would want to distinguish between "about a mile" and "about two miles." Measurement, as we interpret it here, is above all as literal as it can be, and the ambition of the measurer is to create finer and finer distinctions and broader and broader usage.

To illustrate breadth and depth, consider the measurement of the tides. From certain basic properties of the earth and moon, one can generate tables that tell us what the depth of tide will be at various places at various times, with precision, in feet, out to the first or second decimal place. A contrast is some statement about the number of pedestrians killed in a city during a month; little useful information is to be culled from this statistic alone.

But one might wish to say that statistical data of the last type which describe the number, or rate, or relative frequency of events may be *suggestive* in other contexts. "Suggestive" means "evocative, presented partially rather than comprehensively."[4] To make this suggestive definition more precise, we need to depict, or model, the thought process of the information receiver. We assume that he has one or more purposes (goals, ends, objectives), and that the receipt of information in some way affects his capability of attaining these. The information is absorbed into the receiver's "relevant picture of the world," which is modified in one way or another by the information.

For example, a traveler consults an air line guide to determine when planes leave from San Francisco to Washington. The information in the guide is, from the point of view of the user, suggestive. Of course the guide is not suggesting that a plane might conceivably leave at 9:15 AM; rather it is suggesting times of departure that might or might not fit into the traveler's plans. Indeed, the air line guide assumes that the traveler has a fairly well worked out plan of what he wants to do. The item in the guide helps him to fill out one unknown of this almost completed plan. It is not the responsibility of the guide publishers to question the advisability of a traveler's taking a specific trip.

In these terms we can now describe the four types of information listed above. Rather than speak of bits of information, e.g., numbers or descriptors, we need to consider an information system and its relationship to a potential user. Suggestive information systems make only very weak assumptions about what the user wants and how he should get it. Predictive information systems go a step further and tell the user what would happen if he were to do so-and-so. Decisive information systems go further still and model the user as a decision maker within a bounded system, where the boundaries are given (e.g., by the user). Finally, systemic information systems attempt to relate the bounded decision making to other "higher level" considerations.

Thus in the examples given above, an information system which generates statistics about fatalities in a factory makes only a weak assumption about what a user should do; it's entirely up to him whether he closes down the plant, puts on a safety campaign, or does nothing at all. Of course, the suggestive information system makes *some* assumption about the user, because it vaguely assumes that its information is relevant to the user's decision making. An example of a predictive information system is one that tells the user that if the workers were to wear the available safety equipment religiously, the accidents would go down 20%. This information does not necessarily imply any action on the part of the user, but if the information is relevant, then clearly a class of possible actions is implicitly assumed by the information system. For example, the predictive information seems to be saying that the user might seriously consider a safety campaign.

Decisive information systems go much further towards depicting the user's problem. They recognize that safety by itself is only part of the picture; reducing accidents or accident potential, in the decisive system, must be coupled with other objectives, e.g., production or, in the case of highways, "through put." The coupling consists of finding a common dimension for these partially conflicting objectives so that the user is aware of the relative merit of alternative plans or programs. Thus a cost-benefit description of an accident reduction program aids the user in deciding whether to implement the program. The broader systemic information system enables the user to place safety programs in context with other "efficiency" or "cost reduction" activities.

Although my main interest in this paper is to assess the potentials of decisive and systemic information in the area of safety, I do not mean to denigrate either suggestive or predictive information. Most information in today's culture is suggestive, e.g., the information to be found in newspapers, books, TV, "data banks," libraries, Census Bureau, etc. I daresay that up to a short time ago, most industrial safety information was suggestive. This is well borne out in the minutes of the 1966 National Safety Congress. I shall argue later on that all indices are essentially suggestive rather than decisive or systemic, and there was a great deal of interest in the Congress in the development of indices. On the other hand, the attention paid by the Congress to the "critical incident technique"[5] indicates an ambition to go beyond correlations, which tend to be suggestive, to cause-effect models, which are predictive. And the interest of the Congress in costs of accidents and accident reduction programs is a step towards decisive information.

The point to be made about suggestive information is that it is cheap, and, perhaps more important to safety programs, the information system can be quite limited in what it assumes about the real world. In areas which deal primarily with rare events whose consequences are so difficult to evaluate, this restricted assumption making can have its advantages. But of course someone eventually has to make a decision and whoever he is, he will have to make the assumptions.

"Decisive" means "determining, . . . putting an end to a controversy, . . . resolute, determined." The difference between suggestive and decisive information can best be illustrated by one of the classical puzzlers of safety: the ratio or index. For example, in transportation there has long been the debate as to whether fatality per passenger mile is a better or worse index of performance than, say, fatality per trip. Now all ratios of these types are suggestive; the decision maker has to fill in the gap by what he assumes about the world. The relevant question for the decision maker is how a mile or a trip contributes to his values. It's probably the case that manned space travel is one of the safest modes of travel based on fatality per passenger mile, but no one would view it as being especially "safe."

Ratios are essentially suggestive types of information; the numerator represents one kind of value and the denominator another, partially conflicting value. If we measure accidents per man hour in a plant, we are comparing two opposing values: the value of safety and the value of production. But the ratio does not tell us which is the more important value. In the case of an army battalion in a war, we need not be shocked if this ratio is relatively high, unless we feel the war is a mistake. Thus the meaning of a ratio depends on some value system of the decision maker.

Decisive information is rarely expressed as an index. Instead, all the goals are described along one, unifying value scale, e.g., dollars or utility. In the example given at the beginning of this paper, the cost and benefit of a piece of safety equipment are both expressed in dollar terms. The decision maker, in this bounded production system, can then evaluate what a certain policy (enforcing the wearing of masks) would be for him. The "controversy" has been ended, so to speak. This does not mean that all doubt is removed, of course, because all measurement is subject to error. Indeed, some estimate of the reasonable bounds of benefit minus cost should be given by the decisive information system.

Returning to the transportation illustration, we see that neither fatality per mile or per trip is decisive. To become decisive, the information system must say something definite about the value return to a passenger when the transportation system produces one unit for him. Whether this unit is a mile or a trip or something else depends on the purposes of the decision maker. If he is a cab driver and is paid in terms of the number of miles he drives, then mile may be appropriate. If he is a consultant, and is paid in terms of the number of trips he makes, then trip may be appropriate. I say "may be," because value analysis is always complicated and simple scales are rarely appropriate.

I am hinting, of course, that safety engineers should be trying to establish decisive measures, but I should also point out the extreme difficulties and pitfalls of this attempt. For one thing, if a program starts to move into this area, it gives up its own identification. Specifically, in the decisive mode one cannot really speak of safety as such, as a separate and identifiable aspect of a system. Instead, we have to think of safety as an inseparable element of a more comprehensive measure. We have to recognize that people do not want just to be safe, as their use of freeways and jets attest. Indeed, very great concern with one's own bodily safety may be a sign of neurotic or even pathological behavior.

To some extent, the attempt to find decisive measures of safety may seem inappropriate, because safety seems so fraught with intangibles. Many people are shocked by the attempt to express the loss of a limb, or a life, in dollar terms. Such dollar measures are often obtained by calculating the lost income which an accident produces. But lost income may not at all reflect the real pain, shock, or grief. On this method of accounting, an old man turns out to be worthless, or even costly, so that a few induced accidents among the aged might seem to be a good thing.

However, such a superficial economic benefit-cost analysis is really no more than suggestive. The point to be made is that none of the goals of the decision maker are really "intangible," but they may very well be hidden. Various techniques have been suggested for revealing them.[6] All of these techniques are based on the reflection that when a decision maker finally decides in a rational manner, he is directly comparing various goals. Indeed, if one of his goals is dollar income, then *in principle* all the other goals can be expressed in dollars if his choice is rational; because behavior choices indicate how much of dollar income he is willing to sacrifice for each of the goals. In other words, if an information system classifies a goal as "intangible," what is meant is that the system does not intend to touch it, not that it is "untouchable."

If industrial safety programs move into decisive information, I should expect to see the emergence of manuals for each industry which indicate the probable benefit of a specific safety program, minus the probable cost, where benefit and cost are estimated in terms of the value systems of the clients of the industry (customers, stockholders, workers, managers, public). "Probable" implies that the manual will report sources of error, as well as error estimates.

But if such manuals come into being, their introductory material should emphasize how strong a role judgment has played in shaping the data. Judgment is a central aspect of decisive information, just because so much needs to be assumed about the user.

I believe that a movement in the direction of decisive information systems for safety is a realistic program for the next decade. But if such a movement occurs, its success will be greatly enhanced by a consideration of what will follow. One of the most challenging of all stories about the future, be it 1984 or 2000, is to estimate what the future will take its future to be. My guess, in the area of information, is systemic information systems. Today, these are bound to appear unrealistic, and even idealistic, but taking them seriously may be the most important aspect of designing realistic systems.

Systemic information systems have no "data," if by "data" one means "what is given." Put otherwise, the ambition of a systemic system is to remove the necessity of externally induced instructions; obviously, there will be varying degrees of success in attaining this ambition.

A first step away from decisive towards systemic information will be a self-conscious one, in which the cost of measuring is included as an aspect of the information system. That is, the question, "Why measure?", will be meaningful. But this is a mere beginning, as is the attempt to relate benefit-minus-cost to the "next higher level" of the whole system. In the latter case, one is trying to evaluate a safety program, say, against other cost reduction programs of a company. The systemic information system is interested in the next higher level, e.g., as a basis for budgeting, but this is only a step towards its more comprehensive ambition, which is information about the "whole system."

The history of measurement in astronomy makes a reasonably good model of the progress from suggestive to systemic measurement. Early navigators could plot their course by the stars, but had no sound predictive method; the development of Ptolemaic, Copernican, Keplerian and Newtonian theories provided the predictive measurements of the solar system. Then the fixed stars became unfixed, and no longer just plain stars, but a whole genus and species of matter in motion. The whole system is still way out there in the mysterious vastness of an expanding universe.

The lesson of this bit of history is that the systemic information system, unlike the decisive, is never closed and final. Proponents of decisive measures, e.g., cost-benefit analysis and program budgeting, often refer to their method as the "systems approach," but of course it is not in any comprehensive sense. The aim of the decisive information is to bring controversy to an end, to bring action into being, to supply enough information to enable the decision maker to be resolute. It accomplishes this aim by arbitrarily setting "feasible" boundaries on the system. The aim of systemic information systems, on the other hand, is to keep controversy alive, to use action as experiment, to create problems whose study will increase the scope of understanding. Measurement is no longer the servant of decision making; it is the raison d'être of decision making. One decides in order to measure the better. This no doubt seems fantastic to an age so caught up in the practical, but even today one might say that some social decisions—e.g., those of the recent U.S.A. Supreme Court—had experiment in mind as much as welfare: to understand what people want and how they behave one needs to decide things in a certain way.

If the reader's fancy is caught by this advertisement, I'd like to close by depicting the eternal life of a systemic information system. If the reader's fancy has not been hooked, he can stop here and spend the saved time contemplating the possibility of a practical decisive information system.

The systemic information system is no different from any other in its collecting the rudiments of its information: it counts and questions, listens and smells, using whatever instruments seem appropriate. But it never regards these rudiments as givens. Instead, they have a tentative existence. Each set of rudimentary information is interpreted, by means of a model of reality, to be a description of some aspect of reality. Now for any aspect of reality, there must exist significantly different ways of describing it, e.g., if we are describing the safety of a piece of machinery, we can interview workers, take past records, use the critical incident technique, do an engineering analysis. Each one of these methods provides the information system with rudimentary information which is then interpreted as describing the specific aspect of reality. The systemic information system then compares these "adjusted" pieces of information. If they differ significantly, the system tries to alter or enrich its model of reality to explain the differences and arrive at a set of information that is consistent. If the information is all exactly alike, the system refines the rudimentary set, e.g., by inventing instruments that read out to one more decimal place. If the information differs, but not significantly, the system seeks to find another model of reality which also produces a consistent description of the aspect of reality. That is, the system seeks to find an equally plausible explanation of the "facts," the facts themselves being created out of the model and the rudimentary information. Once an alternative explanatory model is found, the original model and its newly created "deadly enemy" fight out their battle in a series of "crucial experiments," until one or both are defeated, and the system looks for another model. Part of the central strategy of the system is the selection of those "aspects of reality" which provide it with the best measure of its progress. The guide line is the one suggested at the beginning of this paper: choose those aspects of reality which have the largest inferential power to the user in different contexts and times.

Such an eternally restless system might remind us of a neurotic compulsive—or else a God: "Behold, he that keepeth Israel shall neither slumber nor sleep."[7]

ENDNOTES

1. See Chapter 5, C. West Churchman, *Prediction and Optimal Decision*, Englewood Cliffs, New Jersey: Prentice-Hall, Inc., 1961.

2. See, for example, S. S. Stevens in C. W. Churchman, P. Ratoosh, *Measurement: Definitions and Theories*, New York: John Wiley & Sons, Inc., 1959.

3. For example, the efforts of the various sections of the American Society for Testing Materials.

4. All definitions are drawn from *The Random House Dictionary*, New York: Random House, 1967, Jess Stein, Editor-in-Chief.

5. See "Applying Measurement Concepts to the Appraisal of Safety Performance," by W. E. Tarrants.

6. For a review, see Chapter 2 of Vol. 1, R. L. Ackoff (ed.), *Progress in Operations Research*, New York: John Wiley & Sons, Inc., 1961.

7. Psalm 121, Paragraph 4.

Questions for Study and Discussion

1. How is Churchman's typology of measurements relevant to the design of a management information system? (This question is taken up by Mason in the following article, but you might well consider your own thoughts first, before reading further.)

2. Note that for Churchman a measurement assumes its significance in part through the linguistic form in which it is expressed. Consider the following illustrative statements:

    (i) "John is a better tennis partner than Bill, and they are both equally available."

    (ii) "If tuition were abolished, approximately $72 million dollars would have to be replaced in the university budget."

    (iii) "The Bruins shot 55% in the first half against Washington State last Saturday, but sank only 10 of 36 for 27% in the second stanza, its lowest shooting percentage in a half this season."

    (iv) "Chemistry course 1A increased from 836 to 1,036 students from fall 1972 to fall 1974."

    (v) "Our statistics indicate that graduates with a 3.5 or better GPA (grade point average) will earn at least $100 more per month in starting salary than those with less than a 3.0 GPA."

    (vi) "What you learn in school is worth twice as much to you in the long run as anything your GPA itself will earn you."

How would you classify these according to Churchman's typology? What is the rationale for each of your classifications?

3. Churchman mentions the "critical incidence technique" as a means of measurement. What is this technique, and how has it been applied? (See, for an example, Flanagan and Burns, 1955.)

4. Select a feature article in a management periodical (e.g., *Wall Street Journal*) and study the statements made by the author in terms of the various measurements included. What are the implications of these measurements with respect to the management issues involved in the article?

5. In terms of Churchman's typology, what type of statement is the claim made by the Department of Motor Vehicles that a clerk needs ten minutes to process a drivers' license application? Within the context of the dispute in which the claim was made, construct examples of the three other types of statements.

BASIC CONCEPTS FOR DESIGNING MANAGEMENT INFORMATION SYSTEMS

Richard O. Mason

INTRODUCTION

Management information systems should supply the basic information that managers need in order to make decisions. The more closely the information provided is attuned with the decision-maker's needs the better the decisions that will be made. This means that the designer of an information system must carefully analyze decision processes as well as existing information flows. For, in a *management* information system the two are essentially inseparable.

All too frequently, however, the approach used by designers has been limited to a study of existing forms, files, reports and procedures and an effort to determine ways in which they might be simplified, expanded, integrated and improved. Sometimes many useful and economical results are realized from this kind of study; but, they are generally in the area of increased efficiency of data flows or reduction in clerical staff, *not* in improved quality of decisions made.

In the decision-oriented approach the designer begins by identifying the range of alternatives open to the decision-maker, and the resources at his disposal. He then determines the kinds of data inputs which are necessary for choosing the best course of action and lays out a program for collecting, processing and disseminating that data to the appropriate decision-making party.

The decision-oriented approach raises two important and closely related questions which the designer must answer:

1. What is the best point of articulation between the information system and the decision-maker? That is, where should the information system leave off and the decision-maker begin?

2. What is the nature of the assumptions which are incorporated in the information system and which consequently influence the user's decision-making? Are they consistent with the decision-maker's needs?

Depending on how the designer resolves these questions a qualitatively different kind of information system will be specified. The designer's choice centers on the

Accounting Information Systems (AIS), Research Paper No. 8, Graduate School of Management, University of California, Los Angeles, October 1969.

sequence of activities which begins with the state of the business itself and ends with the actual taking of a decision. This sequence of activities can be summarized as follows.

1. A *source* consisting of the physical activities and objects which are relevant to the business.

2. The observation, measurement and recording of *data* from the source.

3. The drawing of *inferences* and *predictions* from the data.

4. The evaluation of inferences with regard to the *values* (objectives or goals) of the organization and the *choosing* a course of action.

5. The *taking* of a course of *action*.

The first natural point of articulation between the information system and the decision-maker occurs when they are separated between the process of collecting data (Item 2) and that of drawing inferences (Item 3). This design is sometimes referred to as the databank or data base approach.[1]

DATABANKS

Graphically, the databank design appears as illustrated in Fig. 1:

FIGURE 1

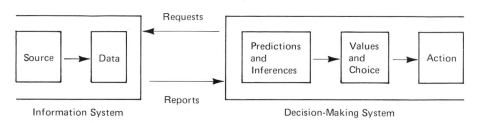

This design assumes the weakest link between the information system and the decision-maker. The responsibility of the information system is just to observe, classify and store any item of data which might be potentially useful to the decision-maker. It is incumbent on the user to request the data items he needs and to determine what their implication is for the decision problem he faces.

The information system's designer must specify the data inputs required for a variety of subsequent uses. For example, he might specify the various master files to be used in several applications. He then collects the master file data into a single pool that is keyed to the lowest common denominator of detail required for each of the decision-making applications. The information system, however, leaves off at this point.

The decision-maker utilizes the data pool by accessing those data items that are relevant to the problem at hand. He must determine which items he needs and secure them by placing retrieval requests or by establishing periodic reporting programs. This means that the databank information system is only a "fact generator." The decision-maker must determine what "meaning" the data has for his decision problem and then act accordingly.

The databank approach makes a lot of sense for some kinds of applications, especially in the general area of management control. Often, management control activity centers around queries in which the manager seeks to ask questions about the relationships between conditions and events occurring in one area and those in another, or between one particular point in time and some other time period. Since any combination or permutation of these data items might be requested (this results in an astronomical number of possibilities) it is not very efficient, if it is feasible at all, to program all of these possibilities into the system. In this case, it is better to let the decision-maker determine the kinds of predictions and inferences he wants to make and simply to inquire directly for the data he needs to do this.

Thus, in situations where the nature of the required inferences is not known with any precision beforehand, or where the structure of relationships and the assumptions about the system's preferences are changing rapidly, the databank approach is most effective. Moreover, it can prove to be economical as well. If properly implemented in an organization, a single databank can service a wide variety of decision-makers who face different decision problems and who have different but overlapping data requirements.

Used in this manner, the potential results from a well-conceived databank can be phenomenal. For example, a large railway company has installed a communications and computer network that provides accurate and immediate data on the status of every railroad car on its lines. Dispatchers use this data to spot pileup areas and to determine which cars are available for reassignment. The dispatcher can then make a judgment as to which cars can be dispatched in order to economically or rapidly fulfill incoming demands. The car status databank aids him in making the associations necessary for arriving at these decisions. By means of the better dispatching decisions that this databank provides, the company expects to substantially reduce its investment in railroad cars—enough to more than recoup its $30 million expenditure for data processing and transmission equipment.

The railroad car status system serves to illustrate why databanks are, in Churchman's words, merely "suggestive." The manager who receives these car status reports must determine the cause and effect relationships between his actions and system and make judgments about which of the possible outcomes is preferred. He must, for example, trade off the economic cost incurred in moving cars with the possible benefits gained by improving customer service. The databank does not make these predictions or decisions for him but by its very nature and availability it tends to *suggest* certain desirable alternatives to him.

It should be pointed out that most of the current discussions on databanks have centered on their implementation with computerized systems. The new third generation computers and the advent of relatively inexpensive mass memories have made it possible to consolidate highly fragmented data sources into a common data base that could be shared by many different computer programs. But in the broader sense in which the term is used in this paper, databanks are widespread and have been around for a long time. Almost all accounting systems are in reality databanks. The criterion of objectivity—"Verifiable, objective evidence has therefore become an important element in accounting and a necessary adjunct to the proper execution of the accounting function of supplying dependable information."—has virtually assured this.[2] Following this criterion traditional accounting systems have incorporated little in the way of predictions or decision recommendations into the information system. Financial statements display data; the user determines what it means for him.

There are many other familiar examples of databanks. The large federal databanks being accumulated by the IRS and the Bureau of Census are exemplary of this design. So too, for that matter, is much of the information found in libraries, books, newspapers and most data storage and retrieval systems.

Two potential drawbacks pertain to databank systems and the designer should take them into account:

1. A failure to properly relate the databank to the decision process will result in both the collection of too much irrelevant data and the omission of many important, relevant items for decision-making. Moreover, a lack of decision orientation will result in data being collected which is not in the appropriate form for its subsequent use.

2. The decision-maker is left with the burden of performing the calculations and evaluations necessary for determining predicted outcomes and the best course of action. Quite often these manipulations are complex and illusive for the manager's unaided intuition; but, frequently they are amenable to a systematic logical inquiry and, eventually, programmable. When this situation occurs, predictive or higher order information systems can be designed.

PREDICTIVE INFORMATION SYSTEMS

The next class of information system extends the system forward from the activities of pure data collection and filing to include the drawing of the inferences and predictions that are relevant for decision-making. Prediction and inference making occur when the information system's processing passes from the basic data to conclusions about the source. In this process certain evidential relationships are assumed to exist. The decision-making system in effect inquires as to "what if?" certain actions are taken and these assumptions are true. The system responds in the vein of "if" he does that "then" this is what he can expect to occur. No attempt is made to evaluate the outcome. Diagrammatically a predictive information system is characterized as Fig. 2 demonstrates.

FIGURE 2

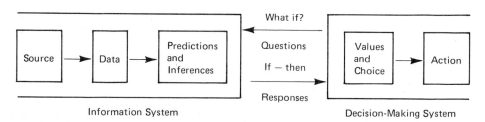

Information System   Decision-Making System

Much of the recent development in information systems tends toward this type. Financial planning simulation models are a good case in point.

Through the use of financial simulation techniques and timeshared computing technology it is possible for the manager of a business firm to sit down at a teletype console and call for the current status of his organization (as depicted by such data-bank type items as financial statements and charts of accounts). He then assumes forecasted levels for certain important economic indicators which affect his business such as population and GNP. He also assumes certain structural relationships between such items as sales and expenses, accounts receivable and collections, etc., and suggests internal policies for coping with them. For example, one policy might be to finance through equity and another to finance through borrowing. His considerations might include choices as to which divisions of the company will manufacture what products and by what methods they will distribute them. Alternative manufacturing techniques and their attendant cost equations might also be considered. Given these assumptions the simulation model then *predicts* the levels of sales, cost of materials and other variables by means of econometric methods and mathematical relationships. Then the program *infers* what the impact of these conditions will be on future financial statements and produces pro forma statements.

These simulations inform the decision-maker as to what is predicted to happen under a given set of circumstances. The decision-maker may, of course, pose as many different conditions to the model as he thinks will be useful and obtain their separate implications. However, an evaluation of the outcomes—by applying the criterion or objective function which ranks one potential outcome as being more preferable than another—remains with the decision-maker. It is not committed to the model. The decision-maker makes the ultimate choice based on predictions he receives about the alternatives tested.

It should be mentioned that predictive information systems need not be thought of strictly in computer or simulation terms. The president's advisory staff group, or a corporate market research group are also examples of predictive information systems embodied in the organizational design. The role of such organizational entities historically has been to intercede between the organization's databank and the final decision-making body for the explicit purpose of selecting and summarizing the data and drawing its implications. Most generally only the inferences are communicated to the manager.

This last observation leads to a consideration which is the underlying principle of this classification scheme. *As one moves from source to action (left to right on the diagram) more assumptions are introduced into the information/decision-making system.* And, at each step the assumptions built in are qualitatively different.

The predictive information systems require that additional aspects of the decision-maker's "relevant picture of the business" or "world view" be incorporated in the model. Relationships must be assumed. Specifically in the financial simulation illustration presented above the model has to include assumptions about the functional form of the forecasting equations, the cause and effect relationships between various activities within the firm and the functional form of the transformation from period to period. These assumptions are in addition to the assumptions built into the databank itself.

The advantages and disadvantages of the predictive information system center on the nature of the assumptions made. The predictive information system is particularly advantageous in those situations where the number of data items to be considered is large and their interrelationships are complicated (such as is the case with financial simulation). The resulting predictive model relieves the decision-maker of the burden of making these calculations and thereby frees him to consider other more important things. A well designed predictive system should be able to take into account more data items, make more accurate calculations, and produce predictions faster than the unaided manager's intellect permits. Moreover, it allows him to test many more alternatives quickly and economically than would be possible at the databank level.

Even if the required calculations are comparatively simple, the need for rapid response may marshal in favor of the predictive system. The investor who is contemplating a new stock purchase would like to know the effect of this action on his portfolio composition, on his projected cash flow and on his tax liability rather quickly. So, too, does the manager who is considering the effect of a proposed merger or acquisition want to know the impact of this move on his firm's future financial statements and reports of corporate performance. When the appropriate assumptions are incorporated in the information system design, these kinds of predictions can be obtained rapidly and they can substantially improve the quality of decision-making.

But there are also some serious dangers connected with use of predictive information systems. Predictive systems are realizations of what March and Simon refer to as "uncertainty absorption." "Uncertainty absorption takes place when inferences are drawn from a body of evidence (i.e., a databank) and the inferences, instead of the evidence itself, are then communicated."[3]

The danger lies in the possibility that the inferences are based on assumptions that are not in accord with the best judgment of the decision-maker and that these assumptions are "hidden" from him by the information system design. This point is of sufficient importance that an entire section will be devoted to it later in this paper.[4] For now, let us turn to the next class of information systems.

DECISION-MAKING INFORMATION SYSTEMS

Moving up the continuum, the next class of information systems includes those in which the organization's value system and the criteria for choice are incorporated into the information system itself. These can be referred to as *decision-making information systems* and are portrayed in Fig. 3.

FIGURE 3

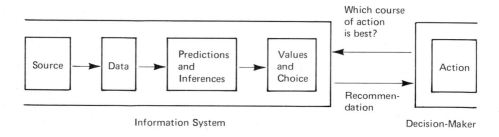

The long range goal of many ardent practitioners of operations research and management science is to produce decision-making information systems. This kind of information system epitomizes these disciplines' major concern. But, it is only realizable when a full databank and prediction system supports an optimizing model.

A linear program for, say, production scheduling is one example of a decision-making information system. In developing this model the designer begins by specifying a group of functional relationships (e.g., "constraints") about machine output rates, cost coefficients, market demands, etc. This is the predictive or implicative aspect of the information system. But now the objective function (in this case to maximize profits) is added to the problem specification and it is built into the information system. In effect (although this is not precisely how the algorithms work) the objective function serves to "rank" the predicted outcome from each alternative and select the best or "optimal" policy. For this LP example the objective function determines the most profitable product mix for the company to produce.

Mathematical programming models are not the only form that decision-making information systems can take. They are examples of what I have referred to elsewhere as "expert advice."[5] Their output is a single recommended course of action. The decision-maker retains just a "veto" power. In effect he either acts on the recommendation or he does not, although in some cases he may modify the original recommendation. There are several organizational entities that essentially operate in this manner. One is the "cost-effectiveness" study group; another is the decision-maker's advisory board.

An illustration of an advisory board form of decision-making information system was the operation of the National Security Council under President Eisenhower. Eisenhower believed that "good staff work means that the President should not be required to choose from among alternative policies, so that his job can instead be that of saying 'yes' or 'no' to the policy his advisors recommend to him."[6] Consequently, the National Security Council was used in this manner during the Eisenhower Administration. "Well-staffed" papers which argued for a single recommended course of action were the order of the day.

Cost-effectiveness studies have much the same flavor. Their mission is to determine benefits gained as compared with the resources expended for each alternative. If the benefits exceed cost an alternative is recommended or, alternatively, that alternative which gives the greatest contribution to effectiveness per unit of resource is advised.

The major difficulty facing all cost effectiveness studies is the problem of choosing the appropriate measure of effectiveness.[7] This same problem pervades every attempt to design a decision-making information system. *Most decision-making information systems assume the knowledge of a uni-dimensional scale for ranking the value of alternatives.*[8] Thus, decision-making information systems require the specification of an *acceptable* measure of value for the organization. If the proper measure is not found the decision-making information system's recommendations will be dysfunctional. They will be turned down or, worse yet, implemented blindly. One plausible answer to this problem is for the system to revert back to a predictive information system. A case history will serve to demonstrate the usefulness of this reversion strategy.

Several years ago a large corporation instituted a formal capital investment analysis procedure as part of their corporate planning function. Every proposed investment over $50,000 was to undergo a thorough discounted rate of return-on-investment analysis before it was presented to the board of directors for approval. The procedure was set up so that if that rate exceeded some benchmark rate, which reflected the corporation's cost of capital, the project would be recommended for action. In this particular decision-making information system the board received a comprehensive description of the technical aspects of the project but only the results of the discounted rate of return calculation.[9]

But much to the dismay of the board most of the discussion and debate about a proposed investment centered on questions of value. They found that there were many dimensions to these decisions which could not be specified in advance or adequately summarized on a single scale of value such as ROI. Questions on the possible effect of the proposed project on corporate image, management development and social responsibility arose.

One special concern, for example, was the timing of cash receipts and how it dovetailed with other corporate cash requirements. But, this information was not presented in the original recommending document. An acceptable solution to this problem was found when the corporate planning group decided to present the board with a summary report showing the key factors affecting the flow of cash receipts and disbursements and of expected profit for each period of the planning horizon. These predictions were performed for each of a variety of assumptions concerning costs, market demands, and alternative uses of the technology. The discounted ROI was still calculated but it became a less important factor in this new, predictive information system.

The principle illustrated by this case is that where some dimensions of the organization's value system can be specified but a single scale of value cannot be determined (or is unacceptable), a predictive information—one which shows the impact in each dimension of value for each of several alternatives—may be the most appropriate design. The information system designer must make this judgment for each individual case.

The basic reason that the decision-making information system was deplored by the board of directors (i.e., the decision-makers) is that they had no *confidence* in the objective function it assumed. They also had some reservations about the assumptions underlying its predictions. Whenever general agreement and confidence in an objective function is present a decision-making information system may be converted into a decision-taking system.

DECISION-TAKING INFORMATION SYSTEM

A decision-taking information system is one in which the information system and the decision-maker are one. Management is so confident in the assumptions incorporated in the system that it sees fit to relegate even its veto power to the information system. For the sake of completion the schema for a decision-taking information system is presented in Fig. 4.

Process-control computer applications represent good examples of decision-taking information systems. The computer is programmed to know the preferred state of, say, a petroleum cracking process. For a rather large number of situations that can occur in the process the computer can "decide" which course of action to take and initiate action. It can, for example, change the temperature or regulate the

FIGURE 4

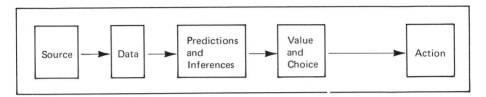

Information (and Decision-Making) System

flow of input materials. There is relatively little human intervention because the managing body for the organization has confidence in the premises upon which the computer acts.

The domain in which a process control computer operates, however, is rather small compared with the decision domain for the organization as a whole. Other attempts at decision-taking information systems are generally restricted to similarly small domains of influence. Some systems automatically initiate a purchase order when inventory has dropped below the reorder point, or send a dunning letter to a customer when he has been overdue for some prespecified period of time, or automatically create loans for bank customers who are overdrawn. But these are really trivial decisions within the overall context of management decision-making.

In a very real sense, decision-taking information systems are the computer scientist's dream for all of the decision-making process is relegated to the technology. But they will continue to escape his grasp until he determines a reliable and trustworthy method of incorporating management's values and basic underlying assumptions into his computer models. Unfortunately, or fortunately, this day is probably a long way off.

The road toward the development of decision-taking information systems has been opened up through the notion of *feedback* or of cybernetics. This idea is sufficiently unique so as to warrant special treatment.

FEEDBACK (CYBERNETIC) INFORMATION SYSTEMS: A SPECIAL CASE

Feedback or cybernetic systems can be formed through combinations of databank, predictive, decision-making and decision-taking information systems. The basic cybernetic model commences with some norm or target being set by a decision-making information system. Then action is taken pursuant to this goal. Subsequently, observations are made to measure the effect that the action has upon the source, and the resulting "feedback" is recorded in a databank. These databank items are then compared with the target to generate a variance, error or mismatch signal which shows the degree of deviation. (These signals are also databank type items.) The mismatch signal is, in turn, processed through the predictive-inferential and decision-making stages. Finally, action is taken with the intent of reducing the deviation to zero. This cycle is repeated to maintain the system "on course" (i.e., to keep the deviation from the goal near zero). A generalized diagram of a feedback system is presented in Fig. 5.

Various combinations of the components shown in the diagram above can be dedicated to the information system while the remaining are assigned to the decision-maker. In the classical example of a feedback system—James Watt's ball governor for controlling the speed of steam engines—all functions are assigned to the information system making it a complete decision-taking information system. The basic purpose of the steam engine, in terms of the equilibrium speed it is to achieve, is crystallized and built into the system. The system collects data and takes automatic action to achieve that speed thereafter. Servomechanisms and much in the way of automated equipment operate on this principle.

There are, however, several familiar examples of decision-making and databank information systems which also employ feedback. For example, most inventory control systems determine a "recommended" reorder quantity but the decision-maker has final veto power and the responsibility to take the action. Thus, they are decision-making information systems. Several managerial techniques provide what is in reality a kind of sophisticated databank information by relating current data to some previous goal. For example, budgetary planning systems produce data which describe the variance between budgeted and actual. But it is up to the decision-maker to make the appropriate predictions and inferences from this data and to reconsider the organizational values that apply before taking corrective action. Quality control methods are similar in this respect. The control chart reports the occurrence of an out-of-control state. The decision-maker must determine the cause of this deviation and then weigh the cost and benefits of several alternatives before taking action.

The designer of a feedback control system, as is true of the designer of any in-

FIGURE 5

Cybernetic Systems

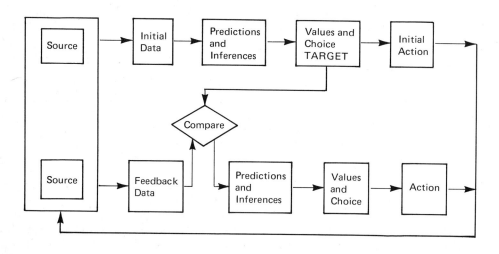

formation system, has a choice as to where the decision-maker/information system interface will be placed. He may develop a databank, a predictive, a decision-making, or a decision-taking information system. His choice depends on the confidence he has in the assumptions upon which the decision-maker's ultimate action should be based. This concern leads us to a last category of information systems—systemic information systems.

SYSTEMIC INFORMATION SYSTEMS

Systemic information systems are those which apprise the manager or the information systems designer about the assumptions or view-of-the-world which underly decisions. They are intended to test his judgment about the "whole system"; what it is and how it is to be defined. The purpose of a systemic information system is to expose these assumptions so that they may be examined and reconsidered.

Consideration of the other classes of information systems suggests the need to examine assumptions carefully. One point of emphasis in each of the preceding classes of information systems centers on the extent and kind of assumptions which are intrinsic to the information system. The key differentiating distinction between a databank information system and a predictive one is that additional managerial assumptions are built in to the predictive system. The same principle holds as one moves along the continuum until in the decision-taking information system essentially all assumptions concerning the domain of choice are contained within the information system itself.

Each class of information system has quantitatively different kinds of assumptions incorporated. These differences are summarized in Fig. 6.

The diagram also reveals that all information systems contain assumptions. Since each step in the information/decision process uses the product of the previous step as its basic input, an assumption, once made, influences the subsequent operations and ultimately, the action taken. An illustration will serve to demonstrate the point.

Consider the accounting system for a financial institution such as a bank. Of the vast panorama of events that occur within the bank only those which are identifiable, objective, verifiable and which represent economic transactions measurable in monetary terms are observed and recorded. Furthermore, they are recorded as entries into a *pre-set* chart of accounts which reflects the aspects and distinctions among these items that the bank feels are important. (The degree of liquidity of an asset, for example.) These constitute some of the assumptions about "item entry" that underlie the bank's databank.

It should be noted that the databank can be manipulated and summarized in various ways so as to produce financial statements and also certain status and performance indicators such as the loan to deposit ratio and the earnings per share. But these manipulations do not essentially change the databank quality.

The bank's management may, however, want to predict the effect that certain strategies and policies will have on future financial statements. Using the accounting system databank as a base, the bank might now begin to build a model which shows the assumed cause and effect relationship between actions taken and their outcome. This would include the effect of adding new loans, buying securities, adding or re-

FIGURE 6

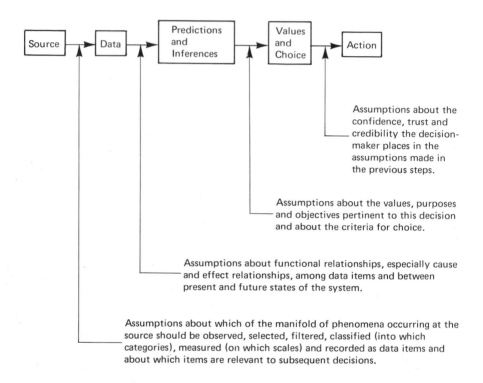

ducing deposits, etc. Using this model the bank may now set parameters to reflect a particular policy (e.g., make an increased percentage of new loans as commercial loans). The model then predicts the effects of these policies on the financial statements. These predicted financial outcomes are based on the databank and in conjunction with assumptions made about available alternative policies, future environmental conditions and the accounting relationships between policy actions and future financial statements.

But this kind of model is so far only predictive. If in addition, however, the model is designed to find that particular policy which maximizes an assumed objective function, such as earnings per share, then this becomes a decision-making information system because it yields just a single recommended course of action. Whenever the decision-maker has complete confidence in the assumptions underlying the model's recommendation and acts automatically on its conclusions, the information system becomes a decision-taking one.

Assumptions, however, are the product of management's judgment. They are not analytical nor can they be proven. But they may be *wrong*. And, incorrect assumptions lead to poor decisions. A systemic information system is one that attempts to guard against inappropriate assumptions. Its mission is to continue to apprise the manager of the assumptions that are being made by his existing information system.

Very little is known about the best design for systemic information systems, but current research suggests that one approach offers promise.[10] The approach is dialectical and is based on the premise that "good" judgments on assumptions are derived in an atmosphere of opposition. An information system is said to be dialectical if it examines data completely and logically with at least two different and opposing sets of assumptions or from two different points of view. It is the conflict between the assumptions representing one point of view and those of the other that aid the manager in learning about his system, and hence, in developing new, more appropriate assumptions.

The dialectical model follows the scheme set forth by Hegel. The designer begins by identifying the existing information/decision system and asks, "What set of assumptions or view-of-the-world would make the existing information system an 'optimal' one"? To return to the banking example he might inquire, "How would one define the whole business of banking, this bank, its liquidity, its customers, its assets, its alternatives, its threats, etc., so that this information system is the best one for its users"? This question should penetrate each of the classes of assumptions underlying the databank, predictive, decision-making and decision-taking systems.

The intent of this inquiry is to develop the strongest argument as to why, say, earnings per share (if that is the stated objective of the bank) is more important than, for example, the number of individuals served (weighed perhaps as to their need). That is, the argument would show in what view of the bank, its customers, suppliers and investors EPS was the best objective to pursue. The argument would go on to show in what view of the banking processes and of banking environment this basis for prediction and for data collection is best. The resulting set of arguments becomes the *thesis*.

The *antithesis* is developed by asking whether or not another opposing but credible conceptualization of a bank's business can be found. For example, a bank might be thought of as an information processor rather than a money depositor and lender. Or, it may define its objectives in terms of its contributions to society and its community (a goal for long-run survival) rather than strictly in economic terms (which is perhaps a short-run goal). It may also define honored concepts such as liquidity in terms of the number of days required to generate levels of cash (through cash on hand, sales or securities, loans, etc., and net of losses) rather than by means of a loan to deposit ratio. The conclusion of this *counter-argument* is that a different set of assumptions are best and consequently a different kind of information system should be designed.

In the dialectical design of a systemic information system these arguments and counter-arguments are presented to the manager via a *structured debate*. An advocate for each side presents his view of the business and argues for it. Hegel's theory, however, leads us to predict that the manager—observer of the conflict—will integrate and form a new and expanded world view, a better set of assumptions—the *synthesis*. The new insights gained from the synthesis serve as the premises for the design of a new data collection, prediction, evaluation, choice and action component of the management system.

What should the primary focus of the arguments and counter-arguments in a systemic information system be? I would propose that they should center around corporate or organizational strategy. A strategy is the most basic of organizational assumptions. It is a "pattern of objectives, purposes, or goals" that serves to define "what business the company is or is to be in and the kind of company it is or is to be."[11] As such it dictates kinds of assumptions about values, predictions and data collection that are appropriate for the organization. *In short, a statement of strategy is the unifying theme around which a management information system is based.*

One final comment about systemic information systems should be made. Their purpose is to promote learning. Contrary to decision-making and decision-taking information systems whose purpose is to bring closure to the debate about the appropriate course of action to be taken, systemic information systems serve to open these questions for a new examination. They are aimed at identifying the kinds of changes in environmental conditions, changing values and new conceptualizations that require new management assumptions. In this sense they are restless and never-ending. This may be a somewhat difficult role for the computer-oriented information scientist or the "green eyeshade" style of accountant who is accustomed to the certainty and security that the closure aspects of his technology provide. But he must reconsider, for change is the way of life in the business world.

CONCLUSION

The major thrust of this paper has been to clarify the differences between several alternative designs for management information systems. However, it is important to stress the point that the designer must consider *all* aspects of the information/decision process. He then chooses the particular combination of designs which is best suited to the decision situation for which it is intended.

A design study for a management information system should proceed essentially in the reverse order of the decision sequence developed above. In the decision-oriented approach the researcher starts by examining the manager's action alternatives and the criteria for choosing from among them. He then specifies the kinds of predictions, forecasts, inferences and measurements that are required in order to render a choice. This, in turn, determines the nature of the data to be collected and recorded.

Throughout this process, however, the designer *and* the manager must continue to examine the assumptions being built into the system. Together they must strive for a structure of assumptions or *Weltanschauung* that integrates the system into one, coherent, cohesive whole—one which reflects the basic values of the participants involved. Without such an integrating structure a collection of data is little more than a pot-pourri of isolated fragments. The only way to interpret and interrelate such fragments is through some theory that binds them and gives them meaning.

For the business enterprise or government agency the central integrating theme is its strategy. A statement of strategy includes the values and purposes of the organization and identifies the critical and pivotal decisions the manager must make. Systemic information systems have as their purpose the development of strategy and an understanding of the assumptions which underly it. Hence, the manager and the designer need to engage in the systemic information system process as a prerequisite to management information systems design. It is the only way to insure that the design is relevant to the problems at hand.

ENDNOTES

1. This classification and subsequent development derives from an interpretation of a paper on measurement by C. West Churchman entitled "Suggestive, Predictive, Decisive and Systemic Measurements" which was prepared for the Second Congress on Industrial Safety, 1969.

2. Paton, W. A., and A. C. Littleton; *An Introduction to Corporate Accounting Standards;* New York: American Accounting Association 1940, page 18.

3. March and Simon, Organizations: New York: John Wiley & Sons, 1958, page 165.

4. See the later section on Systemic Information Systems.

5. Mason, Richard O., "A Dialectical Approach to Strategic Planning," *Management Science,* Vol. 15, No. 8, April 1968.

6. Gordon, Bernard, K., "The Top of Policy Hill," *Bulletin of the Atomic Scientist,* Volume XVI, No. 7, September 1960, p. 289.

7. See for example, Morse, P. M. and G. E. Kimbal, *Methods of Operations Research,* Cambridge, Mass., MIT, 1951, pp. 52–53.

8. Or, what amounts to much the same thing, they require some "decision rule" such as the minimax criterion or the "sure thing" principle.

9. Actually for some projects the firm went so far as to estimate the probability distribution over various parameters of the project and then to calculate a cumulative distribution of rate of return. The procedure was similar to that described in David Hertz's article" Investment Policies that Pay Off," *Harvard Business Review,* Jan–Feb 1968, pp. 96–108.

10. This approach is discussed in more detail in "A Dialectical Approach to Strategic Planning," Mason, *op cit.*

11. Quoted from Learned, Christensen, Andrews and Guth, *Business Policy: Text and Cases,* Homewood, Ill.: Richard D. Irwin, 1965, p. 17.

Questions for Study and Discussion

1. "The most sophisticated type of management information system is that based upon a data bank approach." In consideration of the point of view argued by Mason, would you tend to agree or disagree with this proposition?

2. What is the role of judgement in the use of a management information system?

3. In their book on decision support systems, Keen and Scott Morton (1978) draw distinctions between structured, unstructured, and semistructured problems. A fully structured problem is one in which rules exist to resolve all three decision phases—intelligence, design, and choice. A wholly unstructured problem is one in which decision rules are completely absent. In the case of a semistructured problem, certain decision rules exist in one or more phases, providing a basis for computer-based support; however, managerial judgement is required for resolution. Illustrate each of the three problem types. What is the role of measurement in each of the illustrations?

CHAPTER **FIVE**

"The nutritional content of the average bank of UCLA vending machines is near zilch according to a survey by a student research group, the Office of Environmental and Consumer Affairs (OECA)," reported the University of California, Los Angeles, campus paper, the *Summer Bruin* on August 22, 1975. The OECA reportedly maintains a check which gives food credit (in points) for its "valuable nutrients," and subtracts credit for potentially harmful ingredients. Ratings are based on a system of valuation established by Dr. Michael Jacobson in his book, *Nutritional Scoreboard: Your Guide to Better Eating.* Assorted sandwiches, cottage cheese, and nonfat milk achieved point ratings in the sixties. Orange juice received the highest rating, 74 points. A bagel and cream cheese was worth 18 points. Most soft drinks rated minus 61 points, and gum was seen as most harmful at −98 points. Defending the types of food sold in the UCLA vending machines was the manager of the service, who is quoted as responding, "We sell a hell of a lot of nutritional food. I can buy the same in a supermarket."

The above story is illustrative of many attempts to measure the *value* of things in modern society. The term "value" is understood in this sense to be the quality that makes a thing more or less desirable, useful, estimable, or important. A measure of quality is thus a measure of *worth*.

The measurement of worth is fundamental to management. The classic example is the assessment of the "net worth" of the corporate enterprise. How this net worth ought to be computed is an issue continually under discussion. For example, a recent Securities and Exchange Commission ruling requires corporations to value their plant, equipment, and inventories according to their replacement costs, for "10-K" reporting purposes. The *Wall Street Journal* reports that this procedure produces "flaky figures" for many companies (May 23, 1977). According to the *Wall Street Journal*, Alcan Aluminum Ltd. posted a "respectable" pretax profit of $96 million in 1976, using traditional accounting procedures. But then, required to value its plant, equipment, and inventories at today's inflated prices, Alcan discovered that its allowances for depreciation soared 140% and its cost of sales increased by 2%, resulting in a "loss" of $109 million.

According to the SEC, replacement cost data are needed because "unsupplemented historical-cost-based data do not adequately reflect current business economics." Critics counter that the required estimates involve a managerial decision which is highly unlikely: the replacement of everything at once. Further, the beneficial effects of inflation on long-term debts are ignored. Lastly, the data is said to be costly to produce. Texas Instruments, for example, reported that it spent $400,000 to generate its replacement cost data.

Ideally the resolution of the present replacement cost issue would be based on some accepted theory of accounting measurement. However, the root problem of what is to be meant by "net worth" persists, given current accounting practice. In the section on organization measurement that follows, this subject will be examined further. Here the foundations of the problem in economic theory will be presented in an essay by Kenneth Boulding, who puts the question succinctly, "(suppose we) add an elephant and take away a grand piano from a stock of goods—has the stock increased or decreased?"

The Boulding article ranges far in its examination of the theory of value, providing a brief introduction to utility theory as well as the valuation of the firm.

In addition to the assessment of worth, the manager is also faced continually with judgments of *uncertainty*. The measurement of a *probability* is thus common to modern organizational decision making. Interestingly, *information* is often defined as that which reduces uncertainty. The source of this definition is the mathematical theory of communication developed by Claude Shannon. (This theory has also been called "information theory," though to some this is a misnomer.) The second article in this subsection, by the psychologist George Miller, provides an introduction to this theory which demonstrates its applicability beyond the original context of its development. For the purposes of this book, the important feature of the theory is its *measure* of information or uncertainty reduction.

The third article, by the late Jacob Marschak, integrates the measurement of utilities and probabilities into a single, elegant theoretical structure, that of *decision theory*. While Marschak says in his introduction that he "tried to appeal to the reader's intuition and cater to his laziness," in the exposition of the theory the argument is unusually rigorous, in a qualitative way, and demands close reading. Such a reading is rewarded, however, by an understanding of one of the most sophisticated of modern management measures, *expected utility*.

SOME CONTRIBUTIONS OF ECONOMICS TO THE GENERAL THEORY OF VALUE

Kenneth E. Boulding   *READING 7*

There is a famous character in one of Oscar Wilde's plays who knew the price of everything and the value of nothing. An economist wonders uneasily if the reference is not to him. The word "value" occurs in economic writings with high frequency, the frequency of meanings being almost as great as the frequency of occurrence. It has been the occasion of long and bitter disputes, some on the semantic level, some more substantive. What I want to accomplish in this paper is a relatively humble task—to examine some of the concepts and related systems in economics which seem to be relevant to the general problem of value, and to see how far and in what directions they might be safely generalized. I do not claim that economics, even when generalized to the full, gives us a complete theory of value. Many of the most important and most difficult questions in value theory cannot be answered within the framework which I shall set up. But economics can, I hope, provide something of a foundation on which to build, or at least a launching platform from which to send off our philosophical rockets.

The simplest and perhaps most basic value concept in economics is that of *transformation coefficient or ratio*, of which the most familiar example is the price in a purchase or sale. Almost all the events of the economic universe can be described as *asset transformations*—the replacement of a quantity of one asset by a quantity of another. Thus, suppose I go to a store and buy three pounds of apples for 45 cents. Immediately after the moment of purchase my balance sheet shows a diminution of 45 cents in the cash item and an increase of three pounds in the apples item; the store's balance sheet shows an increase of 45 cents in cash and a decrease of three pounds of apples. The *price* of the apples is the transformation ratio—45 cents for three pounds, or 15 cents a pound. It is clear that a price is a special case of a more general concept of an *exchange ratio* —that is, the transformation ratio of any two exchangeables in exchange. A price is simply an exchange ratio in which one of the assets exchanged is money.

It is less frequently recognized that the cost concept is likewise a special case of the asset transformation, and that *unit cost* or *average cost* is a transformation ratio strictly analogous to the price or ratio of exchange concept. We see this most simply in the case of a "pure marketer" whose economic operations consist in the buying

From *Philosophy of Science*, January 1956. Vol. 23, No. 1, pp. 1–14.©1956, The Williams and Wilkins Co., Baltimore.

and selling of commodities or securities. Thus, when a wheat speculator buys wheat he transforms money into wheat, and the ratio of money given up to wheat acquired is the average cost, to him, of the wheat. The "producer", however, is doing exactly the same kind of thing as the "marketer", except that instead of transforming assets through exchange he is transforming them through *physical transformations* (production). Thus, suppose a milller grinds 1000 tons of wheat into 990 tons of flour. The event is recorded in his balance sheet as a diminution of 1000 tons in the wheat item and an increase of 990 tons in the flour item. The result is exactly the same as if he has exchanged 1000 tons of wheat for 990 tons of flour in the market. The "wheat cost" of the flour is 1000/990 tons of wheat per ton of flour in both cases.

Production, of course, is seldom so simple an operation as the physical transformation of one asset into another; usually many assets are involved in the overall transformations. Thus in the case of our miller, in order to add 990 tons to the flour item in his physical balance sheet he would have to subtract not only 1000 tons from the wheat item, but something from cash for wages, something from machinery for depreciation and wear and tear, something from oil for oiling the machines, and so on. The "physical cost" of the 990 tons of flour in this case is the list of all the items which have diminished as a result of the addition of the 990 tons to the "flour" item. We will return later to the problem of the *evaluation* of this list—that is, its measurement.

The problem of the determinants of the system of "transformation ratios" is one thing which has been known in economics as the "theory of value". We ask the question "why" are apples 15 cents per pound, meaning by this "under what circumstances would the price have been different?". In asking this question we always imply "significantly" different, the "significant" difference being determined by our range of vision and level of abstraction. Thus the apples might have been 14 cents a pound rather than 15 cents because the storekeeper liked numbers divisible by 7, or liked apples, or didn't like apples, or regarded apples (subconsciously, of course) as a Freudian symbol, or as a symbol of the Fall Of Man, or for any of the hundreds of reasons or unreasons which the psychologist might give. All this is out of the economist's somewhat telescopic focus. But if we ask, why are apples 15 cents a pound and not 30 cents a pound, the economist is pretty sure that no psychological explanations amount to very much, and that explanations must be sought in terms of apple blight or large changes in public taste.

The first classical exposition of a "theory of value" in the above sense was Adam Smith's great discussion of deer and beaver.[1] I shall give a modern interpretation of this model as a very simple illustration of the technique of the economist, and also incidentally as a demonstration of the continuity of economics, modern economics being a generalization from the classical special case. Let us suppose, then, that we have a "society of hunters" in which there are only two commodities, deer and beaver. We suppose first that the resources of this society are in some way *limited*. This limitation, or scarcity of resources, is one of the basic concepts of the economic theory of value. This limitation of resources can be expressed in terms of the physical product of the society by supposing that there is an *opportunity boundary function* dividing the set of *possible* combinations of quantities of deer and beaver from the *impossible* combinations. In Fig. 1 we measure quantities of deer and beaver produced in given time on the vertical and horizontal axes respectively. Then the line *DB* represents the "possibility boundary" or "opportunity boundary" dividing those com-

FIGURE 1   FIGURE 2

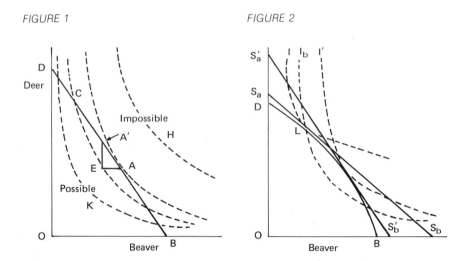

binations of quantities of deer and beaver which can be obtained (within the triangle *ODB*) from those which can not be obtained (beyond this triangle). Thus, if the society devoted all its efforts to producing deer, it could produce *OD* deer; if it devoted all its efforts to producing beaver it could get *OB* beaver, and if it divided its efforts between the two "industries" it could get some intermediate combination of quantities (as at point *A*), but it could never within its given resources get a combination of quantities lying above and to the right of the boundary *DB*, e.g. at point *H*. If it gets a combination lying within the triangle *ODB*, such as *K*, the society is operating in some sense at less than capacity output, all combinations on the line *DB* representing capacity operation.

The slope of the line *DB* at any point is the production transformation ratio or alternative cost of deer for beaver (assuming capacity operation); it is the number of deer which must be given up in order to gain an additional beaver, or which can be gained if one beaver is sacrificed. Thus, if we move from *A* to *A'* we give up *AE* beaver and gain *EA'* deer; the slope of the line *AA'* is *EA'/AE*, or the number of deer gained per beaver sacrificed.

Now let us suppose that in this society there is a market place in which deer and beaver are exchanged one for another, and suppose that there is an exchange ratio in the market which is *not* equal to the alternative cost. Suppose the alternative cost is 2 beaver per deer, and the market ratio is 3 beaver per deer. Then if a beaver producer gives up producing 2 beaver and instead produces 1 deer, and takes this deer to the market place, he can get 3 beaver for it. That is, he can get 3 beaver by producing deer with the same resources with which he could get only 2 beaver in the swamp. It is clear that deer hunting will increase and beaver hunting decline; as this goes on more deer are brought to market and less beaver, and the price of deer will fall and of beaver will rise, thus decreasing the divergence between the market ratio and the alternative cost. This process will go on until this divergence has disappeared and the market ratio and the production transformation ratio are equal. The same process will occur if the price of deer in the market is less than the alternative cost in the field; then it will pay to produce deer indirectly by getting beaver and exchanging them, rather than directly in the forest. Now deer hunting will decline and beaver hunting increase until once more the incentive for this change is removed by equalizing the market price with the alternative cost.

This can be represented in the figure by supposing that at each combination of outputs there is a corresponding market price ratio which can be represented by the slope of a line. We have then a family of curves such as the dotted curves in Figure 1 (*"market ratio curves"*), having the property that at each point the slope of the curve through that point, at that point, is the market price ratio corresponding to the amounts of production symbolized by the point. The equilibrium position is given by the point *A*, assuming capacity operation, where the possibility boundary is touched by a market ratio curve, as this is the only point on the possibility boundary where the market price is equal to the alternative cost.

Suppose now there is a "shift in tastes"; suppose that beaver hats become very fashionable and deerskin cloaks somewhat despised. This is reflected in a "steepening" of the market ratio curves at each point; with a *given* quantity of deer and beaver produced beaver will become dearer and deer cheaper. More deer per unit of beaver must be given in the market in order to persuade people to take the less-wanted deer and to refrain from taking the more-wanted beaver. At the point *A*, therefore, the market ratio curve will now cut the line *DB*, and will be steeper than it. We must move down the curve *DB* in the direction of *B*, therefore, to find the new point of equilibrium where the line *DB* is touched by the new system of market ratio curves. The shift in tastes towards beaver and away from deer has resulted, as we should expect, in a rise in the production of beaver and a fall in the production of deer; resources have been transferred out of the deer into the beaver industry.

Now, however, we notice an interesting fact. If the possibility boundary is a straight line, as in Figure 1, this shift in tastes does *not* produce any change, neither in the production transformation ratio itself, nor in the equilibrium market price, which is equal to the production transformation ratio. This is the classical case of "constant costs", and illustrates the proposition that under constant costs "value" (i.e. the equilibrium market ratio) is not determined at all by "demand" (the structure of tastes) but only by the (constant) production transformation ratio or alternative cost. All that a shift in demand does is to change the structure of relative outputs without changing the structure of relative prices.

Suppose now, however, that alternative cost is *not* constant. This is shown in Figure 2. Here we have "increasing cost" for each industry. This is quite probable, even in our "nation of hunters". As the deer industry expands deer become scarcer, hunters have to go farther afield, and more resources per deer have to be expended. As the beaver industry contracts beaver become more plentiful, they can be obtained nearer and nearer home, and so on. As we move up the possibility boundary *DB* then from *B* to *D*, the beaver-cost of deer rises, the deer-cost of beaver falls, and the slope of the line declines. The opposite is also possible (decreasing cost); as the deer industry grows it may develop specializations and skills which would not be possible in a small industry, so that it may actually be easier to get a lot of deer than a few. If both industries show decreasing cost the possibility boundary will be convex to the origin. Where we do not have constant cost it is clear that the structure of tastes is a determinant not only of relative outputs but also of relative prices. Thus, suppose the system is originally in equilibrium at *L*, the market ratio curve *IL* touching the possibility boundary *DLB*. The ratio of exchange is the slope of the tangent

S_dLS_b, or OS_d/OS_b deer per beaver. If now tastes shift away from deer and towards beaver the market ratio curve through L becomes steeper, I_1L, and we must move to L', the point where one of the new market ratio curves, $I'L'$, touches the possibility boundary. At L', however, the ratio of exchange is the slope of the tangent $S'_dL'S'_b$, or OS'_d/OS'_b. Beaver have become relatively dearer and deer relatively cheaper as the beaver industry has expanded to higher cost levels and the deer industry has contracted to lower cost levels. This effect of a change in demand, however, is determined by the nature of the *possibility* function, not by the nature of the preferences or tastes.

What I have outlined above is essentially a "field theory", of which many examples are to be found in the physical sciences. In such a theory we first define a set of variables (in this case, outputs of deer and beaver); then we define a "product space" which consists of all *conceivable* combinations of variable quantities or "positions" of the system. Then we impose on this product space (the area in the figures) a "possibility boundary" which divides the space into a possible and an impossible set or sector. Then we postulate a field function such as our market ratio curves which has the property that *change* in the system will always take place from positions which have a "lower" value of this function to positions which have a "higher". Then the equilibrium position of the system is that at which the field function is maximized, subject to the constraint of the possibility boundary. That is, to return to Figure 1, suppose that the dotted lines represent the contours of the three-dimensional surface or "mountain" rising above the plane of the paper, the height of the mountain at any point being represented by some number U. Then the system behaves as if it "wanted" to maximize U. If we think of the possibility boundary as a "fence" running across the U-mountain the system moves to a position as high up the mountain as the fence permits; this is the point A in Figure 1 where the "fence" is tangent to one of the U-contours. This is because we have simply defined U in a way that "bigger than" *means* "moves towards"; the system moves by definition of U from a position where U is smaller to a position where U is bigger, as long as the second position is within the possibility boundary.

Now we come to the really big question in value theory—the leap which carries us from the positive to the normative. The U-function as defined above is strictly positive—that is, it is a mere description of the dynamic potentialities of the system; it tells us how the system will in fact behave under certain circumstances. As such it is simply a "physical" system, whether it refers to physical or social variables. In the leap to the normative we define a *welfare* function as a function which orders all the positions in the field according to a scale of "betterness" or "worseness". That is to say, we assign each position of the system a number, W, (which does not, incidentally, have to be a cardinal number like 23; it can be an ordinal number like 23rd) such that any position is regarded as "better than" positions with smaller W's than its own, "worse than" positions with larger W's, and "as good as" positions with equal W's. The critical question is then whether any U-function can be regarded as identical with any W-function. Many attempts have been made to establish such identification—i.e. to establish an empirical or positive basis for value judgements. All these have failed. What we are perhaps justified in saying is that there are many U-functions which are *similar* to W-functions, but we can never be sure that any U-function is *identical* with a W-function.

An illustration may make the meaning clearer. Returning again to Figure 1, suppose that this now represents the situation of a single individual in a market situation, and that the axes now measure *stocks* of beaver and deer. We suppose that the initial position of the individual is C, and that he is faced with a "market opportunity" described by the line DCB. The slope of this line is the ratio of exchange or price with which he is faced, and we suppose that the market is "perfect" in the technical sense that the ratio of exchange does not vary with the quantity exchanged—that is, the exchange opportunity boundary is a straight line through C. If the individual moves from C towards B he is giving up beaver and getting deer; if he moves from C towards B he is giving up deer and getting beaver. Now suppose that the dotted lines are the contours of his "welfare function" or "preference function"; these are then what the economist calls *"indifference curves"*. Each one represents all those points in the field to which the individual is indifferent—i.e. which he regards as "equally good". Movement upward and to the right carries us to "higher" levels of preference—any point on the curve through H represents a preferred or "better" position to any point on the curve through K. If now we say that the individual always moves towards a preferred position, the equilibrium of the system is again at A where the possibility boundary touches an indifference curve; this is as far "up" the preference mountain the individual can get as long as he cannot trespass beyond the line BD.

In this case it would certainly seem plausible to identify the "positive" U-function which simply describes the dynamics of the system with the normative W-function which describes its "ethics". An individual will always presumably move *from* positions which he believes at the time are "worse" (i.e. lower on the W-function) *to* positions which he believes at the time are "better". Hence the U-function is identical with his W-function *as then perceived* by him. Now, however, a host of competing W-functions raise their indignant voices. The snag, of course, lies in the qualifying phrase "as then perceived by him". There may very well be a W_r, or "had-I-but-known" function (r for regret). He may have gone to A under the belief that there was going to be a beaver famine, that the price of beavers was going to rise, and hence it was going to be profitable to have a lot of beaver. This expectation may be disappointed; there may in fact be a deer famine, all he will be caught holding beavers that nobody wants. In such a case, the W_r-function, if he *had* known it, would have sent him towards D rather than towards B. Nor is this the end. Even if his expectations were correct, so that even had he known the future he would still have kept to the old W-function, there may still be a W_s, or "I think you are a skunk" function. That is to say I (or you, or anyone else) may *disapprove* of his W-function and say that his choices are "wrong". There are likely to be a great many W_s functions, indeed as many as he has neighbors. There may even be W_n, or I-as-psychiatrist-think-you-are-neurotic function, as in the famous story of the man who loved pancakes and kept trunks full of them in his attic.

The situation gets much worse when we move from the single individual towards society. Economists have been much occupied in the past generation with trying to answer the question "what is economically good for society". Attempts have been made, for instance, to identify the market ratio curves or things like them—i.e. the U-functions which describe the market dynamics—as welfare functions or *"community indifference curves"*, and to show from this that some condition such as perfect competition maximizes economic welfare. These attempts have usually run up against the problem of *"interpersonal comparisons"*. That is, if a change from one position of society to another moves one individual from a less to a more preferred position, and another from a more to a less preferred position, how do we evaluate the net gain or loss; how, that is to say, do we compare the losses or gains of one person with those of another? An attempt has been made to get around this difficulty by means of a "weak" maximization criterion, called *the "Paretian" optimum* after its inventor, Pareto. As long as a society can move to positions which make no individual worse off, and some better off in their own estimations, it is not at the Paretian optimum. The Paretian optimum, then, is that set of positions from which no movement is possible without making at least one person worse off in his own estimation. A surprising number of propositions follow from this weak assumption. Nevertheless the Paretian optimum exhibits some fatal flaws. In the first place, it falls heir to all the defects of the individual preference function, already noted. Even if we accept the proposition that the individual preference function is a satisfactory welfare function, however, there are still difficulties in the Paretian optimum, mainly because it does not define a unique maximum but a set of positions. Imagine, for instance, that the "Welfare Mountain" is a long ridge running north and south. The Paretian optimum is, say, the ridge itself; as long as we can go only east or west, any point on the ridge is an optimum. But it is perfectly possible for a point which is not on the ridge to be higher than one that is; a point just east or west of the peak of the mountain may be far above the low points on the ridge. There seems to be no escape from the conclusion, then, that in order to say anything definite about "the good" a welfare function must be postulated, and that this welfare function cannot be derived from any field function which is descriptive of empirical systems.

In spite of the impossibility of validating any particular welfare function by reference to the empirical world, neither the theoretical nor even the empirical study of particular welfare functions and choice situations need be abandoned. There is first the possibility of developing an analytic framework for the discussion of generalized welfare functions. Models can be constructed and situations envisaged which are applicable to large groups of welfare functions, and hence conclusions can be drawn which do not depend on the specification of welfare functions but which hold whatever particular welfare function we adopt, within broad limits. Empirical study can also fruitfully be devoted to clarifying both the possibility boundaries and the internal consistency of the welfare functions which are implicit in actual choice patterns. I shall conclude the paper therefore with some illustrations of the way in which the apparatus of the generalized welfare function can be used to explore problems and clarify issues.

THE "EVALUATION PROBLEM"

A problem which frequently crops up in discussions of value is that of the measurement or evaluation of heterogeneous aggregates. This is basically *the problem of index construction*. Thus we find in accounting that the physical balance sheet or position statement of a firm consists of a number of heterogeneous items—tons of this and pounds of that, dollars of money and debt, buildings and machines and so on. One of the principal problems of the accountant is to reduce this heterogeneous mass to a single figure of *"net worth"*. He does this by "valuing" all the heterogeneous components in terms of some common "measure of value" such as the dollar. Valuation in this sense means finding the *equivalent* in dollars of some physical item—say, a machine or 1000 tons of coal. The ratio of the dollar value to the physical quantity is the *valuation coefficient.* Unless we have a set of valuation coefficients, changes in physical aggregates cannot be measured, even as to direction. Thus suppose we ask ourselves the question: add an elephant and take away a grand piano from a stock of goods—has the stock increased or decreased? There is no answer to this unless an equivalence between elephants and grand pianos can be established. If we are interested merely in the weight of the stock and we know that one elephant weighs as much as ten grand pianos, then we know the stock has increased by the weight of 9/10 elephants or 9 grand pianos. If, however, we are interested in the *value* of the stock we must know, for instance, that one elephant is "worth" n grand pianos before we can tell whether the stock has increased or decreased; it will have increased, remained constant, or decreased as $n \gtrless 1$.

Very difficult, and, indeed, theoretically insoluble problems arise in accounting, both private and national, when we try to measure changes in *physical* stocks or flows when the valuation coefficients are changing. The difficulty is illustrated in the case of our simple deer-beaver society in Figure 3. Suppose A and B represent two positions of the deer-beaver stock (the argument applies equally well to flows or income). A represents a lot of deer (OH_a) and a little beaver (OK_a) B a lot of beaver (OK_b) and a little deer (OH_b). The question is which position represents a "larger" total stock. To evaluate the total stock we must be able to express the equivalence between beaver and deer. Then let the slope of AA_1 (or the parallel line BB_1) represent a valuation coefficient (the number of deer equivalent to one unit of beaver). H_aA_1 is then the deer-equivalent of H_aA beaver, and the deer-equivalent of the total stock of A is $OH_a + H_aA_1$ or OA_1. Similarly the deer-equivalent of the total stock at B is OB_1. At this valuation coefficient A is the larger stock. Suppose, however, the valuation coefficient were higher—say equal to the slope of the line AA_2 or BB_2. Now A is the larger stock. There will be some valuation coefficient, equal to the slope of the line AB itself, at which the two stocks are equal. Suppose now that positions A and B represent the situation at two different times, and that the slope of AA_1 (or BB_1) is the valuation coefficient at time 1 and the slope of AA_2 (or BB_2) is the valuation coef-

FIGURE 3   FIGURE 4

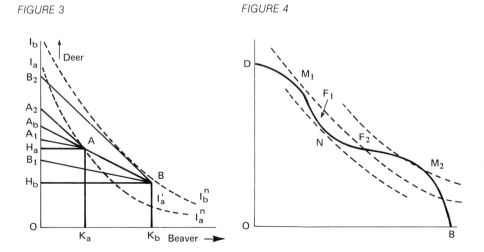

ficient at time 2. The answer we get to the question as to *whether* the total stock has increased or decreased (even without regard to "by how much") depends on which of these valuation coefficients we select, and there is no clear reason why we should select one rather than the other.

Exactly the same difficulty manifests itself in measurements of the national income, of the price level, of net worth, or of profits. Indeed the only reason why we have any impression that these aggregates *can* be expressed as a single number is that in fact the valuation coefficients do not change very much in, say, ten years, although they may change a great deal in a century. Similarly the stability of relative outputs or relative stocks of goods is great enough so that we have some sense of a price level for output or for inventories). The basic difficulty is reflected in the struggles of accountants with the misleading nature of accounts in periods of inflation and deflation, as represented in current controversies over "LIFO" versus "FIFO" methods of inventory accounting, or in original versus replacement cost in the valuation of fixed capital. It should be observed in passing that the valuation coefficient concept is not the same as that of a ratio of exchange, even though valuation coefficients are usually derived from ratios of exchange. Buildings and machinery, for instance, are not generally valued in accounts at market price.

It is interesting to observe, then, that any theoretical "solution" of this fundamental problem of accounting involves a welfare function. Only if we can locate the points A and B in a field of indifference or "equivalue" curves can we say with confidence whether A is larger or smaller than B. Thus in a very real sense we can say that there is an ethical problem, capable only of approximate solution, as the base of all our accounting procedures, both private and national. Suppose that AI_a, BI_b are equivalue curves, contours of a welfare function. Then, and only then, can we say that B is a "better" position than A, with the curves as drawn. Even now it is not possible to say without ambiguity by how much B is better than A, unless we have a cardinal measure of welfare. We can however measure the difference between the two equivalue lines roughly in terms of quantities of deer and beaver. Thus, if the equivalue curves cut the deer axis at I_a and I_b, we can say that B is better than A by an amount equivalent to $I_a I_b$ deer, when there are no beaver, or, say by an amount equivalent to $I_a'B$ deer when there are OK_b beaver, and so on. There is no guarantee, of course, that $I_a I_b = I_a'B$.

INCREASING RETURNS AND THE PROPHETIC VISION

A problem of great interest and generality is illustrated in Figure 4. Here the solid line again represents a deer-beaver possibility curve, as in Figures 1 and 2, but it is drawn with a peculiar but significant shape. From D to F_1 there are "diminishing returns" as in Figure 2, implying that as the production of deer diminish deer can be obtained more easily, and as the production of beaver increases they are harder to get. From F_1 to F_2, however, this tendency reverses itself. Suppose, for instance, that when the beaver industry got to a certain level of output all sorts of improvements became possible which were not possible at smaller outputs, so that instead of beaver becoming harder to get as the beaver industry expanded they actually became easier to get. At F_2 giving up a deer releases resources which can obtain a great many beaver; the curve is almost flat. Then beyond F_2 this "increasing returns" tendency exhausts itself and the old diminishing return sets in again, and giving up deer yields less and less beaver. Suppose then the dotted lines represent both market ratio curves and equivalue curves of a welfare function. Then M_1 is a true position of equilibrium, and so is M_2. N is an "unstable" equilibrium. Between D and N the system moves to M_1; between N and B the system moves to M_2. M_2 is a "superior" point to M_1—i.e. is on a higher equivalue curve. Nevertheless the system will be stable "in the small" at M_1—that is, any small movement from M_1 will result in a worsening of the position of the system. If, however, the system can be induced to "worsen" its position as far as N it will then move up to a superior position at M_2 under the impetus of its own dynamics.

This model has many applications. Suppose, for instance, that OD measures agricultural and OB industrial output in a society. There may be a low-level equilibrium at M_1 from which any small move worsens the position of the society. If, however, by subsidy, tariff, or general monkeyshines the government can push the society down towards N, the expansion of industry then creates its own draft, improvement reverberates back to agriculture, and the society may find a new equilibrium at M_2. This is the classical "infant industry" argument in favor of tariffs. Whether the possibility curve in fact has this shape in any case is of course a "positivistic" question which only experience can answer. If it has this shape, however, an argument of this sort may be sound. It is interesting to note that the "prophetic" strain in religion, especially in Judeo-Christian religion, has much this model in view; M_1 is the equilibrium of this world; M_2 the superior equilibrium of Mount Zion. To get from M_1 to M_2, however, involves a willingness to sacrifice, to go downhill at least for a while to apparently worse positions before turning the corner. OD in this case, let us say, measures "worldly" goods and OB "spiritual" goods. The proposition that those who seek first the Kingdom of Heaven have the "other things" added unto them is thus seen to be a clear expression of the principle of increasing returns.

ETHICAL DILEMMAS

The apparatus of welfare maximization subject to the constraint of a possibility function has applications to problems of choice and dilemmas far beyond the traditional sphere of economics. The slope of an equivalue curve in any plane measures the relative valuation of the variables measured by the coordinates of the plane. Thus in Figure 4, if the equivalue curves are "flat" it means that the proprietor of the welfare function values D highly and B little, for getting a little D will compensate him for losing a lot of B. If the curves are "steep" it means that B is valued highly and D little. Thus in the worldliness-spirituality case the spiritually minded person will have steep equivalue curves and is much less likely to get stuck in the dip at N—he will move straight to a position close to B. Similarly, it must in all fairness be admitted, that the thoroughly worldly minded person whose equivalue curves are flat will likewise not get stuck in the dip but will move to a cheerful damnation at D. It is the half-and-half sinner who needs to be bailed out by the prophets.

As another illustration in which the model of Figure 4 may prove illuminating, suppose OD measures military security and OB measures national income. This relationship may also exhibit an "increasing returns" over a period; the transfer of resources to productive capacity in general from armaments may not yield much return in highly militarized societies, but may yield strongly increasing returns at lower levels of armament.

If now the slope of the equivalue curves and of the possibility boundary are similar over a range, the model may be highly *sensitive*—that is, a slight shift in the underlying conditions will give rise to a large shift in the position of equilibrium. This model illustrates the problem of *ethical confusion*. It is particularly likely to arise under conditions of increasing returns in the possibility functions. Under the conditions of Figure 2 where the curvatures of the possibility boundaries and of the equivalue curves are in opposite directions the maximum position is insensitive—fairly large changes in either of the curves will not cause a great change in the maximum position. If, however, the situation is like Figure 4, the equivalue curves might even coincide with the possibility boundary for some distance, in which case all such points of coincidence would be equally "good" and small differences in welfare functions would enable people to draw entirely different conclusions.

An example of this type of analysis is shown in Figure 5. Let us suppose that the variables in the system are "tolerance of subversive elements" and "danger of subversion". We may postulate a possibility boundary shaped somewhat like $M_0M_1M_2M_3M_4$ in Figure 5. The assumption here is that with no tolerance at all (complete intolerance) at O there will be some danger, OM_0, because of the rigidities and strains which such a system sets up. As tolerance rises, danger at first falls—the system becomes more adaptable, less subject to revolution, but that beyond a certain point M_2 danger begins to rise again and with complete tolerance the danger of subversion is again noticeable. This gives us the U-shaped curve of the figure. I have further supposed that the bottom of the U is very flat—that is, that there is a certain range of tolerance over which the danger does not change very much. Now let us postulate various welfare functions. Suppose first a man who thinks any increase in tolerance is bad but who does not care anything about the danger. His equivalue curves will be vertical, the highest being the axis OM_o. M_o will therefore be his preferred position; this is the absolutely intolerant position. Likewise at the other extreme, if we care nothing about the danger but think any increase in tolerance is good, the equivalue curves will again be vertical, but the highest is TM_4, where T is the position of complete tolerance; M_4 is the optimum point. This is the absolutely tolerant position.

Then we have the man who cares nothing about tolerance, but thinks any increase in danger is bad. His equivalue curves will be horizontal, like L_2M_2, going to higher values as we move toward lesser danger. The highest equivalue curve he can attain is L_2M_2 as long as he sticks to the possibility line, and the optimum point is M_2 where danger is minimized.

Intermediate cases are shown at M_1 and M_3. If the equivalue lines are like L_1M_1, an increase in tolerance must be offset by a decrease in danger. This man actually disapproves of tolerance, though not much—increase in tolerance, danger being constant, moves him to somewhat lower equivalue curves. He is sharply concerned about danger. His optimum is at M_1, where danger is almost minimized and tolerance is low; he will not go on to minimize danger completely at M_2 because he actively disapproves of the amount of tolerance involved. Conversely, if the equivalue lines are like L_3M_3 an increase in danger is accepted if there is a small increase in tolerance. This man approves of tolerance as such, but again not very much; his main concern is still with danger. His position of equilibrium is M_3, where tolerance is greater, and danger only slightly greater than at M_2.

We see here that if the possibility function exhibits this property of having about

FIGURE 5   FIGURE 6

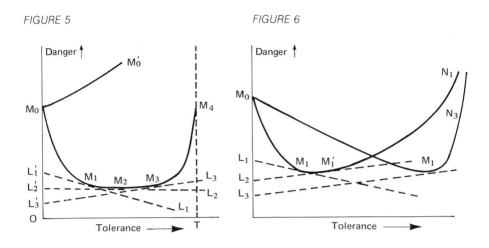

the same degree of danger over a wide range of tolerance, then if people do not care very much about tolerance one way or the other, but care a good deal about the danger, then quite small differences in the welfare function—from slight approval of tolerance to slight disapproval—can result in large differences in the degree of tolerance regarded as optimum. A shift from highly intolerant to highly tolerant positions may be the result of small shifts in the welfare (or in the possibility) function. This example illustrates how difficult it may be to deduce the nature of the welfare function or value system of an individual from his attitudes or opinions. Indeed, unless we know something about the possibility function with which he is working, his recorded attitudes may be quite misleading. People may have identical attitudes with widely differing value systems (welfare functions), if their possibility functions are different. Thus a man may have a tolerant attitude either because he gives a high value to tolerance as such, or because he thinks toleration is harmless. These may represent very different value systems.

A complicating factor here is that frequently the subjective possibility functions are themselves determined in part by the welfare function. A person whose welfare function is "absolutely intolerant" is likely to believe in a possibility function like $M_0M'_0$, where danger increases right from the start with any increase in tolerance. The absolutely tolerant person is likely to believe that danger diminishes with every increase in tolerance. This tendency is likely to lead to greater stability in the attitudes of the individual, up to a point. Once judgment starts to change, however, there can easily be a revolution in attitudes, following rather small changes in the welfare function, because the subjective possibility function follows the change in the welfare function. Thus, suppose that the man with the equivalue curve L_1M_1, because of his slight dislike of tolerance, believed that danger increased rather sharply with increase in tolerance soon after the point M_1 was passed, as $M_0M_1N_1$ in Figure 6. His own equilibrium would look very stable; a shift, say, to the "mild tolerance" position with equivalue curves such as $L_3'M_1$ would change his optimum position very little—only to M_1'. If, however, the shift to "mild tolerance" resulted in a shift in his subjective possibility curve to $M_0M_3N_3$, with the minimum danger point at a high level of tolerance, there would be a marked shift in his optimum point from M_1 to M_3. The relation, if it exists, between subjective possibility functions and welfare functions is likely, therefore, to accentuate the sensitivity of these systems, and increases the difficulty of discovering the underlying welfare functions.

Examples of this type of analysis might be multiplied almost indefinitely. It is clear that we have in this type of field theory a powerful instrument of analysis which is capable of giving formal structure to the whole range of problems involving dynamic systems and choice patterns on the one side, and value systems on the other. No amount of analysis of this type can answer the great fundamental and unanswerable questions which it is the magnificent business of philosophy to ask—questions of right and validity, duty and obligation, the summum bonum and the categorical imperative. Nevertheless, it can provide a framework which may help to clarify the nature of the systems in which we are involved and of the choices, even the great choices which we have to make. It may seem undignified to take a system of analysis which was first devised for the discussion of the choice between ham and eggs, and to use it for a discussion of the choices between freedom and security, justice and mercy, peace and war, good and evil. But put the matter the other way around and we see that the humblest choice is affected with ethical interest, and that the one great pattern of maximization under constraints reverberates over the whole gamut of human life, and even beyond.

ENDNOTES

1. "If among a nation of hunters, for instance, it usually costs twice the labor to kill a beaver which it does to kill a deer, one beaver should naturally exchange for or be worth two deer." Adam Smith, *The Wealth of Nations*, Book 1, Chapter 6, p. 47 (Modern Library).

Questions for Study and Discussion

1. It is Boulding's conclusion that "in a very real sense we can say that there is an ethical problem capable of only approximate solution, as the base of all our accounting procedures, both private and public." Do you agree? (Note that an issue of measurement is at stake, according to Boulding.) What are the implications for the accounting profession, in your view?

2. Consider the establishment of an information utility which provides computer-based consumer reference services. What transformation coefficients might characterize the operation of this utility?

3. How does the notion of value inherent in economic utility theory differ from the notion of value reflected in the nutritional rating system described in the introduction to this group of readings?

WHAT IS INFORMATION MEASUREMENT?

George A. Miller

In recent years a few psychologists, whose business throws them together with communication engineers, have been making considerable fuss over something called "information theory." They drop words like "noise," "redundancy," or "channel capacity" into surprising contexts and act like they had a new slant on some of the oldest problems in experimental psychology. Little wonder that their colleagues are asking, "What is this 'information' you talk about measuring?" and "What does all this have to do with the general body of psychological theory?"

The reason for the fuss is that information theory provides a yardstick for measuring organization. The argument runs like this. A well-organized system is predictable—you know almost what it is going to do before it happens. When a well-organized system does something, you learn little that you didn't already know—you acquire little information. A perfectly organized system is completely predictable and its behavior provides no information at all. The more disorganized and unpredictable a system is, the more information you can get by watching it. Information, organization, and predictability room together in this theoretical house. The key that unlocks the door to predictability is the theory of probability, but once this door is open we have access to information and organization as well.

The implications of this argument are indeed worth making a fuss about. Information, organization, predictability, and their synonyms are not rare concepts in psychology. Each place they occur now seems to be enriched by the possibility of quantification. One rereads familiar passages with fresh excitement over their experimental possibilities. Well-worn phrases like "perceptual organization," "the disorganizing effects of emotion," "knowledge of results," "stereotyped behavior," "reorganization of the problem materials," etc., begin to leap off the pages.

In the first blush of enthusiasm for this new toy it is easy to overstate the case. When Newton's mechanics was flowering, the claim was made that animals are nothing but machines, similar to but more complicated than a good clock. Later, during the development of thermodynamics, it was claimed that animals are nothing but complicated heat engines. With the development of information theory we can expect to hear that animals are nothing but communication systems. If we profit from history, we can mistrust the "nothing but" in this claim. But we will also re-

From *The American Psychologist* 8 (1953), pp. 3–11. Copyright 1953 by the American Psychological Association. Reprinted by permission.

member that anatomists learned from mechanics and physiologists profited by thermodynamics. Insofar as living organisms perform the functions of a communication system, they must obey the laws that govern all such systems. How much psychology will profit from this obedience remains for the future to show.

Most of the careless claims for the importance of information theory arise from overly free associations to the word "information." This term occurs in the theory in a careful and particular way. It is not synonomous with "meaning." Only the *amount* of information is measured—the amount does not specify the content, value, truthfulness, exclusiveness, history, or purpose of the information. The definition does not exclude other definitions and certainly does not include all the meanings implied by the colloquial usages of the word. This garland of "nots" covers most of the objectionable exaggerations. In order to demonstrate some properly constrained associations to the word "information," we need to begin with definitions of some basic concepts.

BASIC CONCEPTS

Amount of information. A certain event is going to occur. You know all the different ways this event can happen. You even know how probable each of these different outcomes is. In fact, you know everything about this event that can be learned by watching innumerable similar events in the past. The only think you don't know is exactly which one of these outcomes will actually happen.

Imagine a child who is told that a piece of candy is under one of 16 boxes. If he lifts the right box, he can have the candy. The event—lifting one of the boxes—has 16 possible outcomes. In order to pick the right box, the child needs information. Anything we tell him that reduces the number of boxes from which he must choose will provide some of the information he needs. If we say, "The candy is not under the red box," we give him just enough information to reduce the number of alternatives from 16 to 15. If we say, "The candy is under one of the four boxes on the left end," we give more information because we reduce 16 to 4 alternatives. If we say, "The candy is under the white box," we give him all the information he needs—we reduce the 16 alternatives to the one he wants.

The amount of information in such statements is a measure of how much they reduce the number of possible outcomes. Nothing is said about whether the information is true, valuable, understood, or believed—we are talking only about *how much* information there is.

Bit. A perfectly good way to measure the amount of information in such statements (but not the way we will adopt) is merely to count the number of possible outcomes that the information eliminates. Then the rule would be that every time one alternative is eliminated, one unit of information is communicated.

The objection to this unit of measurement is intuitive. Most people feel that to reduce 100 alternatives to 99 is less helpful than to reduce two alternatives to one. It is intuitively more attractive to use ratios. The amount of information depends upon the fraction of the alternatives that are eliminated, not the absolute number. In order to convey the same amount of information, the 100 alternatives should be reduced by the same fraction as the two alternatives, that is to say, from 100 to 50.

Every time the number of alternatives is reduced to half, one unit of information is gained. This unit is called one "bit" of information. If one message reduces k to

k/x, it contains one bit less information than does a message that reduces k to $k/2x$. Therefore, the amount of information in a message that reduces k to k/x is $\log_2 x$ bits.

For example, if the child's 16 boxes are reduced to two, then x is 8 and $\log_2 8$ is three bits of information. That is to say, 16 has been halved three times: 16 to 8, 8 to 4, and 4 to alternative outcomes.

Source. The communication engineer is seldom concerned with a particular message. He must provide a channel capable of transmitting any message that a source may generate. The source selects a message out of a set of k alternative messages that it might send. Thus each time the source selects a message, the channel must transmit $\log_2 k$ bits of information in order to tell the receiver what choice was made.

If some messages are more probable than the others, a receiver can anticipate them and less information needs to be transmitted. In other words, the frequent messages should be the short ones. In order to take account of differences in probability, we treat a message whose probability is p as if it was selected from a set of $1/p$ alternative messages. The amount of information that must be transmitted for this message is, therefore, $\log_2 1/p$, or $- \log_2 p$. (Note that if all k messages are equally probable, $p = 1/k$ and $- \log_2 p = \log_2 k$, which is the measure given above.) In other words, some messages that the source selects involves more information than others. If the message probabilities are $p_1, p_2, \ldots, p_k$, then the amounts of information associated with each message are $- \log_2 p_1, - \log_2 p_2, \ldots, - \log_2 p_k$.

Average amount of information. Since we want to deal with sources, rather than with particular messages, we need a measure to represent how much information a source generates. If different messages contain different amounts of information, then it is reasonable to talk about the average amount of information per message we can expect to get from the source—the average for all the different messages the source may select. This expected value from source x is denoted $H(x)$:

$$H(x) = \text{the mean value of } (- \log_2 p_i)$$

$$= \sum_{i=1}^{k} p_i (- \log_2 p_i)$$

This is the equation that occurs most often in the psychological applications of information theory. $H(x)$ in bits per message is the mean logarithmic probability for all messages from source x. In all that follows we shall be talking about the average amount of information expected from a source, and not the exact amount in any particular message.

Related sources. Three gentlemen—call them Ecks, Wye, and Zee—are each making binary choices. That is to say, Ecks chooses either heads or tails and simultaneously Wye also makes a choice and so does Zee. They repeat their synchronous choosing over and over again, varying their choices more or less randomly on successive trials. Our job is to predict what the outcome of this triple-choice event will be.

With no more description than this we know that there are eight ways the triple-choice can come out: HHH, HHT, HTH, HTT, THH, THT, TTH, and TTT. Thus our job is to select one out of these eight possible outcomes. If all eight were equally probable, we would need three bits of information to make the decision.

Now suppose that Ecks tells us each time what his next choice is going to be.

With Ecks out of the way we are left with only four combinations of double-choices by Wye and Zee, so we can gain one bit of information about the triple-choice from Ecks. Similarly, if Wye tells us what his choice is going to be, that can also be worth one bit of information. Now the question is this: If Ecks and Wye both tell us what they are going to do, how much information do we get?

Case I: Suppose that it turns out that Ecks and Wye are perfectly correlated. In other words, if we know what Ecks will do, we also know what Wye will do, and vice versa. Given the information from either one of them, the other one has no further information to add. Thus the most we can get from both is exactly the same as what we would get from either one alone. Note that if Ecks and Wye always make the same choice, there are actually only four possible outcomes: HHH, HHT, TTH, and TTT, so we need only two bits to select the outcome.

Case II: Next, suppose that Ecks and Wye make their choices with complete independence. Then a knowledge of Ecks' choice tells us absolutely nothing about what Wye is going to do, and vice versa. None of the information from one is duplicated by the other. Thus, if we get one bit from Ecks and one bit from Wye, and if there is no common information at all, we must get two whole bits of information from both of them together.

Case III: Finally, suppose that, as will usually be the case when we apply these ideas, Ecks and Wye are partially but not perfectly correlated. If we know what Ecks will do, we can make a fairly reliable guess what Wye will do, and vice versa. Some but not all of the information we get from Ecks duplicates the information we get from Wye. This case falls in between the first two: the total information is greater than either of its parts, but less than their sum.

The situation in Case III is pictured in Fig. 1. The left circle is the information we get from Ecks and the right circle is the information from Wye. The symbols $H(x)$ and $H(y)$ denote the average amounts of information in bits per event expected from sources Ecks and Wye respectively. The overlap of the two circles represents the common information due to the correlation of Ecks and Wye and its average amount in bits per event is symbolized by T. The left half of the left circle is information from Ecks alone, and the right half of the right circle is information from Wye alone. The symbols $H_y(x)$ should be taken to mean the average amount of information per event that remains to be gotten from source Ecks after Wye is already known. The total area enclosed in both circles together represents all the information that both Ecks and Wye can provide. This total amount in bits per event is symbolized by $H(x,y)$.

$H(x)$ is calculated from the probabilities for Ecks' choices according to the equation given above. The same equation is used to calculate $H(y)$ from the probabilities for Wye's choices. And the same equation is used a third time to calculate $H(x,y)$ from the joint probabilities of the double-choices by Ecks and Wye together. Then all the other quantities involved can be calculated by simple arithmetic in just the way Fig. 1 would suggest. For example:

$$H_y = H(x,y) - H(y)$$

or

$$T = H(x) + H(y) - H(x,y)$$

It will be seen that T has the properties of a measure of the correlation (contingency, dependence) between Ecks and Wye. In fact, 1.3863 nT (where n is the num-

FIGURE 1.   Schematic representation of the several quantities
of information that are involved when messages are received
from two related sources.

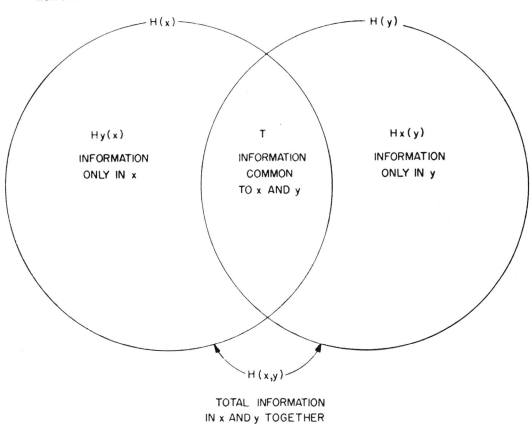

$H(x)$ $H(y)$

$H_y(x)$ T $H_x(y)$

INFORMATION   INFORMATION   INFORMATION
ONLY IN x   COMMON   ONLY IN y
                   TO x AND y

$H(x,y)$

TOTAL INFORMATION
IN x AND y TOGETHER

ber of occurrences of the event that you use to estimate the probabilities involved)
is essentially the same as the value of chi square you would compute to test the null
hypothesis that Ecks and Wye are independent.

These are the basic ideas behind the general theory. There are many ways to
adapt them to specific situations depending on the way the elements of the specific
situation are identified with the several variables of the theory. In general, however,
most applications of the theory seem to fall into one or the other of two types. I shall
refer to these two as the *transmission situation* and the *sequential situation*.

THE TRANSMISSION SITUATION

When information is communicated from one place to another, it is necessary to
have a channel over which it can travel. If you put a message in at one end of the
channel, another message comes out the other end. So the communication engineer

talks about the "input" to the channel and the "output" from the channel. For a good channel, the input and the output are closely related but usually not identical. The input is changed, more or less, in the process of transmission. If the changes are random, the communication engineer talks about "noise" in the channel. Thus the output depends upon both the input and the noise.

Now we want to identify the variables in this transmission situation with the various quantities of information pictured in Fig. 1. In order to do this, we let x be the source that generates the input information and let y be the source that generates the output information. That is to say, y is the channel itself. Since x and y are related sources of information, the overlap or common information is what is transmitted. $H(x)$ is the average amount of input information, $H(y)$ is the average amount of output information, and T is the average amount of transmitted information. (To keep terms uniform, we might refer to T as the average amount of "throughput information.")

What interpretation can we give to $H_y(x)$ and $H_x(y)$? $H_y(x)$ is information that is put in but not gotten out—it is information *lost* in transmission. $H_y(x)$ is often called "equivocation" because a receiver cannot decide whether or not it was sent. Similarly, $H_x(y)$ is information that comes out without being put in—it is information *added* in transmission. $H_x(y)$ is called "noise" with the idea that the irrelevant parts of the output interfere with good communications.

Finally, $H(x,y)$ is the total amount of information you have when you know both the input and the output. Thus $H(x,y)$ includes the lost, the transmitted, and the added information,

$$H(x,y) = H_y(x) + T + H_x(y),$$

equivocation plus transmission plus noise.

This interpretation of the basic concepts of information theory is ordinarily used with the object of computing T, the amount of information transmitted by the channel. A characteristic of most communication channels is that there is an upper limit to the amount of information they can transmit. This upper limit is called the "channel capacity" and is symbolized by C. As the amount of information in the input is increased, there comes a point at which the amount of transmitted information no longer increases. Thus as $H(x)$ increases, T approaches an upper limit, C. This situation is shown graphically in Fig. 2, where T is plotted as a function of $H(x)$.

The obvious psychological analogy to the transmission situation is between the subject in an experiment and a communication channel, between stimuli and inputs, and between responses and outputs. Then $H(x)$ is the stimulus information, $H(y)$ is the response information, and T measures the degree of dependence of responses upon stimuli. It turns out that T can be considered as a measure of discrimination, and C is the basic capacity of the subject to discriminate among the given stimuli. That is to say, C can be interpreted as a sort of modern version of the traditional Weber-fraction.

In order to explain how T and C measure the discriminative abilities of the subject, a simple example is useful. Imagine a subject can discriminate perfectly among four classes of stimuli. Any two stimuli in the same class are indistinguishable to him, but two stimuli from different classes are never confused. If we pick the stimuli carefully from different classes, therefore, he can distinguish perfectly which one of two, of three, or of four alternative stimuli we present. However, there is no way

*FIGURE 2.   Illustrative graph showing the amount of
transmitted information as a function of the amount of input
information for a system with a channel capacity of 2 bits.*

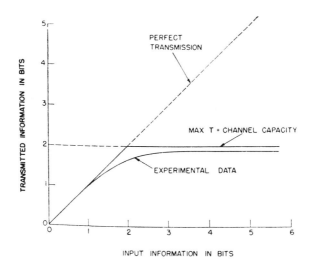

INPUT INFORMATION IN BITS

we can pick five or more stimuli so that he can discriminate them without any mistakes; at least two must be from the same class and so will be confused. If we select
k stimuli to test him with, the best he can do is to reduce *k* to *k*/4 by saying which of
his four classes each stimulus belongs in. He can never reduce the range of possible
inputs to less than *k*/4. Thus his channel capacity, *C*, is $\log_2 4$, or 2 bits, and this is
the maximum value of *T* we can get from him. Since 2^C is the maximum number of
discriminably different classes of stimuli for this subject, *C* is a measure of his basic
discriminative capacity.

Another psychological analogy to the transmission situation arises in mental testing. A test is a device for discriminating among people, with respect to some psychological dimension. Each person who takes the test has some true value on this
dimension. The result of the test is a score that will, with more or less accuracy, tell
us what this value is. So we can think of the test as a communication channel. The
true values are the input information, and the test scores are the output information.
If it is a good test, if *T* is large and the noise, $H_x(y)$, is small, then the test may discriminate rather accurately among the people who take it. In other words, 2^T would
tell us how many classes of people we can distinguish by using this test.

It requires only a slight extension of this analogy to see the similarity between
any process of measurement and the transmission situation. Nature provides the input, the process of measurement is the channel, and the measurements themselves
are the output. In this context, the information of the communication engineer is
quite similar to the information that R. A. Fisher defined many years ago and used
as the foundation for his development of a theory of statistical inference. Considered
in this sense, the possible applications of information theory are as broad as scientific measurement itself.

For the psychologist interested in the construction of scales of measurement, information theory will be a valuable tool. He will find that most of the things it tells him he could have learned just as well by more traditional statistical procedures, but the analogy to the transmission situation will undoubtedly stimulate insights and suggest new approaches to old problems.

THE SEQUENTIAL SITUATION

In all that has been said so far it has been implicitly assumed that successive occurrences of the event are independent. When we are dealing with behavioral processes, this assumption is never better than a first approximation. What we are going to do is conditioned by what we have just done, whether we are carrying out the day's work, writing a letter, or producing a random sequence of digits.

Although any behavioral sequence can be analyzed to discover its conditional probabilities, the most interesting example is our own verbal behavior. To take an obvious case, imagine that you are typing a letter and that you have just typed, "I hope we will see you again very." You need at least one more word to complete the sentence. You cannot open the dictionary at random to get this next word. The whole context of the sentence constrains your freedom of choice. The next word depends on the preceding words. Your most probable choice is "soon," although you might choose "often" or "much." You will certainly not choose "bluejay," or "the," or "take," etc. The effect of these constraints built into normal English usage is to reduce the number of alternatives from which successive words are chosen. We have already seen that when the number of possible outcomes of a choice is reduced, some information has been communicated. That is to say, by reducing the range of choice, the context gives us information about what the next item is going to be. Thus when the next words occurs, some of the information it conveys is identical with information we have already received from the context. This repeated information is called "redundancy."

How can the variables in this sequential situation be identified with the various quantities of information pictured in Fig. 1? In order to relate them we let x be the source that generates the context and let y be the source that generates the next word. Since x and y are related sources of information, the overlap or common information from x and y is the redundancy. $H(x)$ is the average amount of information in the first $n - 1$ words (the context), $H(y)$ is the average amount of information in the nth word, and T is the average amount of redundant information. $H_y(x)$ is the average amount of information in the context that is unrelated to the next word. $H_x(y)$ is the average amount of information in the next word that cannot be obtained from the context. $H(x,y)$ is the total amount of information we have when all n words, the context plus the next word, are known.

When this interpretation of the basic concepts is used, the quantity of major interest is ordinarily $H_x(y)$, the average amount of information per word when the context is known. $H_x(y)$ can be thought of as the additional information we can expect from each new word in the sequence. Thus $H_x(y)$ is closely related to the *rate* at which information is generated by the source; it measures the average number of bits per unit (per word).

If the successive units in a sequence are chosen independently, then the redundancy T is zero and the context tells us nothing about the next unit. If the next unit is completely determined by the context—for example, in English a "q" is always followed by "u"—then the new information $H_x(y)$ is zero and the occurrence of the next unit adds nothing to what we already know.

Sequences of letters in written English have been studied with this model. It has been estimated that a context of 100 letters will, on the average, reduce the effective number of choices for the next letter to less than three possibilities. That is to say, $H_x(y)$ is about 1.4 bits per letter in standard English. We can compare this result with what would happen if successive letters were chosen independently; then each letter would be chosen from 26 alternatives and would carry $\log_2 26$, or about 4.7 bits of information. In other words, we encode about one-fourth as much information per letter as we might if we used our alphabet more efficiently. Our books seem to be about four times as long as necessary.

It is reasonable to ask why we are so redundant. The answer lies in the fact that redundancy is an insurance against mistakes. The only way to catch an error is to repeat. Redundant information is an automatic mistake-catcher built into all natural languages. Of course, if there is no chance of error, then there is no need for redundancy. The large amount of redundancy that we seem to insist on reflects our basic inefficiency as information-handling systems. Compared with the thousands or millions of bits per second that electronic devices can handle, man's performance figures (always less than 50 bits per second and usually much lower if memory is involved) can charitably be called puny. By making our languages redundant we are able to decrease the rate, $H_x(y)$, to a point where we can cope with what is being said.

Knowledge of the redundancy of English is knowledge about our verbal habits. Since so much of man's behavior is conditioned by these verbal habits, any way to measure them should interest a psychologist. For example, a verbal learning experiment might compare the memorization of ten consonant-vowel-consonant nonsense syllables (30 letters in all) with the memorization of a 30-letter sentence from English text. Since the successive letters in the nonsense syllables are effectively independent, the learner faces many more possible sequences than he does if he knows that the 30 letters are English text. Since he has already learned the redundancies of English, he is required to assimilate less new information from the sentence than from the nonsense syllables. A knowledge of the information in sequences of letters in English text thus gives us an independent, quantitative estimate of previous learning. In short, the sequential application of information concepts enables us to calibrate our verbal learning materials and so to control in a quantitative way factors that we have always discussed before in qualitative terms.

It is not necessary to confine the sequential interpretation to verbal behavior. It can be applied whenever an organism adopts a reasonably stable "course of action" that can be described probabilistically. If the course of action is coherent in such a way that future conduct depends upon past conduct, we say the behavior is predictable or, to some degree, stereotyped. In such cases, the redundancy T can be used to measure the stereotypy. Arguments about the degree of organization in emotional behavior, for example, might be clarified by such a measure.

Taken together, the sequential and the transmission situations suggest a wide range of possible applications in psychology. The idea of reviewing some of the applications already made by psychologists is tempting, but space prevents it here. The reader who wants to follow up these ideas in more concrete terms should find the annotated references given below a good starting point.

SELECTED REFERENCES

The following is not a complete bibliography, but should include most of the papers of direct interest to psychologists.

Aborn, M., & Rubenstein, H. Information theory and immediate recall. *J. exp. Psychol.*, 1952, **44**, 260–266. Artificial languages with varying degrees of contextual constraint were constructed and passages from these languages were memorized. For the less organized languages, the amount of information remembered was a constant.

Cherry, E. C. A history of the theory of information. *Proc. Inst. elect. Engineers*, 1951, **98**, 383–393. This scholarly and interesting paper puts the theory in historical context and contains a valuable bibliography.

Dolansky, L., & Dolansky, M. P. *Table of $\log_2 1/p$, $p \log_2 1/p$, and $p \log_2 1/p + (1 - p) \log_2 1/(1 - p)$*. Cambridge: Technical Report No. 227, Research Laboratory of Electronics, Massachusetts Institute of Technology, 1952. This table is quite useful in any computation of amounts of information.

Fano, R. M. Information theory point of view in speech communication. *J. acous. Soc. Amer.*, 1950, **22**, 691–696. This paper presents a nonmathematical discussion of the theory and uses it to estimate the rate of transmission of information in speech communication.

Fano, R. M. *The transmission of information.* Cambridge: Technical Reports No. 65 and No. 149, Research Laboratory of Electronics, Massachusetts Institute of Technology, 1949 and 1950. The basic theorems are developed in a different way than Shannon used, and more attention is given to the problem of finding the optimal coding scheme to reduce equivocation.

Frick, F. C., & Miller, G. A. A statistical description of operant conditioning. *Amer. J. Psychol.*, 1951, **64**, 20–36. The sequential interpretation is used to analyze the behavior of rats in a Skinner box during preconditioning, conditioning, and extinction. Here T is used as a measure of stereotypy.

Garner, W. R., & Hake, H. W. The amount of information in absolute judgments. *Psychol. Rev.*, 1951, **58**, 446–459. This paper contains an excellent description of the method of calculation of T in the transmission form of the theory, and points out the similarity between T and the contingency coefficient.

Hake, H. W., & Garner, W. R. The effect of presenting various numbers of discrete steps on scale reading accuracy. *J. exp. Psychol.*, 1951, **42**, 358–366. Subjects who estimated the position of a pointer along a linear interval had the same channel capacity C for discriminating positions even though they were given different instructions and made different kinds of errors.

Hartley, R. V. The transmission of information. *Bell Syst. tech. J.*, 1928, **17**, 535–550. Mostly of historical interest today, this paper contains most of the basic ideas so elegantly developed by Shannon twenty years later.

Hick, W. E. Information theory and intelligence tests. *Brit. J. Psychol.*, 1951, **4**, 157–164. Answering test questions is broadly interpreted as a communication problem, and ways of designing tests to maximize the transmission are considered theoretically.

Hick, W. E. On the rate of gain of information. *Quart. J. exper. Psychol.*, 1952, **4**, 11–26. Information measurement is applied to a choice-reaction-time experiment. The amount of information in the choice divided by the reaction time gives a constant—about five bits per second.

Hick, W. E. Why the human operator? *Trans. Soc. Instrument Technology*, 1952, **4**, 67–77. The relative efficiency of men and machines is discussed in terms of their capacities to handle information. Several kinds of evidence are reviewed and an upper limit for men of about 15 bits per second (probably too low) is estimated.

Jacobson, H. Information and the human ear. *J. acous. Soc. Amer.*, 1951, **23**, 464–471. The author calculates that 10,000 bits per second is the maximum capacity of the ear, but argues that the brain can utilize less than one per cent of this information.

Laemmel, A. E. *General theory of communication.* Report R—208–49. Brooklyn: Microwave Research Institute, Polytechnic Institute of Brooklyn, 1949. Reviews the general theory and extends it for engineering applications.

MacKay, D. M. Quantal aspects of scientific information. *Phil. Mag.*, 1950, **41**, 289–311. An attempt is made to distinguish "structural" from "quantitative" information and to relate the work of Fisher, Gabor, and Shannon.

Marks, M. R., & Jack, O. Verbal context and memory span for meaningful material. *Amer. J. Psychol.*, 1952, **65**, 298–300. A repetition of the Miller-Selfridge experiment using the span of immediate memory failed to confirm the results of the previous study. Memory span measurements generally fail to show any constancy in the amount of information retained.

Miller, G. A. *Language and communication.* New York: McGraw-Hill, 1951. In this book an attempt is made to use information theory to integrate and interconnect a review of psycho-linguistics.

Miller, G. A. Language engineering. *J. acous. Soc. Amer.*, 1950, **22**, 720–725. Suggestions are made for the use of information theory in the design of special languages for special uses, e.g. an international language for aviation.

Miller, G. A. Speech and Language. In S. S. Stevens (Ed), *Handbook of experimental psycholgoy.* New York: Wiley, 1951. The first half of this chapter relates some of the standard studies of verbal behavior to the sequential form of information theory.

Miller, G. A., & Frick, F. C. Statistical behavioristics and sequences of responses. *Psychol. Rev.*, 1949, **56**, 311–324. The sequential form of the theory is developed in an elementary manner and used to define an index of behavioral stereotypy.

Miller, G. A., Heise, G. A., & Lichten, W. The intelligibility of speech as a function of the context of the test materials. *J. exp. Psychol.*, 1951, **41**, 329–335. The transmission form of the theory was used to show the effect of increasing the input information upon the per cent of spoken words correctly perceived.

Miller, G. A., & Selfridge, J. A. Verbal context and the recall of meaningful material. *Amer. J. Psychol.*, 1950, **63**, 176–185. The sequential interpretation of the theory was used to construct learning materials with varying amounts of contextual constraint. Thus the passages differed in average amount of information per word. To a rough approximation, the amount of information recalled was constant for all passages.

Newman, E. B. Computational methods useful in analyzing series of binary data. *Amer. J. Psychol.*, 1951, **64**, 252–262. In addition to a description of an interesting tabulating device for use with binary data, this paper contains a table of $-p \log_2 p$ that is quite useful to computers.

Newman, E. B. The pattern of vowels and consonants in various languages. *Amer. J. Psychol.*, 1951, **64**, 369–379. The measure of redundancy is used to compare the predictability of vowel-consonant sequences in eleven written languages.

Newman, E. B., & Gerstman, L. S. A new method for analyzing printed English. *J. exp. Psychol.*, 1952, **44**, 114–125. A coefficient of constraint is defined and used to obtain results that can be compared to Shannon's estimates of the redundancy in printed English.

Parke, N. G., & Samson, E. W. *Distance and equivalence in sequence space.* Report E4080. Cambridge: Air Force Cambridge Research Laboratories, 1951. Develops the notion suggested by Shannon that the information from two sources x and y be called equivalent if $H_x(y) + H_y(x)$ are zero and that the "distance" between any two nonequivalent sources be defined as $H_x(y) + H_y(x)$.

Ruesch, J., & Bateson, G. *Communication, the social matrix of psychiatry.* New York: Norton, 1951. This book stresses the importance of communication in psychiatric problems, makes some use of information theory and suggests many more.

Samson, E. W. *Fundamental natural concepts of information theory.* Report E5079. Cambridge: Air Force Cambridge Research Station, 1951. The intuitive nature of the concepts of expectation, surprise, and uncertainty is stressed.

Senders, V. L., & Sowards, A. Analysis of response sequences in the setting of a psychophysical experiment. *Amer. J. Psychol.*, 1952, **65**, 358–374. The sequential model is used to analyze response dependencies in a psychophysical experiment.

Shannon, C. E. Communication in the presence of noise. *Proc. Inst. Radio Engineers*, 1949, **37**, 10–21. A geometrical representation is developed for the communication of continuous functions disturbed by noise interference.

Shannon, C. E. A mathematical theory of communication. *Bell Syst. tech. J.*, 1948, **27**, 379–423, 623–656. These two articles comprise the first systematic presentation of the concepts of information measurement. Although the mathematics are difficult for most psychologists, this is still the basic reference in this field. Reprinted in 1949 with an article by Weaver by the University of Illinois Press.

Shannon, C. E. Prediction and entropy of printed English. *Bell Syst. tech. J.*, 1951, **30**, 50–64. A clever device is developed for estimating upper and lower bounds for the redundancy of English and used to estimate the relative efficiency of English text at about 25 per cent.

Weaver, W. Recent contributions to the mathematical theory of communication. In Shannon, C. E., and Weaver, W., *The mathematical theory of communication.* Urbana: Univer. of Illinois Press, 1949. This nonmathematical exposition is an expansion of an article in *Scientific American*, July 1949, and is intended as an introductory orientation that can be read before one tackles the more mathematical aspects of the theory. Weaver suggests ways to generalize the theory to the broader problems of social communication.

Wiener, N. *Cybernetics.* New York: Wiley, 1948. One chapter of this pioneering volume expounds the author's discoveries in information theory. For most psychologists, this volume is more stimulating than intelligible.

Wiener, N. *The human use of human beings.* Boston: Houghton Mifflin, 1950. In a less mathematical form, the social consequences of the ideas in *Cybernetics* are emphasized and explained in highly readable prose.

Woodbury, M. A. On the standard length of a test. *Psychometrika*, 1951, **16**, 103–106. A parameter called "the standard length" is defined in such a way that a test of standard length gives one unit of information. This paper suggests one way of employing information theory in the analysis of mental tests.

Questions for Study and Discussion

1. Miller cautions in his article that the term "information," as employed in information theory, is not to be taken as synonymous with "meaning." How then should the measure of information described by Miller be interpreted? What property of what types of empirical systems may be said to be represented by this measure?

2. In what sense may a process of measurement be said to be analogous to a channel of transmission?

3. Since its inception information theory has received widespread attention in a variety of intellectual fields. That it should possess such general applicability may or may not be obvious to the reader. For example, can you imagine how information theory might be applied to accounting? (See Theil, May 1969.)

TOWARD A PREFERENCE SCALE
FOR DECISION-MAKING

Jacob Marschak

One strategy is better than another if it brings the player more. More of what? Clearly, one uses some criterion of "utility," of something that is being maximized. Moreover, since the opponent's response or the future in general is uncertain, the player does not know a unique result of his strategy but rather expects various possible results, some with greater, some with smaller degrees of belief or "(subjective) probabilities."

If utilities and probabilities could be merely ranked (like degrees of patriotism) but not also scaled (like degrees of temperature), the theory of games could say rather little. Accordingly, von Neumann and Morgenstern revived the eighteenth century concept of a player who is concerned with his subjective status (so called "moral wealth"—the modern "utility"], a number which, under uncertainty, is a random one, and whose average (the "moral expectation"—the modern "expected utility") the player tries to maximize. A lively discussion developed.[1] The most elegant restatement of the relevant postulates of rational behavior and a rigorous proof of the implied "Bernoulli theorem" was given by Herstein and Milnor.[2] In this discussion, the necessarily subjective nature of the probabilities was somewhat neglected. But this latter aspect (actually also traceable back to the eighteenth century) was revived by Ramsey and De Finetti and in L. J. Savage's *Foundations of Statistics*.[3]

The following exposition tries to appeal to the reader's intuition and cater to his laziness more than it would be permissible in a mathematical paper. A proof is merely sketched. It may be added, however, that the substance of the proof, too, is simpler than in my earlier papers on the subject.[4]

I shall often use the second person pronoun. In discussing rational behavior as in discussing logic, appeal is made to the reader's reasonable self: given time to think, how would you decide? I don't deal with another, quite a different question (as different as psychology is from logic): how often do you decide hurriedly and foolishly?

THE CASE OF THREE OUTCOMES

Suppose you, the reader, have to choose between two decisions (actions): to build or not to build a bomb-proof shelter for yourself and your family. To make the example drastic, let us suppose that you are rich but that the shelter would cost you practically the whole of your fortune; and that such a shelter is both indispensable and sufficient for life preservation in the case of war. Thus your two alternative decisions and the two alternative states of the world (war or peace) combine into the following "payoff matrix":

	States of World	
Decisions	**Peace**	**War**
Build shelter	Alive and poor (r_2)	Alive and poor (r_2)
Don't build shelter	Alive and rich (r_3)	Dead (r_1)

This is oversimplified indeed. Especially, we have neglected the difference between being alive and poor in peace, and being alive and poor in war (with shelterless neighbors dead). I need this particular simplification in order to have in my example just three possible outcomes. This will be a convenient introduction to more complicated cases. The three outcomes, or results, I have denoted by r_1 = "dead"; r_2 = "alive and poor"; r_3 = "alive and rich." I suppose you prefer r_3 to r_2 and r_2 to r_1. This ranking of results is sufficient to determine your choice of action if you are certain about the future. If you are certain that there will be war, you choose to build the shelter (because you prefer r_2 to r_1); if you are sure that there will be peace, you choose not to build the shelter (because r_3 is better than r_2).

But suppose you do not know whether there will be war or peace. Yet you have to take a decision! You will still choose not to build a shelter if your *degree of belief* in peace and your *degree of preference* for wealth relative to survival are sufficiently large. (Note that we now speak of degrees and not of mere ranks! Summer is warmer than spring, and spring is warmer than winter: this is ranking; but we can also measure degrees of temperature in each of the three seasons.)

The statement I have just made, about the degrees of your beliefs and preferences that will make you decide not to build a shelter though you are uncertain about the future, must be made more precise. Denote the degrees of belief (also called subjective probabilities) that you assign to peace and war, respectively, by p and $1 - p$. Calibrate your thermometer of preferences, or "utilities" as follows: assign utility zero to the worst of the three outcomes, and utility one to the best. Thus

$$u(r_1) = 0; \quad u(r_3) = 1$$

Then, since r_2 is better than r_1 and worse than r_3,

$$0 < u(r_2) < 1$$

Subject to these inequalities, you are still free to assign any number $u(r_2)$ to the outcome r_2. I now suggest that you can, without incurring any logical contradiction, determine the number $u(r_2)$ in such a way as to satisfy the following principle: "*of any two decisions, the one you (the reader) choose is the one that, in your opinion, results in the higher, or at least not lower, average utility.*" The average utility that results from the decision "don't build" is defined as the weighted average of $u(r_3)$ and $u(r_1)$, the weights being the corresponding degrees of belief, which we have denoted above by

p and $1 - p$, respectively. Thus the average utility that results from "not building shelter" is

(1) $u(r_3) \cdot p + u(r_1) \cdot (1 - p) = 1 \cdot p + 0 \cdot (1 - p) = p$

On the other hand, the average utility that results from the decision "to build" is

$u(r_2) \cdot p + u(r_2) \cdot (1 - p) = u(r_2)$

Now, suppose you have chosen to build. According to the above principle of choosing in favor of the decision that results in the higher average utility, your actual choice will imply that, in your opinion [and still using the scale where one had fixed $u(r_3) = 1$ and $u(r_1) = 0$],

$u(r_2) \geq p$

On the other hand, if you had chosen not to build, the above principle would imply [still using the same scale]

$u(r_2) \leq p$

You can now perform on yourself a mental experiment, by varying the number p and asking: "with this degree of belief into persistence of peace, do I still prefer to build (or not to build)?" You may come close enough to a value of p, at which you will be *indifferent* between building and not building. Call this hypothetical value: $p = p_0$. Then both statements are true: $u(r_2) \geq p_0$ and $u(r_2) \leq p_0$. That is

$u(r_2) = p_0$

You have now attached numerical utilities to all three outcomes considered. You have also attached numerical average utilities to the two alternative decisions, to build and not to build. Call these two decisions (actions) a_1 and a_2, respectively. Thus

$u(r_1) = 0; \ u(r_2) = p_0; \ u(r_3) = 1;$

average utility if a_1 is taken $= p_0$

average utility if a_2 is taken $= p$,

Remember that p is your actual degree of belief in peace; while p_0 is that degree of belief in peace that would make you indifferent between the two decisions. If you have decided to build, this implies that, in your opinion, $p \geq p_0$. If you have decided not to build, this implies that, in your opinion, $p \leq p_0$.

We have had occasion to discuss your preferences between results (for example, better to be alive and poor than to be dead: choice between r_2 and r_1) as well as between decisions (better to build than not to build: choice between a_1 and a_2). It is thus natural to extend the concept of utility accordingly, and speak, not only of a utility of a result, but also of a utility of a decision. In fact a "result" can be regarded as a special case of a "decision," viz., a decision which can have only one result. Such was in fact the decision a_1 in our example; its unique result was r_2. Accordingly we might simply assign to it the utility $u(a_1) = u(r_2)$. On the other hand, decision a_2 is identified with a bundle of results (r_3 and r_1), each with a respective degree of belief (p and $1 - p$). We can call such a bundle a "prospect": it is a (subjective) probability distribution of results, a lottery. A prospect promising—as in the case of a_1—

a single result, may be called a sure prospect. It is, in fact, *also* a (subjective) probability distribution, with one of the results having probability one. Thus, when you compared the two decisions, you did, in fact, compare the following two probability distributions (or prospects).

Decision:	Probability of		
	r_1	r_2	r_3
a_1	0	1	0
a_2	$1 - p$	0	p

One can say that, of two decisions (or of two corresponding prospects), you have chosen the one with a higher, or at least not lower, utility. If you choose a_1, then $u(a_1) \geq u(a_2)$. The principle of choosing the decision that results in a higher average utility can, then, be rephrased as follows: "the utility of a decision is the higher, the higher the average utility resulting from it." It will therefore not contradict this principle if you simply equate $u(a_1)$ and $u(a_2)$ with the corresponding average utilities. That is

$$u(a_1) = p_0 ; \quad u(a_2) = p$$

You have thus scaled the utilities of prospects, sure as well as non-sure ones:

$$u(r_1) = 0; \quad u(r_2) = u(a_1) = p_0 ; \quad u(a_2) = p; \quad u(r_3) = 1$$

It will prove more convenient to use a notation that unifies the sure and non-sure prospects, by listing the alternative results and their corresponding probabilities. In this notation, the equations just given become

$$u(r_1, r_2, r_3 ; 1, 0, 0) = 0;$$

$$u(r_1, r_2, r_3 ; 0, 1, 0) = u(r_1, r_2, r_3 ; 1 - p_0, 0, p_0) = p_0$$

$$u(r_1, r_2, r_3 ; 1 - p, 0, p) = p;$$

$$u(r_1, r_2, r_3 ; 0, 0, 1) = 1$$

It is easily checked that each of these equations satisfies the principle "utility of a prospect equals its average utility," i.e., the average of the utilities of the component outcomes (sure prospects) promised by the prospect in question.

Note that the zero and the unit of the scale of utilities were chosen arbitrarily, by assigning utility 0 to the worst, and utility 1 to the best of the results considered. To this extent, the scale is arbitrary, just as is a temperature scale. If, for example, we had to put $u(r_1) = -10$ and $u(r_3) = +100$, the principle of choosing the decision with the higher average utility would yield [compare equations (1)]:

$$u(r_3) \cdot p + u(r_1) \cdot (1 - p) = 100 \cdot p - 10 \cdot (1 - p) = 110p - 10$$

as the average utility for the decision a_2; the latter we have also denoted by $(r_1, r_2, r_3; 1 - p, 0, p)$. Thus if, as before, p_0 denotes the probability of peace that would make you indifferent between the two actions, our new scale will be (using both of the suggested notations):

$$u(r_1) = u(r_1, r_2, r_3; 1, 0, 0) = -10;$$

$$u(r_2) = u(a_1) = u(r_1, r_2, r_3; 0, 1, 0) = u(r_1, r_2, r_3; 1 - p_0, 0, p_0) = 110p_0 - 10;$$

$$u(a_2) = u(r_1, r_2, r_3; 1 - p, 0, p) = 110p - 10;$$

$$u(r_3) = u(r_1, r_2, r_3; 0, 0, 1) = 100$$

We see that, to convert from the old to the new utility scale, one has to perform a "linear transformation": that is, to multiply by a constant (110) and to add a constant (-10); just as we do in converting from Fahrenheit degrees to centigrades or from altitudes measured in feet over Lake Michigan level to altitudes in meters over sea level. In this sense, the utility scale that interprets your choices among decisions is "determinate up to an arbitrary linear transformation." (Even measurements of geometrical distances or of physical weights are determinate up to an arbitrary linear transformation, although in those cases only the multiplying constant is arbitrary: the "unit of measurement.")

So far, we have treated a case in which only three alternative outcomes (r_1, r_2, r_3) are possible. What have we shown? We have shown that your decisions are consistent with a scale of utilities that satisfies the following principle: *choose the decision that results, on the average, in the highest utility*. After fixing arbitrarily the utilities of two of the outcomes (assigning a higher utility to the better one), the application of this principle results in a definite utility number for the third outcome, and also in definite utility numbers for all prospects that promise the three outcomes with preassigned probabilities.

THE GENERAL CASE: "BERNOULLI NORM"

Let us now relax the strait jacket of "three outcomes only." Let there be any (finite) number of outcomes, also called "sure prospects." Let us generalize even further, by considering prospects which promise, with preassigned probabilities, not only certain outcomes, but possibly also prospects. The case where a prospect is a lottery promising certain outcomes rather than a lottery promising certain lotteries is clearly a special one, with certain probabilities shrinking to zeros.

So far, the letters a_1, a_2 stood for decision or action, and each corresponded to a certain prospect. We shall continue to denote prospects by $a_1, a_2, \ldots$, but it will be convenient also to use the subsequent letters of the alphabet ($b, c, \ldots$) and also x. For probabilities, we shall use, as before, p; but q and π will also be needed.

I want to convince the reader that it will be possible for him to set up a scale of his utilities of all prospects, sure and otherwise, this scale satisfying the following property: if a prospect x is a lottery promising the prospects $a_1, a_2, \ldots, a_n$ with subjective probabilities $\pi, \ldots, \pi_n$, then

$$(2) \quad u(x) = \sum_{i}^{n} u(a_i)\pi_i$$

That is, again: the utility of a prospect should equal the average of promised utilities.

If it is possible to interpret your behavior as satisfying (2), we shall say that you obey the "Bernoulli Norm": see "Historical Note," below.

The technical term for "average of values of a variable, weighted by probabilities of their occurrences" is "mathematical expectation" of that variable, or, more briefly its "expected value." The expression on the right-hand side of (2) is, then, the "expected value of utility of the prospect x," or, still more briefly, "expected utility of x." What we try to show is: there exists a numerical scale of utility for all prospects, with the following property: the utility of a prospect equals its expected utility. Since you will decide in favor of a prospect with higher utility in preference to one with lower utility, you will choose a decision that maximizes the utility of a prospect; and, by the principle just mentioned (and that we are going to prove), this implies that you maximize the expected utility of a prospect.

Let a and b be two prospects (either sure or uncertain) facing the reader, and let him regard b as better than a. Consider the following classes of prospects:

1. a and b

2. all prospects that promise a or b

3. all prospects that are not better than b and not worse than a [Obviously (1) and possibly (2) are included in (3).]

4. all prospects that are better than b

5. all prospects that are worse than a.

The utilities in class (1) will be assigned arbitrarily, except for the condition that a is worse than b. We put $u(a) = 0$, $u(b) = 1$. [If classes (4) and (5) were empty, a might stand for "agony" and b for "bliss"!]

The utilities in class (2) will all lie between (and excluding) 0 and 1, for the following reason: Let a lottery c promise b if a possible event s happens, and a if it does not happen. Therefore, if you acquire c and s happens, you get something better than a; while if s does not happen you get a. Hence c is better than a. Similarly, c is worse than b. For, if you acquire c and s happens you get b; but if s does not happen you have something worse than b. Hence $u(a) < u(c) < u(b)$ and therefore $0 < u(c) < 1$, i.e., $u(c)$ is some proper fraction.

Moreover compare two lotteries in class (2): c_1 and c_2, where c_1 promises b if the event s_1 happens. Let p_1 be the probability of s_1 and suppose $p_1 < p_2$. Then $u(c_1) < u(c_2)$, for the following reason. The lottery c_2 promises b with larger probability than does lottery c_1; but with smaller probability than does a direct offer of b. Therefore c_2 can be conceived of as a lottery that promises c_1 and b with certain probabilities.[5] Hence, by a reasoning similar to the one made before, c_2 must be better than c_1 and worse than b.

It follows that you will rank the utilities of the various prospects in class (2) by assigning increasing proper fractions as the probability p of getting b increases.

It is permissible therefore to choose as the utility number for a lottery the fraction p if the lottery promises b with probability p. We have thus scaled all prospects of class (2), and this scale fits with the boundary values $u(a) = 0$ and $u(b) = 1$, since a and b can themselves be called lotteries, with $p = 0$ and $= 1$, respectively.

Before proceeding to the remaining classes of prospects, let us satisfy ourselves that our scale, so far, has the desired property. Let a prospect x be a lottery promising prospects [belonging to classes (1) and (2)] $c_1, \ldots, c_n$ with probabilities $\pi_1, \ldots, \pi_n$. Show that

(3) $\quad u(x) = \sum_i^n \pi_i u(c_i)$

To prove (3), we replace $u(x)$ by the probability with which the lottery x promises b. This probability is compounded from $p_1, \ldots, p_n$, where p_1 is the probability with which c_1 promises b.

Hence $u(x) = \sum_i^n \pi_i\, p_i$. But we have seen that $u(c_i) = p_1$.
Hence (3) is true.

Consider now the class (3) of prospects. It includes class (1); and we have seen that it also includes class (2); but it includes more. We have covered those of the members of (3) that are a or b or lotteries promising a or b; and we were able to assign to each of these lotteries a utility p equal to the probability with which that lottery promises b. Of course, p ranges from 0 (the utility of a itself) to 1 (the utility of b itself). Now the utility of any member of class (3) must lie between 0 and 1 since it consists of prospects that are not better than b and not worse than a. Hence, any member of class (3)—say, d_1—that is not a lottery promising a or b has a utility that is equal to that of one of those lotteries—call it c_1—i.e., to some p, $0 \le p \le 1$. If we now form a lottery y that promises various members $d_1, \ldots, d_n$ of class (3) with probabilities $\pi_1, \ldots, \pi_n$, then y has the same utility as the lottery x considered in equation (3). For, the event s_1 (with probability π_1) will give the subject the prospect d_1 if he had chosen y; and the prospect c_1 if he had chosen x. And so for $s_2, \ldots, s_n$. But since we have seen each d_1 to have the same utility as the corresponding c_1 (this utility being equal to the probability with which c_1 promises b), it follows that the subject is indifferent between y and x. Thus (3) is extended to all members of the class (3), since $u(y)$ can replace $u(x)$ and each $u(d_1)$ can replace $u(c_1)$.

This would complete the proof if we could assume that there exists for each subject a worst and a best prospect, "agony" and "bliss" (a and b). If this is not the case, i.e., utility is not bounded and classes (4) and (5) are not empty, equation (3) still holds good. To show this, it suffices to pick the worst and the best prospect—say, a' and b'—among those composing the particular lottery x[i.e., a' and b' will be among the $c_1, \ldots, c_n$ in (3)], and use a' and b' in the same way in which a and b were treated previously; i.e., create a new scale of utilities—say, u'—with $u'(a') = 0$, $u'(b') = 1$, $u'(a) = p < q = u'(b)$, where p and q are certain probabilities; a and b having, respectively, the same utilities as certain two lotteries, each promising a' or b'. We see by former reasoning, that in terms of this new scale, (3) will be valid, that is

(4) $u'(x) = \sum \pi_i\, u'(c)_i$

But this latter equation remains valid also if the function u' is replaced by any linear transform of it, $\alpha u' + \beta$ (this can be easily verified by substitution). Now, the functions u' and u are, in fact, linear transforms of each other, with (for any c) $u'(c) = (q - p)u(c) + p$ [i.e., the scale u' is obtained from the scale u by shifting the origin by p and multiplying the utility unit by $q - p$]. Hence the validity of (4) entails the validity of (3) for any prospects,[6] i.e., the validity of (2).

HISTORICAL NOTE

Suppose that you apply the utility scale just described to various amounts of monetary wealth, and discover that, for you, the utility can be regarded as proportional to money amount. Should your tastes happen to be of this kind then (since you have agreed that your choices are as described by the Bernoulli Norm and you therefore maximize the mathematical expectation of utility) you are a maximizer of the mathematical expectation of monetary wealth. And remember that this mathematical expectation was computed on the basis of your subjective probabilities.

Now, the idea that a consistent decision-maker chooses a bet that gives him the maximum expected monetary wealth, computed on the basis of his subjective probabilities, can be traced back to Thomas Bayes (eighteenth century). Daniel Bernoulli who lived in that same century was not so clear about the subjective nature of the probabilities that can be said to underline human choice. He assumed people to know the true odds in a game, and neglected the case when a man has no sufficient theory or no large sample to compute the odds with precision. But, on the other hand, Bernoulli was emphatic (as Bayes was not: remember that Bayes dealt with money instead of utilities) about the subjective nature of preferences. Unless your tastes are of a peculiar character, utilities are not proportional to money amounts (and moreover they can and should be attached to many other objects of choice besides money!), and one must be careful to state that the consistent decision-maker maximizes his expected utility, not his expected monetary wealth. This is what we called the Bernoulli Norm. In stating it, we did describe the probabilities used as subjective and called them sometimes degrees of belief. But we did not say how they too (like the equally subjective utility numbers) can be derived as characterizing a consistent decision-maker's behavior. This was done by the late Frank Ramsey in 1926, and more recently by De Finetti and by L. J. Savage. Their approach will be outlined in our concluding section.

THE RAMSEY NORM

I shall now try to convince you that your decision, if consistent, can be interpreted in the following manner: there exist utility numbers, attached to outcomes of your actions, and there exist degrees of belief, attached to the future states of the world, with the following property: if for each of your possible actions the expected utility (i.e., the mathematical expectation of utility of outcomes) were computed on the basis of your degrees of belief, then the action chosen by you would be the one with the highest expected utility. We may call this the Ramsey Norm.

Imagine that the following eight actions $a_1, \ldots, a_8$ will have one of the two outcomes, Death (D) or Life (L), depending on whether the world will be in the state s_1 or s_2 or s_3 (mutually exclusive), as shown in the following table which, as you can convince yourself, exhausts all possible triplets of L- and D-symbols:

Actions	STATES OF World			Group
	s_1	s_2	s_3	
a_1	D	D	D	1
a_2	L	D	D	
a_3	D	L	D	2
a_4	D	D	L	
a_5	D	L	L	
a_6	L	D	L	3
a_7	L	L	D	
a_8	L	L	L	4

I assume that you prefer Life to Death. Then you will prefer a_8 to a_7 because a_8 has a better outcome than a_7 in state s_3, and the same outcome as a_7 otherwise. By this reasoning, you will prefer the action a_8 to any of the actions in group 3; you will prefer any action in 3 and any one in 2 to the action a_1.

Now suppose, in addition, that you happen to be indifferent between a_2, a_3, and a_4. If this is the case we shall say that your degrees of belief in the occurrence of each of the states s_1, s_2, s_3 are $\frac{1}{3}$, $\frac{1}{3}$, $\frac{1}{3}$; and we shall assign to the occurrence of the state s_1 or s_2 (and similarly: of the state s_1 or s_3; and s_2 or s_3) the degree of belief $\frac{2}{3}$. Moreover: would it be reasonable for you to be indifferent within group 2 and not to be indifferent within group 3? Would this not mean that you grant the three possible future states of the world an equal degree of belief as long as rewards or punishments are attached to them in a certain way, but revise your beliefs when the rewards and punishments are interchanged? This would be unreasonable.

We thus have:

$$u(a_1) < u(a_2) = u(a_3) = u(a_4) < u(a_5) = u(a_6) = u(a_7) < u(a_8)$$

We now proceed to scale these utilities. We are free to fix the utility of Life (like the utility of "bliss" in an earlier part of the paper) at 1, and the utility of Death at 0. Then the utilities of prospects will also fall in their places, being equal to the probability of Life as promised in a given prospect. That is, we obtain $u(a_1) = 0$; $u(a_8) = 1$; $u(a_2) = u(a_3) = \frac{1}{3} < u(a_5) = u(a_6) = u(a_7) = \frac{2}{3}$. We shall find as before that this utility scale is consistent with your being a maximizer of expected utility.

Thus, not only your utilities but also your degrees of belief can be derived from your behavior—including the indifference which you have shown in choosing within group 2 of actions (and also—as consistency required—within the group 3 of actions).

We have thus shown that it was possible to interpret your choices as consistent with the existence of utilities and subjective probabilities and with the maximization of expected utility. Granted that the example was a special one. It can be easily extended to n (instead of 3) states of the world, and degrees of belief $0, \frac{1}{n}, \frac{2}{n}, \ldots,$ $n - 1$, 1 can then be defined—if one can catch you as being indifferent within a certain group of decisions. How to arrange for a demarkation of states of the world that would make this possible requires a more complete and rigorous logical analysis. (This has been done by L. J. Savage.) Here we have had to content ourselves with a mere sketch.

ENDNOTES

1. For example, at the colloquium on risk in econometrics, held in 1952; its Proceedings published by the Centre National de la Recherche Scientifique, Paris, 1953.

2. I. N. Herstein and John Milnor, "An Axiomatic Approach to Measurable Utility," *Econometrica*, 1953.

3. John Wiley and Sons, 1954.

4. *Econometrica*, 1950; and Second Berkeley Symposium, ed. by J. Neyman, 1951.

5. Let these probabilities be q and $1 - q$, respectively. q is easy to find (though it is not really necessary for our purpose) by posing

$$q \cdot p_1 + (1 - q) \cdot 1 = p_2$$

since p_2, the chance of obtaining b, must be equal to the chance (in the new lottery) of getting it by virtue of having gotten c_1, *plus* the chance of getting it directly. We have $q = 1 - p_2/1 - p_1$.

6. With $u(a) = 0$ and $u(b) = 1$, the utility $u(e)$ of a member of class (4) and the utility of $u(f)$ of a member of class (5) are easily shown to be

$$u(e) = \frac{1}{q} > 1; \quad u(f) = 1 - \frac{1}{r} < 0$$

where q and r arc probabilities defined as follows: the subject is indifferent between b and a lottery promising e or a with respective probabilities q and $1 - q$; and he is indifferent between a and a lottery promising f or b with respective probabilities r and $1 - r$. It is easily verified that with these definitions,

$u(e) \cdot q + u(a) \cdot (1 - q) = u(b)$ and
$u(f) \cdot r - u(b) \cdot (1 - r) = u(a)$

Questions for Study and Discussion

1. Marschak characterizes the utility scale derived under uncertainty as "determinate up to an arbitrary linear transformation." What level of scale is this, within the classification system of Stevens? (See Table 2.3, p. 37)

2. If a decision-maker is certain about the future, a ranking of the results of alternative actions is said to be sufficient for purposes of choice. Why is this so? Illustrate by an example formulated as a special case of decision making under uncertainty. What level of scaling is required for a utility measure based on certainty? When economists say that such measures do not reflect "intensity of preferences," what do they mean?

3. What is measured by an expected utility?

4. The practical application of decision theory involves the construction of *utility functions* reflecting the risk-taking preferences of the decision-maker. A superb introduction to the construction and interpretation of these functions is found in Raiffa (1968), Chapters 1–4. Another source, in the form of a single article, is Swalm (1966). The following review problem assumes the reader is familiar with such an introduction. Suppose you are given $10,000 to invest in one of three mutual funds for a period of one year. At the conclusion of this period, the value of the investment is yours to keep. The "future of the market" is estimated as follows:

m_1: "up strongly"	$p(m_1) = .10$
m_2: "up"	$p(m_2) = .15$
m_3: "no change"	$p(m_3) = .25$
m_4: "down"	$p(m_4) = .35$
m_5: "down strongly"	$p(m_5) = .15$

The estimated decision situation, with outcomes represented in terms of the dollar value of the investment, is the following:

	m_1 (.10)	m_2 (.15)	m_3 (.25)	m_4 (.35)	m_5 (.15)
f_1	$30K	$20K	$12K	$6K	$2K
f_2	$25K	$15K	$10K	$9K	$6K
f_3	$18K	$13K	$10K	$10K	$8K

Assume you wish to maximize your expected utility. Which fund would you select? Provide an interpretation of the shape of your utility-of-investment curve. Interpret three points on the curve in terms of a lottery. What is the expected value of perfect information to you, in this situation? ("Perfect information" means that the future of the market is known with certainty.)

5. Note in the above problem that decision theory provides a framework within which the value of information may be measured. How does this measure differ fundamentally from that of information theory, for decision-support purposes?

6. The utility assessment procedure followed in Problem 4 presumes that the consequences of a particular decision are characterized by a single attribute, that is, monetary income. When more than one attribute is necessary to describe the significant aspects of consequences, the consequences are termed *multiattributed*. An example is the determination of a blood bank inventory ordering policy, described by Keeney (1972). Significant attributes of policy consequences cited in this example include amount of outdated blood, amount of unsupplied demand, age of transfused blood, and total blood intake of the blood bank. Procedures are currently being developed to construct multiattributed utility functions to support decision making in circumstances comparable to the blood bank example. (See Keeney and Raiffa, 1976.) What measurement implications are associated with the existence of multiattributed consequences, with respect to the construction of a multiattributed utility function?

7. What type of computer-based decision support system might be designed to assist in situations where uncertainty and multiattributed consequences prevail? Should the DSS be tailored to the specific problem at hand? (For examples of experimental applications, see Dyer, 1973, and Wehrung *et al.*, 1976).

THE MEASUREMENT OF ORGANIZATIONAL PERFORMANCE

PART THREE

Russell Ackoff (1972) makes a useful distinction between organisms and organizations. Both are purposeful systems in the sense that each can willfully change its goals under constant environmental conditions. The difference is that organisms are comprised of organs which function only to serve the goal of the collective system, whereas organizations are comprised of purposeful subsystems which may choose either to serve the organization's goals or to pursue individual goals. In some cases these individual goals may be diametrically opposite to the organization's goals.

This distinction is the source of much of the difficulty in measuring organizational performance. The question, "How well is the organization doing?" refers not to a single goal but to a complex, hierarchical goal structure. There are multiple goals for the organization as a whole, and multiple—some perhaps divergent—goals for each of its entities. Consequently, the measurement system must differentiate among the dimensions of the organization's goal structure, and it must integrate these into a response to the scorekeeping question. A difficult task!

Many methods have been developed to help practicing managers cope with this complex problem of measuring organizational performance. One new approach, called the "critical success factor method," (Rockart, 1979) is illustrative. The approach involves an initial structured interview of about two hours with a manager. During the interview the manager's goals and best judgment on the factors leading to their successful accomplishment are identified. An effort is then made to combine, eliminate, restate, and otherwise clarify the factors. Finally some preliminary measures are specified.

The interviewer then studies the results of the first session in order to refine the factors and to further develop the measures of performance. The result of the interviewer's analysis is fed back to the manager in a second session. This session focuses primarily on the measures. The availability of data, their degree of quantification, and their cost of acquisition are explored. At the end of this session, a set of "prime measures" is specified for each critical success factor.

The results of applying this approach at Microwave Associates (Rockart, 1979) are instructive. Seven success factors were identified (see Fig. 1.). These factors refer to the organization's success as a financial entity, its ability to sell its product, its ability to maintain the contribution of its employees, and its ability to allocate its internal resources effectively. Underlying these success factors are several critical measurement issues:

FIGURE 1

CSF's developed to meet Microwave Associates' organizational goals

Critical Success Factors	Prime Measures
1. Image in financial markets	Price/earnings ratio
2. Technological reputation with customers	Orders/bid ratio Customer "perception" interview results
3. Market success	Change in market share (each product) Growth rates of company markets
4. Risk recognition in major bids and contracts	Company's years of experience with similar products "New" or "old" customer Prior customer relationship
5. Profit margin on jobs	Bid profit margin as ratio of profit on similar jobs in this product line
6. Company morale	Turnover, absenteeism, etc. Informal feedback
7. Performance to budget on major jobs	Job cost budget/actual

Source: Rockart (1979)

1. How successful is the organization in an exchange economy? This question deals with the organization's ability to trade effectively with other entities and to create collective value under conditions of relative scarcity. The unit of analysis is the transaction and the unit of measure is typically a monetary one. Accounting serves as the principal measurement system used to measure the degree of scarcity involved in an economic exchange. Profitability, return on investment, and market share or penetration are the common measurement concepts employed.

2. How successful is the organization in securing abundance from nature? This is the problem of production. The purpose is to create use value. The criterion is efficiency. Analysis focuses on the jobs, tasks or roles performed, and the amount of resources consumed in order to win beneficial outputs from nature. Cost and productivity are the common measurement concepts employed.

3. How successful is the organization's measurement system for guiding the activities of its purposeful entities towards its collective goals? This issue refers to the behavioral dimensions of the measurement system involved, and emerges from the fact that each subsystem in the organization has a choice in pursuing either the organization's goals or some other goals. The point is that the measurement system *itself* may either promote the achievement of exchange value or use value goals or it may actually inhibit the achievement of those goals, depending on how people interpret the measures and how they adjust their behavior to them.

These three issues dictate the organization of this part of the book. The first section deals with accounting systems and profitability measurement. The second section deals with productivity measurement. The third section discusses the concept of performance measurement systems that attempt to integrate and extend financial and productivity measures. Finally, the fourth section brings the human factor into the measurement system and deals with some of the problems encountered when people are the measurers, the users of measures, and the objects of measurement.

ACCOUNTING SYSTEMS AND PROFITABILITY MEASUREMENT

CHAPTER **SIX**

At the end of its business year 1968, Trans World Airlines appeared headed toward reporting a financial loss after recording nearly $40.8 million profit in 1967. TWA's response to the crisis was to change its accounting procedures. It extended the depreciable life of most of its fleet by several years and took down more of its available investment tax credit in computing deferred income taxes. The result was that the potential loss converted into a $21.2 million profit. The basis for measurement had been changed again. In response some financial analysts complained, "Just what is financial accounting measuring?"

This issue still plagues the accounting profession, a field some people refer to as the "measurement profession." Financial accounting was conceived as a measurement system designed to keep track of the results of exchange transactions among economic entities. Its basic unit of measure is a monetary unit expressed as a price. Hence each measurement reveals something about the relative purchasing power of the organization. The purpose of accounting is to answer the question, "How well is the organization doing in an exchange economy?" by keeping track of the relative scarcity value of items transacted. But to accomplish this purpose properly, there should be a standard set of rules for measurement. The TWA case and others like it raise this fundamental issue of standardizing measurement practice.

It is interesting to note that while accounting has a long history, dating at least to Luca Paciolo's *Summa* in 1494, accountants have yet to reach full agreement on the profession's measurement premises.

Indeed, today the controversy is rather heated. As recently as 1976, the Financial Standards Board released a review document entitled, *Conceptual Framework for Financial Accounting and Reporting: Elements of Financial Statements*, which was proposed as a constitution for establishing consistent standards of financial reporting. Among other things the document describes the attributes of economic entities to be measured and the units to be employed in their measurement.

The *Conceptual Framework* discusses five attributes for measuring and presenting various classes of assets and liabilities. Each of these attributes makes critical measurement assumptions about the points in time at which the measure is to be focused, and the expected action to be taken by the economic entity whose property is being measured. The five attributes are:

1. Historical cost. Historical cost records the price actually paid for property. This assumes that the relevant time for measurement is the time the property was actually exchanged. No other course of action is contemplated.

2. Current cost. Current cost records the cost that would have to be paid to purchase the property at the current market price. This assumes that the relevant time for measurement is the present. The assumed course of action underlying the expectation is a hypothetical purchase.

3. Current market (exit) value. Current market value records the cost as the amount that could be realized by means of the orderly liquidation of the assets. The assumed time is the present. The course of action is to sell the asset.

4. Expected exit value. Expected exit value records the total amount of cash into which an asset is expected to be converted in the due course of business, less the direct costs necessary to make that conversion. This is sometimes referred to as "net realizable value." The assumed time is the future. The assumed course of action is to continue to use the asset according to a business plan or normal business practice.

5. Present value of expected cash flows. The present value of expected cash flows records the discounted present value of future cash inflows into which an asset is expected to be converted in the due course of business, less the present value of outflows necessary to obtain those inflows. The assumed time is the future as discounted into the present. The assumed course of action is to continue to use the asset according to plan or normal business practice. Further, it is assumed that the entity will forego opportunities to obtain interest on the monetary value of the asset throughout the period.

No one of these five approaches is agreed upon by all accountants.

The conceptual framework controversy goes to the heart of many fundamental measurement issues in accounting. Who are the users of financial data and what is their role in establishing the measurement system? What is the meaning of the criterion of usefulness of accounting data? What is the proper measurement unit—current dollars or past dollars? How do the traditional criteria of objectivity and reliability relate to the choice of concepts? The first reading in this section, by Ijiri and Jaedicke, explicitly addresses this last question, in terms which have wider implications.

The conceptual framework also raises another fundamental issue in accounting measurement. What time perspective should be used for measuring financial transactions? Should we measure what has happened in the past, or, alternatively, what will happen in the future? In "The Past's Future," Churchman frames seven prototype responses to these questions and develops their implications for accounting measurements.

Finally, in "Measurement and Misrepresentation," Chambers takes up the issue of measuring profit—profit being defined as "the residue from a series of transactions whose individual effects are expressed in terms of initial price." He argues that misrepresentation such as that described in the TWA case above can be avoided. His argument deals with some of the same issues the *Conceptual Framework* addresses. He also offers some suggestions for improving the relevance of accounting for its users.

RELIABILITY AND OBJECTIVITY OF ACCOUNTING MEASUREMENTS

Yuji Ijiri • Robert K. Jaedicke

Accounting is a measurement system which is plagued by the existence of alternative measurement methods. For many years, accountants have been searching for criteria which can be used to choose the best measurement alternative. Generally, it is conceded by most accountants that the purpose for which the data are to be used (usefulness) is an important criterion to be considered in the choice of accounting method.[1] However, the use or purpose of the data still leaves much to be desired as a criterion since different accounting measurement methods are frequently suggested as being appropriate for a single user or group of users having the same purpose. For example, in a roundtable discussion on "The Measurement of Property, Plant, and Equipment in Financial Statements" the participants agreed that usefulness would be one of the criteria for evaluating different accounting measurement methods. This general criterion ". . . was applied in the sense of *usefulness to investors who are willing and competent to read financial statements carefully and with discrimination for the purposes of assistance in arriving at rational investment decisions.*"[2] In the above statement, the user group and the purpose for which data will be used are both clearly identified. Yet, according to the moderator and reporter, three alternative measurement methods (for fixed asset accounting) represented by three different groups emerged from the discussion. One group would continue to use historical cost. "Some advocates of historical cost will continue to hold to this view unless they are given convincing evidence that an alternative will produce markedly *more useful results.*"[3]

A second group favored retention of historical cost, supplemented with statements where the data have been adjusted for general price-level changes. Yet a third group believed that in certain situations acquisition cost should be replaced with a market value or a specific price-index measurement in order to reflect changes in specific prices and assets. Well-informed accountants and businessmen presumably disagree on what is the most useful measurement method even after the purpose for which the data are to be used and the user group are specified. When this happens, the use or purpose of the data is simply too broad and general a criterion to be of much help.

Usefulness is made up of many factors. Data must be timely, reliable, accurate, relevant, material, etc., to be useful. Our purpose here is not to deny the importance

---

From *The Accounting Review*, July, 1966 pp. 474–483. Reprinted by permission.

of usefulness as a criterion but rather to analyze one important aspect of usefulness. This aspect, we shall refer to as *reliability*. Our two main purposes will be (1) to develop the concept of reliability as it relates to accounting and (2) to show how the criterion of reliability is related to the widely accepted criterion of objectivity. The concept of objectivity is first discussed.

THE CONCEPT OF OBJECTIVITY

Objectivity (like usefulness) of accounting measurements is usually regarded as an important criterion for choosing among measurement methods. For example, Paton and Littleton state, "Verifiable, objective evidence has therefore become an important element in accounting and a necessary adjunct to the proper execution of the accounting function of supplying dependable information."[4] Similarly, Moonitz writes, that "changes in assets and liabilities, and the related effects (if any) on revenues, expenses, retained earnings, and the like, should not be given formal recognition in the accounts earlier than the point of time at which they can be measured in objective terms."[5] Still another example, Fertig concludes " . . . that a high degree of verifiable evidence is necessary as support for financial statement representations because accountants must always be in a position to assure their readers that financial statements are what they are represented to be."[6]

In spite of fairly common agreement that objectivity is important as a criterion for selecting accounting measurement methods, there is a surprising lack of agreement on just what the concept should mean and how it should be applied. On the one hand, Moonitz defines objective evidence as being subject to verification by a competent investigator. Thus the measurements have a meaning which is separate and apart from the measurer.[7] Paton and Littleton's definition of objectivity is similar to Moonitz's.[8] However, Arnett, in an article, "What Does Objectivity Mean to Accountants," points out that the recognition that some useful measures are not objective has caused a loosening of the strict definition of objectivity as expressed by Moonitz and Littleton. He concludes that ". . . data still needs to be impersonal in order to be objective. However, 'impersonal' is now much more flexible in its application than under the strict construction."[9] Fertig joins those who want to broaden the definition of objectivity when he states, "First we will attempt to demonstrate that a more useful, less misleading definition of 'objectivity' is in terms of the measurements sought by accountants, rather than solely in terms of the verifiability of accounting evidence."[10] Of course, at the extreme, there are accountants who would contend that if the measurement is useful, further justification is unnecessary.[11] This latter viewpoint advocates dropping objectivity as a criterion for at least some accounting measurements.

Objectivity as a property of accounting measurements does have appeal. However, it is a difficult concept to define and in some cases leads to confusion and disagreement.

The Winston Simplified Dictionary (College Edition) defines the term "objective" as "existing outside of the mind; having a separate or independent existence." In other words, objectivity refers to the external reality that is independent of the persons who perceive it. However, the precise nature of the separate existence of the external reality is not clear, at least as it relates to accounting. For example, what is meant by the objective income figure of a given firm for a given period? If the above definition is used, it must be something that exists separately and independently from the accountants who measure it. While it may be convenient to assume the existence of such an objective income figure, it is impossible to ascertain what this value is without going through the thinking process of those accountants who made the measurement.

Therefore, rather than basing the definition of objectivity on the existence of objective factors that are independent of persons who perceive them, it is far more realistic to define objectivity to mean simply the *consensus* among a given group of observers or measurers. For example, we can say that the amount of cash in a cash box can be measured more objectively than the annual income of a firm. That is, if we asked a group of accountants to measure both the cash in the cash box and the income of the firm we would expect a higher degree of consensus on the former measure than the latter.[12] We will elaborate on the precise nature of consensus as applied to accounting by means of the following model of measurement.

There are three factors involved in measurement. They are: (1) an object whose property is to be measured; (2) a measurement system which consists of a set of rules and instruments, and; (3) a measurer. These three factors collectively produce a quantity called a measure. (See Figure I.) If the measurement rules in the system are specified in detail, we would expect the results to show little deviation from measurer to measurer. On the other hand, if the measurement rules are vague or poorly stated, then the implementation of the measurement system will require judgment on the part of the measurer; hence the output of the measurement system is more likely to show a wider deviation from measurer to measurer. In other words, the measurement system and the measurer's judgment are complementary with each other. Objectivity of a measurement system gives the degree of consensus in the results (output) or the degree to which the output of the system depends on the measurer.

The degree of consensus depends not only on the measurement system but also on the objects whose property is to be measured. For example, given two measurement systems for measuring income, the first may show a greater degree of consensus when the income of service firms is the object of measurement; however, the second may have a greater degree of consensus when the income of manufacturing firms is being measured. This could happen because the first measurement system contains vague measurement rules for inventory treatment which shows up as a lack of objectivity (consensus) when inventory becomes important.

Further, the objectivity of a measurement system depends upon a particular group of measurers. For example, in measuring the income of a firm, a group of

FIGURE I   *Measurement Process.*

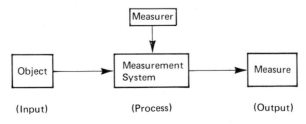

(Input)   (Process)   (Output)

experts in accounting will produce a higher degree of consensus than a group of lay-men. That is, accounting education tends to homogenize the way in which a group of measurers will measure income. In such a case, an income figure which is highly objective from the viewpoint of the experts may be much less objective in the eyes of laymen. Therefore, in defining the objectivity of a measurement system, we must specify which group of measurers (i.e., which reference group) we are concerned with.

Finally, another important point to be noted here is that objectivity is not a black-or-white issue. There are various degrees of objectivity and we should argue whether one measurement is more objective (or less objective) than another and not whether a measurement is objective or not. We shall, therefore, elaborate on how the *degree* of the objectivity can be measured.

A Measure of Objectivity

Let us consider a group of n measurers who are asked to measure a given object, such as income of a given firm for a given period, under a specified measurement system. Let x_i be the quantity that the ith measurer ($i = 1, 2, \ldots, n$) reports by using the specified measurement system. We are now concerned with the degree of unanimity or the degree of variability of x_i's. One commonly used statistical measure of the variability of a set of observations is the variance. We may, therefore, use this as an indicator of the degree of objectivity of the given measurement system in measuring the given object. Namely, objectivity, V, may be defined to be:

$$(1) \quad V = \frac{1}{n} \sum_{i=1}^{n} (X_i - \bar{X})^2,$$

where n is the number of measures in the reference group, x_i is the quantity that the ith measurer reports, and $\bar{x}$ is the average of x_i's over all measurers in the reference group.[13]

Next, we must note the fact that the above measure of variability depends upon a particular object. We must find a way to state the degree of objectivity of a mea-surement system independently from a particular object. This may be done by con-sidering a set of all objects that are to be measured under the measurement system and taking an average (weighed, if necessary) of the above measure associated with the measurement of each object in the set.

One final remark before we move on to the discussion of reliability. If a measure is a highly objective one, it is irrelevant who in the measurement group has actually measured it, since most of the people in the group would have produced an identi-cal (or a similar) result. This is the virtue of objectivity. That is, the measurement is relatively free from personal feelings or prejudice of the measurer if it is objective. Therefore, the decision maker can use the measurement without being concerned about who the measurer is.

However, this does not mean that objectivity is the same as usefulness. For ex-ample, a highly objective measure, such as the cash balance, the number of shares of capital stock, etc. may not be as useful in predicting the future market price of a firm's stock as a highly subjective statement made by the president of the firm as to his expectation of the future stock price. Furthermore, a measure that is very useful for one purpose may not be useful at all for other purposes. Therefore, *the usefulness of a measure cannot be determined until a specific use is given, whereas the objectivity of a measure can be determined independently of its use.*

THE CONCEPT OF RELIABILITY

Let us now move on to the discussion of the reliability of an accounting measurement. In general, a system is said to be reliable if it works in the way it is supposed to work.[14] For example, a barometer is said to be reliable if it reflects accurately the actual barometric pressure, since this is what a barometer is supposed to do. Similarly, a reliable man is one that will do what he is supposed to do, or, in other words, he can be "counted on."

However, there is another aspect of reliability which is especially important in dealing with reliability of an accounting information system. Consider the following question about the barometer example given above: "Is the barometer a reliable indicator of tomorrow's weather?" In this case, the question is not whether the barometer indicates the actual barometric air pressure, but rather whether the barometer reading can be used for predicting tomorrow's weather. This type of question is more user-oriented. It is also the type of question which is of importance in evaluating the reliability of accounting measurements.

How can the degree of reliability be determined and measured when the barometer is used for forecasting the weather? Consider a case where the forecaster is simply interested in forecasting whether it is going to rain or not, i.e., the prediction contains two categories, "Fair" and "Rain." Similarly, suppose the barometer has only two readings, one for "Fair" and the other for "Rain," instead of a more detailed calibration. If the barometer points to Fair, the forecaster expects the weather tomorrow to be Fair, and if the barometer points to Rain, he expects rain.

On the other hand, the relationship can also be reversed. That is, if it is fair today the expectation is that the barometer reading yesterday was "Fair"; if it rains today, the expectation is that the barometer reading yesterday was "Rain." If, on the contrary, yesterday's reading was "Rain" when today is fair, or if the reading yesterday was "Fair" when today is rainy, the barometer gives a wrong indicator. If this occurs many times the barometer would be considered unreliable for predicting the weather.

The degree of reliability of the barometer as used in predicting the weather may, therefore, be measured by the proportion of the total readings which are "right." Likewise the degree of unreliability can be measured by the proportion of readings which are "wrong." This relationship is shown in diagram form in Figures II and III.

If the above concept of reliability is to be used in accounting, the simple "right-or-wrong" classifications must be replaced with a detailed classification by introducing a finer calibration (or measurement). This can be done in the barometer example by using a method similar to the one discussed in dealing with objectivity. That is, reliability can be thought of as the degree of closeness to being right. However, there is one difference to be noted; the degree of closeness to "being right" depends

FIGURE II. *Barometer Reading and Actual Weather.*

		Actual Weather Today	
		Fair	Rain
Barometer Reading Yesterday	Fair	Right	Wrong
	Rain	Wrong	Right

FIGURE III. *The Degree of Reliability of Barometers: Barometer A is more reliable than Barometer B.*

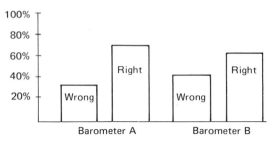

primarily upon the way in which the user uses the indicator (barometer reading). This is something that was not observed in the discussion of objectivity. In fact, the point was made that the degree of objectivity could be measured independent of the manner in which the measurement is to be used.

The relation between the reliability of the measurement and the manner in which the user uses the measurement can be seen by further examination of the barometer example. Assume, for example, that a user wants to use the barometer reading for predicting the amount of rain for the following day. In doing so he creates in his own mind a relationship between today's barometer reading and the amount of rain tomorrow. However, this relationship that the user has determined (perhaps by past experiences) may not coincide exactly with the actual (real) relationship between today's barometer reading and tomorrow's rainfall. For example, assume that the actual and forecaster's relationships are as given in Figure IV. If the barometer reading is b then the forecaster would predict the amount of rainfall to be r. If the barometer reading is b', then r' amount of rain would be predicted. However, the actual relationship between the barometer reading and the rainfall is given by the line A. That is, if the reading is b the actual amount of rainfall is r'', and if the reading is b' the actual amount of rainfall is r.

However, in spite of the actual relationship, if the actual amount of rainfall is r, a right barometer reading from the forecaster's viewpoint is b and not b'. That is, if the actual amount of today's rainfall is r, the forecaster alleges that yesterday's

FIGURE IV. *Actual and Forecaster's Relationships Between Today's Barometer Reading and Tomorrow's Rainfall.*

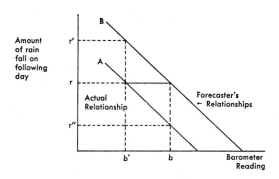

barometer reading should have been at b and not a b'. Let b (in this example) be called the alleged value. The alleged values will depend on the manner in which the forecaster uses the barometer readings for predicting rainfall. In the above example, the set of alleged values for various values of r (the rainfall) is represented by the line B.

The degree of "closeness to being right" is then represented by the difference between b and b'. As in the derivation of the objectivity measure, we may use this difference as a basis of the reliability measure, and by taking a suitable "represent-ative" value of such differences at various levels of rainfall we can define the relia-bility measure of the barometer.

Reliability of Accounting Measurements

Let us now consider the problem of reliability of accounting measurement. For a user of accounting data, the accounting measurement is only a means to an end. In other words, a user of accounting measurements is interested only insofar as the measurements give data which are helpful in his decision process. To make the ar-gument more concrete, let the variable y be a factor which the decision maker wants to determine or predict based on the accounting measure. For example, the variable y may be the price of the firm's stock at a certain point in the future; or, y may be the dividend that the firm will pay at the end of the year; or y may represent the average income of the firm during the next five years. Of course, it is also possible for y to represent an event which has occurred in the past, such as the amount of income tax paid in the previous period, the amount of total sales during the last two years, etc.

Now, let x be the value of the accounting measurement which results from the application of a particular set of measurement rules. A user of x uses the measure only if he thinks he can determine the value of the variable y from the value of the variable x. In deriving the value of the variable y from the value of the variable x, the user develops a formula (or a function) by which he can associate the two vari-ables. This is done through his experience or by education. That is, he may learn the relationship between the variable x and y by observing the value of the two variables for a number of past periods, or he may be taught the relationship between the two. In any event, y and x are related by some function such as $y = f(x)$.

To illustrate, assume that a decision maker is interested in the amount of the fu-ture dividend per share of stock. He has discovered that the dividend in time period $t+1$ is usually about 1/2 of the per-share income reported in time period t. Thus, he uses the relationship: $y = .5x$, where y is the expected per-share dividend in time $t+1$ and x is the per-share income reported in time period i, calculated by using a certain specified set of accounting measurement rules.

If income reported in time period t is $10, then the decision maker, using his relationship $= .5(x)$, would estimate the per-share dividend in time period $t+1$ to be $5. Once a user of accounting data develops his own function f, he expects (and hopes that) the relationship between the variables x and y to be stable during the future periods.

If, in the above example, the dividend in time period $t+1$ actually turns out to be $4 when reported income for time period t is $10, this event decreases the degree of his reliance upon the reported per-share income in estimating the future dividend.

If the dividend on the stock turns out to be $4, then the decision maker may say that the reported per-share income should have been $8. In other words, he *alleges* that the reported per-share profit should have been $8, now that the dividend on the stock is $4. This is his *alleged value* given his decision function and given that the actual dividend was $4. We may use this difference between the actual value ($10) and the alleged value ($8) as a basis for a reliability measure in the following manner.

The Measure of Reliability

First, we introduce the fact that the actual value ($10) depends upon the measurers. Under a given set of measurement rules an accountant may derive $12 as the income figure whereas another accountant may give $8. Therefore, we must average the differences between the actual value and alleged value over all measures in the reference group in the same manner as in the case of objectivity measure. Since we used the average of the square of the difference between the value derived by the measurer (x_i) and the mean of the values derived by all measures ($\bar{x}$) in defining the objectivity measure, we shall use the same average of the square of the difference between the value derived by the measurer (x_i) and the alleged value (x^*) in defining the reliability measure R. Namely,

$$(2) \quad R = \frac{1}{n} \sum_{i=1}^{n} (x_i - x^*)^2.$$

This formula is exactly the same as that of Mean-Square-Error, another measure commonly used in statistics.[15]

Since the above reliability measure depends upon a particular object to be measured, we must apply the same averaging method as the one explained in connection with the objectivity measure in order to derive an expression for the reliability of a measurement system.[16]

Now notice the similarity and difference between the measure of reliability (Equation (2)) and the measure of objectivity (Equation (1)). The degree of reliability of an accounting measurement system depends upon how close the actual measurements (x_i's) are to the alleged value (x^*), whereas the degree of objectivity depends upon how close the actual measurements (x_i's) are to the mean value ($\bar{x}$). A comparison of equations (1) and (2) shows this essential difference between objectivity and reliability. Note that the degree of reliability (R) as given in (2) can be rewritten as follows:

$$(3) \quad R = \frac{1}{n} \sum_{i=1}^{n} \{ (x_i - \bar{x}) + (\bar{x} - x^*) \}^2.$$

By squaring out the expression inside the brackets, we have

$$(4) \quad R = \frac{1}{n} \sum_{i=1}^{n} \{ (x_i - \bar{x})^2 + 2(x_i - \bar{x})$$

$$\cdot (\bar{x} - x^*) + (\bar{x} - x^*)^2 \}.$$

$$= \frac{1}{n} \sum_{i=1}^{n} (x_i - \bar{x})^2 + \frac{2}{n} (\bar{x} - x^*)$$

$$\cdot \sum_{i=1}^{n} (x_i - \bar{x}) + 1 \frac{1}{n} \sum_{i=1}^{n} - x^*)^2.$$

Since the (unsquared) sum of the deviations of any variable from its mean is zero,

$$\sum_{i=1}^{n} (x_i - \bar{x})$$

in the second term of the above expression is zero and this entire term drops out. Hence:

(5) $R = \dfrac{1}{n} \sum_{i=1}^{n} (x_i - \bar{x})^2 + \dfrac{1}{n} \sum_{i=1}^{n} (\bar{x} - x^*)^2.$

Since the second term in (5) does not depend on i, it reduces to $(\bar{x} - x^*)^2$, and we have

(6) $R = \dfrac{1}{n} \sum_{i=1}^{n} (x_i - \bar{x})^2 + (\bar{x} - x^*)^2.$

By using Equation (1), and lettering $B = (\bar{x} - x^*)^2$, we have

(7) $R = V + B.$

From (7) it is clear that the degree of reliability is the degree of objectivity plus a term, B, which may be called a "reliance bias" or simply a "bias." This means that R is always greater than or equal to V. R is equal to V if and only if the alleged value is equal to the mean of all measured values. Although several parts of the method would have to be more precisely specified to make it practically operational (such as how to choose the set of accounting measurers), Equation (7) is an interesting and highly useful way to conceptualize the essential relationship between objectivity and reliability. These relationships are discussed below in detail.[17]

Reliability and Objectivity

Equation (7) shows that the concept of reliability is not independent of objectivity. If the bias factor, B, can be held constant, the degree of reliability can be improved by improving the degree of objectivity. This is shown in the diagram below:

FIGURE V.   Reliability and Objectivity I.

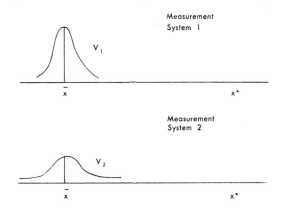

Measurement System 1 is more reliable than System 2, since $(\bar{x} - x^*)^2$ is the same for both methods but $V_2 > V_1$.

On the other hand, Equation (7) shows that the most objective measure is not necessarily the most reliable measure. This is so because the measurement system

FIGURE VI.   Reliability and Objectivity II.

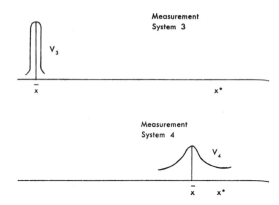

with the higher degree of objectivity (smaller V) may have a mean, $(\bar{x})$, which is quite far from the alleged value, such that $V+B$ will be greater for a system with a small V than for a system where V is large but $(\bar{x}-x^*)^2$ is very small. This is shown in the diagram above. System 4 is more reliable than System 3 despite the fact that $V_4 > V_3$, i.e., System 4 is less objective than System 3.[18]

If there is any misunderstanding on the part of the accountant as to what the user of the accounting data needs and wants, the mean of the reported values $(\bar{x})$ may be quite far from the alleged value (x^*). Even though the degree of objectivity of a measurement method can be determined independently of the use of the measurement, it does not make sense to think of the degree of reliability of an accounting measurement without studying how the measure will be used, how well the user understands the accounting process by which the measurement is made, and (above all), how, *in reality*, the variable x (the reported value) is related to the variable y which is of primary interest to the user of the data.

SUMMARY AND CONCLUSIONS

The reliability of accounting measurements was defined as the degree of objectivity plus a bias factor. This relationship shows that the degree of objectivity can be measured without regard for the use of the measure but reliability cannot because the bias depends on the alleged value which in turn is related to the particular use of the measure.

This conceptual relationship, which depends on the variance of measurement observations from their mean and the distance of this mean from the alleged value, gives valuable insights into some of the possible steps which can be taken by the members of the accounting profession to improve the reliability of accounting measurements.

First, accountants ought to cooperate to the fullest possible extent with the users of accounting data to search for and define those factors or quantities which will be useful in decision processes. These factors were designated as y's. Accountants must then undertake to develop measurements which will produce accounting measurements (x's) that will give good predictions of these decision variables (y's). Both of these research efforts should help to reduce the bias, B. Accountants should also attempt to educate the users of the accounting data as well as be educated in the manner described above. If users of accounting data can be more effectively educated, they might change their function for relating x and y and this change can also result in decreasing the bias and improving reliability. Hence, reliability is definitely a two-way street. It may be that the reliability of a measurement can be improved by changing the measurement system; on the other hand, the reliability of the system may also be improved by changing the manner in which the output from the system is used.

Another way to improve the degree of reliability may be to sacrifice objectivity, if the bias can be made much smaller as a result of sacrificing the objectivity. The recent attempts by the 1964 Concepts and Standards Committees to include holding gains and losses in financial reports may be considered as an attempt to improve the reliability of an accounting measure by decreasing the bias factor even though the new measure may also decrease the degree of objectivity but, hopefully, to a lesser extent.[19]

Also of importance—the degree of reliability can be increased by operating on the degree of objectivity as well as by operating on the bias. Hence, accountants should constantly try to improve the degree of objectivity if the bias does not increase at a faster rate than the improvement in the degree of objectivity. Once the accounting profession finds what alleged values are to be measured, the degree of objectivity might be improved by establishing and more fully specifying a set of accounting measurement principles and procedures. These principles and procedures will, hopefully, produce measurements which are less dependent on the measurer than the situation we now have.

We must note that objectivity per se should not be the sole criterion for selecting accounting measurement systems. On the other hand, it is nearsighted to say that objectivity should be discarded altogether in favor of a vague and poorly defined notion of "usefulness." The degree of reliability (which encompasses objectivity) is the important criterion and it will ultimately determine the extent to which the decision-making public will accept and use accounting measurements.

ENDNOTES

1. See, for example, *The Measurement of Property, Plant, and Equipment in Financial Statements*, Robert T. Sprouse, Reporter, Harvard University, Graduate School of Business Administration, 1964, p. 20.

2. Ibid., p. 21. Italics supplied.

3. Ibid., p. 63. Italics supplied.

4. W. A. Paton and A. C. Littleton, *An Introduction to Corporate Accounting Standards* (American Accounting Association Monograph No. 3, 1940), p. 18.

5. Maurice Moonitz, "The Basic Postulates of Accounting," *Accounting Research Study No. 1* (American Institute of CPA's), p. 41.

6. Paul E. Fertig, "Current Values and Index Numbers, The Problem of Objectivity," *Research in Accounting Measurement* (American Accounting Association, 1966).

7. Moonitz, op. cit., p. 41.

8. Paton and Littleton, op. cit., p. 18.

9. Harold E. Arnett, "What Does Objectivity Mean to Accountants?", *Journal of Accountancy*, May 1961, p. 68.

10. Fertig, op. cit.

11. W. B. McFarland, "Concept of Objectivity," *Journal of Accountancy*, Sept. 1961, p. 29.

12. This definition of objectivity agrees with that normally held by accountants, (i.e., verifiability by an independent party) if we interpret the independent party to mean a representative of a given group of accountants. See, for example, the above quotations from Moonitz.

13. Obviously, there are many other ways of measuring the variability of observations. For example, we may use the average of $[x_i - \bar{x}]$ instead of $(x_i - \bar{x})^2$. Relvariance, i.e., the variance divided by the square of the mean $V/\bar{x}^2$, is another common measure of variability used in statistics. The latter measure has an advantage in that it does not depend upon the measurement unit of the $\bar{x}_i$'s, although difficulty arises as the mean $(\bar{x})$ becomes closer to zero.

14. Reliability is also not a black-or-white issue as we shall soon see later. But here we are using the term loosely.

15. Both the objectivity measure V given by (1) and the reliability measure R given by (2) actually indicate the degree of "subjectivity" and the degree of "unreliability." That is, the degree of objectivity of the measurement system becomes greater as V gets smaller. Conversely, larger values for V (or R) are associated with lower degrees of objectivity (or reliability). The measurement system is *perfectly objective* if $V = 0$ and is *perfectly reliable if $R = 0$*.

16. We may also consider a distribution of x^* based on the various uses of the measure or various users of the measure and apply the same averaging method to derive a reliability measure for a given set of uses or users.

17. In the above discussion, it is assumed that the alleged value is unique for each object that is measured. If it is not unique, we may define the bias factor B to be the smallest value of $(\bar{x} - x^*)^2$ among all alleged values x^*'s in the measurement of a given object.

18. For years, the advocates of, for example, market values have been urging a trade-off between usefulness and objectivity in favor of usefulness. In fact, it is usually agreed that the key problem in the selection of accounting methods is to achieve the proper balance between objectivity and usefulness. (See, for example, Robert T. Sprouse, op. cit., p. 65.) To the extent that reliability constitutes an important part of usefulness, (materiality and timeliness of the data are also important), Equation (7) is an effective way to characterize this trade-off using the statistical concept of variance and mean-squared-error.

19. American Accounting Association, Committee on Concepts and Standards— Long-lived assets, "Accounting for Land, Building, and Equipment," Supplementary Statement No. 1, THE ACCOUNTING REVIEW, July 1964, pp. 693–699; and 1964 Concepts and Standards Research Study Committee, "The Realization Concept," THE ACCOUNTING REVIEW, April 1965, pp. 312–322.

Questions for Study and Discussion

1. What are the sources of bias in accounting measurement, from the viewpoint of Ijiri and Jaedicke?

2. Kerlinger (1964, p. 430) suggests three approaches to defining reliability, reflected in the following questions:

    (i) If we measure the same set of objects again and again with the same or comparable measuring instrument, will we get the same or similar results?

    (ii) Are the measures obtained from the measuring instrument the 'true' measures of the property measured?

    (iii) How much random or chance error is produced by the measuring instrument itself?

How do these concepts of reliability relate to Ijiri and Jaedicke's notion?

3. In proposing the variance or mean-square error as a measure of objectivity and reliability, what assumptions are Ijiri and Jaedicke making about the scale used to measure the x_i's?

4. In a consideration of the philosophical foundations of management science, C. West Churchman (1971, pp. 95–127) discusses the concept of a Lockean community—a community of minds that agrees about its sensory responses to stimuli. In a Lockean community elementary observations are verified by means of a social organization which seeks agreement and consensus on the data. Compare this notion with the use made of the concept of consensus by Ijiri and Jaedicke. Are there any other ways to guarantee the properties of observations?

5. Suppose a relationship $y = f(x)$ is alleged, as characterized by Ijiri and Jaedicke. Subsequently y' not equal to y is observed. What measurement problems could have led to this difference? Is it fair to assume that $x' = f^{-1}(y')$ and therefore x' rather than x was the proper value of the argument?

6. Maurice Moonitz (1969) offers the following definition of accounting:

> The function of accounting is (1) to measure the resource held by specific entities; (2) to reflect claims against and the interests in those entities; (3) to measure the changes in those resources, claims, and interests; (4) to assign the changes to specifiable periods of time; and (5) to express the foregoing in terms of money as a common denominator.

    (i) How do Ijiri and Jaedicke's notions relate to this definition?

    (ii) How does the definition apply to the concept of replacement cost accounting discussed in the introduction?

7. Is replacement cost accounting objective or reliable in the sense of Ijiri and Jaedicke?

8. In an article two decades ago William Vatter (1958) notes that "One of the more recent innovations in the application of accounting measurements to the problems of management is that of measuring deviations from established norms in so-called variance accounts." Many organizations now use this concept to measure the performance of their departments and managers by means of a budgeting and performance review process. Actual expenditures are compared to budgeted expenditures and significant "variances" are identified. What are the important characteristics of this measure of performance? What assumptions does it make about the manager's "disposition to act"? How do the semantic (scientific) measurement issues relate to the pragmatic (managerial) issues in designing this type of measurement system? What roles does the "reliability and objectivity of accounting measurements" play in implementing variance reporting?

Make a list of all the factors which may result in a variance being reported. What conclusions may be drawn if actual equals budgeted?

9. Vatter (1958) states that, ". . . the only test of validity (of an accounting measure) is prediction." Do you agree? Comment.

THE PAST'S FUTURE

C. West Churchman

Reading the papers to be presented at this conference was an impressive experience for me as a philosopher. It might be accurate to say the theme of the conference is as much the philosophy of accounting as it is accounting theory, since so many of the speakers have dipped into philosophical literature and philosophical concepts.

I need not apologize, therefore, because this paper also takes on so strong a philosophical tone. But, in addition to the philosophical discussion, I also have a very practical question to raise about the strategy of the practicing accountant.

My philosophical question has to deal with the role of the future in attempts to describe the past. The practical translation of this problem is the extent to which the accountant per se needs to become involved in some form of forecasting.

Common sense provides a rather ready answer to the question of the role of the future in the attempts to describe the past; the future has no role. That is to say, the practicing accountant need not concern himself with forecasting; perhaps one might want to go so far as to say that the practicing accountant, especially the CPA, is obligated to keep himself free of forecasts.

Built into this commonsense reply to the question is a preconception. Many of us have come to recognize how treacherous commonsense preconceptions can become, especially as they dig themselves like ticks into the living flesh of a scientific discipline. A student of mine has been conducting what he terms "black box experiments." The subject has a black box whose theory he is supposed to describe. He gets his information by putting four numbers into the box, then observing the four-digit output. In one of the black boxes the output is the time of day. It takes many of the subjects quite a bit of effort to realize that there is no relationship between what they are putting in and what is coming out, because the time of day is not one of their preconceptions for such a black box. This is just illustrative of the kind of fix that our preconceptions can get us into. Professors often tell their students to write down all of their preconceptions, but this piece of advice may be of little value, because if one could write down his inmost preconceptions then they would not be inmost. In this conference, however, it is possible that an outsider, joining in a serious discussion with theoreticians and practitioners, may perform some service by

From *Foundations of Accounting Theory*, W. E. Stone, ed. University of Florida Accounting Series No. 7, 1971, pp. 138–148. Copyright 1971 by the State of Florida, Department of General Services. Reprinted by permission of University Presses of Florida, 15 N.W. 15th Street, Gainesville, Florida 32603.

writing down what he observes to be some common preconceptions which seem to be the foundation of accounting theory. In a way, it is the broad task of philosophy to shatter the old tablets, so to speak. As Nietzsche said, "All the secrets of your foundation must come to light; when you are uprooted and broken in the sun, your lie will be separable from your truth."[1]

Suppose we begin with the commonsense preconception just mentioned. This is the preconception of a mind bound to the past. For such a mind, the past is sure; it is a fact, a firm foundation, value-free. The future, however, is unknown, uncertain, vague, treacherous, and threating, and, if you wish, value-loaded. For the past-bound, we all know how we have lived. But what can we know of life in the future or life after death?

Two historical examples will suffice. David Hume in his famous treatise argues that the future is not known in the sense that direct experience is known. Indeed, from Hume's point of view, the kind of knowledge that arises from experience and memory is totally different from the kind of knowledge that is entailed in forecasting. Hume believes that it is natural for people to try to forecast. Anyone having seen a flash would expect that the noise of an explosion will occur, or having seen the heat on the stove, that it will cause a sensation of warmth. But this is expectation based on habit, and is totally different from the kind of knowledge which we acquire from observation. If we were to plot a chart in which the ordinate shows certainty and the abscissa shows time, then up to the moment of the time of the experience, there is no certainty at all. At the time of the experience, there is a sense impression, and, if it is intense enough, there is considerable certainty attached to it. After this point in time, said Hume, there will be a decay of certainty as memory enters in and begins to distort what has been directly observed.

A second example comes from the story of historical method in the nineteenth century when von Ranke made the distinction between official records, where one can obtain objectivity, and the subjective accounts of eyewitnesses and other individuals. Von Ranke was arguing that the historian's job is to sift out the subjective accounts that have no real objectivity and to devote his time to assimilating and accurately recording historical events as they are written down in various kinds of records. The similarity between von Ranke's philosophy and the one that many accountants hold seems notable. The operating statement and the balance sheet are frequently regarded as the results of the official records of the company, are carefully examined by the accountant, and are not based on subjective impressions of managers and other individuals.

In order to look carefully at the commonsense preconception that the future plays no role in the past, suppose we write out four propositions for consideration. In order to do this, we need to say something about systems and especially their components. In systems science a system is conceived as a set of components which play the role of serving the basic purposes of the whole system. In designing such systems, the systems scientist has to pay due regard to the way in which the effectiveness of one component is related to the effectiveness of another.

In the simplest case, we say that one component A is separable from another component B if the effectiveness of A does not depend in any way on the effectiveness of B. If we could write down the relationship in mathematical terms, we would say that A's effectiveness is measured by variables which are causally independent of the activities occurring in B.[2] For example, if two workers are engaged in digging a ditch, it may happen that the effectiveness of one worker is largely independent of the effectiveness of the other. Even in this simple case, however, one might suspect that pure separability does not occur. Indeed, it is safe to say that pure separability never occurs in social systems.

Now let us look at a system the purpose of which is to tell as nearly as possible the accurate story of what has happened, as well as what will happen. In such a system we could identify two activities, one of which devotes itself primarily to telling as accurately as possible what has happened (or is happening), and the other to telling what will happen.

The four propositions are the following:

1. *The activity of estimating what has happened in the past is separable from the activity of estimating what will happen in the future.* An abbreviated statement of this proposition might be, "past reckoning is separable from future reckoning."

2. *Future reckoning is separable from past reckoning.*

3. *Any specific activity of estimating what has happened in the past can be evaluated along an effectiveness scale ranging from 0 or a negative number to some maximum positive number.* In other words, this proposition states that it is possible to describe what has happened in the past, and one can do so with more or less effectiveness. The proposition does *not* state one can describe the past with complete accuracy; it only states that there is a worse and a better method of describing the past. A brief restatement would be, "knowledge of the past is possible."

4. *Knowledge of the future is possible.* Here, as in proposition 2, I have used the abbreviated form.

Now we can bring in a logician to consider our four propositions; he will tell us that these can be accepted or denied, each one in turn, and that the result of such acceptances and denials are sixteen possible positions. Thus, one can accept all four of the propositions, or one could accept the first three and deny the fourth, etc. However, there is a consideration which reduces the list of possible opinions which these four propositions express. Suppose, for example, that you believe that proposition 4 is false; that is, you do not believe that knowledge of the future is possible. In the way in which I have expressed the meaning of proposition 4, your denial amounts to your saying that any activity involving an attempt to study the future will be absolutely ineffective. Hence, you believe there is no effectiveness measure associated with such an activity. If now we look at proposition 2, which in its complete form says that the activity of estimating what will happen in the future is separable from the activity of estimating what has happened in the past, we see that the proposition is largely meaningless if one has already accepted the idea that knowledge of the future is not possible. What the logician suggests at this point is a vacuous stipulation regarding the concept of separability, i.e., a kind of arbitrary decision as to what is to be done when an activity has no effectiveness measure associated with it. The arbitrary decision made here will be that if one argues that an activity has no effectiveness with respect to the total system, then one arbitrarily states such an activity is nonseparable from all other activities.[3]

If we make our arbitrary stipulation, it therefore follows that, if one denies proposition 4, he will also deny proposition 2. Stated otherwise, if he accepts proposition

2, he is committed to accepting proposition 4. This means that one cannot under the arbitrary stipulation consistently accept proposition 2 and deny proposition 4. Similarly, one cannot accept proposition 1 and deny proposition 3.

One final minor point rules out another two possibilities; a position which asserts that knowledge of the past is possible (accepts 3) but is nonseparable from the knowledge of the future (denies 1), and goes on to say that knowledge of the future is impossible (denies 4) would be a ridiculous position to take. A similar remark can be made for the "dual" of this in which past and future are interchanged.

What remains are seven consistent proposals as follows (we use the convention that an apostrophe after the number represents the denial of the proposition):

1,2,3,4:—"Separated past and future"

1,2',3,4:—"Forecasting from the past"

1',2,3,4:—"Past reckoning from the future"

1,2',3,4':—"Past but no future reckoning"

1',2,3',4:—"Future but no past reckoning"

1',2',3,4:—"Integrated past and future"

1',2',3',4':—"Skepticism"

With appropriate apologies for this logical exercise, suppose now we examine these seven consistent statements, or rather, all of them except the last. I assume that in this audience there can be no real interest in skepticism, because, if one were to adopt it, the whole activity of the accounting profession becomes a kind of sardonic joke.

In this examination, as I hinted at the beginning, I would like to take both an epistemological and a strategic look at the propositions. By a strategic look, I mean that a practitioner might agree, for example, that the future can be predicted, but assert that it is none of his business to predict it. I gather this feeling has entered into some of the policies regarding CPA's. I will be interested in both the epistemological and the strategic discussion of the propositions.

At the outset I mentioned what I thought would be a common preconception; namely, that one could tell the past but one could not tell the future, or strategically it is none of his business to tell the future. This is expressed in the fourth of the list of positions which I have dubbed "Past but no future reckoning." It is a series of propositions that has often been accepted by strong positivists, or individuals in disciplines like history who have felt that man can know what his past has been like, but is completely incapable of predicting the future even approximately. We'll see as we progress in the discussion that this particular piece of common sense has many shades of meaning.

The opposite of the commonsense position is the one I have called "Future but no past." This says that one can tell very well what is going to happen, but one cannot tell what did happen. For example, a man whose wife has just told him that she is going to divorce him and marry the iceman believes he can predict what will happen, but does not have any idea what did happen. However, there is no discipline of science that I know of which would accept this combination of assertions and denials. The past has always been such a fundamental part of scientific inquiry that to deny the possibility of saying anything sensible about it would seem to aim at the very heart of the scientific method itself.

The position, however, that I want to argue most strongly for, and which is the deadly enemy of the commonsense preconception, is the one called "Integrated past and future." This position, too, has many different shades of meaning, depending on how the future enters into the determination of the past. I want to give its strongest possible meaning, and for this purpose I will turn to operations research.

Professor Chambers in his paper makes a distinction between a report and a physical fact. He illustrates this in the case of inventory, where, he says, the report contains the items described by numbers, whereas the physical facts are the items actually in inventory that can be observed. From this illustration one might infer, as did Hume in the discussion above, that the direct observation of the physical condition of inventory is more reliable than the report, the report corresponding to Hume's term "decay in memory."

But the question that faces the operations researcher is the meaning of "reliable." The operations researcher's task is to assist the decision-maker in controlling inventory; he will do this by trying to decide on the optimal amounts to be ordered into inventory at various points of time.

Now what are the appropriate data that the operations researcher should use in making his study in order to assist the decision-maker? An obvious reply to this question, a reply that is contained in many operations research texts, is to say that the operations researcher should examine past invoices. The student is told to make a frequency chart, using certain intervals of time, e.g., a day, a week, or a month. This provides the basis of his inferring the probability distribution of demand on inventory. He is also cautioned to observe trends in time, e.g., seasonal fluctuations or gradually rising or falling sales demand and to extrapolate into the future on the basis of these trends.

These recommendations to the operations research student, in fact, are based on what I labelled "Future reckoning from the past," i.e., the recommendations are based on the assumption that past reckoning is independent of future reckoning but not vice versa. But a moment's reflection shows the weakness of this position. Suppose, for example, that there is a seasonal fluctuation of demand. Then it may be very sensible during the off-season to reduce prices and increase advertisement in order to smooth the demand curve. If this were done, then obviously the use of very careful statistical analysis of past data and an extrapolation of seasonal fluctuations into the future would be largely irrelevant because a new kind of demand system would have been created. In the language of systems science discussed above, it is quite obvious that the demand system is not separable from the inventory system. If one does use past demand and makes the kinds of extrapolations mentioned above, he is making a very strong systemic judgment, namely, that nothing can be changed about the demand system, e.g., because the managers are reluctant to make such changes or else because the customers are fixed in their patterns of purchasing.

The same remarks apply to the determination of cost by operations researchers. Obviously, in the case of inventory, it is necessary to determine the cost of holding items in inventory. This cost is an opportunity cost. It is an inference as to how a dollar released from inventory could best be spent in some other activity of the firm. Opportunity costs are what some philosophers of science call "counterfactual conditionals."[4] The counterfactual conditional has the form, "If X were to occur, then Y would occur." In the case of the cost of holding inventory, for example, the counterfactual conditional is "If inventory were to be reduced by such and such an amount, then the released funds could optimally be used to yield P percent return." It is to be noted that the demand on inventory is also an opportunity demand, i.e., based on counterfactual conditional of the form, "If such and such were to be done to the demand system, then the demand function would be so and so."

What is it that the operations researcher observes in order to provide information for decision-making purposes? We have heard a good deal at this conference about how information should be generated for decision-making, so that the question is quite relevant: what does one observe in order to verify a counterfactual conditional? At first glance, the problem seems impossible to solve; how can I observe anything in order to judge what would happen (but never does)? This is why Goodman uses the term "counterfactual." Their premises never, in fact, occur in nature. So it begins to appear as though operations researchers must be spinning their wheels.

But the situation is not hopeless. If one were willing to make a judgment about the future of the whole system, then on the basis of this judgment he would be justified in using a certain kind of data. Suppose, for example, that one makes a judgment that nothing can be changed about the demand system. Then, on the basis of this judgment and the additional judgment that the system will exist in essentially the same environment as it has in the past, one would be justified in taking past invoices and performing the exercise specified above, i.e., extrapolating into the future and using these extrapolations as the basis for calculating optimal inventory policy. In other words, if a strong systemic judgment is made, then a certain kind of data bank, based on past observation, can be said to be authorized. If no systemic judgment seems sensible to make, then of course the operations researcher must regard the problem as intractable.

We see that information for decision-making is really a compound of at least two kinds of activities: the one concerned with authorizing a certain set of data for use on the analysis and the other in the collection of the data itself. But the authorization procedure is essentially a forecast about the future, because it makes a judgment about the characteristics the system will or would have. It is, in fact, much more than a simple forecast, because it must be a model which permits one to say what would happen if certain things were to occur. In this regard the systemic judgment is much more like a set of differential equations in physics, where the boundary conditions can be changed and one can infer which events would occur under these changes.

It is clear that the authorization of a data bank is future reckoning. We can now understand how past reckoning is inseparable from future reckoning, because we need to make very strong and effective judgments about the future in order to be able to use the past effectively. I might add that the reverse is also clear; that is to say, effective reckoning of the past is essential, because effective judgments about the future of the system must somehow draw on past experience. Hence, future reckoning is nonseparable from past reckoning, and vice versa. From these remarks we can conclude that the operations researcher must adopt the position I labelled "Integrated past and future."

What relevance has all of this discussion for the accountant? At this conference we have been swinging between two positions: the one in which there is chiefly a concern with the practicing accountant and his problems of collecting information and the other with the broader question of the accountant as an information collector and as an aid to the decision-maker. I would say that the distinction between the two positions is essentially the strategic question as to whether or not the accountant should be involved in what I called authorization of data banks, i.e., whether the accountant should be involved in the very difficult problem of making adequate systemic judgments. One might adopt the position that the accountant essentially gathers the data, and the authorization is made by the managers or by the legal system. This position would argue for a separability of the information system from the decision-making system, where the accountant does one kind of job and the managers or lawyers do the other kind of job. I think the position is undoubtedly weak in terms of system design. But the real issue depends, so to speak, on the ambition of the accounting profession. Does it wish to become involved in authorizing data banks and hence in making strong systemic judgments?

I have argued elsewhere[5] that information becomes measurement if the information is widely usable in a variety of contexts. I gather from some of the papers in this conference, e.g., Sprouse and Rappaport, that at least some accountants do regard their data in terms of the user and his characteristics and are seeking to make accounting a measurement process. If so, then I would infer that these accountants are strongly involved in considerations of the authorization of data banks based on strong systemic judgments.

In concluding, I would like to make several general remarks about the "Integrated past and future" position. We are going through an age where we are reconsidering many of our traditional human values. From the point of view of the science of the last century, precision, rigor, and clarity were desiderata. The scientist, it was believed, should become clear and precise about his position, and his position should essentially be a consistent one. These values led the scientists to regard descriptions of the past in terms of the "quality of the reports." Reports should be specific, concrete, and unobjectionable. According to this past value system, when we look at the most vital event in the life of a company, namely a sale, one would tend to regard dollar amount and quantity ordered as representing the highest quality a report can attain. We note, however, in terms of our earlier discussion, that the quality of being clear and precise may be at variance with the quality of best serving the user. What does the stockholder think when he reads the item "gross sales"? If he is sensible, he will wonder "What might sales have been?" He is, indeed, raising the counterfactual question again. And the answer to his question must be based on a strong systemic judgment, which, I believe, will inevitably be ambiguous, not clear and precise, and certainly not unobjectionable. We live in a world where we have to make strong systemic judgments in order to make our decisions, but if we are honest we will see that we will forever fail to find the unobjectionable basis for these systemic judgments that authorize the use of certain data banks. So the quality of the report as a concept has changed in terms of a new set of values. On the positive side, this new set of values represents a willingness to be as honest as possible about the basis of our decision-making. Along with this willingness goes, by necessity, the need to accept ambiguity, vagueness, and incomplete consensus as essential qualities of our reports.

I would like to close with a very general philosophical opinion, about which I hope there will be considerable debate, for debate is the essence of everything I have discussed in terms of systemic judgment.

I realize, as Norton Bedford has, that we have been developing a culture which pays more and more respect to the future—to what it will be or should be—in 1984, 2000, or 10,000. But in this paper I have really been putting in a plea for our respect to the past, to what it was and might have been. It is really quite disrespectful for us to assume that the past was simple and easy to describe. What was it like to be alive in the year 1800? No amount of historical data could possibly probe the depth and complexity of such a question. The past is as deep an uncertainty and ambiguity as is the future.

While I appreciate the urge for accounting to limit and define its task, I also appreciate the need for it to expand its horizons and to identify its allies who are all those who are devoting their lives to the worship of the past. There was a time when basic science regarded itself as one form of the adoration of God. The ritual of this form of worship of God by worshipping the past entails the enormous and heroic task of telling the future.

ENDNOTES

1. F. Nietzsche, *Thus Spoke Zarathustra*, trans. M. Cowan, Gateway ed. (Chicago: Regnery Publishing Co., 1958), p. 93.

2. The concept is often expressed by saying that the total system's separability can be represented in a linear form, i.e., as a linear function of the effectiveness of each of the components. In this regard, it should be noted that one could not arrive at such a judgment of linearity without having taken a look at the larger system and made some judgment about it. So, even in the case where the systems scientist arrives at a linear function, some nonlinearities have probably crept into his considerations.

3. The situation is very much like the one pertaining to the so-called null class in Boolean algebra, where the logician has to decide whether a class that has no members belongs or does not belong to other classes. In logic, it has been customary to say that the null class belongs to all classes; this rule produces certain conveniences in the calculus.

4. See Nelson Goodman, *Fact, Fiction and Forecast* (Cambridge, Mass.: Harvard University Press, 1955).

5. C. West Churchman, *Prediction and Optimal Decision* (Englewood Cliffs, N.J.: Prentice-Hall, 1961).

Questions for Study and Discussion

1. For each of Churchman's "seven consistent positions regarding the knowledge of past and future," can you cite an example, basing each of the examples on a single management problem of your own choosing?

2. Why is it necessary, according to Churchman, to "authorize" a data bank? In your view, should the accounting profession involve itself in such authorization?

3. R. J. Chambers, a noted accounting theorist, "takes uncompromisingly the position that accounting is concerned strictly with the past and present, but so that it is always relevant to the future. To mix measurements with expectations is to confuse an already complicated present. To make measurements is the business of the accountant as such; to form expectations is the business of actors. Only if the two functions are carefully distinguished will actors be able to pursue their goals with informed skills" (1965, p. 33). By "actors," Chambers means managers or other decision makers. Which of Churchman's seven consistent positions regarding the knowledge of past and future does Chambers recommend to the accounting profession?

In the same article Chambers advances the concept of "current cash equivalent" as a measurement principle for accounting. What is the rationale behind this principle? Is it consistent or inconsistent with Chamber's position regarding the knowledge of past and future?

4. Churchman's paper explictly raises the issue of the time dimension in measurement. C. W. Thornthwaite (1953) relates the following story about the role of time in decision making. On a large pea farm tension mounted as the harvest approached. When the peas began to mature at a rapid rate the managers marshaled their harvest machinery and tried to keep pace, sometimes working twenty-four hours a day with double crews and giant floodlights. "But that solution had its difficulties. For one thing, harvesting so fast led to a pile-up of the product in the factory, overtaxing the freezer capacity, and eventually getting behind in the harvest, so that some peas were overmature and of poor quality" (p. 34).

Thornthwaite's analysis of the problem was that the managers were basing their decision on calendar time, when what was needed was a way of relating the crop's rate of growth and development to some climatic factors. ". . . something that was independent of the plant, that could be measured, and that would provide an indication of the stage of development and the approach toward the final date of maturity; in other words something to indicate the date of harvest after the date of planting has been established" (p. 34).

The solution was to calibrate the growth of a pea "as it comes up and forms a node, and so on" (p. 35). The rate of node development was translated into "growth units." A pea was ready for harvest after an interval of about 1680 growth units. This "biological clock" was used by Thornthwaite to stagger the planting of peas so that they matured for harvest in amounts per day equal to the capacity of harvest machinery and the processing factory.

What other kinds of "clocks" can you think of that would influence accounting procedures or the measurement of organizational performance?

MEASUREMENT AND
MISREPRESENTATION

R. J. Chambers

The conventional concept of economic man, of whom the businessman is the arche-type, endows him with the capacity for and the habit of careful, informed and cal-culated action. It is a commonplace, on the other hand, that businessmen are in-formed within limits and calculate within limits. These limits may be data to the macro-economist, or they may impose restraints on the validity of his generaliza-tions. The situation of the "business metrologist," concerned with the design of sys-tems for accumulating, processing and communicating information, is quite differ-ent. When he assumes the role of expert, he assumes the responsibility for ensuring that the information supplied is, within his field, complete, pertinent and, as far as possible, objective. That the information may be ignored or misused does not relieve him of this responsibility. Though it has been said that "without measurement there can be no science", it does not follow that the possibility of measuring creates a basis for optimal action. Many widely used business measurements and calculations are inadequate or invalid; their failure to meet the criteria mentioned above offers a chal-lenge to administrative science.

The challenge is only perceived if one finds it necessary to take a more sophisti-cated view of the criteria of business action than the common traditionalist view. The common view arises out of the limited, sporadic and often poorly-evaluated experi-ences of participants in business—of investors, financiers and businessmen them-selves. By constant usage and the unconsidered transmission of commercial and fi-nancial "lore," tests which had significance and an easily discernible meaning in a less complex environment continue to serve; radical changes in the form and milieu of business have had no impact on them, except perhaps to knit them more securely into the fabric of commercial practice.

The oldest form of information processing in business is accounting, based on a monetary scale of measurement; this paper will deal primarily with accounting methods and concepts. But, first, some observations on its scope. Accounting is con-cerned with the measurement and representation of transactions and events; the ef-fects of the majority of these can be measured readily at the time of their occurrence. It does not follow, though it is generally taken as axiomatic, that simple arithmetical manipulation of the measurements of separate events will give a clear and unambig-uous representation of the effects of an extensive series of such events. Growth in

From *Management Science*, January, 1960, Vol. 6, No. 2, pp. 141–142. Reprinted by permission.

the variety and number of events to be described creates the need for rules, if only to ensure consistent recording. These rules may be justified on grounds related to the recording process or on grounds related to the real operations represented. In the sense that rules reduce the area for the exercise of opinions or judgment at the point of recording, the resulting summaries may be considered as objective statements of what has transpired. But to the extent that rules incorporate widely held beliefs, judgments or criteria of the information processors, the result is not independent of the processors; it loses in objectivity and may communicate signals which are irrelevant to real operations.

One's conception of the nature of a business unit will affect what is envisaged as the ideal product of information processing. At any time a business unit has some of the features of an organism. It has purposes or goals to which its parts are expected to contribute. Criteria and measures of the effectiveness of the whole are therefore required. If its parts or its sub-goals are considered piecemeal—for convenience or ease in considering potential actions and their consequences—measures of the effectiveness of the parts and of the whole should have a consistent basis. But a business unit also has some of the features of a system of separate cooperating instruments and organisms. Though the unit as such may continue in existence for a long period, its separate machines, plants, properties, financiers, investors and other contributors may change or be changed as the market values of their separate contributions to the goals of the unit change. Consequently, the contemporary market value of any feature of the unit is the relevant basis of any system the purpose of which is to inform the actions of participants. If, on the other hand, its components are considered to be irrevocably committed or tied to the unit, a different basis of measuring operations and results will be adopted. This assumption is among the foundations of contemporary accounting; with consequences which will be demonstrated.

It is commonly held that the most important piece of information yielded by the accounting process is net income or profit. But what is profit and what in fact does a calculated profit represent? The profit from a single venture promptly consummated is easy to conceive and to measure. The profit from a series of diverse transactions consummated in a relatively short period is similarly easy to conceive and measure. Out of such simple circumstances arose the general idea of profit and its acceptance as a simple measure of the effectiveness of a business operation. But the intermediaries and intermediate functions and operations which characterize modern business have increased the complexities of calculation and rendered the primitive concept of profit irrelevant. Profit as it is now computed, and (by corporations) publicly reported, is a conventional residue, determined periodically from a series of completed and uncompleted operations; and determined in such diverse ways that its amount may differ widely according to the views of those who compute it and the wishes of those responsible for its publication.

Consider first the influence of those who compute profit. Profit may be conceived to be a monetary measure of the residue from a series of transactions (including service-flows) whose individual effects are expressed in terms of initial price. This is not far removed from the primitive concept of profit; it is simple to compute and is the concept underlying most contemporary accounting. But it is appropriate only in limited circumstances; for example, where the enterprise is of a short-term liquidating nature, or where price and market value are equivalent (i.e., money has a constant purchasing power through time), or where the function of the accounts is deemed to be the representation of a true trusteeship operation. Most businesses fall outside this categories. Alternatively, profit may be conceived as a monetary measure of the residue from a series of transactions whose individual effects are represented by value; transactions would be measured in common value terms related to but not necessarily the same as the prices at which bargains were made. As value at the time of action, rather than price at some other time, is relevant to action, this concept is relevant for continuing businesses in a changing economic climate. But it is not an easy concept to evaluate; the simpler notion continues to be used, though it misrepresents the enterprise, in that the effects of changes in the context of operations are ignored. Even when the rate of change in technology or in price is small, the misrepresentation over a period of years may be material.

Typically, business operations are continuous, and reporting is periodical; this creates problems in timing the recognition of transactions. One may adopt as the criterion for allocating transactions to specific periods the dates on which legal claims, by or on the subject enterprise, arise. This satisfies a legalistic view of the rights and obligations of the enterprise and because of historical emphasis on the legal position it has become generally accepted. But a business firm is not simply a congeries of legal rights and liabilities; it is also an economic instrument; and other ways of viewing its operations can be envisaged. Transactions could be accounted for according to the dates on which cash flows take place; or according to the dates on which value is deemed to be created, whether or not there is a simultaneous change in rights and obligations. Each of the these methods would express a reality no less significant than the legal position. For some purposes they are in fact used, but not for the purpose of providing a general measure of performance such as profit is expected to be. The consequence of adopting the legalistic viewpoint is to shift the recognition of profit from the period in which value is created to the period in which its creation is finally realized by sale. This shift may be quite inconsistent with the scale of aggregate operations in consecutive periods; it will misrepresent the operations of those periods.

Whatever basis is adopted for evaluating and timing transactions, certain figures entering profit determination must be computed, because there is no market transaction in the period from which an objective price or value can be obtained. The principal figures of this sort are depreciated allowances and inventory values. The ways of evaluating are manifold, each with its justification. Some of them derive their popularity from their sanction for taxation purposes; and practices which at one time lack favor and support have often found supporters "on theoretical grounds" once they have received the *imprimatur* of the courts or the legislature. But the tax-paying obligation has no necessary relation to the basic economic function of business; profits computed on the basis of taxation rules cannot be expected to represent business operations as such.

There are other possibilities of distortion. The processing of information is (in any firm except the smallest) performed by many people. Their separate opinions about the treatment of different items may have contrasting justifications, and the profit figures of any firm for consecutive periods may have different meanings, because methods having quite contrary effects are concurrently accepted in the business community. Further, there are no rigid rules governing the broad lines of profit computation by different firms, and profits of different firms may differ in kind as well as in degree. The effects of computational differences cannot be dissociated by any interested party from the effects of efficiency, or from the impact of external factors on each firm. Comparison of the results of a given firm in consecutive years, or comparison of a single year's data for several firms (even within the same industry) cannot fail to mislead, except in the most improbable combination of circumstances.

These strictures arise from the nature of the processing operation, an area where there are some generally accepted rules. But profit figures may be deliberately distorted, quite obviously in some cases. Company A published its profit, a six-digit figure, for three consecutive years, with a range of only four units; this in spite of the fact that it is an operating company, a holding company and an investment company, a combination which suggests far greater potential variation. Company B published its profit, again a six-digit figure, for three consecutive years showing an identical sum, this in spite of the fact that five of the six separate items shown in the income statement were different from year to year.

The difficulties of making informed decisions are compounded by the fact that profit calculation is a prior operation to the determination of the rate of profit on capital or resources employed. In some circumstances marked differences between methods may arise. Accounting on a price basis will, in inflationary periods, give a higher profit and a lower capital employed than accounting on a value basis. Both tend to give a higher rate of return on a price basis than on a value basis. Now, one of the functions of a profit rate is to suggest profit expectations; and the function of profit expectations is to direct the flow of funds available for investment into the most profitable projects, firms and industries. This function is improperly performed unless profit rates represent economic efficiency. The price basis of accounting does not have this effect. By its nature it shows better profit rates for well-established firms than for newly-established firms through periods when price levels are steadily rising; or looking at the other side of the coin, it permits older firms to decline in efficiency as prices rise without indicating the decline. It puts the established firm and the established management beyond criticism (or at least gives them a distinct advantage, as far as external support is concerned, over new firms and their managements). In deflationary periods the opposite occurs; and in neither circumstance has the capital market a valid means of assessing real efficiency.

Much of the above argument assumes that profits and profit rates are in fact used by investors in business securities. As there is some evidence to the contrary, this assumption should perhaps be justified. Lay persons (all not thoroughly familiar with the process of profit computation, including many managers) tend to accept profit and profit rates as carefully calculated and unequivocal figures. They have in mind the primitive concept of profit; they expect what is described as profit now to have some relationship to that concept. This is perhaps natural. It is common to rely on precise-looking figures, when so many other things bearing on one's judgments are difficult or impossible to quantify. And it is convenient to have one or few figures which may be taken to represent a very complex unit and its operations. This tendency is strengthened by the fact that financial statements, used to present profits, carry the signed reports of experts; and the fact that comparative figures are given in such statements carries a strong implication that the figures are consistently calculated and strictly comparable. It may be thought that institutional investors (through which much of the money for industrial investment passes) would take a less naive view. A tendency to use cash flow analyses may suggest that they do not depend on too precise a measurement of profit. But this is evidence of the importance to them of the liquidity of the firms in which they invest; it does not involve or imply abandonment of the profit test. One does hear of investment companies which do not make searching analyses of profit records, but invest on the general reputation of a security in the market. This is "guessing about other people's guesses;" it is not the outcome of reasoned and informed decision-making. Aggregate operations of such companies may be profitable, but only because of satisfactory hedging or averaging.

It is possible to show that conventional methods are misleading in other ways. Some of the commonly used indicators of liquidity are open to criticism on the ground that they contemplate a going concern whereas the primary indicators of liquidity do not suggest the real rate at which liquid assets will become available. And the capital gearing or leverage have been so significantly misrepresented by accounting reports that, when new capital was to be sought, restatements of assets values have been prepared on a large scale, where regulatory provisions have not restrained the practice. Misrepresentation of profit is only illustrative of the wider scale on which the products of conventional methods may mislead.

To external supporters, published profit and financial position are bases for appraising success and prospective success. For this reason the published figures and the conditions they indicate occupy the attention of managers. Being in a position to know a firm's condition in more detail, managers would presumably be able to appraise performance by more efficacious methods than those available to outsiders; so that even if the allocation of resources between firms is less than the optimum, the allocation of resources within a firm may be efficient. By budgeting, costing, project planning and other techniques, efficiency is pursued; but are these methods, in themselves, efficient?

The value of budgets, standard costs and other anticipatory calculations is said to lie in the fact that they give measures of what is expected in the period for which they are prepared: they are thus more rigorous bases for appraising performance than recorded measures of performance during a prior period would be. They may still be misleading. They frequently conform to accounting patterns, following conventional classification, cost allocation, inventory and fixed asset valuation methods. Comparison of subsequently recorded achievements with budgeted operations is useful, and comparison is facilitated, if the forecast and the record have the same formal arrangement. But this can be taken too far. It is not uncommon to find elaborate budgetary methods in which, due to routine adoption of conventional overhead cost allocation methods, monthly figures create unfavorable impressions which are contradicted by the annual result. If adaptive behavior is based on recent short period statements, it may clearly be inappropriate to the real conditions. (There are numerous accepted methods of overhead cost allocation, yielding quite different measures of divisional performance. Divisional performance may be made to appear better or worse simply by changing the method, a further example of slackness in information processing which results in misrepresentation.)

On the other hand, some argue that budgets and cost estimates may be prepared without regard for the restraints of conventional accounting and in accordance with operationally relevant concepts and values. (Note that this carries an implicit admission of a deficiency in accounting information.) The consequence of a difference in concepts used in accounting and budgeting is that there will be two scales in use for appraising performance, one by external parties and one by management. Which, then, represents the enterprise? Unless the methods of accounting and of the auxiliary devices are reconciled, management thinking may imperceptibly or unwittingly shift from one point of view to another. There is a loophole through which the chance of consistent pursuit of efficiency may escape. At the same time it is obviously improper for external parties to judge the efficiency of an enterprise and its management on the basis of information of one kind when the enterprise is being managed on the basis of information of another kind. As was observed above, what is operationally relevant is also relevant to external supporters.

To many accountants the charges against conventional methods may be well known; and these charges have been challenged. Rebuttal has been attempted by multiplying justifications. But the contemporary use of the horse and buggy can be justified only on decorative or sentimental grounds; no one would claim that they provide an efficient means of transportation in the modern urban configuration of living, working and shopping areas. This is not simply a picturesque analogy. There are real and critical differences between the nature and operations of business units today and two generations ago; every new form of combination of businesses, every new method of financing operations, every new intermediary in the processes between the conception of new products and their consumption, creates the possibility of new differences arising and a potential need for new kinds of information. Rebuttal of the emphasis given to profit rates in this paper may be attempted on the grounds that no single profit figure can serve the informational needs of all participants. This is only a way of avoiding the difficulties of definition. Belief that there is a single relevant concept and the emphasis here given are derived from the inherent nature of a market economy. Profit is the price paid for the use of capital; if the profit test is abandoned, what alternative is there? That a price must be paid for the use of capital is one thing that remains constant, within an entrepreneurial context, no matter how production and distribution are arranged. To deny the importance of knowing the price, simply because of the present confusion of concepts, is to throw out baby, bath-water and bath.

Because they have as yet had little impact on practices, the foregoing charges against conventional information processing methods are worth repeating. The following consequences of faulty measurement and misrepresentation are pervasive: (a) Averaging persists (in cost determination, in inventory valuation, in investment policies). Reliance on averages prevents the refinement of decision-making processes. (b) Economic ill-fare results; securities and money change hands through poorly informed bargains; and the privileged few benefit to the disadvantage of the technically ignorant majority. Such inequity is not conducive to maintenance of the system. (c) Industrial and commercial power is held by firms or managements beyond the point where it is warranted by real performance; errors of judgment, loss of skill and sheer inertia, are masked by the very processes which should reveal them. (d) General economic inefficiency may result through funds flowing in directions other than where they could be used most efficiently (profitably). (e) Insofar as the defects of one system for providing guides to action are perceived, auxiliary systems arise, leading at least to duplication of effort and waste of resources, and possibly to confusion, indecision and error.

What may be prescribed to eliminate or reduce the effects of contemporary methods?

(a) The firm should be viewed as an organic unity, inasmuch as every sectional operation has effects on the whole, and any external factor which affects the whole affects sectional operations. These effects arise from the conscious actions of participants, employed and independent, whose cooperation is activated by a communication system. The factor unifying these viewpoints is the market; the communication system must therefore convey signals relevant in the market place—signals based on contemporary values. Conventional or private values are inappropriate bases, as the market alone provides the tests of continuity or dissolution.

(b) Some signals originate from within the firm; they are the production of information processing systems. No single measure is adequate to represent the various facets of the firm. A pattern of measures is required: the pattern will be suggested by the tests in current use in the market.

(c) The pattern of measures must be self-consistent. If there are several information processing systems (e.g. financial accounting, cost accounting, budgeting) their basic criteria and methods must be consistent.

(d) The pattern of measures may be considered to comprise at least three layers: *primary measures,* the aggregates, differences, etc., resulting directly from processing systems; *secondary measures,* relationships (ratios, percentages, etc.) between the primary measures; and *tertiary measures,* rates and directions of change in primary or secondary measures. The latter are at least as significant as the other measures.

(e) As, in respect of certain matters, only estimates of market values are available, it should be indicated that primary aggregates and differences are selected values within a band of possible or probable values; and an attempt might be made to indicate the limits of the band, at least for administrative purposes. (Given consistent calculation on a market value basis, the band would be much narrower than under the varied alternatives now permissible.)

(f) As increasing efforts are made to quantify, as computational aids increase and as methods of selecting optimal courses of action are developed, an equally serious effort should be made to clarify key concepts; if maximizing profit or minimizing cost are objectives, it is necessary to know what concepts of profit and cost are operationally relevant in particular problem settings.

Some final comments. The misrepresentation contemplated in this paper is not deliberate in the sense of planned deception. The use of conventional accounting methods, however, is deliberate, and is vigorously defended on traditional and legalistic grounds; but the consequences of conventional methods are not widely understood. Hence the conventional patterns persist. The case under consideration demonstrates what may happen in any field, if methods of measurement become institutionalized; they cease to yield the independent and objective information which is their *raison d'être.* The preceding observations are not to be understood as overemphasizing financial aspects of business. But if more efficacious methods of accounting were developed, participants in business would be able to place greater reliance on formal measures of success and would have less need to fall back on unquantified or unquantifiable considerations.

Questions for Study and Discussion

1. According to Chambers, "Accounting is concerned with the measurement and representation of transactions and events; the effects of the majority of these can be measured readily at the time of their occurrence. It does not follow, though it is generally taken as axiomatic, that simple arithmetical manipulation of the measurements of separate events will give a clear and unambiguous representation of the effects of an extensive series of such events." *Why* does it not follow? Explain in terms of several examples.

2. If "profit," as currently computed and publicly reported by corporations, may be said to be a "conventional residue," to use Chambers's term, how should it be interpreted from a measurement point of view?

3. What basic assumptions about the nature of a firm as an organization underlie Chambers's argument that "the contemporary market value of any feature of the unit is the relevant basis of any system the purpose of which is to inform the actions of participants."

4. An example of a DSS designed to support financial planning and budgeting is the MAPP (Managerial Analysis for Profit Planning) System developed and installed at Citibank, and described by McLean and Riesing (1977). MAPP serves a cost accounting function within the organization: "It establishes a discipline for defining products; it identifies the costs which are incurred in producing these products; it allows for analysis to determine how resources might be shifted among products; and finally, it helps to prepare the budgets for the departments or divisions which produce these products." The product definition feature is a particularly significant feature of MAPP, given that in a bank, as in other service organizations, the nature of a product is typically not well defined. What is the basic measurement problem addressed by MAPP, in terms of the concept of measurement illustrated in Fig. 2.1, p. 30. What assumptions about decision-making at Citibank are necessary in order that the MAPP System be effectively utilized? (See the discussion by McLean and Riesing of the actual use of the system.)

5. May the market price of a share of publicly traded common stock be interpreted as a measure of corporate profitability? If so, upon what assumptions would this interpretation be based? If not, why not?

CHAPTER **SEVEN**

Profitability is a measure of how well an organization is doing in its market environment. Productivity, on the other hand, is a measure of how well an organization is doing in its physical environment. Productivity measures the efficiency with which an organization converts physical resources into physical output.

The concept of productivity is especially important for informing the management decisions which must be made in product flow and conversion systems. These systems begin with some original raw material and proceed through a series of stages in which the material is transformed. In the final stage distinguishable "end products" are produced by the system. For example, in the petroleum industry crude oil eventually emerges as gasoline, motor oil, lubricants, and chemicals of various kinds. In the steel industry iron ore eventually emerges as ingot or as specific steel products. In banking, dollars in the form of deposits and trusts eventually result in returns on loans and investments.

In order to manage the flow of materials through these systems more effectively, managers need common units of measurements that are consistent between the various stages. In the petroleum industry BTUs are commonly used. In mining an assayed percentage of pure metal is frequently used. In financial systems "yields" and the present value of the expected future flow of funds are used as common measures.

These common units of measure are necessary to apply the law of the conservation of matter as it pertains to product flow systems. The law requires that the quantity of inputs must equal the quantity of outputs. Managers rely on this law for several purposes: (1) to allocate resources throughout the product flow systems, (2) to assign costs and values to the various stages and intermediate products in the system, and (3) to evaluate the overall performance of the system.

One product flow system for which no single satisfactory measure exists for applying the law of conservation is the forest products industry. Since about 1846 the industry has employed a measurement procedure known as the Scribner scale to form its basic standards. The Scribner scale is essentially an estimation technique that attempts to measure the net volume of one-inch boards that can be cut from a log. The measure is based on a projection of the cylinder specified by the small-end diameter of the log, and the result is expressed in "board feet." This unit of measure ignores chips, sawdust, and other nonlumber products which may come from a log. It also ignores some of the useful, sound wood within the cylinder that is insufficient to make boards of the prescribed dimensions.

The primary advantage of the Scribner scale is that it informs buyers and sellers of logs how much end product lumber each log contains. Indeed, that was its initial purpose. Accordingly the scale is useful for some marketing and product-planning decisions. However, the scale has several disadvantages as well. It does not estimate the amount of nonlumber end products the log may yield. In the years since the scale's inception these by-products have taken on far more economic and social value. Nor does the scale permit the reconciling of inputs to outputs during most of the early stages of the conversion process. Finally, the scale is not very useful for making important production decisions with regard to the resource requirements for falling, bucking, yarding, loading, transporting, sorting, processing, and storing logs and their intermediate products. Consequently, from the point of view of decision support systems, the Scribner scale is lacking. While it helps to inform decisions in the end product lumber market, it does not adequately support production management decisions and related financial control decisions. Nor does it pertain to decisions involving pulp, paper and other by-products.

In order to overcome this deficiency some forest products companies employ a "cubic volume of wood fiber" measure. It is calculated by measuring the average diameter and length of the log and, adjusting for the taper of the log, using these data to determine the log's gross volume. This measure may be supplemented by classifying the cubic volume by percentage components of different qualities (percent sound, clear lumber wood; percent defective wood useful for pulp; percent chips; percent sound knotty construction wood, etc.). One advantage of the cubic volume measure is that it can obey the law of conservation. Thus it can be used to determine how much wood fiber went into a process and how this quantity is distributed into outputs such as lumber, chips, veneer, bar, sawdust, or waste. Another advantage is that many of the costs associated with timber production tend to be a function of the volume of wood fiber handled. Thus, for management accounting and control purposes, cubic volume is the most relevant measure. The primary disadvantage of the cubic measure is that it does not relate well to end products and decisions taken in their markets.

It should be pointed out that in the forest products industry some form of measurement of a log's wood content is necessary in order to employ several different computer-based decision support models. The major companies in the industry use linear programming models from the timber stand to final product market conversion process, to inform their long-range planning activities. Many firms use inventory models to estimate optimal buffer stocks for each stage in the process. Also, transportation models are used to help identify the most cost effective routes for transporting materials. All of these models require appropriate measures of the log's wood content to be used as their coefficients. End product measures such as the Scribner scale are called for when market valuation is at issue. Gross volume measures such as the cubic volume measure are called for when production, cost, and financial control problems are at issue.

The problem of measuring a log's wood content illustrates some of the measurement problems encountered in measuring the output of an organization. The concept of productivity further attempts to relate output to the level of resources required to produce it. Consequently the measurement of productivity raises some issues beyond those of measuring physical output alone. These include the questions of how inputs are measured and how to devise a standard unit which relates qualitatively different inputs and outputs to each other. Finally, there is the question of what role financial units, such as the dollar, may play in moving from individual physical units of measurement to more general units.

The articles in this section address these broad questions. In "A General Systems Theory of Productivity," Mason lays out the dimensions of the problem of measuring productivity and describes some of the alternative approaches available. Craig and Harris offer a particular approach to the measurement of productivity at the firm level. In doing so they raise the question of the role of financial units in productivity measurement systems.

A GENERAL SYSTEMS THEORY
OF PRODUCTIVITY

Richard O. Mason

SYSTEMS CONCEPTS AND PRODUCTIVITY

Productivity is a systems concept. It measures the level of output a system has generated in relation to the input resources consumed during the production process. In the narrow sense, productivity is a ratio of outputs over inputs, output/input. In a broader sense, however, it concerns the overall efficiency of a system. The rational manager of a system generally achieves efficiency by following three steps: (1) calculating the productivity of the existing productive processes; (2) comparing the result with alternative processes and; (3) reallocating resources to change those processes which are less efficient or are wasteful. The route to efficiency, therefore, starts with the calculation of productivity; but, on what basis are these calculations to be made?

There are a staggering number of productivity calculations which can be made. In order to establish a rationale for selecting appropriate calculations, it is useful to look at the properties of systems themselves and see what these properties imply in terms of providing a basis for meaningful calculations.

Generally speaking, a system is a set of coordinated components. It accepts inputs and engages in processes which yield outputs. According to Churchman (1968, 1971) the study of systems involves five basic considerations.

1. The total system objectives, purposes and measures of performance.

2. The system's resources: the means used for performing the system's tasks and yielding its outputs.

3. The system's environment: the fixed constraints.

4. The components (elements) of the system including their activities, goals and measures of performance.

5. The system's management which acquires the resources and allocates them in order to achieve the system's objectives. Management encompasses the system's decision processes.

Reprinted from International Journal of General Systems, Vol. 5, No. 1, 1979, pp. 17–30, with the permission of Gordon and Breach, Science Publishers, Inc.

An understanding of the system's goals and objectives reveals which of the system's outputs are important for productivity analysis. Essentially the system's goals and objectives define the "functional class" of outputs which it is the purpose of the system to produce (Ackoff and Emery, 1972; Churchman, 1971). This specifies the numerator of the productivity ratio. A thorough recording of the system's resources describes the means which may be employed in producing the output. The cataloging of resources influences the specification of the denominator in the productivity ratio; however, the basis upon which resources are evaluated depends on the nature of the system's environment. The more dynamic the environment the more relevant opportunity concepts are to the evaluation of resources.

In order to develop a systems concepts of productivity it is necessary to draw on a theory of systems' environments. For this purpose I have chosen the causal texture theory of Emery and Trist (1963). In the following section each of their four "ideal type" environments will be summarized and its implications for productivity measurement drawn.

ENVIRONMENTAL TYPE AND PRODUCTIVITY

Type 1: Placid, Randomized Environment

In the simplest type, goals and noxiants are relatively unchanging in themselves and randomly distributed. A critical property from the organization's viewpoint is that there is no difference between tactics and strategy, and organizations can exist adaptively as single, and indeed quite small, units.

The implication of this environment for a system is that it makes it stable and relatively unchanging. The productive function may be characterized as a stable channel through which inputs and outputs flow. An appropriate measure of productivity is a measure of the efficiency of the system for converting inputs into outputs. Thus, the traditional measure, output/input, is applicable. I call this a measure of *process* or *flow productivity*.

Type 2: Placid, Clustered Environments

The next type is also static, but goals and noxiants are not randomly distributed; they hang together in certain ways. Now the need arises for strategy as distinct from tactics. Under these conditions organizations grow in size, becoming hierarchical and tending towards centralized control and coordination.

The clustering aspects of this type of environment give rise to a concentration of resources and the development of a "distinctive competence" which limits the system's output productive capacity. Yet, the placid nature of the environment means that the constraints on the system are not changing rapidly. What a system *could* do with its resources rather than what it *is* doing is the relevant concern. Failure to utilize the system's full or most efficient capacity results in waste and inefficiency and is indicative of an improper concentration of resources. The relevant measure becomes a comparison of actual with potential output. Because it focuses on the constraints imposed by the system's particular concentration of resources, I call this measure *bounded productivity*.

Type 3: Disturbed, Reactive Environments

The third type is dynamic rather than static. It consists of a clustered environment in which there is more than one system of the same kind, i.e., the objects of one organization are the same as, or relevant to, others like it. Such competitors seek to improve their own chances by hindering each other, each knowing the others are playing the same game. Between strategy and tactics there emerges an intermediate type of organizational response—what military theorists refer to as operations. Control becomes more decentralized to allow these to be conducted. On the other hand, stability may require a certain coming-to-terms between competitors.

The reactive nature of this third type of environment means that there are competitors and that the system must consider that what it knows and can produce can also be known and produced by others. The fact that the environment is disturbed and changing means that there are always new opportunities being created in the system's environment which permit it to restructure itself in order to respond to the actions of competitors and others. The critical facility for long-run survival is the system's manager's ability to reach out into the environment, acquire new resources, alter the productive function and the flow of inputs and outputs and to reconfigure a new system with new capacity. Failure to configure the best possible system results in waste and inefficiency. The relevant measure becomes a comparison between the existing system and the best possible system. Since it involves the concepts of investment and the reconfiguring of the system, I call this a measure of *systemic productivity.*

Type 4: Turbulent Fields

The fourth type is dynamic in a second respect, the dynamic properties arising not simply from the interaction of identifiable component systems but from the field itself (the 'ground'). The turbulence results from the complexity and multiple character of the causal interconnections. Individual organizations, however large, cannot adapt successfully simply through their direct interactions. An examination is made of the enhanced importance of values, regarded as a basic response to persisting areas of relevant uncertainty, as providing a control mechanism, when commonly held by all members in a field.

At this fourth level of environment the concept of efficiency is superseded by the concepts of survival and effectiveness. The functional class of outputs is no longer well defined. Thus, the relevant managerial issue becomes the choosing of the "domains" (McWhinney, 1970) in which the system will operate. In this context resources may be radically reoriented to produce new outputs; and, indeed, many resources may be kept idle, in reserve for some yet to be identified new domain. The *value* of efficiency is important; but, a stable measure of productivity cannot be defined.

Thus, there are three idealized environments in which productivity measures are relevant. Generally as the system becomes more open and dynamic with respect to its environment, the appropriate productivity measure changes from a purely internal measure to a comparative externally based measure. In the more complex environments the measures appropriate for a more stable environment may be usefully calculated. However, they must be interpreted in the context of the productivity measure defined for the environment in which the system finds itself.

With this background on the role of systems theory for defining productivity measures, we turn next to an explication of process, bounded and systemic productivity.

PROCESS PRODUCTIVITY

Process productivity is the concept of productivity most generally used in economic theory. It is measured by calculating the ratio of what is produced by the system (output) to what the system consumes in producing it (resource input). This notion of productivity leads to a deceptively simple formula for process productivity, O/I. Difficulties in applying this formula result when units of output and input must be defined and units of measure specified. This has led to much confusion in the economic literature. To sort these problems out it is useful to view process productivity by means of a systems model.

DIAGRAM 1

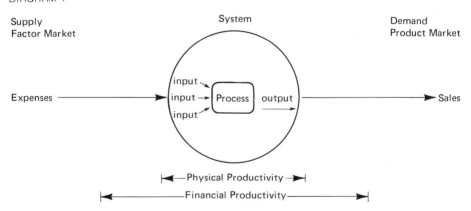

The system's manager seeks to maintain both the technical efficiency of the system and the market and environmental viability of the system. For the former the manager is concerned with the physical relationships between input and output. The latter is concerned with the monetary relationship between expenses (outgo) and sales (income or revenue).

a. Physical Process Productivity

To measure physical process productivity outputs are expressed in physical, tangible units of goods or services. Number of items, tons, kilowatt hours, gallons, square feet, etc. are typical units of measure used. Inputs are expressed in terms of actual amount of resources consumed in producing the output and are usually classified into labor, materials, energy, capital and other factors of production.

From a system's point of view the relevant measure of productivity is a ratio of output to *all* associated inputs. This is generally referred to as a "total factor productivity" measure and it reflects the overall efficiency of the systems processes for converting inputs into outputs. The association of inputs to outputs is accomplished by means of an activity analysis. A full scale activity analysis of a multiple technology system would yield an activity matrix A. The A matrix takes the form:

$$I_{1,1} \; ; \; I_{2,1} \ldots I_{n,1} \; ; \; O_1$$

$$I_{1,2} \; ; \; I_{2,2} \ldots I_{n,2} \; ; \; O_2$$

$$I_{1,m} \; ; \; I_{2,m} \ldots I_{n,m} \; ; \; O_m$$

Process productivity measures deal with only the rows of this A matrix. As will be discussed in a subsequent section, bounded productivity measures permit comparisons to be made among the rows.

A major difficulty in developing a total factor productivity measure is to identify a common unit of measure for diverse inputs and to devise a weighting scheme for converting them into a single measure. In practice some unit of time is often used as a starting point and man-hours, machine hours, kilowatt hours, etc. are identified. However, many inputs such as raw materials are not necessarily measurable in terms of time and some method must be devised to relate these to the other inputs. Next, the inputs are accumulated by a linear weighting function into a single resource input measure of the form: $I = w_1 I_1 + w_2 I_2 + \ldots + w_n I_n$. The approach used most frequently to obtain weights is to perform an activity analysis on the technical relationships in the production process during a base period. The results are used to create a full resource "bill of labor and materials" for a unit level of output. The result is a technological weighting vector W. Its coordinates represent the inputs and outputs associated with the operation of the system's process technology at a unit output level.

Assuming that W^b is a row vector of weights and R^b is a column vector of the input resources consumed during a base period, b, then the functional production relationship for the system is given by the equation:

$$O^b = W^b \bullet R^b$$

Hence in a subsequent period, t, the level of input is given by the equation $I^t = W^b \bullet R^t$ and the process productivity period, t, is given by the formula O^t/I^t.

The most useful information is obtained from process productivity measures if they are calculated and tracked over time. A change in the relationship between output and a measure of all resources consumed indicates whether efficiency is rising or falling as a whole. The general approach is to construct an index number of the form:

$$\frac{O^t \,/\, I^t}{O^b \,/\, I^b}$$

However, when the activity analysis procedure is used as described above $O^b = I^b$ and hence $O^b/I^b = 1$. Consequently, the use of the base year weight vector W^b results in the productivity measure

$$\frac{O^t}{W^b \cdot R^t}$$

becoming in effect an index of productivity.

It is important to point out that many changes in the system's conversion processes may explain the changes observed in a total factor productivity measure. New technology, reorganization, new management, new materials, changes in labor skills and many other factors may account for increases or decreases in the ratio.

Partial productivity measures help identify some of the sources of productivity change and are easier than total measures to operationalize. A partial productivity measure is the ratio of output to a single or limited set of elements of input. It takes the form,

$$\frac{O^b}{I_i^b}$$

for a base year, where I_i^b represents the ith element(s) of input. An index of the form

$$\frac{O^t / I_i^t}{O^b / I_i^b}$$

can also be calculated for any comparative period t.

Output per man-hour is the most frequently used partial measure. In fact it is so commonplace that many people define "productivity'" exclusively as output per man-hour. For many systems this is a reasonable measure to use since labor is a major input factor and because labor efficiency has been a historical focal point for managerial concern. A partial measure such as output per man-hour actually reflects changes in the performance of the system as a whole including the overall efficiency with which resources are used, the average quality of labor, the quality and availability of materials and the methods of organization and work flow.

An illustration of the sensitivity of output per man-hour to systemic changes is found in some recent studies of productivity in the Federal Government. At the behest of Senator Proxmire and the U.S. Congress, the Federal Government initiated a Joint Financial Management Improvement Program (JEMIP) with the cooperative efforts of G.A.O., O.M.B., Civil Service and National Commission on Productivity. The JEMIP undertook an effort to measure the productivity of as many of the functions of government as possible. Among the activities studied was the check and bond preparation processes in the Division of Disbursement, Bureau of Accounts in the Treasury Department (U.S. Government, 1972). During the period 1949 to 1962 the total number of checks and bonds prepared per man-year for the division rose from about 60,000 to nearly 200,000. However, 10 different methods were used to prepare checks during the period. When the output was analyzed in terms of the different technologies it was discovered that the increase in productivity was due entirely to the installation of automatic check processing equipment. Productivity figures for EDP, Semi Electronic and other mechanized check processing procedures improved substantially over the period while output per man-year for manually typed checks and manual transfer posted checks actually decreased.

A similar case is reported by Gerald Peck, Executive Vice President of the National-American Wholesale Grocer's Association (NAWGA). NAWGA provides a productivity measurement service for its members and subscribers as part of a warehouse cost control system (WCCS). The system collects distribution center warehousing data from subscribers, analyzes it and compares it to past performance. Separate WCCS reports are developed for similar operations. Since warehousing primarily involves the moving of merchandise, tons moved per man-hour of direct labor was selected as the appropriate (partial) productivity measure for the receiving and shipping functions. Early experience with the measurement system was successful. Soon, however, changes were experienced in the productivity of car unloading that seemed to be unexplainable. These anomalies were found to be correlated with the increased use of unitized freight shipping. When output was separated into these two subfunctions (i.e., technological options for receiving) the measures revealed that the productivity for car unloading under the unitized technology was much larger (about four times larger) than car unloading using manual methods. This substantially accounted for the higher productivity of the larger warehouses which used unitized freight.

There are a couple of observations to make from these illustrations. One is that the cases demonstrate that partial productivity measures, such as output per man-hour, do reflect changes in the system as a whole and hence serve as signals which may help explain the causes of change. Secondly, they demonstrate the principle that the same output produced by different technological processes often should be considered as different outputs of different producing subsystems, especially if the multiple technologies exist in the same system.

There is a deep social value underlying the use of a physical process productivity measure. In essence it is a measure of society's ability to overcome the forces of nature. More output or use-value per unit of input is a measure of a system's and, hence, man's increasing ability to create "plenty" and abundance. This is the concern of the producer, the engineer, the technologist, and the manager. There is a long history in economic literature for this concern. The primary focus of this concern has been on labor input.

Adam Smith argued that "every man is rich or poor according to the degree in which he can afford to enjoy the necessaries, conveniences, and amusements of human life." This led him to place the value of a commodity as "equal to the quantity of labour which it enables him to purchase or command." Outputs and inputs in this view should be measured in terms of their exchange or market value not in physical terms. In this view a system's outputs and inputs are valued in terms of their "scarcity" value.

David Ricardo, however, disagreed with Adam Smith. The fundamental system's problem was to secure abundance from nature. The proper value is "use" value. The value of an output is not inherent in the quantity of labor purchased or commanded from others in terms of its scarcity; but, rather in the physical quantity of labor which was consumed in the process of producing the output. Ricardo thereby gave rise to the labor theory of value, a theory in which output per man-hour is a central notion. Karl Marx was to extend this notion.

The labor and use theories of value are also the basis of much of contemporary industrial engineering. Time and motion study and scientific management, as developed by Frederick W. Taylor, are notable examples. Taylor sought to reduce the gap between what workers actually turned out and what they might comfortably turn out. His approach was to study the processes of work in detail. The amount of time required to accomplish a task using one method was compared to the amount required using other methods until the most efficient method was found. In his studies Taylor identified three forms of measurement which were essential to scientific management: a measure of the quantity of physical output (e.g., pounds, tons, bushels), a measure of the quality of physical output (e.g., grades, errors), and the productivity measure of man-hours per unit of output required to produce the output. Taylor's objective was to solve the engineering problem of improving a worker's capacity by discovering better methods. He also sought to solve the psychological problem of improving his willingness to work by developing incentive systems. The goal of these solutions was to increase output per man-hour. This tradition, frequently called Taylorism, has continued through much of industrial engineering and management science.

Physical process productivity measures do ignore scarcity, however. A system's manager is also concerned with the financial viability of the system in a market and monetary economy. In a monetarized economy, prices are a measure of the relative scarcity of goods and factors. Indeed, since John Stuart Mill first formulated the monetary measure of value, most of the focus of economics has been on the monetary or price side of systems. Most systems are compared in terms of their relative financial performance.

Productivity analysts have used monetary data extensively for their studies. There are several reasons for this. One is that some analysts firmly believe that a measure of sales or income to expenses is the relevant measure of efficiency for a system. Another prevalent reason is the availability of dollar data for most elements of production. Since the dollar is a common unit of measure among goods and factors, prices are often used as a surrogate for physical relationships. A third explanation, of course, is that they have confused the use value premises, which underly physical relationships, with the scarcity and exchange value premises, which underlie price-market relationships.

b. Financial Process Productivity

For a business enterprise, profit is the purest measure of management's ability to operate efficiently in the market place. It is generally calculated as Sales (Income or Revenue) minus Expenses, that is, Income-Outgo. Sales or Income are normally used as the output measure in the private sector. Revenue is normally used in the public and not-for-profit sectors. This relation may be expressed as a ratio S^b/E^b. The ratio is greater than one when the firm is profitable or the non-profit organization has an excess of revenue over expenses. The ratio is less than one when outgo exceeds income. Trends can then be established by comparing a base period ratio with subsequent periods by means of an index.

While a productivity type measure of the form S/E can be calculated, the more typical measure is the profitability rate, $(S-E)/S$. This is just one of several financial ratios which are used to measure the financial productivity of an organization. Return on investment or return on assets,

$$\frac{\text{Profit}}{\text{Investment}} = \frac{S-E}{A},$$

and the capital turnover ratio,

$$\frac{\text{Revenue}}{\text{Investment}} = \frac{S}{A}.$$

and other variations of investment based ratios are also frequently employed for financial analysis.

These financial measures—profit rate, return on investment and capital turnover—are the purest reflection of the organization's ability to cope with problems of scarcity in a monetarized and market economy where a monetary unit (such as dollars) is the medium of exchange. These financial measures are not normally considered to be productivity measures, but rather measures of financial performance. However, they form one end of a continuum of measures running from pure financial measures on one end to pure physical measures of productivity on the other end. The middle of this continuum contains many "mixed" measures in which prices and financial inputs and outputs are co-mingled with measures of physical inputs and outputs.

Two frequently used measures which mix financial and physical dimensions are cost per unit of output and revenue per man-hour. Cost per unit of output is the fundamental notion of cost accounting. It is the result of dividing all relevant financial input costs by the number of units of physical output,

$$\frac{P_1 I_1 + P_2 I_2 \cdots P_n I_n}{O}.$$

P_i = the factor price for the ith input, I_i = the quantity of the ith input, and O = the physical quantity of output. Cost per unit is influenced not only by the technical efficiency of the organization's conversion processes but also by the supply forces affecting its input factors and the organization's skills and relative power in the factor input market. Consequently, cost per unit is a measure of how well the organization has been able to acquire scarce resources from its environment and convert them to physical output.

Sales or Revenue per man-hour is the converse of cost per unit. It is calculated by dividing sales by man-hours $S/I_e = O \cdot M / I_e$ (where M = the product market price of output O and I_e is the physical amount of labor input). (Actually, a measure of sales per total factor input can be calculated, but its use is rare. Some firms use a related measure, however, in which the total sales or revenue for a product are divided by the direct, traceable costs of producing the product.) Many industrial firms use the measure sales (or revenue) per man-hour as indication of their overall productivity. One reason given for its use is that most employees and managers understand it and because its behavior is believed to be correlated with purer financial and physical measures in the range in which the firm is operating. The partial financial measure Sales (or Revenue) per dollar of labor expense (or, sometimes, just direct labor expense) is used for the same purpose. Sales per man-hour is a measure of the organization's ability to employ its physical inputs to satisfy demand and scarcity requirements in its product market. It is influenced not only by the technical efficiency of the organization, but also by the social demand for its output, the relative scarcity of the output, and the organization's skill and relative power in the output product market.

Some productivity analysts have attempted to reduce some of the effects of scarcity factors on financial measures by using "value added" rather than sales as a financial output measure. Value added is the market price of the output minus the cost of materials purchased from others. Gross value added reflects the cost of labor, taxes, profit, interest, rent and capital depreciation. Net value added excludes capital depreciation. Value added per man-hour has the advantage of not being distorted substantially by the extent to which a system processes its output through all stages of production from basic raw materials to finished product. Hence, it is useful for comparing productivity between organizations with different degrees of plant integration. Value added per man-hour is a measure of the organization's ability to apply its physical labor to the raw and semiprocessed materials it acquires and to add scarcity or market value to them. It is frequently used in industry level productivity studies to compare one firm with another.

One method for moving financial measures closer to physical measures is to employ price deflators. Constant dollar sales and expense figures may be obtained by applying a price index which reflects the prices of the particular outputs and inputs the system handles. Value added figures require a "double deflation" for both the value of output and also for the cost of materials. Constant-dollar values may also be obtained directly by multiplying the number of units of output or of input by a unit price calculated for a base period. In productivity measures, these weights are employed in the same manner as the W^b discussed above.

The use of price deflators reduces the effect of price changes on productivity measures. However, it is not without problems. There is a technical difficulty in estimating constant dollars because the appropriate or ideal price index for a given system usually is not available. There is also a conceptual problem in their use as physical measures. Under ideal circumstances they still reflect the relative financial scarcity in the system's market environment during the base period. Despite these problems, price adjusted data is commonly used. For many systems the requisite financial data is more readily available than the physical data and, especially for large and highly complex systems, constant-dollar productivity is most likely the closest approximation to physical productivity that can be obtained.

A recent paper by Craig and Harris (1973) develops one of the most comprehensive approaches to constant-dollar financial productivity in the literature. Craig and Harris define total productivity as

$$\frac{O}{L+C+R+Q} \quad or \quad \frac{O}{I_1+I_2+I_3+I_4}$$

in the symbology described above. O = total output, L = labor factor input, C = capital factor input, R = raw materials and purchased parts factor input, and Q = other miscellaneous goods and services factor input. Output is defined to be the number of units produced (*not* sold) multiplied by their selling price and deflated by a base year price index. Labor is defined to be man-hours worked multiplied by appropriate wage rates for the base year. Raw materials are defined to be the number of units purchased (adjusted for inventory changes) multiplied by base year prices. Miscellaneous goods and services such as utilities, taxes, advertising and administrative overhead are treated similarly.

The unique feature of the Craig and Harris model is the treatment of capital. The authors reject measures of the physical input of capital (such as depreciation which is, admittedly, a poor measure of physical contribution) in favor of a service value of capital concept. They then turn to the financial market to estimate the service value input. The model assumes that the firm has a leasing subsidiary which purchases its land, buildings, equipment, cash and other assets. The capital input defined to be the payment made by the firm to the leasing subsidiary. The payment is calculated as an annuity on the basis of the base year cost of the asset, its assumed productive life and on the desired rate of return to the lessor. The desired rate of return is considered to be the relevant cost of capital to the firm. A weighted average of the percentage elements of the firm's capital structure multiplied by each source's cost factor is suggested for estimating the cost of capital.

The Craig and Harris model has much to commend it; but, it is nevertheless a mixture of physical and financial measures. In addition to the problems of applying price level deflators its treatment of capital is specifically financial in nature. Cost of capital is a monetary measure of the relative scarcity of financial resources. Consequently, it reflects the firm's skills and power in the capital markets and investor expectations about the firm's earning power.

It is not surprising that financial and physical measures become intermixed in measuring productivity performance. They are inherently dialectical in nature. Scarcity considerations of supply and demand occur as man exchanges goods and services with his fellow men. Efficiency considerations occur as man works against nature to increase the abundance of goods and services. Thus, the concepts are at once distinctively different and deeply interwoven. Scarcity is reduced by efficiency. Efficiency is directed and motivated by scarcity. And, hence, our financial measures of scarcity and our physical measures of efficiency in the end are bound to be interrelated.

In constructing a measurement system for the process productivity of a producing system we need not resolve this dialectic. We need only to understand it. In practice both financial and physical measures and their composites should be used. They each tell us something different about the productivity of the system and its ability to survive in its environment. Also, for reasons discussed above, both partial and total measures are appropriate. Consequently, process productivity is probably best measured by a "family" of productivity measures. Such a family of measures, of course, can be quite large. In the case of a simple production system with one output and n inputs there are 2^n-1 total and partial measures of physical productivity. Since there is an equal number of measures of financial productivity, of physical output to financial input and of financial output to physical input, a total of $4(2^n-1)$ measures are possible for each output.

As we have seen, productivity analysis often requires that we distinguish outputs by the different technological processes which produce them and that inputs be categorized into classes according to their contribution to the productive process. Consequently, for any but the most macro analysis a substantial number of theoretical measures is possible. It behooves the systems manager, therefore, to develop a strategy for choosing the subset of measures which will be most useful in dealing with scarcity and efficiency issues.

There is substantial literature on the subject of what is here called process productivity. An introduction to the topic is found in Fabricant's *A Primer on Productivity* (1969). Application to industrial firms is found in Kendrick and Creamer (1965),

Greenberg (1973), and Eilon, Gold and Soesan (1976). Melman (1951, 1956) has done related studies. Process type productivity measures for industry and the national economy are given in Kendrick (1961) and in Denison (1962, 1967, 1974). Bela Gold (1955, 1971) has dealt explicitly with the difference between financial and physical measures of productivity.

With a few exceptions (to be discussed in the next section), the measures in this literature are all process productivity measures as defined at the beginning of this section. The output to input ratios they contain reflect the system's ability to cope with scarcity and efficiency. As the ratio of output per unit of input increases, the system's power over nature and over other systems is improving. But, process productivity only tells the system manager how well the system *is* doing not how well it *could* do. A system which has accumulated resources in a placid, clustered environment must be concerned with how well it could do. Bounded productivity addresses this question of potential and deals explicitly with the system's performance in relation to its capacity and capability.

BOUNDED PRODUCTIVITY

Bounded productivity describes how well the system is doing compared with its potential, given its *existing* resources and technological configurations. It is measured both in relation to output and to input.

Bounded output productivity is the ratio: actual output *divided by* the maximal output that a system with its particular concentration and configuration of resources (capital, labor, supplies, knowledge, etc.) could produce.

Bounded input productivity is the ratio: minimal input resources that should be required by a system of this configuration to produce a given level of output *divided by* the actual input resources consumed to produce that output.

In traditional economic analysis bounded productivity relates productive performance to that which would have occurred with the "frontier production function." A system's frontier production function expresses the maximal output obtainable from the system's particular combination of factors of production (resource inputs) at the existing state of technical knowledge.

There are several approaches to estimating a system's frontier production function output so that it may be used as the denominator in the boundary productivity ratio. These include: (a) determining the "engineered" production function; (b) estimating relationships on the basis of historical input and output flows; and (c) estimating relationships on the basis of external influencing or modifying factors. The most natural method is to use the theoretical function specified by the system's designers and engineers. It is possible to define such an "engineered" production function by consulting current catalogue information and technical analysis of the flow of work to determine the system's achievable output rate.

As an illustration of this approach, consider a system consisting of a typist, a manual typewriter, paper, etc., the purpose of which is to produce correctly typed pages as output. Suppose the system is currently producing at a rate of 3,000 words per man-hour. Three thousand words per man-hour is its "partial" rate of technical productivity. Suppose that, according to technical specifications of the equipment and analysis of standard labor times, the system is designed to produce at a rate of

7,200 words per man-hour. Then its bounded productivity would be 3000/7200 or .4167. Alternatively, since the world record (performed on an Underwood Standard manual machine) is about 8,820 words per man-hour, one might calculate the lower level bounded productivity as 3000/8820 or .3401. Increases in either of these ratios indicate that the system's resources are being more fully utilized and, hence, the system is more productive.

For many systems, especially in complex organizations, it is difficult to arrive at an agreed upon designed, standard or maximal output. This is particularly true in systems which involve substantial administrative or indirect inputs, learning behavior, or which require coordinated interpersonal relations. When this is the case a maximum can be estimated empirically. Such an empirical production function has the advantage that at least some of its points have been observed as outputs of real systems.

One approach for deriving an empirical production function for a system is to collect statistics on inputs and outputs for a group of similar systems (say, all of the firms in an industry). This data is used to infer an average production function. Normally, this will be an appropriately weighted mean of the production function associated with each of the various technologies used by the group of comparable systems. If the system's analyst is willing to assume a linear, homogenous production function, then the input and output data can be processed using ordinary multiple regression methods to yield an average function.

This approach can be employed in a wide variety of contexts. For example, regression models can also be applied to the historical data for an administrative office. A base year is selected and periodic data is collected on the man-hours of input for each period and the number of units of various outputs produced during the period. Examples of output data include inquiries answered, mail processed, tickets issued, and correspondence routed. Regression analysis yields a constant number of man-hours (the intercept value) and a series of weights for each output. Given the set of actual (or projected) outputs for a period, the regression model can be used to predict the number of man-hours which should have been required to produce the particular bundle of outputs observed. The ratio of actual man-hours to the model's predicted man-hours becomes a partial bounded input productivity measure for the system.

An alternative, but related, approach for deriving an empirical production function is that used by M. J. Farrell (1957). Farrell's method estimates the lower bound of the system's production function. The method essentially involves estimating a unit isoquant (points representing the minimum quantities of the resource factors of production required to produce one unit of output with varying factor proportions). An envelope is fit to the data from below where each data element consists of resource input data divided by the total output. The production function is then found by solving a series of simultaneous equations. A similar result can be achieved, however, with regression techniques by forcing the residuals to be positive.

Farrell's approach and also the "best practice" methods suggested by Anne Grosse (1953) are based on relations between internal factors and output. Sometimes these relationships are difficult to establish. This is especially true in information producing and administrative areas. This difficulty has led some organizations to focus on estimating resource input standards as a function of some environmental parameters of the system.

IBM, for example, has found that standard input resource levels for secretaries are more reliably estimated as a function of the number of personnel in the plant, than as a function of the number of reports, amount of correspondence, etc. produced. IBM currently estimates some 110 administrative input standards on the basis of some 28 external environmental variables ("modifiers" in their system).

Standards, whether derived empirically or through engineering analyses, form the basis of a popular form of bounded productivity measure. This is the relation between standard hours or "earned" hours and the actual hours of labor input. Many organizations have calculated a standard for hours (and also for materials) per unit of output. They subsequently calculate the ratio:

$$\frac{\text{Standard input per unit of output} \times \text{Units of output}}{\text{Input actually consumed}}$$

This ratio is a bounded input productivity measure.

Systems theory also suggests an approach for improving productivity as measured by the bounded concept. At any point in time the system's output is limited by just those constraints which are "binding." In the event that a system is achieving less than its maximum, that is, whenever a system's bounded productivity, actual output/maximal output, or its bounded input productivity, minimum input/actual input, is less than one, then some unspecified constraints must be operating. Discovering these phantom constraints and releasing them will aid the system's management in increasing the system's productivity.

The institutional economist, John R. Commons, refers to these binding constraints as "limiting factors" and relates them to "complementary factors." Complementary factors are similar to resources in systems terms. In Commons's words:

> The limiting factor is the one whose control, in the right form, at the right place and time, will set the complementary factors at work to bring about the results intended. A very little potash, if that is the limiting factor, will multiply the grain yield from perhaps five bushels to twenty bushels per acre. The sagacious mechanic is the one who busies himself with control of the limiting factor, knowing that the complementary factors will work out the results intended. The flutter-budget wastes his time on the complementary factors. (1961, pp. 628–629)

In the typing example discussed earlier, it is possible that the factor limiting a typing system to 3000 words per hour when its achievable rate is 7200 words per hour is the skill of the typist. Hence, additional training may improve this limiting factor. Of course, there are many other possibilities. The output could be limited by the motivation of the typist or the implied or negotiated work rules which control the pace of work. The repair of the machine or the kind of paper, or the organization or the flow of work may constitute or contribute to the limiting factor. Or, it is also possible that the typist is not as productive as possible because some effort is devoted to complying with governmental regulations. Whatever their source, identifying the limiting factors is important in productivity analysis.

John Commons correctly points out that in a dynamic or ongoing system the limiting and complementary factors are continually changing place. Thus, an effective management is one that pays attention, sequentially, to the active limiting factors. In the language of management planning, releasing (i.e., converting to complementary) a limiting factor becomes a management *objective*. Consequently, the sequential attention to objectives which Cyert and March (1963) claim describes managerial behavior is also rational as a means of securing improved productivity in a placid, clustered environment. The vast literature on management by objectives is also relevant in this regard.

Some recent work by Charles Kriebel and colleagues (1976) contains an analytical method for searching for limiting factors, especially those of a technical nature. Using a form of activity analysis, Kriebel relates a vector of output rates, Y_j's for services j to a constraint vector X of x_i's. Each x_i represents the capacity service rate of input resource category i measured in resource processing units per unit time. For a given system technology, A, a standard product output mix $y^o = (y_1, y_2 \ldots y_n)$ can be specified as:

$$Ay^o = x^o \leq X$$

The utilization of resources when the inputs employed are x^o can be evaluated using this model. λ^* is defined as the maximal factor by which the amount employed of all resources for the product mix y^o can be increased without violating the capacity constraints. The scalar λ^* is the solution to:

$$\lambda^* = \text{Max}\lambda$$

subject to $\lambda^* x^o \leq X$

If at least one of the resources (the limiting factor) is fully utilized $\lambda^* = 1$ otherwise $\lambda^* \geq 1$. λ^{*-1} then becomes a bounded productivity measure indicating the level of resource utilization in the system. The method appears to be sound whenever the A's and X's refer to technical production systems. The method could be extended however to deal with less tangible resources and constraints such as motivational and regulatory factors.

The search for the maximal output or minimal input for a system may also be facilitated by linear programming. There is a close connection between the activity analysis developed by Koopmans and the simpler method for linear programming developed by George B. Dantzig. As described briefly in the preceding section, the technical knowledge about a system may be represented in an activity analysis model and summarized by a matrix A. When this model is confronted with a given stock of factors of production and a specific objective to be maximized (e.g., output) or minimized (e.g., input), a linear program may be formulated. Linear programming involves finding a non-negative vector which satisfies a series of linear inequalities and which maximizes or minimizes a given linear function. The general forms are as follows:

Maximize Output $= \Sigma wx$
Subject to: $xA \leq b$
$\qquad x \geq 0$

Minimize Input $= \Sigma wy$
Subject to: $yA \geq c$
$\qquad y \geq 0$

where $w =$ a series of relative weights
$\qquad x =$ a vector of system outputs

b = a vector of input constraints
y = a vector of inputs
c = a vector of minimum output requirements

Bounded productivity as described here is important because it serves as a guide to management. It tells the manager how far actual production is from what is achievable with the system's given resources. It spurs the search for limiting factors. Hence, it provides valuable information for the practical and rational decision-maker. Measures similar to the bounded productivity measures developed here are found in various parts of the literature. The rate of return on investment analysis of DuPont and General Motors (Jerome, 1961) relates output to capacity as one of the explanatory variables. Bela Gold (1971) has linked it to more traditional productivity analysis through the equation:

$$\frac{\text{Output}}{\text{Total investment}} = \frac{\text{Output}}{\text{Capacity}} \times \frac{\text{Capacity}}{\text{Fixed investment}} \times \frac{\text{Fixed investment}}{\text{Total investment}}$$

Several studies of productive systems have used a bounded measure as their effectiveness criterion. For example in the Ahmedabad Experiments (1970), A. K. Rice employed engineering techniques to estimate productivity as actual output divided by engineered potential output. M. J. Farrell's original work has been extended by Farrell and Fieldhouse (1962) and Wesley Seitz (1970, 1971). Ann Grosse's "best practices" method (1953) is an alternative to that of Farrell.

The common use of measures of this sort is enough to suggest their usefulness as measures of a system's productivity. However, there is a deeper theoretical sense in which bounded productivity is a relevant measure of the efficiency of a system. A generalization of the economic aspects of thermodynamics as developed by the American Institute of Physics (1975) and applied to energy policy by Barry Commoner (1976) can be used to develop a system's theory of production. Some of the economic underpinnings of this theory have been anticipated by Georgescu-Roegen (1971). The next section develops an argument for bounded productivity from a systems and thermodynamics point of view.

SYSTEMS, THERMODYNAMICS AND BOUNDED PRODUCTIVITY

A system which consumes resources in the production of output is involved in a process of *work*. The output and processes of an unmanaged system is totally determined by external natural forces, which simply move the system blindly and inevitably. The role of system's management, however, is to intercede in this natural flow of forces by means of the exercise of will, volition and intellect. The purpose of the intervention is to change the direction of nature's forces so that different and more desirable outputs result. This is how use-value is created. Indeed early economists, notably Ricardo and Marx, stress the notion that a larger quantity of labor energy is required when nature's resistance is great, then when nature's resistance is weak. For them the "embodied" labor needed to overcome nature became a measure of the value of the resulting output.

Creating use-value by overcoming the resistance of natural forces, such as, say, lifting a one-pound rock one foot in the air, constitutes work. Work, in turn, requires energy. Thus, the concepts of production, work and energy are closely linked.

Energy is consumed in simple tasks such as lifting a rock and in more complex tasks such as, for example, performing the work of typing pages, adding potash to farm land, collecting a city's garbage, or delivering welfare services to clients. In this sense, the concept of energy is fundamental to the economic concepts of production, productivity and management. In essence, then, system's management may be defined as the governance of energy applied to work.

Energy in this context consists of at least three types: physical, physiological and psychic. Physical energy is the normal mechanical energy derived from oil, coal, wood, nuclear, solar or geothermal sources. Physiological energy is that provided by a living organism—people and draft animals. It is frequently called "labor" and is obtained from nutrition, metabolism and "sweat of the brow."

Psychic energy is somewhat more elusive in definition and description, but is nonetheless fundamental. Psychic energy refers to the propelling force behind mental activity. According to Freud it emerges from the id—the reservoir of drives and instincts. Jung valued psychic energy as a system's resource. He considered it to be something which could be dissipated, misdirected, or lost. Psychic energy converts instincts and drives into bodily action. How psychic energy is guided in work situations is the subject of motivation, incentives, job satisfaction and concern for the quality of working life. Ultimately, it concerns the will and volition.

All three of these sources of energy are necessary components in the production of goods and services and, hence, are fundamental to productivity. This suggests that a search for a theory of productivity could well begin by exploring the theory of energy: thermodynamics.

The theory of thermodynamics is based on two fundamental laws. The first law, the so-called law of conservation of energy, states that energy can neither be created or destroyed. The first law implies that for any system energy inputs must equal energy outputs. Thus, following this law, it is natural to measure efficiency in any work system by relating the energy actually applied in useful work (i.e., output) to the energy input. The resulting ratio is analogous to that of process productivity developed above.

The second law, however, states that the entropy of the universe always moves toward a maximum. Nature irreversibly moves toward a state of disorder and chaos; that is, from a placid randomized state toward a more turbulent one. Reversing this process requires energy. For example, the natural (and more probable) state of sand, clay, limestone, and water is to be spread out in disarray. In contrast, these very same elements in the form of, say, a brick and mortar wall are substantially more ordered. However, this ordered state is also much less probable and natural. Energy is required to convert naturally dispersed sand, clay, limestone and water into a brick wall; just as energy is required to counteract all entropic forces of nature and to create order.

In system's terms, order is an expression of the relationship between the properties of the system as a whole and the properties of its components or parts. The extent to which a desired order can be achieved depends on three factors—the set of relationships achievable within the *boundaries* of the system, the amount of energy available to change relationships, and the choices made by the system's management in governing the application of energy.

All of the energy available to a system, however, is not of equal quality. According to thermodynamic theory, energy consists of two types: (a) free energy which is available to do work and (b) bound or latent energy which is not available to do work. The second law also states, in effect, that in every work process some energy is lost, irrevocably, by being converted to bound or latent energy. Taken to its logical conclusion, the law states that the final outcome of the universe is a state in which all energy is bound or latent—the so-called "heat death."

If this is the case, then it behooves the system's management to economize by avoiding the unnecessary creation of bound or latent energy. The manager thereby delays the system's day of irretrievable maximum entropy. Conceptually, the principle for this form of economy is simple and straightforward. The management need only calculate the theoretical minimum amount of energy required to produce a required output and relate the result to the amount of energy actually used. The formula is:

$$\frac{\text{Actual energy (resources) consumed}}{\substack{\text{Minimum possible energy (resources)} \\ \text{which could be used by the same system} \\ \text{producing the same level of system's} \\ \text{output (work)}}}$$

The closer the numerical value of this ratio is to one, the more productive the system is considered to be.

The above principle is based on inputs, but can be expressed alternatively in terms of system's outputs as follows:

$$\frac{\text{Output (work) actually achieved}}{\substack{\text{Maximum possible output (work) which} \\ \text{could be produced by the same system} \\ \text{using the same level of energy input}}}$$

Again, the closer the ratio approaches one, the more productive the system.

The concept of bounded productivity developed here is a generalization of these two ratios. It applies to all resources of a system. The major operational problem in applying the concept to real systems is to estimate the maximal output or minimal input levels. These estimates require a deep understanding of the productive system and are difficult, but not necessarily impossible, to make. A major challenge for researchers in the disciplines of management science, organization theory, economics and operations research is to develop theories and techniques for making these estimates.

To summarize, process productivity is the analog of the first law of thermodynamics applied to production. Bounded productivity is the application of the second law. We turn next to systemic productivity.

SYSTEMIC PRODUCTIVITY

Both process productivity and bounded productivity take the existing system as given. They are measures of how well the system is doing with the resources available to it. Systemic productivity questions the design of the system itself: "Is it living up to its maximum feasible potential?" "Is it doing what it *ought* to do to develop its resources and to pursue opportunities?" In a disturbed, reactive environment these are the salient questions. Strategic planning is the information base for answering these questions. Systemic productivity is the measure. Investment is the action orientation.

Systemic productivity is measured by the ratio: actual output *divided by* maximal output that could be produced by any feasible, designable system of the same functional class. Systems of the same functional class are ones which are either potential or actual producers of outputs which achieve the same end or purpose in their environment. To return to the illustration of the typing system, the actual rate of 3000 words per man-hour using a manual typewriter was related to a design standard (7200) and a world record (8820) for manual machines in order to obtain the bounded productivity measure. The system, however, could be redesigned using an electric typewriter. Electric typewritten pages are of the same functional class (and, in this case, also of the same morphological class) as manually typewritten pages. However, the official world record on an electric machine is 9316 words per man-hour, recorded using an I.B.M. electric. Actually, rates approaching 12,960 have been observed. This would suggest that one basis for calculating systemic productivity would be to relate the actual rate to this potential rate. The systemic productivity then would be

$$\frac{3000}{9316} = .3220 \quad \text{or} \quad \frac{3000}{12,960} = .2315.$$

The investment decision to exchange a manual typewriter for an electric typewriter is a relatively minor system's redesign. Computerized word processing represents a more dramatic reconfiguration within the same functional class. While it is still limited to some form of manual key entry for original data, a word processing system can store, format and organize data so that the net effective output rates can be much higher. For example, it may be possible on current I.B.M. equipment, to achieve as high as 45,000 words per man-hour. The systemic productivity of the manual typing system then would be

$$\frac{3000}{45,000} = .0667.$$

Systemic productivity is an indicator of the long-run survival and viability of the system. It may be applied to work stations, organizations, industries and entire economies, alike. Its application raises questions the other measures miss. For example, it is possible that an industry, such as the U.S. textile industry, has process and bounded productivity measures which are within historically acceptable levels. That is, the industry may be relatively efficient given the turn-of-the-century technology many firms employ. However, in light of the development of new looms and methods in Europe, the industry's systemic productivity may be quite low. This low ratio is a signal to the industry's management that its long-range plans and its investment policy ought to be reevaluated. The firm is in a disturbed environment and eventually its competitors may out-perform it.

Low rates (i.e., below one) of bounded or systemic productivity do not necessarily imply that immediate action should be taken to close the gap. The measure is a signal. It alerts management to conditions which should be understood and explained. For example, a low *bounded* productivity measure calculated on the basis of machine specifications may also be the result of a previously unconsidered constraint such as work rules negotiated in collective bargaining or work conditions imposed by compliance with an OSHA safety rule. Several judgments are possible in this case: (a) accept the imposed rates as binding and scale down the rest of the system to match; (b) attempt to negotiate a new standard; (c) continue to operate the system as is; or (d) seek ways to reconfigure the system within the confines of these constraints. The appropriate action would be determined by the result of a thorough productivity review.

Low *systemic* productivity measures suggest other options. Options for improvement include total redesign of the system, acquisitions of new equipment, or substantial restraining or hiring programs. In short, low systemic productivity is an indication that new investment is required. In terms of managerial action, there is a special relationship between bounded and systemic productivity. Bounded productivity focuses attention within the system to look for solutions; systemic productivity focuses attention without. However, if bounded productivity is low, then the system's management must be very careful in adopting systemic changes such as new equipment or new designs as a solution, unless these new solutions deal specifically with the limiting factor.

This is not unlike the story of the farmer who told the agriculture extension agent, "Shucks, I'm not farming as well as I know how now!" He was essentially saying, "Don't bother me with systemic changes. I'm not working up to my bounded productivity level yet." Consequently, the first order of business for the system's manager is to see that the system's available physical, physiological and psychic energy is freed to do work and that this energy is appropriately directed. This requires the manager to employ a wide range of skills, including organizational development skills.

The difference between bounded and systemic productivity is still relevant however. It is a guide for new investment and the importing of new energy for the system. If a manual typing system has a boundary output rate of 7200 words per man-hour and a systemic output rate of 9316, or of 45,000 words per man-hour, then a potential of between 2116 or 37,800 additional words per man-hour could be realized by an investment in an electric typewriter or a new word processing system. Of course, the system would have to be redesigned so that its energies would be channeled to secure the higher rate. This decision is the primary responsibility of a system's manager, as is any investment or reconfiguration of the system.

SUMMARY

Productivity has been defined in systems terms. It was argued that depending on the assumptions made about the system's environment and management's perceived relation to it, three different concepts of productivity can be identified. Based on a theory of system's environments, notions of process productivity, bounded productivity, and systemic productivity were developed and appropriate measures suggested. These system's concepts also relate to a theory of energy.

REFERENCES

1. R. L. Ackoff and F. F. Emery. *On Purposeful Systems.* Aldine-Atherton, Chicago, 1972.

2. S. Beer. *Brain of the Firm*. Herder and Herder. New York, 1972.

3. C. W. Churchman. *The Systems Approach*. Dell Publishing Co., New York, 1968.

4. C. W. Churchman. *The Design of Inquiring Systems*. Basic Books, New York, 1971.

5. J. R. Commons. *Institutional Economics*. The University of Wisconsin Press, Madison, Wisconsin, 1961, pp. 628–629.

6. C. F. Craig and R. C. Harris. "Total productivity measurement at the firm level." *Sloan Management Review*, **14**, No. 3, Spring 1973.

7. R. M. Cyert and J. G. March. *A Behavioral Theory of the Firm*. Prentice-Hall, Englewood Cliffs, New Jersey, 1963.

8. E. F. Denison. "The sources of economic growth in the United States and the alternatives before us," Committee for Economic Development, New York, 1962.

9. E. F. Denison. *Why Growth Rates Differ*. Brookings Institute, Washington, 1974.

10. E. F. Denison. *Accounting for United States' Economic Growth, 1929–1969*. Brookings Institute, Washington, 1974.

11. S. Eilon, B. Gold and J. Soesan. *Applied Productivity Analysis for Industry*, Pergamon International Library, Oxford, 1976.

12. F. E. Emery and E. L. Trist. "The causal texture of organizational environments," *Human Relations*, **18**, 1963, pp. 20–26.

13. S. Fabricant. *A Primer on Productivity*. Random House, New York, 1969.

14. M. J. Farrell. "The measurement of productive efficiency," *Journal of the Royal Statistical Society*, **120**, Part II, 1957, pp. 253–290.

15. M. J. Farrell and M. Fieldhouse. "Estimating efficient productions under increasing returns to scale," *Journal of the Royal Statistical Society*, **125**, Part II, 1962, pp. 252–267.

16. I. Fisher. *The Nature of Capital and Income*. Macmillan, New York, 1906.

17. Fisher, Irving. *The Nature of Capital and Income*. 1906.

18. Georgescu-Roegen, Nicholas. *The Entropy Law and the Economic Process*. Cambridge: Harvard University Press, 1971.

19. Gold, Bela. *Foundations of Productivity Analysis*, Pittsburg: University of Pittsburg Press, 1955.

20. Gold, Bela. *Explorations in Managerial Economics: Productivity, Costs, Technology and Growth*. New York: Basic Books, 1971.

21. Greenberg, Leon. *A Practical Guide to Productivity Measurement*. Washington, D.C.: The Bureau of National Affairs, Inc., 1973.

22. Grosse, Anne P. "The Technological Structure of the Cotton Textile Industry." In Wassily Leontief, et al., *Studies in the Structure of the American Economy*. New York: Oxford University Press, 1953, Chapter 10.

23. Jerome, William T. *Executive Control—The Catalyst*, New York: John Wiley & Sons, 1961.

24. Kendrick, John W. *Productivity Trends in the United States*. Princeton: Princeton University Press, 1961.

25. Kendrick, John W., and Creamer, Daniel. *Measuring Company Productivity*. New York: The Conference Board, 1965.

26. Kriebel, C.H., et al. "Modeling the Productivity of Information Systems."

(Technical Report No. NSF APR 75—20546/76/TR2) Carnegie-Mellon University, April 1976 (Revised June 1976).

27. McWhinney, William H. "Organizational Form, Decision Modalities and the Environment." *Human Relations*, Vol. 21, No. 3, August 1968, pp. 269-281.

28. Melman, Seymour. "The Rise of Administrative Overhead in the Manufacturing Industries of the United States, 1899-1947." *Oxford Economic Papers*, January 1951, Vol. III, No. 1.

29. Melman, Seymour. *Dynamic Factors in Industrial Productivity*. Oxford: Basil Blackwell, 1956.

30. Rice, A.K. *Productivity and Social Organization*. London: Tavistock, 1970.

31. Seitz, Wesley. "The Measure of Efficiency Relative to a Frontier Production Function." *American Journal of Agriculture Economics*, November 1970, pp. 505-511.

32. Seitz, Wesley D. "Productive Efficiency in the Steam-Electric Generating Industry." *Journal of Political Economy*, July-August 1971, pp. 878-886.

33. Smith, Adam. *An Inquiry Into the Nature and Causes of the Wealth of Nations*. Great Books of the Western World, Vol. 39.

34. Theil, Henri. *Economics and Information Theory*. New York: Rand McNally and Co. and North Holland Publishing Co., 1967.

35. U.S. Government, Joint Economic Committee. *Measuring and Enhancing Productivity in the Federal Sector*. Government Printing Office, August 4, 1972, No. 81-339.

Questions for Study and Discussion

1. What role might the Scribner scale or the cubic volume measure of log yield play in creating a measure of physical process productivity?

2. Consider the following types of property:

    (i)   Corporeal property—tangible property of a material nature, being physical and perceptible by the senses.

    (ii)   Incorporeal property—promises, such as promises to pay money in the future (a debt) or to perform some obligation in the future (a contract).

    (iii)   Intangible property—a subclass of incorporeal property. It has no material being and no direct use or appraisable intrinsic value, and includes patents, copyrights, trademarks, franchises, business goodwill, etc. Intangible property is a right to future rights, such as the right to engage in future beneficial transactions.

What problems do these different types of property created and processed by organizations present for measuring productivity? What are the implications for accounting measurement? What are the implications for process, bounded, and systemic productivity?

3. John Kendrick and Daniel Creamer (1965) ask: "But why measure productivity when that ultimate measure, profit, is available from the usual accounting records?" (p. 7). What is your response?

4. Bela Gold (1955) relates productivity to innovation and technical change. He defines his terms: ". . . 'technical change' or 'innovation' will be used to imply *any changes in input-output relations which is not to be attributed directly to changes in factor prices or variations in the rate or scale of production of the enterprise in question.*" What measurement issues does this approach raise?

5. In economic theory, public goods as opposed to private goods are characterized as (1) indivisible into definable commodities, and therefore subject to joint supply; (2) not subject to the exclusion principle in the sense that once they are produced they are immediately available to many consumers without price-controlled exchange; (3) subject to external economies and diseconomies. What implications does this distinction have for the measurement of productivity, if the organization's output is a public good?

6. In the information age the production and dissemination of information of all kinds has perhaps become more important than the production and distribution of traditional goods and services. Information activities constitute a large part of the GNP and nearly half of the United States workforce is employed in information related jobs. Information involves the means by which one system affects another system. How might the productivity of a system which produces and disseminates information be measured? (For one approach see Mason, 1979.)

TOTAL PRODUCTIVITY MEASUREMENT AT THE FIRM LEVEL

Charles E. Craig • R. Clark Harris

READING 14

INTRODUCTION

Productivity has now become an everyday word. Politicians and economists are concerned with productivity because they feel its movement is integrally related to the nation's general economic health—particularly in relation to inflation control, economic growth, foreign competition, and balance of payments. Corporate managers are concerned with productivity because they feel it is a representative indicator of the overall efficiency of their firms. Recently, productivity measurement at the firm level has become a factor in government-business relations via the Price Commission, and is expected to play a role in Phase III controls. In 1970 the President of the United States named a high-level commission to formulate national policies designed to increase productivity throughout the economy.

In spite of this activity, productivity remains as one of the most elusive concepts in business and economic literature. It remains elusive because of a lack of definitive theoretical work—mainly at the firm level. There has been very little done to develop measurement and calculation procedures that match the information desired with the intended use of that information. Many firm-level productivity measurement and calculation methods are either extrapolations of methods used to determine national productivity indexes or "rules-of-thumb" developed within a firm. These methods were suitable when only a rough guide for year-to-year performance was needed. However, as productivity indexes enter the pricing decision (via formal or informal governmental controls) and the wage decision (via clauses in labor contracts), the manager needs a suitable measurement scheme. This article describes a theoretical framework to firm-level productivity measurement; a framework particularly suitable for supporting the corporate management decision process.

Productivity is one of those words for which everyone has his own meaning, but often no two meanings agree. A brief overview of general productivity concepts will be useful in the discussion which follows.

Productivity is the efficiency with which outputs are produced—the ratio of output to input. In addition, there are least two distinct types of productivity ratios, *total* productivity and *partial* productivity.

Sloan Management Review, Vol. 14, No. 3, Spring 1973, pp. 13–29. Reprinted by permission.

$$\text{Total Productivity} = \frac{\text{Total Output}}{\text{Total Input}}$$

$$\text{Partial Productivity} = \frac{\text{Total Output}}{\text{Partial Input}}$$

A familar example of a partial productivity ratio is the output per manhour ratio—the *labor productivity* index.

Another index sometimes cited is the *value added* index. This ratio does not meet the strict definition of a partial productivity ratio just given. It is calculated by beginning with the total productivity ratio and removing the value of raw materials and purchased parts from the numerator and denominator. The value added index, therefore, equals partial output over partial input.

Many other such measures could be listed. The important point is that numerous partial measures exist, but they rarely are defined to the user as such. All partial measures, however, have certain common characteristics.

Fallacies of Partial Productivity Measures

Many of the productivity indexes quoted by economists and businessmen are labor productivity indexes. Their use can lead to serious misunderstandings. A simple example will demonstrate the potential problem. Assume a company procures a higher quality raw material that significantly reduces the man-hours necessary for processing. The output per man-hour index would naturally rise since a worker now can produce more of the same product in less time. However, suppose that the improved raw material is more costly. To simplify the example, assume that the increase in material cost is equal to the savings from reduced processing man-hours. Using the labor productivity index as a guide, labor and stockholders would note an increase in productivity. Either group could take action to distribute this gain. Labor could bargain for increased wages, and stockholders could expect increased dividends or at least a growth in profits. Customers might expect a price reduction. However, there has been no real gain to the corporation. The apparent increase in labor productivity has already been distributed to the raw material supplier; there is nothing available for distribution to labor, stockholders, or customers. Gains indicated by increased labor productivity may not actually be gains at all. *The cost of generating the increased labor productivity must be considered.*

It should be obvious that this type of fallacy is inherent in all partial productivity measures. Therefore, some measure of *total productivity* must be used for most top-level management decisions. Partial productivity measures should not be used as indiscriminately as they usually are.

TOTAL PRODUCTIVITY

Total productivity of the firm can be stated as follows:

$$P_t = \frac{O_t}{L + C + R + Q}$$

where, P_t = total productivity
L = labor input factor

C = capital input factor
R = raw material and purchased parts input factor
Q = other miscellaneous goods and services input factor
O_t = total output

The output of the firm as well as all inputs must be stated in a common measurement unit. Therefore, to describe the calculation of total productivity for a firm, a definition in *dollars* of all the above factors is required. Also, to make productivity indexes comparable from period to period, each index must be adjusted to a base period value. This simply means that the output and all inputs for any year after (and including) the base year must be stated in terms of base year dollars. This is often referred to as *deflating* the output and input factors. Deflation is used since prices and wages have typically risen each year.

Up to this point the importance of using all input factors when measuring productivity has been stressed. A proper productivity index for management use, however, is dependent not only on considering all factors, but also on how the factors are defined and used. The contention is that much of the previous work on firm-level productivity measurement has taken too little account of the precise definitions and the resultant consequences of the calculated index. The next section therefore is devoted to a definition of the output and input factors necessary for a total productivity calculation.

THE PROPOSED MODEL OF THE FIRM

The model is described as a service flow model. Physical inputs are converted to dollar equivalents which are remunerations for services provided by those inputs. From the manager's viewpoint, productivity is a measure of the efficiency of the conversion process. The manager converts resources into goods and services which provide returns for all input factors. The model will be expanded below.

Output

The output of a firm is usually expressed in units of physical volume, such as pieces, tons, feet, or number of cars. However, if the output is nonhomogeneous, the different products must be weighted in some manner so that they can be added together. For most purposes, the use of selling price (dollars) is the most suitable weighting unit. Therefore, a definition of output is the summation of all units produced times their selling price. Note that the number of units *produced* is used—not units *sold*. Since productivity is concerned with the efficiency of converting inputs to outputs, units sold cannot be used. Some of the units sold could be from a reduction in finished inventory. Such a condition would yield an overstated output. Conversely, units produced but not sold would not be counted, giving an understated output. In-process inventory must be included in the output calculation as well. In effect, in-process inventory is partial units produced. Adjustment of output will generally take the form of multiplying the in-process units by their selling price and their percentage completion as measured in cost terms.

As discussed previously, it is necessary to calculate productivity indexes in base year terms. This can be most satisfactorily accomplished by using the base year selling price in lieu of the current price. Unfortunately, there are two practical pitfalls to this method: new products and quality changes. New products not produced in the base year obviously have no base year selling prices. For those industries that have frequent product and quality changes (e.g., the auto industry) this is a particularly serious issue.

It is impossible to specify an adjustment technique that is universally applicable. Many firms could use an adjustment method based on the ratios of established costs of new and old products. Such a process can be accomplished with reasonable accuracy. If the current product line becomes significantly different from that of the base year, a change in base year is suggested.

Perhaps it also is beneficial to point out now the importance of choosing a normal base year. A normal base year is one in which no serious deviations from average production occurred. A year in which the company experienced a strike of some duration would be an unacceptable base year. Likewise, a year in which the company greatly changed its complexion, such as by acquisition or merger, is an unwise choice.

Another component of total output is revenue received from sources other than production. For example, dividends from securities and interest from bonds and other such sources should be included. The reason for this is that a portion of the input factors is being employed to produce these outputs. Both labor and capital (usually current assets) are employed to produce this revenue. To omit this revenue would understate the total output. Granted, the value of labor and capital may not be great in comparison to production output, but they should be included for completeness. These output components also must be adjusted to base year values. An appropriate cost-of-living index could be used. All forms of windfall profits should be excluded on the reasoning that no input was employed to produce them. For example, income derived from the sale of land not purchased for speculation but discovered to contain valuable minerals should not be included as output.

Sometimes it is possible to use a shortcut for deriving the value of output in any year after the base year. This involves beginning with sales revenue, adjusting it for finished and in-process inventory changes, and then deflating (or inflating) the dollars derived by a suitable index to calculate a value for output in base year terms. It is impossible to generalize what one would lose in accuracy by applying this abbreviated method; it simply is another of the many cost-accuracy trade-offs managers must make every day.

Input

The input calculations will be discussed next. Labor input, typically a large part of total input for a firm, is presented first.

1 Labor

The primary unit of labor input is man-hours worked. The man-hours must be converted into dollars by multiplying total man-hours times an appropriate wage rate ($/hour). Theoretically, each person employed could have a different wage rate. More typically, employees are separated into various job classifications that have more or less identical base wage rates or salaries. In addition to base wages and salaries, fringe benefits must be considered. Therefore, to calculate labor input for the current year in base year dollars, multiply the man-hours worked in each classification by the base year wage rate and/or salary scale for that job classification.

Difficulties similar to those inherent in the output calculation are found in the labor input calculation. Some jobs in the current year will not have been occupied in the base year. Usually, it is not too difficult to estimate what the base year rate for these jobs would have been.

2 Raw Materials and Purchased Parts

Productive material is quite often a significant input to the production process. The physical units of these inputs are tons, feet, pieces, gallons, etc. Adjustment of material costs to base year prices can be accomplished by multiplying the purchased units (adjusted for inventory changes) times base year material prices. If base year prices are not readily available, an appropriate commodity price index can be used to adjust the current year prices.

3 Miscellaneous Other Goods and Services

This group of inputs is comprised of all resources except labor, capital, and raw materials/purchased parts. Typical examples would be utilities (heat, light, power), government services (taxes), advertising, and nonproductive materials (office supplies, etc.). Each of these specific inputs must be adjusted to base year terms by using an appropriate price deflator.

It is important to note that interest payments are not considered as an input. Interest on loans is accounted for in the capital input factor calculation. Indirect business taxes, however, should be included. Even though it is impossible to link a government service directly to a tax, it is rational to consider taxes as quasi-license fees. In other words, if a firm wants to produce and sell certain products, the firm is obligated to pay the related business taxes. That some taxes are passed directly to the consumer simply means they appear directly in the output (through the price) and in the input.

4 Capital

Of all the terms involved in productivity measurement, capital historically has been the most difficult to define. At the same time, capital also is one of the most important resources of any firm. Most previous work in productivity measurement has recommended that capital input be considered as the physical use of the equipment. Depreciation generally is used as the approximation of the capital consumed in the production process. However, there are other ways of viewing capital input.

"At one time it was believed sufficient to measure change in capital input by change in depreciation and other capital consumption changes obtained from accounting records. A later variation of this procedure involved the use of an input-output table to translate the capital consumption charges into labor-input equivalents. Both procedures are deficient, however. It is the *value of the services of capital* that constitutes capital input. This value includes more than capital consumption, and is not necessarily related to capital consumption in any close way . . ."[1]

The deficiency of using a depreciation schedule is caused by the difficulty of representing the actual consumption of an asset. This problem is, of course, not new to accountants.

". . . This question has a long history of lively controversy for two reasons. First, because factual observation does not determine in any precise way the annual depreciation charge for an asset, considerable variation in the charge is possible. Second, the expenditure or sacrifice by a company in connection with a depreciable asset arises out of the purchase decision and not the depreciation decision. Therefore, in contrast with labor or materials expenses, depreciation expense can never be identified uniquely with any given time period. These characteristics of depreciation would make the consideration of how it should be determined practically meaningless without the careful *examination of the objectives to be served.*"[2]

The authors believe that capital input must be represented by a concept of the service value of capital. The service value concept best fulfills the criteria of the model. Furthermore, a concept of lease value is a better form than other service value concepts. To amplify this point, the model assumes that the firm has a leasing subsidiary to buy the land, buildings, and equipment. The leasing subsidiary also supplies current assets (such as cash) and expects a return from them. The capital input term is then the payment made to the leasing subsidiary.

A typical lease is in the form of an annuity. The amount of the annuity depends on three factors: the cost of the asset, the productive life of the asset, and the desired rate of return to the lessor. The cost of the asset is simply the asset's original purchase price plus any capitalized costs necessary to prepare the asset for use. These costs must be stated in base year terms. Adjustments to actual costs can be made by using appropriate capital equipment and building indexes. Productive life (economic life) is the length of time an asset can be expected to be useful prior to either complete physical deterioration or economic obsolescence. This term must be estimated. Time periods currently used for normal accounting practices are probably a good first estimate. The consequences of severely underestimating the life are more serious than those of overestimating.

In this model the lessors are the stockholders and debtors. A proper rate of return for them is derived from the cost of capital theory. The required rate of return is defined as the cost of capital in the base year, where the cost of capital is calculated by a weighted average method. (An example of this is given later.) The cost of capital, of course, varies by firm and industry. Therefore, the capital input factor is defined as the sum of the annuity values calculated for each asset on the basis of its base year cost, productive life, and the firm's cost of capital.

To clarify this important concept, an example is helpful. Assume that $100,000 is supplied for purchasing equipment. The equipment is expected to have a life of five years, and to have no salvage value at the end of that time. A weighted average cost of capital for the firm is calculated from the balance sheet to be 10 percent. The invested $100,000 must earn a 10 percent return on invested capital *and* the entire $100,000 in a five year period to return the proper amount to the investor (the assumed leasing subsidiary). In essence, the manager of this firm must turn over the capital invested *plus* earn a 10 percent return. Therefore, the service cost of using the invested capital is an annual charge that produces this effect. The annual charge can be calculated by using annuity tables. In this case the annual payment (annuity) would be $26,380. Table 1 shows for this example how the investor's (lessor's) money was returned.

Cash, accounts receivable, securities, inventory, and other liquid assets also are part of the capital input factor. The input service cost of these assets is calculated in a manner similar to that just described. The major difference is that liquid assets can be assumed to have an infinite productive life; therefore their costs are calculated on the basis of a perpetuity rather than an annuity. Input costs from these assets are calculated by the general formula $K \times C$, where K is the value of the asset in base year terms and C is the base year cost of capital for the firm. For example, if the firm maintained a cash balance of one million dollars (in base year dollars) and the base year cost of capital were 10 percent, the cash input factor would be one million dollars times 10 percent or $100,000. Adjusting each of these liquid assets to base year value requires an appropriate deflator for each specific type of asset.

Differences from Prior Productivity Calculations

It is important to note that the method just presented for calculating total productivity is different from some other suggested methods. The main differences can be explained by noting that historical productivity calculations have relied on weighted physical concepts. Output generally is defined strictly as weighted physical output (production of goods and services), i.e., interest earned on investments would not be included as an output of the firm. Interest on capital invested is not what the firm produces (as the argument goes), so it should not be included. Likewise, the capital input is related to the physical consumption of capital assets. Usually this estimate comes from normal accounting definitions of depreciation. Federal, state, and local taxes would be inputs on the basis that they are payments for services rendered by the governments. However, advertising may not be interpreted as contributing to the total output in a physical sense.

As such, numbers derived in the manner just described should not be compared directly with industry figures calculated on a pure physical capital, labor, and raw-material (and purchased parts) input basis. However, it is felt that a total productivity approach, as defined here, better suits the manager's needs in that it more accurately describes the efficiency with which *all* inputs are used.

TABLE 1   *Annuity Calculation Example*

Year	Net Capital Invested During the Year	Interest on Invested Capital (10%)	Reduction in Invested Capital		Total Annuity Payment
1	$100,000	$10,000 +	$16,380	=	$26,380
2	83,620	8,362 +	18,018	=	26,380
3	65,602	6,560 +	19,820	=	26,380
4	45,782	4,578 +	21,802	=	26,380
5	23,980	2,398 +	23,982	=	26,380

One more point deserves amplification. It could be argued that certain expenditures such as research and development and advertising have a lagged effect—they contribute to productivity in the future as well as in the current year. As such, these expenditures could be capitalized according to some appropriate time pattern. One cannot generalize—the individual manager should determine the sensitivity of his productivity measure to these issues. If an argument could be made for any given time pattern, then the manager should adjust his inputs accordingly. Once each individual manager understands the consequences of various actions, he is the best judge of what to use in his firm.

Interpretation of Total Productivity Values

Due to the way the model and calculation are stated, the actual value of the total productivity ratio (and not just its relation to other total productivity ratios) has a special significance. A 1.0, or 100 percent, total productivity ratio indicates that the firm produced *exactly* the correct output necessary to return proper amounts to labor, material, suppliers, outside services, and capital. *Proper in this context, means that base year relationships are maintained in total.*

As it is used here, capital is a measure of the firm's contribution to production input. Workers supply labor, outside dealers provide raw materials, and utilities provide heat and light. The company uses all these inputs, receiving services from them, to produce output. The input suppliers outside of the firm always will receive their proper return. Workers and suppliers must be paid before the firm computes its profits. The return to capital is the residual left when all other input factors have been paid for their services. Profit, in effect, is the return to capital. If total productivity is 1.0, the firm breaks even. Should total productivity fall below this level, all outside suppliers of input will be paid (i.e., receive their return), but the return to capital for the firm becomes negative and the firm goes into the red. A value for total productivity greater than 1.0 means that the company is making a profit and that the return to capital is greater than the cost of capital.

Note that the discussion centers around the return to capital as a *residual* value, i.e., all slack in the total productivity is taken in the capital factor. Using the hypothetical leasing subsidiary once again, a value for total productivity less than 1.0 indicates that the firm could not meet the annuity payment to the leasing subsidiary, and a value greater than 1.0 means that the payment could be met and the firm had some earnings left after making the payment.

TOTAL PRODUCTIVITY MEASUREMENT: A CASE STUDY

The following section describes productivity index calculations for an actual manufacturing company. This case study should help demonstrate the method previously described. It should also point out some of the difficulties in making the actual calculations.

Mid-Region Manufacturing is a relatively large, multi-plant manufacturing company. Its primary products are automobile and truck components, although the company does produce some products for other markets such as mechanical devices for aircraft. All the firm's plants are clustered in and around the city in which the company's headquarters are located. All plants and product lines are grouped together, and productivity calculations are made for the company as a whole. Company accounting records were the primary source of data. The base year chosen was 1968, and productivity indexes were calculated each year for the period 1968 through 1971.

Since the accounting records did not contain all of the specific data required, various estimating processes were used to derive the information. The processes used are described briefly below.

Output

Because complete records of units produced were not available, output was calculated from the annual sales revenue. Total calendar year sales dollars for each year were adjusted by a specifically calculated price index. By using information developed for pricing decisions it was possible to estimate the magnitude of price changes caused by increased input factor costs. The effect of these price changes was subtracted from total sales revenue. Adjustments for price changes due to product configuration changes (quality improvements) were not made because of incomplete data.

After deflating sales revenue with price changes an inventory adjustment was made to convert the sales output to a production output. With the help of the production control department, the total inventory value was subdivided into finished, in-process, and raw materials categories. The finished and in-process categories were then converted into a sales dollar value. Once these calculations were completed the annual inventory change could be added to or subtracted from the deflated sales revenue. This process and the resulting output dollars are summarized in Table 2.

Input

The input calculations will be discussed next. Labor input is first.

1 Labor

The labor input factor was calculated as follows: Total man-hours worked in the current year by all hourly paid employees was multiplied by the average per hour wage rate in the base year (1968). The average base year wage rate included vacation pay and all fringe benefit costs. As was noted previously, this calculation method does not properly account for skill-mix changes. However, during the four year period studied, the skill-mix had remained relatively unchanged. Thus very little distortion was expected.

TABLE 2   Output Calculation

	1968	**1969**	**1970**	**1971**
Total sales revenue	384	394	299	486
Minus price change		−1	−4	−13
Adjusted sales revenue	384	393	295	473
± Inventory change	−7	+22	−5	+5
Output in 1968 terms	377	415	290	478

A total head count of all salaried employees in the current year was multiplied by the average annual base salary per person. Current year bonus payments, deflated by a cost of living index, were added to total salary dollars. The average base year salary also included fringe benefit costs. This method also is deficient in accounting for skill-mix changes. But, again, it was estimated that significant changes in salary skill-mix had not occurred. The labor input factor is shown in Table 3.

2 Capital

The annuity lease concept of capital, as previously described, was used for calculating the capital input factor. The company's accounting records were quite adequate for making this type of calculation. The cost of capital was calculated by the weighted average method as shown in Table 4. Note that this is a cost of capital *after* tax considerations. The common stock and retained earnings costs were obtained by using goals established by management for these inputs.

Current year costs of buildings and equipment were deflated to base year dollars by using appropriate construction and wholesale price indexes.[3] The contribution of other assets was calculated by multiplying the base year value of the asset by the cost of capital. A summary of the capital input factor calculations is given in Table 5.

3 Raw Material and Purchased Parts

The material input factor was calculated by deflating the current year productive material expense to base year dollars. The adjustment to base year dollars was ac-

TABLE 3   Labor Input Factor

	1968	1969	1970	1971
Hourly paid	76	76	56	76
Salaried	23	25	25	26
Total	99	101	81	102

TABLE 4   Cost of Capital Calculation

	Percentage of Capital Structure (1)	Cost (2)	Weighted Cost (1)×(2)
Capital Structure			
Current liabilities	25	.04	.010
Long term debt	4	.06	.002
Preferred stock	2	.08	.002
Common stock	4	.12	.005
Retained earnings	65	.12	.078
	100		.097

complished by using purchasing department and accounting records that showed price changes. The resulting value of base year material dollars was further adjusted by material inventory changes. This last adjustment converts the material expenses to material consumed in the production process. A summary of these calculations is shown in Table 6.

4 Miscellaneous Goods and Services

This input factor consists of all other expenses and taxes. Each of these items was deflated to base year dollars. Federal income taxes were deflated by taking the current year profits, before tax, adjusting them by a cost-of-living index, and then multiplying by the base year tax rate. A summary of these calculations is shown in Table 7.

Total productivity can now be calculated as in Table 8.

TABLE 5   Capital Input Factor

	1968	*1969*	*1970*	*1971*
Buildings, land, and equipment	27	30	32	34
Inventory	3	4	4	5
Accounts receivable	4	4	4	3
Cash	2	2	1	2
Total capital input	36	40	41	44

TABLE 6   Material Input Calculation Summary

	1968	*1969*	*1970*	*1971*
Material expenses	139	147	110	184
Minus price increases	____	−4	−7	−12
Base year dollar material expenses	139	143	103	172
± Inventory adjustment	−1	−2	____	____
Material input factor	138	141	103	172

TABLE 7   Miscellaneous Goods and Services

	1968	*1969*	*1970*	*1971*
Miscellaneous expenses	56	66	60	82
Federal income tax	43	37	19	48
Total	99	103	79	130

* 100 percent = 1.0
** Rounded values. 100 percent = 1.0

TABLE 8   Total Productivity Calculation Summary

	1968	1969	1970	1971
Output (1)	377	415	290	478
Input				
Capital	36	$40	41	44
Material	138	141	103	172
Labor	99	101	81	102
Other	99	103	79	130
Total input (2)	372	385	304	448
Total productivity (1) ÷ (2)	101.3	107.8	95.3	106.7
Total productivity in relation to base year	100.0	106.4	94.1	105.3

Interpretation of Total Productivity Results

Refer first to the actual total productivity figures calculated for Mid-Region Manufacturing in Table 8. Using the *residual* notion of capital return discussed earlier, it can be seen that only in 1970 was the total productivity ratio less than 100 percent, and thus 1970 was the only year in which Mid-Region failed to earn the required 9.7 percent (after tax) return to capital.

Here it is important to note again that the residual value of capital is used. For example, in 1969 the material cost could have been 131 (instead of 141) and capital 50 (instead of 40) and the same total productivity would result. This is one more reason for analyzing total productivity and partial productivity together.

Note also at this point that one of the more striking observations about the total productivity ratios is their volatility. Relative to the base year, total productivity varied plus or minus roughly six percent. However, total productivity is less volatile than the major partial productivity indexes.

Analysis of Total Productivity Movement

One way to better analyze total productivity movement is to begin by examining the movement of the various partial productivity measures. Partial productivity, as mentioned earlier, is merely the ratio of total ouput to one or more (but not all) inputs. Figure 1 shows the relationship among total productivity and the various labor productivity (i.e., partial) measures. Figure 2 indicates the relationships among total productivity and the partial productivity of the remaining input factors—capital, material (raw material and purchased parts), and other (miscellaneous goods and services).

In analyzing the movement of total productivity and the various partial productivity ratios it is helpful to consider certain input factors as fixed and others as vari-

FIGURE 1   Total Productivity versus Labor Productivity

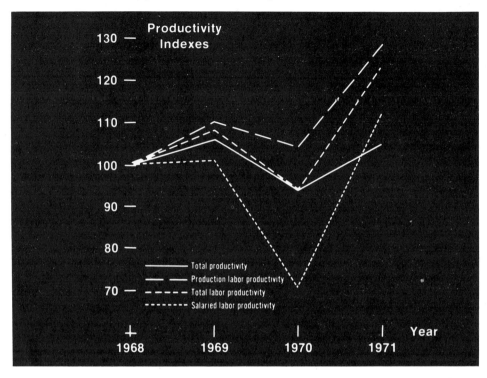

able. Capital, salaried labor, and miscellaneous goods and services tend to be more fixed than the remaining factors. These factors do not vary as significantly with output volume changes as do production labor and raw materials and purchased parts (material).

A further comment is in order relative to the miscellaneous other goods and services input factor. It is inherent in the calculation for total productivity that as output rises, yielding higher profits, the miscellaneous goods and services input factor will rise somewhat disproportionately. This phenomenon is caused by corporate income taxes included in the category. Therefore, this input factor could be considered as a transitional factor between fixed and variable, and is included for the purposes of analysis in the fixed category.

Total Productivity Versus Partial Productivity

In the preceding discussion partial productivity measures were used to help explain the change in total productivity. Such a use of partial productivity indexes obviously is helpful. However, for many types of decisions, only the total productivity index can be used. This point was discussed above but bears repeating.

Suppose that in 1972 Mid-Region raises prices. If *labor* productivity is considered the applicable index, management would be implying that Mid-Region had experi-

FIGURE 2   *Total Productivity versus Remaining Partial Measures*

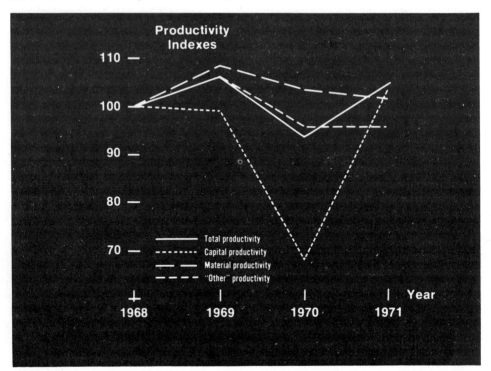

enced a 23 percent gain in productivity relative to 1968. If the production labor index were used, the implied gain would be 27 percent. Use of these labor partial productivity measures would significantly overstate the actual total productivity gain of about five percent. Consequently, either a price increase would not be allowed (under Phase III controls) or the price increase would be substantially less than warranted.

Similarly, if Mid-Region's management were bargaining on wages with its union, equally adverse consequences could arise. If the labor partial productivity indexes were used as the basis for determining reasonable levels of wage increases, the resulting wage settlement could go beyond the company's actual total productivity gain. Increased prices, lower profits, or a combination of both would probably be necessary to accommodate the wage increases.

SUMMARY AND CONCLUSIONS

By far the most important fact for the manager to understand is that for most conditions the total productivity index should be used. Partial productivity measures like labor productivity should be avoided except in the most specific circumstances. Only the total productivity index provides the indication of *real* productivity changes. Therefore, whenever a manager is dealing with productivity, he should insist on a total productivity definition.

As was shown in Mid-Region's case, not all partial productivity measures should show an upward trend. Managers consciously take actions that reduce one partial index (such as material) to increase another (such as production labor). It generally is not even possible to have all partial indexes move upward together. The notion of trade-offs among labor, capital, materials, and "other" almost precludes joint upward movement. Productivity increases and decreases are passed from one area of the firm to another through various managerial decisions. Thus the importance of measuring total productivity to determine managerial efficiency cannot be overestimated.

The method of calculating total productivity is also an important consideration. A service flow model has been used to develop a calculation method that is valid for the manager. This method differs from others in its treatment of capital and the use of all inputs and outputs. A lease service concept of capital was used rather than a physical consumption concept. Also, all revenue items were included as outputs and all cost or expense items are inputs.

Proponents of ratio analysis based on earnings statements and balance sheets may argue that nothing new has been presented. However, earnings statements are based primarily on current dollars, but depreciation is not in current dollars. Likewise, balance sheets include many items purchased by the company in prior years at historical costs. Neither earnings statements nor balance sheets measure efficiency. Selling price fluctuations, for example, can cause a good profit picture *this* year, but a more basic loss of efficiency could be developing.

The method for measuring total productivity presented here ties the firm together for the manager. It forces the firm to show a return on invested capital; it forces a meticulous study of trade-offs such as better material for less labor, more current assets for fewer long-term assets, and so on. The analysis of Mid-Region Manufacturing was more complete than an analysis based on earnings statements and balance sheets. Also, the analysis showed to management the result of trade-off decisions regarding labor, materials, and capital.

REFERENCES

1. Fabricant, S. "Meaning and Measurement of Productivity." In: J. Dunlop and V. Diatchenko (eds.), *Labor Productivity*. New York, McGraw-Hill, 1964.

2. Fuchs, V. *The Service Economy*. New York, Columbia University Press, 1968.

3. Gordon, M. and Shillinglaw, G. *Accounting: A Management Approach*, 4th ed. Homewood, Ill., Irwin, 1969.

4. Kendrick, J.W. *Productivity Trends in the United States*. Princeton, New Jersey, Princeton University Press, 1961.

5. Kendrick, J.W. and Creamer, D. *Measuring Company Productivity*. Studies in Business Economics, No. 89, New York, National Industrial Conference Board, 1965.

6. Van Horne, J.C. *Financial Management and Policy*, 2nd ed. Englewood Cliffs, New Jersey, Prentice-Hall, 1965.

ENDNOTES

1. See Fabricant [1], p. 24 (emphasis supplied).
2. See Gordon and Shillinglaw [3], pp. 321–2 (emphasis supplied).

3. If time had permitted, it would have been possible to develop a more accurate set of equipment deflators from company records. Generally, it is believed that specific deflators unique to each company can be calculated.

Questions for Study and Discussion

1. Is the measure of total firm productivity defined by Craig and Harris a measure of the efficiency of the organizational conversion process, independent of the organization's effectiveness in making marketplace exchanges?

2. In computing the total productivity of the firm, as defined by Craig and Harris, how should the base year be chosen?

3. In Reading 7, Kenneth Boulding concludes that there is an ethical problem underlying the development of accounting measurements. Is there also an ethical problem underlying productivity measurement?

PERFORMANCE MEASUREMENT SYSTEMS

CHAPTER **EIGHT**

"How well is our organization doing?" There are many possible measurement responses to this question.

"The social responsibility of business is to increase its profit," argues Milton Freedman in an article of the same title (*The New York Times Magazine*, September 13, 1970). From this point of view profit is the proper measure of a firm's performance.

"It is not . . . a matter of the amount of profit, but the relation of that profit to the real worth of invested capital within the business," is the response that Alfred P. Sloan might give, based on a quotation from *My Years With General Motors* (p. 49). Sloan advocates return on investment (ROI) as the primary measure of how well a business is doing.

"It is one of our objectives to be first or second in each market," says E. M. de Wendt, chairman and chief executive officer of the Eaton Corporation in a *Wall Street Journal* article (February 3, 1978). This statement reflects the more recently popular view that market share is the most appropriate measure of corporate performance. This position is bolstered by the research findings of the PIMS (Profit Impact of Market Strategy) Program of the Strategic Planning Institute. These studies indicate that as a firm's relative market share increases, its pretax ROI also increases (Schoeffler, Bazzell and Heany, 1974, p. 141).

"A productivity measurement is the best yardstick for comparing management of different units within an enterprise, and for comparing management of different enterprises," states Peter Drucker (1973, p. 111). Drucker might argue for a productivity measure as the firm's primary measure of performance.

". . . An institution must constantly meet the twin tests of legitimacy and relevance by demonstrating that society requires its services and that the groups benefiting from its rewards have society's approval." So state Allan Shocker and S. Prakash Sethi (1974). Their position is that social preferences ought to be taken into account when measuring and evaluating the performance of an organization.

With all of these differing points of view how is an organization's performance to be measured? What is the true "bottom line?" One answer is to develop a *system* of measures which reflects the many different dimensions of performance. One recent example of such a system is that developed for Microwave Associates by means of the "critical success factors" (CSF) method, reported by Rockart (1979), and summarized in the introduction to this part of the book. An earlier, pioneering effort in the development of performance measurement systems occurred at General Electric in the 1950s, and is reported by Robert Lewis in the reading of this section.

211

The design of an organizational performance measurement system is, from the point of view of this book, a design for a decision support system (DSS). The purpose is to "keep score" and direct attention in support of management decision making. The product or service provided is a measurement-based report of the organization's performance. The design answers the necessary system question raised by Churchman (1971): what is the organization's measure of performance?

A MEASUREMENTS PROJECT

Robert W. Lewis

Over the years, many companies have expended considerable effort on the developing of procedures for establishing objectives and measuring the results of operations of their businesses. However, within General Electric the evolution of our organizational philosophy and the establishment of our decentralized management structure indicated a need to take a fresh look at the measurements we had been using to determine two things—first, whether our existing measurements could be improved upon and, second, whether our measurements program was sufficiently broad in scope.

GUIDING PRINCIPLES

Early in our research activity, we developed the following set of principles by which we believed our Measurements Project should be governed:

1. Measurements within the scope of the Project are designed to measure the performance of *organizational components*, not of *individuals*.

2. The Project is concerned with formulating common *indexes* of performance but is not concerned with developing common *standards* of performance. For example, rate of return on investment is an *index* common to all businesses but the *standard* in terms of this index might be ten per cent for one product business, twenty per cent for another, and thirty per cent for a third.

3. Measurements are designed to supplement, not supplant, judgment. Measurements provide a valuable tool to help management make decisions based on a *greater* amount of factual knowledge, but they cannot be substituted for judgment.

4. Measurements must be so constructed as to be useful in appraising both current results and future projections in order that a proper balance may be maintained between immediate results and long-term objectives.

5. Measurements must be kept to a minimum at each level of the organizational structure.

Reprinted from *A Case Study of Management Planning and Control at General Electric Company*, New York: Controllership Foundation, 1955, with permission.

DIVISION OF OVERALL PROJECT INTO SUB-PROJECTS

With these ground rules defined, the Project was then segregated into three major sub-projects:

1. Operational measurements—for example, profitability and market position.

2. Functional measurements—engineering, manufacturing, marketing, finance, employee and plant community relations and legal.

3. Measurements of the work of management—planning, organizing, integrating and measuring.

In approaching the problem of developing operational measurements, we asked ourselves this question: What are the specific areas for which measurements should be designed, bearing in mind that sound measurements of over-all performance require a proper balance among the various functions and among the aspects (planning, organizing, for example) of managing? In seeking an answer to this question, a careful analysis was made of the nature and purposes of the basic kinds of work performed by each function, with the purpose of singling out those functional objectives which were of sufficient importance to the welfare of the business as a whole as to be termed "key result areas".

KEY RESULT AREAS

To check whether a tentative area was sufficiently basic to qualify as a key result area, this test question was applied:

> "Will continued failure in this area prevent the attainment of management's responsibility for advancing General Electric as a leader in a strong, competitive economy, even though results in all other key result areas are good?"

The result of this evaluation produced the following eight key result areas:

1. Profitability.

2. Market position.

3. Productivity.

4. Product leadership.

5. Personnel development.

6. Employee attitudes.

7. Public responsibility.

8. Balance between short-range and long-range goals.

Key Result Area Number 8 is, of course, essentially different in nature from the other seven. The decision to segregate it initially as a separate area is simply to recognize that its significance is so basic that we prefer to risk over-emphasis rather than under-emphasis.

In summary, these eight key result areas constitute the operational measurements sub-project and, in addition, represent the foundation on which we hope to build sound measurements of both functional work and the work of managing.

Now I would like to review briefly our preliminary thinking on each of the key result areas constituting the operational measurements portion of the Project.

PROFITABILITY

I believe we all recognize that profitability is the ultimate measure of business performance in a free competitive economy. Profits alone make possible the funds for expansion of physical facilities, for research, for product development, for the development of a distributive organization and for the many other elements that are the seeds of growth.

Our study of profitability indexes included an evaluation of conventional indexes, such as rate of return on investment and per cent profit to sales and a number of possible other indexes, such as per cent profit to value added. Rate of return on investment, today probably the most widely used index of profitability, is generally considered to be the most significant yardstick available to measure the effectiveness with which capital has been employed. We do not quarrel with this as an abstract principle. If capital has been committed to a given operation, we agree that it makes sense to look at rate of return, and specifically at the elements that contribute to it, to get an indication as to whether operating costs are getting out of line or segments of investment are not being turned over as rapidly as they should be. Or, looking at the future, if you have a list of investment proposals of equivalent risk involving expenditures in excess of the amount available to spend, it makes sense to select those promising the highest rates of return.

WEAKNESSES OF RATE OF RETURN INDEX

However, we have tentatively concluded that in a company as decentralized as General Electric, rate of return possesses several shortcomings which preclude establishing it as the *primary* profitability objective of each of our businesses. It seems to us that the acid test of an index should be its effectiveness in guiding decentralized management to make decisions in the best interests of the company overall, since operating managers efforts naturally will be to improve the performance of their businesses in terms of the index used for evaluation. This test points up the particular weakness of rate of return and of other ratio indexes, such as per cent profit to sales. This weakness is the tendency to encourage concentration on improvement of the *ratios* rather than on improvement in *dollar* profits. Specifically, the business with the better results in terms of the ratios will tend to make decisions based on the effect the decisions will have on the particular business's current *ratios* without consideration of the *dollar* profits involved. This tends to retard incentive to growth and expansion because it dampens the incentive of the more profitable businesses to grow.

What I am saying in brief is that in a decentralized organization it is important to consider the motivating influence of an index. In a centralized organization with control concentrated at the top, or in a small owner-type company where the decisions are made by the owner-general manager, there is no particular need to consider the motivating influence of an index. In a decentralized structure, however, where operating management is given a substantial degree of autonomy, the motivating factor becomes important.

To summarize then, we are seeking in the profitability area to develop an index which will meet the following criteria:

1. Recognize the contribution of capital investment to profits;

2. Recognize the contribution of human and machine effort to profits;

3. Recognize the corporate "facts of life", in the sense that the index is realistic, understandable, equitable and in accord with our organizational philosophy;

4. And, finally, guide operating management's decisions in the best interests of the whole company.

MARKET POSITION

Market position measures the acceptance of a company's products and services by the market and thus reflects the value placed by the market on the quality and prices of the company's products, its distributing and promotional policies and its technological contributions. Sound measurements of market position will provide the best indicators of the success of a business in attaining its twin objectives of growth and leadership.

The first major consideration in designing market position measurements is a determination of what constitutes a product line and what constitutes the market for each product line of a business. A product line may be defined as a grouping of products in accordance with the purposes they serve or the essential wants they satisfy. The definition is somewhat misleading in that a product line may be a broad classification, such as clocks, or it may be a narrow classification, such as alarm clocks, kitchen clocks, or mantel clocks. In addition, product lines may overlap so that a particular product could be included in several product lines. Hence, the actual grouping of products by product lines must be accurately identified.

There may be wide variations in the interpretation of what constitutes the market for a given product line. Therefore, it is important that for each of their lines, our product departments identify such things as:

1. Whether the market includes not only directly competing products but also indirectly competing products (electric ranges vs. electric ranges; electric ranges vs. all types of ranges—electric, gas, oil, and others).

2. Whether the market includes sales by all domestic competitors or only those reporting to trade associations.

3. Whether the market includes imports, if foreign sellers are competing in the domestic market.

4. Whether the market includes export sales.

5. Whether the market includes captive sales.

6. Whether the market is considered to be represented by sales to distributors, or to retailers, or to ultimate users.

In other words, in establishing measurements of market position there should be a clear understanding of precisely what comprises the product line and what comprises the market. The purpose of having sharp definitions of these two items is, of course, to avoid being misled into thinking we are doing better than we actually are simply because of failure to identify the nature and extent of our competition.

After the market has been defined, the second major undertaking becomes measuring performance in that market, based on our relative status in terms of:

1. Sales to the market.

2. Customer satisfaction with our service performance and the quality of our products.

With respect to sales to the market, it appears that our present measurement index—per cent of available business—is as good an index as can be devised. "Market" in this sense is generally expressed in terms of dollars or in terms of units, KVA, or other meaningful terms.

In studying market position in terms of customer satisfaction with our service performance and the quality of our products, we have not been able to design a precise method of expressing the measurement. It appears that the survey technique is the best means of obtaining a reading on service performance and product quality. The mechanics of making the survey would vary depending upon the nature of the business, but the objective in any case would be to determine what the customer expects in the way of quality and service, how we compare with competitors in the areas of quality and service and what the customer would like to have that he does not now get.

PRODUCTIVITY

In a broad economic sense, productivity may be defined as the utilization of men, capital, and natural resources in creating goods or services to satisfy human wants. A measurement of productivity, therefore, is a measurement of the ability of a business to utilize its human, capital, and material resources to the best advantage and in the best balance.

In general, productivity may be measured by relating the *output* of goods and services to the *input* of human effort and of the other factors of production. Accordingly, an improvement in productivity means that *output* is increased without a corresponding increase in *input*.

The indexes of productivity developed for the economy as a whole are computed by relating derivatives of gross national product to total man hours worked. In developing an index of productivity for a specific business, rather than the economy as a whole, we may consider that sales billed is the counterpart of gross national product (or output) and that productivity of an individual business may be expressed as the relationship between its sales billed and the number of man-hours worked by its employees. There are many other factors, however, that may be used to express productivity and, in developing an index for our product business, we propose to examine the merits of all the possible combinations. A listing of these factors includes the following:

Output	*Input*
Sales billed.	Man-hours worked.
Units sold.	Payroll dollars.
Value added.	Equivalent man-hours.
Manufacturing cost.	Floor space.
Units produced.	First cost of plant and equipment.

We have not completely explored the possible indexes, but in our preliminary look we have not been satisfied with the factors commonly used to express either output or input.

We have been seeking to develop an index which will do two things: (1) measure improvement in the productivity of our operations as distinguished from improvement contributed by our suppliers of materials, and (2) broaden the input base so as to recognize that capital as well as labor contributed to improvement in productivity.

In reviewing the factors that might be used to express productivity, we have considered several possibilities. In lieu of sales billed as an expression of output, we have been studying the possibility of using "value added", which may be defined as sales billed less the cost of goods and services purchased from other producers whether incorporated in the end product or consumed in the operation of the business. Another possibility is "contributed value", which is sales billed less only the cost of goods or services actually incorporated in the end product. While "value added", in theory, would reflect the more realistic evaluation of the contribution of the product business, "contributed value" would be easier to compute and would be less subject to differences in definition. On the input side of the ratio we have thought about using payroll dollars plus depreciation dollars as the input factor and, hence, expressing productivity as the ratio of contributed value to the sum of these two items. The use of payroll dollars, rather than hours, is to give effect to differences in the labor skills employed, and the use of depreciation dollars is an attempt to factor in machine effort. Since productivity indexes computed from dollars of output and input would be affected by changes in price and cost levels, it would be necessary to express both output and input in dollars of constant value.

PRODUCT LEADERSHIP

Product leadership is the ability of a business to lead its industry in originating or applying the most advanced scientific and technical knowledge in the engineering, manufacturing and marketing fields to the development of new products and to improvements in the quality or value of existing products.

In our first attempt at measurements of performance in this area, we have tentatively concluded that the measurements most applicable at this time are more of a qualitative than a quantitative nature. By this we mean that we cannot readily place numbers on the factors involved in product leadership but we can measure performance by appraising our existing products to determine:

1. How they compare with competitors' products and with General Electric standards;

2. The source of the research on which the products are based; and

3. Whether the basic product and subsequent product improvements were first introduced by General Electric or by competition.

Each business would conduct an annual product review for the purpose of analyzing its products both intrinsically and in direct comparison with competitors' products. In making this analysis the viewpoints of the engineering, marketing and manufacturing functions would be brought to bear in order to get a balanced evaluation. From such a review, an overall appraisal could be made to determine whether the product has held its own or has lost ground as compared with competitors' products. In addition, the review would provide a convenient occasion to evaluate the opportunities and need for product improvement and to stimulate thinking in terms of the need for new products to replace those that are subject to obsolescence because of engineering advances, changes in manufacturing processes or equipment or changes in the market.

The sources of the research on which the products of our businesses are based may include competitors, universities, the Government, other nations and company components. We think it important that our measurement structure provide for determination of the source of such research. Factual knowledge with respect to sources of research would result in a greater awareness of research status and research needs and stimulate more effective and efficient planning for the future.

The number of new products and product improvements first introduced by the product business as compared with competition would be a significant indicator of product leadership. A listing of "firsts" would include a wide range of products or product improvements, some of which would be much more significant than others. By means of a weighting system, a "first" which did not add appreciably to the volume and stature of a business, or which was marketed before it had been adequately developed, would receive limited or "minus" recognition, whereas one which made a substantial contribution to the growth and prosperity of a business would receive extensive recognition.

In order to bring into focus short-range and long-range objectives, each product business would prepare a projection of new products and product improvements that may be required for the succeeding five or ten-year period together with a program to satisfy these requirements. Such a projection would be facilitated by the three-fold appraisal of our existing products along the lines I have just described because these appraisals would promote a greater awareness of our own deficiencies, the need to provide for overcoming them and the need to be planning ahead to avoid a recurrence in the future. These projections and programs would then be useful as yardsticks for additional measurements in this area. Current performance could be measured by comparing actual accomplishments with planned objectives and with competitive advances as disclosed by the annual product review.

PERSONNEL DEVELOPMENT

We define personnel development as the systematic training of managers and specialists to fill present and future needs of the company, to provide for further individual growth and retirements and to facilitate corporate growth and expansion. It includes programs in each field of functional endeavor, such as engineering, manufacturing, marketing and finance, and broad programs aimed at developing an understanding of the principles of managing. Such programs must be designed to provide a continuous flow of potentially promotable employees in sufficient numbers to permit proper selection and development of individuals for each position. And, at the same time, these programs must encourage competition and initiative for further individual growth.

One approach to measuring the effectiveness of personnel development programs consists of inventorying managers and functional specialists to determine the nature of their training background, that is, whether they were graduates of company-sponsored programs, were hired from outside the company or attained their position without the benefit of a company-sponsored program. Such data if collected on a year to year basis would yield a broad measurement of the success of a company-sponsored educational programs and could be used to measure progress over a period of time.

A more direct measurement of the effectiveness of personnel development programs would be the degree of progress achieved by employees as evidenced by promotions within the department, transfers to higher positions in other components and the number of qualified individuals made available for promotion to higher positions either within the department or in other components.

In order to achieve a balance between short and long-range objectives, it would be necessary to forecast annually the immediate and long-range needs of each department and of the company at all levels and for each function. Such a projection would represent in effect a master timetable of manpower requirements and would take into consideration the department's responsibility for developing managers and technical specialists not only for its own needs but for other company components as well. This forecast of requirements could also be used as a basis for an additional measure of performance in the sense that a comparison of actual accomplishments with the projection would provide an indication as to how accurate a department forecast it needs and how well the needs were met.

A personnel development program is essentially long-range in nature. There is no quick and easy way to measure its effectiveness; our suggestions on possible measurements are not intended to imply otherwise.

EMPLOYEE ATTITUDES

Employee attitudes may be defined as the disposition of the employees to discharge their duties voluntarily to the full extent of their ability and in the best interests of the business. Although employee attitudes are ultimately reflected in productivity and profitability measurements, they are not discernible from the numerous other factors which also contribute to the overall result. Consequently, it is necessary to consider other indicators in order to develop measurements in this area.

In considering measurements of employee attitudes, we have tentatively concluded that two different approaches are required. The first is concerned with those objective factors which are generally accepted as indicators of employee attitudes— labor turnover, absenteeism, safety, and suggestions. The second involves a direct approach to the employees themselves, utilizing surveys which request the answers to specific questions.

In order to use labor turnover rates to measure employee attitudes, it would first be necessary to establish turnover standards based on the optimum turnover desired. The optimum turnover would be determined by the nature of the work, the nature of the work force and other considerations, such as the condition of the labor market. The variation between actual and standard turnover could then be interpreted in terms of employee attitudes. Similarly, in order for absenteeism data to be meaningful, the actual rate must be compared with the normal rate to be expected for the nature of the work force employed. Safety records and suggestion systems may also be useful in measuring employee attitudes. The value of statistics on these items lies in the trends disclosed over a period of time, rather than in the absolute numbers.

As these objective measurements do not show management where action is needed and what it should be, they must be supplemented by a series of employee attitude surveys, focusing on management policies and practices. In order to be effective, such surveys must be conducted with the primary objective of building attitude. Management must convince the employees that it really wants to know their thoughts and opinions and that it is committed to do something about legitimate complaints. It would be necessary for management to report back the results of the survey to the employees, acknowledge legitimate criticisms and tell the employees what was being done to alleviate just complaints. The survey would have to be repeated periodically for an extended period to obtain maximum benefits.

PUBLIC RESPONSIBILITY

In a broad sense, the corporation's obligations to society are three-fold: to render a worthwhile service; to make a profit so that it may continue to render that service; and, while fulfilling these obligations, to conduct its affairs in a manner becoming a good citizen. We feel that the corporation's obligations with respect to rendering service and earning a profit are covered in other key result areas and that in Key Result Area Number 7, *Public Responsibility*, we may confine ourselves to the third obligation of the corporation: to conduct itself as a good citizen within society.

Society is a broad classification and we must identify the elements which comprise it if we are to construct meaningful measurements. For this purpose we have considered that society includes shareowners, customers, employees, vendors, the plant community, the business community, educational institutions and all areas of government.

In considering how we might measure our conduct with respect to each of these elements of society, we have tentatively concluded that responsibilities to shareowners, educational institutions and areas of government are best measured from an overall company viewpoint rather than from the viewpoint of the individual product businesses. In addition, we believe that there would be little point in trying to measure relationships with customers under the heading of "public responsibility". While customers are a social group with which we are vitally concerned, the effectiveness of the way in which the product businesses fulfill their responsibility to their customers is best measured by "market position", which we have set apart as one of the key result areas.

From the viewpoint of the individual product businesses, then, the elements of society for which measurements must be developed are employees, vendors, the plant community and the business community. I will review very briefly specific indicators that might be used to measure performance with respect to these social units.

Significant indicators for evaluating the economic relationship existing between a product business and its *employees* as a social group might include stability of employment, improvement in standard of living, job opportunities and family security. These could be expressed in quantitative indexes prepared from statistical data on such factors as average number of hours worked per week, average number of employees and hourly wages in terms of what they will buy.

The conduct of a product business as it affects its *vendors* could best be determined by means of an attitude survey which would request the vendor's appraisal of the product business as an individual customer and also as compared with its principal competitors.

Comprehensive reaction surveys are probably the most effective device for measuring the effect of the actions of a product business on the *plant community*. These reaction or opinion surveys could be supplemented by quantitative indexes developed from various types of data such as community rate surveys, number of employment applications, volume of local purchases, contributions to local charities and participation of leading employees in civic, church and business organizations.

In considering measurements of a product department's responsibility to the *business community*, we are thinking in terms of its relationships with all components of the business society without regard to geographical location. Suggested measurements of the conduct of a product business with its customers and vendors have been mentioned previously. We believe that qualitative measurements might be developed to appraise the reasonableness of the product business in its dealings with its distribution and dealers and competitors.

BALANCE BETWEEN SHORT-RANGE AND LONG-RANGE GOALS

The balance between short-range and long-range goals has been set out as a separate area in order to emphasize its significance as a factor to be considered in developing any measurements program. The survival and growth of our businesses five, ten and fifteen years hence depend on the major management decisions made today, and the impact of these decisions on the future must not be overlooked.

As a practical matter, we have decided that our approach will be to consider the "balance between short-range and long-range goals" as an integral part of the development of measurements in each of the first seven key result areas, rather than as an area separate and distinct in itself. Upon completion of the measurements program in the other seven areas, we plan to summarize the specific recommendations which relate to the proper balance between goals in order to assure ourselves that consideration has been given to this important factor.

The foregoing material represents our preliminary thinking on measurements in each of the key result areas constituting the operational measurements portion of our Project. These key result areas also represent the foundation on which we hope to build sound measurements of functional work and the work of management in the product businesses of the General Electric Company.

Questions for Study and Discussion

1. It is possible to design a composite measure of performance for General Electric by weighting the measures in each of the eight key result areas, and adding or averaging them? What technical problems are involved? What are the behavioral implications of creating and reporting a composite measure?

2. As is any system, a performance measurement system is subject to examination in terms of the Churchman ideal, the nine necessary conditions which must be met in order to conceive of something, S, as a system. These conditions are discussed in Churchman (1971), and were the basis of the systems view of organizations presented by Mason and Swanson in Reading 1 of this book. What issues about a performance measurement system might arise when it is examined by means of the Churchman conditions? Illustrate in terms of the measurement project at General Electric, or in terms of the "critical success factors" (CSF) method described by Rockart (1979).

3. Daniel Gray (1974) argues: "If 'stretch accountants' want to find sophisticated measurements to deal with external costs and benefits that lie outside the realm of transactions, they will find them only by inventing new kinds of accounting. Such invention will not be possible until there is a new theory from which it can be derived." What implications does this view have for measuring a firm's public (or social) responsibility? Suggest a theory that has the "schemapiric" properties necessary to derive a measure of public responsibility.

4. The period of economic growth following World War I forced large corporations to rethink their organizational philosophy. DuPont and General Motors placed particular emphasis on strategies of divisionalization and on investment-based measures of profitability. Rate of Return on Investment (ROI), the ratio of the amount of profit to the amount of investment, became the primary performance measure for each division of DuPont and General Motors. In his book, *My Years With General Motors*, Alfred P. Sloan offered three reasons for the new approach:

> (It) increases the morale of the organization by placing each operation on its own foundation, making it feel that it is a part of the Corporation, assuming its own responsibility and contributing its share to the final result.

> (It) develops statistics correctly reflecting the relation between the net return and the invested capital of each operating division—the true measure of efficiency—irrespective of the number of other divisions contributing thereto and the capital employed within such divisions.

> (It) enables the Corporation to direct the placing of additional capital where it will result in the greatest benefit to the Corporation as a whole. (p. 50)

In the early 1950s the General Electric Company decided that ROI was too simple a decision rule to use in evaluating projects or divisions, and that the methods of calculating the investment base could lead to misleading information. General Electric developed a *dollar* unit measure called Residual Income (RI). RI is calculated by deducting a capital charge from the divisional profit figure. The capital charge is generally calculated by applying a cutoff interest rate to the amount of assets employed in the division. The rate can be varied according to the type of asset employed. General Electric believes that the RI measure is more consistent and leads to better investment decisions. (See, for example, Anthony and Dearden, 1976).

How do Sloan's three reasons relate to the semantic issue of properly relating the measure to the underlying phenomenon? To the pragmatic one of properly directing managerial behavior? Do they apply equally to both ROI and RI? How do ROI and RI stack up as measures of performance as discussed in the introduction? What role do the accounting measurement issues brought up by Chambers, for example, play in evaluating these two measures?

5. Alter (1980) presents a case describing a decision support system named AAIMS (An Analytic Information Management System). AAIMS is based on the APL programming language and was developed at American Airlines. It consists of a standard data base of industry and company data and a collection of program functions for retrieval, manipulation, and reporting of this data. Industry data are based on those gathered by the Civil Aeronautics Board as part of the regulatory process. Among the ongoing uses of AAIMS is the production of corporate performance indicators. Review the AAIMS case. What design features are desirable in such a system to support the development and use of organizational performance indicators?

CHAPTER **NINE**

There is an old story about Charles Schwab, the first president of Bethlehem Steel, that has become a standard myth in the management culture. It seems that Schwab had the habit of taking a daily inspection tour of his steel-making plant. One day he came upon a team that had just completed pouring ingot for the day. He walked over, counted the ingot, grabbed a piece of black chalk, wrote the number "78" on the hearth, and without saying anything left. On his tour the next day he visited the same location. The "78" had been crossed out and next to it his employees had written the number "80." The following day the "80" was crossed out and an "85" was recorded beside it.

This story illustrates two aspects of the behavioral dimensions of measurement. One, measures are visible. They draw people's attention to some things, while they divert their attention from others. Second, measurement systems tend to evoke maximizing behavior. People like to look good as recorded by the measurement system; consequently, they shift their behavior to get better scores. Sometimes the behavioral change is stimulated by honest motivation consistent with the basic values of the organization. This was presumably the case with the increased production on the part of the Bethlehem steelworkers. Sometimes, however, the maximizing behavior can be dysfunctional. People may cheat or otherwise subvert the basic values of the organization in order to make the measurements come out better.

Peter Blau's (1955) study of two welfare offices is an excellent illustration of this subversive and dysfunctional behavior. The offices set up a performance measurement system based on two monthly statistics—the number of cases closed and the number of cases still pending. The first was to be maximized, the latter minimized. The caseworkers, however, reacted to this measurement system in an interesting way. The highly trained, experienced caseworkers maneuvered to take only the "easy" cases, thereby maximizing their reported performance. The more urgent problem cases were allocated, by default, to the least experienced, least savvy caseworkers. As a result the measurement system encouraged behavior that was counter to the expressed values of the organization. Rather than improve the efficiency and effectiveness with which welfare cases were handled, the measurement system actually encouraged worse handling.

Reprinted from *Administrative Sciences Quarterly*, Vol. 1, No. 2, September 1956, pp. 240–247. Used by permission.

The behavior of the people being measured is an integral part of the measurement system itself. So too are the behavioral and psychological dimensions of the people doing the measuring. This point was brought forcefully to the attention of scientists in 1822 when F.W. Bessel made a unique discovery. He was reviewing the sightings made of astronomical phenomena by several observers. He found that there was a systematic difference between the time that a heavenly body moved across the telescope's cross hairs as recorded by one observer and the time recorded by other observers. That is, A's readings were always earlier than B's, which were always earlier than C's.

Was one reading "right" and the other two "wrong"? Bessel thought not. Rather, he argued that every observer was affected by his or her own "personal equation." Bessel went on to conduct experiments which demonstrated that an observer's "reaction time," which differed systematically among observers, influenced readings. His general conclusion was that the physical dimensions of measurement are inextricably intertwined with the psychological dimensions.

During the second world war, C. West Churchman discovered the presence of a corresponding "organizational equation." In doing quality control work on the hardness of metals for the Frankfort Arsenal, he was surprised to find that although each of several laboratories throughout the United States appeared to be operating within established control limits, end users were experiencing inconsistencies in the hardness of metals received. The explanation was found in the method used for testing, and its implementation at each site. Hardness was measured by dropping a diamond-headed plunger from a known distance onto the metal under test. A set of vertical and horizontal cross hairs were moved over the diamond-shaped indentation and the length and width were measured. The greater the distances, the softer the metal. The problem was that in some organizational units an inside measure was taken; in others, an outside measure was taken. Some units swept the cross hairs in from the right, others from the left, still others from the top, and others from the bottom. The result was that while all of the observers within any one organization used the same procedure, different establishments had implemented different procedures. Consequently metals were being classified inconsistently. In short, Bessel's problem had appeared again this time at the organizational level.

The psychological and behavioral dimensions of measurement raise some important questions of validity. These are summarized in Fig. 9.1.

The diagram portrays first the relationship between an organizational problem situation (the empirical relational system) intended for measurement, and the "focus" of the measurement (the numerical relational system) actually made. Both the problem situation and the measurement focus are represented by circles in the diagram. The focus may be likened to a beam of light intended to illuminate the problem. The intersection area I of the diagram represents that portion of the problem revealed, and is the area of measurement validity. Areas II and III of the diagram represent areas of invalidity. Area II is that portion of the problem unrevealed (termed the "dark figure" by Biderman and Reiss in Reading 26 of this book). Area III is a confounding area and contains aspects of the world which became part of the measurement but which are not part of the intended empirical relational system.

Three types of persons add psychological and behavioral dimensions to the measurement problem: the measurer, the measuree, and the measurement user. Lines A and B depict the relationship between the measurer and the measurement

FIGURE 9.1   Behavioral Dimensions of Measurement Invalidity

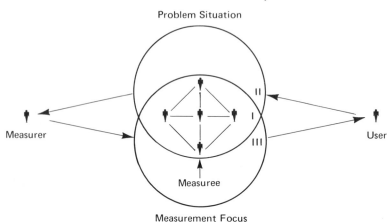

system. The concepts of the personal and organizational equation state that the original observations from the world, A, will always be mediated through the psychology and social structures of the measurer, before a measurement, B, is rendered. Thus the existence of the "dark figure" and of the confounding area are in part a function of the psychology and sociology of the measurers. This constitutes a first important behavioral dimension.

The measuree is that individual whose behavior is intended to be reflected, directly or indirectly, in the measurement made. Managers of investment centers measured by ROI (return on investment) are examples. Measurees are not indifferent to being measured. In some circumstances they may seek to confine their problems to the "dark figure." In other circumstances they may manipulate the measurements by means of extraneous activities. Measurees are thus also sources of measurement invalidities, and a second important behavioral dimension.

Thirdly the user of measurements must be considered. Lines C and D represent the relationship between the user of a measurement and the measurement system. The measurement, C, is reported to the user, who either forms knowledge and opinion about the system or takes action, D. In decision support and management control systems action is taken on the empirical relation system in order to change the ERS in a way that creates more value for the user. Clearly the user also brings personal and organizational equations to the measurement process. No measurement focus is perfect, independent of the user. The user is thus a third source of measurement invalidity, and the third important behavioral dimension.

Each of the three types of individuals—the measurer, the measuree, and the measurement user—may further be expected to anticipate the behavior of the other, and to adapt his or her own behavior accordingly. (It is suggested that the reader think through some examples of this "corrective behavior.") Whether the measurement system is properly focused is a complex matter indeed!

The articles in this section were selected to expand upon the concepts summarized in Figure 9.1. In "Dysfunctional Consequences of Performance Measurement,"

Ridgway describes the great difficulty the designer of a measurement system has creating a single, multiple, or composite measure of organizational performance which does not invite dysfunctional behavior on the part of the measurees.

In the second article, Macy and Mirvis present a standardized set of definitions, measures, and costing methods to be used in measuring behavioral outcomes in organizations. The emphasis is on reducing the "dark figure" of an organizational problem situation by the use of a more sophisticated and better focused measurement system.

Finally, in "Toward a Psycho-Technical Systems Paradigm of Organizational Measurement," Flamholtz focuses on the user of measurements. He argues that the measurement, C, may influence the behavior, D, of the user in four principal ways: criterion function, catalyst function, set function and motivational function. This leads him to consider the behavioral validity and reliability of a measurement, defined in terms of the user.

All the readings in this section deal with human beings as they relate to organizational measurement. Thus this set of readings helps in the transition to the concepts of individual measurements covered in the next part. It also sets the stage for discussing social measurement in Part Five.

DYSFUNCTIONAL CONSEQUENCES OF PERFORMANCE MEASUREMENT

W. F. Ridgway

READING 16

There is today a strong tendency to state numerically as many as possible of the variables with which management must deal. The mounting interest in and application of tools such as operations research, linear programming, and statistical decision making, all of which require quantifiable variables, foster the idea that if progress toward goals can be measured, efforts and resources can be more rationally managed. This has led to the development of quantitative performance measurements for all levels within organizations, up to and including measurements of the performance of a division manager with profit responsibility in a decentralized company. Measurements at lower levels in the organization may be in terms of amount of work, quality of work, time required, and so on.

Quantitative measures of performance are tools, and are undoubtedly useful. But research indicates that indiscriminate use and undue confidence and reliance in them result from insufficient knowledge of the full effects and consequences. Judicious use of a tool requires awareness of possible side effects and reactions. Otherwise, indiscriminate use may result in side effects and reactions outweighing the benefits, as was the case when penicillin was first hailed as a wonder drug. The cure is sometimes worse than the disease.

It seems worth while to review the current scattered knowledge of the dysfunctional consequences resulting from the imposition of a system of performance measurements. For the purpose of analyzing the impact of performance measurements upon job performance, we can consider separately single, multiple, and composite criteria. Single criteria occur when only one quantity is measured and observed, such as total output or profit. Multiple criteria occur when several quantities are measured simultaneously, such as output, quality, cost, safety, waste, and so forth. Composite criteria occur when the separate quantities are weighted in some fashion and then added or averaged.

SINGLE CRITERIA

A single criterion of performance was in use in a public employment agency studied by Peter M. Blau.[1] The agency's responsibility was "to serve workers seeking employment and employers seeking workers." Employment interviewers were ap-

Reprinted from *Administrative Sciences Quarterly*, Vol. 1, No. 2, September 1956, pp. 240–247. Used by permission.

praised by the number of interviews they conducted. Thus the interviewer was motivated to complete as many interviews as he could, but not to spend adequate time in locating jobs for the clients. The organization's goal of placing clients in jobs was not given primary consideration because the measurement device applied to only one aspect of the activity.

Blau reports another case in a federal law enforcement agency which investigated business establishments. Here he found that work schedules were distorted by the imposition of a quota of eight cases per month for each investigator. Toward the end of the month an investigator who found himself short of the eight cases would pick easy, fast cases to finish that month and save the lengthier cases till the following month. Priority of the cases for investigation was based on length of the case rather than urgency, as standards of impartiality would require. This is one of many instances in which the existence of an "accounting period" adversely affects the overall goal accomplishment of the organization.

Chris Argyris also reports this tendency to use easy jobs as fillers toward the end of a period in order to meet a quota.[2] In this case, a factory supervisor reported that they "feed the machines all the easy orders" toward the end of the month, rather than finish them in the sequence in which they were received. Such a practice may lead to undue delay of the delivery of some customers' orders, perhaps the most profitable orders.

David Granick's study of Soviet management reveals how the attention and glory that accrues to a plant manager when he can set a new monthly production record in one month leads to the neglect of repairs and maintenance, so that in ensuing months there will be a distinct drop in production.[3] Similarly, the output of an entire plant may be allowed to fall off in order to create conditions under which one worker can make a production record, when the importance of such a record is considered greater than overall plant production.

Joseph S. Berliner's report on Soviet business administration points out sharply how the accounting period has an adverse effect upon management decisions.[4] The use of monthly production quotas causes "storming" at the end of the month to reach the quota. Repairs and maintenance are postponed until the following month, so that production lags in the early part of the month, and storming must again be resorted to in the following month. This has impact upon the rate of production for suppliers and customers who are forced into a fluctuating rate of operations with its attendant losses and wastes.

Standard costs as a criterion of performance is a frequent source of dissatisfaction in manufacturing plants.[5] The "lumpiness" of indirect charges that are allocated to the plants or divisions (indirect charges being unequal from month to month), variations in quality and cost of raw materials, or other factors beyond the control of the operating manager, coupled with inaccuracies and errors in the apportionment of indirect charges, causes distrust of the standards. A typical reaction of operating executives in such cases seems to be to seek explanations and justifications. Consequently, considerable time and energy is expended in discussion and debate about the correctness of charges. Only "wooden money" savings accrue when charges are shifted to other accounts and there is no increase in company profits. It should be pointed out, however, that having charges applied to the proper departments may have the advantage of more correctly directing attention to problem areas.

Granick discusses two measures of the success of the Soviet firm which have been considered and rejected as overall measures by Soviet industrial leaders and economists.[6] The first, cost-reduction per unit of product, is considered inadequate because it does not provide a basis for evaluating new products. Further, variations in amount of production affect the cost-reduction index because of the finer division of overhead costs, quality changes, and assortment. The second overall measure of a firm's performance, profitability, has been rejected as the basic criterion on the grounds that it is affected in the short run by factors outside the control of management, such as shortages of supplies. Profitability as a measure of success led to a reduction in experimental work and deemphasized the importance of production quantity, quality, and assortment. Neither cost-reduction nor profitability was acceptable alone; each was only a partial index. The Soviets had concluded by 1940 that no single measure of success of a firm is adequate in itself and that there is no substitute for genuine analysis of all the elements entering into a firm's work.

Difficulties with single criteria have been observed in operations research, where one of the principal sources of difficulty is considered to be the choice of proper criteria for performance measurement.[7] The difficulty of translating the several alternatives into their full effect upon the organization's goal forces the operations researcher to settle for a criterion more manageable than profit maximization, but less appropriate. The efficiency of a subgroup of the organization may be improved in terms of some plausible test, yet the organization's efficiency in terms of its major goal may be decreased.

In all the studies mentioned above, the inadequacy of a single measure of performance is evident. Whether this is a measure of an employee at the working level, or a measure of management, attention is directed away from the overall goal. The existence of a measure of performance motivates individuals to effort, but the effort may be wasted, as in seeking "wooden money" savings, or may be detrimental to the organization's goal, as in rushing through interviews, delaying repairs, and rejecting profitable opportunities.

MULTIPLE MEASUREMENTS

Recognition of the inadequacies of a single measure of success or performance leads organizations to develop several criteria. It is felt then that all aspects of the job will receive adequate attention and emphasis so that efforts of individuals will not be distorted.

A realization in the employment office studied by Blau that job referrals and placements were also important led eventually to their inclusion in measuring the performance of the interviewers.[8] Merely counting the number of referrals and placements had led to wholesale indiscriminate referrals, which did not accomplish the employment agency's screening function. Therefore, to stress the qualitative aspects of the interviewer's job, several ratios (of referrals to interviews, placements to interviews, and placements to referrals) were devised. Altogether there were eight quantities that were counted or calculated for each interviewer. This increase in quantity and complexity of performance measurements was felt necessary to give emphasis to all aspects of the interviewer's job.

Granick relates that no single criterion was universally adopted in appraising Soviet management.[9] Some managers were acclaimed for satisfying production quotas while violating labor laws. Others were removed from office for violating quality and assortment plans while fulfilling production quotas. Apparently there is a ranking of importance of these multiple criteria. In a typical interfirm competition the judges were provided with a long list of indexes. These included production of finished goods in the planned assortment, an even flow of production as between different ten-day periods and as between months, planned mastery of new types of products, improvement in product quality and reduction in waste, economy of materials through improved design and changing of technological processes, fulfillment of labor productivity tasks and lowering of unit cost, keeping within the established wage fund, and increase in the number of worker suggestions for improvements in work methods and conditions and their adoption into operation. But no indication of how these indexes should be weighted was given. The preeminence of such indexes as quantity, quality, assortment of production, and remaining within the firm's allotment of materials and fuels brought some order into the otherwise chaotic picture. The presence of "campaigns" and "priorities" stressing one or more factors also has aided Soviet management in deciding which elements of its work are at the moment most important.

Without a single overall composite measure of success, however, there is no way of determining whether the temporarily increased effort on the "campaign" criteria of the month represents new effort or merely effort shifted from other criteria. And the intangibility of some of these indexes makes it impossible to judge whether there has been decreased effort on other aspects. Hence even in a campaign period the relative emphases may become so unbalanced as to mitigate or defeat the purpose of the campaign.

The Soviet manager is working then under several measurements, and the relative influence or emphasis attached to any one measurement varies from firm to firm and from month to month. Profits and production are used, among other measurements, and these two may lead to contradictory managerial decisions. Granick hypothesizes that some managers have refused complicated orders that were difficult to produce because it would mean failure to produce the planned quantities. Acceptance of these orders would have been very profitable, but of the two criteria, production quantity took precedence.

Numerous American writers in the field of management have stressed the importance of multiple criteria in evaluating performance of management. Peter Drucker, for example, lists market standing, innovation, productivity, physical and financial resources, profitability, manager performance and development, worker performance and attitude, and public responsibility.[10] This list includes many of the same items as the list used by Soviet management.

The consensus at a round-table discussion of business and professional men[11] was that although return on investment is important, additional criteria are essential for an adequate appraisal of operating departments. These other criteria are fairly well summed up in Drucker's list above.

Thus we see that the need for multiple criteria is recognized and that they are employed at different levels of the organization—lower levels as in the employment agency, higher levels as considered by Granick and Drucker. At all levels these multiple measurements or criteria are intended to focus attention on the many facets of a particular job.

The use of multiple criteria assumes that the individual will commit his or the organization's efforts, attention, and resources in greater measure to those activities which promise to contribute the greatest improvement to overall performance. There must then exist a theoretical condition under which an additional unit of effort or resources would yield equally desirable results in overall performance, whether applied to production, quality, research, safety, public relations, or any of the other suggested areas. This would be the condition of "balanced stress on objectives" to which Drucker refers.

Without a single overall composite measure of performance, the individual is forced to rely upon his judgment as to whether increased effort on one criterion improves overall performance, or whether there may be a reduction in performance on some other criterion which will outweigh the increase in the first. This is quite possible, for in any immediate situation many of these objectives may be contradictory to each other.

COMPOSITES

To adequately balance the stress on the contradictory objectives or criteria by which performance of a particular individual or organization is appraised, there must be an implied or explicit weighting of these criteria. When such a weighting system is available, it is an easy task to combine the measures of the various subgoals into a composite score for overall performance.

Such a composite is used by the American Institute of Management in evaluating and ranking the managements of corporations, hospitals, and other organizations.[12] These ratings are accomplished by attaching a numerical grade to each of several criteria, such as economic function, corporate structure, production efficiency, and the like. Each criterion has an optimum rating, and the score on each for any particular organization is added to obtain a total score. Although there may be disagreement on the validity of the weighting system employed, the rating given on any particular category, the categories themselves, or the methods of estimating scores in the A.I.M. management audit, this system is an example of the type of overall performance measurement which might be developed. Were such a system of ratings employed by an organization and found acceptable by management, it presumably would serve as a guide to obtaining a balanced stress on objectives.

A composite measure of performance was employed in Air Force wings as reported by K. C. Wagner.[13] A complex rating scheme covering a wide range of activities was used. When the organizations were put under pressure to raise their composite score without proportionate increases in the organization's means of achieving them, there were observable unanticipated consequences in the squadrons. Under a system of multiple criteria, pressure to increase performance on one criterion might be relieved by a slackening of effort toward other criteria. But with a composite criterion this does not seem as likely to occur. In Wagner's report individuals were subjected to tension, role and value conflicts, and reduced morale; air crews suffered from intercrew antagonism, apathy, and reduced morale; organizations and power structures underwent changes; communications distortions and blockages occurred; integration decreased; culture patterns changed; and norms were violated. Some of these consequences may be desirable, some undesirable. The net result, however, might easily be less effective overall performance.

These consequences were observable in a situation where goals were increased without a corresponding increase in means, which seems to be a common situation.

Berliner refers to the "ratchet principle" wherein an increase in performance becomes the new standard, and the standard is thus continually raised. Recognition of the operation of the "ratchet principle" by workers was documented by F. J. Roethlisberger and William J. Dickson.[14] There was a tacit agreement among the workers not to exceed the quota, for fear that the job would then be rerated. Deliberate restriction of output is not an uncommon occurrence.

Although the experiences reported with the use of composite measures of performance are rather skimpy, there is still a clear indication that their use may have adverse consequences for the overall performance of the organization.

CONCLUSION

Quantitative performance measurements—whether single, multiple or composite—are seen to have undesirable consequences for overall organizational performance. The complexity of large organizations requires better knowledge of organizational behavior for managers to make best use of the personnel available to them. Even where performance measures are instituted purely for purposes of information, they are probably interpreted as definitions of the important aspects of that job or activity and hence have important implications for the motivation of behavior. The motivational and behavioral consequences of performance measurements are inadequately understood. Further research in this area is necessary for a better understanding of how behavior may be oriented toward optimum accomplishment of the organization's goals.

ENDNOTES

1. Peter M. Blau, *The Dynamics of Bureaucracy* (Chicago, Ill., 1955).

2. Chris Argyris, *The Impact of Budgets on People* (New York, 1952).

3. David Granick, *Management of the Industrial Firm in the U.S.S.R.:* (New York, 1954).

4. Joseph S. Berliner, A Problem in Soviet Business Management, *Administrative Science Quarterly*, 1 (1956), 86–101.

5. H.A. Simon, H. Guetzkow, G. Kozmetsky, G. Tyndall, *Centralization vs. Decentralization in Organizing the Controller's Department* (New York, 1954).

6. Granick, *op. cit.*

7. Charles Hitch and Roland McKean, "Suboptimization in Operations Problems" in J. F. McCloskey and Flora F. Trefethen, eds., *Operations Research for Management* (Baltimore, Md., 1954).

8. Blau, *op. cit.*

9. Granick, *op. cit.*

10. Peter M. Drucker, *The Practice of Management* (New York, 1954).

11. William H. Newman and James P. Logan, *Management of Expanding Enterprises* (New York, 1955).

12. *Manual of Excellent Managements* (New York, 1955).

13. Kenneth C. Wagner, Latent Functions of an Executive Control: A Sociological Analysis of a Social System under Stress, *Research Previews*, vol. 2 (Chapel Hill: Institute for Research in Social Science, March 1954), mimeo.

14. F. J. Roethlisberger and William J. Dickson, *Management and the Worker* (Cambridge, Mass., 1939).

Questions for Study and Discussion

1. According to Ridgway, the use of a standard time interval in measurement, e.g., a particular accounting period, may lead to the phenomenon of "storming." Cite some examples of this phenomenon and indicate how the dysfunctional effects might be minimized or controlled in each instance.

2. Russell Ackoff (1962, p. 206) states, "There are several possible sources of error in measurement which may contribute to it separately or in combination. There are (1) the observer, (2) the instruments used, (3) the environment, and (4) the thing observed." How does this classification of sources of error relate to the issues raised by Ridgway?

3. How does Ridgway's analysis of multiple and composite measures apply to the General Electric system of performance measures described by Lewis in Reading 15?

4. The following are some considerations concerning the human response to measures of performance.

    (i) *Visibility:* Measures highlight some things, hide others.

    (ii) *Invidious Comparison:* Score "A" collected in Environment E_1, is likely to be compared with Score "B" collected in different Environment E_2.

    (iii) *Gerrymandering:* Power politics is used to change ground rules or the environment so that the scores look better.

    (iv) *Maximizing Behavior:* Shifting behavior to get "good" or "better" scores without regard to basic values. This includes cheating.

How do these four considerations relate to the illustrations used by Ridgway and those in the introduction to this section?

A METHODOLOGY FOR ASSESSMENT OF QUALITY OF WORK LIFE AND ORGANIZATIONAL EFFECTIVENESS IN BEHAVIORAL-ECONOMIC TERMS

Barry A. Macy • Philip H. Mirvis

READING 17

The measurement and assessment of work organizations often focuses on gross financial outcomes. Variables commonly used to represent economic effectiveness include the volume of goods or services produced, the cost of output, and the like. For both practicing managers and organizational researchers, however, these gross measures are not sufficient for interpreting financial changes or assessing organizational performance. Indeed, Katzell and Yankelovitch (1975:99) reported that chief executives and national union leaders hold a broad view of economic effectiveness and regard absenteeism, turnover, work disruptions, and materials handling as important elements of productivity. This paper describes the development of a standardized approach for identifying, defining, and measuring indicators of work performance fitting this broader conception of effectiveness and the methods for expressing these indicators in financial terms. The purpose of the methodology is to complement the usual fiscal evaluations of work organizations with reliable and valid measures pertinent to the longitudinal assessment of organizations.

The importance of standardized assessment has become more salient with the expansion of work humanization or quality of work life experiments and the growth of industrial and governmental interest in this area. Mills (1975) and others have argued that these experiments will improve economic effectiveness. Unfortunately, few evaluation efforts utilize the behavioral and economic criteria necessary to test this contention. An illustration is a recent report (United States Department of Health, Education, and Welfare, 1972) which attempted to make a persuasive case for the economic significance of improvements in the quality of working life. Ash (1972:600) challenged the findings of this report based upon "the adequacy of the data . . . and the validity of its underlying assumptions." For example, in the 34 case studies cited absenteeism was measured in 5 studies, turnover was reported in only 3, and the financial assessments were generally not comparable in conceptual definition, breadth of coverage, or specific measurement operations. Therefore, beyond describing the behavioral-economic methodology, this paper illustrates its use in assessing a quality of work life experiment. A longitudinal assessment of an intervention in a Southern manufacturing and assembly plant is reported.

Reprinted from *Administrative Science Quarterly*, June, 1976, Vol. 21, pp. 212–226. Used by permission.

DEVELOPMENT OF THE METHODOLOGY

Conceptual Framework

The conceptual framework underlying this methodology emphasizes the notion that employees' behavior at work results from choices they make: (1) about being available to work (March and Simon, 1958) and (2) about role performance while on the job (Lawler, 1973). It assumes that employees are more likely to come to work and remain in the organization if they obtain satisfaction from their jobs, and that they are likely to put forth more effort and work more effectively if they expect to be rewarded for their efforts and performance.

The employees' satisfaction and reward expectations are influenced by their work environment and the extent to which it provides valued rewards. The work environment includes the employees' jobs, supervisors, and work groups, and the organizational structure and technology. Implicit in this conceptualization is the assumption, supported in the literature (Lawler, 1973; Porter and Steers, 1973), that work behaviors are to some extent intended products or by-products of the sociotechnical organization. Thus quality of work life experiments which alter organizational characteristics and employees' reward expectations should effect their choices in job-related behavior. These choices, however, are moderated by the external labor and production market, technological constraints, and individual differences.

Despite the noncomparability of conceptualization and measurement in other research, there is ample evidence that work experimentation can affect employees' behavior. For example, Hill and Trist (1962), using a similar causal scheme, noted changes in absenteeism, accidents, and productivity in a coal mine following an intervention. Similarly, Rice (1953) found shifts in productivity and equipment damage in a textile mill and Marrow, Bowers, and Seashore (1967) noted improvements in absenteeism and turnover rates and performance versus an engineered standard in a clothing factory. Unfortunately, these studies and others have used only a few behavioral variables. Further, they have not attempted to measure the financial impact of the behavioral changes.

Selecting, Defining, and Measuring the Behaviors

There is some precedent for assessing organizations in behavioral terms. The definitions and measures used, however, have not been standardized and reviews by Price (1972) and Campbell *et al.* (1974) underscore the need for a methodology using a systematic reporting of behavioral outcomes. Herrick (1975) recognizing this need, identified a group of behavioral variables likely to be influenced by work experiments and stimulated the development of the standardized methodology reported here. Macy and Mirvis (1974) proposed three criteria for selecting a behavior for measurement:

1. It had to be defined so that it was significantly affected by the work structure;

2. It had to be measurable and convertible to significant costs to the organization; and

3. The measures and costs of the behaviors had to be mutually exclusive.

Consistent with these criteria, behavioral definitions were devised, distinguishing behaviors such as absence because of jury duty, funerals, maternity, and so on from those related to the work environment. Behaviors like alcohol consumption were omitted, for though potentially related to working conditions, manifest themselves in the costly behaviors of absenteeism and tardiness.

Four variables were selected relating to member participation: absenteeism, tardiness, turnover, and work stoppages and strikes. Six variables reflecting role performance were chosen: productivity, product or service quality, grievances, accidents and job-related illnesses, unscheduled downtime, and unaccounted-for inventory, material, and supply utilization variances. In constructing the definitions and measures for each behavior, specific conceptual and methodological problems were encountered and should be reviewed.

Absenteeism and Tardiness

Of concern when defining absenteeism were the distinct psychological and organizational implications of absences arising from different causes. Involuntary absence (for example, long-term illness) seemed less likely to reflect intentional or unconscious withdrawal from participation in the organization than voluntary absences (for example, absence for personal reasons). Indeed, these two classes of absences correlate differently with various organizational characteristics (Student 1968; Lyons, 1972). Therefore, voluntary and involuntary absenteeism were distinguished and reported separately. However, since each might be influenced by work experimentation and have a financial effect on the organization, both were included for assessment purposes.

Another problem centered on the measurement of absenteeism. There is contradictory evidence in the literature as to whether absenteeism is best represented in terms of lost time, number of incidences, or an absence rate (Heneman *et al.*, 1961). Latham and Pursell (1975) noted that Huse and Taylor (1962) found intercorrelations between different measures of absenteeism to be quite low, so they suggested computation of an attendance rate as an alternative. In the present research, an absenteeism rate was used, total workforce days absent over total possible workforce days, but this computation can be easily altered to reflect an attendance rate.

Tardiness is analogous to absenteeism in terms of the definition and measurement operations and was treated similarly.

Turnover

Price (1972) defined turnover as movement across the membership boundary of the organization, which excludes promotions and transfers within a firm. In the methodology reported here, voluntary and involuntary turnover were distinguished, predicated on whether or not the employee initiated the action.

Price (1973) reported that measures of turnover generally reflect a "crude separation index" and noted that such measures have been widely criticized. Some alternative measures have included a regeneration rate (McNeil and Thompson, 1971) reflecting the ratio of newcomers to veterans, and a measure of additions to the work force over the total employed (Katzell, Barrett, and Parker, 1961). The measure used in the present study was a turnover rate, total workforce turnovers over the average work-force size (Levine, 1957 and Wright, 1957; Bowers and Seashore, 1966). It was computed on a monthly basis in order to highlight months with significant work-force additions, thus aiding in interpretation of changes in the turnover rate.

Strikes and Work Stoppages

These vary across organizations in terms of their occurrence and economic impact (Chamberlain and Schilling, 1954). There are no standard conceptual schemes for identifying strikes related to working conditions, though Hyman (1972) and The United States Department of Labor, Bureau of Labor Statistics (1971) provide criteria for distinguishing sanctioned and unsanctioned work stoppages. The measure reported here compared the number of strike days with the total available working days.

Accidents and Grievances

These two behaviors are significant indicators of the quality of work life in many organizations, and they often represent substantial costs to an organization (Heinrich, 1941). Student (1968) used the number of reported injuries per work group over the number of group members as an accident rate. Following the introduction of accident reported guidelines (United States Department of Labor, Occupational Safety, and Health Administration [OSHA], 1972), standard reporting categories and measures of major accidents have been devised and were adopted for this methodology. Since firms differ in the extent to which they record minor accidents, this methodology also reported the number of visits and revisits to the plant's first aid facilities and the kinds of injuries that were treated. The minor accident rate was computed using the OSHA formula.

Records of grievances tend to be characteristic to each type of organization (Kaplan, 1950). Labor-management contracts generally define grievable issues and the procedures for resolutions. In this study, grievances were reported as a ratio of individual grievances over the average work-force size. However, this measure treats group grievances as singular ones. Therefore, the methodology can be used to distinguish individual grievances for collective ones.

Productivity Measures

Measurement of productivity represents extraordinary problems arising from the uniqueness of performance in many organizations and the idiosyncrasies of their measurement operations. Nevertheless, since the volume of work performance and the quality of the products or services are so central to the assessment of the organization, a serious effort was undertaken to define and incorporate productivity measurement in this present study.

Productivity is best regarded as a family of measures comparing a set of work inputs with a set of work outputs, along with intervening process indicators or activity measures (Stein, 1971; Greenberg, 1973). A number of researchers have used productivity indicators and for measurement purposes, this family of measures can be divided in the following ways. The amount of output is defined as the quantity of goods or services produced. This may be reported as a measure of productivity when compared against inputs, such as man-hours (Katzell, Barrett, and Parker,

1961) or labor costs (Bowers, 1964). It becomes a measure of efficiency when compared against engineered standards. The quality of the output may be reflected as the number of errors (Parker, 1963), product rejects (Beek, 1964), customer returns (Likert and Bowers, 1969), product rework time, and scrap. Such figures, too, may be compared against standards (Student, 1968). Intervening process measures center on downtime (Beek, 1964), unscheduled machine repair, and material supply, and inventory variation.

The central problem in developing an array of productivity measures is finding a common metric for equating them. Greenberg's (1973) "principle of equivalents" is commonly used. It stated that if one output can be valued, for example in dollars, then dollars can be used to value all other outputs in relative terms. Using this principle, diverse production or service outputs can be brought to a value equivalence and merged in a common scale. The methodology reported here included four productivity indicators measuring productivity, product quality below standard, downtime, and material, supply, and inventory utilization variances all in comparable dollar terms. Appendix A summarizes the general definitions and reporting categories for these performance indicators and the other behavioral variables. Appendix B reports the computational formulas and measures of each.

The 10 variables reported in the methodology will not apply in all organizations. Further, those which do apply may be reported in somewhat different terminology. Indeed, in the demonstration study, voluntary absenteeism and leave days, tardiness, turnover, accidents, grievances, production below standard, and quality below standard were the only measurable variables.

Determining the Costs of the Behaviors

The expression of behavior in financial terms is not a novel idea. A classic article by Brogden and Taylor (1950) addressed the potential for developing on-the-job performance criteria in cost accounting terms. Predating that was the work of Heinrich (1941) determining the costs of industrial accidents. Rather it is the intention to financially quantify a common set of behavioral and performance outcomes that represents a new undertaking.

Traditional cost accounting reflects the productivity measures in financial terms. Following the introduction of human resource accounting costing guidelines (Brummet, Flamholtz, and Pyle, 1968), the other behaviors could be reported in dollar terms, too (cf. Flamholtz, 1973; Alexander, 1971; Gustafson, 1974; Macy and Mirvis, 1974). To accomplish this, human resource accounting asset and expense models had to be distinguished (Mirvis and Macy, 1976a). Asset models are used to reflect the organization's investment in employees. They are directed toward assessing the value of employees, treating them as capitalized resources. In contrast, expense models are oriented toward measuring the economic effects of employees' behavior. As such, an expense model was used here to financially assess the quality of work life experiment.

To measure the financial effects of employees' behaviors, the cost components associated with each behavior had to be identified and their separate and mutually exclusive dollar values computed. The costs could be conceptualized in two ways. One would reflect outlay costs, such as materials used in training new employees, versus time costs, such as supervisor's time allocated to orienting the new staff members. A second distinction would be between variable, fixed, and opportunity costs. An example of a variable cost would be the overtime expense incurred because of absenteeism, a fixed cost would be the salary and fringe benefits for personnel involved in replacing the absent worker, while an opportunity cost would be the profit lost during the replacement process. Those distinctions are important because only variable costs would be directly related to incidents of behavior. Fixed costs are incurred regardless of behavioral occurrences and opportunity costs are realized only if employees put their free time to productive use.

Each behavior has distinct costs to an organization. Included in the costs of absenteeism, for example, are expenses like fringe benefits, lost efficiency, replacement employees, and overtime. To report these costs for a particular behavior, however, they must be separated from their expense accounts. Appendix C illustrates the decision rules used in measuring the costs of absenteeism. A detailed costing procedure for each behavior is available from the authors.

In order to be comprehensive, all the behavioral costs were measured, but special care was taken not to report a cost component under more than one behavior. For example, if the production losses associated with absenteeism were found, they were reported as absenteeism costs and not included in the production figures.

The preceding pages describe the development of the behavioral-economic methodology. The remainder of this paper illustrates the use of this approach in assessing a quality of work life experiment.

IMPLEMENTATION OF THE METHODOLOGY

Sample

The field researchers, working in a unionized manufacturing and assembly plant in the rural South, XYZ Corporation, relied on historical data for the most part in collecting behavioral and financial information. The plant was located in a small community of approximately 8,000 people. The study covered three years and the average work-force size of hourly personnel for the three periods was 652, 884, and 900 persons and the average wage rate for these persons during the periods was $2.67, $2.83, and $3.24 per hour. The average supervisory rate during this time was $6.47, $8.08, and $8.50 per hour. The XYZ work force was composed of 53 percent black and 47 percent white employees; 66 percent of the hourly staff lacking a high school degree. In addition, 55 percent of the work force was over 30 years of age, and 81 percent was raised on farms. The organization's cost accounting system was a typical one for industrial settings, accumulating costs in direct labor cost centers.

Data Collection Procedures

The standardized methodology was devised for assessment of change and, where appropriate, interorganizational comparisons. To ensure that collection of the data was consistent with those purposes, standard procedures were developed. First, the organization's data gathering practices were reviewed with their accountants and engineers. Next, the system was examined by the researchers to assess the measurement operations and their compatibility with the standardized methodology. A series of meetings was held, as necessary, with officials of the organization and modifications and supplements to their present system were proposed and implemented. Lastly, organizational personnel were oriented and trained in the use of the recording forms and computational procedures. The experience indicated that this was practical and resulted in unanticipated benefits to the organization in increased efficiency in data gathering.

Records of employees' absenteeism, tardiness, and turnover were maintained in the personnel department. Incidents of these behaviors were grouped into voluntary and involuntary coding categories on the employees' time cards. These variables were recorded at the individual level, but could be aggregated to work group or organizational levels. These measures were suitable for comparison over time, and since they are calculable in most organizations, they could also be used for interorganizational comparisons.

Records of accidents and grievances were also found in the personnel department. Since this data is more characteristic to the firm, it was suitable only for comparison over time.

Productivity data was found in the accounting department. Ideally, this data is recorded in natural units, such as man-hours and units of output. Unfortunately, the site reflected these variables in monetary terms. To use this data for comparison over time, deflation factors had to be constructed expressing productivity in constant dollar terms. Thus, all production figures were reported using base period dollar valuations, controlling for inflation. Productivity and product quality figures were compared against standards developed and periodically updated by the engineering department. They were reported as a variance, the difference between actual productivity and product quality and their respective standards. Production data was available by the work group and organizational level only.

The costs of the other behaviors were calculated by reviewing variable and fixed expense accounts and allocating the costs among the relevant behaviors. Time savings resulting from a reduction of one incident of a behavior were calculated and the profit contribution associated with that time was reported as the opportunity cost. The costing methodology was designed to measure the costs per incident of behavior, thus involving some averaging, since the cost per incident at a low incidence rate may not be the same at a higher rate.

Findings

Table 1 reports the incidents and rates of absenteeism, turnover, tardiness, accidents, and grievances at the plant over the three time periods. The measures are reported in their standard computational forms.

Table 2 reflects the cost per incident and total estimated costs for each behavior measurable at the plant during the three periods. Costs for the last period represent data from only eight months, except for production and quality below standard, so for reporting purposes, year-end projections were computed. The behavioral costs per incident vary due to fluctuations in the work force size and incident rates. The production quality under standard costs is reported in constant dollar terms.

The major costs measured for the behaviors are: lost productivity, downtime, salaries and benefits paid, costs of a replacement work force, and other expenses associated with hiring and training new personnel. For example, the cost per incident of absenteeism in period one ($55.36) included downtime ($10.03), fringe benefits paid to the missing worker ($5.12), replacement work force costs ($6.29), and underabsorbed fixed costs ($33.92). The production and quality below standard costs are reported in standard direct labor dollars, costs which do not reflect the profit

TABLE 1 Incidents and Rates of Behaviors at XYZ Corporation 1972 to 1975

Behaviors and Performance	Period 1 1972–1973		Period 2 1972–1973		Period 3* 1972–1973	
	Number of incidents	Rate (%)	Number of incidents	Rate (%)	Number of incidents	Rate (%)
Absenteeism*						
Absences	4,420	3.3	9,604	5.19	6,905	3.76
Leave days	—	—	12,486	6.75	13,332	7.25
Accidents						
OSHA						
Hourly work force	251	38.35	316	35.34	208	23.76
Salaried work force	16	17.56	12	10.90	9	7.90
Minor†	3,181	421.80	6,713	706.08	5,559	635.26
Revisits†	1,806	216.99	2,455	258.22	2,028	231.74
Turnover						
Voluntary						
Hourly work force	132	24.10	229	29.59	116	14.57
Salaried work force	18	17.00	29	24.17	4	3.25
Involuntary						
Hourly work force	118	21.40	161	20.80	120	16.08
Salaried work force	—	—	5	4.17	4	3.25
Tardiness† §	48	8.68	—	—	—	—
Grievances§§	57	10.40	40	5.17	41	5.15

*Actual incidents and rates only for eight month period; projection for the period is reported.
†Hourly work force; leave days were instituted in periods 2 and 3 and are measured and computed as absences.
‡Hourly and salary employees combined.
§This is a daily rate; available only in period 1.
§§Hourly work force.

Table 2   Estimated Costs of Behavior at XYZ Corporation 1972–1975

Behaviors and Performance	Period 1 1972–1973		Period 2 1973–1974		Period 3 1974–1975	
	Estimated cost per incident ($)	Estimated total cost ($)	Estimated cost per incident ($)	Estimated total cost ($)	Estimated cost per incident ($)	Estimated total cost ($)
Absenteeism*						
Absences	55.36	$ 286,360	53.15	$ 510,453	62.49	$ 431,494
Leave Days	—	—	55.04	687,229	61.64	821,795
Accidents*						
OSHA	727.39	194,213	698.31	229,046	1,106.52	240,115
Minor	6.64	21,122	5.71	38,331	6.45	35,856
Revisits	6.64	11,992	5.71	14,018	6.45	13,081
Tardiness*†	4.86	56,920	—	—	—	—
Turnover*						
Voluntary	120.59	18,089	131.68	33,973	150.69	18,083
Involuntary	120.59	14,230	131.68	21,859	150.69	18,686
Grievances	32.48	1,851	34.44	1,378	56.10	2,300
Quality below standard‡‡	19,517	663,589	19,517	573,800	19,517	409,857
Production below standard§	22,236	266,838	22,236	335,764	22,236	255,714
Total Costs§§‖		$1,535,204		$2,445,851		$2,246,971

*Costs associated with absenteeism, leave days, accidents, turnover and grievances during the last four months of this period are projections. Product quality and production below standard are actual figures.

†Rates and costs for salaried personnel are assumed to be the same as those for hourly employees (period 1: salaried absence costs—$41,669; salaried accident costs—$11,638; salaried tardiness costs—$9,641; salaried turnover costs—$1,829).

‡Average tardiness time was 27 minutes.

‡‡The costs of rejects and scrap was 3.4% of total sales for period 1. Each .1 reduction is valued at $19,517 per incident. Period 2 costs were 2.94% of total sales; period 3 costs were 2.1% of total sales. A constant dollar equivalency of $19,517 was used in periods 2 and 3 to discount inflation. Nordiscounted cost of quality below standard in period 2 was $677,015 ($23,028 per incident); in period 3, nondiscounted cost was $613,970 ($29,237 per incident).

§Plant productivity for period 1 was 38% of total sales. The production below standard rate is 12%; thus, a reduction of 1% is valued at $22,236 per incident. Plant productivity in periods 2 anc 3 was 84.9% and 83.5% of standard respectively. A constant dollar equivalency of $22,236 was used in periods 2 and 3 to discount inflation. Nondiscounted cost of production below standard in period 2 was $400,567 ($26,528 per incident); in period 3, nondiscounted cost was $405,938 ($25,299 per incident).

§§The total cost in period 1 is $1,470,427 for hourly personnel, $64,777 for salaried personnel.

‖The total cost is reflected in standard labor dollars. The estimated cost in real dollar equivalents in period 1: $1,688,724 or 10.4% of sales in period 2: $2,690,436 or 8.45% of sales, in period 3: $2,471,668 or 10.61% of sales.

realizable through customer sales. Indeed, a significant problem in utilizing the behavioral-economic methodology is its dependence on the measurement and accounting systems at the site. Limitations in these systems at the XYZ Corporation precluded the precise allocation of fixed costs across the behaviors, necessitating some estimation of their relative expense. Further, some salaried personnel records were unavailable, so that the fixed costs were not entirely accounted for. Finally, the firm's profit contribution figures were out of date, so no estimates of opportunity costs were computed. The costs reported in Table 2 combine both fixed and variable expenses, and because of the absence of some data, are conservative.

These tables illustrate the feasibility of reporting the rates and costs of employees' behavior over multiple periods. They indicate a sizable reduction in turnover, OSHA accidents and grievances during the experiment. Absenteeism increased, however, as employees in experimental groups seemed to select leave days, rather than a bonus, as a reward for good performance. Product quality improved over the course of the experiment and in the third period, production levels did too (see Figure 1). Any interpretation of these trends is dependent on the reliability and validity of the behavioral and cost figures. Some steps were undertaken to verify the accuracy of these data.

Reliability and Validity

It is difficult to attest to the reliability of the behavioral and financial data (cf. Mirvis and Macy, 1976a). The volume of record keeping suggests that some mistakes were inevitable. On-site sampling procedures were used to check the accuracy of the behavioral data. Time cards were periodically examined and cooperative ventures into this plant were undertaken with union and management officials to ensure that actual production rates were entered into the company records. In addition, extreme variations in trends were discussed with site personnel to determine whether the data was misrecorded.

The reliability of the cost figures was more difficult to check.

Financial data is inherently unreliable in the sense that the "true cost" of a behavior is never determinable (Committee on Nonprofit Organizations, American Accounting Association, 1975: 17). Any employee action can result in varied financial effects on the organization. It seemed reasonable, therefore, to measure only the recurring behavioral costs, assuming that the more extreme effects would not be representative. All costs were estimated using generally accepted accounting procedures. When dollar components were based on time estimates, such as the amount of time spent in replacing an absent worker, the judgments of a number of supervisors and hourly workers were pooled.

There was no systematic attempt to assess the validity of the behavioral and cost figures reported here. Other research, however, illustrates possible approaches. Flamholtz (1974) reported finding convergent validity between measures of turnover costs, performance, and compensation; Taylor and Bowers (1972) noted the use of attitudinal data in predicting employees' attendance and performance; Hopwood (1972, 1973) presented examples of these relationships using financial data. Similarly, Miller's (1975) follow-up study of Rice's (1953) intervention illustrated the importance of integrating additional and performance information in assessing work experiments. The central problem in validating behavioral and cost data centers on controlling for nonwork-related variation.

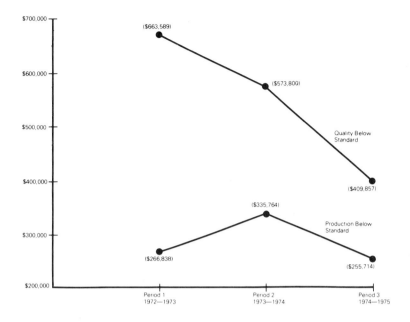

FIGURE 1.   Quality below standard and production below
standard at XYZ Corporation (in dollars).

As such, variables such as the unemployment rate, inflation rate, utilization of
plant capacity, salary changes, and so on should be partialled from the behavioral
and production measures before attempting validation.

Nevertheless, some information was garnered bearing on the validity of this
data. For example, employee satisfaction is often negatively related to turnover: at
the XYZ Corporation, the absence rate was quite low while over 86 percent of the
employees reported that they were satisfied with their jobs.

Employee productivity is related to reward expectations: at the plant, both productivity and quality were below standard while 63 percent of the employees reported that the output demanded from them would be increased if they did their job
well and only 13 percent reported they would receive a bonus or pay increase. Further, 57 percent of the employees reported that their coworkers sometimes worked
slowly, badly, or incorrectly on purpose, 39 percent reported that coworkers sometimes damaged the company's products or equipment, and 21 percent noted that coworkers sometimes stole merchandise or equipment from the plant. This data was
useful in interpreting some of the behavioral costs. Clearly, in future research the
behaviors and costs must be validated through predictive conceptual models.

FUTURE DIRECTIONS

In its present form, the behavioral-economic methodology has wide applications.
First, from the viewpoint of the economy, it provides a means for estimating the
costs of employee absenteeism, turnover, and so on (Kearns, 1970). Dierkes and
Bauer (1973) suggest such financial measures are important economic and social indicators. Second, the methodology can be used to stimulate interest in quality of

work life experiments. Mirvis and Lawler (1976) used this methodology in estimating the cost savings associated with improvements in employee's satisfaction, motivation, and organizational involvement, all concerns in quality of work life experiments. Third, the methodology can be used to assess the costs and benefits of quality of work life experiments (Mirvis and Macy, 1976b), in order to evaluate the cost effectiveness of these programs. Fourth, the behavioral measures can be utilized in the ongoing management of an organization. They have high face validity and can be continuously monitored within the framework of the organization's normal data collection. As such, they can be incorporated into organizational information systems. Fifth, the estimated costs of behaviors can be included in profit-sharing and incentive plans, where financial outcomes are contingent on reduced absenteeism, increased productivity and so on. In the XYZ Corporation, for example, they have initiated a cost-savings program, where employees and management will jointly share the financial benefits associated with increased output and reduced scrap, supply utilization, downtime, and rework. Some of the savings are planned for child care services and social causes.

All of these applications, however, are predicated on the refinement of the methodology. Research is needed to determine whether voluntary absenteeism is more related to the work environment than other absences. The behavioral measures proposed here, and the alternative measures that were discussed, must be empirically tested to determine which best reflects the effect of the working environment on employees. Attention can be given to determine optimal rates of employee behavior. For example, both too little and too much turnover can be costly for the organization. Although the methodology presented here is in its preliminary stages, it has many uses. Research is needed to both revise and refine it for these purposes.

REFERENCES

Alexander, Michael O. 1971 "Investments in people." Canadian Chartered Accountant, July: 1–8.

Ash, Philip. 1973 "Review of *Work in America*." Personnel Psychology, 26: 597–604.

Beek, H. G. 1964 "The influence of assembly line organization on output, quality, and morale." Occupational Psychology, 38: 161–172.

Bowers, David G. 1964 "Organizational control in an insurance company." Sociometry, 27: 230–244.

Bowers, David G., and Stanley E. Seashore 1966 "Predicting organizational effectiveness with a four-factor theory of leadership." Administrative Science Quarterly, 11: 238–263.

Brogden, Hubert E., and Erwin Taylor 1950 "The dollar criterion—applying the cost accounting concept to criterion construction." Personnel Psychology, 3, 133–154.

Brummet, R. Lee, Eric G. Flamholtz, and William C. Pyle 1968 "Human resource measurement—a challenge for accountants." The Accounting Review, April: 217–224.

Campbell, John P., David Bownas, Norman G. Peterson, and Marvin D. Dunnette 1974 The Measurement of Organizational Effectiveness: A Review of Relevant Research and Opinion. Final Technical Report No. TR 75–1, University of Minnesota.

Chamberlain, Neil W., and Jane M. Schilling 1954 The Impact of Strikes. New York: Harper and Brothers.

Committee on Nonprofit Organizations, American Accounting Association 1975 "Report of the committee on nonprofit organizations." The Accounting Review, Supplement to Vol. XLX: 3–39.

Dierkes, Mienoff, and Raymond G. Bauer 1973 Corporate Social Accounting. New York: Praeger Publishers, Inc.

Flamholtz, Eric G. 1973 "Human resource accounting: measuring positional replacement costs." Human Resource Management, spring: 8–16. 1974 Human Resource Accounting. Encino, CA: Dickenson.

Greenberg, Leon 1973 A Practical Guide to Productivity Measurement. Bureau of National Affairs, Inc., Washington, D.C.

Gustafson, H. W. 1974 "Force loss cost analysis." Human Resource Laboratory, Human Resources Development Department, American Telephone and Telegraph Company. New York, January.

Heinrich, Herbert W. 1941 Industrial Accident Prevention, New York: McGraw-Hill.

Heneman, Herbert G., Jr., Carter Comaford, Judson Jasmin, and Roburta J. Nelson 1961 "Standardized absent rate a first step toward comparability." Personnel Journal, July–August: 114–115, 127.

Herrick, Neil Q. 1975 The Quality of Work and its Outcomes: Estimating Potential Increases in Labor Productivity. Columbus, Ohio: The Academy for Contemporary Problems.

Hill, J. M., and E. L. Trist 1962 Industrial Accidents, Sickness, and Other Absences. London: Tavistock Institute of Human Relations, Pamphlet No. 4.

Hopwood, Anthony G. 1972 "An empirical study of the role of accounting data in performance evaluation." In Empirical Research in Accounting: Selected Studies; Supplement to Vol. X, Journal of Accounting Research. 1973 An Accounting System and Managerial Behavior. Lexington, Mass.: Lexington Books, D. C. Heath & Co.

Huse, Edgar F., and Erwin K. Taylor 1962 "The reliability of absence measures." Journal of Applied Psychology, 46:159–160.

Hyman, R. 1972 Strikes. Fontana/Collins: London, England.

Kaplan, A. 1950 Making Grievance Procedures Work. Institute of Industrial Relations. University of California, Los Angeles, Los Angeles.

Katzell, Raymond A., Richard Barrett, and Treadway G. Parker 1961 "Job satisfaction, job performance and situational characteristics." Journal of Applied Psychology, 45:65–72.

Katzell, Raymond A., and David Yankelovich and others 1975 Work, Productivity, and Job Satisfaction: An Evaluation of Policy-Related Research. Final Report to the National Science Foundation, Grant No. SSH 73–07939 A01. Psychology Department, New York University.

Kearns, J. 1970 "Controlling absenteeism for profit." Personnel Journal, January.

Latham, Gary P., and Elliott D. Pursell 1975 "Measuring absenteeism from the opposite side of the coin." Journal of Applied Psychology, 60:369–371.

Lawler, Edward E. III 1973 Motivation in Work Organizations. Monterey, Calif.: Brooks/Cole Publishing Company.

Levine, Eugene 1957 "Turnover among nursing personnel in general hospitals." Hospitals, 31:50–53, 138–140.

Levine, Eugene, and Stuart Wright 1957 "New ways to measure personnel turnover in hospitals." Hospitals, 31:38–42.

Likert, Rensis, and David G. Bowers 1969 "Organizational theory and human resource accounting." American Psychologist, 24:585–592.

Lyons, Thomas F. 1972 "Turnover and absenteeism: a review of relationships and shared correlates." Journal of Applied Psychology, 25:271–281.

McNeil, Kenneth and James D. Thompson 1971 "The regeneration of social organizations." American Sociological Review, 36:624–637.

Macy, Barry A., and Philip H. Mirvis 1974 Measuring Quality of Work and Organizational Effectiveness in Behavioral-Economic Terms. Paper presented at APA Convention, New Orleans.

March, James O., and Herbert A. Simon 1958 Organizations, New York: Wiley.

Marrow, Alfred J., David G. Bowers, and Stanley E. Seashore (eds.) 1967 Management by Participation. New York: Harper and Row.

Miller, Eric J. 1975 "Socio-technical systems in weaving, 1953–1970: a follow-up study." Human Relations, 28:349–386.

Mills, Ted 1975 "Human resources—why the new concern." Harvard Business Review, Vol. 53, No. 2.

Mirvis, Philip H., and Edward E. Lawler III 1976 "Measuring the financial impact of employee attitudes." Journal of Applied Psychology, in press.

Mirvis, Philip H. and Macy, Barry A. 1976a "Human Resource Accounting: A Measurement Perspective," Academy of Management Review (in press). 1976b "Accounting for the Costs and Benefits of Human Resource Development Programs: An Interdisciplinary Approach," Accounting, Organizations, and Society (in press).

Parker, Treadway G. 1963 "Relationships Among Measures of Supervisory Behavior, Group Behavior, and Situational Characteristics," Personnel Psychology, 16:319–334.

Porter, Lyman W., and Richard M. Steers 1973 "Organizational, work, and personal factors in employee turnover and absenteeism." Psychological Bulletin, 80(3):151–176.

Price, James L. 1972 Handbook of Organizational Measurement, Lexington, Mass.: D.C. Heath Co. 1973 The Correlates of Turnover. Department of Sociology, University of Iowa. Working Paper, Series No. 73–1.

Rice, A. K. 1953 "Productivity and social organization in an Indian weaving shed: an examination of some aspects of the sociotechnical system of an experimental automatic loom shed." Human Relations, 6:297–329.

Stein, Herbert 1971 The Meaning of Productivity. Bulletin 1714, United States Department of Labor, September.

Student, Kurt R. 1968 "Supervisory influence and work group performance." Journal of Applied Psychology. 52:188–194.

Taylor, James C., and David G. Bowers 1972 Survey of Organizations. Ann Arbor, Institute for Social Research, The University of Michigan.

United States Department of Health, Education, and Welfare: Report of a Special Task Force to the Secretary 1972 Work in America. Washington, D.C.: G.P.O.

United States Department of Labor, Bureau of Labor Statistics 1971 Work Stoppage—Selected Periods. January, Washington, D.C.: G.P.O.

United States Department of Labor, Occupational Safety and Health Administration 1972 Recordkeeping Requirements: Form 100, Washington, D.C.: G.P.O.

APPENDIX A

Behavioral Definitions and Recording Categories

Definition	*Recording Category*
Absenteeism: Each absence or illness over four hours	Voluntary: short-term illness (less than three consecutive days), personal business, personal leave day, family illness
	Involuntary: long-term illness (more than three consecutive days), short-term leave of absence (jury duty, maternity, military), funerals, out-of-plant accidents, lack of work (temporary lay off), presanctioned days off
Tardiness: Each absence or illness under four hours	Voluntary: same as absenteeism
	Involuntary: same as absenteeism
Turnover: Each departure beyond organizational boundary	Voluntary: resignation
	Involuntary: termination, disqualification, requested resignation, long-term leave of absence, permanent lay off, retirement, death
Strikes and work stoppages: Each day lost due to work strike or stoppage	Sanctioned: union authorized strike, company authorized lockout
	Unsanctioned: work slowdown, walkout, sitdown
Accidents and work related illness: Each recordable injury, illness, or death from a work related accident or from exposure to the work environment	Major: OSHA accident, illness, or death which results in medical treatment by a physician or registered professional person understanding orders from a physician
	Minor: Non-OSHA accident or illness which results in one time treatment and subsequent obsevation not requiring professional care
Grievance: Written grievance in accordance with labor-management contract	Stage: recorded by step (first step—arbitration)
Productivity: Resources used in production of acceptable outputs (comparison of inputs with outputs)	Output: Product or service quantity (units or $)
	Input: Direct and/or Indirect (Labor in hours or $)

Production Quality: Resources used in production of unacceptable output	Resource utilized: Scrap (unacceptable in-plant products in units or $). Customer returns (unacceptable out-of-plant products in units or $). Recoveries (salvageable products in units or $). Rework (additional direct and/or indirect labor in hours or $)
Downtime: Unscheduled breakdown of machinery	Downtime: duration of breakdown (hours or $) Machine repair: nonpreventative maintenance ($)
Inventory, material, and supply variance: Unscheduled resource utilization	Variance: Over-or-under utilization of supplies, materials, inventory (due to theft, inefficiency, and so on)

*Reports only labor inputs

APPENDIX B

Behavioral Measures and Computational Formulas

Absenteeism Rate* (monthly)	$\dfrac{\Sigma \text{ Absence Days}}{\text{Average Work-Force Size} \times \text{Working Days}}$
Tardiness Rate* (monthly)	$\dfrac{\Sigma \text{ Tardiness Incidents}}{\text{Average Work-Force Size} \times \text{Working Days}}$
Turnover Rate (monthly)	$\dfrac{\Sigma \text{ Turnover Incidents}}{\text{Average Work-Force Size}}$
Strike Rate (yearly)	$\dfrac{\Sigma \text{ Striking Workers} \times \Sigma \text{ Strike Days}}{\text{Average Work-Force Size} \times \text{Working Days}}$
Accident Rate (yearly)	$\dfrac{\Sigma \text{ of Accidents, Illnesses}}{\text{Total Yearly Hours Worked}} \times 200,000\dagger$
Grievance Rate (yearly)	Plant: $\dfrac{\Sigma \text{ Grievance Incidents}}{\text{Average Work-Force Size}}$ Individual: $\dfrac{\Sigma \text{ Aggrieved Individuals}}{\text{Average Work-Force Size}}$
Productivity Total	$\dfrac{\text{Output of Goods or Services (Units or \$)}}{\text{Direct and/or Indirect Labors (Hours or \$)}}$
Production below Standard	Productivity (Actual versus Engineered Standard)

Product Quality Total	Scrap + Customer Returns + Rework − Recoveries ($)
Product Quality Below Standard	Product quality (Actual versus Engineered Standard)
Downtime	Labor ($) + Repair Costs or Dollar Value of Replaced Equipment (S)
Inventory, Supply, and Material Usage‡	Variance (Actual versus Standard Utilization) ($)

*Sometimes combined as Σ hours missing/average work force size × working hours
†Base for 100 full-time equivalent workers (40 hours × 50 weeks)
‡Often subsumed under total productivity below standard figure.

APPENDIX C

Measuring the Costs of Absenteeism

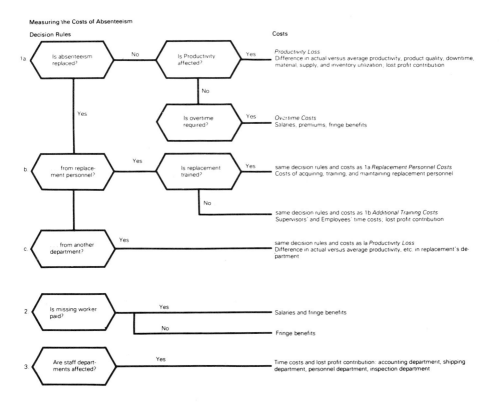

Questions for Study and Discussion

1. How might a decision support system be designed around a set of measurements such as those suggested by Macy and Mirvis? In particular, what design for the utilization of the measurements might be envisioned? What design for the gathering of the necessary data might be recommended?

2. Drawing on some of the concepts developed in the Macy and Mirvis paper, Philip Mirvis and Edward Lawler (1977) have engaged in "measuring the financial impact of employee attitudes." Their approach is to measure attitudes of intrinsic satisfaction, organizational involvement and intrinsic motivation, correlate these with behaviors such as absence or illness, turnover and shortages and then to cost out the financial impacts of the behaviors. From the point of view of the behavioral dimensions of measurement, what problems do you see in using this method? (Consider this question again after reading Part IV of this book.)

3. In introducing a chapter on "Measuring the Human Organization," Edward Lawler and John Rhode (1976) state:

> Measuring the human side of the organization is somewhat like the wonderful morning in the play *Oliver*. It has been the subject of articles, speeches, and discussion for years without being usefully packaged for decision makers.. . . No one has been able to tie up human system measurement and put it in a box in a way that is generally seen as useful.

Do you agree? Why or why not? What special measurement problems must be overcome when the empirical relational system is a human organization? Review Lawler and Rhode's book (especially Chapter 9) and the references cited there.

TOWARD A PSYCHO-TECHNICAL SYSTEMS PARADIGM OF ORGANIZATIONAL MEASUREMENT

Eric G. Flamholtz

READING 18

PURPOSE

The prevailing view of organizational measurement systems is in need of revision. The current paradigm of measurement treats it as a "representational technology," a technique for representing the properties of objects in numerical terms.[1] In contrast, this study proposes that an organizational measurement system must be viewed as a "psycho-technical system" (PTS); that is, as a technology that is intended to perform certain predefined psychological (behavioral) functions rather than to merely represent properties of objects in numerical terms.

The proposed "psycho-technical systems paradigm" is based upon a different conception of the ultimate objective or organizational measurement. While the traditional representation paradigm treats the ultimate objective as numerical representation per se and employs the criteria of representational validity and reliability to assess measurement systems, the PTS paradigm treats the ultimate objective as the behaviors intended to be influenced by the measurement systems rather than the system's numerical output. Stated differently, in an organizational context, measurement systems are intended to influence behavior (i.e., decision); they are not merely intended to measure properties of objects in numerical terms as an end in itself. Yet the traditional measurement paradigm does not reflect this; it operates as though representation were an end in itself. In addition the proposed paradigm implies the need for a different set of criteria to evaluate organizational measurement systems: the criteria of *behavioral validity* and *behavioral reliability*. These notions, which are distinct from representational validity and reliability, will be examined in a subsquent section.

POTENTIAL SIGNIFICANCE TO DECISION SCIENCE

The notion that the present paradigm of organizational measurement needs to be revised to reflect a PTS view is significant to decision science for two basic reasons.

First, decision science is, by definition, concerned with managerial decision behavior. In turn, organizational measurement systems are intended to influence decision behavior in two major ways: (1) by providing quantitative information on

Reprinted from *Decision Sciences* Vol. 10, 1979, pp. 71–84 with permission.

which managers can base decision, and (2) through the act of measurement itself which has certain effects on decisions as well as the decision-making process. The first of these functions of measurement systems may be termed the "informational function." The second may be termed the "process function." Unfortunately, the former function of organizational measurement systems, the informational function, has explicitly or implicitly come to be thought of as the dominant or ultimate purpose of measurement; the latter function, the process function, has been relatively ignored and not subjected to systematic analysis.[2]

This paper focuses on the implications of the *act of measurement* for decision science. Recognition of the importance of the process functions of measurement is one product of the proposed PTS paradigm. Thus our objective is to present a revised paradigm of organizational measurement that will lead to an explicit recognition (by decision scientists and others) of the priority of the process functions of measurement in an organizational context.

The second major aspect of significance of this problem for decision science is that it suggests new lines of inquiry for decision scientists. If the proposed paradigm shift is accepted, decision scientists will have to tease out its implications, identify hypotheses for empirical testing, and perhaps revise aspects of existing decision theory. These issues will be examined further in the section on "Future Research."

ORGANIZATION

The paper is organized into four related parts. First, it examines defects in the traditional measurement paradigm as it relates to organizations and examines the proposed alternative concept of PTS for the development of measurement theory. Second, it develops a framework for analyzing the functions of measurement under a PTS paradigm. The functions of measurement as a PTS are illustrated in the human-resource management process as well as other aspects of management. The paper focuses upon human-resource management as a context for illustrating the PTS view of measurement because it is an organizational activity in which the anomalous effects of the traditional measurement paradigm are revealed most clearly. For as Kuhn [18] states, it is the appearance of anomalies that leads to the revision of paradigms. Third, the paper examines the usefulness of existing criteria for measurement systems and proposes some alternative criteria which are consistent with the PTS perspective. Fourth, it suggests some additional implications of the PTS paradigm for decision science and avenues for future research.

ANALYSIS OF THE PROBLEM

Traditional Measurement Paradigm

The traditional paradigm of measurement is an outgrowth of the historical role of measurement in science, especially the physical sciences [2] [27]. Specifically, as developed in science, measurement was intended as a *representational* process. It was intended to represent the properties or qualities of "objects." Typifying this view, Stevens [27, p. 677] states that "measurement is the assignment of numerals to objects or events according to rules," and Campbell [2, p. 267] asserts: "measurement is the process of assigning numbers to represent *qualities*." Similarly, Grove, Mock, and Ehrenreich [11, p. 220] state:

> The primary purpose of measurement is the establishment of empirical rules of correspondence between a set of empirical objects (A) and a set of numerals (N). The numerals act as surrogates for relevant attributes of the measurement objects.

Historically, the "objects" which measurement was intended to represent were such things as weight, temperature, and velocity.

Defect in Traditional Measurement Paradigm Applied to Organizations

The fundamental problem of measurement in an organizational context is not with the traditional paradigm per se, but with its application to organizational phenomena with little or no adjustment for the differences in purpose. For example, Chambers [4, p. xiii] points out the perceived parallels of measurement in the physical sciences and accounting and implies its utility in both domains:

> The foot (or the meter), the pound (or the gram), the hour, the degree (of an angle or temperature) were neither more nor less "conventional" than the dollar or the pound. Measurements made with reference to these units were combined to yield derived measurements, such as density and velocity; *there are analogous measurements in financial matters*, such as rate of return and gearing [emphasis added].

He does not differentiate between the functions of measurement in science and accounting, even though the latter is an organizational measurement system with a difference in purpose.

In the context of organizations, the role of measurement is *not* merely a technical role of representation; it has social and psychological dimensions as well. The function of accounting measurement systems, for example, is not merely to represent the properties of "wealth" (measured in terms of "assets") and "income"; but rather, to fulfill a complex set of functions which are sometimes in conflict. Accounting measurements are *simultaneously* intended to facilitate the functions of accountability (stewardship), performance evaluation, and motivation as well as to provide information for decision making.

In brief, the primary characteristic that differentiates organizational measurement systems from those in physical science is the degree to which the former are intended to be more than merely a representational process. They are intended to influence human behavior as well as to represent objects. We may hypothesize that the greater the degree to which representation is the function of a measurement system, the more it can be concerned with technical properties.

Need for a PTS View

Once it is recognized that organizational measurement systems, such as accounting, must be concerned with psychological as well as technical representational issues, then a fundamental reconceptualization of the measurement paradigm as it relates to organizations is needed. The proposed solution, as noted above, is to develop a PTS model of the role of measurement.

Under a PTS concept, measurement systems are viewed as having the two different types of functions noted above: (1) process functions, and (2) informational functions. The former are the functions performed by the measurement process, the act of measurement itself, rather than the numbers which are the output of that process. The latter are functions performed by the measurements derived per se.

The subsequent discussion will examine the process function of measurement. It will present a model of the elements (subfunctions) of the process function and will illustrate their role in the human-resource management process. We will not examine the informational function of measurement, because this function is well known.

ELEMENTS OF THE PROCESS FUNCTION OF MEASUREMENT

The intended purpose of measurement systems is to influence various aspects of the process of management—decision making, planning, and control.

The measurement process can influence management behavior through a variety of ways. Four principal ways (or subfunctions of the measurement process) can be identified: (1) the criterion function, (2) the catalyst function, (3) the set function, and (4) the motivational function. Each of these subfunctions is described in turn below.

The Criterion Function

A principal process function of measurement systems is to provide an "operational criterion" or set of criteria to guide decisions. This means that a measurement system *operationally defines the goal of an activity*.

There are three psychological effects of a measurement-system-defined performance criterion. First, it tends to provide a focus or direction for efforts [19, p. 63]. Second, it helps structure thought and analysis. Third, it provides a model of the relevant set of variables to which effort ought to be directed.

The role of the measurement system as a model of the decision maker's "world" may be better appreciated by drawing upon the work of Piaget. In discussing Piaget's ideas, Carroll [3, p. 79] states that

> the unifying theme in the work of Piaget is the gradual unfolding of the individual's ability to construct an internal "model" of the universe around him and to perform manipulations on that model so as to draw conclusions about the probable past history of his environment as the probable results of possible actions that could be taken upon that environment. The ability to do this is the essence of all "thinking" in the nontrivial meaning of the term.

Thus, the measurement system provides an implicit model or set of criteria through which the decision maker organizes thought.

The need for such structured thought is derived from limits on man's cognitive information-processing capacities [10, pp. 23-24]. The psychological role of the criterion function is thus to provide mechanisms to simplify cognitive information-processing requirements [24] [5].

Another way of looking at the criterion function is that it performs the "coding" process described by Katz and Kahn [16, p. 22]: "Through the coding process the 'blooming, buzzing confusion' of the world is simplified into a few meaningful and simplified categories for a given system."

Criterion Function in Human-Resource Management

We can illustrate the role of the criterion function in the context of human-resource management, which, to a very great extent, consists of decision making. Management continuously makes decisions involving the acquisition, development, allocation, and compensation of human resources. For example, since people differ in such qualities as intelligence, skills, motivation, and personality, management must decide what qualities are desirable in people recruited into a firm. It must also evaluate possible job candidates and select people. Similarly, management must decide how to allocate its existing people to roles. It must also decide if the firm should invest in specialized training programs.

Such human-resource management decisions should be based upon some guiding criterion or standard. This means that there should be a measure of a decision's potential consequences for an organization. In other words, what is the utility of this decision for an organization? In addition, it would help if all decisions could be based upon a common criterion so that they could be compared. Unfortunately while the logic of this approach may be obvious, it is typically not feasible to apply it to human-resource decision because of the lack of a well-defined conception of the ultimate goal of such decisions [12, p. 4].

The development of Human Resource Accounting (HRA) measures is, in part, based on recognition of the need for such a criterion [7]. The criterion suggested by HRA is a person's value to an organization. For example in human-resource-acquisition decisions, the criterion used in selecting people should be the expected value of people to the organization. Similarly, in human-resource-development decisions the criterion should be the expected increase in human-resource value, as reflected in the return on investment. In addition, in deciding whom to retain in layoff decisions, the criterion should be the relative value of people to the enterprise. These examples are intended to be illustrative and not exhaustive.

These measures of human-resource value define the goals of the human resource management activity *even if the measures themselves are difficult to operationalize or the measurements derived are subject to error*. Their function is to provide a criterion to guide decisions as much as to provide measurements of the criterion per se. Thus it would be incorrect to apply the traditional criteria for representational validity and reliability to evaluate proposed measures of human-resource value because such measures may perform the criterion function irrespective of their degree of representational validity or reliability.

Another example of the criterion function of measurements is provided by Mirvis and Lawler [21]. They argue that while the behavioral literature contains a large number of studies of the relationship between attitudes and absenteeism, turnover, tardiness, job performance, strikes, and grievances, no study has measured the costs associated with different levels of job satisfaction and motivation. "Thus, psychologists are still unable to talk in dollars and cents terms when they argue for measuring employee attitudes and for improving job satisfaction" [21, p. 1]. Measurements of human resource costs, in spite of errors of estimates, would permit a monetary criterion to be applied to such analyses. Again, the function of measurement is to provide the criterion as well as the measurements (numbers) per se.

The Catalyst Function

Another function of measurement systems is to serve as a catalyst to produce systematic planning. The process of deriving measurements causes systematic consideration of the parameters used to derive the budget measurements. Thus calculation or measurement of a budget is merely a catalyst for systematic financial planning.

Catalyst Function in Human-Resources Management

In the context of human-resource management, the process of measuring human-resource value is also intended to function as a catalyst to produce systematic planning of human resources. In the process of measuring human-resource value, managers are forced to think systematically about human resources. They must project future requirements for people and the tasks they may perform and assess the value of these tasks to the organization. They must also assess the supply of people anticipated to be available, the probabilities that these people will occupy various positions, their need for training and development to enhance promotability, their transferability, and the likelihood that they will remain in the firm. Thus, in the measurement of human-resource value, the numbers produced may not be as important as the process that must be employed to derive those numbers. This suggests that subjectivity involved in measuring such constructs as human-resource value may not be a critical limitation; for even though the numbers derived may be uncertain, the measurement process may cause systematic planning to occur.

The Set Function

Another function of measurement systems is to influence the "set" of managers who are engaged in decision making. The term "set" refers to a cognitive expectation of what a decision maker is "ready" to perceive. Measurements can influence a decision maker's set by providing information about relevant variables to be considered. Thus they can influence the variables or criteria used in decision making.

Set Function in Human-Resource Management

In human-resource management, measurements can be used to influence the manager's set. For example, there is a tendency for decisions to be made without consideration of their effects upon a person's value to the organization. Decisions tend to be made on the basis of short-term benefits and costs, and not with respect to their longer term consequences for the value of human resources.

A recent study [8] suggests how the presence or absence of human-resource value (HRV) measures can influence a decision maker's set. In this study, using a test-retest design, decision makers were asked to choose between two individuals for a job assignment (allocations) in a CPA firm. In the first test, they were presented with traditional performance appraisal data on which to base decisions. The results of their choices are shown in Table 1 (Case A). The decision makers were also asked to indicate their reasons for their choice. Their responses were content-analyzed and found to be primarily concerned with the relative capabilities or value of the people to either (1) serve the firm's current needs or (2) serve the needs of the client. They did *not* consider the needs of the individuals assigned or the effect of the anticipated assignment on their value to the firm. In the second test, they were presented with nonmonetary human-resource valuation data. Specifically, they received estimates of assessments of the expected promotability of the staff and the probability that they would remain in the firm. The results of their revised decisions are shown in Table 1 (Case B). The rationale for these decisions was also content analyzed, and the results indicated that a significantly greater percentage of the reasons concerned the effect of the job assignment upon the individual's value to the firm than to either serve the firm's or client's needs. The third retest presented the subject with monetary data about the individual's expected value, as shown in Table 1 (Case C).

The content analysis indicated a significant change in the set used to reach the decision. In brief, the presence of the HRV measures stimulated a different way of thinking about the decisions; there was a change in the proportion of people using each factor to select each staff accountant for the job assignment from the first to second to third tests.

The Motivational Function

A fourth function of the measurement process is intended to affect both the direction and magnitude of motivation.[3] It is assumed that the presence or absence of measurements of an object or activity influences people's behavior. This assumption has been supported by empirical research. For example, Cammann [1] found that managers concentrated their efforts in areas where the results were measured.

The measurement process functions as a motivational mechanism because it is linked to the process of distributing organizational rewards. In discussing the operation of accounting as a measurement system, Ijiri [14, p. 158] describes how measurement systems may influence a decision maker's motivation:

> Another way an accounting system determines the goals for a manager is by defining an area for him to pay attention to. For example, assume the accountants suddenly report scrap cost for the first time. The manager now creates a goal that specifies his objectives in regard to the control of scrap cost. . . .

TABLE 1   Study of Effects of Human-Resource Measures on Allocation Decisions: Frequencies of Choices of Jackson and Williams in Cases (A), (B), and (C)

Case	Jackson		Williams		Total	
	N	%	*N*	%	*N*	%
A	17	49	18	51	35	100
B	11	31	24	69	35	100
C	11	31	24	69	35	100

The motivational function of the measurement process has also been recognized by Ridgeway [23, p. 247], who argues that "Even where performance measures are instituted purely for purposes of information, they are probably interpreted as definitions of the important aspects of their job or activity and hence have important implications for the motivation of behavior."

Motivational Function in Human-Resource Management

The measurement process can also play a motivational role in the content of the human-resource management process. For example, measures of human-resource value may be used to motivate human-resource development and conservation. If the value of human resources under a manager's stewardship is measured, we anticipate that the manager will pay attention to, and be concerned about, changes in human-resource value. For example, if one factor used in evaluating the performance of managing partners in local CPA firm offices is the change in human-resource value attributable to development, we may expect that a greater degree of attention will be devoted to the development process. The manager may begin to ask himself: "How can I utilize this person in a way that will enhance his value to the firm?" Thus the measurement process rather than the numbers per se influence the decisions of managers in this situation.

MEASUREMENT'S MEDIUM AS ITS MESSAGE

The prior analysis of the subfunctions of the measurement process has been based on the notion of measurement as a PTS. It has been proposed that the measurement process has certain built-in psychological functions for decision makers.

An alternative explanation of the psychological effects of measurement system can be found in the thought of Marshall McLuhan [20]. Drawing upon McLuhan, one can argue that the medium of measurement is its message. *The very fact that an organization is measuring some object may convey a meaning to people in an organization beyond the numbers derived from the measurement system.* This means that the measurement process is itself part of the stimulus as well as the measurements produced.

In the context of human-resource management, a recent experiment by Schwan [25] suggests how measurements of investments in human resources may convey a meaning to decision makers (investors) beyond the numbers generated as the output of that measurement process. Schwan provided two sets of financial statements to managers and analysts employed in investment, credit, and trust departments of nine large banks. In Set A, human resource costs were treated as a period cost (expensed as incurred), while in Set B they were treated as assets. Subjects were required to rate the management of the firms and to make predictions of operating revenues and income. Subjects were also asked an open-ended question about the reasons for their ratings of management.

Their responses to the question suggest that the very fact that "firm B" was measuring investment in human resources had an effect on the subjects' decision processes. It led to different perceptions of the firms and their managements. Some of the subjects specifically referred to human resources as reasons for their judgments of management and noted that the firm measuring human resources was "more progressive."

Similarly, some firms have recognized the possible use of the measuring process for signaling management's concern for the management of human resources. For example, Lester Witte & Company, Certified Public Accountants, a medium-sized national CPA firm, has applied a system of accounting for the value of this firm's human resources in five of its offices as a pilot study [9]. The firm is explicitly trying to use HRV to increase the awareness throughout the firm that people are valuable organizational resources. They want to use the process of measuring human resource value to communicate the message that "People are valuable organizational resources, and we are measuring their value in order to determine if it has increased, decreased, or remained unchanged." Thus, the medium of measurement is its message.

IMPLICATIONS OF PSYCHO-TECHNICAL SYSTEMS VIEW OF MEASUREMENT FOR DECISION SCIENCE

What are the implications of a PTS view of measurement? There are three basic implications:

1. There is a need to develop a broader concept of measurement theory to reflect the existence of measurement's process functions;

2. There is a need to reflect this revised view of measurement in decision science; and

3. Given the existence of such process functions, there is a need to review the traditional criteria used to evaluate organizational measurement systems.

Need for Broader Concept of Measurement Theory

A PTS view of measurement is based on the notion that the very existence of a measurement system can have effects on human behavior in organizations regardless of the numbers which are the output of that system.[4] Yet traditional measurement theory deals with it as a representational process, and does not reflect its psychological effects. Thus we need to develop a framework for measurement that reflects this broader concept of its role in organizations. The framework described above represents a preliminary effort at such a PTS view of measurement. There is, of course, a need for further research in this area.

The recognition that measurement influences human behavior is not new. What is different in this paper, however, is treatment of the behavioral aspects of measurement as more than merely "unintended dysfunctional consequences" or aberrations; rather, they are treated as an integral part of the measurement process. As Hopwood [13, p. 103] states:

> . . . while an enormous amount of attention has been devoted to describing the dysfunctional consequences [of measurement systems] surprisingly little consideration has been given to studying their precise determinants. The approach has been pathological rather than diagnostic. Yet a deeper understanding of the reasons and underlying processes is essential for anyone who is concerned with the intelligent management of change and improvement.

Implications for Decision Sciences

At present, we tend to treat the dysfunctional effects of measurement systems on decisions as anomalies [23]. We have not recognized or appreciated the need for a paradigm shift.

The power of a paradigm [18] is that is helps us see things differently. It helps us see things that might otherwise been overlooked or invisible. Taking an example from chemistry, Joseph Priestley was the first to isolate a gas that was later to be recognized as a distinct species—oxygen. However, Priestley's acceptance of the Phlogiston paradigm of chemistry made him fail to see a broader significance of the discovery of oxygen per se, but an oxygen theory of combustion, which, as Kuhn [18, p. 56] states: ". . . was the keystone for a reformulation of chemistry so vast that it usually called the chemical revolution."

Similarly, the PTS paradigm suggests a different way of looking at the role of measurement in management decisions. Although the specific implications are not yet fully developed, the new paradigm may lead to a reformulation of aspects of decision science. This is obviously an avenue for future research.

Revised Criteria of Measurement Systems

Given the presumed function of measurement as a representational process, the criteria of validity and reliability of measurement are undoubtedly appropriate. The notion of "validity" refers to the extent a measurement represents what it purports to present [17]. "Reliability" refers to the reproducibility of the measurement. It is the extent to which repeated measurements of the object will yield the same results.

With recognition of the broader role of measurement, these traditional criteria for measurement systems are insufficient (and perhaps irrelevant) in the context of human-resource management systems.

Too much emphasis has been placed upon the technical perfection of measures, without a sufficient appreciation that the measurement process functions in ways that are more diverse and complex than can be captured in the traditional criteria of validity and reliability. For example, a measure may be "subjective," and, in turn, lack reliability; however, it may facilitate the catalyst function. Similarly, a measure may not be valid in the strictest sense—such as return on investment—but may be useful in performing the criterion function.

This view of the need for a broader set of criteria for measurement systems is reflected in Alfred P. Sloan's [26, p. 140] discussion of the role of return on investment as criterion for decisions:

> A word on rate of return as a strategic principle of business. I am not going to say that rate of return is a magic wand for every occasion in business. There are times when you have to spend money just to stay in business, regardless of the visible rate of return. . .And in times of inflation, the rate of return comes up against the problem of assets undervalued in terms of replacement. Nevertheless, no other principle with which I am acquainted serves better than rate of return as an objective aid to business judgment.

In his book, *My Years With General Motors* [26, 139–140], Sloan also argues that the rate of return was used to help implement the philosophy of decentralized management. The key was to find a method by which the firm could exercise effective control over the whole organization consistent with the philosophy of decentralization. Through the use of the ROI measure, the firm found a means of reviewing and judging the effectiveness of operations while leaving execution of operations to the people responsible for them. In brief, the basic point is not to argue for the merits of ROI, but to suggest that the role of measurements and the measurement process transcends the validity and reliability of measures per se. Thus ROI may be imperfect as a representational measure, but it may still facilitate the criterion function by providing a guide to business decisions and a means of reviewing their effectiveness.

Although the investigation of measurement under a PTS view is still in its early stages, some tentative criteria to supplement traditional criteria may be suggested: (1) behavioral validity and (2) behavioral reliability. These are examined below.

Behavioral Validity

This construct refers to the extent to which a measurement process leads to the behavior it is intended to produce.[5] It does not concern itself with the issue of whether the measure represents the object being measured in a valid way; but, rather, whether the intended effects (or behaviors) occur.

A measurement process may lead to intended or unintended consequences. A behaviorally valid measure is one that leads to intended consequences and the degree of behavioral validity is the extent to which this occurs. For example, the behavioral purpose of a measurement system may be to motivate managers to pay attention to human resource development as well as to current period productivity. If however, the organization only measures current period productivity, managers may suboptimize by ignoring employee development (which is unmeasured) and maximizing the measured variable of productivity. (Certified Public Accounting firms are a case in point. They measure "chargeable hours" rather than employee development.) It may not be possible to develop a measure of employee development that has a high degree of representational validity and/or reliability. Yet it may be possible to develop a measure that has behavioral validity. By simply measuring employee development in some manner, decision makers may be motivated to pay attention to it (the motivational function).

Behavioral Reliability

This construct refers to the extent to which the behavioral outcomes produced by the measurement process are consistently produced. It does not concern itself with the representational reliability of measures, but rather, with the degree to which its behavioral effects are replicated. For example, to what extent does the measurement of employee development in a specified manner consistently lead decision makers to efforts to enhance this variable.

Relation Between Behavioral Validity and Reliability

The constructs of behavioral validity and reliability are, in principle, independent. A measurement system may lead to behavior it purports to lead to, but do so unreliably. Alternately, it may lead to invalid behaviors quite consistently.

FUTURE RESEARCH

This paper has argued that we need to look at measurement theory in an organizational context as more than merely a representational technology, and that previous recognition of "behavioral aspects" of measurement systems has viewed them as aberrations or pathologies rather than as natural phenomena of measurement which are an integral part of measurement systems. If the present view is accepted, it will require a reconceptualization of measurement theory to deal with more than technical criteria for measurement.

The framework presented in this paper attempts a preliminary approach to this problem. The potential contribution of such a framework was examined in the context of human-resource management, though it may be generalized to other areas as well. As we begin to reconceptualize the role of measurement in organizational processes such as human-resource management, theory and empirical research are necessary to test, refine, and articulate this perspective.

The proposed constructs of behavioral validity and reliability also require future research. One question that must be resolved is: Do we need to develop ways to measure behavioral validity and/or reliability, or is it simply sufficient that we be aware of them? (The medium may be the message here, too.) If we must measure them, then future research will also be required to deal with this area.

To the extent that decision science is concerned with the behavior of decision makers, the implications of the PTS paradigm of measurement need to be recognized and incorporated into decision theory.

ENDNOTES

1. The term "technology" as it is used here means something different from machine technology. It is used in the sense proposed by Jacques Ellul [6]. Thus "technology" refers to any complex of standardized means for attaining a predetermined result.

2. The "behavioral effects" of measurement systems have been recognized but treated as aberrations [23] rather than as positive functions of measurement per se. This is a subtle but significant difference.

3. Prakash and Rappaport [22] have used the term "inductance" to refer to the type of process that has been described in this paper as the motivational function of measurement.

4. This implies that the *act of measurement* ought to be viewed as a management intervention whose intention is to affect the decision system, regardless of the numerical results of the measurement process.

5. The construct behavioral validity should not be confused with the notion of predictive validity. The latter deals with the prediction from a measurement (numbers per se) to a criterion, while the former deals with the effect of the *act* of measurement on behavior, irrespective of the numbers that result.

REFERENCES

1. Cammann, C. "The Impact of a Feedback System on Managerial Attitudes and Performance." New Haven, Conn.: Yale University, 1974. (Unpublished Ph.D. thesis.)

2. Campbell, N. R. *Foundations of Science.* New York: Dover Publications, Inc., 1957.

3. Carroll, J. B. *Language and Thought.* Englewood Cliffs, N.J.: Prentice-Hall, Inc., 1964.

4. Chambers, R. J. *Accounting, Evaluation, and Economic Behavior.* Lawrence, Kans.: Scholars Book Co., 1974.

5. Driver, M. J., and T. J. Mock. "Human Information Processing, Decision Style Theory, and Accounting Information Systems." *The Accounting Review,* Vol. 50 (July 1975), pp. 490–508.

6. Ellul, J. *The Technological Society.* New York: Alfred A. Knopf, Inc., 1964.

7. Flamholtz, Eric. *Human Resource Accounting.* Encino, Calif.: Dickenson Publishing Company, 1974.

8. Flamholtz, Eric. "The Impact of Human Resource Valuation on Management Decisions: A Laboratory Experiment." *Accounting, Organizations, and Society,* Vol. 1, No. 2/3 (1976), pp. 153–165.

9. Flamholtz, E., and T. S. Lundy. "Human Resource Accounting for CPA Firms." *The CPA,* Vol. 45 (November 1975), pp. 45–51.

10. Gardner, W. R. "Attention: The Processing of Multiple Sources of Information." *Handbook of Perception, Vol. II: Psychophysical Judgement and Measurement.* Edited by E. Carterette and M. Friedman. New York: Academic Press, 1974, pp. 23–59.

11. Grove, H., T. J. Mock, and K. Ehrenreich. "A Review of HRA Measurement Systems from a Measurement Theory Perspective." *Accounting, Organizations, and Society,* Vol. 2, No. 3 (1977), pp. 219–236.

12. Haire, M. "Coming of Age in the Social Sciences." The second Douglas M. McGregor Memorial Lecture of the Alfred P. Sloan School of Management. Cambridge: Massachusetts Institute of Technology, 1967.

13. Hopwood, A. *Accounting and Human Behavior.* Englewood Cliffs, N.J.: Prentice-Hall, 1974.

14. Ijiri, Yuji. *The Foundations of Accounting Measurement.* Englewood Cliffs, N.J.: Prentice-Hall, Inc., 1967.

15. Ijiri, Yuji. *Theory of Accounting Measurement.* Studies in Accounting Research #10. Sarasota, Fla.: American Accounting Association, 1975.

16. Katz, D., and R. L. Kahn. *The Social Psychology of Organizations.* New York: John Wiley and Sons, Inc., 1966.

17. Kerlinger, F. N. *Foundations of Behavioral Research.* New York: Holt, Rinehart and Winston, 1964.

18. Kuhn, T. *The Structure of Scientific Revolutions.* 2nd ed. Chicago, Ill.: University of Chicago Press, 1970.

19. March, J. G., and H. A. Simon. *Organizations.* New York: John Wiley and Sons, 1958.

20. McLuhan, M. *Understanding Media: The Extensions of Man.* New York: McGraw-Hill Book Company, 1964.

21. Mirvis, P. H., and E. E. Lawler. "Measuring the Financial Impact of Employee Attitudes." *Journal of Applied Psychology,* Vol. 62, No. 2 (1977), pp. 1–8.

22. Prakash, P., and A. Rappaport. "Information Inductance and Its Significance for Accounting." *Accounting, Organizations, and Society.* Vol. 2, No. 1 (1977), pp. 29–38.

23. Ridgeway, V. F. "Dysfunctional Consequences of Performance Measurements." *Administrative Science Quarterly,* Vol. 1 (September 1956), pp. 240–247.

24. Schroeder, H. M.; and M. J. Driver; and S. Streufert. *Human Information Processing.* New York: Holt, Rinehart and Winston, 1967.

25. Schwan, E. S. "The Effects of Human Resource Accounting Data on Financial Decisions: An Empirical Test." *Accounting, Organizations, and Society.* Vol. 1, No. 2/3 (1976), pp. 219–237.

26. Sloan, A. P. *My Years With General Motors.* New York: Macfadden-Bartell Corporation, 1965.

27. Stevens, S. S. "On the Theory of Scales of Measurement." *Science,* No. 103 (1946) pp. 677–680.

Questions for Study and Discussion

1. In what ways is Flamholtz's notion of a "psycho-technical" measurement system similar and different from the measurement for management decision perspective taken in this book?

2. Gerald Hurst (1977) presents the following list of desirable characteristics of performance measurement:

(i) Controllable—measuree has control over all aspects of performance which go to make up the measure.

(ii) Useful—the measurement has utility for the overall organization of which the measured person or subunit is a part.

(iii) Measurable—there is a procedure for applying a metric and obtaining values.

(iv) Unequivocal—the outcome or value of the performance measurement cannot be misinterpreted.

(v) Reproducible—the outcome is not spurious; other measurers measuring the same performance would obtain the same result.

(vi) Accurate—the measure is not subject to random or systematic biases.

(vii) Objective—the measure is not based on human judgment, but on some external or easily agreed upon criterion.

(viii) Understandable—the measure is understood by the person being measured.

(ix) Choosable—the measure has some influence over the means by which his performance is measured.

Critique this list from the point of view of each of the articles in Part Three. What characteristics would you add? Delete? Redefine?

Hurst argues that there are trade-offs among these criteria, and that improvements in one are often achieved only by sacrificing some degree of another. Review some of the possibilities of trade-offs among these criteria. (Churchman's article, Reading 2, "Why Measure," may be useful in this regard.)

3. Harold Wilensky (1967) describes the criteria for "organizational intelligence" as follows:

High-quality intelligence designates information that is clear because it is understandable to those who must use it; timely, because it gets to them when they need it; reliable because diverse observers using the same procedures see it the same way; valid because it is cast in the form of concepts and measures that capture reality (the tests include logical consistency, successful prediction, congruence with established knowledge or independent sources); adequate because the account is full (the context of the act, event or life of the person or group is described); and wide ranging because the major policy alternatives, promising a high probability of attaining organizational goals, are posed or new goals suggested. (p. ix)

How do Wilensky's criteria for evaluating intelligence relate to the problem of measuring organizational performance? How do the behavioral dimensions impact on these criteria?

MEASUREMENT OF THE INDIVIDUAL

PART FOUR

The summer of 1979 marked a difficult period in the administration of President Jimmy Carter. For more than a week the president secluded himself at Camp David and sought the counsel of various representatives of the American people in an attempt to give new direction to his leadership, which polls indicated was ranked dismally low. A shakeup of the cabinet followed the president's return to Washington.

As part of the shakeup, a "White House Report Card" was distributed by Chief of Staff Hamilton Jordan to cabinet members and senior aides to use in evaluating the work of cabinet officials and other members of the staff (Figure 4.1). The evaluation form comprised thirty items, covering such attribute classes as "work habits," "personal characteristics," "interpersonal relations," and "supervision and direction." Measurement scales were employed throughout.

Use of the White House report card created a commotion among members of the government and received widespread public attention. Criticism of the evaluation form was strong. "Scoring people on 'flexibility' and 'brightness' is diddlypoo," Representative Thomas J. Downey (Democrat, New York) is reported to have said. "This would be an embarrassing personality test for the lower-level employment interviewer at a department store" (*Los Angeles Times*, July 20, 1979). However, use of the form was staunchly defended by the president.

The case of the White House report card is perhaps a classic in the history of measurement of the individual, in support of management decision making. In your judgment, was the notoriety achieved by the form deserved? What would be appropriate criteria on which to judge the form? In this portion of the book, we turn our attention to the measurement of the individual, within the overall framework of measurement for management decision. In doing so, we seek to establish some basis for answering questions such as those just raised.

The individual in modern society assumes a variety of roles, e.g., student, employee, customer, consumer, club member, vehicle driver, property owner, taxpayer, voter, and citizen. The formalization of these roles is often associated with measurement of the individual in support of management decision making.

Two forms of individual measurement predominate. The first is concerned with decisions made with respect to particular individuals in roles. Personnel selection and placement is perhaps the organizational function in which this concern is most classically expressed. The second form is concerned with decisions which relate to particular populations of individuals. Consumer surveys are a well-known example of individual measurement of this type. Measures of this type may also be tied di-

Office _____

Name of Rater _____

Please answer each of the following questions about this person

Name _____ Duties _____

Salary _____

Position _____

Work Habits

1. On the average when does this person
   arrive at work _____
   leave work _____

2. Pace of Work
   1 2 3 4 5 6
   slow   fast

3. Level of Effort:
   1 2 3 4 5 6
   below   full
   capacity   capacity

4. Quality of Work
   1 2 3 4 5 6
   poor   good

5. What is he/she best at? (rank 1-5)
   ____ Conceptualizing
   ____ Planning
   ____ Implementing
   ____ Attending to detail
   ____ Controlling quality

6. Does this person have the skills to do the job
   he/she was hired to do?
   yes
   no
   ?

7. Would the slot filled by this person be better
   filled by someone else?
   yes
   no
   ?

Personal Characteristics

8. How confident is this person? (circle one)
   x   x   x   x   x
        confident   cocky

9. How confident are you of this person's
   employment?
   1 2 3 4 5 6
   confident   very
                    confident

10. How mature is this person?
    1 2 3 4 5 6
    immature   mature

11. How flexible is this person?
    1 2 3 4 5 6
    rigid   flexible

12. How stable is this person?
    1 2 3 4 5 6
    erratic   steady

13. How frequently does this person come up
    with new ideas?
    1 2 3 4 5 6
    seldom   often

14. How open is this person to new ideas?
    1 2 3 4 5 6
    closed   open

15. How bright is this person?
    1 2 3 4 5 6
    average   very bright

16. What are this person's special talents?
    1. _____
    2. _____
    3. _____

17. What is this person's range of information?
    1 2 3 4 5 6
    narrow   broad

Interpersonal Relations:

18. How would you characterize this person's
    impact on other people? (for example,
    hostile, smooth, aggressive, charming, etc.)
    1. _____
    2. _____
    3. _____

19. How well does this person get along with
    Superiors   1 2 3 4 5 6
    Peers   1 2 3 4 5 6
    Subordinates   1 2 3 4 5 6
    Outsiders   1 2 3 4 5 6
                   not well   very well

20. In a public setting, how comfortable would
    you be having this person represent
    you or your office 1 2 3 4 5 6
    uncomfortable   comfortable

21. Rate this person's political skills.
    1 2 3 4 5 6
    naive   savy

Supervision and Direction

22. To what extent is this person focused on
    accomplishing the:
    Administration's goals   ____ %
    personal goals   ____ %
                              100 %

23. How capable is this person at working
    toward implementing a decision with
    which he/she may not agree?
    1 2 3 4 5 6
    reluctant   eager

24. How well does this person take direction?
    1 2 3 4 5 6
    resists   readily

25. How much supervision does this person
    need?
    1 2 3 4 5 6
    a lot   little

26. How readily does this person offer to help
    out by doing that which is not a part of
    his/her "job"?
    1 2 3 4 5 6
    seldom   often

Summary

27. Can this person assume more responsibility?
    yes ____
    no ____
    ? ____

28. List this person's 3 major strengths and
    3 major weaknesses
    Strengths 1 _____
    2 _____
    3 _____
    Weaknesses 1 _____
    2 _____
    3 _____

29. List this person's 3 major accomplishments.
    1 _____
    2 _____
    3 _____

30. List 3 things about this person that have
    disappointed you.
    1 _____
    2 _____
    3 _____

FIGURE 4.1
Source: San Francisco Chronicle, Fri., July 20, 1979.

rectly to organizational and societal measurement. For example, an organization may measure the value of its human resources (Flamholtz, 1974), or a society may utilize an index of consumer sentiment. Both examples may be constructed on measurements of the individual.

Measurements concerned with decisions made about individuals in roles may themselves be classified into two groups. The first seeks to assess the individual's *potential* with respect to a role. Examples are many. The would-be college student is assessed by means of the Scholastic Aptitude Test (SAT) administered by the Educational Testing Service (ETS). The aspiring public employee is assessed by the Civil Service Examination. The military recruit receives a battery of exams designed to assess skills and interests. A job interviewee is sometimes given a psychological test by a prospective employer seeking to assess "management potential."

The second group of measurements is concerned with actual *performance* in a role. Students receive grades. Employees receive performance reviews. Drivers of automobiles acquire records of accidents and violations. Consumers receive credit ratings. Professors enumerate their publications. Golfers utilize a handicap and bowlers an average to reflect their achievements.

Actual performance in a role also serves as an indicator of potential performance. (Recall the "Peter Principle," whereby the individual who performs successfully in a role receives successive promotions up to the "level of his or her incompetence." This sometimes results in perplexing situations for the individual. For example, the consumer seeking credit may not be able to get it without a good credit record. But one has to start somewhere!

All these examples are based on management's need for decision support. The readings of Part Four are intended to explore this subject in more depth.

The first section reviews the subject of work measurement, which has its roots in the first conceptions of a "scientific management" (Taylor, 1911). The reading in this section, by Elliott Jaques, presents an original, radical measurement basis on which to pay individuals for their work.

The second section explores the establishment of individual performance criteria relative to organizational roles. Two articles from the 1950s are representative of attempts to deal with this issue. In the first Bryant Nagle presents guidance for criterion development, based on the ideal of the ultimate criterion. In the second, H.E. Brogden and E.K. Taylor propose a dollar criterion, which relates criterion measurement to cost accounting.

The third section is concerned with rating systems as bases for individual measurement. Here the reading reflects the more current tendency toward multiple-dimensional approaches to problem formulation and resolution. Edward Lawler's subject is the multitrait-multirater approach to measuring managerial job performance.

In the fourth section, psychological measurement is discussed—in particular, psychological testing as a basis for individual performance prediction. The subject of construct validity is explored in the reading by Lee Cronbach and Paul Meehl.

Part Three concludes with a brief discussion of consumer measurement. The reading, by Paul Green and Yoram Wind, demonstrates the applicability of the new technique of conjoint measurement to this problem area.

CHAPTER **TEN**

The following item appeared some years ago in the "People" section of the *International Herald Tribune*, written by Samuel Justice (December 6, 1972):

"Scalpel, forceps, No. 2 wood . . ." According to an article in the American consumers publication National Bureau Report, a measuring unit of surgical work—the hernia equivalent (HE)—has been developed to measure the operative workloads of general surgeons in the United States. A hernia equivalent is defined as the amount of surgical work equal to that involved in performing a unilateral adult inguinal herniorraphy. The first application of HE in measuring surgical workloads involved the determination of the annual in-hospital surgical workload of a population of 19 general surgeons practicing in a suburban community in the New York metropolitan area. The median workload in the population—assuming 48 work weeks per year—was 3.1 HE, and the mean was 4.3 HE per week. A consensus of general surgeons from a number of practice settings estimated that 10.0 HE per week would comprise a surgical workload sufficiently large to maintain operative skills and still leave adequate time for other professional and personal activities. This, of course, raises the question, what were the surgeons doing with the remainder (6.0 to 7.0 HE) of their professional time per week? To answer this question, a time-motion study of the 19 surgeons' work was carried out by a fourth-year medical student, Frederick V. Lorenzo. Although analysis of his data is still preliminary, it appears that many surgeons work considerably less than five days per week. No, uh, kidding.

What is a "fair day's work?" How much time should it take a trained employee to perform a certain job? These questions have long motivated the practitioners of *work measurement*, an early established form of measurement of the individual in the organization. Training in this discipline has traditionally been associated with the study of industrial engineering. *Time and motion study* is the term which has been applied by industrial engineers to "the systematic study of work systems with the purposes of (1) developing the preferred system and method—usually the one with the lower cost; (2) standardizing this system and method; (3) determining the time required by a qualified and properly trained person working at a normal pace to do a specific task or operations; and (4) assisting in training the worker in the preferred method," (Barnes, 1968). The time determined by the analyst as necessary for the worker to do the specific task or operation is commonly referred to as the *time standard*.

Time standards have been of use to management in planning and work scheduling, cost estimation, labor cost control, and as bases for wage incentive systems, (Barnes, 1968). Stopwatch timing of work has often been involved in determining the standard, and the spectre of the stealthy analyst, stopwatch in hand, making clandestine observations of recalcitrant factory workers for the purpose of raising the standard, has been the subject of several popular portrayals (e.g., the British film, "I'm All Right, Jack"). No doubt the methods analyst is not often a popular person. One wonders, for example, how medical student-turned-analyst Lorenzo fared during his final years of study.

Much of the work subjected to time and motion study has been of the manual assembly type. In determining standards for this type of work, pioneers in the field developed analytic systems which identified the "elementary subdivisions" of any cycle of hand motions. Perhaps the earliest system was that developed by Frank B. Gilbreth in the 1920s. Gilbreth identified seventeen "therbligs" (Gilbreth spelled backward) as "fundamental hand motions": search, select, grasp, transport empty, transport loaded, hold, release hold, position, pre-position, inspect, assemble, disassemble, use, unavoidable delay, avoidable delay, plan, and rest for overcoming fatigue (Barnes, 1968, p. 136). Time standards were later developed for application to therbligs under varying work circumstances. Work could then be measured indirectly, without the use of a stopwatch. Time standards set in this way are often referred to as *predetermined times.*

One of the best-known systems for the determination of predetermined times is Methods-Time Measurement (MTM), developed at Westinghouse Electric in the 1940s (Nance and Nolan, 1971; Maynard, Stegemerten and Schwab, 1948). Basic motions of manual operations were recorded by camera, and because the times associated with these motions were so small (e.g., 0.00002 hours, or 0.072 seconds), the developers of MTM defined a new unit of measurement called the Time Measurement Unit (TMU), equal to 0.00001 hour, for use in standard setting. Basic motions could thus be associated with whole number measurements, which were regarded as much easier to remember and work with. A professional association, the MTM Association of Standards and Research, was also formed, and given all rights to MTM data and its development.

The rise of white-collar work in modern society has presented a new challenge to advocates of work measurement (Nance and Nolan, 1971). Stopwatch studies have "generally proved psychologically unacceptable to office personnel." Instead systems of predetermined times have been recommended. One such system, Master Clerical Data (MCD), is said to cover "95 percent of all clerical activities performed in the office (Nance and Nolan, 1971; Birn, Crossan and Eastwood, 1961).

Another technique which has found application in office measurement is *work sampling.* At the simplest level, termed *ratio delay,* random observations are made to determine whether the employee is working or not working. Other forms of measurement are based on enumeration of the various tasks included in the work, and the determination of the relative frequencies of their performance. Presumably some variation of this technique was applied to the study of surgeons described earlier.

PAY SYSTEMS

The measurement of a "fair day's work" inevitably leads to questions of a "fair day's pay." In the factory, *piece rate systems* have sometimes been established which link the two directly, the worker being paid at a fixed unit output rate. On the whole, with this and other wage incentive systems, management seeks to make its labor factor as cost-effective as possible—for example, paying somewhat more sometimes to achieve a corresponding increase in productivity.

However, in modern society pay systems are often products of negotiation with organized labor. Questions of *equity* often predominate, and simple work measurements may carry little weight where the comparison is with those whose work involves a different product or service. (Comparability of work performed and payment received, whether in the public versus the private sectors of the economy, or in one geographical location versus another, or by those of different sex, is always an issue in negotiated pay systems.)

Nevertheless the motivation to measure work in support of management decision persists. In the reading that follows Elliott Jaques presents a new approach, based on a new measure, called the *time span of discretion.*

OBJECTIVE MEASURES FOR PAY DIFFERENTIALS

Elliott Jaques

- Does the lack of objective methods for settling payment disputes cause mistrust, stress, and leadership failures?

- Is it time to give up the notion that employees regard pay differentials solely in the primitive manner that economic theory often suggests?

- Can the fruits of labor be distributed in such a way that justice is done, and can be *seen* to be done by all concerned?

My answer to each of these questions is *yes*. I believe that a radically new policy is needed for setting pay scales, and I shall outline the principles of that policy in this article. My proposals will be found, I am sure, to have disadvantages as well as advantages for an economy as complex as that of the United States. I hope to demonstrate, however, that this revolutionary approach deserves serious consideration by policy-making businessmen, labor executives, and government leaders.

SOUND PRINCIPLES NEEDED

All industrial disputes concerning payment are differential in character. They arise over the question of how much one group is getting as compared with others. For instance, is one group suffering more than others because of inflation in the cost of living. This important social fact was clearly stated by Keynes: ". . . the struggle about money-wages primarily affects the distribution of the *aggregate* real wage between different labor groups. . . . The effect of combination on the part of a group of workers is to protect their *relative* real wages."[1]

Failure to regulate differential payment is one of the fundamental sources of disruption in modern society. Today the problem is dealt with in most industrial nations by a complex of bargaining and arbitration procedures built up by custom and practice, and carried out within a broad framework of labor law. The arbitration procedures are intended to bring some order into the working of the labor market on those occasions when, if left to bargaining alone, the market mechanism would lead to chaos.

But this framework of rules is primitive. The bargaining rests upon the relative

Harvard Business Review, January–February 1962, Vol. 40, No. 1 Copyright © 1961 by the President and Fellows of Harvard College; all rights reserved.

power of the contending sides. Arbitration, when used, is based on the wisdom and personal good sense of the particular individual who has been chosen to arbitrate. The fundamental problem is not even overcome by successful bargaining or arbitration procedures, or by such mechanisms as sliding-scale agreements or arrangements to increase payment in relation to local or national productivity. All these devices leave the pattern of differentials either unchanged or vicariously changed. And the problem is the differential pattern of payment, not the absolute levels.

What is required? We need to supplant custom and practice and *ad hoc* procedures by principle—or at least to give negotiation procedures a firm footing in principle. We need to bring the sophistication of the rule of law into an area of social and economic life where rule-of-thumb judgments largely prevail.

Using principles to resolve the problem of pay differentials calls for the recognition of one fundamental notion: equity demands that a man be rewarded for the level of work which he is employed to do. The question of how much any given section of the population should receive in wages or salaries cannot be *equitably* settled by reference to productivity, efficiency, profitability, strength of union organization, or capacity of an industry to pay. It is the responsibility of those who direct an enterprise to ensure that its work is organized efficiently, to determine what work it can afford to undertake, and to reward its employees at an equitable level for the work they do.

A NEW YARDSTICK

If the foregoing notions are accepted, the next problem is to develop an objective yardstick for measuring the level of work in any job. Such a yardstick has, I believe, been discovered in the course of extensive research for a light engineering firm located near London, England—the Glacier Metal Company. My knowledge of other industries in England and the United States leads me to believe that what I shall report about this firm is almost universally true in the organizations of both countries.

The use of this yardstick has unexpectedly brought to light the existence of an unrecognized system of norms of what constitutes fair payment for any given level of work. Employees share these norms regardless of the type of work they are doing. The findings suggest a national wage and salary policy based on equity and applying to all levels of work from the managing director to the shop floor worker.

The most important discovery is that level or weight of responsibility in a job (which I shall hereafter refer to simply as level of work) can be measured by determining the maximum period of time during which the work assigned by a manager requires his subordinate to exercise discretion, judgment, or initiative in his work without that discretion being subject to review by the manager. This measure rigorously excludes all those aspects of work which are prescribed or regulated by policies, administrative routines, or physical controls, to which the subordinate must conform or be guilty of negligence. I have termed this measure the *time span of discretion,* and have described it in detail in a book recently published.[2]

To illustrate, here are a few of the measured ranges of time span of discretion that I have obtained for various jobs:

- *Low-level manual and clerical jobs*—a half day to a full day.

- *So-called skilled craft jobs* (e.g., machine tool fitting work)—one week to a few months.

- *Foreman positions*—six months to a year, depending on the responsibilities connected with work throughout, forward orders, and forward planning for work input.

- *Research technologist jobs*—weeks, months, or years, depending on the maximum length of the project assigned to the research worker.

- *Sales management*—months to years, depending on the time required to cover territories, to open markets, to introduce new products, and so on.

- *Top management roles* (or "managing director" roles, in British parlance)—several to many years.

Generally speaking, the higher the position is in an executive system, the longer is its time span because of the increased connection with longer term planning.

To avoid any misimpression, let me emphasize here that these time spans do not mean that there is no managerial intrusion at all during the periods covered.

Making the Measurements

In the calculations of time span, not all exercises of discretion are taken into account. For instance, obvious forms of substandard work and negligence are not included; they are subject to review at any time during the period in question. The measurements extend only to reasonable and marginally substandard exercises of discretion; that is, substandard work which would become noticeable to senior managers only over a period of time, and not in any particular instance.

While I shall not try in the scope of this article to give a detailed explanation of how to carry out time-span measurements, I must warn against loose attempts to calculate time spans "off the cuff," or to think up hypothetical jobs. It is necessary to use real data drawn up in the form of a time-span chart. The conclusions to be described presently are all based on careful use of the time-span instrument in measuring actual and not hypothetical jobs.

It is worth noting that the yardstick is not itself affected by such factors as supervisory whims, personalities, or company "politics" except so far as these factors bring about real changes in the level of work in a job. When shifts of this kind do occur, the yardstick can be used to identify and measure the amount of difference. Bear in mind, too, that, as is the case with any measuring instrument, time-span-of-discretion results are purely quantitative. Left out of account, for instance, are such questions as the "importance" of the job being measured to management or to the firm. However, my experience suggests that time-span figures accurately reflect qualities that are usually related to feelings about the importance of the work or the level of responsibility represented.

Wide Application

The time span of discretion can be measured in any position in any executive hierarchy. Analyses that have been carried out in a large international trading company, an advertising agency, a large motor corporation, an oil company, and in other types of organizations have proved that every job has its own time characteristic, and that this property can be measured. Moreover, because the measure refers only to the time dimension of work, and not to job content, it can be used for direct comparison of work levels between any jobs, regardless of the industry or content of the work.

EQUITABLE PAY SCALES

The major significance of the time span of discretion in relation to payment lies in the finding that individuals in jobs having the same level of work (as measured in terms of time span) privately state the same wage or salary bracket to be fair for the work they are doing. Their opinions are not affected by the income taxes they pay. After putting the data together, I was able to construct a scale of what was considered to be fair payment for given time-span levels. I have called this pattern of payment the *equitable work-payment scale.*

To be sure, my findings were made in Great Britain. However, I have evidence from another type of analysis which suggests that, generally speaking, the equitable work-payment scale obtained for Great Britain should also apply to the United States. This evidence is derived from data which show that individual earning progressions (corrected for wage-index movements) of persons employed in industry in the United States follow the same pattern as do those of people employed in Great Britain.[3]

The relationship between time span and equitable payment is shown in Exhibit I, which is based on analyses of about a thousand jobs of all types and at all levels, with additional confirmatory findings from a heavy engineering firm, a food factory, a bank, and a chemical concern. The annual scale in pounds sterling has been con-

EXHIBIT I. Relation between time span of discretion and what employees consider equitable work payment

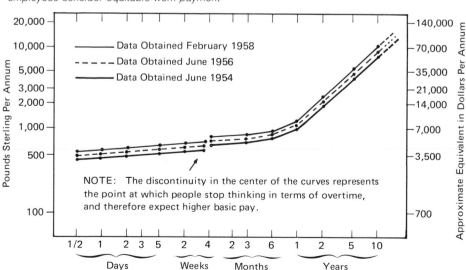

Level of Responsibility as Measured by Time Span

verted to dollars by multiplying by 7. This factor of 7 has been obtained by taking 2.8 for the current exchange value, and 2.5 to correct for differences in the standard of living ($2.8 \times 2.5 = 7$). Thus, we consider a person earning £3,000 per year in Great Britain to be enjoying about the same standard of living as someone earning $21,000 per year in the United States.

As Exhibit I suggests, the pay levels considered to be equitable tend to change roughly in step with movements in the wage index.

Pattern of Response

When individuals' reactions to their payment are considered in the light of their work level as I have defined it, a characteristic pattern of responses is found. A person whose compensation is at the equitable level feels that it is a fair payment, relative to the pay of others, although he may also feel that the economy as a whole ought to provide a higher standard of living for all. By contrast, deviations in payment *below* the equitable level are usually accompanied by feelings of dissatisfaction, which become stronger as the deviation is greater. For example, deviations at the minus 10% level lead to an active sense of grievance, complaints, or the desire to complain and, if no redress is given, to an active desire to change jobs or to take collective action if an organized group is involved; these reactions become *very* strong at the minus 15% to 20% deviation level.

On the other hand, deviations *above* the equitable level are accompanied by feelings of being relatively well off as compared with others; and at the plus 10% to 15% deviation level there is a strong sense of receiving preferential treatment, which may harden into bravado, with underlying feelings of unease about how long the relatively advantageous position can be maintained.

These results suggest that it is not necessarily true that each worker is out to get as much as he can for his work. Instead, workers appear to have strong desires that each one should earn the right amount—a fair and reasonable amount relative to others.

Understanding Wage Troubles

The existence of an unwritten pattern of pay differentials which employees feel to be equitable—a set of standards based on the idea of the "right rate for the job"—helps to explain why there is not greater chaos than there is in the field of wage and salary negotiations. The laws of supply and demand, and the wielding of power, do not function unfettered; they do not produce the trends, concentrations, and interminable shifting suggested by economic theory. Instead, the laws are constrained by standards of what is intuitively regarded as fair. Our findings—e.g., reactions to deviations actual pay from the equitable work-payment scale—suggest that the actual payment levels in a high proportion of jobs in any given occupational group must deviate by more than 10% from equity to cause severe disequilibrium; granted that much deviation, however, upset will result regardless of the relative power of the contending sides, or of the state of the market for the type of labor in question.

In connection with the chronic pattern of recurring wage demands, early findings from the time-span analyses of hourly rated jobs tend to support the view that, although some manual and clerical jobs are paid above equitable levels, a significantly large proportion are underpaid at the present time by amounts ranging from 5% to 12% as compared with technical work of equivalent time-span level. This deviation is sufficient to cause chronically recurring unrest. Conversely, I wonder if the presence of unrest may not suggest inequitable payment as the cause (granting, of course, that it is not by any means the only possible cause of disturbance). For instance, may not the chronic wage troubles in the United States and Great Britain indicate that there is widespread over-equity and under-equity payment?

DANGEROUS ASSUMPTIONS

The importance of the time span of discretion in employee's thinking about jobs and pay levels means that executives should critically reappraise many common assumptions about compensation scales. I shall mention just a few examples of ideas that need to be challenged. (All figures have been converted from pounds sterling to dollars, and are only approximately accurate.) Thus:

- It is a commonplace in arguments about pay—in Great Britain as much as in the United States—to hear it said that one job is obviously worth more than another because the other is "merely routine." A dangerous thing to take for granted!

  A job in a chemical works was called "routine laboring." It was described as lifting certain components into an acid bath for etching, and taking them out again. The operator was being paid the equivalent of $1.65 per hour. He complained that the job required much more skill than was recognized, and considered himself to be $0.20 an hour underpaid.

  Analysis of the job revealed that the operator had the responsibility for deciding when the etching was "just right." Substandard work could pile up for two to three days without review. Accordingly, the equitable payment bracket was indeed higher—$1.85 to $2.00.
- Jobs with the same title and similar work content are usually held to be worth the same pay. However, this is not *necessarily* so.

  In two adjacent drawings offices men were doing the same types of design work and were subject to the same salary range of $100 to $120 per week. In the first office, all work was reviewed by the chief designer before the drawings were approved for use. The calculated time-span-of-discretion range was four weeks to three months; the equitable pay range was from $110 to $120; the actual pay range was nearly consistent with equity.

  But in the second office the designs were not scrutinized before the parts were manufactured, review taking place at the time of testing of the parts. Here the actual time-span range was from three to nine months; the equitable pay range was from $120 to $150; and the actual salary range was well below equity. The people in this office sensed the discrepancy (without the benefit of our analysis) and were disgruntled.
- Technologists often change jobs because increases in the level of their work go unrecognized. For instance, a firm lost a research physicist. It advertised the job at $9,000 per year, the same rate of pay as had been given before. No suitable candidates were found. The job was readvertised at $10,500. The same result followed. The position was advertised again at $12,500 and this time filled, the extra $3,500 being considered payment "for scarcity value."

Analysis showed that the discretion required for the job had increased during the tenure of the previous occupant from a time-span bracket of six months to one year ($6,500 to $9,500), to a bracket of eighteen months to two years ($12,000 to $17,500). Hence the old rate had become inequitable. If the change in level of work had been recognized, the technologist who had helped to create the job might not have been lost.

In my experience, even the most technically advanced firms are not always sufficiently alive to changes in the discretion level of technological work.

The foregoing are examples of everyday occurrences, not of rarities. These occurrences demonstrate that before a "reasonable" rate of pay for different occupational categories—whether engine drivers, bus drivers, engineers, chemists, or teachers—can be discussed, a common yardstick is required. In the absence of a yardstick, and of any common language for talking meaningfully about work, such questions as what is fair compensation utterly defy constructive resolution.

CONCLUSION

Widespread application of the new principles I have described would require a complete reorientation to the question of work and payment. It would call for giving up that part of economic theory and practice which regards labor—whether manual, clerical, technical, or managerial—as a commodity to be sold under market conditions; and it would demand giving up the notion that human behavior with regard to payment must be as primitive as economic theory often suggests.

A new type of policy would emerge—a policy of fixing wage or salary brackets in connection solely with level of work. The scale of differential payment would be fixed nationally; the principle to be followed would be that of a genuine "rate for the job" system of payment in which everyone would receive the given rate for any given level of work, regardless of executive level, occupation, or industry. Applying this national scale would require extensive analysis of jobs in term of time span, a program that would in turn require a radical reorientation and reorganization of personnel work and much revision of work study.

Important Gains at Stake

What I am urging is a compensation policy based, as many other industrial relations policies are, on a "rule of law," meaning, in this case, norms of equity in payment that are based on objective study and precedent. Such a policy would subject everyone in industry—senior executive and unskilled worker alike—to the same scale of value for the work he does. Individual progress in earnings relative to other employees could be obtained only by progress in the level of work performed, either within the work bracket in a person's existing job, or by gaining promotion to a job carrying a higher level of responsibility. If pay increases were based on these conditions, employees would, in my opinion, have a genuine incentive to improve their skills.

Moreover, the proposed program would mitigate the problem of wage inflation and the inhibiting effect of inflation on industrial expansion. The burdens of a nonabundant economy would be more equitably shared, and increases in national productivity would be reflected in an upward shifting of the whole scale of payment.

The cost of such a program would have to be weighed against the gain in productivity to be obtained from sound and systematic organization and manning of work. In some cases the cost might be in the very nature of the enterprise itself; that is, some firms might not be able to afford to pay equitably without concentrating more on profitable lines of business. Payment below equity must be recognized as equivalent to requiring employees to invest a portion of their wage or salary in the industry.

We do not have objective methods for settling payment levels in a manner that is manifestly equitable. There is plenty of evidence that this lack causes an abdication of executive leadership and stirs up widespread envy, mistrust, socioeconomic rivalry, and stress. But we do not know how the human outlook would change if the distribution of the fruits of labor were arranged in such a manner that people could recognize justice based on equity and *could* see its being accomplished. Our research on work levels and payment suggests that very powerful forces of social construction and cooperative effort lie waiting to be released.

ENDNOTES

1. John Maynard Keynes, *The General Theory of Employment, Interest, and Money* (New York: St. Martin's Press, 1954), p. 14.

2. Elliott Jaques, *Equitable Payment* (New York: John Wiley & Sons, Inc., 1961); see also Elliott Jaques, *Measurement of Responsibility* (Cambridge, Harvard University Press, 1956).

3. For a fuller discussion of this point see Elliott Jaques, *Equitable Payment*, op. cit., pp. 291–296.

Questions for Study and Discussion

1. An example of a computer-based decision support system based on work measurement is described by Swanson (1974). The system, named ARIS ("Activity Reporting Information System"), is employed by a production quality control department of more than 200 employees in a large electronic equipment manufacturing plant. The large staff consists primarily of engineers and technicians, supplemented by clerical support. The allocation of staff time, both current and planned, is regarded as a significant management problem. ARIS gathers data on the actual and planned work activity of departmental personnel and makes them available to management on a "need to know" basis, through terminal-based inquiry. A query language facilitates the generation of reports in unanticipated forms.

Two data files are maintained online by ARIS. The first, the Activity Status File, contains work activity data from the most recent thirteen weeks, at a level of detail which includes the activity records of individual employees. The second file, derived from the first, maintains a eighteen-month summary of work activity at the department level. This second file is referred to as the Activity History File. Both files are relatively simple in structure. Despite the limited nature of the ARIS files, there is no practical limit to the number of unique reports which can be produced. Some examples:

(i) A summary of man-hours charged to a given product type during a recent month, broken down by employee skill code.
(ii) An exception listing of those product types for which the actual man-hours charged exceed the budgeted man-hours, for each month over a one-year period.
(iii) A profile of the man-hours charged by a given employee to various work activity types during each week of the current month.
(iv) A listing of man-hours charged by a given department to various product types, for each month during the most recent six months.

What measurement issues underlie the data upon which ARIS is based?

2. Recall the work measurement system of the University of California, from which faculty-student contact hours were computed (discussed in the introduction to this book). Data for this system were gathered each term, a process administered at the academic department level. Each faculty member was asked to complete a form indicating the average number of hours spent weekly in teaching activities. What data gathering alternatives should be considered in the redesign of this measurement system? What are the relative strengths and weaknesses of each?

3. In implementing the system described by Elliott Jaques, how should the time span of discretion be measured? What issues may arise?

4. Measuring the productivity of the individual worker is often an important element in productivity measurement as a whole. An example is the measurement of computer programmer productivity at the Standard Bank of South Africa, described by Crossman (1979). Programmer productivity in the development of new systems is measured in terms of the number of man-hours spent on development divided by the number of functions in all the programs in the system. A function is defined as "that section of the program that performs only one activity, such as initializing fields, computing values, setting up a print line, validating a record, etc; has one entry point and one exit point; conforms to the permitted logic structures of structured programs; and has about 5 to 50 source statements." What management decisions are potentially supportable by this productivity measure? What behavior on the part of individual programmers is likely to be motivated, in each case?

CHAPTER **ELEVEN**

The essence of traditional work measurement is its concentration on improving the productivity of the individual employee. Labor time is considered the scarce resource, and the objective of time and motion study is the optimization of this resource's use in the completion of some productive operation. The output of a factory worker, relative to established time standards, thus offers one *criterion* for the evaluation of individual job performance.

Performance criteria represent the bases for assessing the success or failure of the individual's performance in the organization. They are also the bases for the evaluation of the organization's personnel decisions, as Guion (1965) has noted:

> Every personnel decision is an implied prediction of future on-the-job behavior. A decision to hire one applicant in preference to another is logically based on the belief that the first applicant, if hired, is more likely to exhibit behavior desirable in certain pertinent respects than is the other. (p. 91)

Measures of an individual's actual performance in an organizational role are thus necessary to validate the usefulness of *predictors* of the same performance.

Performance criteria are often classified as objective or subjective, depending on whether certain *judgment methods* are used to generate the measurements. Examples of objective measures based on production data include output rates (e.g., the sales volume generated by a salesman); quality rates (e.g., as determined by scrap and rework charges in a factory operation); and trainability indicators (e.g., as determined from output rate progression over time, compared against a standard learning curve). Examples of objective measures based on personnel data include absence rates, promotion rates, accident rates, and accumulated tenure. Clearly, considerable judgment may be required to interpret an individual's performance based on such objective data. (The reader should offer an example of how the data might mislead, for each of the above measures.) For this reason, subjective measures are often developed, which permit this interpretation to be incorporated into the criteria. For example, a manager may simply rate the quality of an employee's work on a one-to-five point scale ranging from "low" to "high."

However, subjective measures of performance do not really absorb all uncertainty associated with their interpretation, in spite of their design. In fact, *rating methods* for subjective measurement present some new difficulties for the manager. These will be discussed following the readings of the present subsection.

Ideally a performance criterion, whether objective or subjective in terms of measurement construction, seeks to satisfy the values of scientific objectivity. Its purpose is to establish performance actually achieved, and its adequacy in meeting this purpose is a matter for scientific resolution. Or is it? The following story reports the existence of a "double standard" of performance measurement which has arisen in the educational system of the state of California.

HIGH SCHOOL GRADUATION TESTING

In an article entitled "Graduation Testing: Will Scoring be Fair?" (*Los Angeles Times*, March 14, 1977), writer Robert Fairbanks reports that the state of California is expected to implement a double standard in its measurement of students' knowledge of reading, writing, and arithmetic fundamentals:

> SACRAMENTO—California employers may be pleased to know that the state's high schools are beginning to test all potential graduates for their knowledge of the fundamentals (reading, writing and arithmetic) and will be denying diplomas to those who fail.
>
> But the passing grades for these tests are creating a remarkable anomaly.
>
> For reasons having to do with the politics of public education, the passing grades for fourth year students (seniors) will in all likelihood be much lower than the passing grade for a test now given to students who want to graduate at the end of their second or third years.
>
> Furthermore, the test given to fourth year students almost certainly will be much less difficult than the one being given to others.
>
> In other words, the more time a student spends in school, the less he or she is expected to know.

How has such a state of affairs come to be? Two state laws are responsible. One, passed in 1972, authorized the graduation of students before the completion of their fourth year of studies, based on the passing of a proficiency test. Any student sixteen or older may take the test. Those who pass receive a "certificate of proficiency," which is the legal equivalent of a high school diploma. Implementation of the program was designed to assist students who were "uncomfortable" in high school and on the verge of dropping out, as well as those who wanted an early start in college. In setting standards for the test, it was decided that students who leave school early should do at least as well on this test as the average high school senior, according to bill author Arlen Gregorio. Thus, if the test were given to all high school seniors, half would fail.

> Why set the standards there?
>
> "Politically, there was no other way we could do it," Gregorio said, explaining that any easier standard would have generated too much opposition from too many persons.
>
> These would include, he said, school officials who would lose state aid as attendance declines and labor leaders who don't want former students competing in the job market and parents who don't want their children around.

"Essentially, there's a helluva lot of people who want to pay professional educators to take the kids out of their hair," he said.

The Gregorio test has been given twice annually since its start in December, 1975, but only about 5% of eligible students have taken it.

At a news conference last month, Gregorio suggested that the low turnout might result from school district "reluctance" to tell students about the test because of its potential for causing lower attendance and a loss of funds.

The more recent law, enacted in 1976, requires all school districts in California to adopt standards for knowledge of the fundamentals, and to deny diplomas to students who cannot pass a test based on these standards. Test standards are currently being designed (as of the date of the article), and few districts are reported to be choosing standards as high or higher than those required for early graduates. According to Alex Law, a member of the Department of Education, "I just have a hunch that most governing boards will not set a standard that is sufficiently rigorous that they will not graduate a substantial number of students."

An education special on the staff of Legislative Analyst A. Alan Post echoed Law.

"The pressure is on to keep standards low. They figure that the first student denied a diploma is their first lawsuit," she said.

Some employers of high school graduates are reported to be aware of the double standard now being implemented, and are deliberately seeking the early graduates. These include recruiters for the United States armed forces and various apprentice training programs.

THE "FOR KEEPS" PHENOMENON

The testing of high school graduates is not a scientific exercise. It is "for keeps." It matters very much to educators, parents, and employers, not to mention students, how the performance criterion is established. In this sense, it is a true measurement for management decision, made ultimately for pragmatic purposes.

When a measurement is made "for keeps," especially a measurement of an individual, it is to be expected that those with a stake in the decision will seek to influence the outcome. The scientific community may be one of these "stakeholders," but it has relatively weak claim to final authority on the matter. The dilemma of criterion measurement is that it is a means not only for the evaluation of performance, but a potential means for other individual, organizational, and social purposes within the context in which it is organized.

THE IDEAL CRITERION

What would be the ideal criterion in individual performance measurement, and what would be its characteristics? In the first article of two which address this question, Bryant Nagle discusses the problem of criterion development in terms of the concept of the *ultimate criterion*. In the second article, H. E. Brogden and E. K. Taylor make the argument that a *dollar criterion* is the appropriate basis for the construction of an overall measure of worker effectiveness.

Both articles, written in the early 1950s, are now somewhat dated from the perspective of modern psychological and personnel theory. The ideal of a single criterion has given way to approaches based on multiple performance criteria (see, for example, Guion, 1961). However, the two articles are important for their clear orientation to measurement for managerial purposes. Useful lessons may still be drawn by the contemporary reader. These lessons will receive emphasis in the questions for study and discussion following each reading.

CRITERION DEVELOPMENT

Bryant F. Nagle

READING 20

THREE CRITERION CONSIDERATIONS

Inherent in the phase 'given a criterion' are many of the pitfalls of psychological research. This phrase, so common in the literature 10 years ago, overcame the problem of criterion development by ignoring it. The problem is no longer ignored. During World War II American psychologists were forced to exert a considerable portion of their efforts toward the construction and selection of criteria.

It is the purpose of this paper to survey the criterion literature published during the past 10 years and to suggest a systematic procedure for the development of criteria. The review of criterion literature has been organized about three theoretical considerations: relevancy, reliability, and combination of measures.

Before continuing it would be well to define what a criterion is. Horst says, "The measure of success or failure in an activity is what is technically known as a criterion" (17, p. 20). Similarly, Bechtoldt defines a criterion as, ". . . a means of describing the performance of individuals on a success continuum" (4, p. 357). As Brogden and Taylor see it, "The criterion should measure the contribution of the individual to the overall efficiency of the organization" (8, p. 139). Also representing the industrial bent is the definition given by Ghiselli and Brown, "By criterion is meant any attribute or accomplishment of the worker that can be used as an index of his serviceability or usefulness to the organization that employs him" (14, p. 62). We may say, then, that for a given activity, the criterion is an index by which we can measure the degree of success achieved by various individuals. Criteria are also used in industrial psychology to measure the success of an organization or of a program. This discussion is centered around the use of criteria to measure the success of individuals in the industrial situation.

How do criteria fit into the prediction process? Prediction might be thought of as consisting of two steps: validation and selection. In validation predictor variables are tested against a criterion. The criterion will give a metrical ordering of subjects in terms of success on the given activity. The predictor variables are matched against this metrical ordering to determine their relationship to success on the given activity. When one or more predictor variables shows a satisfactory relationship, such predictor variables are used to select those individuals likely to achieve success on the given activity. This last step is what is known as "selection."

From *Personnel Psychology*, 1953, 6, pp. 271–289. Reprinted by permission.

It must be pointed out here that, while the goal of this process is prediction, the predictors themselves can never be anything but subsidiary to the criterion, for it is from the criterion that the predictors derive their significance. If the criterion changes, the predictors' validity is necessarily affected. If the predictors change, the criterion does not change for that reason. Likewise, it can be seen that if no criteria are used, one would never know whether or not the predictors were selecting those individuals likely to succeed. Research can be no better than the criteria used. One must, therefore, approach the prediction process in a logical fashion, developing criteria first, analyzing them, and then constructing or selecting variables to predict the criteria. When one or more variables show a satisfactory relationship to the criteria, such variables may be used as selection instruments.

Three of the fundamental problems of criteria will be discussed here. These are: 1. The relevance of the criterion, 2. The reliability of the criterion, and 3. The combination of criterion measures into a composite score. The exclusive emphasis on these three problems should not be interpreted as meaning that these are the only problems of criterion construction and selection. These three seem to the author to be the primary theoretical problems involved.

Relevancy

Relevancy, a term which seems to have been used first by Bechtoldt (4) and later by Ghiselli and Brown (14), Thorndike (28) and many others, refers to the extent to which an index of success (criterion) is related to the 'true' order of success in the given activity. In this respect relevancy is akin to validity, but to avoid confusion, use of the term relevancy seems desirable. Thorndike (28) has been helpful in clarifying this problem. He has spoken of the 'ultimate criterion', which may be thought of as the properly weighted embodiment of all the elements making for success in the activity. This is the 'true' order of success in the activity. Relevancy is the hypothetical correlation coefficient between the criterion used and the ultimate criterion.

In the preceding sentence an important point is introduced. Relevancy (validity of the criterion) is the *hypothetical* correlation coefficient between the criterion used and the ultimate criterion. It is hypothetical because one is forced to judge the relevance of the criterion used to the ultimate criterion. For example, in attempting to develop an index of success (criterion) for automobile driving, we may lay out a trial driving course and give a rating on the subject's proficiency in navigating the course. In laying out this course we must endeavor to duplicate the activity of driving in the non-experimental situation as closely as possible. Here we make judgments as to how closely our driving course approximates the everyday conditions of driving. Here also we must instruct the judge to look for certain things upon which to base his rating. We have made judgments that certain things constitute success in driving and tell him to look for those things. In all cases, when one accepts a measure as a criterion, he has judged that the measure has a certain degree of relevance to the ultimate criterion. Oftentimes investigators fail to realize that they are making a judgment. Because they have a measure available which is somehow related to the given activity they are satisfied. What must be realized is that when a measure, or measures, is adopted as the criterion, one is implying that it is synonymous with success in the activity. By adopting certain measures the investigator has, consciously or unconsciously, judged them to be relevant to success in the activity.

Here would seem to be perhaps the greatest stumbling block to obtaining a 'true' criterion measure—one may only judge the validity of the criterion. Anyone familiar with the validity and reliability of judgments knows how serious is this shortcoming.

To have high relevancy, the systematic, non-error sources of variance in the criterion must be the same as those in the ultimate criterion. The systematic, non-error sources of variance will not be the same if the criterion does not include some variance present in the ultimate criterion, or if the criterion includes variance not present in the ultimate criterion. In other words, the criterion can suffer from omission of pertinent elements, or from inclusion of extraneous elements. These situations may be referred to as "criterion deficiency" and "criterion contamination" respectively (7).

If the criterion omits pertinent elements, predictive efficiency may not be as high as the correlation between the predictors and the criterion indicates. This will happen because the criterion, in its deficient form, is used to represent the ultimate criterion in the validation process. If we obtain a correlation of .90 between the predictors and the deficient criterion, and if the hypothetical correlation between the criterion and the ultimate criterion were .50, then the predictive efficiency will probably be less than .90.

If the criterion includes extraneous elements, predictive efficiency may not be as high as the correlation between the predictors and the criterion indicates. In cases where criterion contamination occurs, the predictors may correlate with the relevant variance in the criterion, or they may correlate with the extraneous elements in the criterion, or the predictors may correlate with both. To the extent to which the predictors correlate with the extraneous elements of the criterion, the validity coefficient will overestimate the predictive efficiency. In the extreme case where all the correlation is between extraneous elements and the predictors, subjects will be selected without regard to their chances of success in the activity. Therefore, extraneous elements in the criterion are a much greater handicap if they are predictor correlated. Inclusion of extraneous elements which do not correlate with the predictors only increases the error of measurement.

Bellows (5), Brogden and Taylor (7), and Thorndike (28) give numerous examples of criterion contamination. The research individual should be constantly on guard against these sources of criterion contamination. When one is aware that a certain extraneous element is likely to occur in a criterion, the influence of the extraneous element can usually be controlled experimentally or statistically. The real problem lies in anticipating the occurrence of such extraneous variables. This further emphasizes the need for careful consideration of the criterion measure or measures before such data are gathered.

Reliability

As we have seen, there is almost never a quantitative statement of criterion relevancy because it is usually not possible to compare the criterion with a more representative measure of the given activity. But when it comes to reliability of criterion scores, there is a very definite possibility of obtaining a measure. Because one is able to measure the reliability of a criterion, there seems to be a tendency for writers to overemphasize its importance. This is not to imply that it is not important, but it must be remembered that high reliability, while desirable is not sufficient.

What is the relationship of criterion reliability to the validation process? First, the relevancy, as defined by correlation coefficient (since relevancy is admittedly subjective, it does not seem realistic to analyze it as a correlation coefficient), cannot exceed the square root of the reliability coefficient of the criterion. This should emphasize the necessity of reasonably high reliability. Second, the obtained validity coefficient between the criterion and the predictor cannot exceed the square root of the product of the reliability coefficients of the predictor and the criterion (1). A reasonably high criterion reliability is necessary if any predictors are to show a significant relationship with the criterion.

The sources of criterion unreliability have received considerable attention in the literature (4, 14, 19, 28, 31). Among the most importance influences upon criterion reliability are:

1. The size of the sample of performance.

2. The range of ability among the subjects.

3. Ambiguity of instructions.

4. Variation in conditions during measurement period.

5. The amount of aid provided by instruments.

The inherent instability of the given activity is a prime limitation on reliability. Careful consideration of the above sources of unreliability can lead to reliabilities which more closely approximate the reliability of the activity.

In addition to these sources of unreliability, there are several which are peculiar to the situation in which ratings are used as criteria:

1. The competency of the judges.

2. The simplicity of the behavior.

3. The degree to which the behavior is overt.

4. The opportunity to observe.

5. The degree to which the rating task is defined.

Spuriously high reliabilities are found frequently when criterion contamination occurs. Such reliabilities are termed spurious because the reliability contribution of the extraneous elements is meaningless, since the extraneous elements can add nothing in the way of relevancy. One cannot afford to ignore this spurious reliability, for if the reliability contributed by the extraneous elements were removed, surely some criterion reliabilities would become insignificant. Until such spurious reliability is eliminated, one does not know the reliability of the criterion. Whenever extremely high reliability is found in a criterion measure, one should be on guard for the presence of extraneous elements. It is also possible, though not so common, for extraneous elements to lower the reliability of a criterion.

Combination of Criterion Measures

Since ultimate criteria are usually of a complex nature, it is usually necessary to use a multi-dimensional criterion to approximate the ultimate criterion. Seldom, however, can one criterion measure correspond to this multi-dimensional nature. The researcher is frequently faced, therefore, with the problem of using several criterion measures.

The use of several criterion measures raises the problem of whether scores should be left separate or combined into a single criterion score. The author is inclined to agree with Toops (29) that when several measures are to be used a unitary criterion score is indispensable. Use of a single criterion score may tend to minimize the number of predictors necessary and aid in the interpretation of predictor scores.

When several criterion measures are to be combined into a single criterion score there are two problems which arise:

1. Comparability of units along a scale.

2. Comparability of units from scale to scale.

Let us first consider equality of units along a scale. In an excellent treatment of the subject, Brogden and Taylor state, "From the criterion point of view, the scale-unit problem reduces to one of establishing units which represent equal increments in terms of the overall efficiency of the organization" (7, p. 180). When units along the scale are not equal one is assigning different weights to the various portions of the criterion continuum. Thus, if the real difference between ratings of 5 and 6 is four times that of the difference between ratings of 2 and 3, then one is in effect weighting the difference between ratings 2 and 3 four times as heavily as that between 5 and 6. In the area of ratings this scale unit problem is an especially knotty one. There seems to be no acceptable method for judging the presence or absence of scale unit bias (7). In the matter of production data, the scale unit problem often disappears. Production data can be translated into dollars or work units which represent equal increments in terms of the overall efficiency of the organization. The thirteenth part scrapped represents just as great a loss to the organization as the first.

Comparability of units from scale to scale refers to weighting the various criterion measures so that the criterion composite will correspond to the ultimate criterion. When criterion measures are so combined, the individual criterion scales are usually referred to as sub-criteria and the combined scales as a criterion composite. Edgerton and Kolbe (10) suggest a number of ways of combining sub-criteria into a composite. These will be listed and discussed.

1. Weighting sub-criteria according to judgments of 'experts'. This method was first proposed by Toops (29). He had competent judges assign bids to the various traits in question. The experts are really called upon to analyze the nature of the ultimate criterion, then analyze the nature of the various sub-criteria, and weight the sub-criteria so that their composite will correspond as closely as is possible to what is believed to be the composition of the ultimate criterion. This amounts to weighting the sub-criteria on their judged relevancy.

2. Weighting in proportion to reliability (27). This reflects the undue emphasis that has often been placed upon reliability of criteria. The effect of this approach is to obtain the most reliable possible combination of the sub-criteria, without regard to relevancy.

3. Weighting in proportion to average correlation with other variables. This method tends to exaggerate the influence of any general factor there may be in the various sub-criteria. Again, relevancy is not considered.

4. Weighting so as to obtain maximum correlation with the predictors (18, 23). Both the sub-criteria and predictors are weighted to obtain the maximum possible correlation. This represents a perversion of the validation process. In the validation process the predictors are weighted to predict the criterion composite. The predictors should have no influence on the composition or weighting of the sub-criteria.

5. Extracting by factor analysis parts of criterion variates which may be due to the same factor. The purpose of this approach seems to be to include in the criterion composite just one measure of each factor. This is a desirable approach, but the problem remains of weighting the factors.

6. Weighting variates so that discrimination between all possible pairs of individuals will be as great as possible. This method is advocated by Edgerton and Kolbe (10). They state that, "Any method for combining several criterion variates into a single composite assumes that they are measures of the same thing" (10, p. 183). From this, the authors say one should expect, ". . . the differences among the variate values for any individual, expressed in standard scores, to be small" (10, p. 183). The method gives the same results as Horst's method (16). The process assumes that the sub-criteria are measures of the same thing in a statistical sense (one factor). But the correct assumption is that the sub-criteria are measures of the same thing in a psychological sense (measures of success). This method may have some use when success is composed of one factor.

Other methods which have been discussed in the literature (14) are equal weighting of the sub-criteria, and multiple cutoffs. To this writer it seems that the only defensible method of combining sub-criteria is on the basis of relevancy. The more relevant the sub-criterion, the greater should be its weight. And since the relevancy must be judged, so the weights of the sub-criteria must be assigned by judgments. All weighting of sub-criteria on a relevancy basis is subjective.

When weights are assigned to the sub-criteria one must consider the influence of the standard deviations on the weights assigned. Should the weights given by judges to the sub-criterion variables be applied to the raw scores of the individual sub-criteria, or should they be applied to the standard score transformations? If the weights are applied to raw scores, the effective weights of the sub-criteria will differ from those assigned by the judges because of the influence of the varying standard deviations among the sub-criteria. But if the weights are to be applied to the standard scores of the sub-criteria, will the judges be able to think of the sub-criteria in terms of standard scores when they weight them? The problems reduces to one of what are the judges' conceptions of the sub-criteria as they stand before weighting. At present this seems an unanswerable problem. Many arguments can be advanced for both approaches, but this writer prefers to apply the sub-criterion weights to the standard scores of the sub-criteria.

The judge's job of weighting the sub-criteria will be simplified and made more meaningful if the sub-criteria are as independent as possible of each other. Factorially complex measures are difficult to analyze on a judgmental basis.

Brogden and Taylor (8) have proposed a new approach to the problem of combining sub-criterion measures which solves many of the difficulties discussed above. This new approach is applied in an industrial setting. It amounts to changing the scale units of all sub-criteria into dollar units. Their basic premise is that, "The general objective of industrial firms is to make money" (8, p. 139). Therefore, the contribution of an individual to the efficiency of the industrial organization is evaluated on a dollar basis. The individual worker's output, spoilage, accidents, damage to equipment, etc., can be expressed in dollar units. This approach solves the problem of scale unit differences. The fiftieth dollar saved is just as important as the sixth. This approach also solves the problem of weighting the sub-criteria. If an error costs six times as much to correct as the cost of producing one satisfactory piece, then each error is weighted six times as heavily as a satisfactory piece by virtue of the cost incurred. The scores obtained by an individual on each sub-criterion scale are directly additive to obtain a criterion composite. This dollar criterion solves the problems of combining subcriterion measures, but it may be argued that the method does not include all relevant variables—those contributions to success which cannot be evaluated in terms of dollars and cents.

CRITERION DEVELOPMENT

The preceding three sections have dealt with some of the considerations involved in evaluating criteria. There remains the problem of where and how does one obtain criteria. It is the purpose of this section to present an approach to this problem.

Many writers have urged that in the development of criteria one go beyond the state of asking for ratings of good and poor performers and try to determine the 'why' and 'how' aspects of success in the activity. Fiske (11) would first establish the goal of the organization and then specify the purpose of each position in the organization before asking why are some people successful. In the field of learning criteria, Brownell (9) says that in the more complex learning situations one should analyze the goal of the learning process and develop criteria to measure the attainment of the goal. The criteria are found by analysis of the purpose or goal of the learning process. Thorough-going analysis of the process should indicate the more specific goals. The problem then becomes one of developing measures of these specific goals. Other writers have also emphasized the need to seek the real reasons for success. What is suggested, then, by these authors is that one specify the purposes, goals, or objectives of the behavior first and then ask the question of why are some persons successful and others not.

Using this type of approach this writer has developed a four step procedure for criterion development:

1. *Definition of the problem.* In what type of activity are we seeking to determine success? The activity must be as closely defined as is possible if confusion is not to arise in subsequent steps.

2. *Activity Analysis.* The second step in this procedure is an analysis of the activity. This activity analysis may be subdivided into four parts. First a statement of the purposes of the activity should be made. What are the goals of the activity? Second, the types of behavior called for should be described. What does a man working at this activity have to do? Third, standards of performance in the activity should be stated. What levels of performance are required in the various behaviors of the activity? Fourth, the relative importance of the various behaviors must be indicated. What is the relative importance of each behavior called for in the activity?

The similarity of the above activity analysis to job analysis is quite apparent. The use of a thorough job analysis done by a well-trained job analyst would be an appropriate way in which to complete this step. In this respect, Flanagan has written, ". . . the problems of job definition, job requirements, and criteria of success necessarily reduce to one and the same problem, at least with regard to their major outlines" (12, p. 40). The advancement of criterion research is limited to some extent, therefore, by the advancement of a more objective job analysis procedure.

3. *Definition of Success.* What must an individual do to be successful in the activity? What are we trying to develop here is a list of elements of any activity which will differentiate a successful individual from an unsuccessful one. The resultant group of elements when weighted may be thought to be equivalent to what has been spoken of as the ultimate criterion.

In this step we must ask the question of why are some persons successful and others not. By thoughtful analysis of the activity description in step 2 and by research, we should be able to identify the elements of the activity which are related to success. Ryans' work (26) suggests the possible use of the critical incident approach in this step.

When the success elements of the activity have been identified they should be weighted in accordance to their importance to success in the activity. It should be noted that the success elements are being weighted here, not sub-criteria. The sub-criteria are later combined in accordance with the weights established here. The effect of this is to place the weighting step in a more basic position.

There are several ways in which this weighting of success elements can be accomplished. Success elements could be weighted according to their dollar value. If a critical incident approach were used, the success elements might be weighted according to frequency of occurrence. Still another approach would be to have the experts who analyzed the activity weight the success elements. This author favors the latter approach. The use of a judging approach does not preclude the use of fiscal information as an aid to making such judgments.

4. *Development of sub-criteria to measure the elements of success.* The last step in this criterion development procedure is the development of sub-criteria to measure each of the elements of success. In some cases the sub-criterion measures developed will be identical to the elements of success. For example, an element of success on an industrial job may be infrequent absence. The number of times absent could be used as a sub-criterion measure for the success element, infrequent absence. To measure success elements for which there are no objective data, ratings will often have to be used. In such cases, the success element which the rater is called upon to rate should be carefully defined for him. Sometimes success elements may not be amenable even to ratings.

It is in this step that the sub-criterion measures are subjected to analysis of the matter of relevancy and reliability to determine their acceptability. When we are unable to develop sub-criteria for some success elements, criterion deficiency occurs—the criterion omits some of the variance found in the ultimate criterion. On the other hand, sub-criterion measures designed to measure success elements may be contaminated with extraneous variance. In such a case criterion contamination occurs—a sub-criterion designed to measure a success element includes extraneous variance. Prolonged reflection upon the likely sources of contamination in a measure before the measure is developed is required. With ratings this problem is acute and difficult to diagnose. In the rating situation, therefore, the task of the rater should be carefully explained to him. Wherever the possibility of contamination exists the researcher must turn his thoughts toward experimental and statistical control of the sources of contamination. It is here, also, that we inquire into the reliability of the sub-criterion measure. Every effort must be made to obtain as reliable a measure as possible through consideration of the sources of unreliability previously listed.

When all the measurable sub-criteria are assembled they should be weighted according to the weights assigned to the success elements they are supposed to measure. The weights should be applied to the standard score transformations of the sub-criteria. For some success elements there may be no sub-criterion measures. Then we will have to temporarily leave out these elements, but still weight the other sub-criteria according to the original weights assigned to their respective success elements. When sub-criterion measures eventually are developed for the omitted success elements, these sub-criterion measures can be added to the composite criterion score according to the weights of their respective success elements.

Thus, this approach includes four steps:

1. Define the activity

2. Analyze the activity
   a. purposes of the activity
   b. types of behavior called for
   c. standards of performance in the activity
   d. relative importance of the various behaviors

3. Define success
   a. find the elements of success
   b. weight the elements of success

4. Develop sub-criteria to measure each element of success
   a. relevancy of each sub-criterion to its success element
   b. reliability of each sub-criterion
   c. combination of the sub-criteria

The importance of a thorough analysis of the activity and of a careful definition of success cannot be overemphasized. These steps must be done by psychologically trained persons well acquainted with the activity.

Does this approach seem too laborious? Couldn't a simple rating to determine "good" and "poor" performers do just as well? It must be admitted that considerable work is involved. Certainly an overall rating would be much easier and less time consuming. But it is felt that the procedure outlined here will lead to criteria of much higher relevancy than that achieved by overall ratings. There are two other major advantages of this four step approach as contrasted with an overall rating. First, this procedure holds out the hope for continued improvement of the criterion to increase relevancy. Second, the success elements provide a useful diagnostic instrument. These success elements can be invaluable in indicating training needs and serving as a counseling aid. On the other hand, practicality must be the deciding factor in many instances. Perhaps the activity in question is not important enough to warrant the expense of the more comprehensive criterion approach. Perhaps the simple, overall rating is good enough. The researcher who comes to this conclusion must realize that he is avoiding important problems, that he is settling for something easy but not quite so good, that the criterion for his criterion has become expediency.

It has been suggested that one might identify the elements of success by,

". . . a factorial analysis of a set of criterion measures" (4, p. 364). While much can be said for this approach, it has two limitations. First, the factors obtained may not have psychological meaning and not exist as separate entities, and second, possible success elements for which we have no criterion measures will not be identified in the factorial analysis. In effect, step 3, definition of success, has been overlooked, and we are dealing only with the available criterion measures and forgetting about the success elements for which we have no criterion measures.

Bechtoldt has pointed out realistically that, "The development of an acceptable criterion is, in actual practice, accomplished by a series of successive approximations" (4, p. 379). When one obtains a criterion composite, it is not time to sit back and relax, forgetting the criterion and its origin. The present inadequacies of job or activity analysis make it necessary to try repeatedly to analyze further the activity which was first done in step 2. The definition of success should also be subjected to periodic scrutiny to insure that all the elements of success have been obtained, that no false elements have been included, and that the proper weights have been assigned. The sub-criteria must be constantly watched to determine if extraneous elements are creeping into them. Also, sub-criteria will be subjected to more exacting tests as our knowledge of the nature of psychological measurements is expanded.

There have been a number of recent studies reported in the literature which deal primarily with analyses of criterion data. This seems to reflect an increased awareness of the crucial role of the criterion in research. Among the more important of these studies are two by Rothe (24, 25) analyzing the output rates of butter wrappers and chocolate dippers, one by Lawshe and McGinley (20) concerned with the independence and reliability of criterion measures for proofreaders, one by Gaier (13) about the criteria of success in medical school, and one by Hemphill and Sechrest (15) analyzing aircrew criteria and providing an example of how objective information may influence ratings.

While this paper is directed principally toward criterion development in the personnel selection field, most of what is said here can be used in criterion development in other areas (evaluation of training, marriage, organizations, equipment, personal adjustment, etc.). It is believed that the general methodology of criterion development, though not well systematized, is present now, but that the basis on which success is to be determined is still undecided and, in large measure, unexplored. A recent article by Bass (3) urges that the concept of success be extended beyond the confines of productivity to include the satisfaction derived from the activity by the individual and the contribution of the activity to society. While this is not a new idea, it reflects a growing awareness of and interest in the effects of an activity on the participants and society. As the basis of success is extended to include individual satisfaction and value to society, the psychologist will be faced with more complicated and more subjective methods of criterion measurement.

REFERENCES

1. Adkins, Dorothy. *Construction and analysis of achievement tests.* Washington: U.S. Government Printing Office, 1947.

2. Anastasi, Anne. The concept of validity in the interpretation of test scores. *Educ. psychol. Measmt.*, 1950, 10, 67–78.

3. Bass, B. M. Ultimate criteria of organizational worth. *Personnel Psychol.*, 1952, 5, 157–174.

4. Bechtoldt, H. P. Problems of establishing criterion measures. In D. B. Stuit (Ed.), *Personnel research and test development in the Bureau of Naval Personnel.* Princeton, N.J.: Princeton Univer. Press, 1947, pp. 357–380.

5. Bellows, R. M. Procedures for evaluating vocational criteria. *J. appl. Psychol.,* 1941, 25, 499–513.

6. Bellows, R. M. *Psychology of personnel in business and industry.* New York: Prentice-Hall, 1949.

7. Brogden, H. E., and Taylor, E. K. The theory and classification of criterion bias. *Educ. psychol. Measmt.,* 1950, 10, 159–186.

8. Brogden, H. E., and Taylor, E. K. The dollar criterion—applying the cost accounting concept to criteria construction. *Personnel Psychol.,* 1950, 3, 133–154.

9. Brownell, W. A., Criteria of learning in educational research. *J. educ. Psychol.,* 1948, 39, 170–182.

10. Edgerton, H. A., and Kolbe, L. E. The method of minimum variation for the combination of criteria. *Psychometrika,* 1936, 1, 183–187.

11. Fiske, E. W. Values, theory and the criterion problem. *Personnel Psychol.,* 1951, 4, 93–98.

12. Flanagan, J. C. Job requirements. In W. Dennis (Ed.), *Current trends in industrial psychology.* Pittsburgh: U. Pittsburgh Press, 1949, pp. 32–54.

13. Gaier, E. L. The criterion problem in the prediction of medical school success. *J. appl. Psychol.* 1952, 36, 316–322.

14. Ghiselli, E. E., and Brown, C. W. *Personnel and industrial psychology.* New York: McGraw-Hill, 1948.

15. Hemphill, J. K., and Sechrest, L. B. A comparison of three criteria of aircrew effectiveness in combat over Korea. *J. appl. Psychol.,* 1952, 36, 323–327.

16. Horst, P. Obtaining a composite measure from a number of different measures of the same attribute. *Psychometrika,* 1936, 1, 53–60.

17. Horst, P., et al. *The prediction of personal adjustment.* Soc. Sci. Res. Coun. Bul., 48, 1941, pp. 20–36.

18. Hotelling, H. The most predictable criterion. *J. educ. Psychol.,* 1935, 26, 139–142.

19. Jenkins, J. G. Validity for what? *J. consult. Psychol.,* 1946, 10, 93–98.

20. Lawshe, C. H., and McGinley, A. D. Job performance criteria studies I. The job performance of proofreaders. *J. appl. Psychol.,* 1951, 35, 316–320.

21. Otis, J. L. The criterion. In W. H. Stead, and C. L. Shartle (Eds.), *Occupational counseling techniques.* New York: American Book Co., 1940, pp. 73–94.

22. Patterson, C. H. On the problem of the criterion in prediction studies. *J. consult. Psychol.,* 1946, 10, 277–280.

23. Peel, E. A. Prediction of a complex criterion and battery reliability. *Brit. J. Psychol., Statis. Sect.,* 1948, 1, 84 94.

24. Rothe, H. F. Output rates among butter wrappers: I Work curves and their stability. *J. appl. Psychol.,* 1946, 30, 199–211.

25. Rothe, H. F. Output rates among chocolate dippers. *J. appl. Psychol.,* 1951, 35, 94–97.

26. Ryans, D. G. A study of criterion data (a factor analysis of teacher behaviors in the elementary school). *Educ. psychol. Measmt.,* 1952, 12, 333–344.

27. Thomson, G. H. Weighting for battery reliability and prediction. *Brit. J. Psychol.,* 1940, 30, 357–366.

28. Thorndike, R. L. *Personnel selection.* New York: John Wiley, 1949.

29. Toops, H. A. The selection of graduate assistants. *Personnel J.*, 1928, 6, 457–472.

30. Toops, H. A. The criterion. *Educ. psychol. Measmt.*, 1944, 4, 271–297.

31. Van Dusen, A. C. Importance of criteria in selection and training. *Educ. psychol. Measmt.*, 1947, 7, 498–504.

Questions for Study and Discussion

1. On what fundamental considerations does the choice of a criterion measure of employee job performance rest?

2. What criterion measures of job performance might plausibly be established for the following individuals:

   (i)   a case worker in a social welfare agency
   (ii) a computer programmer
   (iii) an assembly line worker in an automotive firm
   (iv) an inspector of manufactured electronic parts
   (v)   a secretary

What questions of criterion deficiency and criterion contamination might be raised in each case?

3. According to Nagle, "Spuriously high reliabilities are found frequently when criterion contamination occurs". Why might this tend to be the case?

4. In principle the establishment of a criterion measure of job performance cannot take place independently of the establishment of a criterion measure of organizational performance. Would you tend to agree? Why or why not?

5. An "objective" measure of a student's performance in school is his or her grade point average. (It is objective in the sense that it is data taken from the transcript, rather than a subjective judgment made by, say, an interviewer.) Until recently the University of California system for assigning grade points to the letter grades of students was:

   A: 4
   B: 3
   C: 2
   D: 1
   F: 0

A "plus" or a "minus" carried no weight. Now, however, a "plus" is worth 0.3 of a point, and a minus," –0.3. (Thus for example, a B+ is worth 3.3 grade points.) What might have motivated the change in this measurement system? What are the relative strengths and weaknesses of the former and present approaches?

6. In approximating the ultimate criterion, the problems of the use of multiple criterion measures arises. Should these be combined into a single criterion score? Nagle answers in the affirmative, calling such a unitary score "indispensable." Others disagree, e.g., Ghiselli (1956), and Guion (1961). For a summary of the opposing viewpoints, see James (1973). What are the arguments for and against the use of a single criterion score? On balance, which approach would you favor?

THE DOLLAR CRITERION

H. E. Brogden • E. K. Taylor   *READING 21*

I. INTRODUCTION

It is generally agreed that the most important problem facing the industrial psychologist interested in test validation is devising adequate criteria of industrial efficiency. In spite of this, little effort is usually expended in criterion development. The criteria used are too frequently those most immediately available rather than those which would be most desirable.

This paper emphasizes the need for a common metric for sub-criterion variables, such that the measures obtained reflect the contribution of the individual to the objectives (or, usually to the overall efficiency) of the hiring organization. The principles to be discussed are pertinent to a number of possible common metrics. It is proposed in particular, however, that dollar units, determined on a cost accounting basis, will be found the most desirable units for many criterion purposes. For convenience this discussion will be confined to such monetary units—since the authors believe these to be most generally useful for criterion purposes. In addition, it is their opinion that the cost accounting criterion makes possible a more definitive solution of related problems in the area of personnel selection and differential placement.

The criterion problem under discussion in this paper is the development of an overall index of an employee's value to the hiring organization. The authors are not here concerned with the criterion problems arising in the choice or development of part criteria to be used in validation of predictors devised for measurement of particular job elements.

The Major Criterion Problems

To provide background for the discussion to follow, we will consider, briefly, some of the major criterion problems and indicate the relationship between these problems and the concept we are proposing. The principal problems encountered in the criterion construction are, we believe, included in the following discussion.

1. *Definition of the Job.* Before any type of criterion construction can be undertaken, the job involved must be defined in order to identify a group of workers homo-

From *Personnel Psychology*, 3 (1950), pp. 133–154. Reprinted by permission.

geneous with respect to their job duties. The cost accounting concept may sometimes be relevant in shedding light on discrepancies between apparently similar jobs. This is particularly true where two jobs have common elements but where the relative importance of these elements is quite different in terms of their value to the organization.

2. *"What it is" that Criterion Elements Should Measure.* Definition of the nature of criterion elements is one of the basic problems in criterion construction. The solution to this problem is intimately related to the underlying logic of the cost accounting concept.

3. *Isolation of all Essential Sub-Criterion Elements.* There is probably no practical means of securing a criterion which will take *all* criterion elements into consideration. The writers believe that the cost accounting criterion procedures aid in judging which of the job elements are most essential.

4. *Devising Means of Measuring the Sub-Criterion Variables' Reliability.* The cost accounting concept proposed offers no solution to the problem of reliability.

5. *Avoiding Inclusion of Irrelevant Factors (criterion contamination).* The approach under consideration bears indirectly on certain types of criterion contamination.

6. *Developing a Procedure for Combining Sub-Criterion Measures.* This is the area in which the cost accounting criterion makes its major contribution.

7. *Developing Equal Scale Units.* The procedure proposed aids in the solution of this problem.

8. *Meaningful Units.* A direct solution to this problem is provided.

9. *Sponsor Acceptability.* The procedure by its very nature should yield a criterion that is meaningful and fully acceptable to management.

10. *Demonstrable Significance.* In addition to the foregoing the authors feel that a full consideration of criterion problems requires the introduction and discussion of the requirement that the criterion composite and its individual elements possess *demonstrable significance.*

In constructing predictor variables, the research investigator need not directly justify the use of any type of measure, since the responsibility for determining usefulness of the predictors rests on the criterion, and, of course, on the design of the research study.

In constructing criterion variables, however, it must be possible to demonstrate (by means other than the usual correlational techniques of validation studies) that the on-the-job behaviors measured do contribute to the objective of the sponsoring organization. If use of a criterion is justified only by showing its relationship to a better established criterion, the essential criterion problem will not have been solved. Justification of the second criterion is then required. This shift of responsibility cannot become an infinite regress. The criterion must, in the last analysis, be directly justifiable on logical grounds. To solve the criterion problem, it must be possible to show, as the authors would phrase it, that the criterion possesses demonstrable significance or, if you wish, *"logical validity."*

II. THE THEORETICAL SIGNIFICANCE OF COST ACCOUNTING UNITS TO THE SOLUTION OF THE CRITERION PROBLEM

In discussing the theoretical significance of cost accounting units, two approaches are possible. It will be profitable, we believe, to consider both.

The first grew out of a search for a common denominator or a common metric for combining various sub-criterion measures which are apparently quite different in nature. Suppose that for a typing job, the number of pages of typed copy produced is one sub-criterion variable and number of errors is a second criterion element. How can these two be combined to give an overall measure of typing proficiency suited to the needs of a particular hiring organization? One possible solution was suggested by Otis (6) in the handling of two corresponding criterion elements obtained on key punch operators. In the given work situation, errors were found and corrected by a verifier. The total number of correctly punched cards could not be directly obtained. It was discovered, however, that something over 13 cards could be punched by the key punch operator while the verifier corrected a single error. To obtain an overall criterion measure, 13 times the number of erroneous cards was subtracted from the total number of cards punched.

In this instance the *time* required for two different work units was employed as a means of expressing both measures in comparable units. The time required to correct an error was found to be 13 times that required to punch an original card. The implicit and obvious assumption in this combining procedure is that man-hours required for a given production unit is a fundamental measure of the degree of contribution to the efficiency of the organization. If the principle illustrated in this example is carried further, the possibility of converting man-hours required into the cost of punching a card or correcting an error becomes obvious. Without taking the time to elaborate too far at this point, the reader will note that with conversion to monetary units it would be possible to make allowance for possible differences in salary between key punch operators and verifiers. While in this example such salary differences would probably be small, other cases could be cited where salary differences are greater and assume considerable importance. It would also be possible, for example, to obtain as a criterion measure the amount of supervisory time required by different workers in a given job assignment. Here, man-hours used as a common denominator would obviously fail properly to weight card punching, errors in punching, and supervisory time required into a composite defensible as a measure of the effect of workers in that job on the overall efficiency of the organization.

It should also be apparent that monetary units allow the expression of a considerable variety of additional factors in the same metric. Material wastage, accidents, overhead, etc., can, where they are important factors, be expressed in dollar units and combined to give an overall evaluation. A logical basis is thus obtained for combining elements which were orginally expressed in units having no obvious relation to each other.

The second approach to the cost accounting criterion grew out of the previously mentioned close relationship between this concept and the criterion problem, "What is it that the criterion should measure?" The authors believe that a definition of "what it is that the criterion should measure" must stress that the only functions of the criterion are (1) to establish the basis for choosing the "best" battery from the experimental predictors, and (2) to provide an estimate of the validity of that battery.

Logically, then, the question of "what it is that the criterion should measure" is subsidiary to the question of "what it is that the predictors should predict." Since, in practice, the predictors operate as selection instruments, the question can be rephrased again to ask "what is it that the selection process should accomplish?"[2]

Since the selection instruments determine which of a group of applicants will be admitted to an organization, the characteristics measured by the instruments must be related to the general objective of that organization. The instruments contribute to that objective to the degree that they select those applicants who will contribute most to the general objective of the organization.

In statistical processing, a battery of selection instruments is chosen through validation data to provide numerical scores having as close agreement with the criterion scores as possible. The battery is evaluated according to the degree of that relationship. A perfect relationship indicates perfect validity. Disregarding considerations such as time and expense, the criterion should, then, constitute the most perfect predictor obtainable and should, theoretically at least, be capable of effecting selection of those applicants who would contribute most to the general objective of the organization.

This line of reasoning leads to the authors' opinion to a definite answer to the question of "what it is that the criterion should measure." *The criterion should measure the contribution of the individual to the overall efficiency of the organization.*

To say that the criterion should measure the contribution of the individual to the overall efficiency of the organization leads next to a definition of the objectives of the organization. The general objective of industrial firms is to make money. This statement carries no implication of an undesirable materialistic attitude. Even in the case of governmental agencies, and nonprofit organizations, it is desired to render service as efficiently as possible—and efficiency is measured in terms of monetary outlay. Monetary saving, being the objective of the organization, is the logical measure of the degree to which on-the-job activity of the individual contributes to or detracts from this overall objective. Only after we have succeeded in evaluating on-the-job performance in these terms can we be sure that our criterion measures conform to the objectives of the organization. It seems apparent that examination of the way in which a given employee affects overall efficiency requires that we determine the way in which his on-the-job activities produce objects or services of monetary value and the ways in which his errors, accidents, spoilage of materials, etc., result in monetary outlay.

While this paper is not primarily concerned with the nature of or techniques required to identify the component variables of a composite criterion, it might be noted that cost-accounting weights may be applied only to certain types of variables. Such variables must be expressed in units that can be evaluated in dollar terms. An object produced, an error or an accident can be evaluated in dollar terms; units of rating scales (as ordinarily constructed) cannot be so evaluated. It is believed, however, that unless criterion elements are of such a nature that they can be expressed in dollar units, their use as criterion measures cannot be directly justified and do not satisfy the requirement of logical face validity previously discussed.

This does not mean that the authors propose to leave important areas of job success unmeasured. In practice it is better to employ scales of questionable validity and approximate weighting than to ignore an important area of job success entirely.

III. THE RELATIONSHIP BETWEEN THE COST ACCOUNTING CONCEPT AND TECHNIQUES OF CRITERION CONSTRUCTION

With this overall justification of the cost accounting concept, we will proceed to relate the general concept to techniques of criterion construction. In showing the relationship to these techniques, the concept can be further clarified. Techniques deriving from the cost accounting concept will be introduced in the course of this discussion.

As in the case of all criteria, the variables of a cost accounting criterion must be identified by means of some form of job analysis. In the development of cost accounting criteria, however, it is necessary in the analysis of the job to go beyond the mere identification of the component criterion variables and to determine the manner and extent to which the products or behaviors measured affect the efficiency of the organization. In this additional process, information basic to the construction of cost accounting criteria is obtained. Considerable attention will consequently be devoted to discussion of this phase of criterion construction.

Before proceeding to a discussion of this additional process, we should like to stress one point important in use of job analysis for identification of component criterion variables.

In job analysis for criterion purposes we believe that a clearcut distinction must be made between the end products of a given job and the job processes that lead to these end products. It may be pertinent to such other legitimate objectives of job analysis as training or position classification, to study the exact sequence of operations in the production of the finished product. The skills needed, the tools used, and the methods employed may all be needed for this purpose. Such information does not, however, give a direct answer to the major question, "how much does the employee produce and how good is it?" The criterion problem centers primarily in the quantity, quality and cost of the finished product. While work sequences and such factors as skill undoubtedly do indirectly affect efficiency of the organization, any attempt to demonstrate such effect will lead, first of all, to a demonstration of the way in which skill affects productivity and finally to a *tracing out* of the effect of the objects produced to determine what happens in the organization as a consequence of the production of errors, accidents or finished products. Such factors as skill are latent; their effect is realized in the end product. They do not satisfy the logical requirements of an adequate criterion.[3]

A tracing out of the exact nature and importance of the *effect* of each sub-criterion variable on the efficiency of the organization is the essential step which differentiates the dollar criterion from the more conventional techniques. This technique will, in our opinion, be found useful to the technician in the early stages of criterion construction in which job analysis is ordinarily employed. Its usefulness lies in the possibility provided of obtaining an early estimate of the relative importance of the various criterion elements, and a selection of those elements of most importance in arriving at a practicable approximation to a measure of the total effect of the individual on the efficiency of the organization. Evaluation in dollar units is one of the two variables determining the importance of the given criterion element to overall value to the organization. The second variable is the standard deviation of the given component criterion measures. From cost accounting evaluation and such rough estimates of the standard deviation as can be made before actual criterion measurement, the relative importance of the various possible sub-variables can be estimated. On this basis an intelligent and more exact judgment can be made as to which elements it is necessary to evaluate in constructing the criterion for the actual validation study.

Let us illustrate the tracing out process by taking as an example the criterion variables resulting from actual analysis of the job of a carpenter laying underflooring. We will assume that the criterion variables isolated are: (1) square feet of lumber wasted, (2) damage to equipment, (3) time of other personnel consumed, (4) accidents, (5) quality of finished product, (6) errors in finished product and (7) square feet of underflooring laid for a given time unit.

To trace out the effect of square feet of lumber wasted on the efficiency of the organization, we need only determine the cost of lumber. Records might be kept or supervisors might be questioned regarding individual differences in wastage and the value of the lumber wasted. These estimates will provide a basis for deciding whether or not to include lumber usage as a sub-criterion variable. If it were found that the cost of lumber used varied considerably from carpenter to carpenter, the variable would be included as a criterion element. If the cost of lumber were so little as to be of no consequence or if the amount wasted were practically the same for all carpenters, no measures of this variable would need to be obtained in the actual validation study.

If the equipment were supplied by the company, it would be necessary to determine the cost of repair and replacement. If this amount were significant, it would then be necessary to estimate the extent of individual differences in such costs. The magnitude of these two factors would determine whether or not to include this as a criterion element.

.In tracing out the effect of "time of other personnel consumed" we need only determine the salaries of the various individuals concerned. The actual component criterion variable, weighted in dollar terms, would be the total salary of all individuals concerned for the total amount of time wasted by the individual whose criterion score is being computed. Such a variable would, of course, receive negative weighting.

It is realized that some difficulties may arise in assigning responsibility for time consumed. It may also be true in the case of supervisors that their sole function is supervision and that their time can be utilized for no other useful purpose. No general rule can be given for handling problems such as these.

If overhead is an appreciable factor in the total cost of the product it should be considered in evaluating the dollar value of the contributions of the subjects of the criterion study. Overhead costs, it should be stressed, are not properly prorated equally to each subject. The overhead cost per object produced is much less for an efficient worker than for an inefficient worker.

To trace out the effects of accidents, an evaluation of the cost of repairing the resulting damage would be required. Time of other personnel lost because of the accident, damage paid by the company because of personal injury, etc., would also enter into the cost accounting evaluation. Individual differences in frequency of accidents may, however, be found to be too small to warrant its consideration as a criterion variable in the case of carpenters. In this particular instance, also, the reliability of any possible criterion variable would bear close inspection.

Evaluation of quality and errors in the finished product would require the most laborious "tracing out." Here it would be necessary to determine by observation of, or interviews with, follow-up workers, the additional amount of their time required because of errors or deficiencies in quality. Such a follow-up, if made with complete thoroughness, might involve a large number of different types of subsequent workers and might even lead to the effect of such errors or variations in quality on the final evaluation of the finished structure. In any event the errors, etc., would be classified, and the average additional labor entailed as their consequence, determined. It would be neither feasible nor theoretically desirable to trace the effect of each individual error, since in doing so we would be allowing individual differences in efficiency of follow-up workers differentially to influence the criterion estimates of different subjects of the validation study. It can be seen that such tracing out may become complex since inadequacies in laying the underflooring may not only increase the time requirements for subsequent operations but may cause inadequacies in these subsequent operations which would have to be evaluated in turn.

Deficiencies in the final structure would present a special problem involving salability of the structure and reputation of the construction company. Some overall arbitrary judgment would probably have to be made by the administrators with necessary background for such a judgment.

Square feet of underflooring completed within a given time unit can be converted to dollar units by determining units completed per time interval by all carpenters in that given job classification, and dividing this into total wages for the time involved. In effect, we thus determine the cost of laying a square foot of underflooring or its value to the organization.

Given the cost accounting evaluations of the individual criterion elements and the best available estimates as to individual differences, the importance of each criterion element can now be estimated as the product of these two figures. In the example under discussion it would probably be found that effect of equipment damage is negligible. Thus, this variable may well have been eliminated at the outset or at least after interviewing a construction supervisor. Lumber wasted may also be found unimportant because all workers use about the same amount. Quality of the finished product might possibly have too little significance to justify its evaluation. Whether or not these variables were included, the number of production units would probably be found most important.

It is believed that the tracing out of possible sub-criteria to their end effect on the efficiency of the organization will often lead to results at considerable variance with judgmental evaluations that the technician or management might have made without benefit of this additional information. In the case of the correction of punch-card errors referred to above, it took over 13 times as long, it will be recalled, to correct an error as to punch an original card. It is doubtful if a technician constructing a composite criterion would have judged errors to be so costly.

If the effect of such errors were traced further, it would be found, probably, that the number of errors escaping all checks is a function of the number of initial errors made. Such errors may in some organizations be extremely costly. Some may require effort equivalent to redoing a complete accounting job in addition to their effects on other scheduled work and on the reputation and morale of the organization. If the cost of correcting an initial error by a bank teller, for example, is 50¢ and one in every two hundred errors escaped initial detection and cost $100 on the average to find and correct, the total dollar weighting for each error would be one dollar instead of 50¢. In other words, the weighting would, on the average, be doubled. Experience with the cost of errors in statistical analysis suggests that such a finding would not be unusual.

A single clerical error, to cite an extreme example in another type of work, in the computation of the amount of lead ballast in a ship being sold by the government for scrap resulted in a loss of several hundred thousand dollars to the seller.

This general approach of evaluating importance, in cost accounting terms, leads to consideration of elements that are important to evaluation of overall efficiency but which would probably be generally ignored by usual methods. If, for example, a good IBM tabulator operator produced twice as many usable reports as a poor one, it should be noted that even if they are paid on piecework basis, the rental of the machine is the same in both cases. In a cost accounting criterion, this cost would be taken into account along with many other such items. In the usual rating element or production record criteria, this factor would usually be ignored.

It may be helpful to list factors which will probably have to receive consideration in the proposed cost accounting type of employee evaluation. The following listing of such factors is not intended to be all-inclusive; a careful analysis of each job in relation to the organization will undoubtedly disclose factors peculiar to each.

1. Average value of production or service units.

2. Quality of objects produced or services accomplished.

3. Overhead—including rent, light, heat, cost depreciation or rental of machines and equipment.

4. Errors, accidents, spoilage, wastage, damage to machines or equipment through unusual wear and tear, etc.

5. Such factors as appearance, friendliness, poise, and general social effectiveness, where public relations are heavily involved. (Here, some approximate or arbitrary value would have to be assigned by an individual or individuals having the required responsibility and background.)

6. The cost of the time of other personnel consumed. This would include not only the time of the supervisory personnel but also that of other workers.

So far, we have considered briefly the relation of job analysis to the isolation of criterion variables and have discussed in some detail the nature and importance of the "tracing out" process to the construction of the cost accounting criterion. Given the criterion elements and the dollar weights obtained as a result of the "tracing out" process, the problems of technique of measurement for each criterion element and of combination of the measured elements still remain.

Both of these problems need only very brief consideration. Problems of technique of measurement, while of general importance to the criterion problem, bear no intimate relation to the concept of criterion construction under consideration. As we have indicated earlier, the measurements obtained must be in production unit form for ready application of the cost accounting procedures. Possible adaptations to rating measurement will be discussed later. Other important problems in technique of measurement, such as that of eliminating bias and that of obtaining adequate reliability, would be approached in the same manner as in any criterion construction problem.

The problem of weighting needs only brief consideration because its solution has in effect already been presented. Given the cost of production units, errors, etc., with all criterion units translated into dollar terms, the weighting problem is solved. All variables are expressed in a common denominator and may be directly summed to obtain an overall composite.

In the opinion of the authors, the most significant contributions of the cost accounting approach to criterion construction emerge in the combining of the criterion elements to yield an overall measurement of the workers' contribution to the effectiveness of the organization. Two distinct advantages of the cost accounting technique may be identified: (1) all measures are made in or translated into a single, meaningful metric—the dollar contribution to or detraction from the overall objective of the sponsoring organization; and (2) the resultant determination of the importance of each element in terms of its standard deviation. These two characteristics of the cost accounting approach completely solve the problem of combining criterion elements. The cost accounting units common to all elements make them directly additive; the reflection of importance directly as the standard deviation makes possible appropriate weighting by merely adding of raw score values of the several elements.

IV. SIGNIFICANCE OF COST ACCOUNTING UNITS TO RELATED SELECTION AND CLASSIFICATION PROBLEMS

It has been stressed in the introduction to this paper that the cost accounting approach to the criterion problem makes its most significant contribution, not only in converting the criterion variables to units most meaningful and satisfactory to an industrial sponsor of validation research, but also in offering a sound theoretical solution to a number of important problems in this general area of selection and classification. The ways in which cost accounting units offer a solution to problems internal to criterion construction have already been considered.

An evident extension of the usefulness of dollar units in combining component criterion variables is suggested in obtaining an integration of training cost, turnover, and on-the-job productivity into a single index showing the total picture of the potential value of an applicant. In relating cost of training to other criterion measures, it is evident that the employee whose services are terminated during training represents a loss to the company equal to the cost of selection and training. For the remaining employees, cost of training would have to be prorated over the time spent in the assignments toward which the training was directed. Turnover or attrition assume importance, then, when selection and/or training is costly. Of course, efficiency during the on-the-job training or warm-up should be considered along with formal training.

In a follow-up study of applicants selected by a given battery of predictors, training, attrition and production on-the-job (expressed in dollar terms) could be readily and logically integrated into a single value showing the total value or loss to the organization for the entire period of employment of a given individual. Cost of training would simply be subtracted from the total dollar value of his productivity during the period of his employment.

Elsewhere (2), one of the authors has shown how various statistical constants lend themselves to interpretations which should greatly aid the psychologist in convincing the sponsor of research studies of the appropriateness and adequacy of the criterion measures and the value of the resulting selection procedures. Thus, saving effected per selected individual is given by the mean of the criterion scores of the selected group minus the mean of the population of applicants. The coefficient $r_{xy}\sigma_y$ gives the increase in dollar saving per unit increase in standard (z) predictor scores. In this formula r_{xy} is the validity coefficient and σ_y is the standard deviation in dollar terms of the criterion.

The validity coefficient itself gives the ratio of dollars saved by use of the predictors to select a given number of workers to the saving that would have resulted if selection of the same number of workers could have been made on the criterion itself; that is, it gives the per cent of perfect prediction achieved by use of a given set of selector instruments.

Criterion measures expressed in dollar terms allow determination of the interrelations of the cost of testing, the selection ratio, the standard deviation of the dollar criterion and the validity coefficient. Equations and graphs showing these interrelations have been presented elsewhere (3). When test administration is expensive, the advantage that is expected from a highly favorable selection ratio is sharply diminished. In general, the role of the selection ratio in saving effected by testing undergoes considerable reevaluation.

Possibly the most important of the several related problems to be considered in this section arises in connection with differential classification. Even though regression weights of members of a test battery for predicting success in several assignments have been adequately established, the relative importance of amount of production, number of errors, etc., in the several assignments must still be considered in deciding upon the disposition of any given applicant.

Even though an applicant's predicted criterion score is equally high in both of two assignments, it does not follow that his placement in either of the jobs will be equally profitable to the company. Obviously a man who could do equally well as a janitor or as a manager would contribute much more to the objectives of the organization in the latter capacity. If the criteria for these two jobs were expressed in dollar units, the monetary benefits of this placement would be accurately estimated. In general, the use of dollar units for the criteria of all jobs provides a common denominator which makes it possible to compare an applicant's potential contribution in each of the several positions for which he might be hired.

When the predicted dollar criterion scores taken as deviations from the mean of the applicant population are added for all selected individuals for a given job, this sum is an expression of the dollar saving realized as a result of the selection process.

The sum of such predicted criterion scores for the selected cases (when expressed as deviations from the mean of applicants) gives the total saving expected from one of the several jobs under consideration. Furthermore, sums obtained in this way for each of several assignments are in comparable units and are directly additive. Thus, a "sum of sums" will indicate the total saving resulting from differential placement into several assignments. If the total saving is divided by total assigned cases, the average saving per selected individual may be obtained. This *index of average saving* will serve to show advantages of differential placement and may be used as a basis for determining optimal differential placement procedures.

V. DISCUSSION

A number of investigators have published procedures for weighting sub-criterion variables into a composite. Horst (5) and Edgerton-Kolbe (4) both proposed weighting to give the most reliable and "most predictable" composite. Such procedures are believed by the authors to be unjustifiable unless the criterion measures involve only a single factor. Neither group nor specific factors can be neglected. Since such procedures provide the first principal axis of the configuration of criterion variables, some aspects of the job will most certainly be neglected or minimized. It might be noted in addition that in those situations where the supposition of a single factor would appear reasonable, weighting to provide the first principal axis would afford too little improvement over an equally weighted composite to justify the labor entailed.

Richardson (7) has proposed a weighting procedure which has since been used in combining the sub-criterion variables so that they contribute equally to the covariance of the overall composite. His procedure provides an interesting contrast to the above maximum reliability procedure. By Richardson's procedure the weights are large if the given criterion variable has low average correlation with the remaining sub-criterion variables; by the maximum reliability procedure, the weights are relatively small under these conditions.

We might stress here that weighting according to effect on overall efficiency as in use of dollar units is quite independent of the degree of correlation between the criterion elements. *If it costs 13 times as much to correct an error in card punching as to punch a card, the weights should be 13 and one regardless of whether the correlation between them is high and positive, negligible or high and negative.* If the correlation between two variables is very high, it may be considered expedient to obtain measures of one only and to employ it as a substitute for or as a predictor of the sum. If this is done, however, the substitute for the sum should be made to have the same dollar unit standard deviation as would the sum.

Toops (8) has proposed combining sub-criterion variables according to "guessed beta's" or evaluations by qualified judges of the importance of each sub-criterion variable to overall on-the-job efficiency. His procedure attempts, in part at least, to achieve by pooled judgment the same end that would be achieved by cost accounting criteria—assignment to each element a weight proportionate to the extent of its contribution to overall efficiency. It is difficult, however, in requesting judgments as to importance of a criterion variable to overall efficiency to disentangle the effect of the standard deviation of the sub-criterion variables from the value or importance of a unit of production, an error or some other unit of measurement of a criterion variable. Guessed beta's, in addition, are dependent upon the judgment of the person(s) doing the guessing.

These arguments will not be pressed too strongly; they are mentioned to emphasize the point that the obtained judgments are subjective and are not buttressed by analysis demonstrating the nature and importance of the ultimate effect on the organization of the individual production units, errors, etc., which enter into the final composite. When ratings are employed as criteria, it is probable that judgments such as that provided by guessed beta's will offer the most practicable rational basis for criterion combination.

It is suggested, however, that the procedure might be improved by explaining to the persons providing the judgment, how overall efficiency is best defined in terms of the effect on efficiency of operation of the organization, illustrating with a few examples the way in which various sub-criterion variables have their effect. In effect, then, an estimate would be obtained of the outcome of a cost accounting analysis.

VI. IMPLICATIONS OF THE COST ACCOUNTING CONCEPT FOR USE OF RATINGS

Within the limited resources usually available for validation studies, it is doubtful that all phases of production, errors, accidents, etc., can be economically evaluated through direct observation. Limitations as to time of completion and the intangible nature of certain important sub-criterion variables may, together with the above consideration, require frequent use of ratings to evaluate a number of the sub-criterion variables involved.

Application of the cost accounting procedure to ratings presents certain special problems. With current rating procedures, the significance of the mean and standard deviation of the obtained ratings is questionable. It is probably more desirable, however, to include a rating with inaccurate scale units and weighting than to exclude any important criterion variable for lack of more objective evaluation procedure, since to exclude it entirely would be tantamount to estimating its weight as zero.

In many validation studies, ratings may have to be employed in evaluating all aspects of performance on the job. It is believed that the basic rationale of the proposed procedure does have implications, as yet quite untested, for procedures and format of such criterion ratings. Briefly the reasoning is as follows. Criterion ratings are substitutes for direct observations of effectiveness expressed in dollar units. The adequacy of ratings is, consequently, a function of the accuracy with which they estimate the measures for which they are substitutes. An obvious approach to the problem would be to state explicitly the objectives in the directions to the raters and to have the ratings themselves made in terms of the monetary value of individual differences in the area being measured. The disadvantage of this approach is that it assigns two judgments to the rater: first, he must evaluate the performance of the employee on the behavior under consideration; and secondly, the rater must make a second judgment in assigning a monetary value on that behavior.

What appears to be a more promising technique is that of determining in the tracing out process the continuum on which critical behaviors in a given area occur and to have raters evaluate in terms of these behaviors. If the dollar value of these several steps had also been determined in the tracing out process, these values could then be centrally applied during statistical processing to the ratings. The latter would then put greater stress on recording of observations and less on value judgments on the part of the raters.

In the absence of research data on the effect of such a modification in rating format and procedure on reliability, intercorrelations, and ease of administration, no claim of advantage can be made. It would be desirable, where production records are to be obtained for validation purposes, to collect ratings by both the proposed and some conventional procedure in order that their comparative merits may be determined by showing the accuracy with which they predict the production records.

ENDNOTES

1. The opinions expressed are those of the authors and do not necessarily reflect official Department of the Army policy.

2. This may appear paradoxical in that the predictors are generally considered subsidiary to the criterion. The paradox is easily resolved, however, if the reader will bear in mind the distinction between the problem of establishing content of the predictor battery and that of understanding the objectives of the validation process. In establishing content, predictors are in practice subsidiary to the criterion. In relation to the objectives of the predictors and the criterion, understanding of the objectives of the criterion is subsidiary to understanding of the objectives of the predictors and of the selection process.

3. It is recognized that the relationship between job-process and job-product vary widely from job to job. There are, thus, some situations in which, after establishing the existence of a high correlation, job processes (because they may be easier to observe than job products) may be substituted as a criterion. They satisfy the logical requirement of criterion variables, however, only because of their demonstrated relationship to job products.

REFERENCES

1. Bellows, R. M. Procedures for evaluating vocational criteria. *Journal of Applied Psychology*, 1941, **25**, 499–516.

2. Brogden, H. E. On the interpretation of the correlation coefficient as a measure of predictive efficiency. *Journal of Educational Psychology*, 1946, **37**, 65–76.

3. _____When testing pays off. *Personnel Psychology*, 1949, **2**, 171–183.

4. Edgerton, H. A. and Kolbe, L. E. The method of minimum variation for the combination of criteria. *Psychometrika*, 1936, **1**, 183–187.

5. Horst, Paul. Obtaining a composite measure from a number of different measures of the same attribute. *Psychometrika*, 1936, **1**, 53–60.

6. Otis, Jay in Stead, Shartle et al. *Occupational Counseling Techniques*. New York: American Book Co., 1940.

7. Richardson, M. W. The combination of measures. In Horst, Paul, ed. *The Prediction of Personal Adjustment*. Social Science Research Council, New York: 1941, 377–401.

8. Toops, H. A. The selection of graduate assistants. *The Personnel Journal*, 1928, **6**, 457–472.

Questions for Study and Discussion

1. Compare the "dollar criterion" proposed by Brogden and Taylor to other alternatives for the weighting of multiple performance criteria. (Several of these alternatives are described by Nagle in the preceding reading.) What are the relative strengths and weaknesses of the dollar criterion?

2. Is the choice of a criterion measure of job performance a scientific problem? Or is it a managerial one?

3. Are the tenets of human resource accounting (as proposed, for example, by Flamholtz, 1974) consistent with those of the dollar criterion? What basic assumptions are common to both? What assumptions are not?

4. How does the design of a decision support system interact with the choice of a criterion measure of job performance for its users? (In answering this question it is suggested that the Portfolio Management System originally designed by Gerrity, 1971, and described in detail in Keen and Scott Morton, 1978, be used as an illustration.)

CHAPTER **TWELVE**

Measurement of the individual in organizations is often formalized by means of a *rating system*. A rating is a judgment made about the individual by a qualified observer. The judgment may be relative to actual job performance or to potential performance, as illustrated by the following example.

THE "GOOD BOOK"

Professional football teams conduct annual drafts of eligible college players, and making good choices in these drafts is fundamental to the future success of each team. Sportswriter Bob Oates interviewed Don Klosterman, general manager of the Los Angeles Rams, to ascertain the reasoning behind the Rams' choices. (*Los Angeles Times*, February 4, 1975.) Klosterman reported that the Rams maintain a "Good Book," a compilation of reports on 325 college football players rated by Rams scouts.

As reported by Oates:

"It is possible to evaluate and compare halfbacks against tackles," Klosterman believes. "You can take a measure of their God-given ability. For example, if you see enough film on any player, you can tell whether or not he has happy feet."

Happy what?

"Feet," says Klosterman. "There's never been a great football player in any position who didn't have quick feet."

Is this the first thing you measure?

"It's one of the first things. Regardless of a man's size, 185 or 285, the question is whether he is clumsy or quick. Players with the happiest feet are apt to get prominent places in the Good Book."

When the Rams draft each year, does the club's master list match the page-by-page evaluations in this book?

"Yes, and also the Mid Book—which appraises the next best 250 players. We give every player in the country a grade—a 9 or 8 is high, a 2 or 1 low—and we draft strictly according to these categories. When it's our turn, we never draft a player in the 6 category, if there's a 7 left on the board."

Suppose the 6 is a defensive back—a player you need—and the 7 is a defensive end. You don't need any more defensive ends.

"We take the 7, regardless, because, we feel there's no substitute for quality. We take quality every time. I don't like to use a meat-market analogy, but it's the same thing there. You're going to take the highest-grade meat they have. If their pork chops are top-grade and their steak second-grade, you buy the pork chops even if you want steak."

If you have the money.

"In the draft, we never think of money—of what a player might want. We only consider quality."

The "Good Book" of the Rams contains reviews by Rams scouts of an average of eighteen film reports on each player, plus an "indefinite" number of practice reports, game reports, and personal interviews with the player, his coaches, teachers, and others.

Specifically, what are you trying to find out about college players?

"We have detailed lists of things our scouts look for in films and inquire about in person. They're the usual football things. For instance, does the player sustain his block? Does he appear to have overall speed? How does he tackle in the open field? Does he pass-protect well? Is he a good drive blocker? What about his foot speed on pass protection? Will he catch the ball in a crowd? If he's a defensive lineman or linebacker, does he shed blockers well? Does he have happy feet? Does he pursue aggressively? Does he play with intensity? There are dozens of things like this to check each time. If you see enough film and follow up with a personal visit or two, you can get a good line on the football ability of any player. A good portrait emerges."

A good portrait of a college player, you mean. How do you project this to his NFL potential?

"Well, we're really trying to find out five things about him, and if he grades well in all five we're pretty sure he'll fit the Ram mold?

What do you mean by Ram mold?

"This is a player who has ability, character, toughness, foot speed and preferably good size for his position. If you have those five things you fit the Ram mold."

And after you have all this information, you assign him a final grade of 9, 8, 7 or whatever.

"Yes."

By the way, what does each of those numbers signify?

"A 9 is a cinch to be a starter his first year unless he's a quarterback. O.J. Simpson was a 9. Some years there aren't any. A player in the 8 category is a cinch to make the squad and should make the starting team his first year. A 7 will make the squad and has the ability to start eventually. Players in the 6 category will make an NFL 40-man squad. Those graded 5 have better than an even chance to make a 47-man squad in the NFL. A 4 is well worth bringing to camp. He has a chance to make some club but its doubtful if he has the potential ever to become a Ram starter. A 3 has a slim chance. He's above average in college ability but may lack one or more physical qualifications. We don't feel he can make it now but we don't rule out the possibility that he could develop someday."

Are the 2s and 1s players you don't want?

"Yes, a 2 is a reject with one redeeming quality—size, maybe, or speed, or the ability to do one thing well. A 1 is a reject. Goodby."

Is the grading more or less automatic in an operation of this kind—or is it difficult arranging the players in categories?

"After we have the information, the discussions and arguments are endless. We spend a lot of time fitting each guy into just the right category. Nothing in scouting is more important. Working out the final list—1 to 350 or whatever—is not significant. It's hard to tell whether a Michigan tackle might be the 27th or 28th best player in the country. But it is possible to place him in the right category, an 8 or a 7—or, in a few cases, a 7 plus or minus. The thing that upsets a football scout the most is to assign an 8 to a guy who turns out to be a 6—or vice versa. Categories are everything in scouting.

JUDGMENT METHODS

Judgment methods in evaluating performance may be grouped into three major types. The first, *rating scale methods*, requires the rater to evaluate the individual on a set of specific scales, with respect to various attributes of, say, job performance. The second, *employee comparisons*, requires the rater to compare one individual to another, or to a group of others, usually on an overall performance basis. The third, *checklist techniques*, requires the rater to describe the behavior of the individual, by indicating the applicability of a set of descriptive statements. Each group of methods is reviewed in detail in Guion (1965).

Rating scale methods are often used for diagnostic purposes, relative to various aspects of job performance. Individual scales may exist for quality of work, speed, and regularity of attendance, for example. Scales may assume various graphical forms, an example of which is the following familiar construction:

Quality: High ⌊_⌊_⌊_⌊_⌊_⌊_⌊_⌋ Low

An odd number of scale divisions is typically employed, so that "average" occupies a middle position.

Rating scales have several weaknesses. *Conspect reliability*, that is, interrater agreement, is often low. The *halo effect*, a tendency to rate a person the same way on all attributes because of one general, overall impression, may undermine the diagnostic purpose. *Leniency*, the tendency to give a skewed distribution of ratings favorable or unfavorable, and *central tendency*, restricted variability around the center of the scale, also introduce systematic error into the evaluation.

Employee comparisons may avoid the latter three error sources mentioned above. An ordinal ranking of employees on overall performance is the usual method. *Alternation ranking* is one procedure—the rater identifies the best and worst performers iteratively until the ranking is complete. The *method of paired comparisons* may also be used, in which the performance of each employee is compared with that of each of the others or a sample of the others. The final rank order may further be converted to an interval scale by *normalizing* methods. A *forced distribution* comparison method may also be employed, such as the one used by teachers to grade students "on the curve."

Checklists are common to a variety of judgment methods. With the *method of summated ratings*, the rater indicates the applicability of a set of items describing desirable or undesirable employee behavior. Several response categories, such as "always," "often," "sometimes," "seldom," and "never," are employed and weighted, e.g., 1 to 5. An overall rating is the sum of the response weights for the individual items on the checklist. Thurstone's *method of equal appearing intervals* may also be used. Judges are employed to rate candidate statements according to a 7-, 9-, or 11-point scale based on the statements' reflection of job performance. Means and variances of judges' ratings are computed. Statements with a high variance are considered ambiguous. Unambiguous statements representing the full range of the scale are assembled into a checklist for rating. The overall rating is the sum of the scale values of the items check. *Forced-choice* methods may similarly be applied to checklists. Statements can be arranged in groups from which the rater chooses the statement most descriptive of the individual being rated. The grouping is typically based on pairs of statements of equal "favorableness" but substantially different discriminative ability. It is presumed, for example, that if a rater must give a favorable rating to an ineffective performer, he or she will tend to choose the "nice" statement that can be made of everyone. The purpose of this procedure is to encourage greater rater objectivity, through the avoidance of the leniency effect.

Many variations of the judgment methods mentioned above have been developed, each with its own advantages and disadvantages. Other methods exist. A full discussion is beyond the scope of the book. The reader is referred to any of several authoritative sources on the subject, e.g., Nunnally (1959), Guion (1965), and Green and Tull (1970).

RATING MANAGERIAL PERFORMANCE

Rating systems have frequently been applied to management performance appraisal. Criticism of these systems, early versions of which often focused on personality traits, was voiced by McGregor (1957) who concluded that the approach, "places the manager in the untenable position of judging the personal worth of his subordinate, and of acting on these judgments. No manager possesses, nor could he acquire, the skill necessary to carry out this responsibility effectively" (p. 94). Because of the respect we hold for the inherent value of the individual, McGregor argued, we are uncomfortable when placed in a position of "playing God" with respect to our fellows. As an alternative approach McGregor recommended the now popular "management by objectives" (MBO) technique, which places major responsibility for setting performance goals on the subordinate manager. A similar approach is recommended by Patton (   ).

Nevertheless the use of rating systems in management persists. Edward E. Lawler, in the following article, describes an alternative rating system which, he argues, might be appealing to organizations of the McGregor-Theory Y type.

THE MULTITRAIT-MULTIRATER APPROACH TO MEASURING MANAGERIAL JOB PERFORMANCE

Edward E. Lawler III

It has become increasingly stylish in the last 10 years to be critical of industrial psychology's favorite measure of job performance, the superior's global rating of his subordinate's performance. It is often pointed out that more objective measures are needed and that it is time to become more sophisticated in performance measurement. However, despite impressive pleas for new approaches, the superior's evaluation is still the most frequently used measure where criteria are needed either for research purposes or for personnel decision-making purposes. That is, whether a criterion is needed against which to validate a test, measure the impact of a training program, or whether a criterion is needed upon which to base a promotion or a pay raise, the superior's rating is still the most frequently used measure of job performance. For example, in Vroom's (1964) review of the studies relating job satisfaction and job performance, he found that 16 studies had used ratings while 7 had used objective measures of performance. A review of the criteria used for test validation as cited by Guion (1965) indicates that superiors' ratings are used about twice as frequently as more objective measures and that peer ratings are seldom used.

The superior's evaluation has probably enjoyed its greatest popularity at the management level. The reasons for this are obvious: management jobs are often multidimensional and hard to define; thus performance in them is difficult to quantify and make objective. This is not to say that attempts to get more objective criteria have not been made. Hulin (1962) and others (e.g., Bingham & Davis, 1924; Gifford, 1928; Williams & Harrel, 1964) have used salary as a criterion while others (e.g., Henry, 1948; Starch, 1942) have used organizational level achieved as a criterion. The problems with these indicators are in most cases even more severe than those associated with superiors' ratings. Salary, for instance, is easily quantifiable, but it is a result of a subjective rating to begin with, and then is further contaminated by the economic market value of managerial skills and a number of company policies. Thus, it is not surprising to note that several studies have concluded that salary level in management jobs is not necessarily closely related to merit (Lawler, 1966a; Meyer, Kay, & French, 1965). The same severe problems that exist for salary as a criterion are equally relevant with respect to promotion rate. As Stark (1959) has pointed out,

From *Journal of Applied Psychology*, Vol. 51, No. 5, Part 1 of 2 Parts, October 1967, pp. 369–381. Copyright 1967 by the American Psychological Association. Reprinted by permission.

promotion is a subjective decision that is made on the basis of factors that are often irrelevant as far as managerial effectiveness is concerned.

Organizational decentralization offers the opportunity in many cases for companies to establish profit centers against which to evaluate a manager's performance. This method does appear to have promise; however, it will probably never be possible to evaluate all managers in an organization on the basis of their own profit center. In addition, there is some evidence that unless profit center measures and other objective measures are taken over long periods of time, they can be highly unreliable. Also, there is always a very real question as to whether profit and other objective measures are an accurate measure of the goals that managers should try to achieve in order to perform their jobs effectively. Further, many objective and seemingly relevant criteria may be completely beyond the control of the manager.

In-basket and other business games also have been suggested as potential criteria. They do possess some face validity and may be potentially very useful. However, there has been relatively little research on the relationship between how a manager behaves in a game and his behavior in an actual decision situation. The behavior of a manager in a business game may be quite different from his behavior on the job where the rewards and punishments are much larger. Further, business games tend to deemphasize the interpersonal dimension in managerial performance, while many management jobs appear to emphasize it heavily.

The multitrait-multirater approach to measuring performance has received relatively little attention, but it appears to be potentially quite valuable since it has some of the advantages of the more objective measures and some of those of the more subjective ones. For example, with this approach it is possible to assess the criterion by determining its convergent and discriminant validity, and it is not necessary to depend on an objective indicator such as profits or sales that may miss the essence of the job. The focus of the present paper, therefore, will be upon considering the potential usefulness of this approach both where research criteria are needed and where criteria are needed for personnel decision making. In addition, some empirical data will be presented relative to the usefulness of this method.

The first questions that arise when the multitrait-multirater approach is used concern who is going to participate in the multirater aspects of the approach and what traits are going to be included in the multitrait aspect. One must look first at the potential raters that are available for evaluating managerial job performance. The obvious constraint here is that the rating should not be done by ratees who are unfamiliar with the aspects of the individual's performance that they are to rate. Otherwise, the ratings tend to be more likely to be affected by the halo tendency (Bescoe & Lawshe, 1959) and tend to be unreliable. Thus, the most likely raters for a given manager would be his superior, his peers, his subordinates, and the manager himself. A good argument can be made that each of these raters typically has an adequate view of the manager's performance, although admittedly a slightly different one.

Superior ratings have traditionally been included because it is assumed that the superior has the best overview of the situation and knows best how the manager's job behavior contributes to the overall goals of the organization.

Peer evaluations are relevant because peers are best situated to evaluate how a manager performs in terms of the lateral relationships in working toward organization goals. Further, peers often see the manager at times when his superior is not viewing his behavior and, therefore, they may see aspects of his behavior of which the superior is not aware.

Subordinate ratings are relevant since subordinates are able to determine the superior's impact on what has been called by Likert (1961) the human resources of the organization. The subordinate is also often in a position to observe more of his superior's behavior than are either peers or superiors.

Self-ratings are relevant because the individual's self-perceptions are important determinants of his future behavior, in addition to the fact that he probably has more information about his own behavior than anyone else.

There are many potential traits that could be used in the multitrait aspect of the approach. Unfortunately, there is no easy rule that allows one to state that a certain list of traits can always be rated reliably and validly. The evidence seems to indicate that it is easy to err on the side of providing too many traits upon which to make ratings. On the other hand, as Dunnette (1963a, 1963b) and others have pointed out, the concept of a single criterion is unrealistic, and job performance is a function of a number of dimensions so that one needs to think in terms of partial criteria. The evidence from factoranalytic studies (e.g., Ewart, Seashore, & Tiffin, 1941; Grant, 1955; Rush, 1953) indicates that somewhere around three to five factors is a reasonable number. The question still remains, however, as to the kinds of traits upon which ratings should be obtained. One rating that probably should be included is a global one on quality of job performance. This statement is based partially upon Whitlock's (1963)[2] impressive series of studies on the psychological basis of performance judgments. His data suggest that when people are asked to make global ratings they act in a very predictable way, as efficient processors of critical-incident data from their observations of the individual's performance over the past 6 months. As Whitlock points out, judged quality of performance grows as a power function of the ratio of the number of specimens of effective to ineffective performance. Other studies have shown that raters tend to agree upon the weight to be assigned to the different behavior specimens; thus, interrater reliability is possible. This suggests that simple global-performance ratings may yield a reasonable approximation of what would be obtained by using a more extensive critical-incident or other type of checklist. The factor-analytic studies of ratings have also invariably produced a job-performance factor. In addition, Hollingworth's (1922) data on what traits can be rated reliably suggest that performance dimensions can be reliably rated.

A second reason for including a global rating is that it may help to reduce the halo effect that often comes from overall performance when other ratings are given. The assumption is that including the global rating allows raters to get their overall positive feelings toward the ratee out of their systems.

The question of what other traits should be included in addition to a global one is difficult to answer. The answer depends on the purpose of the study and on the particular types of behavior that characterize the important functions of the job. It may be necessary to develop partial criteria that are ratings of traits or factors like supervising, planning, and others which Hemphill's (1960) studies seem to indicate are the functions that make up a managerial job. The traits that are included should be clearly defined and carefully distinguished from the global-performance measure and from each other. Perhaps one operational way of determining whether a trait can be specified exactly enough is to see if a behavior-description-anchored rating scale can be developed for it. Barrett, Taylor, Parker, and Martens (1958) have found that formats incorporating behavioral description of scale steps were of superior reliability to numerically anchored scales. One test of how adequately a trait can be observed and conceptualized may be whether a behavior description can be developed for the scale points. Smith and Kendall (1963) have used behavioral descriptions provided by employees as anchors for rating scales and they report that excellent discrimination and high scale reliability were obtained. Further evidence in support of adding verbal description to scale points comes from a study by Peters and McCormick (1966) which showed that job-task-anchored rating scales are more reliable than numerically anchored scales.

One important perspective that has been too often overlooked where multitrait ratings systems are created is the development first of a theoretical point of view about what the determinants of effective performance are. This does not mean a theory of whether performance consists of quality, productivity, turnover, or absenteeism, but rather attention to a model like the one that specifies that performance = f(Ability × Motivation). This model points out that job performance has two components—ability (a) and motivation (m)—and suggests that unless separate measures of these are obtained, errors are likely to appear in evaluating the effectiveness of ability tests and in evaluating the motivational systems of organizations. For example, a study that measures the effects of a pay plan by including only measures of performance (e.g., output, quality) would appear to be in danger of missing the impact of the pay program. Output measures are affected by ability as well as situational factors and they might mask the increased effort the workers are putting forth under the new plan. The real test of the plan should be whether or not it increases motivation.

A similar problem can occur in test validation. Ability tests are often evaluated against output and performance measures alone without including measures of motivation. A situation may occur where test scores are uncorrelated with performance measures because motivation is low. The model clearly points out that unless motivation is high, ability will not be related to performance. Thus, the wrong conclusion in this instance would be to assume that the ability measure is no good and to stop testing. A more realistic approach would be to keep testing despite low validity and to try to increase the motivational level of the employees so that the ability differences will manifest themselves. Since there is considerable evidence (Fleishman, 1958; French, 1957; Lawler, 1966b; Vroom, 1960) that indicates the performance = f(a × m) model has general validity, this would appear to be a good place to start. Specifically, it would appear to be reasonable to get ratings on a few factors like effort and ability that are suggested by the model and to avoid the traditional approach of giving a long list of traits including such dimensions as adaptability, friendliness, consideration, etc., which cannot be rated reliably (Hollingworth, 1922). Some support for the belief that the ability factor is a reasonable one upon which to obtain ratings comes from the Ewart, Seashore, and Tiffin (1941) study where an ability factor appeared in their factor analysis of rating scales.

USE FOR RESEARCH CRITERIA

At this point it seems appropriate to turn to the question of what the researcher can gain from using the multitrait-multirater approach, and to present some data concerned with the use of this approach in establishing research criteria. The primary gain from a research point of view is that this approach allows the researcher to develop a much more sophisticated understanding of his criteria than is possible where it is not employed. This understanding can come about partially as a result of being able to determine the discriminant and convergent validity (Campbell & Fiske, 1959) of the ratings.[3]

Convergent validity is demonstrated by the correlations between the same traits as rated by different raters being significantly different from zero. Discriminant validity is demonstrated by three criteria. First, a validity diagonal correlation value should be higher than the values lying in its column and row in the heterotrait-heterorater triangles. That is, a trait measure should correlate more highly with another measure of the same trait than with any other variable having neither trait nor rater in common. Second, a trait measure should correlate higher with an independent effort to measure the same trait than with measures designed to get at different traits which employ the same rater. For a given variable, this involves comparing its values in the validity diagonal with its values in the heterotrait-monorater triangles. Third, it is desirable for the same pattern of trait interrelationships to be shown in all of the heterotrait triangles of both the monorater and the heterorater blocks.

Campbell and Fiske (1959) point out that most studies do not report criterion measures that even begin to approach all the requirements for convergent and discriminant validity. The major problem, however, at this stage in the development of criterion measures for managerial positions, is not so much that ratings often fail to meet the requirements for either convergent or discriminant validity, but that in most studies presented in the literature, it is impossible to assess the convergent and discriminant validity of the criteria used. Given this absence of information, it is impossible to determine if one set of raters, or perhaps one trait, is performing particularly well, and therefore should be the central focus of the study. It is also difficult to eliminate certain traits or raters in order to sharpen criterion measurement for future studies. In effect, where either one rater is used or where ratings are obtained on only one trait the validity of criteria must be taken on faith. If insignificant results are obtained, it is impossible to know whether the problem lies in the criterion or in the predictor.

It should also be pointed out at this time that it is possible for ratings to have convergent and discriminant validity and still not be what would be normally called valid measures of the dimension that is to be measured. For example, peer and superior rankings of a group of managers may agree perfectly so that convergent and discriminant validity are obtained. However, both the peers and superiors may be simply making the same incorrect inferences from observing the individual's behavior. A manager who is seldom in his office and rarely available for meetings may be seen as low in commitment to the organization, in comparison with others, by both his peers and superiors. However, it may be that, unknown to the others, he is spending all his waking hours working on an innovation that will significantly help the organization. This would suggest that despite the existence of convergent and discriminant validity for the ratings on commitment, the ratings would be invalid. However, it is probable that this kind of situation is sufficiently rare to permit placing considerable faith in ratings that obtain convergent and discriminant validity. Still, this example clearly illustrates the point that it is impossible to ever finally validate a criterion. All that can ever be done is to gain information about what it measures.

With the requirements of convergent and discriminant validity in mind, two examples where the multitrait-multirater approach has been used can be considered. The first is shown in Table 1 and was taken from an article by Tucker, Cline, and Schmitt (1967). They had superiors, peers, and subordinates rate research scientists on four traits. Unfortunately, they did not report the correlations for the subordinates' ratings, although they do mention that they did not agree with the peer and superior ratings. Table 1 shows that the peer and superior ratings do not tend to agree on the validity diagonal (circled correlations) highly enough to argue that convergent validity exists. In addition, the data do not appear to satisfy the requirements for discriminant validity either. What is evident from the correlations is that a large halo tendency exists and that the superiors and peers are seeing quite different things.

Admittedly, at this point the researchers are not on completely firm ground with

TABLE 1   Criterion Intercorrelation from Tucker, Cline, and Schmitt (1967)

Traits	Superior Ratings				Peer Ratings			
	A_1	B_1	C_1	D_1	A_2	B_2	C_2	D_2
Superior								
A_1								
B_1	.83							
C_1	.79	.71						
D_1	.91	.86	.83					
Peers								
A_2	(16)	.04	.13	.15				
B_2	.30	(27)	.26	.29	.66			
C_2	.16	.07	(24)	.15	.75	.59		
D_2	.18	.09	.18	(16)	.94	.71	.80	

Note.—$N = 79$.

respect to their criteria, but they can now make more sensible interpretations of their data than if they had used only one set of raters or obtained ratings on only one trait. For example, the variable that the researchers were interested in was creativity. Had they obtained ratings of only creativity, they might have erroneously assumed that this is what they were measuring and gone on to say that their data showed that certain variables were related to creativity. In the present case, because multi-trait data were collected, it is possible to look further at the creativity measures and to determine that they probably reflect the general positive halo of the individual which may be influenced by his creativity.

The second example of the use of a multitrait-multirater approach comes from some data recently collected by the author from a group ($N = 113$) of middle- and top-level managers in a manufacturing organization. Superior, peer, and self-ratings were obtained on quality of job performance, ability to perform the job, and effort put forth on the job. The superiors and peers were asked to do rankings and these were converted to standardized score equivalents of percent position for the purposes of the data analysis. Table 2 presents the correlation matrix for these data. It shows that the superior and average peer ratings have good convergent validity and it shows that they meet two of the three criteria for discriminant validity. The validity diagonal is higher than the correlations found in the heterotrait-heterorater tri-

TABLE 2   *Intercorrelations among Ratings*

Traits	Superior			Peers			Self		
	A_1	B_1	C_1	A_2	B_2	C_2	A_3	B_3	C_3
Superior									
A_1									
B_1	.53								
C_1	.56	.44							
Peers									
A_2	.65	.38	.40						
B_2	.42	.52	.30	.56					
C_2	.40	.31	.53	.56	.40				
Self									
A_3	.01	.01	.09	.01	.17	.10			
B_3	.03	.13	.03	.04	.09	.02	.43		
C_3	.06	.01	.30	.02	.01	.30	.40	.14	

Note.—$N = 113$.

angles (dotted lines) and the same pattern of trait interrelationship is shown in all of the heterotrait triangles, even though there are some differences in the general level of correlations involved. The third requirement for discriminant validity that the validity diagonal correlations be higher than the values in the heterotrait-monorater triangles (solid lines) comes close to being met. This is a rather stringent requirement which as Gunderson and Nelson (1966) point out is seldom met by behavior-trait data. The fact that some evidence for convergent and discriminant validity has been obtained is a significant point since it suggests that ratings of managerial job performance can achieve a level of measurement that is aspired to, but infrequently obtained.

A recent study by Gunderson and Nelson (1966) also obtained evidence for peer and superior ratings on three traits that indicates that they obtained convergent, and to some extent discriminant, validity. Forehand (1963) has found that forced-choice ratings of innovative behavior show considerable promise with respect to convergent and discriminant validity but that ratings obtained on 7-point rating scales do not. Fiske and Cox (1960) also have found that ratings on certain traits can achieve promising levels of convergent and discriminant validity. Thus, it would appear that ratings with a good degree of discriminant and convergent validity might be generally obtainable where well-defined traits are used, where the raters have good knowledge of the managers' job performance, and where appropriate rating scales are used.

Less encouraging are the self-ratings' data presented in Table 2. These data offer little evidence of either convergent or discriminant validity, as the self-ratings appear to be relatively unrelated to the superior and peer ratings. At this point the researcher is in the position of not knowing how to interpret the self-ratings. One possibility is that they are reflecting different, but nevertheless valuable, views of the same traits on which superiors and peers agree. A less charitable view is that they are simply totally invalid. It is true that the self-ratings are ratings rather than rankings and that because of this they are generally inflated. However, they may still be valid despite the leniency tendency if the relative position of the managers stays the same. Kirchner (1966) has found some low but significant relationships between self and superior multitrait ratings; however, he did not report enough data to allow the discriminant validity of the ratings to be determined.

The question of how subordinates' ratings are related to superiors', peers', and self-ratings, of course, cannot be answered from these data. At this point it would seem to be entirely appropriate to focus on this topic in an empirical investigation. A reasonable prediction is that they would probably correspond more closely to the superior and peer ratings than to the self-ratings.

The use of the multitrait-multirater approach offers another benefit to the researcher since it enables him to explore a potentially quite fruitful research area. With this approach it is possible to begin to answer questions such as: what are the factors associated with managers being evaluated differently by their superiors, peers, and selves? This can be accomplished by looking at the off-quadrants in the relationship between the different raters' ratings and looking for moderator variables (Ghiselli, 1963). The data reported in Table 2, when combined with some additional data gathered from managers in four government and social welfare agencies, offer a sample of managers on whom to attempt this kind of analysis. These data are particularly appropriate since job-satisfaction measures and demographic data were also collected for each manager. For the purpose of this data analysis, it was decided to focus on the ratings of job performance. Two off-quadrant groups (a low-high group and a high-low group) and an on-quadrant group were established for the relationship between the superior and the peer ratings, for the relationship between the superior and the self-ratings, and for the relationship between the peer and the self-ratings.

Table 3 presents the mean scores for the two off-quadrant groups and for the one on-quadrant group where the comparison is between the superior and peer ratings. The data were gathered from questionnaires that each manager completed at a group meeting where the researcher explained that the data were being collected for a university research project and that their responses would be confidential. As can be seen in Table 3, they were asked to indicate their age, how long they had been in the same position, their education, and their seniority. Where possible, these data were checked with company records and typically proved to be correct.

Table 3 also presents mean dissatisfaction scores for the three groups in five need areas. The 13 items used here are those originally used by Porter (1961) and contain two parts. The manager is asked to indicate on a 7-point scale how much of a given factor there is now associated with his job, and then he is asked to indicate how much there should be associated with his position. The rationale is that the larger the difference between his feelings of how much there is and his feelings of how much there should be, the greater the dissatisfaction. Thus, the larger the numbers in Table 3, the greater the dissatisfaction.

Two trends appear in the data presented in Table 3. The first trend appears in

TABLE 3   Mean Scores on Demographic and Need-Dissatisfaction Variables for the Two Off-Quadrant Groups and the On-Quadrant Group in Superior- and Peer-Ratings Comparison

	Lower by Peers than Superior (N = 33)	Same by Superior and Peers (N = 82)	Higher by Peers than Superior (N = 32)
Demographic variables			
Time in present position (% longer than 3 yr.)	42.4	37.4	64.5
Time with company (% longer than 10 yr.)	39.4	47.6	59.4
Age (% older than 40)	36.4	56.1	71.9
Education (% with college degree)	66.7	60.0	53.1
Needs			
Security (1 question)	.5	1.3	1.5
Social (2 questions)	.4	.5	.8
Esteem (3 questions)	.5	.8	1.3
Autonomy (4 questions)	.8	1.1	1.2
Self-Actualization (3 questions)	1.0	1.4	1.7

the demographic data which show that the off-quadrant group which is rated lower on job performance by their peers than by their superiors is composed of the younger ($p<.01$), lower seniority ($p<.10$), more highly educated managers (*ns*) than is the group that is rated higher by peers than by superiors. Thus, the off-quadrants appear to contain two different but rather identifiable groups. What may be happening in these organizations is that peers, perhaps through a sense of rivalry, are downgrading the young, bright lights in the organization. This tendency undoubtedly has been accentuated in several of these organizations since they recently have made special efforts to revitalize by bringing in new managers. This finding suggests that when peer ratings are used in a situation such as the one existing in these organizations, an attempt should be made to consider the degree to which they reflect rivalries and resistance to new managers.

The second trend that is apparent from Table 3 is related to the satisfaction data. Those managers who are rated higher by their superiors than by their peers are better satisfied across the need areas than are those managers who are rated higher by their peers than they are by their superiors ($p<.01$).[4] An indication of the reason for this finding can be found in the responses of the managers to the question of how much is there now, which was asked for each of the 13 need-satisfaction items. Analysis of these responses showed that those managers who were rated higher by their superiors than by their peers felt that they were getting more in terms of need satisfaction than were those rated higher by their peers. This, of course, would be expected in an organization, since the superiors control the opportunities that managers have for obtaining many kinds of need satisfaction. Apparently, being rated more highly by the boss than by one's peers is not bad because one still gets rewarded, but being rated highly by peers and not the boss is disturbing because not only does one not get rewarded, one is likely to think that he should.

Table 4 presents the data from the comparison between the self- and the superior ratings. First, with respect to the demographic variables, the off-quadrants appear to be characterized as being made up of the extremes on the time dimension. The higher-by-superior-than-self quadrant in comparison to the lower-by-superior-than-self is made up of the younger managers. (Time in position is the only significant difference, $p<.10$.) Again, what may be happening is that the superiors are relatively more favorable toward their younger than toward their older subordinates.

Table 4 also shows that there is a tendency for those managers who are rated lower by their superiors than by themselves to be more highly dissatisfied than are those managers who are rated lower by themselves than by their superiors ($p<.05$). An analysis of the managers' responses to the two questions that made up the satisfaction measure shows that the difference between two off-quadrant groups comes largely on the managers' answers to the question concerned with how much they should get. Those managers who were rated higher by their superiors than by themselves tended to have lower expectations about how much of the reward they should get than did those managers who were rated higher by themselves than by their superiors.

Table 5 presents the data from the comparison between the peer and self-ratings. Not surprisingly, since the peer and superior ratings are substantially correlated, the results for the peer-self rating analysis are similar to those obtained for the superior-self rating comparison although none of the differences on the demographic variables is significant. High satisfaction appears where self-ratings are lower than peer

TABLE 4   *Mean Scores on Demographic and
Need-Dissatisfaction Variables for the Two Off-Quadrant
Groups and for the On-Quadrant Group in Superior- to
Self-Ratings Comparison*

	Lower by Superior than Self (N = 40)	**Same by Superior and Self (N – 81)**	**Higher by Superior than Self (N – 33)**
Demographic variables			
Time in present position (% longer than 3 yr.)	52.5	40.8	33.3
Time with company (% longer than 10 yr.)	47.5	48.1	42.4
Age (% older than 40)	60.0	54.3	45.5
Education (% with college degree)	50.0	67.9	57.6
Needs			
Security	1.3	1.3	.8
Social	.6	.6	.3
Esteem	1.1	1.0	.6
Autonomy	1.3	1.1	.8
Self-Actualization	1.6	1.4	1.2

TABLE 5   *Mean Scores on Demographic and
Need-Dissatisfaction Variables for the Two Off-Quadrant
Groups and for the On-Quadrant Groups in the Peer- to
Self-Ratings Comparison*

	Lower by Peers than Self (N = 46)	**Same by Peers and Self (N = 68)**	**Higher by Peers than Self (N = 56)**
Demographic variables			
Time in present position (% longer than 3 yr.)	56.5	35.3	38.9
Time with company (% longer than 10 yr.)	54.4	44.1	47.2
Age (% older than 40)	58.7	54.4	52.5
Education (% with college degree)	50.0	73.5	52.8
Needs			
Security	1.3	1.3	.8
Social	.7	.5	.4
Esteem	.9	1.0	.7
Autonomy	1.1	1.1	.9
Self-Actualization	1.6	1.3	1.1

ratings, and low satisfaction appears where peer ratings are lower than self-ratings ($p<.05$). As was the case with the superior-self rating comparison, this came about because of the difference among the groups on the managers' expectation of what they should receive. Higher self-ratings were associated with higher expectations.

In summary, the data show that the demographic variables of age, seniority, and time in position do tend to identify the off-quadrant groups in this sample. Managers with less seniority tend to be rated higher by their superiors than their peers and to be rated higher by their peers and superiors than by themselves. Older managers with high seniority tend to be rated lower by their superiors than by their peers and to be rated lower by their peers and superiors than by themselves. The data also show consistent relationships between satisfaction and the managers' positions in the on- and off-quadrant groups. High dissatisfaction appears where managers are rated lower by superiors than by peers and where managers are rated higher by themselves than by their peers and superiors. Low dissatisfaction occurs where managers are rated higher by superiors than by peers and where managers are rated lower by themselves than by their peers and superiors. These differences between the on- and off-quadrant groups are important because they can contribute substantially to the researcher's understanding of the basis upon which the ratings are made. Thus, a good argument can be made that, in addition to looking at the convergent and discriminant validity of ratings, off-quadrant analyses should be performed.

IMPLICATIONS FOR PERSONNEL DECISION MAKING

So far the focus has been upon the potential gains to a researcher from using the multitrait-multirater approach. There are also some advantages in using it for personnel decision making. Just as the opportunity to establish the convergent and discriminant validity of ratings is important for the researcher, it is important for the decision maker. This approach allows the decision maker to gain a real grasp of the adequacy of the superiors' ratings that have traditionally been used as a basis for personnel decisions. The expectation, therefore, would be that the opportunity to see the degree of relationship among the different trait ratings and the different raters' ratings will add significantly to the decision maker's understanding of what the ratings indicate. The result of this increased understanding is likely to be that decisions will be of a higher quality than if just superiors' ratings are relied upon. Further, the decision maker now has the opportunity of doing off-quadrant analyses which should lead to an increase in his understanding of the factors influencing performance appraisal in his organization. Thus, the same gains that are likely to accrue to the researcher from using this approach are also likely to come to the personnel decision maker if he uses this approach.

There are several important additional advantages that the decision maker gains from this approach, that lie in the multirater aspect of the method. Personnel decision making is at best a rather complex set of trade-offs and compromises, whether it involves promotion, raises, or dismissals. By obtaining subordinate, peer, and self-evaluations, many of the trade-offs inevitably will become much clearer in several important areas, perhaps the most important of these being motivation. It is the stated policy of most organizations that they attempt to reward merit with pay raises and promotions; yet there is also evidence that indicates many managers do not believe that merit is heavily rewarded in their organizations (Adams, 1965; Lawler, 1966a). One of the problems here may be that organizations have not taken careful enough account of peer and subordinate opinion when they have dispensed rewards in the past. Every time an organization gives a reward, it communicates to the members something about the payoff matrix of the organization. Unless an organization knows the perceptions of all its members with respect to the other members of the organization, it can never be sure what it is communicating when it dispenses rewards.

There is one final reason why decision quality can be improved through the use of more than one rater. This advantage accrues from the fact that an individual's peers and subordinates are often in a better position to judge his performance and potential for other jobs than is his superior. Thus, improved decision quality may be expected from the additional relevant evaluations offered by other observers. The evidence with respect to subordinate ratings suggests that they may be valid but the evidence is not extensive. Mann and Dent (1954) have found that subordinates could identify some characteristics of promotable supervisors, and Patinka (1962) reported that less than 10% of those superiors who were presented with their subordinates' ratings of them thought they were invalid.

A rather large body of literature has now accumulated on the ability of peer ratings to predict other criteria, much of it contributed by Hollander (1954, 1956, 1957, 1964, 1965), and the evidence is consistently favorable. It has been demonstrated that after a relatively short period of time reliable test-retest ratings are obtained. Williams and Leavitt (1947) have found that peer ratings were better predictors of long-term success in the Marine Corps than were superiors' ratings. Roadman (1964) has found that peer ratings have validity as predictors of promotion in IBM, and Weitz (1958) found that peer ratings of salesmen during training correlated about .40 with superiors' ratings once the salesmen began work. Hollander (1965) and others (e.g., Wherry & Fryer, 1949) have also established that peer ratings do not tend to become popularity contests.

Perhaps the most important problem with respect to use of peer ratings for personnel decision making is the problem of the research set versus the administrative set. Most of the studies that have been done utilized the research set in getting their positive results. A good argument can be made that if the rater knows it is "going to count," ratings may lose their validity, particularly if a situation exists where an individual's self-interests might be best served by distortion of the peer ratings. However, a study by Hollander (1957) seems to indicate that peer ratings can be reliable and valid even when given with an administrative set. Undeniably, this is a topic that needs further research before wide use of peer ratings for administrative purposes would be advisable.

Leavitt (1964) has pointed out that peer ratings (the same would also appear to be true for self- and subordinate ratings) can be an important tool for allowing participation in personnel decision making, but that they will be effective only when integrated with a participative mood and participative practices in other areas. This relationship is illustrated and elaborated upon in Figure 1. It shows that the validity and reliability of a rating system for personnel decision making is not a simple function of the objective characteristics of the system, such as who does the rating or what characteristics are rated, but that individual differences as well as organizational characteristics modify this relationship. Under individual differences two di-

FIGURE 1   Illustration of the factors that affect the validity of ratings.

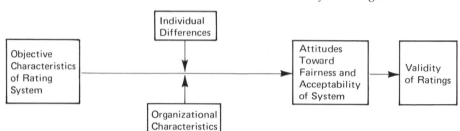

mensions appear to be important in determining reactions to rating systems. The first dimension concerns the strength of the need for feedback and the second is the authoritarian personality dimension. Presumably the more need an individual has for feedback and the less authoritarian he is, the more acceptable will be peer and subordinate ratings.

The assumption, with respect to organizational characteristics, is that in a Theory Y or participative organization, peer, self-, and subordinate ratings will be more acceptable than they will be in a Theory X organization. Attitudes toward the equity and acceptability of a rating system then are functions not only of the system itself but also of organizational and individual characteristics. The final part of the figure shows that the attitudes toward the system will dictate the validity of the ratings obtained. It is assumed that where negative attitudes exist among the raters toward the system, it will be impossible to get valid ratings. Perhaps the key point illustrated in Figure 1 is that a rating system does not exist in a vacuum and because of this no one system will be appropriate for all situations.

If one assumes for a moment that it is possible to establish the kind of organization in which peer ratings and perhaps even self-ratings can be valid, then an off-quadrant analysis approach would appear to be particularly useful. Such an analysis would identify those managers about whom consensus does not exist and then these appraisal differences could be openly considered. For example, if a subordinate evaluates himself more highly than does his superior, he could openly discuss this with his superior and have the opportunity to point out to the superior what data he might be overlooking or perhaps misinterpreting. The results of this kind of interaction might well be a situation where few off-quadrant individuals can be found, but more importantly it could lead to a situation where each individual has more confidence in the evaluation situation because he has not only a feeling for how it operates but also has a chance to participate in it.

ENDNOTES

1. Revised version of a paper presented at the Executive Study Conference, Sterling Forest, N.Y., May 1966. The author would like to thank C. Argyris and L. W. Porter for their helpful comments on an earlier version of this paper.

2. G. H. Whitlock, Performance Evaluation through Psychophysics. Unpublished paper, University of Tennessee, 1965.

3. Campbell and Fiske (1959) consider the multitrait-multimethod approach rather than the multitrait-multirater approach; however, they point out that use of

raters that occupy different organizational positions relative to the ratee can reasonably be considered to be measurement by more than one method.

4. A sign test was used in a manner similar to that done by Porter (1962). For each question the mean score for the lower-by-peers-than-superior group was compared with the mean score for the equal group. An increase was considered a plus and a decrease was considered a minus. A similar comparison was made for the equal group versus the higher-by-peers-than-superior group. Out of 13 questions there were 22 pluses, 3 ties, and 1 minus.

REFERENCES

Adams, J. S. *A study of the exempt salary program.* Crotonville, N.Y.: General Electric, Behavioral Research Science, 1965.

Barrett, R. S., Taylor, E. K., Parker, J. W., & Martens, L. Rating scale content: I. Scale information and supervisory ratings. *Personnel Psychology*, 1958, **11**, 333–346.

Bescoe, R. O., & Lawshe, C. H. Foremen leadership as perceived by superiors and subordinates. *Personnel Psychology*, 1959, **12**, 573–582.

Bingham, W. V., & Davis, W. T. Intelligence test scores and business success. *Journal of Applied Psychology*, 1924, **8**, 1–22.

Campbell, D. T., & Fiske, D. W. Convergent and discriminant validation by the multitrait-multimethod matrix. *Psychological Bulletin*, 1959, **56**, 81–105.

Dunnette, M. D. A modified model for test validation and selection research. *Journal of Applied Psychology*, 1963, **5**, 317–323. (a)

Dunnette, M. D. A note on the criterion. *Journal of Applied Psychology*, 1963, **47**, 251–254. (b)

Ewart, E. S., Seashore, S. E., & Tiffin, J. A factor analysis of an industrial merit rating scale. *Journal of Applied Psychology*, 1941, **25**, 481–486.

Fiske, D. W., & Cox, J. A., Jr. The consistency of ratings by peers. *Journal of Applied Psychology*, 1960, **44**, 11–17.

Fleishman, E. A. A relationship between incentive motivation and ability level in psychomotor performance. *Journal of Experimental Psychology*, 1958, **56**, 78–81.

Forehand, G. A. Assessments of innovative behavior: Partial criteria for the assessment of executive performance. *Journal of Applied Psychology*, 1963, **47**, 206–213.

French, E. G. Effects of interaction of achievement, motivation and intelligence on problem-solving success. *American Psychologist*, 1957, **12**, 339–400. (Abstract)

Ghiselli, E. E. Moderating effects and differential reliability and validity. *Journal of Applied Psychology*, 1963, **47**, 81–86.

Gifford, W. W. Does business want scholars? *Harpers Magazine*, 1928, **156**, 669–674.

Grant, D. L. A factor analysis of managers' ratings. *Journal of Applied Psychology*, 1955, **39**, 283–286.

Guion, R. M. *Personnel testing.* New York: McGraw-Hill, 1965.

Gunderson, E. K. E., & Nelson, P. D. Criterion measures for extremely isolated groups. *Personnel Psychology*, 1966, **19**, 67–80.

Hemphill, J. K. *Dimensions of executive positions.* Research Monograph No. 98, Bureau of Business Research, Ohio State University, 1960.

Henry, W. E. Executive personality and job success. *AMA Personnel Series*, 1948, No. 120.

Hollander, E. P. Buddy ratings: Military research and industrial implications. *Personnel Psychology,* 1954, **7,** 385–393.

Hollander, E. P. The friendship factor in peer nominations. *Personnel Psychology,* 1956, **9,** 425–444.

Hollander, E. P. The reliability of peer nominations under various conditions of administration. *Journal of Applied Psychology,* 1957, **41,** 85–90.

Hollander, E. P. *Leaders, groups, and influence.* New York: Oxford University Press, 1964.

Hollander, E. P. Validity of peer nominations in predicting a distance performance criterion. *Journal of Applied Psychology,* 1965, **49,** 434–438.

Hollingworth, H. L. *Judging human character.* New York: Appleton, 1922.

Hulin, C. L. The measurement of executive success. *Journal of Applied Psychology,* 1962, **5,** 303–306.

Kirchner, W. K. Relationships between supervisory and subordinate ratings for technical personnel. *Journal of Industrial Psychology,* 1966, **3,** 57–60.

Lawler, E. E., III. Ability as a moderator of the relationship between job attitudes and job performance. *Personnel Psychology,* 1966, **19,** 153–164. (a)

Lawler, E. E., III. Managers' attitudes toward how their pay is should be determined. *Journal of Applied Psychology,* 1966, **50,** 273–279. (b)

Leavitt, H. J. *Managerial psychology.* Chicago: University of Chicago Press, 1964.

Likert, R. *New patterns of management.* New York: McGraw-Hill, 1961.

Mann, F. C., & Dent, J. K. The supervisor: Member of two organizational families. *Harvard Business Review,* 1954, **32,** 103–112.

Meyer, H. H., Kay, E., & French, J. R. P. Split role in performance appraisal. *Harvard Business Review,* 1965, **43,** 123–129.

Patinka, P. S. Rate your supervisor program. *Social Science Research Reports.* New York: Standard Oil Company, 1962.

Peters, D. L., & McCormick, E. J. Comparative reliability of numerically anchored versus job-task anchored rating scales. *Journal of Applied Psychology,* 1966, **1,** 92–96.

Porter, L. W. A study of perceived need satisfactions in bottom and middle management jobs. *Journal of Applied Psychology,* 1961, **45,** 1–10.

Porter, L. W. Job attitudes in management: I. Perceived deficiencies in need fulfillment as a function of job level. *Journal of Applied Psychology,* 1962, **46,** 375–384.

Roadman, H. E. An industrial use of peer ratings. *Journal of Applied Psychology,* 1964, **48,** 211–214.

Rush, C. H. A factorial study of sales criteria. *Personnel Psychology,* 1953, **6,** 9–24.

Smith, P. C., & Kendall, L. M. Retranslation of expectations: An approach to the construction of ambiguous anchors for rating scales. *Journal of Applied Psychology,* 1963, **47,** 149–157.

Starch, D. An analysis of the careers of 150 executives. *Psychological Bulletin,* 1942, **39,** 435.

Stark, S. Research criteria of executive success. *Journal of Business,* 1959, **32,** 1–14.

Tucker, M. F., Cline, V. B., & Schmitt, J. R. Prediction of creativity and other performance measures from biographical information among pharmaceutical scientists. *Journal of Applied Psychology,* 1967, **51,** 131–138.

Vroom, V. H. *Some personality determinants of the effects of participation.* Englewood Cliffs, N.J.: Prentice-Hall, 1960.

Vroom, V. H. *Work and motivation*. New York: Wiley, 1964.

Weitz, J. Selecting supervisors with peer ratings. *Personnel Psychology*, 1958, **11**, 25–35.

Wherry, R. J., & Fryer, D. H. Buddy ratings: Popularity contest or leadership criteria? *Personnel Psychology*, 1949, **2**, 147–159.

Whitlock, G. H. Application of the psychophysical law to performance evaluation. *Journal of Applied Psychology*, 1963, **1**, 15–23.

Williams, F. J., & Harrell, T. W. Predicting success in business. *Journal of Applied Psychology*, 1964, **48**, 164–167.

Williams, S. B., & Leavitt, H. J. Group opinion as a predictor of military leadership. *Journal of Consulting Psychology*, 1947, **11**, 283–291.

Questions for Study and Discussion

1. How might the job performance measurement approach described by Lawler be applied within
   (i)   a public accounting firm
   (ii)   a sales organization
   (iii) a research and development organization
   (iv)   a computer software development organization
   (v)   a police department

In which of these organizations would you expect Lawler's approach to have the greatest chance of success? The least chance of success? Why? In general, what would be the major determinants of success for this approach?

2. In general, for what types of measurement systems do the issues of convergent validity and discriminant validity arise? Do these issues arise in the case of the "Good Book" system employed by the Los Angeles Rams for the drafting of football prospects?

3. How might the "Good Book" system of the Los Angeles Rams be validated, on the whole?

4. Rating systems are particularly susceptible to the "for keeps" phenomenon, discussed earlier on p. 285. In some situations raters will seek to "beat the system." For example, consider a performance rating system where (1) a forced ranking is used, so that a high ranking for one person means that someone else must necessarily be ranked lower; (2) merit pay decisions are based on rankings; (3) older members of the work group have reached the top of their pay grade. Such a system is described in Guion (1965). What correlation between ratings and length of service might be expected in such a case? In what ways, if any, is the multitrait-multirater approach described by Lawler susceptible to similar difficulties when used administratively?

CHAPTER **THIRTEEN**

Psychological measurement of individuals is a basic tool of personnel selection in organizations. In contrast to criterion measures of job performance, psychological measures serve fundamentally as predictors. Measures of an individual's intelligence, attitudes, knowledge and personality have all been employed for this purpose. Psychological testing is the basis of measurement in each case.

The history of psychological measurement has shown rapid development since the nineteenth century. Boring (1961) identifies four components of this history: (1) psychophysics, pertaining to the measurement of the discriminatory capacity of the senses; (2) reaction time measurement, based upon the concept of the "personal equation" as the basis of human variability; (3) the measurement of learning or remembrance, based in experimentation, and leading to the concepts of reinforcement and operant conditioning; and (4) the measurement of individual differences, mostly by means of the mental test.

The father of the mental test in psychology was Francis Galton, whose commitment to measurement has beem amusingly described by Boring:

> Galton was an indefatigable measurer. His classical *Inquiries into Human Faculties and Its Development* of 1883 is packed full of measurements and attempts at measurement of the phenomena that he met as he lived his life. He used to carry a paper cross and a little needlepoint, arranged so that he could punch holes in the paper to keep count of whatever he was at that time observing. A hole of the head of the cross meant greater, on the arm equal, and on the bottom less. He "measured" individual differences in imagery in all the sense departments. He carried a "Galton" whistle on a cane to poke through the bars at the Zoo to see how high a pitch the different animals can perceive. He measured many abilities in sensory discrimination and motor precision and proposed to inventory the English nation for their capacies as tested in this manner. Thus he was really the inventor of the mental test, although the term was coined in America by Cattell (1890) in an article to which Galton appended an approving note. (p. 252)

Apparently few individuals could cross Galton's path without being measured!

While Galton sought in his time to test the capacities of the English nation, modern measurers have generally pursued more modest aims, following, however, in the same tradition. A plethora of mental tests now exists, and is widely used in the assessment of individual capacities to serve in various organizational and social positions. The citizen who would avoid such tests is hard put to do so, and would have to forego a formal education and driving a car, among other widely pursued social activities.

PSYCHOLOGICAL TYPE AND DECISION SUPPORT

Psychological measurement has also been suggested as a tool for use in the design and implementation of management information systems. The rationale for this suggestion is reflected in a definition proposed by Mason and Mitroff (1973):

> An information system consists of at least one *person* of a certain *psychological type* who faces a *problem* within some *organizational context* for which he needs *evidence* to arrive at a solution, where the evidence is made available through some *mode of presentation*. (p. 475, authors' emphasis)

This definition identifies the key variables which comprise an MIS or a decision support system. A design for such a system would relate these variables in a particular way, and the suitability of this design would be dependent on various central assumptions. Included among these assumptions would be the nature of the psychological types represented, and the appropriateness of the evidence and modes of presentation for these particular types.

Designers of a DSS may thus be motivated to measure the psychological types of persons for whom the system is intended. Mason and Mitroff suggest that the psychological typology of Carl Gustav Jung is the appropriate basis for this measurement, and that the Myers-Briggs Type Indicator (1962) is a suitable instrument to employ for this purpose. Bariff and Lusk (1977) suggest that two aspects of psychological type are most relevant to user behavior: cognitive style and implementation apprehension. In an exploratory study of the design of a nursing evaluation information system, a battery of standard psychological tests was employed by Bariff and Lusk to measure these two aspects. It was found that reports with minimal complexity would be most suitable to the users' cognitive structures, and that anxiety and resistance to change posed no problems in this case. Driver and Mock (1975) propose a Decision Style Theory which accounts directly for the amount of information used by a decision maker as well as the degree of "focus" exhibited in the use of this data. Instruments to measure these attributes of decision style have been developed and tested.

The pervasiveness of the impulse to measure is thus demonstrated once again. A user of a DSS is a user of measures as has been argued. But the user is also of a particular psychological type, which receives and acts upon the measure, and thus determines the pragmatic consequences of the process. The designer thus turns his or her measurement attention back to the user. Use a measure and you may in turn be measured!

VALIDATION OF PSYCHOLOGICAL TESTS

An important issue in the development of a psychological test is its validation. In the following article, Lee J. Cronbach and Paul E. Meehl review the basic types of validation and offer a theoretical basis for one of these, *construct validity*.

CONSTRUCT VALIDITY IN PSYCHOLOGICAL TESTS

Lee J. Cronbach • Paul E. Meehl

READING 23

Validation of psychological tests has not yet been adequately conceptualized, as the APA Committee on Psychological Tests learned when it undertook (1950–54) to specify what qualities should be investigated before a test is published. In order to make coherent recommendations the Committee found it necessary to distinguish four types of validity, established by different types of research and requiring different interpretation. The chief innovation in the Committee's report was the term *construct validity.*[2] This idea was first formulated by a subcommittee (Meehl and R. C. Challman) studying how proposed recommendations would apply to projective techniques, and later modified and clarified by the entire Committee (Bordin, Challman, Conrad, Humphreys, Super, and the present writers). The statements agreed upon by the Committee (and by committees of two other associations) were published in the *Technical Recommendations* (59). The present interpretation of construct validity is not "official" and deals with some areas where the Committee would probably not be unanimous. The present writers are solely responsible for this attempt to explain the concept and elaborate its implications.

Identification of construct validity was not an isolated development. Writers on validity during the preceding decade had shown a great deal of dissatisfaction with conventional notions of validity, and introduced new terms and ideas, but the resulting aggregation of types of validity seems only to have stirred the muddy waters. Portions of the distinctions we shall discuss are implicit in Jenkins' paper, "Validity for what?" (33), Gulliksen's "Intrinsic validity" (27), Goodenough's distinction between tests as "signs" and "samples" (22), Cronbach's separation of "logical" and "empirical" validity (11), Guilford's "factorial validity" (25), and Mosier's papers on "face validity" and "validity generalization" (49, 50). Helen Peak (52) comes close to an explicit statement of construct validity as we shall present it.

FOUR TYPES OF VALIDATION

The categories into which the *Recommendations* divide validity studies are: predictive validity, concurrent validity, content validity, and construct validity. The first two of these may be considered together as *criterion-oriented* validation procedures.

From *Psychological Bulletin,* Vol. 52, No. 4, July 1955, pp. 281–302. Copyright 1955 by the American Psychological Association. Reprinted by permission.

The pattern of a criterion-oriented study is familiar. The investigator is primarily interested in some criterion which he wishes to predict. He administers the test, obtains an independent criterion measure on the same subjects, and computes a correlation. If the criterion is obtained some time after the test is given, he is studying *predictive validity*. If the test score and criterion score are determined at essentially the same time, he is studying *concurrent validity*. Concurrent validity is studied when one test is proposed as a substitute for another (for example, when a multiple-choice form of spelling test is substituted for taking dictation), or a test is shown to correlate with some contemporary criterion (e.g., psychiatric diagnosis).

Content validity is established by showing that the test items are a sample of a universe in which the investigator is interested. Content and validity is ordinarily to be established deductively, by defining a universe of items and sampling systematically within this universe to establish the test.

Construct validation is involved whenever a test is to be interpreted as a measure of some attribute or quality which is not "operationally defined." The problem faced by the investigator is, "What constructs account for variance in test performance?" Construct validity calls for no new scientific approach. Much current research on tests of personality (9) is construct validation, usually without the benefit of a clear formulation of this process.

Construct validity is not to be identified solely by particular investigative procedures, but by the orientation of the investigator. Criterion-oriented validity, as Bechtoldt emphasizes (3, p. 1245), "involves the *acceptance* of a set of operations as an adequate definition of whatever is to be measured." When an investigator believes that no criterion available to him is fully valid, he perforce becomes interested in construct validity because this is the only way to avoid the "infinite frustration" of relating every criterion to some more ultimate standard (21). In content validation, *acceptance* of the universe of content as defining the variable to be measured is essential. Construct validity must be investigated whenever no criterion or universe of content is accepted as entirely adequate to define the quality to be measured. Determining what psychological constructs account for test performance is desirable for almost any test. Thus, although the MMPI was originally established on the basis of empirical discrimination between patient groups and so-called normals (concurrent validity), continuing research has tried to provide a basis for describing the personality associated with each score pattern. Such interpretations permit the clinician to predict performance with respect to criterion which have not yet been employed in empirical validation studies (cf. 46, pp. 49–50, 110–111).

We can distinguish among the four types of validity by noting that each involves a different emphasis on the criterion. In predictive or concurrent validity, the criterion behavior is of concern to the tester, and he may have no concern whatsoever with the type of behavior exhibited in the test. (An employer does not care if a worker can manipulate blocks, but the score on the block test may predict something he cares about.) Content validity is studied when the tester *is* concerned with the type of behavior involved in the test performance. Indeed, if the test is a work sample, the behavior represented in the test may be an end in itself. Construct validity is ordinarily studied when the tester has no definite criterion measure of the quality with which he is concerned, and must use indirect measures. Here the trait or quality underlying the test is of central importance, rather than either the test behavior or the scores on the criteria (59, p. 14).

Construct validation is important at times for every sort of psychological test: aptitude, achievement, interests, and so on. Thurstone's statement is interesting in this connection:

> In the field of intelligence tests, it used to be common to define validity as the correlation between a test score and some outside criterion. We have reached a stage of sophistication where the test-criterion correlation is too coarse. It is obsolete. If we attempted to ascertain the validity of a test for the second space-factor, for example, we would have to get judges [to] make reliable judgments about people as to this factor. Ordinarily their [the available judges'] ratings would be of no value as a criterion. Consequently, validity studies in the cognitive functions now depend on criteria of internal consistency . . . (60, p. 3).

Construct validity would be involved in answering such questions as: To what extent is this test of intelligence culture-free? Does this test of "interpretation of data" measure reading ability, quantitative reasoning, or response sets? How does a person with A in Strong Accountant, and B in Strong CPA, differ from a person who has these scores reversed?

Example of Construct Validation Procedure

Suppose measure X correlates .50 with Y, the amount of palmar sweating induced when we tell a student that he has failed a Psychology I exam. Predictive validity of X for Y is adequately described by the coefficient, and a statement of the experimental and sampling conditions. If someone were to ask "Isn't there perhaps another way to interpret this correlation?" or "What other kinds of evidence can you bring to support your interpretation?", we would hardly understand what he was asking because no interpretation has been made. These questions become relevant when the correlation is advanced as evidence that "test X measures anxiety proneness." Alternative interpretations are possible; e.g., perhaps the test measures "academic aspiration," in which case we will expect different results if we induce palmar sweating by economic threat. It is then reasonable to inquire about other *kinds* of evidence.

Add these facts from further studies: Test X correlates .45 with fraternity brothers' ratings on "tenseness." Test X correlates .55 with amount of intellectual inefficiency induced by painful electric shock, and .68 with the Taylor Anxiety scale. Mean X score decreases among four diagnosed groups in this order: anxiety state, reactive depression, "normal," and psychopathic personality. And palmar sweat under threat of failure in Psychology I correlates .60 with threat of failure in mathematics. Negative results eliminate competing explanations of the X score; thus, findings of negligible correlations between X and social class, vocational aim, and value-orientation make it fairly safe to reject the suggestion that X measures "academic aspiration." We can have substantial confidence that X does measure anxiety proneness if the current theory of anxiety can embrace the variates which yield positive correlations, and does not predict correlations where we found none.

KINDS OF CONSTRUCTS

At this point we should indicate summarily what we mean by a construct, recognizing that much of the remainder of the paper deals with this question. *A construct is some postulated attribute of people, assumed to be reflected in test performance.* In test validation the attribute about which we make statements in interpreting a test is a construct. We expect a person at any time to possess or not possess a qualitative attribute (amnesia) or structure, or to possess some degree of a quantitative attribute (cheerfulness). A construct has certain associated meanings carried in statements of this general character: Persons who possess this attribute will, in situation X, act in manner Y (with a stated probability). The logic of construct validation is invoked whether the construct is highly systematized or loose, used in ramified theory or a few simple propositions, used in absolute propositions or probability statements. We seek to specify how one is to defend a proposed interpretation of a test; *we are not recommending any one type of interpretation.*

The constructs in which tests are to be interpreted are certainly not likely to be physiological. Most often they will be traits such as "latent hostility" or "variable in mood," or descriptions in terms of an educational objective, as "ability to plan experiments." For the benefit of readers who may have been influenced by certain eisegeses of MacCorquodale and Meehl (40), let us here emphasize: Whether or not an interpretation of a test's properties or relations involves questions of construct validity is to be decided by examining the entire body of evidence offered, together with what is asserted about the test in the context of this evidence. Proposed identifications of constructs allegedly measured by the test with constructs of other sciences (e.g., genetics, neuroanatomy, biochemistry) make up only *one* class of construct-validity claims, and a rather minor one at present. Space does not permit full analysis of the relation of the present paper to the MacCorquodale-Meehl distinction between hypothetical constructs and intervening variables. The philosophy of science pertinent to the present paper is set forth later in the section entitled, "The nomological network."

THE RELATION OF CONSTRUCTS TO "CRITERIA"

Critical View of the Criterion Implied

An unquestionable criterion may be found in a practical operation, or may be established as a consequence of an operational definition. Typically, however, the psychologist is unwilling to use the directly operational approach because he is interested in building theory about a generalized construct. A theorist trying to relate behavior to "hunger" almost certainly invests that term with meanings other than the operation "elapsed-time-since-feeding." If he is concerned with hunger as a tissue need, he will not accept time lapse as *equivalent* to his construct because it fails to consider, among other things, energy expenditure of the animal.

In some situations the criterion is no more valid than the test. Suppose, for example, that we want to know if counting the dots on Bender-Gestalt figure five indicates "compulsive rigidity," and take psychiatric ratings on this trait as a criterion. Even a conventional report on the resulting correlation will say something about the extent and intensity of the psychiatrist's contacts and should describe his qualifications (e.g., diplomate status? analyzed?).

Why report these facts? Because data are needed to indicate whether the criterion is any good. "Compulsive rigidity" is not really intended to mean "social stimulus value to psychiatrists." The implied trait involves a range of behavior-dispositions which may be very imperfectly sampled by the psychiatrist. Suppose dot-counting does not occur in a particular patient and yet we find that the psychiatrist has rated him as "rigid." When questioned the psychiatrist tells us that the patient was a rather easy, free-wheeling sort; however, the patient *did* lean over to straighten out a skewed desk blotter, and this, viewed against certain other facts, tipped the scale in favor of "rigid" rating. On the face of it, counting Bender dots may be just as good (or poor) a sample of compulsive-rigidity domain as straightening desk blotters is.

Suppose, to extend our example, we have four tests on the "predictor" side, over against the psychiatrist's "criterion," and find generally positive correlations among the five variables. Surely it is artificial and arbitrary to impose the "test-should-predict-criterion" pattern on such data. The psychiatrist samples verbal content, expressive pattern, voice, posture, etc. The psychologist samples verbal content, perception, expressive pattern, etc. Our proper conclusion is that, from this evidence, the four tests and the psychiatrist all assess some common factor.

The asymmetry between the "test" and the so-designated "criterion" arises only because the terminology of predictive validity has become a commonplace in test analysis. In this study where a construct is the central concern, any distinction between the merit of the test and criterion variables would be justified only if it had already been shown that the psychiatrist's theory and operations were excellent measures of the attribute.

INADEQUACY OF VALIDATION IN TERMS OF SPECIFIC CRITERIA

The proposal to validate constructual interpretations of tests runs counter to suggestions of some others. Spiker and McCandless (57) favor an operational approach. Validation is replaced by compiling statements as to how strongly the test predicts other observed variables of interest. To avoid requiring that each new variable be investigated completely by itself, they allow two variables to collapse into one whenever the properties of the operationally defined measures are the same: "If a new test is demonstrated to predict the scores on an older, well-established test, then an evaluation of the predictive power of the older test may be used for the new one." But accurate inferences are possible only if the two tests correlate so highly that there is negligible reliable variance in either test, independent of the other. Where the correspondence is less close, one must either retain all the separate variables operationally defined or embark on construct validation.

The practical user of tests must rely on constructs of some generality to make predictions about new situations. Test X could be used to predict palmar sweating in the face of failure without invoking any construct, but a counselor is more likely to be asked to forecast behavior in diverse or even unique situations for which the correlation of test X is unknown. Significant predictions rely on knowledge accumulated around the generalized construct of anxiety. The *Technical Recommendations* state:

It is ordinarily necessary to evaluate construct validity by integrating evidence from many different sources. The problem of construct validation becomes especially acute in the clinical field since for many of the constructs dealt with it is not a question of finding an imperfect criterion but of finding any criterion at all. The psychologist interested in construct validity for clinical devices is concerned with making an estimate of a hypothetical internal process, factor, system, structure, or state and cannot expect to find a clear unitary behavior criterion. An attempt to identify any one criterion measure or any composite as *the* criterion aimed at is, however, usually unwarranted (59, p. 14–15).

This appears to conflict with arguments for specific criteria prominent at places in the testing literature. Thus Anastasi (2) makes many statements of the latter character: "It is only a measure of a specifically defined criterion that a test can be objectively validated at all . . . To claim that a test measures anything over and above its criterion is pure speculation" (p. 67). Yet elsewhere this article supports construct validation. Tests can be profitably interpreted if we "know the relationships between the tested behavior . . . and other behavior samples, none of these behavior samples necessarily occupying the preeminent position of a criterion" (p. 75). Factor analysis with several partial criteria might be used to study whether a test measures a postulated "general learning ability." If the data demonstrate specificity of ability instead, such specificity is "useful in its own right in advancing our knowledge of behavior; it should not be construed as a weakness of the tests" (p. 75).

We depart from Anastasi at two points. She writes, "The validity of a psychological test should not be confused with an analysis of the factors which determine the behavior under consideration." We, however, regard such analysis as a most important type of validation. Second, she refers to "the will-o'-the-wisp of psychological processes which are distinct from performance" (2, p. 77). While we agree that psychological processes are elusive, we are sympathetic to attempts to formulate and clarify constructs which are evidenced by performance but distinct from it. Surely an inductive inference based on a pattern of correlations cannot be dismissed as "pure speculation."

Specific Criteria Used Temporarily: The "Bootstraps" Effect

Even when a test is constructed on the basis of a specific criterion, it may ultimately be judged to have greater construct validity than the criterion. We start with a vague concept which we associate with certain observations. We then discover empirically that these observations covary with some other observation which possesses greater reliability or is more intimately correlated with relevant experimental changes than is the original measure, or both. For example, the notion of temperature arises because some objects feel hotter to the touch than others. The expansion of a mercury column does not have face validity as an index of hotness. But it turns out that (*a*) there is a statistical relation between expansion and sensed temperature; (*b*) observers employ the mercury method with good interobserver agreement; (*c*) the regularity of observed relations is increased by using the thermometer (e.g., melting points of samples of the same material vary little on the thermometer; we obtain nearly linear relations between mercury measures and pressure of a gas). Finally, (*d*) a theoretical structure involving unobservable microevents—the kinetic theory—is worked out which explains the relation of mercury expansion to heat. This whole process of conceptual enrichment begins with what in retrospect we see as an extremely fallible "criterion"—the human temperature sense. That original criterion has now been relegated to a peripheral position. We have lifted ourselves by our bootstraps, but in a legitimate and fruitful way.

Similarly, the Binet scale was first valued because children's scores tended to agree with judgments by schoolteachers. If it had not shown this agreement, it would have been discarded along with reaction time and the other measures of ability previously tried. Teacher judgments once constituted the criterion against which the individual intelligence test was validated. But if today a child's IQ is 135 and three of his teachers complain about how stupid he is, we do not conclude that the test has failed. Quite to the contrary, if no error in test procedure can be argued, we treat the test score as a valid statement about an important quality, and define our task as that of finding out what other variables—personality, study skills, etc.—modify achievement or distort teacher judgment.

EXPERIMENTATION TO INVESTIGATE CONSTRUCT VALIDITY

Validation Procedures

We can use many methods in construction validation. Attention should particularly be drawn to Macfarlane's survey of these methods as they apply to protective devices (41).

Group Differences

If our understanding of a construct leads us to expect two groups to differ on the test, this expectation may be tested directly. Thus Thurstone and Chave validated the Scale for Measuring Attitude Toward the Church by showing score differences between church members and nonchurchgoers. Churchgoing is not *the* criterion of attitude, for the purpose of the test is to measure something other than the crude sociological fact of church attendance; on the other hand, failure to find a difference would have seriously challenged the test.

Only coarse correspondence between test and group designation is expected. Too great a correspondence between the two would indicate that the test is to some degree invalid, because members of the groups are expected to overlap on the test. Intelligence test items are selected initially on the basis of a correspondence to age, but an item that correlates .95 with age in an elementary school sample would surely be suspect.

Correlation Matrices and Factor Analysis

If two tests are presumed to measure the same construct, a correlation between them is predicted. (An exception is noted where some second attribute has positive loading in the first test and negative loading in the second test; then a low correlation is expected. This is a testable interpretation provided an external measure of either the first or the second variable exists.) If the obtained correlation departs from the expectation, however, there is no way to know whether the fault lies in test A, test B, or the formulation of the construct. A matrix of intercorrelations often points out profitable ways of dividing the construct into more meaningful parts, factor analysis being a useful computational method in such studies.

Guilford (26) has discussed the place of factor analysis in construct validation. His statements may be extracted as follows:

"The personnel psychologist wishes to know 'why his tests are valid.' He can place tests and practical criteria in a matrix and factor it to identify 'real dimensions of human personality.' A factorial description is exact and stable; it is economical in explanation; it leads to the creation of pure tests which can be combined to predict complex behaviors." It is clear that factors here function as constructs. Eysenck, in his "criterion analysis" (18), goes farther than Guilford, and shows that factoring can be used explicitly to test hypotheses about constructs.

Factors may or may not be weighted with surplus meaning. Certainly when they are regarded as "real dimensions" a great deal of surplus meaning is implied, and the interpreter must shoulder a substantial burden of proof. The alternative view is to regard factors as defining a working reference frame, located in a convenient manner in the "space" defined by all behaviors of a given type. Which set of factors from a given matrix is "most useful" will depend partly on predilections, but in essence the best construct is the one around which we can build the greatest number of inferences, in the most direct fashion.

Studies of Internal Structure

For many constructs, evidence of homogeneity within the test is relevant in judging validity. If a trait such as *dominance* is hypothesized, and the items inquire about behaviors subsumed under this label, then the hypothesis appears to require that these items be generally intercorrelated. Even low correlations, if consistent, would support the argument that people may be fruitfully described in terms of a generalized tendency to dominate or not dominate. The general quality would have power to predict behavior in a variety of situations represented by the specific items. Item-test correlations and certain reliability formulas describe internal consistency.

It is unwise to list uninterpreted data of this sort under the heading "validity" in test manuals, as some authors have done. High internal consistency may *lower* validity. Only if the underlying theory of the trait being measured calls for high item intercorrelations do the correlations support construct validity. Negative item-test correlations may support construct validity, provided that the items with negative correlations are believed irrelevant to the postulated construct and serve as suppressor variables (31, p. 431–436; 44).

Study of distinctive subgroups of items within a test may set an upper limit to construct validity by showing that irrelevant elements influence scores. Thus a study of the PMA space tests shows that variance can be partially accounted for by a response set, tendency to mark many figures as similar (12). An internal factor analysis of the PEA Interpretation of Data Test shows that in addition to measuring reasoning skills, the test score is strongly influenced by a tendency to say "probably true" rather than "certainly true," regardless of item content (17). On the other hand, a study of item groupings in the DAT Mechanical Comprehension Test permitted rejection of the hypothesis that knowledge about specific topics such as gears made a substantial contribution to scores (13).

Studies of Change over Occasions

The stability of test scores ("retest reliability," Cattell's "N-technique") may be relevant to construct validation. Whether a high degree of stability is encouraging or discouraging for the proposed interpretation depends upon the theory defining the construct.

More powerful than the retest after uncontrolled intervening experiences is the retest with experimental intervention. If a transient influence swings test scores over a wide range, there are definite limits on the extent to which a test result can be interpreted as reflecting the typical behavior of the individual. These are examples of experiments which have indicated upper limits to test validity: studies of differences associated with the examiner in projective testing, of change of score under alternative directions ("tell the truth" vs. "make yourself look good to an employer"), and of coachability of mental tests. We may recall Gulliksen's distinction (27): When the coaching is of a sort that improves the pupil's intellectual functioning in school, the test which is affected by the coaching has validity as a measure of intellectual functioning; if the coaching improves test taking but not school performance, the test which responds to the coaching has poor validity as a measure of this construct.

Sometimes, where differences between individuals are difficult to assess by any means other than the test, the experimenter validates by determining whether the test can detect induced intra-individual differences. One might hypothesize that the Zeigarnik effect is a measure of ego involvement, i.e., that with ego involvement there is more recall of incomplete tasks. To support such an interpretation, the investigator will try to induce ego involvement on some task by appropriate directions and compare subjects' recall with their recall for tasks where there was a contrary induction. Sometimes the intervention is drastic. Porteus finds (53) that brain-operated patients show disruption of performance on his maze, but do not show impaired performance on conventional verbal tests and argues therefrom that his test is a better measure of planfulness.

Studies of Process

One of the best ways of determining informally what accounts for variability on a test is the observation of the person's process of performance. If it is supposed, for example, that a test measures mathematical competence, and yet observation of students' errors shows that erroneous reading of the question is common, the implications of a low score are altered. Lucas in this way showed that the Navy Relative Movement Test, an aptitude test, actually involved two different abilities: a spatial visualization and mathematical reasoning (39).

Mathematical analysis of scoring procedures may provide important negative evidence on construct validity. A recent analysis of "empathy" tests is perhaps worth citing (14). "Empathy" has been operationally defined in many studies by the ability of a judge to predict what responses will be given on some questionnaire by a subject he has observed briefly. A mathematical argument has shown, however, that the scores depend on several attributes of the judge which enter into his perception of *any* individual, and that they therefore cannot be interpreted as evidence of his ability to interpret cues offered by particular others, or his intuition.

The Numerical Estimate of Construct Validity

There is an understandable tendency to seek a "construct validity coefficient." A numerical statement of the degree of construct validity would be a statement of the proportion of the test score variance that is attributable to the construct variable. This numerical evidence can sometimes be arrived at by a factor analysis, but since present methods of factor analysis are based on linear relations, more general methods will ultimately be needed to deal with many quantitative problems of construct validation.

Rarely will it be possible to estimate definite "construct saturations," because no factor corresponding closely to the construct will be available. One can only hope to set upper and lower bounds to the "loading." If "creativity" is defined as something independent of knowledge, then a correlation of .40 between a presumed test of creativity and a test of arithmetic knowledge would indicate that at least 16 per cent of the reliable test variance is irrelevant to creativity as defined. Laboratory performance on problems such as Maier's "hatrack" would scarcely be an ideal measure of creativity, but it would be somewhat relevant. If its correlation with the test is .60, this permits a tentative estimate of 36 per cent as a lower bound. (The estimate is tentative because the test might overlap with the irrelevant portion of the laboratory measure.) The saturation seems to lie between 36 and 84 per cent; a cumulation of studies would provide better limits.

It should be particularly noted that rejecting the null hypothesis does not finish the job of construct validation (35, p. 284). The problem is not to conclude that the test "is valid" for measuring the construct variable. The task is to state as definitely as possible the degree of validity the test is presumed to have.

THE LOGIC OF CONSTRUCT VALIDATION

Construct validation takes place when an investigator believes that his instrument reflects a particular construct, to which are attached certain meanings. The proposed interpretation generates specific testable hypotheses, which are a means of confirming or disconfirming the claim. The philosophy of science which we believe does most justice to actual scientific practice will now be briefly and dogmatically set forth. Readers interested in further study of the philosophical underpinning are referred to the works by Braithwaite (6, especially Chapter III), Carnap (7; 8, pp. 56–69), Pap (51), Sellars (55, 56), Feigl (19, 20), Beck (4), Kneale (37, pp. 92–110), Hempel (29; 30, Sec. 7).

The Nomological Net

The fundamental principles are these:

1. Scientifically speaking, to "make clear what something *is*" means to set forth the laws in which it occurs. We shall refer to the interlocking system of laws which constitute a theory as a *nomological network.*

2. The laws in a nomological network may relate (*a*) observable properties or quantities to each other; or (*b*) theoretical constructs to observables; or (*c*) different theoretical constructs to one another. These "laws" may be statistical or deterministic.

3. A necessary condition for a construct to be scientifically admissible is that it occur in a nomological net, at least *some* of whose laws involve observables. Admissible constructs may be remote from observation, i.e., a long derivation may intervene

between the nomologicals which implicitly define the construct, and the (derived) nomologicals of type *a*. These latter propositions permit predictions about events. The construct is not "reduced" to the observations, but only combined with other constructs in the net to make predictions about observables.

4. "Learning more about" a theoretical construct is a matter of elaborating the nomological network in which it occurs, or of increasing the definiteness of the components. At least in the early history of a construct the network will be limited, and the construct will as yet have few connections.

5. An enrichment of the net such as adding a construct or a relation to theory is justified if it generates nomologicals that are confirmed by observation or if it reduces the number of nomologicals required to predict the same observations. When observations will not fit into the network as it stands, the scientist has a certain freedom in selecting where to modify the network. That is, there may be alternative constructs or ways of organizing the net which for the time being are equally defensible.

6. We can say that "operations" which are qualitatively very different "overlap" or "measure the same thing" if their positions in the nomological net tie them to the same construct variable. Our confidence in this identification depends upon the amount of inductive support we have for the regions of the net involved. It is not necessary that a direct observational comparison of the two operations be made—we may be content with an intranetwork proof indicating that the two operations yield estimates of the same network-defined quantity. Thus, physicists are content to speak of the "temperature" of the sun and the "temperature" of a gas at room temperature even though the test operations are nonoverlapping because this identification makes theoretical sense.

With these statements of scientific methodology in mind, we return to the specific problem of construct validity as applied to psychological tests. The preceding guide rules should reassure the "toughminded," who fear that allowing construct validation opens the door to nonconfirmable test claims. *The answer is that unless the network makes contact with observations, and exhibits explicit, public steps of inference, construct validation cannot be claimed.* An admissible psychological construct must be behavior-relevant (59, p. 15). For most tests intended to measure constructs, adequate criteria do not exist. This being the case, many such tests have been left unvalidated, or a finespun network of rationalizations has been offered as if it were validation. Rationalization is not construct validation. One who claims that his test reflects a construct cannot maintain his claim in the face of recurrent negative results because these results show that his construct is too loosely defined to yield verifiable inferences.

A rigorous (though perhaps probabilistic) chain of inference is required to establish a test as a measure of a construct. To validate a claim that a test measures a construct, a nomological net surrounding the concept must exist. When a construct is fairly new, there may be few specifiable associations by which to pin down the concept. As research proceeds, the construct sends out roots in many directions, which attach it to more and more facts or other constructs. Thus the electron has more accepted properties than the neutrino; *numerical ability* has more than *the second space factor*.

"Acceptance," which was critical in criterion-oriented and content validities, has now appeared in construct validity. Unless substantially the same nomological net is accepted by the several users of the construct, public validation is impossible. If A uses *aggressiveness* to mean overt assault on others, and B's usage includes repressed hostile reactions, evidence which convinces B that a test measures *aggressiveness* convinces A that the test does not. Hence, the investigator who proposes to establish a test as a measure of a construct must specify his network or theory sufficiently clearly that others cannot accept or reject it (cf. 41, p. 406). A consumer of the test who rejects the author's theory cannot accept the author's validation. He must validate the test for himself, if he wishes to show that it represents the construct as *he* defines it.

Two general qualifications are in order with reference to the methodological principles 1–6 set forth at the beginning of this section. Both of them concern the amount of "theory," in any high-level sense of that word, which enters into a construct-defining network of laws or lawlike statements. We do not wish to convey the impression that one always has a very elaborate theoretical network, rich in hypothetical processes or entities.

Constructs as Inductive Summaries

In the early stages of development of a construct or even at more advanced stages when our orientation is thoroughly practical, little or no theory in the usual sense of the word need be involved. In the extreme case the hypothesized laws are formulated entirely in terms of descriptive (observational) dimensions although not all of the relevant observations have actually been made.

The hypothesized network "goes beyond the data" only in the limited sense that it purports to *characterize* the behavior facets which belong to an observable but as yet only partially sampled cluster; hence, it generates predictions about hitherto unsampled regions of the phenotypic space. Even though no unobservables or high-order theoretical constructs are introduced, an element of inductive extrapolation appears in the claim that a cluster including some elements not-yet-observed has been identified. Since, as in any sorting or abstracting task involving a finite set of complex elements, several nonequivalent bases of categorization are available, the investigator may choose a hypothesis which generates erroneous predictions. The failure of a supposed, hitherto untried, member of the cluster to behave in the manner said to be characteristic of the group, or the finding that a nonmember of the postulated cluster does behave in this manner, may modify greatly our tentative construct.

For example, one might build an intelligence test on the basis of his background notions of "intellect," including vocabulary, arithmetic calculation, general information, similarities, two-point threshold, reaction time, and line bisection as subtests. The first four of these correlate, and he extracts a huge first factor. This becomes a second approximation of the intelligence construct, described by its pattern of loadings on the four tests. The other three tests have negligible loading on any common factor. On this evidence the investigator reinterprets intelligence as "manipulation of words." Subsequently it is discovered that test-stupid people are rated as unable to express their ideas, are easily taken in by fallacious arguments, and misread complex directions. These data support the "linguistic" definition of intelligence and the test's claim of validity *for* that construct. But then a block design test with pantomime instructions is found to be strongly saturated with the first factor. Immediately the purely "linguistic" interpretation of Factor I becomes suspect. This finding, taken together with our initial acceptance of the others as relevant to the background concept of intelligence forces us to reinterpret the concept once again.

If we simply *list* the tests or traits which have been shown to be saturated with the "factor" or which belong to the cluster, no construct is employed. As soon as we even *summarize the properties* of this group of indicators—we are already making some guesses. Intensional characterization of a domain is hazardous since it selects (abstracts) properties and implies that new tests sharing those properties will behave as do the known tests in the cluster, and that tests not sharing them will not.

The difficulties in merely "characterizing the surface cluster" are strikingly exhibited by the use of certain special and extreme groups for purposes of construct validation. The P_d scale of MMPI was originally derived and cross-validated upon hospitalized patients diagnosed "Psychopathic personality, asocial and amoral type" (42). Further research shows the scale to have a limited degree of predictive and concurrent validity for "delinquency" more broadly defined (5, 28). Several studies show associations between P_d and very special "criterion" groups which it would be ludicrous to identify as "*the* criterion" in the traditional sense. If one lists these heterogeneous groups and tries to characterize them intensionally, he faces enormous conceptual difficulties. For example, a recent survey of hunting accidents in Minnesota showed that hunters who had "carelessly" shot someone were significantly elevated on P_d when compared with other hunters (48). This is in line with one's theoretical expectations; when you ask MMPI "experts" to predict for such a group they invariably predict P_d or M_a or both. The finding seems therefore to lend some slight support to the construct validity of the P_d scale. But of course it would be nonsense to *define* the P_d component "operationally" in terms of, say, accident proneness. We might try to subsume the original phenotype and the hunting-accident proneness under some broader category, such as "Disposition to violate society's rules, whether legal, moral, or just *sensible*." But now we have ceased to have a neat operational criterion, and are using instead a rather vague and wide-range class. Besides, there is worse to come. We want the class specification to cover a group trend that (nondelinquent) high school students judged by their peer group as least "responsible" score over a full sigma higher on P_d than those judged most "responsible" (23, p. 75). Most of the behaviors contributing to such sociometric choices fall well within the range of socially permissible action, the proffered criterion specification is still too restrictive. Again, any clinician familiar with MMPI lore would predict an elevated P_d on a sample of (nondelinquent) professional actors. Chyatte's confirmation of this prediction (10) tends to support *both*: (a) the theory sketch of "what the P_d factor is, psychologically"; and (b) the claim of the P_d scale to construct validity for this hypothetical factor. Let the reader try his hand at writing a brief phenotypic criterion specification that will cover both trigger-happy hunters and Broadway actors! And if he should be ingenious enough to achieve this, does his definition also encompass Hovey's report that high P_d predicts the judgments "not shy" and "unafraid of mental patients" made upon nurses by their supervisors (32, p. 143)? And then we have Gough's report that *low* P_d is associated with ratings as "good-natured" (24, p. 40), and Roessell's data showing that high P_d is predictive of "dropping out of high school" (54). The point is that all seven of these "criterion" dispositions would be readily guessed by any clinician having even superficial familiarity with MMPI interpretation; but to mediate these inferences explicitly requires quite a few hypotheses about dynamics, constituting an admittedly sketchy (but far from vacuous) network defining the genotype *psychopathic deviate.*

Vagueness of Present Psychological Laws

This line of thought leads directly to our second important qualification upon the network schema. The idealized picture is one of a tidy set of postulates which jointly entail the desired theorems; since some of the theorems are coordinated to the observation base, the system constitutes an implicit definition of the theoretical primitives and gives them an indirect empirical meaning. In practice, of course, even the most advanced physical sciences only approximate this ideal. Questions of "categoricalness" and the like, such as logicians raise about pure calculi, are hardly even statable for empirical networks. (What, for example, would be the desiderata of a "well-formed formula" in molar behavior theory?) Psychology works with crude, half-explicit formulations. We do not worry about such advanced formal questions as "whether all molar-behavior statements are decidable by appeal to the postulates" because we know that no existing theoretical network suffices to predict even the *known* descriptive laws. Nevertheless, the sketch of a network is there; if it were not, we would not be saying *anything* intelligible about our constructs. We do not have the rigorous implicit definitions of formal calculi (which still, be it noted, usually permit of a multiplicity of interpretations). Yet the vague, avowedly incomplete network still gives the constructs whatever meaning they do have. When the network is very incomplete, having many strands missing entirely and some constructs tied in only by tenuous threads, then the "implicit definition" of these constructs is disturbingly loose; one might say that the meaning of the constructs is underdetermined. *Since the meaning of theoretical constructs is set forth by stating the laws in which they occur, our incomplete knowledge of the laws of nature produces a vagueness in our constructs* (see Hempel, 30; Kaplan, 34; Pap, 51). We will be able to say "what anxiety is" when we know all of the laws involving it; meanwhile, since we are in the process of discovering these laws, we do not yet know precisely what anxiety is.

CONCLUSIONS REGARDING THE NETWORK AFTER EXPERIMENTATION

The proposition that x per cent of test variance is accounted for by the construct is inserted into the accepted network. The network then generates a testable prediction about the relation of the test scores to certain other variables, and the investigator gathers data. If prediction and result are in harmony, he can retain his belief that the test measures the construct. The construct is at best adopted, never demonstrated to be "correct."

We do not first "prove" the theory, and then validate the test, nor conversely. In any probable inductive type of inference from a pattern of observations, we examine the relation between the total network of theory and observations. The system involves propositions relating test to construct, construct to other constructs, and finally relating some of these constructs to observables. In ongoing research the chain of inference is very complicated. Kelly and Fiske (36, p. 124) give a complex diagram showing the numerous inferences required in validating a prediction from assessment techniques, where theories about the criterion situation are as integral a part of the prediction as are the test data. A predicted empirical relationship permits us to test all the propositions leading to that prediction. Traditionally the proposition claiming to interpret the test has been set apart as the hypothesis being tested, but actually the evidence is significant for all parts of the chain. If the prediction is not confirmed, any link in the chain may be wrong.

A theoretical network can be divided into subtheories used in making particular predictions. All the events successfully predicted through a subtheory are of course evidence in favor of that theory. Such a subtheory may be so well confirmed by voluminous and diverse evidence that we can reasonably view a particular experiment as relevant only to the test's validity. If the theory, combined with a proposed test interpretation, mispredicts in this case, it is the latter which must be abandoned. On the other hand, the accumulated evidence for a test's construct validity may be so strong that an instance of misprediction will force us to modify the subtheory employing the construct rather than deny the claim that the test measures the construct.

Most cases in psychology today lie somewhere between these extremes. Thus, suppose we fail to find a greater incidence of "homosexual signs" in the Rorschach records of paranoid patients. Which is more strongly disconfirmed—the Rorschach signs or the orthodox theory of paranoia? The negative finding shows the bridge between the two to be undependable, but this is all we can say. The bridge cannot be used unless one end is placed on solider ground. The investigator must decide which end it is best to relocate.

Numerous successful predictions dealing with phenotypically diverse "criteria" give greater weight to the claim of construct validity than do fewer predictions, or predictions involving very similar behaviors. In arriving at diverse predictions, the hypothesis of test validity is connected each time to a subnetwork largely independent of the portion previously used. Success of these derivations testifies to the inductive power of the test-validity statement, and renders it unlikely that an equally effective alternative can be offered.

Implications of Negative Evidence

The investigator whose prediction and data are discordant must make strategic decisions. His result can be interpreted in three ways:

1. The test does not measure the construct variable.

2. The theoretical network which generated the hypothesis is incorrect.

3. The experimental design failed to test the hypothesis properly. (Strictly speaking this may be analyzed as a special case of 2, but in practice the distinction is worth making.)

For Further Research

If a specific fault of procedure makes the third a reasonable possibility, his proper response is to perform an adequate study, meanwhile making no report. When faced with the other two alternatives, he may decide that his test does not measure the construct adequately. Following that decision, he will perhaps prepare and validate a new test. Any rescoring or new interpretative procedure for the original instrument, like a new test, requires validation *by means of a fresh body of data.*

The investigator may regard interpretation 2 as more likely to lead to eventual advances. It is legitimate for the investigator to call the network defining the construct into question, if he has confidence in the test. Should the investigator decide that some step in the network is unsound, he may be able to invent an alternative network. Perhaps he modifies the network by splitting a concept into two or more portions, e.g., by designating types of *anxiety*, or perhaps he specifies added conditions under which a generalization holds. When an investigator modifies the theory in such a manner, he is now required to *gather a fresh body of data* to test the altered hypotheses. This step should normally precede publication of the modified theory. If the new data are consistent with the modified network, he is free from the fear that his nomologicals were gerrymandered to fit the peculiarities of his first sample of observations. He can now trust his test to some extent, because his test results behave as predicted.

The choice among alternatives, like any strategic decision, is a gamble as to which course of action is the best investment of effort. Is it wise to modify the theory? That depends on how well the system is confirmed by prior data, and how well the modifications fit available observations. Is it worth while to modify the test in the hope that it will fit the construct? That depends on how much evidence there is—apart from this abortive experiment—to support the hope, and also on how much it is worth to the investigator's ego to salvage the test. The choice among alternatives is a matter of research planning.

For Practical Use of the Test

The consumer can accept a test as a measure of a construct only when there is a strong positive fit between predictions and subsequent data. When the evidence from a proper investigation of a published test is essentially negative, it should be reported as a stop sign to discourage use of the test pending a reconciliation of test and construct, or final abandonment of the test. If the test has not been published, it should be restricted to research use until some degree of validity is established (1). The consumer can await the results of the investigator's gamble with confidence that proper application of the scientific method will ultimately tell whether the test has value. Until the evidence is in, he has no justification for employing the test as a basis for terminal decisions. The test may serve, at best, only as a source of suggestions about individuals to be confirmed by other evidence (15, 47).

There are two perspectives in test validation. From the viewpoint of the psychological practitioner the burden of proof is on the test. A test should not be used to measure a trait until its proponent establishes that predictions made from such measures are consistent with the best available theory of the trait. In the view of the test developer, however, both the test and the theory are under scrutiny. He is free to say *to himself privately*, "If my test disagrees with the theory, so much the worse for the theory." This way lies delusion unless he continues his research using a better theory.

Reporting of Positive Results

The test developer who finds positive correspondence between his proposed interpretation and data is expected to report the basis for his validity claim. Defending a claim of construct validity is a major task, not to be satisfied by a discourse without data. The *Technical Recommendations* have little to say on reporting of construct validity. Indeed, the only detailed suggestions under that heading refer to correlations of the test with other measures, together with a cross reference to some other sections of the report. The two key principles, however, call for the most comprehensive type of reporting. The manual for any test "should report all available information which will assist the user in determining what psychological attributes account for variance in test scores" (59, p. 27). And "The manual for a test which is used primarily to assess postulated attributes of the individual should outline the theory on which the test is based and organize whatever partial validity data there are to show in what way they support the theory" (59, p. 28). It is recognized, by a classification as "very desirable" rather than "essential," that the latter recommendation goes beyond present practice of test authors.

The proper goals in reporting construct validation are to make clear (*a*) what interpretation is proposed, (*b*) how adequately the writer believes this interpretation is substantiated, and (*c*) what evidence and reasoning lead him to this belief. Without *a* the construct validity of the test is of no use to the consumer. Without *b* the consumer must carry the entire burden of evaluating the test research. Without *c* the consumer or reviewer is being asked to take *a* and *b* on faith. The test manual cannot always present an exhaustive statement on these points, but it should summarize and indicate where complete statements may be found.

To specify the interpretation, the writer must state what construct he has in mind, and what meaning he gives to that construct. For a construct which has a short history and has built up few connotations, it will be fairly easy to indicate the presumed properties of the construct, i.e., the nomologicals in which it appears. For a construct with a longer history, a summary of properties and references to previous theoretical discussions may be appropriate. It is especially critical to distinguish proposed interpretations from other meanings previously given the same construct. The validator faces no small task; he must somehow communicate a theory to his reader.

To evaluate his evidence calls for a statement like the conclusions from a program of research, noting what is well substantiated and what alternative interpretations have been considered and rejected. The writer must note what portions of his proposed interpretation are speculations, extrapolations, or conclusions from insufficient data. The author has an ethical responsibility to prevent unsubstantiated interpretations from appearing as truths. A claim is unsubstantiated unless the evidence for the claim is public, so that other scientists may review the evidence, criticize the conclusions, and offer alternative interpretations.

The report of evidence in a test manual must be as complete as any research report, except where adequate public reports can be cited. Reference to something "observed by the writer in many clinical cases" is worthless as evidence. Full case reports, on the other hand, may be a valuable source of evidence so long as these cases are representative and negative instances receive due attention. The report of evidence must be interpreted with reference to the theoretical network in such a manner that the reader sees why the author regards a particular correlation or experiment as confirming (or throwing doubt upon) the proposed interpretation. Evidence collected by others must be taken fairly into account.

VALIDATION OF A COMPLEX TEST "AS A WHOLE"

Special questions must be considered when we are investigating the validity of a test which is aimed to provide information about several constructs. In one sense, it is naive to inquire "Is this test valid?" One does not validate a test, but only a principle for making inferences. If a test yields many different types of inferences, some of them can be valid and others invalid (cf. Technical Recommendation C2: "The manual should report the validity of each type of inference for which a test is recommended"). From this point of view, every topic sentence in the typical book on Rorschach interpretation presents a hypothesis requiring validation, and one should validate inferences about each aspect of the personality separately and in turn, just as he would want information on the validity (concurrent or predictive) for each scale of MMPI.

There is, however, another defensible point of view. If a test is purely empirical, based strictly on observed connections between response to an item and some criterion, then of course the validity of one scoring key for the test does not make validation for its other scoring keys any less necessary. But a test may be developed on the basis of a theory which in itself provides a linkage between the various keys and the various criteria. Thus, while Strong's Vocational Interest Blank is developed empirically, it also rests on a "theory" that a youth can be expected to be satisfied in an occupation if he has interests common to men now happy in the occupation. When Strong finds that those with high Engineering interest scores in college are preponderantly in engineering careers 19 years later, he has partly validated the proposed use of the Engineer score (predictive validity). Since the evidence is consistent with the theory on which all the test keys were built, this evidence alone increases the presumption that the *other* keys have predictive validity. How strong is this presumption? Not very, from the viewpoint of the traditional skepticism of science. Engineering interests may stabilize early, while interests in art or management or social work are still unstable. A claim cannot be made that the whole Strong approach is valid just because one score shows predictive validity. But if thirty interest scores were investigated longitudinally and all of them showed the type of validity predicted by Strong's theory, we would indeed be caviling to say that this evidence gives no confidence in the long-range validity of the thirty-first score.

Confidence in a theory is increased as more relevant evidence confirms it, but it is always possible that tomorrow's investigation will render the theory obsolete. The Technical Recommendations suggest a rule of reason, and ask for evidence for each *type* of inference for which a test is recommended. It is stated that no test developer can present predictive validities for all possible criteria; similarly, no developer can run all possible experimental tests of his proposed interpretation. But the recommendation is more subtle than advice that a lot of validation is better than a little.

Consider the Rorschach test. It is used for many inferences, made by means of nomological networks at several levels. At a low level are the simple unrationalized correspondences presumed to exist between certain signs and psychiatric diagnoses.

Validating such a sign does nothing to substantiate Rorschach theory. For other Rorschach formulas an explicit a priori rationale exists (for instance, high $F\%$ interpreted as implying rigid control of impulses). Each time such a sign shows correspondence with criteria, its rationale is supported just a little. At a still higher level of abstraction, a considerable body of theory surrounds the general area of *outer control*, interlacing many different constructs. As evidence cumulates, one should be able to decide what specific inference-making chains within this system can be depended upon. One should also be able to conclude—or deny—that so much of the system has stood up under test that one has some confidence in even the untested lines in the network.

In addition to relatively delimited nomological networks surrounding *control* or *aspiration*, the Rorschach interpreter usually has an overriding theory of the test as a whole. This may be a psychoanalytic theory, a theory of perception and set, or a theory stated in terms of learned habit patterns. Whatever the theory of the interpreter, whenever he validates an inference from the system, he obtains some reason for added confidence in his overriding system. His total theory is not tested, however, by experiments dealing with only one limited set of constructs. The test developer must investigate far-separated, independent sections of the network. The more diversified the predictions the system is required to make, the greater confidence we can have that only minor parts of the system will later prove faulty. Here we begin to glimpse a logic to defend the judgment that the test and its whole interpretative system is valid at some level of confidence.

There are enthusiasts who would conclude from the foregoing paragraphs that since there is some evidence of correct, diverse predictions made from the Rorschach, the test as a whole can now be accepted as validated. This conclusion overlooks the negative evidence. Just one finding contrary to expectation, based on sound research, is sufficient to wash a whole theoretical structure away. Perhaps the remains can be salvaged to form a new structure. But this structure now must be exposed to fresh risks, and sound negative evidence will destroy it in turn. There is sufficient negative evidence to prevent acceptance of the Rorschach and its accompanying interpretative structures as a whole. So long as any aspects of the overriding theory stated for the test have been disconfirmed, this structure must be rebuilt.

Talk of areas and structures may seem not to recognize those who would interpret the personality "globally." They may argue that a test is best validated in matching studies. Without going into detailed questions of matching methodology, we can ask whether such a study validates the nomological network "as a whole." The judge does employ some network in arriving at his conception of his subject, integrating specific inferences from specific data. Matching studies, if successful, demonstrate only that each judge's interpretative theory has some validity, that it is not completely a fantasy. Very high consistency between judges is required to show that they are using the same network, and very high success in matching is required to show that the network is dependable.

If inference is less than perfectly dependable, we must know which aspects of the interpretative network are least dependable and which are most dependable. Thus, even if one has considerable confidence in a test "as a whole" because of frequent successful inferences, one still remains as an ultimate aim to the request of the Technical Recommendation for separate evidence on the validity of each type of inference to be made.

RECAPITULATION

Construct validation was introduced in order to specify types of research required in developing tests for which the conventional views on validation are inappropriate. Personality tests, and some tests of ability, are interpreted in terms of attributes for which there is no adequate criterion. This paper indicates what sorts of evidence can substantiate such an interpretation, and how such evidence is to be interpreted. The following points made in the discussion are particularly significant.

1. A construct is defined implicitly by a network of associations or propositions in which it occurs. Constructs employed at different stages of research vary in definiteness.

2. Construct validation is possible only when some of the statements in the network lead to predicted relations among observables. While some observables may be regarded as "criteria," the construct validity of the criteria themselves is regarded as under investigation.

3. The network defining the construct, and the derivation leading to the predicted observation, must be reasonably explicit so that validating evidence may be properly interpreted.

4. Many types of evidence are relevant to construct validity, including content validity, interitem correlations, intertest correlations, test- "criterion" correlations, studies of stability over time, and stability under experimental intervention. High correlations and high stability may constitute either favorable or unfavorable evidence for the proposed interpretation, depending on the theory surrounding the construct.

5. When a predicted relation fails to occur, the fault may lie in the proposed interpretation of the test or in the network. Altering the network so that it can cope with the new observations is, in effect, redefining the construct. Any such new interpretation of the test must be validated by a fresh body of data before being advanced publicly. Great care is required to avoid substituting a posteriori rationalizations for proper validation.

6. Construct validity cannot generally be expressed in the form of a single simple coefficient. The data often permit one to establish upper and lower bounds for the proportion of test variance which can be attributed to the construct. The integration of diverse data into a proper interpretation cannot be an entirely quantitative process.

7. Constructs may vary in nature from those very close to "pure description" (involving little more than extrapolation of relations among observation-variables) to highly theoretical constructs involving hypothesized entities and processes, or making identifications with constructs of other sciences.

8. The investigation of a test's construct validity is not essentially different from the general scientific procedures for developing and confirming theories.

Without in the least *advocating* construct validity as preferable to the other three kinds (concurrent, predictive, content), we do believe it imperative that psychologists make a place for it in their methodological thinking, so that its rationale, its scientific legitimacy, and its dangers may become explicit and familiar. This would be preferable to the widespread current tendency to engage in what actually amounts to construct validation research and use of constructs in practical testing, while talking an "operational" methodology which, if adopted, would force research into a mold it does not fit.

ENDNOTES

1. The second author, Paul E. Meehl, worked on this problem in connection with his appointment to the Minnesota Center for Philosophy of Science. We are indebted to the other members of the Center (Herbert Feigl, Michael Scriven, Wilfrid Sellars), and to D. L. Thistlethwaite of the University of Illinois, for their major contributions to our thinking and their suggestions for improving this paper.

2. Referred to in a preliminary report (58) as *congruent validity.*

REFERENCES

1. American Psychological Association. *Ethical standards of psychologists.* Washington, D.C.: American Psychological Association, Inc., 1953.

2. Anastasi, Anne. The concept of validity in the interpretation of test scores. *Educ. psychol. Measmt.,* 1950, **10,** 67–78.

3. Bechtoldt, H. P. Selection. In S. S. Stevens (Ed.), *Handbook of experimental psychology.* New York: Wiley, 1951. Pp. 1237–1267.

4. Beck, L. W. Constructions and inferred entities. *Phil. Sci.,* 1950, 17. Reprinted in H. Feigl and M. Brodbeck (Eds.), *Readings in the philosophy of science.* New York: Appleton-Century-Crofts, 1953. Pp. 368–381.

5. Blair, W. R. N. A comparative study of disciplinary offenders and non-offenders in the Canadian Army. *Canad. J. Psychol.,* 1950, **4,** 49–62.

6. Braithwaite, R. B. *Scientific explanation.* Cambridge: Cambridge Univer. Press, 1953.

7. Carnap, P. Empiricism, semantics, and ontology. *Rev. int. de Phil.,* 1950, II, 20–40. Reprinted in P. P. Wiener (Ed.), *Readings in philosophy of science,* New York: Scribner's, 1953. Pp. 509–521.

8. Carnap, R. *Foundations of logic and mathematics. International encyclopedia of unified science,* I, No. 3. Pages 56–69 reprinted as "The interpretation of physics" in H. Feigl and M. Brodbeck (Eds.), *Readings in the philosophy of science.* New York: Appleton-Century-Crofts, 1953. Pp. 309–318.

9. Child, I. L. Personality. *Annu. Rev. Psychol.,* 1954, **5,** 149–171.

10. Chyatte, C. Psychological characteristics of a group of professional actors. *Occupations,* 1949, **27,** 245–250.

11. Cronbach, L. J. *Essentials of psychological testing.* New York: Harper, 1949.

12. Cronbach, L. J. Further evidence on response sets and test design. *Educ. psychol. Measmt.,* 1950, **10,** 3–31.

13. Cronbach, L. J. Coefficient alpha and the internal structure of tests. *Psychometrika,* 1951, **16,** 297–335.

14. Cronbach, L. J. Processes affecting scores on "understanding of others" and "assumed similarity." *Psychol. Bull.,* 1955, **52,** 177–193.

15. Cronbach, L. J. The counselor's problems from the perspective of communication theory. In Vivian H. Hewer (Ed.), *New perspectives in counseling*. Minneapolis: Univer. of Minnesota Press, 1955.

16. Cureton, E. E. Validity. In E. F. Lindquist (Ed.), *Educational measurement*. Washington, D. C.: American Council on Education, 1950. Pp. 621–695.

17. Damrin, Dora E. A comparative study of information derived from a diagnostic problem-solving test by logical and factorial methods of scoring. Unpublished doctor's dissertation, Univer. of Illinois, 1952.

18. Eysenck, H. J. Criterion analysis—an application of the hypothetico-deductive method in factor analysis. *Psychol. Rev.*, 1950, **57**, 38–53.

19. Feigl, H. Existential hypotheses. *Phil. Sci.*, 1950, **17**, 35–62.

20. Feigl, H. Confirmability and confirmation. *Rev. int. de Phil.*, 1951, **5**, 1–12. Reprinted in P. P. Wiener (Ed.), *Readings in philosophy of science*. New York: Scribner's 1953. Pp. 522–530.

21. Gaylord, R. H. Conceptual consistency and criterion equivalence: a dual approach to criterion analysis. Unpublished manuscript (PRB Research Note No. 17). Copies obtainable from ASTIA-DSC, AD-21 440.

22. Goodenough, Florence L. *Mental testing*. New York: Rinehart, 1950.

23. Gough, H. G., McClosky, H., & Meehl, P. E. A personality scale for social responsibility. *J. abnorm. soc. Psychol.*, 1952, **47**, 73–80.

24. Gough, H. G., McKee, M. G., & Yandell, R. J. Adjective check list analyses of a number of selected psychometric and assessment variables. Unpublished manuscript. Berkeley: IPAR, 1953.

25. Guilford, J. P. New standards for test evaluation. *Educ. psychol. Measmt.*, 1946, **6**, 427–439.

26. Guilford, J. P. Factor analysis in a test-development program. *Psychol. Rev.*, 1948, **55**, 79–94.

27. Gulliksen, H. Intrinsic validity. *Amer. Psychologist*, 1950, **5**, 511–517.

28. Hathaway, S. R., & Monachesi, E. D. *Analyzing and predicting juvenile delinquency with the MMPI*. Minneapolis: Univ. of Minnesota Press, 1953.

29. Hempel, C. G. Problems and changes in the empiricist criterion of meaning. *Rév. int. de Phil.*, 1950, **4**, 41–63. Reprinted in L. Linsky, *Semantics and the philosophy of language*. Urbana: Univer. of Illinois Press, 1952. Pp. 163–185.

30. Hempel, C. G. *Fundamentals of concept formation in empirical science*. Chicago: Univer. of Chicago Press, 1952.

31. Horst, P. The prediction of personal adjustment. *Soc. Sci. Res. Council Bull.*, 1941, No. 48.

32. Hovey, H. B. MMPI profiles and personality characteristics. *J. consult. Psychol.*, 1953, **17**, 142–146.

33. Jenkins, J. G. Validity for what? *J. consult. Psychol.*, 1946, **10**, 93–98.

34. Kaplan, A. Definition and specification of meaning. *J. Phil.*, 1946, **43**, 281–288.

35. Kelly, E. L. Theory and techniques of assessment. *Annu. Rev. Psychol.*, 1954, **5**, 281–311.

36. Kelly, E. L., & Fiske, D. W. *The prediction of performance in clinical psychology*. Ann Arbor: Univer. of Michigan Press, 1951.

37. Kneale, W. *Probability and induction*. Oxford, Clarendon Press, 1949. Pages

92–110 reprinted as "Induction, explanation, and transcendent hypotheses" in H. Feigl and M. Brodbeck (Eds.), *Readings in the philosophy of science.* New York: Appleton-Century-Crofts, 1953. Pp. 353–367.

38. Lindquist, E. F. *Educational measurement.* Washington, D. C.: American Council on Education, 1950.

39. Lucas, C. M. Analysis of the relative movement test by a method of individual interviews. *Bur. Naval Personnel Res. Rep.*, Contract Nonr-694 (00), NR 151-13, Educational Testing Service, March 1953.

40. MacCorquodale, K., & Meehl, P. E. On a distinction between hypothetical constructs and intervening variables. *Psychol. Rev.*, 1948, **55,** 95–107.

41. MacFarlane, Jean W. Problems of validation inherent in projective methods. *Amer. J. Orthophyschiat.*, 1942, **12,** 405–410.

42. McKinley, J. C., & Hathaway, S. R. The MMPI: V. Hysteria, hypomania, and psychopathic deviate. *J. appl. Psychol.*, 1944, **28,** 153–174.

43. McKinley, J. C., Hathaway, S. R., & Meehl, P. E. The MMPI: VI. The K scale. *J. consult. Psychol.*, 1948, **12,** 20–31.

44. Meehl, P. E. A single algebraic development of Horst's suppressor variables. *Amer. J. Psychol.*, 1945, **58,** 550–554.

45. Meehl, P. E. An investigation of a general mortality or control factor in personality testing. *Psychol. Monogr.*, 1945, **59,** No. 4 (Whole No. 274).

46. Meehl, P. E. *Clinical vs. statistical prediction.* Minneapolis: Univer. of Minnesota Press, 1954.

47. Meehl, P. E., & Rosen, A. Antecedent probability and the efficiency of psychometric signs, patterns or cutting scores. *Psychol. Bull.*, 1955, **52,** 194–216.

48. *Minnesota Hunter Casualty Study.* St. Paul: Jacob Schmidt Brewing Company, 1954.

49. Mosier, C. I. A critical examination of the concepts of face validity. *Educ. psychol. Measmt.*, 1947, **7,** 191–205.

50. Mosier, C. I. Problems and designs of cross-validation. *Educ. psychol. Measmt.*, 1951, **11,** 5–12.

51. Pap, A. Reduction-sentences and open concepts. *Methodos,* 1953, **5,** 3–30.

52. Peak, Helen. Problems of objective observation. In L. Festinger and D. Katz (Eds.), *Research methods in the behavioral sciences.* New York: Dryden Press, 1953. Pp. 243–300.

53. Porteus, S. D. *The Porteus maze test and intelligence.* Palo Alto: Pacific Books, 1950.

54. Roessel, F. P. MMPI results for high school drop-outs and graduates. Unpublished doctor's dissertation, Univer. of Minnesota, 1954.

55. Sellars, W. S. Concepts as involving laws and inconceivable without them. *Phil. Sci.*, 1948, **15,** 287–315.

56. Sellars, W. S. Some reflections on language games. *Phil. Sci.*, 1954, **21,** 204–228.

57. Spiker, C. C., & McCandless, B. R. The concept of intelligence and the philosophy of science. *Psychol. Rev.*, 1954, **61,** 255–267.

58. Technical recommendations for psychological tests and diagnostic techniques: preliminary proposal. *Amer. Psychologist*, 1952, **7,** 461–476.

59. Technical recommendations for psychological tests and diagnostic techniques. *Psychol. Bull. Supplement*, 1954, **51,** 2, Part 2, 1–38.

60. Thurstone, L. L. The criterion problem in personality research. *Psychometric Lab. Rep.*, No. 78. Chicago: Univer. of Chicago, 1952.

Questions for Study and Discussion

1. According to Cronbach and Meehl, the development of a particular psychological measure may result in a "bootstraps effect" whereby, "even when a test is constructed on the basis of a specific criterion, it may ultimately be judged to have greater construct validity than the criterion." Why may this process be both "legitimate and fruitful," in the authors' words? Under what circumstances might the effect be misleading and dysfunctional?

2. If you were to apply for a job as a computer programmer, you might be asked to take the well-known Programmer's Aptitude Test (PAT). (For a characterization and critique of this test see Weinberg, 1971, pp. 170–176.) Suppose you were asked to undertake an independent investigation of this test to assist the management of an organization in deciding whether to adopt it for placement purposes. What basic questions might be raised in assessing the validity of the test? (For another view of programming aptitude testing, see Wolfe, 1969.)

3. What experimentation might be undertaken to establish construct validity in the use of the Myers-Briggs test to assess psychological types associated with the use of decision support systems?

4. Bariff and Lusk (1977) propose that "the measurement and evaluation of users' cognitive styles and related personality traits may provide an effective means for attaining successful MIS modifications" (p. 822). Such a methodology is described further as "more systematic and objective" than traditional approaches to the determination of user information requirements. What barriers to the successful adoption of the Bariff and Lusk proposal might be anticipated in a particular organizational setting? (For further reading, see Benbasat and Taylor, 1978.)

5. The concept of construct validity is applied by Cronbach and Meehl to psychological testing. Might the concept also be applied to the choice of a criterion measure of job performance? (For one view on this issue, see James, 1973.)

CHAPTER **FOURTEEN**

There is an old story told about a survey conducted to determine the market potential of pay television. The survey made use of personal interviews of prospective consumers. One interviewer's travels took him to the far reaches of Maine, where he encountered a farmer. "What do you think of pay television?" the interviewer asked hopefully. The farmer pondered the question for a moment, smiled, and responded, "Sounds like a fine idea. How much will they pay me to watch it?"

Consumer measurement is one of the more pervasive forms of individual measurement in our society. Consumers are understood in this sense to be the recipients of public as well as private goods and services. Thus public opinion polling falls to some extent within the scope of this subsection. A poll on the desirability of providing a new rapid transit system is an example of consumer measurement, in this sense.

Consumer measurements are usually made of a sample group of persons, since it is not the individual who is of primary interest, but rather some population of which the individual is one representative. This is true whether a firm is studying the limited market potential of one of its new products, or whether a society is studying the attitudes of its entire citizenry.

CONSUMER SENTIMENT

Measures of consumer sentiment are examples of social measurement based on individual measurement. The problems of measuring at the societal level will be discussed more fully in the sections that follow, but it is of interest to note here that alternative indices of consumer sentiment exist, and that these may not always be consistent with each other, as noted in the January 16, 1978, issue of the *Wall Street Journal*:

> NEW YORK—Polls of consumer confidence are giving off conflicting signals.
>
> The Conference Board's index of consumer confidence rose to 100.4 in December, its highest level since late 1972 and 10 points above November.
>
> Last week, however, the University of Michigan's Survey Research Center reported that its index of consumer sentiment in the fourth quarter fell to 83.1 the lowest level since early 1976. And Sindlinger & Co.'s confidence index, which it calls "household money supply," rose sharply in the fourth quarter—but has been falling sharply since then.

The differences may stem from timing and polling methods. The Conference Board, a business research organization with headquarters here, bases its index on a mail poll conducted for the board by National Family Opinion Inc. of Toledo, Ohio. Polling was done in December.

The Survey Research Center's index is based on telephone interviews conducted in November and December. Sindlinger & Co., Media, Pa., polls consumers continuously by telephone.

Polling methods are components of the measurement process, in computing an index such as those discussed above. Telephone interviews are subject to potential bias in terms of inability to include nonsubscribers as well as subscribers who are not listed, or who have moved. Mail interviews are plagued by the problem of nonresponse, which introduces bias in that respondents tend to be those who feel more strongly about the subject. Mail interviews also lack the facility for conversational exchange, to insure that questions are understood and answers properly recorded.

MARKET RESEARCH

Market research is the organizational activity which makes the most extensive use of consumer measurement. Psychological tests are commonly employed, as in personnel selection. However, the management decision involved is of an entirely different character. In personnel selection, the choice pertains to the individual measured. In consumer measurement, the choice pertains to products and services offered in the marketplace.

One of the more interesting approaches to consumer measurement deals with the *multiple attributes* of products and services. The problem here is to identify those attributes which make a decisive difference in consumer acceptance of the product or service. This may be of assistance in design and development of the product or service, or in its marketing. In the article that follows, Paul E. Green and Yoram Wind introduce the technique of *conjoint measurement* applied to this problem area.

NEW WAY TO MEASURE CONSUMERS' JUDGMENTS

Paul E. Green • Yoram Wind

Taking a jet plane for a business appointment in Paris? Which of the two flights described below would you choose?

- A B-707 flown by British Airways that will depart within two hours of the time you would like to leave and that is often late in arriving in Paris. The plane will make two intermediate stops, and it is anticipated that it will be 50% full. Flight attendants are "warm and friendly" and you would have a choice of two movies for entertainment.

- A B-747 flown by TWA that will depart within four hours of the time you would like to leave and that is almost never late in arriving in Paris. The flight is non-stop, and it is anticipated that the plane will be 90% full. Flight attendants are "cold and curt" and only magazines are provided for entertainment.

Are you looking for replacement tires for your two-year-old car? Suppose you want radial tires and have the following three options to choose from:

- Goodyear's, with a tread life of 30,000 miles at a price of $40 per tire; the store is a 10-minute drive from your home.

- Firestone's, with a tread life of 50,000 miles at a price of $85 per tire; the store is a 20-minute drive from your home.

- Or Sears's, with a tread life of 40,000 miles at a price of $55 per tire; the store is located about 10 minutes from your home.

How would you rank these alternatives in order of preference?

Both of these problems have a common structure that companies and their marketing managers frequently encounter in trying to figure out what a consumer really wants in a product or service. First, the characteristics of the alternatives that the consumer must choose from fall along more than a single dimension—they are multiattribute. Second, the consumer must make an overall judgment about the relative value of those characteristics, or attributes; in short, he must order them according to some criterion. But doing this requires complex trade-offs, since it is likely that no alternative is clearly better than another on every dimension of interest.

Harvard Business Review, July–August 1975, Vol. 53, No. 4 Copyright © 1975 by the President and Fellows of Harvard College; all rights reserved.

In recent years, researchers have developed a new measurement technique from the fields of mathematical psychology and psychometrics that can aid the marketing manager in sorting out the relative importance of a product's multidimensional attributes.[1] This technique, called conjoint measurement, starts with the consumer's overall or global judgments about a set of complex alternatives. It then performs the rather remarkable job of decomposing his or her original evaluations into separate and compatible utility scales by which the original global judgments (or others involving new combinations of attributes) can be reconstituted.[2]

Being able to separate overall judgments into psychological components in this manner can provide a manager with valuable information about the relative importance of various attributes of a product. It can also provide information about the value of various levels of a single attribute. (For example, if price is the attribute under consideration, conjoint measurement can give the manager a good idea of how sensitive consumers would be to a price change from a level of, say, 85¢ to one of 75¢ or one of 95¢.) Indeed, some models can even estimate the psychological trade-offs consumers make when they evaluate several attributes together.

The advantages of this type of knowledge to the planning of marketing strategy are significant. The knowledge can be useful in modifying current products or services and in designing new ones for selected buying publics.

In this article, we first show how conjoint measurement works from a numerical standpoint. We then discuss its application to a variety of marketing problems, and we demonstrate its use in strategic marketing simulations. The Appendix provides a brief description of how other research tools for measuring consumer judgments work, and how they relate to conjoint measurement.

HOW CONJOINT MEASUREMENT WORKS

In order to see how to apply conjoint measurement, suppose a company were interested in marketing a new spot remover for carpets and upholstery. The technical staff has developed a new product that is designed to handle tough, stubborn spots. Management interest centers on five attributes or factors that it expects will influence consumer preference: an applicator-type package design, brand name, price, a *Good Housekeeping* seal of endorsement, and a money-back guarantee.

Three package designs are under consideration and appear in the upper portion of *Exhibit I*. There are three brand names under consideration: *K2R, Glory,* and *Bissell.* Of the three brand names used in the study, two are competitors' brand names already on the market, whereas one is the company's present brand name choice for its new product. Three alternative prices being considered are $1.19, $1.39, and $1.59. Since there are three alternatives for each of these factors, they are called three-level factors. The *Good Housekeeping* seal and money-back guarantee are two-level factors, since each is either present or not. Consequently, a total of $3 \times 3 \times 3 \times 2 \times 2 = 108$ alternatives would have to be tested if the researcher were to array all possible combinations of the five attributes.

Clearly, the cost of administering a consumer evaluation study of this magnitude—not to mention the respondents' confusion and fatigue—would be prohibitive. As an alternative, however, the research can take advantage of a special experimental design, called an *orthogonal array*, in which the test combinations are selected so that the independent contributions of all five factors are balanced.[3] In this way

EXHIBIT I Experimental design for evaluation of a carpet cleaner

Package designs

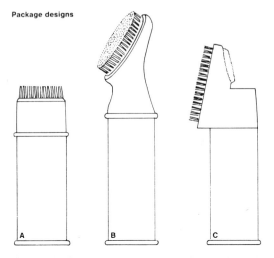

Orthogonal array

	Package design	Brand name	Price	Good Housekeeping seal?	Money-back guarantee?	Respondent's evaluation (rank number)
1	A	K2R	$1.19	No	No	13
2	A	Glory	1.39	No	Yes	11
3	A	Bissell	1.59	Yes	No	17
4	B	K2R	1.39	Yes	Yes	2
5	B	Glory	1.59	No	No	14
6	B	Bissell	1.19	No	No	3
7	C	K2R	1.59	No	Yes	12
8	C	Glory	1.19	Yes	No	7
9	C	Bissell	1.39	No	No	9
10	A	K2R	1.59	Yes	No	18
11	A	Glory	1.19	No	Yes	8
12	A	Bissell	1.39	No	No	15
13	B	K2R	1.19	No	No	4
14	B	Glory	1.39	Yes	No	6
15	B	Bissell	1.59	No	Yes	5
16	C	K2R	1.39	No	No	10
17	C	Glory	1.59	No	No	16
18	C	Bissell	1.19	Yes	Yes	1*

*Highest ranked

each factor's weight is kept separate and is not confused with those of the other factors.

The lower portion of *Exhibit I* shows an orthogonal array that involves only 18 of the 108 possible combinations that the company wishes to test in this case. For the test the researcher makes up 18 cards. On each card appears an artist's sketch of the package design, A, B, or C, and verbal details regarding each of the other four factors: brand name, price, *Good Housekeeping* seal (or not), and money-back guarantee (or not). After describing the new product's functions and special features, he shows the respondents each of the 18 cards (see *Exhibit I* for the master design), and asks them to rank the cards in order of their likelihood of purchase.

The last column of *Exhibit I* shows one respondent's actual ranking of the 18 cards; rank number 1 denotes her highest evaluated concept. Note particularly that only *ranked* data need be obtained and, furthermore, that only 18 (out of 108) combinations are evaluated.

Computing the Utilities

Computation of the utility scales of each attribute, which determine how influential each is in the consumers' evaluations, is carried out by various computer programs.[4] The ranked data of a single respondent (or the composite ranks of a group of respondents) are entered in the program. The computer then searches for a set of scale values for each factor in the experimental design. The scale values for each level of each factor are chosen so that when they are added together the *total* utility of each combination will correspond to the original ranks as closely as possible.

Notice that two problems are involved here. First, as mentioned previously, the experimental design of *Exhibit I* shows only 18 of 108 combinations. Second, only rank-order data are supplied to the algorithms. This means that the data themselves do not determine how much more influential one attribute is than another in the consumers' choices. However, despite these limitations, the algorithms are able to find a *numerical* representation of the utilities, thus providing an indication of each factor's relative importance.

In general, more accurate solutions are obtained as the number of combinations being evaluated increases. Still, in the present case, with only 18 ranking-type judgments, the technique works well. *Exhibit II* shows the computer results.

As can be observed in *Exhibit II*, the technique obtains a utility function for each level of each factor. For example, to find the utility for the first combination in *Exhibit I*, we can read off the utilities of each factor level in the five charts of *Exhibit II*: U (A) = 0.1; U (K2R) = 0.3; U ($1.19) = 1.0; U (No) = 0.2; U (No) = 0.2. Therefore the total utility is 1.8, the sum of the five separate utilities, for the first combination. Note that this combination was ranked only thirteenth by the respondent in *Exhibit I*.

On the other hand, the utility of combination 18 is 3.1 (0.6 + 0.5 + 1.0 + 0.3 + 0.7); which is the respondent's highest evaluation of all 18 combinations listed.

However, as can be easily seen from *Exhibit II*, if combination 18 is modified to include package Design B (in place of C), its utility is even higher. As a matter of fact, it then represents the highest possible utility, even though this specific combination did not appear among the original 18.

EXHIBIT II   Results of computer analysis of experimental data
of Exhibit I

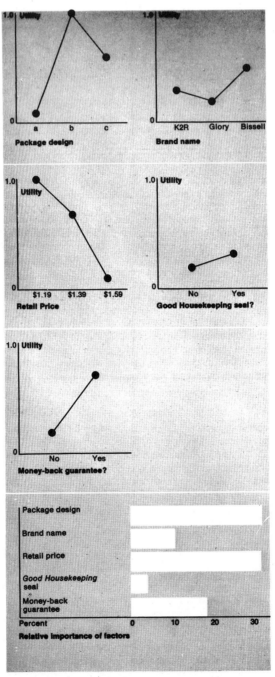

Importance of Attributes

By focusing attention on only the package design, the company's marketing researchers can see from *Exhibit II* that Design B displays highest utility. Moreover, all utility scales are expressed in a common unit (although their zero points are arbitrary). This means that we can compare utility ranges from factor to factor so as to get some idea of their relative importance.

In the case of the spot remover, as shown in *Exhibit II,* the utility ranges are:

- Package design $(1.0 - 0.1 = 0.9)$

- Brand name $(0.5 - 0.2 = 0.3)$

- Price $(1.0 - 0.1 = 0.9)$

- *Good Housekeeping* seal $(0.3 - 0.2 = 0.1)$

- Money-back guarantee $(0.7 - 0.2 = 0.5)$

How important is each attribute in relation to the others? The lower portion of *Exhibit II* shows the relative size of the utility ranges expressed in histogram form. As noted, package design and price are the most important factors, and together they account for about two thirds of the total range in utility.

It should be mentioned that the relative importance of a factor depends on the levels that are included in the design. For example, had price ranged from $1.19 to a high of $1.89, its relative importance could easily exceed that for package design. Still, as a crude indication of what factors to concentrate on, factor importance calculations provide a useful by-product of the main analysis regardless of such limitations.

Managerial Implications

From a marketing management point of view the critical question is how these results can be used in the design of a product/marketing strategy for the spot remover. Examination of *Exhibit II* suggests a number of points for discussion:

- Excluding brand name, the most desirable offering would be the one based on package Design B with a money-back guarantee, a *Good-Housekeeping* seal, and a retail price of $1.19.

- The utility of a product with a price of $1.39 would be 0.3 less than one with a price of $1.19. A money-back guarantee which involves an increment of 0.5 in utility would more than offset the effect of the higher price.

- The use of a *Good Housekeeping* seal of approval is associated with a minor increase in utility. Hence including it in the company's product will add little to the attractiveness of the spot remover's overall offering.

- The utility of the three brand names provide the company with a quantitative measure of the value of its own brand name as well as the brand names of its competitors.

Other questions can be answered as well by comparing various composites made up from the utilities shown in *Exhibit II*.

The Air Carrier Study

What about the two Paris flights you had to choose between? In that study, the sponsor was primarily interested in how air travelers evaluated the B-707 versus the B-747 in transatlantic travel, and whether relative value differed by length of flight and type of traveler—business versus vacation travelers. In this study all the respondents had flown across the Atlantic at least once during the preceding 12 months.

Exhibit III shows one of the findings of the study for air travelers (business and vacation) flying to Paris. Without delving into details it is quite apparent that the utility difference between the B-707 and the B-747 is very small. Rather, the main factors are departure time, punctuality of arrival, number of stops, and the attitudes of flight attendants.

The importance of type of aircraft did increase slightly with length of flight and for business-oriented travelers versus vacationers. Still, its importance to overall utility was never greater than 10%. It became abundantly clear that extensive replacement of older aircraft like the B-707 would not result in major shifts in consumer demand. On the contrary, money might better be spent on improving the scheduling aspects of flights and the attitudes and demeanor of flight personnel.

The air carrier study involved the preparation of some 27 different flight profiles (only two of which appear at the beginning of the article). Respondents simply rated each flight description in terms of its desirability on a seven-point scale. Only the order properties of the ratings were used in the computer run that resulted in the utility scales appearing in *Exhibit III.*

The Replacement Tire Study

The conjoint measurement exercise in the replacement tire study was part of a larger study designed to pretest several television commercials for the sponsor's brand of steel-belted radial tires. The sponsor was particularly interested in the utility functions of respondents who expressed interest in each of the test commercials.

The respondents considered tread mileage and price as quite important to their choice of tires. On the other hand, brand name did not play an important role (at least for the five brands included in the study). Not surprisingly, the most popular test commercial stressed tread mileage and good value for the money, characteristics of high appeal to this group. What was surprising was that this group represented 70% of the total sample.

This particular study involved the preparation of 25 profiles. Again, the researchers sorted cards into seven ordered categories. The 25 profiles, also constructed according to an orthogonal array, represented only one twenty-fifth of the 625 possible combinations.

POTENTIAL USES OF CONJOINT MEASUREMENT

The three preceding studies only scratch the surface of marketing problems in which conjoint measurement procedures can be used. For example, consumer evaluations can be obtained on:

• New product formulations involving changes in the physical or chemical characteristics of the product

EXHIBIT III   Utility functions for air travelers to Paris

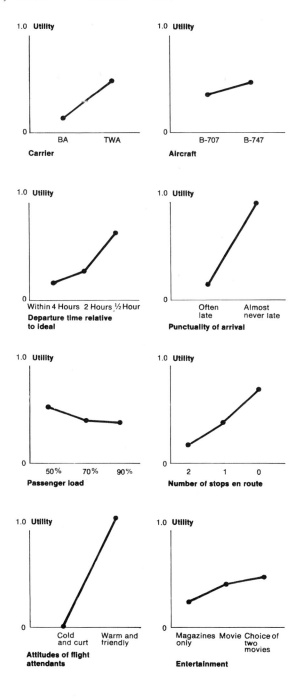

- Package design, brand name, and promotional copy combinations

- Pricing and brand alternatives

- Verbalized descriptions of new products or services

- Alternative service designs

Moreover, while the three preceding examples emphasized preference or likelihood-of-purchase orderings, any explicit judgmental criterion can be used. For example, alternatives might be ordered by any of these criteria:

- Best value for the money

- Convenience of use

- Suitability for a specified type of consumer or for a specified end use

- Ruggedness, distinctiveness, conservativeness, and other "psychological images"

Designing Bar Soaps

In one recent study researchers related the psychological imagery of physical characteristics of actual bars of soap to end-use appropriateness; this study was conducted for the laboratory and marketing personnel of a diversified soap manufacturer.

While the designing of a bar of soap—by varying weight, size, shape, color, fragrance type and intensity, surface feel, and so on—may seem like a mundane exercise, the fact remains that a cleverly positioned bar soap (for example, Irish Spring) can rapidly become a multimillion-dollar enterprise. Still, the extent of knowledge about the importance of such imagery is woefully meager. The researchers formulated actual bars of soap in which color, type of fragrance, and intensity of fragrance were constructed according to a design in which all possible combinations of the experimental factors appeared. All the other characteristics of the soap were held constant.

Respondents examined the soaps and assigned each bar to the end use that they felt best matched its characteristics—moisturizing facial soap, deep-cleaning soap for oily skin, woman's deodorant soap, or man's deodorant soap. The data were then analyzed by conjoint measurement techniques, leading to a set of psychophysical functions for each of the characteristics.

The study showed that type of fragrance was the most important physical variable contributing to end-use appropriateness. Rather surprisingly, the type of fragrance (medicinal) and color (blue) that appeared best suited for a man's deodorant soap were also found to be best for the deep-cleaning soap, even though deep-cleaning soap had been previously classed for marketing purposes as a facial soap. On the other hand, fragrance intensity played a relatively minor role as a consumer cue for distinguishing among different end uses.

In brief, this study illustrated the feasibility of translating changes in various physical variables into changes in psychological variables. Eventually, more detailed knowledge of these psychological transformations could enable a laboratory technician to synthesize color, fragrance, shape, and so forth to obtain soaps that conjure up almost any desired imagery. Moreover, in other product classes—beers, coffees, soft drinks—it appears possible to develop a psychophysics of taste in which such elusive verbal descriptions as "full-bodied" and "robust" are given operational meaning in terms of variations in physical or chemical characteristics.

Verbalized Descriptions of New Concepts

In many product classes, such as automobiles, houses, office machines, and computers, the possible design factors are myriad and expensive to vary physically for evaluation by the buying public. In cases such as these, the researcher usually resorts to verbalized descriptions of the principal factors of interest.

To illustrate, one study conducted among car owners by Rogers National Research, Inc. employed the format shown in *Exhibit IV*. In this case the researchers were interested in the effects of gas mileage, price, country of manufacture, maximum speed, roominess, and length on consumer preferences for new automobiles. Consumers evaluated factor levels on a two-at-a-time basis, as illustrated in *Exhibit IV*. Market Facts, Inc. employs a similar data collection procedure.[5]

In the Rogers study it was found that consumer evaluations of attributes were highly associated with the type of car currently owned and the type of car desired in the future. Not surprisingly, gas mileage and country of manufacture were highly important factors in respondent evaluations of car profiles. Somewhat surprising, however, was the fact that even large-car owners (and those contemplating the purchase of a large car) were more concerned with gas economy than owners of that type of car had been historically. Thus, while they fully expected to get fewer miles per gallon than they would in compact cars, they felt quite strongly that the car should be economical compared to others in its size class.

Organizations as Consumers

Nor is conjoint measurement's potential limited to consumer applications. Evaluations of supply alternatives by an organizational buyer are similar to benefits sought by the consumer. Thus, one can argue, these evaluations are among the most important inputs to industrial marketing strategy.

As an illustration, the management of a clinical laboratory was concerned with the problem of how to increase its share of laboratory test business. It had a study conducted to assess how physicians subjectively value various characteristics of a clinical laboratory in deciding where to send their tests.

Each physician in the study received 16 profiles of hypothetical laboratory services, each showing a different set of characteristics, such as reliability of test results, pick-up and delivery procedures, convenience of location, price range of services, billing procedures, and turnaround time. Utility functions were developed for each of these factors. On the basis of these results the management of the laboratory decided to change its promotion by emphasizing a number of convenience factors in addition to its previous focus on test reliability.

MARKETING STRATEGY SIMULATIONS

We have described a variety of applications of conjoint measurement, and still others, some in conjunction with the other techniques outlined in the Appendix, could

EXHIBIT IV A two-at-a-time factor evaluation procedure

What is more important to you?

There are times when we have to give up one thing to get something else. And, since different people have different desires and priorities, the automotive industry wants to know what things are most important to you

We have a scale that will make it possible for you to tell us your preference in certain circumstances - for example, gas mileage vs. speed. Please read the example below which explains how the scale works and then

tell us the order of your preference by writing in the numbers from 1 to 9 for each of the six questions that follow the example

Example:
Warranty vs. price of the car

Price of car	Years of warranty		
	3	2	1
$3,000	1		
$3,200			
$3,400			

Procedure:
Simply write the number 1 in the combination that represents your first choice. In one of the remaining blank squares, write the number 2 for your second choice. Then write the number 3 for your third choice, and so on, from 1 to 9.

Step 1 (Explanation)

You would rather pay the least ($3,000) and get the most (3 years). Your first choice (1) is in the box as shown.

Step 2

Your second choice is that you would rather pay $3,200 and have a 3-year warranty than pay $3,000 and get a 2-year warranty.

Price of car	Years of warranty		
	3	2	1
$3,000	1	3	
$3,200	2		
$3,400			

Step 3

Your third choice is that you would rather pay $3,000 and have a 2-year warranty than pay $3,400 and get a 3-year warranty.

Price of car	Years of warranty		
	3	2	1
$3,000	1	3	6
$3,200	2	5	8
$3,400	4	7	9

Sample:

This shows a sample order of preference for all possible combinations. Of course, your preferences could be different.

For each of the six questions below, please write in the numbers from 1 to 9 to show your order of preference for your next new car.

Price of car	Miles per gallon		
	22	18	14
$3,000			
$3,200			
$3,400			

Maximum speed	Miles per gallon		
	22	18	14
80 mph			
70 mph			
60 mph			

Roominess	Miles per gallon		
	22	18	14
6 passenger			
5 passenger			
4 passenger			

Made in	Miles per gallon		
	22	18	14
Germany			
U.S.			
Japan			

Length	Miles per gallon		
	22	18	14
12 feet			
14 feet			
16 feet			

Made in	Price of car		
	$3,000	$3,200	$3,400
Germany			
U.S.			
Japan			

be mentioned.[6] What has not yet been discussed, and is more important, is the role that utility measurement can play in the design of strategic marketing simulators. This type of application is one of the principal uses of conjoint measurement.

As a case in point, a large-scale study of consumer evaluations of airline services was conducted in which consumer utilities were developed for some 25 different service factors such as on-ground services, in-flight services, decor of cabins and seats, scheduling, routing, and price. Moreover, each utility function was developed on a route (city-pair) and purpose of trip basis.

As might be expected, the utility function for each of the various types of airline service differed according to the length and purpose of the flight. However, in addition to obtaining consumers' evaluations of service profiles, the researchers also obtained information concerning their *perceptions* of each airline (that is, for the ones they were familiar with) on each of the service factors for which the consumers were given a choice.

These two major pieces of information provided the principal basis for developing a simulation of airline services over all major traffic routes. The purpose of the simulation was to estimate the effect on market share that a change in the service configuration of the sponsor's services would have, route by route, if competitors did not follow suit. Later, the sponsor used the simulator to examine the effect of assumed retaliatory actions by its competitors. It also was able to use it to see what might happen to market share if the utility functions themselves were to change.

Each new service configuration was elevated against the base-period configuration. In addition, the simulator showed which competing airlines would lose business and which ones would gain business under various changes is perceived service levels. Thus, in addition to single, ad hoc studies, conjoint measurement can be used in the ongoing monitoring (via simulation) of consumer imagery and evaluations over time.

PROSPECTS AND LIMITATIONS

Like any new set of techniques, conjoint measurement's potential is difficult to evaluate at the present stage of development and application. Relatively few companies have experimented with the approach so far. Capability for doing the research is still concentrated in a relatively few consulting firms and companies.

Conjoint measurement faces the same kinds of limitations that confront any type of survey, or laboratory-like, technique. First, while some successes have been reported in using conjoint measurement to predict actual sales and market share, the number of applications is still too small to establish a convincing track record at the present time.

Second, some products or services may involve utility functions and decision rules that are not adequately captured by the models of conjoint measurement. While the current emphasis on additive models (absence of interactions) can be shifted to more complex, interactive models, the number of combinations required to estimate the interactions rapidly mounts. Still, little is known about how good an approximation the simpler models are to the more elaborate ones.

Third, the essence of some products and services may just not be well captured by a decomposition approach that assumes that the researcher can describe an alternative in terms of its component parts. Television personalities, hit records, movies, or even styling aspects of cars may not lend themselves to this type of reductionist approach.

While the limitations of conjoint measurement are not inconsequential, early experience suggests some interesting prospects for measuring consumer trade-offs among various product or service characteristics. Perhaps what is most interesting about the technique is its flexibility in coping with a wide variety of management's understanding of consumers' problems that ultimately hinge on evaluations of complex alternatives that a choice among products presents them with.

APPENDIX: OTHER TECHNIQUES FOR QUANTIFYING CONSUMERS' JUDGMENTS

Conjoint measurement is the latest in an increasing family of techniques that psychometricians and others in the behavioral and statistical sciences have developed to measure persons' perceptions and preferences. Conjoint measurement can often be profitably used with one or more of the following:

Factor Analysis

Factor analysis in marketing research has been around since the 1940s. However, like all the techniques to be (briefly) described here, factor analysis did not reach any degree of sophistication or practicality until the advent of the computer made the extensive computations easy to carry out. A typical input to factor analysis consists of respondents' subjective ratings of brands or services on each of a set of attributes *provided by the researcher*. For example, a sample of computer systems personnel were asked to rate various computer manufacturers' equipment and services on each of the 15 attributes shown in *Table I*.

The objective of factor analysis is to examine the commonality across the various rating scales and find a geometric representation, or picture, of the objects (computers), as well as the attributes used in the rating task. As noted in *Table I*, International Business Machines (IBM) was ranked highest on virtually all attributes while Xerox (XDS), a comparatively new entrant at the time of the study, National Cash Register (NCR), and Central Data Corporation (CDC) were not perceived as highly as the others with regard to the various attributes of interest to computer users.

The tight grouping of the attribute vectors also suggests a strong "halo" effect in favor of IBM. Only in the case of price flexibility does IBM receive less than the highest rating, and even here it is rated a close second. Thus as *Table I* shows, factor analysis enables the researcher to develop a picture of both the things being rated (the manufacturers) and the attributes along which the ratings take place.

Perceptual Mapping

A somewhat more recent technique—also abetted by the availability of the computer—is perceptual mapping. Perceptual mapping techniques take consumer judgments of *overall* similiarity or preference and find literally a picture in which objects that are judged to be similar psychologically plot near each other in geometric space (see *Table II*). However, in perceptual mapping the respondent is free to choose his *own* frame of reference rather than to respond to explicitly stated attributes.

The perceptual map of the 11 automobiles shown was developed from con-

TABLE I   *Factor Analysis of Average Respondent Ratings
of Eight Computer Manufacturers' Images on Each of
15 Attributes*

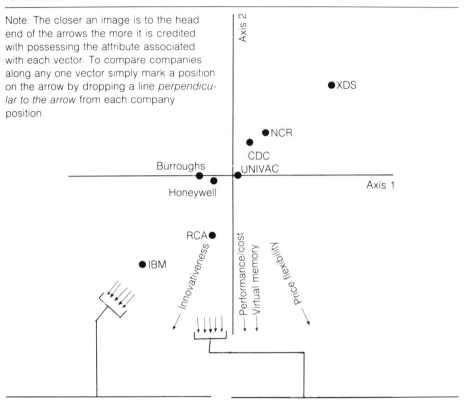

Note: The closer an image is to the head
end of the arrows the more it is credited
with possessing the attribute associated
with each vector. To compare companies
along any one vector simply mark a position
on the arrow by dropping a line *perpendicu-
lar to the arrow* from each company
position.

Reliability
Software extensiveness
Education/Training
Technical backup
Sales presentations
Systems personnel acceptance

Programming language
Ease of changeover
Service after sale
Time sharing
Overall preference

sumers' judgments about the relative similarity of the 55 distinct pairs of cars that
can be made up from the 11 cars listed. The dimension labels of *luxurious* and *sporty*
do *not* come from the technique but rather from further analysis of the map, once it
is obtained from the computer. Ideal points I and J are shown for two illustrative
respondents and are fitted into the perceptual map from the respondents' preference
judgments. Car points near a respondent's ideal point are preferred to those farther
away. Thus respondent I most likes Ford Thunderbird, while respondent J most
likes Chevrolet Corvair. In practice, data for several hundred respondents might be
used to find regions of high density for ideal points.

Cluster Analysis

Still another way to portray consumers' judgments is in terms of a hierarchical tree structure in which the more similar a set of objects is perceived to be, the more quickly the objects group together as one moves from left to right in the tree diagram. Thus the words *body* and *fullness* are perceived to be the two most closely associated of all of the descriptions appearing in *Table III* that characterize hair. Note further that smaller clusters become embedded in larger ones until the last cluster

TABLE II   *Perceptual Mapping of Respondents' Judgments of
the Relative Similarity of 11 Cars and Two Respondents'
Preference Orderings*

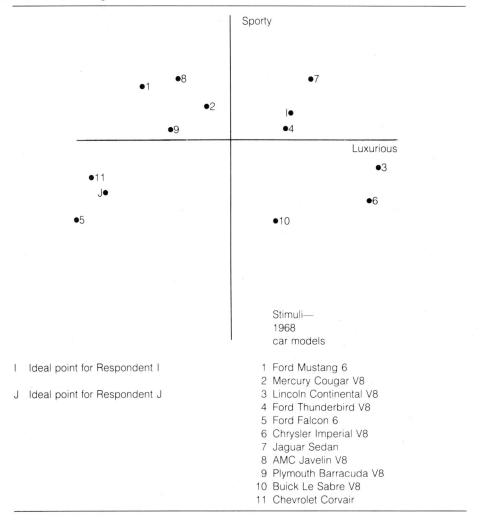

| I | Ideal point for Respondent I |
| J | Ideal point for Respondent J |

Stimuli—
1968
car models

1 Ford Mustang 6
2 Mercury Cougar V8
3 Lincoln Continental V8
4 Ford Thunderbird V8
5 Ford Falcon 6
6 Chrysler Imperial V8
7 Jaguar Sedan
8 AMC Javelin V8
9 Plymouth Barracuda V8
10 Buick Le Sabre V8
11 Chevrolet Corvair

on the right includes all 19 phrases. The words in this example were based on respondents' free associations to a set of 8 stimulus words. The researchers assumed that the more a stimulus evoked another word, the more similar they were.

Relationship to Conjoint Measurement

These three methods are best noted for their complementarities—both with each other and with conjoint measurement. Factor analysis and perceptual mapping can

TABLE III   *Hierarchical Cluster Analysis of 19 Phrases Evoked in a Free Association Task Involving Women's Hair Shampoos*

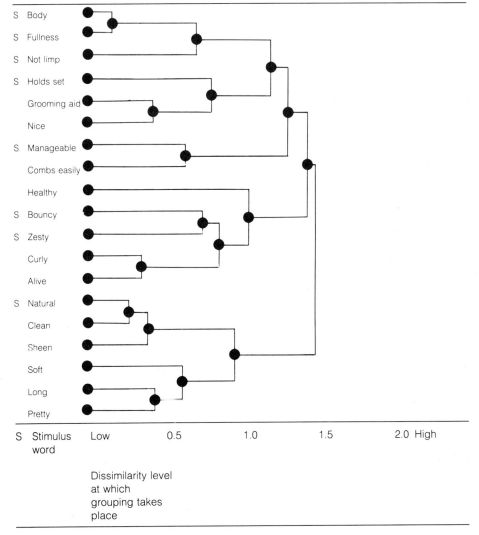

S   Stimulus
    word

Low   0.5   1.0   1.5   2.0 High

Dissimilarity level
at which
grouping takes
place

be used to measure consumers' perceptions of various products or services, while conjoint measurement can be used to quantify how consumers trade off some of one attribute to get more of another. Cluster analysis can be used in a variety of ways, either as a comparison technique for portraying the similarities of various objects or as a basis for grouping people with common perceptions or preferences. In short, all these techniques can—and frequently are—applied in the *same* study. As such, their combined use can heighten different aspects of the same general types of input data.

ENDNOTES

1. R. Duncan Luce and John W. Tukey, "Simultaneous Conjoint Measurement: A New Type of Fundamental Measurement," *Journal of Mathematical Psychology*, February 1964, p. 1.

2. The first marketing-oriented paper on conjoint measurement was by Paul E. Green and Vithala R. Rao, "Conjoint Measurement for Quantifying Judgmental Data," *Journal of Marketing Research*, August 1971, p. 355.

3. A nontechnical discussion of this special class of designs appears in Paul E. Green, "On the Design of Experiments Involving Multiattribute Alternatives," *Journal of Consumer Research*, September 1974, p. 61.

4. As an illustration, see Joseph B. Kruskal, "Analysis of Factorial Experiments by Estimating Monotone Transformation of the Data," *Journal of the Royal Statistical Society*, Series B, March 1965, p. 251.

5. Richard M. Johnson, "Trade-Off Analysis of Consumer Values," *Journal of Marketing Research*, May 1974, p. 121.

6. Paul E. Green and Yoram Wind, *Multiattribute Decisions in Marketing: A Measurement Approach* (Hinsdale, Ill.: Dryden Press, 1973).

Questions for Study and Discussion

1. In conjoint measurement, the utility scales associated with the relevant attributes are computed on the basis of rank-ordering data expressing overall preferences. According to Green and Wind, "This means that the data themselves do not determine how much more influential one attribute is than another in the consumers' choices. However, despite these limitations, the algorithms are able to find a *numerical* representation of the utilities, thus providing an indication of each factor's relative importance." In terms of the classification of scales of measurement presented in Table 2.3, p.37, what level of scale is present in a utility computed by means of conjoint measurement?.

2. Green and Wind discuss applications of conjoint measurement to the consumer evaluation of commercial plane flights, automobile tires, and carpet cleaners, as well as various other products and services. For such applications to be successful, alternative products or services must be describable in terms of their component characteristics. Do information systems and services lend themselves to being described in this way? What is the potential for application of conjoint measurement to user evaluation of information systems and services?

3. Might an interactive computer-based DSS for conjoint measurement applications be envisioned? What would be some useful features to include in a design for such a system?

SOCIAL MEASUREMENT

PART FIVE

Most people believe in the use of social statistics. Because of this acceptance, social statistics play a dominant role in modern society. They are, of course, principal means for monitoring the state of the economy. But they serve further to support management decisions in every area of social concern, including health, education, and law enforcement.

THE WIZARD OF ID
by Brant parker and Johnny hart

In democracies, leaders are chosen statistically by the deceptively simple process of counting votes. Because of the decisive nature of this process, the probing of "public opinion" has also become a central preoccupation of our society. The "polls" have thus provided decision makers with new forms of social statistics, designed in part to reflect the "bottom line" of the vote.

Statistics is a word derived from the word "state" and originally meant, "facts relating to the constitution, resources and policies of the various states of the world." Statistics enable us to grasp many large scale, complex social phenomena which would otherwise be incomprehensible. This capability makes statistics indispensable to social decision making. Statistics, however, can also be misleading, causing the mind to grasp something quite different from what is really there. Statistics often mislead because of a tendency for statistical operations to focus on just those aspects of a social issue which are measurable, to choose the most politically acceptable measurement procedure, and to downplay the level of bias and inaccuracy in the methods. For example, public understanding of the Vietnam War was formed through the reporting of body counts and kill ratios without sufficient concern for the relevance, comprehensiveness, accuracy, or validity of the numbers. The public's current understanding of inflation, unemployment and poverty may suffer from the same problems. As a result, a misplaced belief in any social statistic and the story it tells can lead to serious, even tragic, consequences.

On his resignation from government, Arthur M. Ross summed it up well: "One or two dimensions, which happen to be measurable, serve as a shadow representation of something with numerous, perhaps innumerable, dimensions." For the unaware user, this shadow replaces substance." (*Washington Post*, June 30, 1968.)

This shadow versus substance dilemma resides even in the apparently simplest issues of social measurement. Consider the issue, "How many people are there in the United States, your congressional district, or your city?" The quest for an answer to this question stirs a $34 billion controversy.

The context is the 1980 census. Since the founding of this country the census has been an integral part of the nation's policy-making structure. Article I of the United States Constitution calls for an enumeration of the population at least every ten years. Since the adoption of the Constitution census figures have been relied on for policy making. However, as Nathan Keyfitz (1979) remarks, when the results of the 1980 census are reported, "The courts and the public will be treated to a fireworks display of forensic, statistical, and demographic exposition, with a generous mixture of truth and fallacy." Why? The reasons go to the very heart of measurement for management decision at the societal level.

The measurement process of census taking involves a simple count, an enumeration. But as pointed out in Part Four, when the item being measured is a person, new sources of error are introduced into the measurement process. In the case of the census the primary concern is one of failing to count people who are really there—the so-called underenumeration problem.

Why should the possibility of underenumeration create all of this excitement? It is because the political and economic stakes are high. Census data are used to allocate seats in the House of Representatives, to distribute more than $34 billion dollars of revenue-sharing funds to some 38,000 political entities, and to set standards for many local and national social programs.

One source of underenumeration is pure random variation. If several censuses were taken at the same time using the same procedures, they would undoubtedly come up with different results. This is because, for example, "The Census Bureau's preferred evidence is the person's being described on a return-mail questionnaire containing plausible answers. Equally convincing, although more expensive, is being mentioned to an enumerator by self, spouse, or landlady in a follow-up of those for whom no questionnaire is returned. A neighbor saying that he/she is sure two persons live in a certain dwelling, even though repeated calls fail to find them at home, is another kind of evidence that the Census Bureau accepts" (Keyfitz, 1979, p. 48). Such measurement procedures are sure to introduce random error in an active, democratic, mobile society. The error potential is exacerbated by pervasive social changes such as new living arrangements and the increased number of working women.

A more perplexing source of underenumeration however is bias—the systematic failure to count some segment of the population. In the United States strong claims are made that certain minorities are systematically undercounted, thereby costing them representation and their share of government payments. For example, "The Bureau of Census has estimated that of the 5.3 million persons omitted in 1970, some 3.4 million were white and 1.9 million nonwhite. The percentage of whites omitted 1.9, of nonwhites 6.9"—a fact which evokes demands for statistical revision on the part of blacks and the Hispanic population.

How might the measurement process be improved? Several proposals have been made. These proposals and the principal arguments on their behalf are summarized below:

1. Report the census count as it emerges from the conventional measurement process and do not adjust the results at all.
   This measurement option is supported for a variety of reasons.
   a. It is said to be objective.
   b. It is preferable for statistical analyses.
   c. It does not jeopardize credibility of the census. "So far, the courts have sustained the census in virtually all cases in which its numbers have been challenged." (p. 55)

2. Report the census count as adjusted for estimated racial underenumeration in each category.
   This option would be crude and perhaps less valid, but is supported because:
   a. It removes some bias.
   b. It is simple and understandable. "No one will mistake it for anything other than a means to remove gross bias in allocation of funds." (p. 48)

3. Report the census count as further modified by age and sex, individual state corrections, information on differential underenumeration by income and other indirect and even qualitative evidence.
   This option is the most subjective of the three but is supported for the following reasons:
   a. It is more valid in the long run.
   b. It is more precise.

How should this measurement problem be resolved? It can only be resolved with a thorough understanding of the technical and social issues involved. This concluding part of the book addresses these issues.

The Census Bureau controversy highlights one of the central issues of measurements at the societal level. Social measurement is used to allocate resources. Consequently, accuracy and validity take on special meaning with respect to economic data. This theme is central to the section which follows on "The Measurement of Economic Activity."

Social measurement can also be "attention-getting" and serve to focus concern on critical social problems. The second section explores this theme.

Effective economic and social measurement requires the design and implementation of social information systems. This theme is covered in the third section.

Underlying all social measurement is the deep question of values. What social purposes should guide the measurement process? How do the values inherent in a measure influence social decision making? These questions are explored in the section on Social Values.

Finally, in the concluding section of Part Five, the basic assumptions of the measurement process are reconsidered. Positions on the role of dialogue, quantification and mood are developed.

THE MEASUREMENT OF
ECONOMIC ACTIVITY

CHAPTER **FIFTEEN**

The measurement of economic activity is perhaps the most pervasive form of societal measurement for management decision. Measures of national production, employment, prices, and productivity dominate discussions of economic policy and are well known to the public. In this section attention is focused on certain issues of measurement particular to this important area.

UNEMPLOYMENT

Perhaps no single economic indicator receives more attention from the news media, politicians, and economists than the monthly unemployment figure published by the Bureau of Labor Statistics. The figure is expressed as an unemployment *rate* and is intended to be used to guide a "full employment" policy. But as President Carter's secretary of labor, Ray Marshall points out, the measure can be deceiving. "Many statistics are designed for public consumption, but not to make decisions with. The numbers don't tell you what you have to do to get these people jobs." (*Wall Street Journal*, February 16, 1977.)

Of special concern is the fact that unemployment is not a well-defined concept, and that the standard measure is regarded by many to be severely biased. Basically, this measure considers an individual to be unemployed if he or she is sixteen years of age or older, out of work, looking for a job, and available to begin work immediately.

Some people argue that the current statistics understate real joblessness because many "discouraged" workers who have dropped out of the labor force are ignored. In 1977 the AFL-CIO estimated that this results in a reported jobless rate of 7.8% instead of an "actual" rate of 10.7%. Others argue that the statistic overrates joblessness because the Bureau of Labor Statistics defines adults as everyone aged sixteen or older. They argue that many students and teenagers who do not desire to be in the regular work force are incorrectly counted as unemployed.

Some severe reservations are also expressed by people who believe that the bureau's procedures do not objectively identify job seekers. Currently the bureau takes the word of any adult respondent at face value. Respondents who report that they have filled out a job application, answered a help-wanted ad or have been in touch with their former employer concerning the possibility of reemployment are classified as unemployed. Thus the self-report of job seeking without regard to one's qualifications or the sincerity of one's job search is taken as evidence of unemployment.

Because of differing views on unemployment and its measurement, the bureau currently publishes quarterly figures showing what the jobless rate would be under six alternative definitions. However, while these alternative measures "assuage the soul of statistician," Sar Levitan, chairman of a committee to study the figures for possible revision, concludes, ". . . there's only one number in the headlines, and that's the number that determines policy, so we have to decide what is the best single number." (*Wall Street Journal*, December 20, 1977.)

From a policy-making point of view, an important issue is the interpretation of any particular *level* of unemployment. Historically, a social goal has been the achievement of "full employment." But at what level shall we reach this goal? Here again, conceptual differences are a source of problems. If "full employment" means jobs for all those willing and able to work, this translates to a 3% jobless rate among adults as currently measured, according to some economists. Alternatively, if the goal is interpreted as the lowest jobless rate possible without generating inflation through tight labor markets, a 4–5½% rate might be implied. (*Wall Street Journal*, February 16, 1977.) Going further still, taking into account voluntary joblessness, the target rate might approach 7%, according to Herbert Stein. (*Wall Street Journal*, September 14, 1977).

Well, no one said public policy making was easy!

With such large political and economic consequences at stake, it behooves the user of unemployment and other economic statistics to be skeptical before basing decisions on this data. But what sorts of questions might be asked of the data? What should the policy maker look for? Oskar Morgenstern addresses these questions in the selection that follows. He reviews the problems of securing control over the data acquisition process, and the problems of dealing with errors, lying, and falsification of data on questionnaires.

SOURCES AND ERRORS OF
ECONOMIC STATISTICS

Oskar Morgenstern

1. LACK OF DESIGNED EXPERIMENTS

Economic statistics are not, as a rule, the result of designed experiments, although one of the earlier great economists, J. H. von Thünen, conducted careful experiments in administering his estate, kept extensive records of his operations which he then analyzed, thereby anticipating much of the later marginal utility theory. But in general, economic statistics are merely by-products or results of business and government activities and have to be taken as these determine. Therefore, they often measure, describe, or simply record something that is not exactly the phenomenon in which the economist would be interested. They are often dependent on legal rather than economic definitions of processes.

A significant difference between the use of data in the natural and social sciences is that in the former the *producer* of the observations is usually also their *user*. If he does not exploit them fully himself, they are passed on to others who, in the tradition of the sciences, are precisely informed about the origin and the manner of obtaining these data. Furthermore, new data have to be fitted into a vast body of data that have been tested over and over again and into theories that have passed through the crucible of application. Also, the quality of the work of the observers is well known, and this contributes to establishing a level of precision of and confidence in the information. In the natural sciences, even the most abstract theorists are exceedingly well informed about the precise nature, circumstances, and limitations of experiments and measurements. Indeed, without such knowledge their work would be entirely impossible or meaningless.

In the social sciences the situation is quite different. It is not often feasible to be aware of the detailed nature of the data. Summarization of data is often performed by widely separated statistical workers who are likewise far removed from the later users. And finally, the tradition has simply not yet fully established itself for the users to insist upon being fully informed about all steps of the gathering and computing of statistics. Anyone who has used economic statistics, even when prepared by the finest economic-statistical institutions, knows how exceedingly difficult it is to reestablish the conditions under which they were collected, their domain, the pre-

Excerpt from "Characteristics of Sources and Errors of Economic Statistics," in Oskar Morgenstern, *On the Accuracy of Economic Observations*, 2nd. rev. ed. (copyright © 1963 by Princeton University Press): pp. 13–32. Reprinted by permission of Princeton University Press.

cise activity they define, etc., although it may be decisive to be fully informed about these various stages. One of the main reasons for this difficulty is that economic data as a rule have to cover long periods of time in order to be useful. It is rarely the case that single pieces of information, not concerned with processes that extended into the past and are likely to continue into an indefinite future, are of value for economic analysis. Thus economic data are normally time series, i.e., numbers of the same kind of event, say the price of bread, strung out over time. When the series are long, as they ought to be, it is often exceedingly difficult to know how the data were obtained in the past and to what extent temporal comparability is assured.

Many producers of primary statistics make a considerable effort to inform the reader of the details of composition, stages of classification, and all other characteristics of the statistics. There are too many cases, however, where this description is sketchy and where large gaps remain. Sometimes this is due to negligence and the belief and the authority of the reporting agency is great enough to inspire full confidence in the statistics. Such authority never exists for scientific purposes. On the other hand, the great detail involved in the collection of most economic information makes it virtually impossible physically to produce the entire background of the descriptive detail each time that some figures are given or used. Sometimes the official commentary to statistical tables is exceedingly lengthy and fills volumes, impossible to absorb in a manner that would lead to a correction of the given numbers by the user. By swamping the user with hosts of footnotes and explanations, the makers of statistics try to absolve themselves from the need to indicate numerical error estimates. Thus a dilemma exists that could only be overcome by the development and indication of a quantitative measure expressing the error. As will be seen, such numerical expressions are lacking at the present time; in some cases they may never become available.

The deficiency of information on procedures of data-gathering is usually less striking when *sampling* methods are used to obtain economic statistics. Although a sample may sometimes be bad and though there may be other objectionable features, their construction is subject to scientific scrutiny, and the problems that must be solved in setting up a good sample are very well known. The solutions are a function of the state of sampling theory and its application in the given case. Sampling statistics in economics—a technique that we do not discuss here any further—are fortunately gaining in importance. They suggest themselves in particular when great aggregates have to be measured, such as the determination of the volume of industrial output, share of market, sales, foreign trade, and so on. Sampling is also highly valuable in constructing price statistics. In general, it can be said that the possibilities of sampling procedures have not yet been fully utilized in economics. Wherever estimates are necessary, and often they are the only possible way to arrive at some aggregates, sampling is indispensable. This is true, for example, in estimating items in the balance of payments, such as travelers' expenditures abroad, etc., where a direct approach to totals is clearly out of the question. In addition, sampling statistics can be used as checks on complete counts in order to improve the latter. Unfortunately, not enough use is made of this opportunity.

Sampling, however, is a possible additional source of error when mistakes are made in the application of the technique. Such mistakes are sometimes exceedingly difficult to avoid and some striking instances are known, as revealed by special investigations. Furthermore, sampling statistics are susceptible to the other kinds of error derived from faulty classification, time discrepancies, poor recording, etc. Sampling errors, of course, can be estimated and are usually stated. Although they do not account for the entire error or provide a way to its numerical evaluation, the indication of this component is extremely valuable.

Even though sampling procedures are being more widely introduced, the largest masses of economic statistics simply accrue without any overall scientific design or plan. It would probably be impossible to make general plans for collecting statistics without violating some basic principles of the free exchange economy. Thus the development of economics is dependent to a very high degree upon an agglomeration of statistics that in the main is rather accidental from the point of view of economic theory.

The interplay between theory, measurement, and data collection should be as intimate in economics as it is in physics, but we are far from having reached this condition. However, the signs are multiplying that economics is moving in this direction.

2. HIDING OF INFORMATION, LIES

There is overly often a deliberate attempt to hide information. In other words, economic and social statistics are frequently based on evasive answers and *deliberate lies* of various types. These lies arise, principally, from misunderstandings, from fear of tax authorities, from uncertainty about or dislike of government interference and plans, or from the desire to mislead competitors. Nothing of this sort occurs in nature. Nature may hold back information, is always difficult to understand, but it is believed that she does not lie deliberately. Einstein has aptly expressed this fact by saying: "Raffiniert ist der Herr Gott, aber boshaft ist er nicht."[1] In that, he follows Descartes and Bacon and adheres to the classical idea of the *"veracitas dei."* The difference between describing a statistical universe made up of physical events exclusively and one in which social events occur can be, and usually is, profound. We observe here a significant variation in the structure of the physical and social sciences, provided it is true that nature is merely indifferent and not hostile to man's efforts to finding out truth—it certainly not being friendly. We shall assume indifference, though proof is, I believe, lacking.

The fact, all too frequently occurring, that statistics are sloppily gathered and prepared at the source, for example, by the firms giving out the requested information, is a different matter altogether; it is less serious than the fact of evasion, which may or may not be present at the same time. It will be seen that the lie can also take the form of handing out literally "correct," but functionally and operationally meaningless or false statistics.

Deliberately untrue statistics offer a most serious problem with broad ramifications in the realm of statistical theory, where, however, the nature and consequences of such statistics do not seem to have been explored sufficiently. It is frequently to the advantage of business to *hide* at least some information. This is easily seen—if not directly evident—from the point of view of the theory of games of strategy. Indeed, the theory of games finds a very strong corroboration in the indisputable fact that there *are* carefully guarded business secrets. Law cannot always force correct information into the open; on the contrary, it often makes some information even more worth hiding (e.g., when taxes are imposed). The incentive to lie, or at least to hide, is also strongly influenced by the competitive situation: the more prevalent are monopolies, quasi-monopolies, or oligopolies, the less trustworthy are many statistics deriving from those industries, especially information about prices because of secret rebates granted to different customers. Consequently, statistics derived from this kind of basic data suffer greatly in reliability. For example, where national income or personal income distribution is computed on the basis of income tax returns, the results will be of widely different accuracy for different countries, tax rates, tax morale, price movements, etc. It is well known that income tax returns for France and Italy, and probably many other countries, have only a vague resemblance to the actual, underlying income patterns of those countries. Yet it is on the basis of tax returns that important and elusive problems, such as the validity of the "Pareto distribution" explaining the inequality of personal incomes, are minutely studied. For sales—an item of primary importance in input-output studies—it must be remembered that sales prices constitute some of the most closely guarded secrets in many businesses. The same is often true for inventories. A prime example is the distilling industry. There it is vital for one company not to let any other know what its stock is, lest it suffer in the inevitable price and market struggle.

Governments, too, are not free from falsifying statistics. This occurs, for example, when they are bargaining with other governments and wish to obtain strategic advantages or feel impelled to bluff. More often, information is simply blocked for reasons of military security, or in order to hide the success or failure of plans. In Fascist and Communist totalitarian countries the suppression of statistics is often carried very far. For example, foreign trade data are considered secret in some eastern European countries with capital punishment threatened for disclosure! Even in the United States incomplete figures are released in the field of atomic energy, although the known total appropriations for the Atomic Energy Commission indicate that this is one of the largest American industrial undertakings. The same applies to this field to all present (and will apply to all future) atomic powers. The budget for the Central Intelligence Agency, unquestionably running into hundreds of millions of dollars, is hidden in a multitude of other accounts in the Federal budget, invalidating also those accounts. The Russian defense budget is only incompletely known. An example of government falsification of statistics is Nazi Germany's stating its gold reserves far below those actually available, as was revealed by later information. Or, more subtly, indexes of prices are computed and published from irrelevant prices in order to hide a true price movement. Central banks in many countries, the venerable Bank of England not excepted, have for decades published deliberately misleading statistics, as, for example, when part of the gold in their possession is put under "other assets" and only part is shown as "gold." In democratic Great Britain before World War II, the Government's "Exchange Equalization Account" suppressed for a considerable period all statistics about its gold holdings, although it became clear later that these exceeded the amount of gold shown to be held by the Bank of England at the time. This list could be greatly lengthened. If respectable governments falsify information for policy purposes, if the Bank of England lies and hides or falsifies data, then how can one expect minor operators in the financial world always to be truthful, especially when they know that the Bank of England and so many other central banks are not?

A special study of these falsified, suppressed, and misrepresented government statistics is greatly needed and should be made. The probably deliberate over- and understatements of needs and resources in the negotiations concerned with the international food situation, the Marshall Plan, etc., offer vast opportunities for such investigations—if the truth can be found out.

When the Marshall Plan was being introduced, one of the chief European figures in its administration (who shall remain nameless) told me: "We shall produce any statistic that we think will help us to get as much money out of the United States as we possibly can. Statistics which we do not have, but which we need to justify our demands, we will simply fabricate." These statistics "proving" the need for certain kinds of help will go into the historical records of the period as true descriptions of the economic conditions of those times. They may even be used in econometric work!

The true or imagined purpose of statistics often has a great influence upon the answers (especially in designed statistics). In undeveloped areas there is often an important element of "boasting," beside a general desire to give the questioner the kind of answer he would like to hear, however remote it might be from the truth.[2]

A very modern and unusually important instance of the problem of obtaining data is the problem of inspection in arms control. There, sampling would have to be used in order to discover possible evasions through secret production of arms, secret atomic tests, etc. An international inspection team would encounter great difficulties not yet resolved by modern statistics. A theory of "sampling in a hostile environment" is now under development; it would be applicable to many other situations in the social world.

Where such conditions prevail, the designer may have to hide the purpose of the statistic and the nature of the statistical procedure from the subject, who, in his turn, tries to hide the truth. This is the precise setup of a nonstrictly determined two-person game where both sides have to resort to mixed or "statistical" strategies. It is an ironic circumstance that in order to get good statistics, "statistical strategies" may have to be used.

Proper techniques of questioning will have to be worked out to produce a minimum of error under these conditions. These phenomena may also be viewed as disturbances of the subjects interrogated. They are familiar to anthropologists who find that conditions in primitive societies have changed after these have previously been visited by other anthropologists. Conditions of disturbances occur also in physical experiments, where in some well-defined cases in quantum mechanics it has been shown impossible on *principle* to obtain certain types, or rather certain combinations, of information.

The undeniable existence of an unknown but undoubtedly substantial amount of deliberately falsified information presents a unique feature for the theoretical social sciences, totally absent in the natural sciences, whether historical or theoretical.

History too has to cope with this difficulty. Falsifications are notorious there and can be found everywhere. Therefore source criticism is a highly developed technique that every student of history has to learn in detail. A large literature exists in this field and many eminent historians have contributed to it. Without this tradition, the writing of history would be entirely worthless. Clearly, it is not simple to establish a "historical fact" or else there would be little need to rewrite history as often as this is done (quite apart, of course, from the ever-changing evaluation of the past).

A good illustration of the difficulty in determining the true value of historical claims is given in the classical work of Hans Delbrück,[3] who has carefully examined most military battles fought over the centuries with a view to determining the strength of the opposing forces. It is clear that the victors have always stated the defeated to have been much stronger then they were in order to make victory impressive, and the losers vice versa in order to make defeat excusable; this often creates figures that are impossible for the same occasion. Delbrück has found, for example, that if the Greek claims regarding the strength of the Persians at Thermopylae were true, there would not even have been room for the Persian troops to occupy the battlefield. Or, given the roads of the time, the last Persian troops would have just crossed the Bosporus when the first already had arrived in Greece. In this manner it goes throughout history, even up to most recent times; and what really happened is very difficult to find out.

Other instances from fields of social statistics or fact-finding are suicide statistics. They are notoriously bad because lay coroners so frequently disagree with medical men, and because great efforts have always been made to keep the fact of suicide secret.[4] This applies also to medical statistics; for generations it was considered improper to die of cancer, hence little mention of this disease. This shows up in the very limited value of statistics of death (the records of insurance companies notwithstanding). Time series, in particular, suffer from the fact that many diseases in former years were entirely unknown to medical science, although people died of them. Thus, the "growth" of certain diseases is perhaps simply their better identification. This is notorious for mental illness. For example, there are many more mental cases in Sweden per 100,000 of population than in Yugoslavia. But this is simply due to the fact that in the former country the patient is taken care of in a hospital, whereas in the latter he vegetates as the village idiot and is not recorded as a mental case. Death certificates are very difficult to make out when death is due, as is often the case, to several causes, e.g., pneumonia following upon some other affliction. Only a few countries demand autopsies in every case; and even then death cannot always be uniquely attributed to a single cause.

The difficulties of finding out what "facts" are can clearly be seen in legal procedure. Evidence is placed before juries but the outcome of their fact-finding is notoriously uncertain. In general, the experience is that the chances of establishing a fact as such before a court of law are very small and that a prediction of the outcome of a law suit is hazardous. Many witnesses lie, sometimes perjury is discovered. Even when witnesses are truthful, or trying to be truthful, their statements are subject to all the doubts and limitations that have been brought out in a vast literature on the psychology of witnesses and the reliability of memory. It would lead too far afield to deal further with these matters here, though they do illuminate some of the difficulties of fact-finding encountered also in economics.

Without knowing the extent of the falsifications that actually occur in economic statistics, it is impossible to estimate their influence upon economic theory. But the peculiar feature remains that, if economic theory is based on observations of facts (as it ought to be), these are not only subject to ordinary errors, but in addition to the influences of deliberate falsifications. If for no other reasons, this is a severe restriction on the operational value of economics as long as the magnitude of this factor has not been fully investigated. Here is a field where thorough studies are required; they will be difficult to make, but they promise important results. The theory of games takes full cognizance of the phenomenon wherever it becomes relevant.

Falsification is difficult when it is attempted in a system of organization that is well described and understood. It is virtually impossible in a small mechanical system, though for large systems there are already doubts as to its working beyond a certain degree of reliability. To introduce a false circuit in an electronic computer would be foolish, since it is bound to be discovered. But social organizations are not nearly as well described as physical systems. Hence their working behavior cannot be predicted as precisely. This means that there are degrees of freedom of behavior that are compatible with alternative, equally plausible descriptions of the system. They need not differ profoundly. In addition, it should be noted, it is possible to prove that *there can be no complete formalization of society.* Consequently, a lie or falsification relating to some part or component of the system is exceedingly hard to discover, except by chance. Yet the chance factor itself is a necessary, constituent element of every social system. Without it "bluffing," a perfectly sound move in strategic behavior by elements (persons or firms) of a social organization, would be impossible. But it is a daily occurrence. Bluffing is an essential feature of rational strategies.

So we see that a lie or falsification has to be related to the degree of our knowledge of the framework within which it is attempted.

To give an illustration: Our knowledge of the population of a country, as established by a series of population counts, to which is added our knowledge of human reproductive ability makes it difficult to introduce in the next census willful distortions that would go beyond a certain measure. Lies—or other, ordinary errors—can be discovered, though this may be laborious. An economy is much less understood, and when a government, for example, reports to be in the possession of x millions of gold instead of the true y millions, this is very hard, if not impossible, to contradict, since both x and y may be compatible with our understanding of the economy and its workings. Experiments with individual firms have shown that many falsifications of production records cannot be discovered, even by means of the most minute money accounting controls. When it comes to the recording of prices, movement of goods (especially in international trade, inventories, etc.), the possibilities are substantially widened. Even in production the wide substitutability of one material for another makes great variations plausible. Of course, nobody would believe that a large country could have doubled its steel capacity within one year—but we do not consider such crude matters.

When an economy is in the throes of a great development, coupled with a rapidly changing technology, the scope for misrepresentation is correspondingly widened. Our knowledge of dynamic processes is necessarily inferior to our ability to describe stationary conditions. Yet the economies we deal with are now and have been for decades in a period of active, dynamic development.

In summarizing, we see that there are three principal sources of false representation: First, the observer, by making a selection as to what and how much to observe, introduces a bias that it is impossible to avoid, because a complex phenomenon can never be exhaustively described. This bias, common to all science, is of no concern here. Second, the observer may deliberately hide information or falsify his findings to suit his hypotheses or his political purposes. This occurs in historical writings, even in physical science in exceptional cases of fraud, and more frequently when economic and social statistics are used or abused in the hands of unscrupulous persons or institutions. Reference to some cases has been made above. Third, the observed distinction between social and physical observations; in the latter, this factor is absent no matter how difficult it may be to discover the facts. To account for this additional character of observations in the social field, new ideas concerning the foundations of statistics are necessary, as has been indicated above. The distinction applies to both measureable and (for the time being) nonmeasurable information or observations.

3. THE TRAINING OF OBSERVERS

Economic statistics, even when planned in detail, are frequently not gathered by highly trained observers but by personnel collected ad hoc. This is a source of the most serious kind of mass errors. Even trained census-takers and many others engaged in field work are not "observers" in a strict scientific sense. A scientific observer is the astronomer at his telescope, the physicist recording the scatter of mesons, the biologist determining the hereditary behavior of some cells, etc.; all are themselves scientists; they do not operate through agents many times removed. Except where experiments are involved, the social sciences will never get into an equivalent position as far as the basic raw material of observations is concerned. Because of the masses of data needed this would be physically impossible. We cannot place technically trained economists or statisticians at the gates of factories in order to determine what has been produced and how much is being shipped to whom at what prices. We will have to rely on business records, kept by men and, increasingly, by machines, none of them part of the ideally needed scientific setup as such. If properly engineered (and costs of processing are a minor consideration), these data can be useful. In the future we will be able to rely more on automatic recording devices and computers, thereby improving, but also modifying, the picture.

It is well known from sampling experience (where, if properly done, one deals with strictly, though not always *well* designed statistics!) that the response is very different depending upon the type of observer, even if the latter is trained[5] and should be—miraculously—free of bias. Detailed knowledge of how much improvement in statistics could be obtained by training, or more training (at greater expense) is difficult to come by. Hence, the phenomenon, well known from experimental physics and astronomy, of the "personal equation" assumes very much larger proportions with less definite controls and perhaps even fundamentally different characteristics.

It could perhaps be argued that it should be possible to explore the nature of lies and the influence of training and bias of the observer thoroughly in controlled experiments. In other words, a sample would be designed which would be studied to the utmost degree; from the information thus gained one could then arrive at an evaluation of these factors, even in cases where no thorough exploration would be possible. It is to be doubted, however, that such a program can be carried out at the present state of affairs; it may even encounter systematic difficulties of a nature too deep to be discussed here.

4. ERRORS FROM QUESTIONNAIRES

Designed economic and social statistics often require the use of questionnaires. Some are presented orally; others require written answers. Some of the latter may at times contain several hundred questions directed to the same firm or individual. Errors can and do derive from the setting up of the questionnaires and from the answers. The questions should always be so formulated that unique answers are possible. But this is often not the case, for, on the contrary, many questions are not stated unambiguously or they require more intelligence for correct answers than is possessed by the person questioned. When large numbers of questions are involved, the possibility that contradictions will occur in the answers may be great, while at the same time significant omissions may be made. Often words are used that have emotional or political connotations and prejudice the answer, depending on the individual to whom they are presented. Some questions invite evasion, lies, and, when very numerous, a summary response (sometimes capricious) in order to save time, money, and generally to avoid bother and trouble. It also makes a great deal of difference whether the same questions are presented orally, in writing, by mail, and so forth.

As is well known, each form of interrogation produces its own kind of bias. The process of asking questions and getting answers is a delicate psychological one. Apart from lying and refusal to give information, there is forgetfulness, prompting by the questioner with its own consequent bias, lack of comprehension of the question, etc. These phenomena have been studied in the literature.[6] Certain investigations of business decisions by means of questionnaires have produced results contradictory to expectations. In these cases, however, it is difficult to arrive at a conclusion, largely because it need not be assumed that businessmen always are able to interpret their own actions. A human being, though a living organism, is not necessarily able to describe his own functioning; yet he has a formidable "experience" of living. It takes several sciences to describe the process of living and to tell how the human body functions, and these sciences clearly have not yet come to the end of their questions and the search for answers.

The field of questionnaires is comparatively new in statistics, and the theory covering it is far from completely developed. Indeed, it is doubtful that even the qualitative description and enumeration of its characteristics are complete. Here we merely point to its existence and emphasize its enormous importance, especially for those large data collections connected with input-output studies of industry and business, determination of incomes, spending habits, etc.

The difficulties of preparing good questionnaires and using them properly are, indeed, formidable but not appreciated by the public. The simple fact is that it is not easy to ask good questions and to ensure that intelligent, reliable, and honest answers will be given. Science is, after all, nothing but a continuing effort to find the right questions, followed by the search for answers. And the question is often more important than the answer. It is not different in drawing up questionnaires for economic matters. Progress in science has often been blocked by having asked the wrong questions. When a field such as economics depends so largely on asking human rather than inanimate nature, the problem of the right question assumes new importance.

There is one requirement that can and should be fulfilled, whatever the state of the theory that covers the problems arising from the design and use of questionnaires: whenever questionnaires are used (or questions are asked orally), their precise text, with instructions for use, should be published together with the final results and interpretation. A mere paraphrasing of the question is insufficient because it may involve subtle changes in the meaning and undertones. In that respect, however, many producers of primary statistics, including government agencies, fail to comply and give only the vaguest kind of information about the underlying questions. This circumstance deprives the user of the results of a great deal of their value. Publicly used statistics for which the user does not have access to this information should be rejected, no matter how interesting and important the particular field may be. On the other hand, the publication of the frequently very numerous and complicated questions does not make the use of the answers any easier, because the reader is supposed to accomplish a difficult task of interpretation and evaluation for which he may not always be prepared.

Countless examples could be given of poorly designed questionnaires and samples. But we are not looking for the inadequate in economic statistics. Rather we try to assess the presumably best and to find out how much confidence can be placed in the work of the most renowned institutions. When troublesome errors are found there we have to conclude that elsewhere they will not be much different.

An interesting example, pertaining to questionnaires but pointing toward wider problems, is the following: In 1953, the British Ministry of Labor and National Service conducted an inquiry into household expenditure by questionnaire and by interview. A total of 20,000 households were asked to list all their expenditures over a period of three weeks. Of the returns, only 12,911 were usable. The figures were broken down in many ways, one way being expenditure on various items by household against income of head of household. We can extract from Table 9 of the "Report of an Enquiry into Household Expenditure in 1953–54," (H.M.S.O., London), the figures indicated in our Table 1. We note the huge figure for weekly expenditure on women's outer clothing for the richest group (over £ 50). However, a footnote gives the reason for this: "One member of a household in this group spent £ 1903 on one item during the period"—the item presumably being a very expensive fur coat. This fur coat keeps reappearing throughout other tables and each time provides us with a ridiculous figure. There is nothing *wrong* with the data; and the statisticians who wrote the report have been perfectly honest, but their results would have been more useful if the coat had been left out.

This example shows, incidentally, with what great care certain statistical phenomena have to be treated. When they are encountered and recognized, they give rise to refinements in statistical methodology that constitute a progress of our understanding of such situations. They also make it clear that there always have existed errors of a more elusive kind which now can be avoided. But the approach to these problems also puts ever-increasing demands on the user of statistics that cannot always be met.

Specifically, the above example shows that it is dangerous to break down results of surveys into many, very small groups. The number of "subjects" lying in some of these will be small, and the results will be inaccurate. These "outlyers" are rare events (in terms of the sample) and probably belong to a different statistical distribution than the one encountered. They can mislead badly and will do so unless there is an immediate, intuitive reason to recognize the circumstances, as in the case of the fur coat. Even if its value had only been one-tenth it would still have biased the statistics, but this would not have been as obvious.

Techniques for the rejection of outlyers have been developed. They show that

TABLE 1 Weekly Income of Head of Household

	£ 50 or more		£ 30 to £ 50		£ 20 to £ 30		£ 14 to £ 20		£ 10 to £ 14		£ 8 to £ 10		£ 6 to £ 8		£ 3 to £ 6		Under £ 3	
Number in sample falling in this group	58		111		291		1003		2705		2770		2472		1589		1843	
	s.	d.	s.	d.	s.	d.	s.	d.	s.	d.	s.	d.	s.	d.	s.	d.	s.	d.
Weekly expenditure on women's outer clothing	225	6.3	11	4.9	13	9.3	9	8.2	6	2.0	4	9.6	4	11.7	4	8.9	3	5.7

(s = shillings, d = pence)

outlyers appear in many statistics and can lead to important inaccuracies, unless good methods for their rejection are used. Poor methods can produce other biases, hard to discover.

We have introduced this matter in order to show that one may sometimes spot an obvious or striking fact and recognize it as an error or distortion; but behind it there usually are many more of the same kind, yet hidden and elusive. They can be brought to light only by sophisticated statistical theory.

ENDNOTES

1. Inscription on the mantle of a fireplace in Fine Hall in Princetown University: "The Lord God is sophisticated, but not malicious."

2. It is reported that in Russia in the early 1930s the central statistical authorities had worked out "lie-coefficients" with which to correct the statistical reports according to regions, industries, etc. Nothing definite is known, but quite recently Khrushchev has accused especially Russian agricultural circles of reporting grossly false statistics.

3. *Geschichte der Kriegskunst in Rahmen der Politischen Geschichte* (Berlin, 1900). A brief extract is found in his (now very rare) *Numbers in History, How the Greeks Defeated the Persians* (London, 1913).

4. Accidents are another case where great doubts often prevail as to cause and effect. Probably most murders go undetected. For example, a very large proportion of hunting accidents are apparently murders; an investigation showing this was suppressed, however.

5. For example, population statistics often show concentrations at the rounded-off ages of 20, 25, 30, etc. which are in clear contradiction to earlier information. In other words, people prefer to indicate these ages, rather than their true ones which lie in between. The response to questions about attendance at college depends to a high degree upon the social status of the questioned and that of the investigator. If he appears to belong to the college-educated class, he will more often than not hear that the questioned went to college too, and vice versa. Some of these answers are also motivated by the fact that the questioned wishes to please the interrogator.

6. Compare F. F. Stephan, "Sampling Opinions, Attitudes and Wants," *Proceedings of the American Philosophical Society*, Vol. 92 (February 1943), pp. 387–98; and F. F. Stephan and P. J. McCarthy, *Sampling Opinions. An Analysis of Survey Procedures* (New York 1958), which gives a comprehensive and up-to-date discussion of the difficulties and the current ways to overcome them.

A particularly interesting work is S. L. Payne, *The Art of Asking Questions* (Princeton, 1951; Rev. Ed., 1955) which shows the many ambiguities in questions asked, the different associations they evoke, and what dangerous manipulations are possible.

Questions for Study and Discussion

1. How do Morgenstern's three principal sources of falsification apply to the problem of getting an accurate estimate of the United States population? Unemployment?

2. People deceive, nature doesn't. Do you agree? Comment.

3. Morgenstern states, "The true or imagined purpose of statistics often has a great influence upon the answers." Do you agree? Provide illustrations. How does this statement relate to the behavioral dimensions of measurement discussed in Part Three?

4. Monthly unemployment figures released by the Bureau of Labor Statistics are seasonally adjusted. What is the rationale for making such adjustments? What is a rationale opposed to these adjustments? (For one point of view on this, see the *Wall Street Journal*, February 22, 1977.)

5. The source for the unemployment data compiled by the Bureau of Labor Statistics is the Current Population Survey administered by the Bureau of the Census. (For a description of the design of this survey, see Thompson and Shapiro, 1973.) Sources of error in the Current Population Survey have been classified into the following categories:

(i) Sampling errors
(ii) Undercoverage
(iii) Noninterviews
(iv) Nonresponse
(v) Response bias
(vi) Response variance
(vii) Processing errors

How may errors in each of these categories be controlled?

6. In tabulating the unemployed, should a student who is taking fifteen credit hours and looking for a few hours babysitting work on the side be counted? (Currently, such a student, if sixteen years of age or older, *is* counted as unemployed.) Is this a question which should be resolved scientifically? If you were the mayor of Ann Arbor, Michigan, for instance, would you be indifferent to the resolution of this question?

7. In *The Design of Inquiring Systems* (1971) Churchman presents the concept of the "guarantor"— the fundamental belief system which assures one that a statement is valid and true. How does this concept relate to the problem of creating and maintaining the credibility of a social statistic, or as Morgenstern states, the problem of establishing the "belief that the authority of the reporting agency is great enough to inspire full confidence in the statistics"?

8. In an intriguing article entitled "The Case of the Indians and the Teen-age Widows" Ansley Coale and Frederick Stephan (1962) describe how errors were created in the 1950 Census of Population when a relatively small proportion (less than 1%) of the "Persons" cards were punched one column to the right of the proper position in several columns. As a result exaggerated numbers were tabulated in certain *rare* categories—very young widows and divorcés, and male Indians aged 10–14 and 20–24.

For example, the following numbers were reported:

Age	Number of Widowed Males
14	1670
15	1475
16	1175
17	810
18	905
19	630

Apparently, some of the keypunching errors slipped through because the very costly operation of 100% verification was replaced by sample verification. How would you suggest dealing with this source of error?

CHAPTER **SIXTEEN**

"Seventeen million Americans go to bed hungry every night." Citing this statistic, John F. Kennedy called attention to a social problem which was to serve as a main theme of his 1960 campaign for the presidency. The "New Frontier" politics which emerged proposed social programs aimed at improving the situation measured by this statistic.

How did Kennedy know the extent of the hunger problem in the United States? His estimate was based on a 1955 Department of Agriculture study on eating habits. The study assumed that almost all households with low incomes had diets with nutritional deficiencies. The report also indicated that about 13% to 17% of American households with incomes of $10,000 or more also experienced dietary problems. Nutritional deficiency as a definition of hunger, household income as an indicator of nutritional deficiency, and census data as an estimate of the magnitude were the basis for this estimate of hunger in the United States.

"Going to bed hungry" is a potent political image, and one can well understand its use in a presidential campaign. But what is the extent of the problem to be faced by a "War on Poverty?"

POVERTY MEASUREMENTS

The "official" source of information on poverty in the United States is the Current Population Survey conducted monthly by the United States Census. A random sample of 47,000 households (about 100,000 individuals) is taken. A household is "in poverty" if its total money income for the previous year falls below a standard based on family size, member ages, and whether or not it lives on a farm. The standard is updated annually for inflation. In 1976 the official poverty line for a nonfarm family of four was $5,700. The resulting poverty count, based on the survey methodology, was twenty-five million poor persons, one out of eight Americans.

How accurate was this measurement? In a review of recent criticisms of the poverty measure, Frank Levy (*Wall Street Journal*, March 3, 1978) lists the following sources of "error":

1. a bias toward overestimation exists through well-known patterns of underreporting of income, particularly from government payments, an important income source for the poor.

2. a bias toward underestimation may exist in that pretax, rather than after-tax income is assessed.

3. a second bias toward overestimation exists in that only *money* income is considered. "In-kind" income (e.g, food stamps, free school lunches, public rent subsidies, and Medicaid) are not included.

4. poverty may be "transitory" in many situations; researchers at the University of Michigan's Institute for Social Research estimate that over one seven-year period, only one fifth of the poverty population was poor all seven years, though three fourths were poor four years or more.

Applying what he terms "back-of-the-envelope" corrections to the official 1976 poverty count, Levy estimates the number of long-term poor in the United States to be 13.7 million. This, he concludes, is still a significant number deserving of reform.

Was Kennedy's estimate of hungry Americans an adequate basis for guiding social policy? Is the official United States poverty count any better as a measurement for management decision? This section explores questions of this kind. One of the purposes of social measurement is to draw attention to social problems. Kennedy's estimate certainly did that. But a proper measure should also accurately reflect the nature and extent of the problem. Here some important questions should be posed:

1. Is the measure the "true" measure of the phenomenon?

2. Can the measure by validated and tested?

3. If the measured situation improves following the implementation of a policy, when can we infer that the policy led to improvement?

These three questions motivate the choice of articles in this section.

In the first reading Biderman and Reiss discuss the difficulty of measuring all incidents of criminality. They refer to these unobserved and uncounted incidents as the "dark figure" of crime. An important distinction is made between the "realist" approach to measurement which seeks to report every real occurrence of a crime, and the "institutionalist" approach which acknowledges only those incidences of crime for which there is an organized, legitimate social response. The institutionalist uses actual counts such as those appearing on a police blotter, whereas the realist uses additional data to impute and infer the "true" extent of the problem.

The fascinating aspect of Kennedy's seventeen million hungry Americans is that the number took on a life of its own. It was repeated extensively in the media and became *the* definition of the problem. In "The Vitality of Mythical Numbers," Max Singer explores this phenomenon by which measures become unchallenged realities. He alerts us to the dangers of taking these numbers at face value, and suggests some methods for testing the plausibility of such numbers.

In "Reforms as Experiments," Donald Campbell takes up the question of how measures can be used to evaluate the effectiveness of social programs. Drawing on the theory of experimentation, he argues that social programs can be conducted as experiments which successfully deal with threats to the validity of the program's measures of performance.

ON EXPLORING THE "DARK FIGURE" OF CRIME

Albert D. Biderman • Albert J. Reiss, Jr.   *READING 26*

Statistical criminology began with the development of *moral statistics*.[1] No subject has dominated the field of criminal statistics more since its inception than the search for the key moral statistic—a measure of the "criminality" present among a population. This search led increasingly to a concern about the "dark figure" of crime—that is, about occurrences that by some criteria are called crime yet that are not registered in the statistics of whatever agency was the source of the data being used.[2]

The history of criminal statistics testifies to continuing contention between those who sought to bring more of the dark figure to statistical light and those who deplored elements of invalidity in each such attempt. The major object of this contention for over a century was *police statistics*. Both official and scholarly comprehensions of the incidence of crime were almost exclusively based on statistics of *indictments* or *adjudications*. There were those who sought the development of police statistics to supplement, if not supplant, them. The contending arguments were fundamentally between what we can loosely term "realist" as opposed to "institutionalist" emphases.[3] The former emphasized the virtues of completeness with which data represented the "real crime that takes place." The institutionalist perspective emphasized that crime could have valid meaning only in terms of organized, legitimate social responses to it.

The ultimate juristic view is that a given crime is not validly known to have taken place until a court finds someone guilty of that offense. Only at that point in the process has there been an irrevocable decision as to the evidence regarding the objective facts in relation to their legal significance. Outside the United States, there was little resistance to utilizing data from earlier stages in the adjudicatory process, such as prosecution, indictment, arraignment, or even investigation, particularly in legal systems where there are police magistrates.[4] In all countries, however, most criminologists were less ready to credit the competence of the police to make determinations of the objective facts and to classify them validly—police competence being judged in terms of legitimacy, skill, and the adequacy of information available to the police. Presumably, the lower social status of the police than of the bench— and, correlatively, the greater political power of the judiciary—together with the

Reprinted from "On Exploring the 'Dark Figure' of Crime" by Albert D. Biderman and Albert J. Reiss, Jr., Vol. 374, *The Annals of The American Academy of Political and Social Science*, November 1967.

loose fashion in which police systems were for long grafted on the legal-institutional systems, has much to do with these views.[5]

There has been a long contest to gain institutional acceptance for police statistics over opposition from legalistic traditionalism. In England, a plan was worked out for the collection of police statistics on a uniform and national basis in 1856, and they have been a regular part of the annual report of criminal statistics since 1857. While from the outset, police statistics were logically placed prior to judicial statistics in the published volumes, in 1893 they were placed after court statistics with the statement:

> The tables of the results of judicial proceedings, which are at once the most important, the most definite, and the most accurate of all criminal statistics, occupy the first place. The tables as to police action . . . are of less statistical value, and follow in a subordinate position.[6]

Not until 1923 did the argument over their merit abate sufficiently in England so that they were accepted as a valid basis for estimating crime.[7] Even today, in England, police statistics are considered less reliable than judicial statistics.

An additional difficulty inhered in the localistic nature of police organization in the United States. Not only did this make for dubiousness about the judgment and record-keeping capabilities of police in all but the larger jurisdictions, but producing national series also posed formidable problems of standardization and compilation of data from a multitude of jurisdictions having a myriad of laws, definitions, and practices. The present voluntary system of national crime reporting in the United States owed its form and many of its limitations to the fact that the national government cannot (at least not readily) compel local governments to report on their operations.[8]

As police statistics were legitimated, statistics on arrests generally gained acceptance earlier than those based on citizen complaints or reports of offenses known to the police. Arrests involve the legal authority system, while the status of a citizen complaint is moot. Eventually, however, realist perspectives prevailed, and the Uniform Crime Reports (UCR's) from the outset gathered information on all offenses reported or known to the police. Nonetheless, there is a strong disposition to count as offenses only those that are substantiated by police investigation—a process of "unfounding" citizen complaints. Published reports of UCR count only the number of "actual offenses" that survive police "unfounding" procedures.

To a considerable degree, precisely what the institutional view regarded as the vices of police statistics, the realist one regarded as sources of virtue. This was the absence of any "institutional processing" of the data—the selecting, defining, and winnowing of records of events by legitimate organizations of the legal system in accordance with legally established evidentiary and evaluative criteria and procedures. The classical statement for American police statistics by Sellin sums up why police statistics of "offenses known" provide the "best index" of crime:

> In general, it may be said that the value of a crime rate for index purposes is in inverse ratio to the procedural distance between the commission of the crime and the recording of it as a statistical unit. An index based on crimes reported to or known to the police is superior to others, and an index based on statistics of penal treatment, particularly prison statistics, is the poorest.[9]

Each remove from the crime, in terms of official procedures, leaves more of the actual crime taking place in a community submerged in the dark figure. Each procedural step, furthermore, is so selective that the "visible tip of the iceberg of crime" looks progressively different from the huge submerged mass.

The classically realist view in the use of police statistics as an index of criminality attaches greatest emphasis to those police data which are least dependent on agency action. Arrests, which vary with the extent, skill, and discretion of police activity, thus are regarded as a less satisfactory basis for an index of criminality than complaints, reports, and directly observed ("police on-view") "crimes." The realist view, at the same time, held that even police statistics distort the "real crime problem." An "index" of "crime," therefore, was devised that would provide a measure of the "crime problem" least subject to effects of jurisdiction. The UCR annual report states the case:

> Not all crimes come readily to the attention of the police; not all crimes are of sufficient importance to be significant in an index; and not all important crimes occur with enough regularity to be meaningful in an index.[10]

Among all offenses known to the police, those were selected for index purposes for which, in theory at least, the police function most nearly as passive recorders and nondiscretionary classifiers of events that take place. Index crimes are, in each case, offenses which largely come to the attention of the police by complaints from those victimized by the event. Violations which do not involve specific victims, or which largely or wholly come to be registered only as a result of police action, such as disorderly conduct, assaulting an officer, and receiving stolen property, are excluded from the measure. Offenses also deemed unsuitable for an index are those unlikely to be reported to the police either because they involve only persons disinclined toward police action, as is usually the case for gambling, prostitution, and other illegal services, or because the offenses are frequently too trivial to be "worth the bother" of reporting, such as petty larcenies and acts of malicious mischief. An additional criterion of the realist position was that the criminal act should be uniformly classifiable, independently of the varying local laws and practices. Miscegenation, until recently, afforded a clear example of an offense unsuitable for an index.

Realist views in the United States became predominant, first in criminological theory and then in practice, with the establishment in 1929 of the compilation of a national crime statistics series by the Federal Bureau of Investigation from voluntary reports by police agencies. The UCR index of crime that resulted from the application of these "realist" criteria consists of counts of offenses known to the police falling in seven predatory, common-law classifications: homicide, forcible rape, robbery, aggravated assault, burglary, larceny ($50 and over), and automobile theft.

Although police statistics gained acceptance largely as a result of realists' efforts to achieve more comprehensive and less selective indexes than were provided by institutional data, the victory of police statistics had barely begun to be consolidated before some realists attacked these statistics on the same grounds. Police statistics were challenged as not reflecting "the real crime picture." The criticism, as had been the case with older dissatisfactions with court and prison statistics, concentrated on the "real crime" that *escaped* the police data rather than on *invalid* classification of events as crimes. Critics pointed out that police statistics reflected only an unknown and selective portion of "all crime" and that they distorted in many ways the kinds of crime they did reflect. Interestingly, defenses of police statistics have come to rest increasingly on institutionalist arguments, rather than the realist ones to which they largely owe their acceptance. In rebutting criticisms of UCR, for example, Lejins writes:

> The existence of serious offenses not reported in the police statistics should not be accorded exaggerated meaning in the sense of detracting from the significance of the criminal activity that *is* reflected in the *Reports*, since the latter do encompass the bulk of the conventional, serious behavior to which society chooses to react through its public law enforcement agencies.[11]

It is beyond the scope of this essay to recapitulate the many criticisms and defenses that have been made of police statistics, generally, and the Crime Index, in particular.[12] It is important here, however, to formulate the thrust of these criticisms with respect to the misleading social implications that were seen in police statistics.

Because of the partial and selective nature of the police data, comparisons based on them of variations in "actual crime" over time, between places, and among components of the population, are all held to be grossly invalid. Furthermore, because of the fundamental subordination of police statistics to the particular normative perspectives and workings of this institution, it is contended, there are limitations and distortions inherent in the significance drawn from them for social policy.

Barely masked in these contentions regarding statistics have been more fundamental *ideological cleavages*.[13] It is useful to make explicit that much of the argument over appropriate indexes of criminality tends to array on one side those who regard a person's social status as largely a product of his own vices and virtues, and on the other, those who interpret status, as well as vices and virtues, as largely a product of socially conferred advantages and disadvantages. With regard to measures for dealing with crime, the cleavages are, for example, between deterrence and social amelioration, or between punishment and therapy.

Ideological cleavage had clear expression in Sutherland's denunciation of the failure of conventional crime statistics to reflect "white-collar crime." In prevalence and in economic and social effects, Sutherland's denunciation of the failure of conventional crime statistics to reflect *"white-collar crime."* In prevalence and in economic and social effects, Sutherland sought to show, law violations by a person of "the upper socioeconomic class in the course of his occupational activities" were more consequential than the typically lower-class crimes that comprised the index. Something of the same thrust was inherent in the innovation of *self-reporting studies*. The high proportions of middle-class persons who admit having committed serious delicts indicated both that the dark figure of crime must be of vast proportions and, at the very least, that "criminal" behavior was not nearly as exclusively a lower-class property as suggested by arrest and juvenile delinquency statistics.[14]

Despite the great effort devoted to developing and operating a uniform reporting system, the use of the police data for interarea comparisons has also been subject to vigorous criticism on a variety of grounds. One form of criticism pointed to the many instances in which abrupt and vast increases of crime figures for cities occurred when police reforms curtailed the practice of *"killing crime on the books."* Police departments and political administrations controlling them, it is often alleged, frequently have too great a stake in the effects of their crime figures on their "image" to be trusted to report fully and honestly. Beyond these qualms regarding "statistical conflicts of interest," there was evidence that police departments with effective and centralized controls over the reporting by individual officers and divisions reflected more of "true crime" in their communities than did less tightly organized departments.[15]

In recent years, the strongest complaint against police statistics has suggested that much of the rapid and extreme reported increases in the extent of criminality are spurious, being but a surfacing of what has heretofore been in the dark figure. The most general argument takes the form that crime *statistics* are as much (and perhaps more) a product of modern urban social organization as are the so-called urban forms of criminal behavior.[16] For example, it is suggested that the professionalization and bureaucratization of police forces with centralized command and control leads to improved record-keeping and greater use of formal, as opposed to informal, police procedures, with consequent increases in figures of offenses and arrests. And it is maintained that as larger proportions of the population become integrated into the dominant society and come to share its normative conceptions, more people mobilize the police to enforce middle-class norms regarding property, violence, and public deportment. At the same time, these public agencies become less disposed toward a tolerant view and informal processing of deviance.[17]

That improvements in law enforcement frequently have the effect of decreasing the dark figure, and consequently inflating statistics used to judge the magnitude of the crime problem, can be disconcerting for those planning innovational reforms. The President's Commission on Law Enforcement and Administration of Justice (hereinafter referred to as the National Crime Commission), for example, produced a table illustrating reporting-system changes in a dozen major cities that resulted in Crime Index increases of from 27 per cent to more than 200 per cent over the immediately preceding report.[18] The nation's two largest cities, it went on to say, in this way, "have several times produced large paper increases in crime."[19] Current attempts at improving police-community relations conceivably could produce sharp "paper increases" in some classes of crime were they to result in a greater disposition of citizens to report offenses.[20]

But no basis exists for forming proportionate estimates of what kinds of criminal behavior are reported to the police. Primarily with this problem in mind, the National Crime Commission undertook exploration of the use of cross-sectional survey methods.[21] A central idea was that one could discover crimes not known to the police by screening random samples of the population to find the victims of these crimes.

SAMPLE SURVEYS AND THE DARK FIGURE

Given the growth of what is literally a vast citizen-interviewing industry in the United States, it perhaps is surprising that the sample survey had not hitherto been applied to systematic examination of the crime problem.[22] Perhaps, the very availability of the captive populations in correctional institutions (if we include educational institutions as such), and of the neatly compiled agency statistics, diverted attention from such possibilities.

Neglect of the interview survey represents some discontinuity in the history of social research on crime, however. In the nineteenth century, a far more prominent place was accorded surveys of populations for knowledge. Henry Mayhew and Charles Booth, who often are credited with having set the path for the survey movement, were, for example, very conscious that the significance of crime for the poor of the city resided as much in their being its victims as in their being its contributors.[23] Booth's systematic survey sought to investigate "the numerical relation which poverty, misery, and depravity bear to the regular earnings and comparative comfort, and to describe the general conditions under which each class lives."[24]

Although there has been an occasional specific suggestion of using "Gallup Poll" methods[25] as a specific check on official statistics, the current turning to the cross-sectional survey method probably has received greater impetus from recent comments that criminology has been neglecting the victim in its concentration on the criminal. These writings argue that attention in criminology has been misdirected by the usual tendency to regard the victim of crimes as a purely passive and accidental target of the criminal act. A science of "victimology" is proposed to explain social, psychological, and behavioral characteristics that predispose some individuals to victimization, including factors consistently more subtle than such commonly recognized contributing acts as negligence and provocation by which some persons precipitate criminal acts toward themselves.[26]

Attention to the victim has also been urged from a quite different evaluative standpoint. In prefacing the 1963 volume of *Crime in the United States: Uniform Crime Reports*, the Director of the Federal Bureau of Investigation wrote:

> Statistics herein are published in terms of the number of crimes reported and persons arrested. At the same time, they also represent a count of millions of victims. While some of these victims may have been "merely inconvenienced," the vast majority suffered property losses they could ill afford and many lost their physical or mental health while others lost their lives. Nevertheless, many impassioned and articulate pleas are being made today on behalf of the offender tending to ignore the victim and obscuring the right of a free society to equal protection under the law.[27]

In the 123 pages of "general United States crime statistics" in the 1963 *Uniform Crime Reports*, however, the equivalent of only two pages provides any information on the victims of crime—and this only if we include categories of property as "victims." But two tables dealt with persons as victims: one on "Murder Victims [by age]—Weapons Used" and one on "Murder Victims by Age, Sex and Race."

In sponsoring cross-sectional interviewing surveys, the National Crime Commission hoped to be able to develop data on the characteristics of victims that would go considerably beyond the scant information available from police sources. Since the same surveys were directed toward developing data on citizens' behavior and attitudes toward the crime problem and toward law enforcement, it would also be possible to relate such attitudes to actual experience with crime as contrasted with secondary influences such as the mass media.

HOW MUCH CRIME IS THERE?

It should be apparent that the answer to the question of how much crime there is depends to a great extent upon whether one phrases the question from an institutionalist or a realist position. The choice of indicators and their labels, to a great extent, bears marks of these positions. The hallmarks of the realists are the prevalence of criminals and their acts of crime; more recently, of victims. The hallmarks of the institutionalists are the prevalence of only such of these as survive institutional validation.

But there are no rates without some organized intelligence system, whether that of the scientist, the police, or the jurist. The sample survey, the citizen's mobilization of the police, and the pretrial and trial proceedings are all organized intelligence systems that process events and people to determine their crime status. The criteria of knowing, defining and processing lie in organization.

Given the diversity of sources and types of information on crimes, the procedures that one develops for determining whether an event has occurred and who was involved in it must vary. It is doubtful, therefore, whether, logically, any current organized way of knowing makes possible the computation of a measure of crime that can serve equally all purposes and perspectives.

Kitsuse and Cicourel state the purposes and perspectives of a sociologistic institutionalist:

> Indeed in modern societies where bureaucratically organized agencies are increasingly invested with social control functions, the activities of such agencies are centrally important sources and contexts which generate as well as maintain definitions of deviance which produce populations of deviants. Thus, rates of deviance constructed by the use of statistics routinely issued by these agencies are social facts *par excellence*.[28]

This quotation discriminates the use of agency data from the perspective of the institutional processing of observations from that of the realist. Realists use agencies as a tool for observations of realities external to them.

The ideal mechanism for a realist would be a universal surveillance of time and space by recording mechanisms completely sensitive to all pertinent phenomena. Yet any organization confronts technical limitations to observation. Inherent in any observational system are errors from sampling probability, faulty observation and measurement, imperfections in operational translation of observational categories, and impedance to flow and feedback in communication.

Organizations such as the police have their own surveillance purposes. For processors inside the organization, an ideal surveillance mechanism is not an alien concept. However, action and observational mechanisms are inextricably linked one to the other.

From a realist point of view, this linkage makes the organization serve observational purposes poorly. For example, operational organizations such as the police or courts choose not to observe more than they can process with given resources, and they selectively screen observations to fit organizational goals, strategy, and tactics. Furthermore, organizations suffer from their own form of deviance, the subversion of organizational goals by their members. Three strategies are open to realists in overcoming these organizational barriers to information. First, they can insulate the surveillance apparatus from operations, as, for example, through the creation of central communications, intelligence, and records divisions.[29] Second, they can undertake independent surveillance of the operating system, by monitoring through outside observers either the operations or records of the organization.[30] Third, they can develop surveillance completely independent of the organization. The sample survey of the public is one of a variety of such devices.[31] A separate intelligence organization is another.

The deviance of members of the system from system norms, with respect to reporting as well as technical limitations to observation that are errors from a realist point of view, negates the social-choice interpretations of organizational data made by institutionalists. From a radical institutionalist point of view, these errors are treated, in part, as irrelevant, in that the differential sensitivity of surveillance reflects, to a substantial degree, social choices of what it is important to observe. Nonetheless, technical limitations as well as social choice reflect what is responded to. Indeed, realism itself is a system norm for members of organizations.

From the standpoint of a scientific criminology, a defect of the institutionalist point of view is that it uses concepts and data derived exclusively from those employed by formal organizations of the law-enforcement and legal systems. There is more to social life than its formally organized aspects. For scientific purposes, independently organized observations employing appropriate concepts and tools of measurement are necessary.

Thus, attacking the institutionalist point of view, Glaser points out that:

> Variation in the public definition of most predatory crimes is not appreciable, especially outside of so-called "white-collar crimes." The categories of predatory crimes most commonly distinguished in the law—for example, murder, robbery, burglary, theft, fraud, and rape—have almost everywhere and always been employed to denote essentially the same types of behavior as criminal. In almost all societies, they comprise the majority of acts for which severe negative sanctions are imposed.[32]

But, clearly, a large proportion of these "crimes" are "processed," if at all, only by informal mechanisms. "The criminal offense" itself is an important social transaction, quite apart from social transactions that ensure thereafter. It should be evident that police data, whether on offenses or arrests, exaggerate the incidence of those kinds of offenses for which an identifiable person is suspect, in that these are more likely to be reported to the police and processed by the department through investigation.

The neglect of victims in processing by law-enforcement, legal, and correctional agencies is another case in point. Offense rates, today, are based on data from the police; victim rates, on data from independently organized means.

OFFENSE RATES AND VICTIMIZATION RATES

Any simple *incidence rate* consists of but two elements, a population that is exposed to the occurrence of some event (the denominator) and a count of the events (the numerator). Both of these events are measured for a given point or period of time. An *offense rate* states the probability of occurrence of an offense for a given population while a *victimization rate* states the probability of being a victim of some offense.

There is no simple relationship between offense and victimization rates, however. Consider an event occurring that is to be defined as a crime or criminal offense. A single social encounter may involve more than one offense leading to multiple indictments of an offender or offenders in the event. This is the case, for example, when one is charged with larceny of an auto and larceny from an auto or when one is charged with armed robbery and simple assault. A single encounter may involve one or more persons as victims or it may involve no persons as victims. An offense against public order or decency may be observed only by a police officer, while the robbery of patrons in an establishment may involve large numbers of victims. Similarly, the number of offenders may vary, and indeed there may be mutual victimization and offending, as is the case in assaults that give rise to cross-complaints. Furthermore, for a given period of time over which the rate is calculated, any person may be a victim of one or more crime events—one's house may be burglarized on several occasions, for instance.

Given the fact that a single event may produce multiple victimization and multiple offenses and that, over time, there is repeated victimization, it is difficult to calculate *a priori* the relationship between offense and victimization rates. For some types of crimes, the number of crime victims exceeds the number of offenses, particularly if one makes rather simple assumptions that "collective property" *ipso facto* defines "collective victimization." Thus if one defines all members of a household as victims of a burglary, a single breaking and entering of a household involves all of its members as victims. Indeed, it may involve more than members of the household. A breaking and entering, for example, that does damage to property, may involve a landlord as victim of a breaking and tenants as victims of burglary. On the other hand, repeated victimization of a person by offenses over time and multiple offenses against a victim in a single event lead to conditions where the number of offenses exceeds the number of victims.

While, in the aggregate of all crime events, it would appear that the victimization rate should be higher than the offense rate, assuming that the number of crime victims exceeds the number of offenses, it is by no means clear what the magnitude of the difference is. Indeed, much depends upon how one counts the offenses and victims in a situation and upon the time interval over which one is calculating the event. The problem may not be unlike that for morbidity, where, in a relatively short time interval, the number of visits to a physician exceeds the number of persons who are ill.

SALIENCE OF EVENTS AND THEIR RECALL

Applying the sample-survey method to the realist's objective of illuminating the dark figure of crime assumes that events are salient to persons as real experiences and that what appears to be socially salient events, such as crimes, will be readily recalled and recounted. The organized processes of the mind are regarded as providing more valid and reliable information than the organized processes of organizations, the armament of the institutionalists.

Yet, recent research on recall of events assumed to be salient and significant to persons clearly indicates that, even in the very short time interval, there is selective recall of events. There is a significant amount of underreporting noted in studies of hospitalization and visits to doctors, for example.[33] These studies and others where the sample survey is used to recall events that organizations record as having taken place lead to several generalizations. First, underreporting increases with length of time between the event and the interview. Second, the degree of social threat or em-

barrassment is negatively related to rate of reporting. Third, the greater the involvement in institutional processing, the more likely it is to be recalled. Episodes that
involve surgical treatment and long stays are more likely to be recalled, for example.[34] Fourth, respondents report their own experiences better than those of others.
Fifth, the more events to which one has been subject, the more likely one is to report
a known event.

Perhaps the crucial matter is that underreporting is selective among classes of
persons and events, and by time. For analysis, then, the problem of separating truth
from differences in reporting rates is confronted precisely as in any other organizationally processed data. Survey interviewing, in fact, has become an institutionalized
device, with its own meanings for the population. Consequently, rates of mentions
of events can be subject to institutional interpretation. One such interpretation might
be the salience of a type of experience to difference classes of respondents.

The study of crime events makes apparent each of these conditions affecting recall. Indeed, it is likely that institutional processing of an event is an important factor
in recall; yet it clearly is not a sufficient condition, as events where institutional processing occurs—calling the police, for example—prove to be insufficient conditions
for recall. What does seem obvious is that, provided individuals can be brought to
report events to organizations, organizational intelligence is superior to recall. The
weight of the argument, in that sense, lies with the institutionalists.

COMPARABILITY OF POLICE AND SURVEY STATISTICS

Many of the limitations of police statistics, for which the survey has been claimed as
a corrective, are not inherent in the theoretical capabilities of law enforcement as a
system. Indeed, police agencies today collect far more information than they process
statistically or publish. They collect, but rarely publish, information, for example, on
victims, multiple offenders and offenses, suspects, the nature of criminal transactions, and the time and place of their occurrence. It is primarily the failure to process
information, rather than inherent limitations in collection, that renders comparison
between survey and police data difficult.

The survey is generally designed to gain data on victimization, while the police
report data on complaints and observed violations, reporting them as offenses
known to the police. Even when one sets the denominator in an incidence rate—the
exposed population—common to both, it is no simple matter to render the two sets
comparable.

To gain some comparability of victimization rates with police offense rates, it is
necessary to adjust survey data for victimization occurring outside the jurisdiction
sampled (a trivial problem for a national sample); victimization of more than one
person in given incidents; and "false" or "baseless" reports. Furthermore, if one is
interested in comparing survey estimates of offenses with police estimates of them,
the survey estimates should take account of whether or not the respondent reported
the event to the police.

At the same time, police data must be rendered comparable with that from survey sources. Since police data are collected by place of occurrence rather than by
place of residence of the victim, for less than national units, they must be adjusted
for place of residence. Furthermore, police data include offenses against businesses
and other organizations; household samples may not. Finally, if only the adult pop-

ulation is sampled and there is no reporting for others in the household, offenses involving persons not included in the sample must be eliminated.

The fact that the two sides are not altogether comparable should make clear that institutionalist and realist perspectives are built into the data for reasons that derive from these very perspectives. Consider the fact that police statistics are for offenses by place of occurrence of the event. It should be obvious that a law-enforcement system based on a strategy and tactics of deployment of technology and manpower is interested in the location of events—events that dictate proactive and reactive strategies. Such an interest is not incompatible with exploration of the dark figure *per se,* but it is incompatible with the realist ideology of how much crime there is.

VALIDITY OF SURVEY DATA ON CRIME

The crux of the traditional realist-versus-institutionalist controversy involves questions of validity rather than reliability. The cross-section sample survey may represent an extreme pole in the movement from "institutionalist" to "realist" approaches to crime statistics, in its complete dependence on the unsupported verbal testimony of a nonofficial character.

This logical possibility should not obscure the fact that formal organizational processing systems similarly rely primarily on supported oral testimony—the complaints of citizens or officers as witnesses, without other evidence. Indeed, most adjudicatory processes, such as the pretrial hearing or the decision to prosecute, rely heavily on unsupported testimony. Nonetheless, these formal systems, unlike the survey, rest on both the potential of investigation and formal sanctions to reduce fabrication. Technically, the survey might employ many of the same techniques available to the police; but these are alien to its basic premises, and the survey organization lacks formal sanctions.

The survey method, rather, tries to exploit the advantage that no material consequences ensue from testimony. The guarantee of anonymity, the relative absence of sanctions for providing information, and the general absence of consequences in giving information avoid some conditions that give rise to nonreporting to the police and other formal agencies. Such an advantage is of no little consequence in exploring the dark figure of crime.

In exploring the dark figure of crime, the survey generally has several other advantages over other organizationally processed statistics. First, it provides a form of organization that can transcend local practices by providing uniform operational definitions. Second, the survey taps the definitions of victims, independent of organizational processing, and it can compare these with those of formal processing organizations. Third, the survey can identify and compare what is institutionally labeled as crime with that consensually labeled as crime.

Although the data cannot be adduced here, problems of evidence rather than of inference probably predominate statistically in exploring the dark figure. Determining the objective character of events seems more problematic than inferring the motivation and competence that make acts *legally* criminal.

CONCLUSION

Statistical criminology, from its outset, has searched for the key moral statistic, a measure of the "criminality" present among a population. Both "institutionalists" and "realists" have pursued this search. The foregoing discussion has not made explicit our key premise, that is, the question of whether this search has been a scientific one. If pragmatic objectives of criminal statistics are posed, there are no data *par excellence,* nor is there a theory *par excellence.*

Although a neat polar distinction has been employed that pits institutionalist against realist perspective, in practice, neither camp has been comfortable in, and hence rarely consistent with, its position. The neglect of the role of organization in the production of knowledge has led both camps astray On the other hand, the realists neglect the shaping of objective reality by whatever the organizational mode of registering knowledge. On the other, the institutionalists confuse the observational efficacy of organizations with their normative functioning. Realist objectives are best served by special organizational structures for observing and recording events. Institutional goals would be best served by special organizational structures for developing and scientific processing of operational organizational activity. Concepts and operational definitions will differ depending upon formally organized or informal social processes, whether those of science, of operations, or of social policy are the primary objective.

In exploring the dark figure of crime, the primary question is not how much of it becomes revealed but rather what will be the selective properties of any particular innovation for its illumination. As in many other problems of scientific observation, the use of approaches and apparatuses with different properties of error has been a means of approaching truer approximations of phenomena that are difficult to measure.

Any set of crime statistics, including those of the survey, involves some evaluative, institutional processing of people's reports. Concepts, definitions, quantitative models, and theories must be adjusted to the fact that the data are not some objectively observable universe of "criminal acts," but rather those events defined, captured, and processed as such by some institutional mechanism.

ENDNOTES

1. The French are generally credited with the early development of moral statistics. Especially noteworthy is the work of A. M. Guerry, *Essai sur la statistique moral de la France* (Paris, 1833). Guerry calculated rates of crimes against persons and against property for 86 departments of France and age-sex specific crime rates for seventeen crimes against the person and seventeen against property. The rates were presented in tabular, graphic, and cartographic forms.

2. The earliest published discussion of the dark-figure problem that we have been able to find is that of Bulwer. In his two-volume treatise on France, published in 1836, Bulwer devoted an entire chapter to crime in France, based primarily on A. M. Guerry's major work. Bulwer (pp. 174–175) discusses the problem of using either offenses known or of the accused as measures of crime and concludes that, despite their limitations, they are more accurate than calculations based on convictions. See Henry Lytton Bulwer, *France, Social, Literary, Political,* Vol. I. Book I: *Crime* (London: Richard Bentley, 1836), pp. 169–210.

3. William Douglas Morrison stated the distinction rather well in a paper before the Royal Statistical Society in 1897: "If . . . we are anxious to know how the criminal law is being administered, we shall analyse and classify the contents of the statistics from that point of view. If on the other hand we desire to know the movement

of crime, the criminal conditions of the community, and the relative value of the several methods by which these methods are to be ascertained, we shall adopt a somewhat different method of classifying the contents of criminal statistics. I have ventured to classify criminal statistics into police statistics, judicial statistics, and prison statistics because I desire, at least in the first place, to point out the amount of weight to be attached to each of these methods of recording the nature and proportions of crime."—"The Interpretation of Criminal Statistics," *Journal of the Royal Statistical Society*, Vol. LX, Part I (March 1897), pp. 1–24, at pp. 1–2. Also: "But it would be a mistake to suppose that the number of crimes known to the police is a complete index of the total yearly volume of crime. The actual number of offenses annually committed is always largely in excess of the number of officially recorded crimes" (*Ibid.*, p. 4).

4. In France, for example, early statistical compilations of crime provided information on *accusations, accusés, acquités, and condamnés*. See *Recherches statistiques sur la ville de Paris et le department de la Seine* (A Paris de l'Imprimerie Royale, 1821–1830). See also Guerry, *op. cit.*

5. The *Report on Criminal Statistics*, U.S. National Commission on Law Observance and Enforcement (Washington, D.C.: U.S. Government Printing Office, 1931) stated contemporary views in the United States: "If it took the highly centralized English Government 66 years to get its famous and highly efficient police to report correctly crimes known to the police, it is evident that it will be many years before our decentralized and nonprofessional police forces can be induced to make trustworthy reports of crimes known to the police" (p. 55). After more than a third of a century, patience is still being counseled: see Peter P. Lejins, "Uniform Crime Reports," *Michigan Law Review*, 64 (April 1966), pp. 1011–1030.

6. Great Britain, *Judicial Statistics, England and Wales*, 1893, Part I: *Criminal Statistics*, p. 14.

7. *Ibid.*, 1923, p. 5.

8. For a good history and discussion of the problems of uniform crime reporting in the United States during the formative period, see U.S., Department of Justice, *Ten Years of Uniform Crime Reporting, 1930–1939: A report by the Federal Bureau of Investigation* (Washington, D.C.: U.S. Government Printing Office, 1939), esp. chap. v.

9. *Encyclopedia of the Social Sciences*, Vol. 4, p. 565.

10. U.S., Department of Justice, Federal Bureau of Investigation. *Crime in the United States: Uniform Crime Reports* (Washington, D.C.: U.S. Government Printing Office, 1930—[annually]). The above quotation is taken from the annual report for 1964, p. 48.

11. Lejins, *op. cit.*, p. 1010.

12. For recent criticisms, see Daniel Glaser, "National Goals and Indicators for the Reduction of Crime and Delinquency," *Social Goals and Indicators for American Society*, Vol. I, THE ANNALS, Vol. 371 (May 1967), pp. 104–126; Stanton Wheeler, "Criminal Statistics: A Reformulation of the Problem," *Journal of Criminal Law and Criminology*, Vol. 58 (September 1967); Marvin E. Wolfgang, "Uniform Crime Reports: A Critical Appraisal," *University of Pennsylvania Law Review*, Vol. 111 (April 1963), pp. 708–738. For a defense, see Lejins, *op. cit.*, pp. 1011–1130. See also Albert D. Biderman, "Social Indicators and Goals," in Raymond A. Bauer (ed.), *Social Indicators* (Cambridge, Mass: The M.I.T. Press, 1966).

13. Lejins, *op. cit.*, pp. 1029–1030.

14. For a recent summary, see Harwin L. Voss, "Socioeconomic Status and Reported Delinquent Behavior," *Social Problems*, 13 (Winter 1966), pp. 314–324. See also Albert J. Reiss, Jr. and Albert Lewis Rhodes, "The Distribution of Juvenile Delinquency in the Social Class Structure," *American Sociological Review*, 26 (October 1961), pp. 720–732.

15. In U.S., President's Commission on Law Enforcement and Administration of Justice, *The Challenge of Crime in a Free Society*, hereinafter referred to as General Report (Washington, D.C.: U.S. Government Printing Office, 1967), of the two recommendations concerning the measurement of crime, one was that each city adopt centralized procedures for handling crime reports from cities (pp. 27, 293).

16. For a discussion, see Albert D. Biderman, "Social Indicators and Goals," in Bauer (ed.), *op. cit.*, pp. 124–125.

17. John Kitsuse and Aaron Cicourel, "A Note on the Use of Official Statistics," *Social Problems*, 11 (Fall 1963), pp. 131–139.

18. U.S., President's Commission on Law Enforcement and Administration of Justice, General Report, *op. cit.*, p. 25.

19. *Ibid.*, p. 26.

20. Neil Rackham, "The Crime-Cut Campaign," *New Society*, 238 (April 1967), pp. 563–564.

21. Albert D. Biderman, "Surveys of Population Samples for Estimating Crime Incidence," in this issue of THE ANNALS, pp. 16–33. Subsequently, a similar survey was undertaken by the Government Social Survey of Great Britain. The results of this work were not available at the time of writing. (Personal communication from Louis Moss, Director, Great Britain Government Social Survey, July 18, 1967.)

22. A search of the Roper Public Opinion Research Center poll repository disclosed that, until 1964, public opinion surveys had given little attention to crime, except for polling sentiments regarding capital punishment and juvenile delinquency.

23. Henry Mayhew, *London Labour and the London Poor: Cyclopedia of the Conditions and Earnings of Those That Will Not Work* (London: Charles Griffin, 1861); Charles Booth, *Labour and Life of the People* (London: Williams and Norgate, 1891).

24. Booth, *op. cit.*, Vol. 1, p. 6..

25. Inkera Anttila, "The Criminological Significance of Unregistered Criminality," *Excerpta Criminologica*, Vol. 4 (1964), pp. 411–414.

26. See selected bibliography in B. Mendelsohn, "The Origin of the Doctrine of Victimology," *Excerpta Criminologica*, Vol. 3 (May–June, 1963).

27. U.S., Department of Justice, Federal Bureau of Investigation, *Crime in the United States: Uniform Crime Reports*, *op. cit.*, 1963, p. vii.

28. Kitsuse and Cicourel, *op. cit.*, p. 139.

29. For a discussion of this strategy by police chiefs, see David J. Bordua and Albert J. Reiss, Jr., "Command, Control, and Charisma: Reflections on Police Bureaucracy," *American Journal of Sociology*, Vol. 72 (July 1966), pp. 68–76.

30. For an organized observational study of the police, see Donald J. Black and Albert J. Reiss, Jr., "Patterns of Behavior in Police and Citizen Transactions," in Albert J. Reiss (ed.), *Studies in Crime and Law Enforcement in Major Metropolitan Areas*, U.S. President's Commission on Law Enforcement and Administration of Justice Field Survey III (Washington, D.C.: U.S. Government Printing Office, 1967).

31. See Albert D. Biderman, "Surveys of Population Samples for Estimating Crime Incidence," in this issue of THE ANNALS, pp. 16–33.

32. Glaser, *op. cit.*, p. 107.

33. A study of visits to doctors for the National Health Survey showed that 30 per cent of the known visits to doctors during a two-week period prior to the week of interviewing were *not* reported in response to a standard National Health Survey question; 23 per cent remained unreported after three special probe questions had been asked. The study also shows that underreporting was greater for less recent visits, that women reported better than men, and that persons with more serious health conditions and more visits during the two-week period were more likely to report. See Charles F. Cannell and Floyd J. Fowler, "A Study of the Reporting of Visits to Doctors in the National Health Survey," Survey Research Center, University of Michigan, October 1963, p. 8.

The study of hospitalization of persons showed that hospitalized persons in the sample underreported for themselves by 7 per cent, while the rate for both proxy adults and children was twice as high. The underreporting rate was lowest for women reporting the birth of a child, being but 2 per cent. See U.S., National Center for Health Statistics, *Comparison of Hospitalization Reporting in the Health Interview Survey*, U.S. Department of Health, Education, and Welfare Series 2, No. 6 (Washington, D.C.: U.S. Government Printing Office, July 1965), p. 8.

34. U.S., National Center for Health Statistics, *Comparison of Hospitalization Reporting in Three Survey Procedures*, U.S. Department of Health, Education, and Welfare Series 2, No. 8 (Washington, D.C.: U.S. Government Printing Office, July 1965), p. 2.

Questions for Study and Discussion

1. A valid measure of the "criminality" present in a population is inherently more difficult to construct than a valid measure of some purely economic attribute, e.g., "unemployment." Would you tend to agree? Why or why not?

2. From the viewpoint of measurement for management purposes, which perspective makes the most sense, the realist or the institutionalist?

3. The FBI's Crime Index provides a well-known measure of crime incidence in the United States (Biderman, 1966). Based on "crimes reported to the police or coming directly to their attention," it is constructed from reports of seven specific types of serious crime: criminal homicide, forcible rape, robbery, aggravated assault, burglary, larceny (involving property worth $50 or more), and automobile theft. What questions about sources of error and bias might be raised relative to the Crime Index? (See Biderman, 1966, for a critique.)

4. "Serious Crime up 18% in 1st Quarter of 1975, FBI says." So reads the headline of an article in the *Los Angeles Times*, reported by Jack Nelson (July 22, 1975). Excerpts from the article follow:

> WASHINGTON—The FBI, on the eve of announcing an experimental program to assist local police agencies in crime control, reported Monday yet another increase in serious crime in the United States.
>
> In a report released by Atty. Gen. Edward H. Levi, the FBI said that crime had risen 18% during the first three months of 1975 over the same period a year ago. That compares with a 15% increase during the first three months of 1974 over the same period in 1973.
>
> Levi called the latest statistics "one of the terrifying facts of life, which we have come to accept as normal, and which we must not accept as normal." He said the figures demonstrated the need for major new programs at all levels of government.
>
> Levi pointed out that the latest increase in the crime rate was consistent with preliminary figures for all of calendar 1974, which showed that serious crime last year was up 17% over 1973.

Violent crimes increased 18%, with robbery going up 28%, aggravated assault 10%, murder 7% and forcible rape 4%.

Property crimes also increased by 18%, with burglary rising 20%, larceny-theft 19% and motor vehicle theft 6%.

What questions might be raised about this increase in the crime rate, from realist and institutionalist perspectives?

5. What "dark figures" might be of concern in measurement at the organizational level as opposed to the societal level? For example, does it make sense to conceive of a "dark figure of profitability" within a firm? A "dark figure of product demand?" A "dark figure of productivity?"

6. In 1976 a move to end the FBI's control over crime statistics was reported. (*Los Angeles Times*, April 19, 1976.) A plan prepared in the Department of Justice proposed the creation of a central bureau of statistics that would integrate fifty-four existing statistics-gathering programs in the department, including that of the FBI. The proposed bureau would gather and interpret information but have no other operational responsibilities, and thus "no ax to grind." What are the likely strengths and weaknesses of this proposal, from realist and institutionalist perspectives?

7. Biderman and Reiss contend that much of the argument over appropriate indices of criminality is due to an "ideological cleavage" between those who believe that crime is a product of one's own actions and those who believe that crime results from environmental forces and "socially conferred" advantages and disadvantages. Can you cite other examples of ideological cleavages which have resulted in arguments over measurements?

8. How does the notion of the "dark figure" relate to the concept of the "empirical relational system?"

9. What role do traditional measurement criteria such as objectivity, validity, and reliability play in choosing between the realist and institutionalist approaches?

10. What is the "dark figure" of poverty in the United States, and how significant is it?

THE VITALITY OF MYTHICAL NUMBERS

Max Singer

It is generally assumed that heroin addicts in New York City steal some two to five billion dollars worth of property a year, and commit approximately half of all the property crimes. Such estimates of addict crime are used by an organization like RAND, by a political figure like Howard Samuels, and even by the Attorney General of the United States.[1] The estimate that half the property crimes are committed by addicts was originally attributed to a police official and has been used so often that it is now part of the common wisdom.

The amount of property stolen by addicts is usually estimated in something like the following manner:

There are 100,000 addicts with an average habit of $30.00 per day. This means addicts must have some $1.1 billion a year to pay for their heroin (100,000 × 365 × $30.00). Because the addict must sell the property he steals to a fence for only about a quarter of its value, or less, addicts must steal some $4 to $5 billion a year to pay for their heroin.

These calculations can be made with more or less sophistication. One can allow for the fact that the kind of addicts who make their living illegally typically spend upwards of a quarter of their time in jail, which would reduce the amount of crime by a quarter. (*The New York Times* recently reported on the death of William "Donkey" Reilly. A 74 year old ex-addict who had been addicted for 54 years, he had spent 30 of those years in prison.) Some of what the addict steals is cash, none of which has to go to a fence. A large part of the cost of heroin is paid for by dealing in the heroin business, rather than stealing from society, and another large part by prostitution, including male addicts living off prostitutes. But no matter how carefully you slice it, if one tries to estimate the value of property stolen by addicts by assuming that there are 100,000 addicts and estimating what is the minimum amount they would have to steal to support themselves and their habits (after making generous estimates for legal income), one comes up with a number in the neighborhood of $1 billion a year for New York City.

But what happens if you approach the question from the other side? Suppose we ask, "How much property is stolen—by addicts or anyone else?" Addict theft must be less than total theft. What is the value of property stolen in New York City in any year? Somewhat surprisingly to me when I first asked, this turned out to be a diffi-

---

From *The Public Interest*, 23: Spring, 1971, pp. 3–9. Reprinted by permission.

cult question to answer, even approximately. No one had any estimates that they had even the faintest confidence in, and the question doesn't seem to have been much asked. The amount of officially reported theft in New York City is approximately $300 million a year, of which about $100 million is the value of automobile theft (a crime that is rarely committed by addicts). But it is clear that there is a very large volume of crime that is not reported; for example, shoplifting is not normally reported to the police. (Much property loss to thieves is not reported to insurance companies either, and the insurance industry had no good estimate for total theft.)

It turns out, however, that if one is only asking a question like, "Is it possible that addicts stole $1 billion worth of property in New York City last year?" it is relatively simple to estimate the amount of property stolen. It is clear that the two biggest components of addict theft are shoplifting and burglary. What *could* the value of property shoplifted by addicts be? All retail sales in New York City are on the order of $15 billion a year. This includes automobiles, carpets, diamond rings, and other items not usually available to shoplifters. A reasonable number for inventory loss to retail establishments is 2 per cent. This number includes management embezzlements, stealing by clerks, shipping departments, truckers, etc. (Department stores, particulary, have reported a large increase in shoplifting in recent years, but they are among the most vulnerable of retail establishments and not important enough to bring the overall rate much above 2 per cent.) It is generally agreed that substantially more than half of the property missing from retail establishments is taken by employees, the remainder being lost to outside shoplifters. But let us credit shoplifters with stealing one per cent of all the property sold at retail in New York City—this would be about $150 million a year.

What about burglary? There are something like two and one-half million households in New York City. Suppose that on the average one out of five of them is robbed or burglarized every year. This takes into account that in some areas burglary is even more commonplace, and that some households are burglarized more than once a year. This would mean 500,000 burglaries a year. The average value of property taken in a burglary might be on the order of $200. In some burglaries, of course, much larger amounts of property are taken, but these higher value burglaries are much rarer, and often are committed by non-addict professional thieves. If we use the number of $200 × 500,000 burglaries, we get $100 million of property stolen from people's homes in a year in New York City.

Obviously, none of these estimated values is either sacred or substantiated. You can make your own estimate. The estimates here have the character that it would be very surprising if they were wrong by a factor of 10, and not very important for the conclusion if they were wrong by a factor of two. (This is a good position for an estimator to be in.)

Obviously not all addict theft is property taken from stores or from people's homes. One of the most feared types of addict crime is property taken from the persons of New Yorkers in muggings, and other forms of robbery. We can estimate this, too. Suppose that on the average, one person in 10 has property taken from his person by muggers or robbers each year. That would be 800,000 such robberies, and if the average one produced $100 (which it is very unlikely to do), $8 million a year would be taken in this form of theft.

So we can see that if we credit addicts with *all* of the shoplifting, *all* of the theft from homes, and *all* of the theft from persons, total property stolen by addicts in a year in New York City amounts to some $330 million. You can throw in all the "fudge factors" you want, add all the other miscellaneous crimes that addicts commit, but no matter what you do, it is difficult to find a basis for estimating that addicts steal over a half billion dollars a year, and a quarter billion looks like a better estimate, although perhaps on the high side. After all, there must be some thieves who are not addicts.

Thus, I believe we have shown that whereas it is widely assumed that addicts steal from $2–$5 billion a year in New York City, the actual number is *ten* times smaller, and that this can be demonstrated by five minutes of thought.[2] So what? A quarter billion dollars' worth of property is still a lot of property. It exceeds the amount of money spent annually on addict rehabilitation and other programs to prevent and control addiction. Furthermore, the value of the property stolen by addicts is a small part of the total cost to society of addict theft. A much larger cost is paid in fear, changed neighborhood atmosphere, the cost of precautions, and other echoing and re-echoing reactions to theft and its danger.

One point in this exercise in estimating the value of property stolen by addicts is to shed some light on people's attitudes toward numbers. People feel that there is a lot of addict crime, and that $2 billion is a large number, so they are inclined to believe that there is $2 billion worth of addict theft. But $250 million is a large number, too, and if our sense of perspective were not distorted by daily consciousness of federal expenditures, most people would be quite content to accept $250 million a year as a lot of theft.

Along the same lines, this exercise is another reminder that even responsible officials, responsible newspapers, and responsible research groups pick up and pass on as gospel numbers that have no real basis in life. We are reminded by this experience that because an estimate has been used widely by a variety of people who should know what they are talking about, one cannot assume that the estimate is even approximately correct.

But there is a much more important implication of the fact that there cannot be nearly so much addict theft as people believe. This implication is that there probably cannot be as many addicts as many people believe. Most of the money paid for heroin bought at retail comes from stealing, and most addicts buy at retail. Therefore, the number of addicts is basically—although imprecisely—limited by the amount of theft. (The estimate developed in a Hudson Institute study was that close to half of the volume of heroin consumed is used by people in the heroin distribution system who do not buy at retail, and do not pay with stolen property but with their "services" in the distribution system.[3]) But while the people in the business (at lower levels) consume close to half the heroin, they are only some one-sixth or one-seventh of the total number of addicts. They are the ones who can afford big habits.

The most popular, informal estimate of addicts in New York City is 100,000-plus (usually with an emphasis on the "plus"). The federal register in Washington lists some 30,000 addicts in New York City, and the New York City Department of Health's register of addicts' names list some 70,000. While all the people on those lists are not still active addicts—many of them are dead or in prison—most people believe that there are many addicts who are not on any list. It is common to regard the estimate of 100,000 addicts in New York City as a very conservative one. Dr. Judianne Densen-Gerber was widely quoted early in 1970 for her estimate that there would be over 100,000 teenage addicts by the end of the summer. And there are obviously many addicts of 20 years of age and more.[4]

In discussing the number of addicts in this article, we will be talking about the kind of person one thinks of when the term "addict" is used.[5] A better term might be "street addict." This is a person who normally uses heroin every day. He is the kind of person who looks and acts like the normal picture of an addict. We exclude here the people in the medical profession who are frequent users of heroin or other opiates, or are addicted to them, students who use heroin occasionally, wealthy people who are addicted but do not need to steal and do not frequent the normal addict hangouts, etc. When we are addressing the "addict problem" it is much less important that we include these cases; while they are undoubtedly problems in varying degrees, they are a very different type of problem than that posed by the typical street addict.

The amount of property stolen by addicts suggests that the number of New York City street addicts may be more like 70,000 than 100,000, and almost certainly cannot be anything like the 200,000 number that is sometimes used. Several other simple ways of estimating the number of street addicts lead to a similar conclusion.

Experience with the addict population has led observers to estimate that the average street addict spends a quarter to a third of his time in prison. (Some students of the subject, such as Edward Preble and John J. Casey, Jr., believe the average to be over 40 per cent.) This would imply that at any one time, one-quarter to one-third of the addict population is in prison, and that the total addict population can be estimated by multiplying the number of addicts who are in prison by three or four. Of course the number of addicts who are in prison is not a known quantity (and, in fact, as we have indicated above, not even a very precise concept). However, one can make reasonable estimates of the number of addicts in prison (and for this purpose we can include the addicts in various involuntary treatment centers). This number is approximatley 14,000–17,000 which is quite compatible with an estimate of 70,000 total New York City street addicts.

Another way of estimating the total number of street addicts in New York City is to use the demographic information that is available about the addict population. For example, we can be reasonably certain that some 25 per cent of the street addict population in New York City is Puerto Rican, and some 50 percent are Negroes. We know that approximately five out of six street addicts are male, and that 50 per cent of the street addicts are between the ages of 16 and 25. This would mean that 20 per cent of the total number of addicts are male Negroes between the age of 16 and 25. If there were 70,000 addicts, this would mean that 14,000 Negro boys between the ages of 16 and 25 are addicts. But altogether there are only about 140,000 Negro boys between the ages of 16 and 25 in the city—perhaps half of them living in poverty areas. This means that if there are 70,000 addicts in the city, one in 10 Negro youths are addicts, and if there are 100,000 addicts, nearly one in six are, and if there are 200,000 addicts, one in three. You can decide for yourself which of these degrees of penetration of the young Negro male group is most believable, but it is rather clear that the number of 200,000 addicts is implausible. Similarly, the total of 70,000 street addicts would imply 7,000 young Puerto Rican males are addicted, and the total number of Puerto Rican boys between the ages of 16 and 25 in New York City is about 70,000.

None of the above calculations is meant in any way to downplay the importance of the problem of heroin addiction. Heroin is a terrible curse. When you think of the individual tragedy involved, 70,000 is an awfully large number of addicts. And if you have to work for a living, $250 million is an awful lot of money to have stolen from the citizens of the city to be transferred through the hands of addicts and fences into the pockets of those who import and distribute heroin, and those who take bribes or perform other services for the heroin industry.

The main point of this article may well be to illustrate how far one can go in bounding a problem by taking numbers seriously, seeing what they imply, checking various implications against each other and against general knowledge (such as the number of persons or households in the city). Small efforts in this direction can go a long way to help ordinary people and responsible officials to cope with experts of various kinds.

ENDNOTES

1. New York RAND Issue Paper on Drug Addiction Control in New York, 1968; Howard Samuels, Position Paper on Narcotics, 1970; Speech by Attorney General Mitchell, October 6, 1969.

2. Mythical numbers may be more mythical and have more vitality in the area of crime than in most areas. In the early 1950's the Kefauver Committee published a $20 billion estimate for the annual "take" of gambling in the United States. The figure actually was "picked from a hat." One staff member said: "We had no real idea of the money spent. The California Crime Commission said $12 billion. Virgil Petersen of Chicago said $30 billion. We picked $20 billion as the balance of the two."

An unusual example of a mythical number that had a vigorous life—the assertion that 28 Black Panthers had been murdered by police—is given a careful biography by Edward Jay Epstein in the February 13, 1971, *New Yorker*. (It turned out that there were 19 Panthers killed, ten of them by the police, and eight of these in situations where it seems likely that the Panthers took the initiative.)

3. A parallel datum was developed in a later study by St. Luke's Hospital of 81 addicts—average age 34. More than one-half of the heroin consumed by these addicts, over a year, had been paid for by the sale of heroin. Incidentally, these 81 addicts had stolen an average of $9,000 worth of property in the previous year.

4. Among other recent estimators we may note a Marxist, Sol Yurick, who gives us "500,000 junkies" (*Monthly Review*, December 1970), and William R. Corson, who contends, in the December 1970 *Penthouse*, and "today at least 2,500,000 black Americans are hooked on heroin."

5. There is an interesting anomaly about the word "addict." Most people, if pressed for a definition of an "addict," would say he is a person who regularly takes heroin (or some such drug) and who, if he fails to get his regular dose of heroin, will have unpleasant or painful withdrawal symptoms. But this definition would not apply to a large part of what is generally recognized as the "addict population." In fact, it would not apply to most certified addicts. An addict who has been detoxified or who has been imprisoned and kept away from drugs for a week or so would not fit the normal definition of "addict." He no longer has any physical symptoms resulting from not taking heroin. "Donkey" Reilly would certainly fulfill most people's ideas of an addict, but for 30 of the 54 years he was an "addict" he was in prison,

and he was certainly not actively addicted to heroin during most of the time he spent in prison, which was more than half of his "addict" career (although a certain amount of drugs is available in prison.)

Questions for Study and Discussion

1. As Singer's article illustrates, "estimates" are an important component of information generated for social decision making. What is the basic role of estimation in measurement at the societal level? Paraphrasing Churchman, "Why estimate?"

2. How might Singer's approach be used to assess statements such as "seventeen million Americans to go bed hungry every night?" Does it apply to the statement "Los Angeles County must serve seven million people?"

3. The introductory chapters of this book argued that measurement is an application of systems theory. In what ways is Singer's approach an operationalization of systems theory as a method of testing estimates? How might it be extended?

4. In what ways does "the vitality of mythical number" relate to the behavioral dimensions of measurement discussed in Part Three of this book?

5. How might Singer's approach be used to uncover errors such as those described in "The Case of the Indians and the Teenage Widows" (Study question 8, Reading 25)?

REFORMS AS EXPERIMENTS

Donald T. Campbell

The United States and other modern nations should be ready for an experimental approach to social reform, an approach in which we try out new programs designed to cure specific social problems, in which we learn whether or not these programs are effective, and in which we retain, imitate, modify, or discard them on the basis of apparent effectiveness on the multiple imperfect criteria available. Our readiness for this stage is indicated by the inclusion of specific provisions for program evaluation in the first wave of the "Great Society" legislation, and by the current congressional proposals for establishing "social indicators" and socially relevant "data banks." So long have we had good intentions in this regard that many may feel we are already at this stage, that we already are continuing or discontinuing programs on the basis of assessed effectiveness. It is a theme of this article that this not at all so, that most ameliorative programs end up with *no* interpretable evaluation (Etzioni, 1968; Hyman & Wright, 1967; Schwartz, 1961). We must look hard at the sources of this condition, and design ways of overcoming the difficulties. This article is a preliminary effort in this regard.

Many of the difficulties lie in the intransigencies of the research setting and in the presence of recurrent seductive pitfalls of interpretation. The bulk of this article will be devoted to these problems. But the few available solutions turn out to depend upon correct administrative decisions in the initiation and execution of the program. These decisions are made in a political arena, and involve political jeopardies that are often sufficient to explain the lack of hard-headed evaluation of effects. Removing reform administrators from the political spotlight seems both highly unlikely, and undesirable even if it were possible. What is instead essential is that the social scientist research adviser understand the political realities of the situation, and that he aid by helping create a public demand for hard-headed evaluation, by contributing to those political inventions that reduce the liability of honest evaluation, and by educating future administrators to the problems and possibilities.

For this reason, there is also an attempt in this article to consider the political setting of program evaluation, and to offer suggestions as to political postures that might further a truly experimental approach to social reform. Although such consid-

From *American Psychologist*, Vol. 24, No. 4, April 1969, pp. 409–429, as reprinted in Caro, Francis R., Ed., *Readings in Evaluation Research*. N.Y.: Russell Sage Foundation, 1977, 2nd ed. Used by permission.

erations will be distributed as a minor theme throughout this article, it seems convenient to begin with some general points of this political nature.

POLITICAL VULNERABILITY FROM KNOWING OUTCOMES

It is one of the most characteristic aspects of the present situation that *specific reforms are advocated as though they were certain to be successful.* For this reason, knowing outcomes has immediate political implications. Given the inherent difficulty of making significant improvements by the means usually provided and given the discrepancy between promise and possibility, most administrators wisely prefer to limit the evaluations to those the outcomes of which they can control, particularly insofar as published outcomes or press releases are concerned. Ambiguity, lack of truly comparable comparison bases, and lack of concrete evidence all work to increase the administrator's control over what gets said, or at least to reduce the bite of criticism in the case of actual failure. There is safety under the cloak of ignorance. Over and above this tie-in of advocacy and administration, there is another source of vulnerability in that the facts relevant to experimental program evaluation are also available to argue the general efficiency and honesty of administrators. The public availability of such facts reduces the privacy and security of at least some administrators.

Even where there are ideological commitments to a hard-headed evaluation of organizational efficiency, or to a scientific organization of society, these two jeopardies lead to the failure to evaluate organizational experiments realistically. If the political and administrative system has committed itself in advance to the correctness and efficacy of its reforms, it cannot tolerate learning of failure. To be truly scientific we must be able to experiment. We must be able to advocate without that excess of commitment that blinds us to reality testing.

This predicament, abetted by public apathy and by deliberate corruption, may prove in the long run to permanently preclude a truly experimental approach to social amelioration. But our needs and our hopes for a better society demand we make the effort. There are a few signs of hope. In the United States we have been able to achieve cost-of-living and unemployment indices that, however imperfect, have embarrassed the administrations that published them. We are able to conduct censuses that reduce the number of representatives a state has in Congress. These are grounds for optimism, although the corrupt tardiness of state governments in following their own constitutions in revising legislative districts illustrates the problem.

One simple shift in political posture which would reduce the problem is the shift from the advocacy of a specific reform to the advocacy of the seriousness of the problem, and hence to the advocacy of persistence in alternative reform efforts should the first one fail. The political stance would become: "This is a serious problem. We propose to initiate Policy A on an experimental basis. If after five years there has been no significant improvement, we will shift to Policy B." By making explicit that a given problem solution was only one of several that the administrator or party could in good conscience advocate, and by having ready a plausible alternative, the administrator could afford honest evaluation of outcomes. Negative results, a failure of the first program, would not jeopardize his job, for his job would be to keep after the problem until something was found that worked.

Coupled with this should be a general moratorium on ad hominum evaluative research, that is, on research designed to evaluate specific administrators rather than alternative policies. If we worry about the invasion-of-privacy problem in the data banks and social indicators of the future (e.g., Sawyer & Schechter, 1968), the touchiest point is the privacy of administrators. If we threaten this, the measurement system will surely be sabotaged in the innumerable ways possible. While this may sound unduly pessimistic, the recurrent anecdotes of administrators attempting to squelch unwanted research findings convince me of its accuracy. But we should be able to evaluate those alternative policies that a given administrator has the option of implementing.

FIELD EXPERIMENTS AND QUASI-EXPERIMENTAL DESIGNS

In efforts to extend the logic of laboratory experimentation into the "field," and into settings not fully experimental, an inventory of threats to experimental validity has been assembled, in terms of which some 15 or 20 experimental and quasi-experimental designs have been evaluated (Campbell, 1957, 1963; Campbell & Stanley, 1963). In the present article only three or four designs will be examined, and therefore not all of the validity threats will be relevant, but it will provide useful background to look briefly at them all. Following are nine threats to internal validity.

1. *History:* events, other than the experimental treatment, occurring between pretest and posttest and thus providing alternate explanations of effects.

2. *Maturation:* processes within the respondents or observed social units producing changes as a function of the passage of time per se, such as growth, fatigue, secular trends, etc.

3. *Instability:* unreliability of measures, fluctuations in sampling persons or components, autonomous instability of repeated or "equivalent" measures. (This is the only threat to which statistical tests of significance are relevant.)

4. *Testing:* the effect of taking a test upon the scores of a second testing. The effect of publication of a social indicator upon subsequent readings of that indicator.

5. *Instrumentation:* in which changes in the calibration of a measuring instrument or changes in the observers or scores used may produce changes in the obtained measurements.

6. *Regression artifacts:* pseudo-shifts occurring when persons or treatment units have been selected upon the basis of their extreme scores.

7. *Selection:* biases resulting from differential recruitment of comparison groups, producing different mean levels on the measure of effects.

8. *Experimental mortality:* the differential loss of respondents from comparison groups.

9. *Selection-maturation interaction:* selection biases resulting in differential rates of "maturation" or autonomous change.

If a change or difference occurs, these are rival explanations that could be used to explain away an effect and thus to deny that in this specific experiment any genuine effect of the experimental treatment had been demonstrated. These are faults that true experiments avoid, primarily through the use of randomization and control groups. In the approach here advocated, this checklist is used to evaluate specific quasi-experimental designs. This is evaluation, not rejection, for it often turns out that for a specific design in a specific setting the threat is implausible, or that there are supplementary data that can help rule it out even where randomization is impossible. The general ethic, here advocated for public administrators as well as social scientists, is to use the very best method possible, aiming at "true experiments" with random control groups. But where randomized treatments are not possible, a self-critical use of quasi-experimental designs is advocated. We must do the best we can with what is available to us.

Our posture vis-à-vis perfectionist critics from laboratory experimentation is more militant that this: the only threats to validity that we will allow to invalidate an experiment are those that admit of the status of empirical laws more dependable and more plausible than the law involving the treatment. The mere possibility of some alternative explanation is not enough—it is only the *plausible* rival hypotheses that are invalidating. Vis-à-vis correlational studies, on the other hand, our stance is one of greater conservatism. For example, because of the specific methodological trap of regression artifacts, the sociological tradition of "ex post facto" designs (Chapin, 1947; Greenwood, 1945) is totally rejected (Campbell & Stanley, 1963, pp. 240–241; 1966, pp. 70–71).

Threats to external validity, which follow, cover the validity problems involved in interpreting experimental results, the threats to valid generalization of the results to other settings, to other versions of the treatment, or to other measures of the effect:[2]

1. *Interaction effects of testing:* the effect of a pretest in increasing or decreasing the respondent's sensitivity or responsiveness to the experimental variable, thus making the results obtained for a pretested population unrepresentative for the unpretested universe from which the experimental respondents were selected.

2. *Interaction of selection and experimental treatment:* unrepresentative responsiveness of the treated population.

3. *Reactive effects of experimental arrangements:* "artificiality"; conditions making the experimental setting atypical of conditions of regular application of the treatment: "Hawthorne effects."

4. *Multiple-treatment interference:* where multiple treatments are jointly applied, effects atypical of the separate application of the treatments.

5. *Irrelevant responsiveness of measures:* all measures are complex, and all include irrelevant components that may produce apparent effects.

6. *Irrelevant replicability of treatments:* treatments are complex, and replications of them may fail to include those components actually responsible for the effects.

These threats apply equally to true experiments and quasi-experiments. They are particularly relevant to applied experimentation. In the cumulative history of our methodology, this class of threats was first noted as a critique of true experiments involving pretests (Schanck & Goodman, 1939; Solomon, 1949). Such experiments provided a sound basis for generalizing to other *pretested* populations, but the reactions of unpretested populations to the treatment might well be quite different. As a result, there has been an advocacy of true experimental designs obviating the pre-test (Campbell, 1957; Schanck & Goodman, 1939; Solomon, 1949) and a search for nonreactive measures (Webb, Campbell, Schwartz, & Sechrest, 1966).

These threats to validity will serve as a background against which we will discuss several research designs particularly appropriate for evaluating specific programs of social amelioration. These are the "interrupted time-series design," the "control se-ries design," "regression discontinuity design," and various "true experiments." The order is from a weak but generally available design to stronger ones that require more administrative foresight and determination.

INTERRUPTED TIME-SERIES DESIGN

By and large, when a political unit initiates a reform it is put into effect across the board, with the total unit being affected. In this setting the only comparison base is the record of previous years. The usual mode of utilization is a casual version of a very weak quasi-experimental design, the one-group pretest-posttest design.

A convenient illustration comes from the 1955 Connecticut crackdown on speed-ing, which Sociologist H. Laurence Ross and I have been analyzing as a methodo-logical illustration (Campbell & Ross, 1968; Glass, 1968; Ross & Campbell, 1968). After a record high of traffic fatalities in 1955, Governor Abraham Ribicoff instituted an unprecedentedly severe crackdown on speeding. At the end of a year of such enforcement there had been but 284 traffic deaths as compared with 324 the year before. In announcing this the Governor stated, "With the saving of 40 lives in 1956, a reduction of 12.3% from the 1955 motor vehicle death toll, we can say that the program is definitely worthwhile." These results are graphed in Figure 1, with a de-liberate effort to make them look impressive.

In what follows, while we in the end decide that the crackdown had some ben-eficial effects, we criticize Ribicoff's interpretation of his results, from the point of view of the social scientist's proper standards of evidence. Were the now Senator Ribicoff not the man of stature that he is, this would be most unpolitic, because we could be alienating one of the strongest proponents of social experimentation in our nation. Given his character, however, we may feel sure that he shares our interest both in a progressive program of experimental social amelioration, and in making the most hard-headed evaluation possible of these experiments. Indeed, it was his integrity in using every available means at his disposal as Governor to make sure that the unpopular speeding crackdown was indeed enforced that make these data worth examining at all. But the potentials of this one illustration and our political temptation to substitute for it a less touchy one, point to the political problems that must be faced in experimenting with social reform.

Keeping Figure 1 and Ribicoff's statement in mind, let us look at the same data presented as a part of an extended time series in Figure 2 and go over the relevant threats to internal validity. First, *History*. Both presentations fail to control for the effects of other potential change agents. For instance, 1956 might have been a par-ticularly dry year, with fewer accidents due to rain or snow. Or there might have been a dramatic increase in the use of seat belts, or other safety features. The ad-vocated strategy in quasi-experimentation is not to throw up one's hands and refuse to use the evidence because of this lack of control, but rather to generate by in-

FIGURE 1. *Connecticut Traffic Fatalities.*

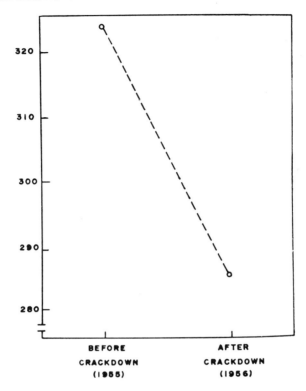

formed criticism appropriate to this specific setting as many *plausible* rival hypotheses as possible, and then to do the supplementary research, as into weather records and safety-belt sales, for example, which would reflect on these rival hypotheses.

Maturation. This is a term coming from criticisms of training studies of children. Applied here to the simple pretest-posttest data of Figure 1, it could be the plausible rival hypothesis that death rates were steadily going down year after year (as indeed they are, relative to miles driven or population of automobiles). Here the extended time series has a strong methodological advantage, and rules out this threat to validity. The general trend is inconsistently up prior to the crackdown, and steadily down thereafter.

Instability seemingly implicit in the public pronouncement was the assumption that all of the change from 1955 to 1956 was due to the crackdown. There was no recognition of the fact that all time series are unstable even when no treatments are being applied. The degree of this normal instability is the crucial issue, and one of the main advantages of the extended time series is that it samples this instability. The great pretreatment instability now makes the treatment effect look relatively trivial. The 1955–56 shift is less than the gains of both 1954–55 and 1952–53. It is the largest drop in the series, but it exceeds the drops of 1951–52, 1953–54, and 1957–58 by trivial amounts. Thus the unexplained instabilities of the series are such

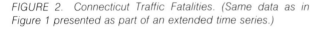

FIGURE 2. *Connecticut Traffic Fatalities. (Same data as in Figure 1 presented as part of an extended time series.)*

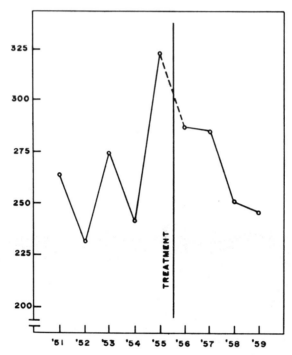

as to make the 1955–56 drop understandable as more of the same. On the other hand, it is noteworthy that after the crackdown there are no year-to-year gains, and in this respect the character of the time series seems definitely to have changed.

The threat of instability is the only threat to which tests of significance are relevant. Box and Tiao (1965) have an elegant Bayesian model for the interrupted time series. Applied by Glass (1968) to our monthly data, with seasonal trends removed, it shows a statistically significant downward shift in the series after the crackdown. But as we shall see, an alternative explanation of at least part of this significant effect exists.

Regression. In true experiments the treatment is applied independently of the prior state of units. In natural experiments exposure to treatment is often a cosymptom of the treated group's condition. The treatment is apt to be an *effect* rather than, or in addition to being, a cause. Psychotherapy is such a cosymptom treatment, as in any other in which the treated group is self-selected or assigned on the basis of need. These all present special problems of interpretation, of which the present illustration provides one type.

The selection-regression plausible rival hypothesis works this way: Given that the fatality rate has some degree of unreliability, then a subsample selected for its extremity in 1955 would on the average, merely as a reflection of that unreliability, be less extreme in 1956. Has there been selection for extremity in applying this treatment? Probably yes. Of all Connecticut fatality years, the most likely time for a crackdown would be after an exceptionally high year. If the time series showed instability, the subsequent year would on the average be less, *purely as a function of that instability*. Regression artifacts are probably the most recurrent form of self-deception in the experimental social reform literature. It is hard to make them intuitively obvious. Let us try again. Take any time series with variability, including one generated of pure error. Move along it as in a time dimension. Pick a point that is the "highest so far." Look then at the next point. On the average this next point will be lower, or nearer the general trend.

In our present setting the most striking shift in the whole series is the upward shift just prior to the crackdown. It is highly probable that this caused the crackdown, rather than, or in addition to, the crackdown causing the 1956 drop. At least part of the 1956 drop is an artifact of the 1955 extremity. While in principle the degree of expected regression can be computed from the auto-correlation of the series, we lack here an extended-enough body of data to do this with any confidence.

Advice to administrators who want to do genuine reality-testing must include attention to this problem, and it will be a very hard problem to surmount. The most general advice would be to work on chronic problems of a persistent urgency or extremity, rather than reacting to momentary extremes. The administrator should look at the pretreatment time series to judge whether or not instability plus momentary extremity will explain away his program gains. If it will, he should schedule the treatment for a year or two later, so that his decision is more independent of one year's extremity. (The selection biases remaining under such a procedure need further examination.)

In giving advice to the *experimental* administrator, one is also inevitably giving advice to those *trapped* administrators whose political predicament requires a favorable outcome whether valid or not. To such trapped administrators the advice is pick the very worst year, and the very worst social unit. If there is inherent instability, there is no where to go but up, for the average case at least.

Two other threats to internal validity need discussion in regard to this design. By *testing* we typically have in mind the condition under which a test of attitude, ability, or personality is itself a change agent, persuading, informing, practicing, or otherwise setting processes of change in action. No artificially introduced testing procedures are involved here. However, for the simple before-and-after design of Figure 1, if the pretest were the first data collection of its kind ever publicized, this publicity in itself might produce a reduction in traffic deaths which would have taken place even without a speeding crackdown. Many traffic safety programs assume this. The longer time-series evidence reassures us on this only to the extent that we can assume that the figures had been published each year with equivalent emphasis.[3]

Instrumentation changes are not a likely flaw in this instance, but would be if recording practices and institutional responsibility had shifted simultaneously with the crackdown. Probably in a case like this it is better to use raw frequencies rather than indices whose correction parameters are subject to periodic revision. Thus per capita rates are subject to periodic jumps as new census figures become available correcting old extrapolations. Analogously, a change in the miles per gallon assumed in estimating traffic mileage for mileage-based mortality rates might explain a shift. Such biases can of course work to disguise a true effect. Almost certainly, Ribicoff's crackdown reduced traffic speed (Campbell & Ross, 1968). Such a decrease in speed increases the miles per gallon actually obtained, producing a concomitant drop in the estimate of miles driven, which would appear as an inflation of the estimate of mileage-based traffic fatalities if the same fixed approximation to actual miles per gallon were used, as it undoubtedly would be.

The "new broom" that introduces abrupt changes of policy is apt to reform the record keeping too, and thus confound reform treatments with instrumentation change. The ideal experimental administrator will, if possible, avoid doing this. He will prefer to keep comparable a partially imperfect measuring system rather than lose comparability altogether. The new politics of the situation do not always make this possible, however. Consider, as an experimental reform, Orlando Wilson's reorganization of the police system in Chicago. Figure 3 shows his impact on petty larceny in Chicago—a striking *increase!* Wilson, of course, called this shot in advance, one aspect of his reform being a reform in the bookkeeping. (Note in the pre-Wilson records the suspicious absence of the expected upward secular trend.) In this situation Wilson had no choice. Had he left the record keeping as it was, for the purposes of better experimental design, his resentful patrolmen would have clobbered him with a crime wave by deliberately starting to record the many complaints that had not been getting into the books.[4]

Those who advocate the use of archival measures as social indicators (Bauer, 1966; Gross, 1966, 1967; Kaysen, 1967; Webb et al., 1966) must face up not only to their high degree of chaotic error and systematic bias, but also to the politically motivated changes in record keeping that will follow upon their public use as social indicators (Etzioni & Lehman, 1967). Not all measures are equally susceptible. In Figure 4, Orlando Wilson's effect on homicides seems negligible one way or the other.

Of the threats to external validity, the one most relevant to social experimenta-

FIGURE 3. Number of Reported Larcenies under $50 in Chicago, Illinois, from 1942 to 1962 (data from Uniform Crime Reports for the United States, 1942–62).

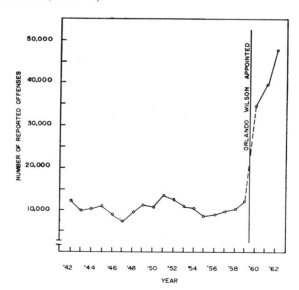

tion is *Irrelevant Responsiveness of Measures.* This seems best discussed in terms of the problem of generalizing from indicator to indicator or in terms of the imperfect validity of all measures that is only to be overcome by the use of multiple measures of independent imperfection (Campbell & Fiske, 1959; Webb et al., 1966).

For treatments on any given problem within any given governmental or business subunit, there will usually be something of a governmental monopoly on reform. Even though different divisions may optimally be trying different reforms, within each division there will usually be only one reform on a given problem going on at a time. But for measures of effect this need not and should not be the case. The administrative machinery should itself make multiple measures of potential benefits and of unwanted side effects. In addition, the loyal opposition should be allowed to add still other indicators, with the political process and adversary argument challenging both validity and relative importance, with social science methodologists testifying for both parties and with the basic records kept public and under bipartisan audit (as are voting records under optimal conditions). This competitive scrutiny is indeed the main source of objectivity in sciences (Polanyi, 1966, 1967; Popper, 1963) and epitomizes an ideal of democratic practice in both judicial and legislative procedures.

The next few figures return again to the Connecticut crackdown on speeding and look to some other measures of effect. They are relevant to the confirming that there was indeed a crackdown, and to the issue of side effects. They also provide the methodological comfort of assuring us that in some cases the interrupted time-series design can provide clear-cut evidence of effect. Figure 5 shows the jump in suspen-

FIGURE 4. *Number of Reported Murders and Nonnegligent Manslaughters in Chicago, Illinois, from 1942 to 1962 (data from Uniform Crime Reports for the United States, 1942–62).*

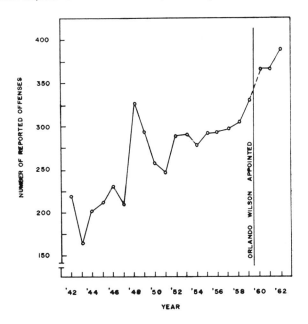

FIGURE 5.   *Suspensions of Licenses for Speeding, as a Percentage of All Suspensions.*

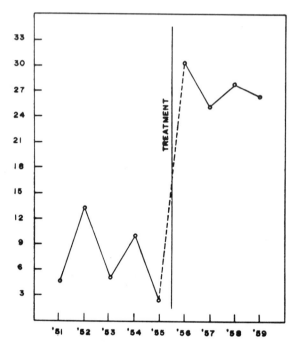

sions of licenses for speeding—evidence that severe punishment was abruptly instituted. Again a note to experimental administrators: with this weak design, *it is only abrupt and decisive changes that we have any chance of evaluating.* A gradually introduced reform will be indistinguishable from the background of secular change, from the net effect of the innumerable change agents continually impinging.

We would want intermediate evidence that traffic speed was modified. A sampling each year of a few hundred five-minute highway movies (random as to location and time) could have provided this at a moderate cost, but they were not collected. Of the public records available, perhaps the data of Figure 6, showing a reduction in speeding violations, indicate a reduction in traffic speed. But the effects on the legal system were complex, and in part undesirable. Driving with a suspended license markedly increased (Figure 7), at least in the biased sample of those arrested. Presumably because of the harshness of the punishment if guilty, judges may have become more lenient (Figure 8) although this effect is of marginal significance.

The relevance of indicators for the social problems we wish to cure must be kept continually in focus. The social indicators approach will tend to make the indicators themselves the goal of social action, rather than the social problems they but imperfectly indicate. There are apt to be tendencies to legislate changes in the indicators per se rather than changes in the social problems.

To illustrate the problem of the irrelevant responsiveness of measures, Figure 9

FIGURE 6. Speeding Violations, as a Percentage of All Traffic Violations.

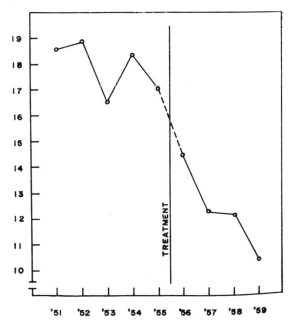

shows a result of the 1900 change in divorce law in Germany. In a recent reanalysis of the data with the Box and Tiao (1965) statistic, Glass (Glass, Tiao, & Maguire, 1971) has found the change highly significant, in contrast to earlier statistical analyses (Rheinstein, 1959; Wolf, Lüke, & Hax, 1959). But Rheinstein's emphasis would still be relevant: This indicator change indicates no likely improvement in marital harmony, or even in marital stability. Rather than reducing them, the legal change has made the divorce rate a less valid indicator of marital discord and separation than it had been earlier (see also Etzioni & Lehman, 1967).

CONTROL SERIES DESIGN

The interrupted time-series design as discussed so far is available for those settings in which no control group is possible, in which the total governmental unit has received the experimental treatment, the social reform measure. In the general program of quasi-experimental design, we argue the great advantage of untreated comparison groups even where these cannot be assigned at random. The most common of such designs is the nonequivalent control-group pretest-posttest design, in which for each of two natural groups, one of which receives the treatment, a pretest and posttest measure is taken. If the traditional mistaken practice is avoided of matching on pretest scores (with resultant regression artifacts), this design provides a useful control over those aspects of history, maturation, and test-retest effects shared by both groups. But it does not control for the plausible rival hypothesis of *selection-*

FIGURE 7.   Arrested while Driving with a Suspended License,
as a Percentage of Suspensions.

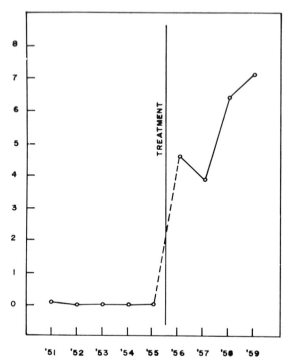

maturation interaction—that is, the hypothesis that the selection differences in the natural aggregations involve not only differences in mean level, but differences in maturation rate.

This point can be illustrated in term of the traditional quasi-experimental design
problem of the effects of Latin on English vocabulary (Campbell, 1963). In the hypothetical data of Figure 10B, two alternative interpretations remain open. Latin may
have had effect, for those taking Latin gained more than those not. But, on the other
hand, those students taking Latin may have a greater annual rate of vocabulary
growth that would manifest itself whether or not they took Latin. Extending this
common design into two time series provides relevant evidence, as comparison of
the two alternative outcomes of Figure 10C and 10D shows. Thus approaching quasi-
experimental design from either improving the nonequivalent control-group design
or from improving the interrupted time-series design, we arrive at the control series
design. Figure 11 shows this for the Connecticut speeding crackdown, adding evidence from the fatality rates of neighboring states. Here the data are presented as
population-based fatality rates so as to make the two series of comparable
magnitude.

The control series design of Figure 11 shows that downward trends were available in other states for 1955–56 as due to history and maturation, that is, due to
shared secular trends, weather, automotive safety features, etc. But the data also

FIGURE 8. *Percentage of Speeding Violations Judged Not Guilty.*

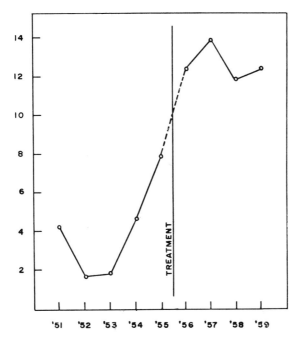

show a general trend for Connecticut to rise relatively closer to the other states prior to 1955, and to steadily drop more rapidly than other states from 1956 on. Glass (1968) has used our monthly data for Connecticut and the control states to generate a monthly difference score, and this too shows a significant shift in trend in the Box and Tiao (1965) statistic. Impressed particularly by the 1957, 1958, and 1959 trend, we are willing to conclude that the crackdown had some effect, over and above the undeniable pseudo-effects of regression (Campbell & Ross, 1968).

FIGURE 9. *Divorce Rate for German Empire, 1881–1914.*

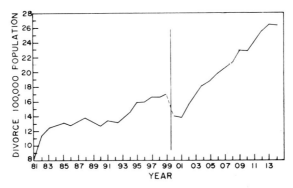

FIGURE 10.   Forms of Quasi-Experimental Analysis for the Effect of Specific Course Work, Including Control Series Design.

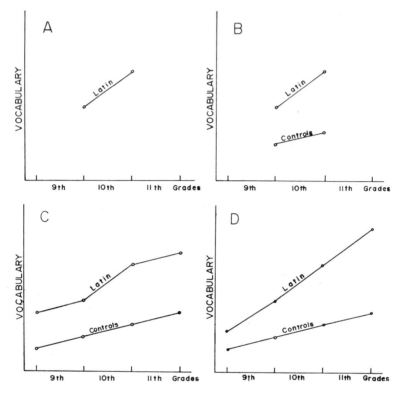

The advantages of the control series design point to the advantages for social experimentation of a social system allowing subunit diversity. Our ability to estimate the effects of the speeding crackdown, Rose's (1952) and Stieber's (1949) ability to estimate the effects on strikes of compulsory arbitration laws, and Simon's (1966) ability to estimate the price elasticity of liquor were made possible because the changes were not being put into effect in all states simultaneously, because they were matters of state legislation rather than national. I do not want to appear to justify on these grounds the wasteful and unjust diversity of laws and enforcement practices from state to state. But I would strongly advocate that social engineers make use of this diversity while it remains available, and plan cooperatively their changes in administrative policy and in record keeping so as to provide optimal experimental inference. More important is the recommendation that, for those aspects of social reform handled by a central government, a purposeful diversity of implementation be envisaged so that experimental and control groups be available for analysis. Properly planned, these can approach true experiments, better than the casual and ad hoc comparison groups now available. But without such fundamental planning, uniform central control can reduce the present possibilities of reality testing, that is, of true social experimentation. In the same spirit, decentralization of de-

FIGURE 11. *Control Series Design Comparing Connecticut Fatalities with Those of Four Comparable States.*

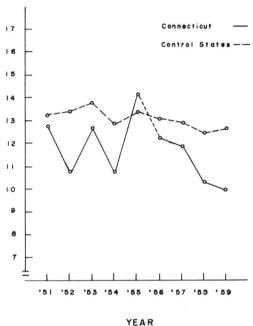

YEAR

cision making, both within large government and within private monopolies, can provide a useful competition for both efficiency and innovation, reflected in a multiplicity of indicators.

One further illustration of the interrupted time series and the control series will be provided. The variety of illustrations so far given have each illustrated some methodological point, and have thus ended up as "bad examples." To provide a "good example," an instance which survives methodological critique as a valid illustration of a successful reform, data from the British Road Safety Act of 1967 are provided in Figure 11A (from Ross, Campbell, & Glass, 1970).

The data on a weekly-hours basis are available only for a composite category of fatalities plus serious injuries, and Figure 11A therefore uses this composite for all three bodies of data. The "Weekend Nights" comprises Friday and Saturday nights from 10:00 P.M. to 4:00 A.M. Here, as expected, the crackdown is most dramatically effective, producing initially more than a 40 per cent drop, leveling off at perhaps 30 per cent, although this involves dubious extrapolations in the absence of some control comparison to indicate what the trend over the years might have been without the crackdown. In this British case, no comparison state with comparable traffic conditions or drinking laws was available. But controls need not always be separate samples of times or stimulus materials (Campbell & Stanley, 1966 pp. 43–47).

A cigarette company may use the sales of its main competitor as a control comparison to evaluate a new advertising campaign. One should search around for the most nearly appropriate control comparison. For the Breathalyser crackdown, com-

FIGURE 11A.   British Traffic Fatalities plus Serious Injuries, before and after Breathalyser Crackdown of October 1967 (seasonally adjusted).

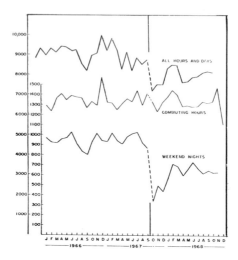

muting hours when pubs had been long closed seemed ideal. (The "Commuting Hours" figures come from 7:00 A.M. to 10 A.M. and 4:00 P.M. to 5 P.M. Monday through Friday. Pubs are open for lunch from 12:00 to 2:00 or 2:30, and open again at 5:00 P.M.)

These commuting hours data convincingly show no effect, but are too unstable to help much with estimating the long-term effects. They show a different annual cycle than do the weekend nights or the overall figures, and do not go back far enough to provide an adequate base for estimating this annual cycle with precision.

The use of highly judgmental category such as "serious injuries" provides an opportunity for pseudo effects owing to a shift in the classifiers' standards. The overall figures are available separately for fatalities, and these show a highly significant effect as strong as that found for the serious injury category or the composite shown in Figure 11A.

More details and the methodological problems are considered in our fuller presentation (Ross, Campbell, & Glass, 1970). One further rule for the use of this design needs emphasizing. The interrupted time series can provide clear evidence of effect only where the reform is introduced with a vigorous abruptness. A gradually introduced reform has little chance of being distinguished from shifts in secular trends or from the cumulative effect of the many other influences impinging during a prolonged period of introduction. In the Breathalyser crackdown, an intense publicity campaign naming the specific starting date preceded the actual crackdown. Although the impact seems primarily due to publicity and fear rather than an actual increase of arrests, an abrupt initiation date was achieved. Had the enforcement effort changed at the moment the Act was passed, with public awareness being built up by subsequent publicity, the resulting data series would have been essentially uninterpretable.

REGRESSION DISCONTINUITY DESIGN

We shift now to social ameliorations that are in short supply, and that therefore cannot be given to all individuals. Such scarcity is inevitable under many circumstances, and can make possible an evaluation of effects that would otherwise be impossible. Consider the heroic Salk poliomyelitis vaccine trials in which some children were given the vaccine while others were given an inert saline placebo injection—and in which many more of these placebo controls would die than would have if they had been given the vaccine. Creation of these placebo controls would have been morally, psychologically, and socially impossible had there been enough vaccine for all. As it was, due to the scarcity, most children that year had to go without the vaccine anyway. The creation of experimental and control groups was the highly moral allocation of that scarcity so as to enable us to learn the true efficacy of the supposed good. The usual medical practice of introducing new cures on a so-called trial basis in general medical practice makes evaluation impossible by confounding prior status with treatment, that is, giving the drug to the most needy or most hopeless. It has the further social bias of giving the supposed benefit to those most assiduous in keeping their medical needs in the attention of the medical profession, that is, the upper and upper-middle classes. The political stance furthering social experimentation here is the recognition of randomization as the most democratic and moral means of allocating scarce resources (and scarce hazardous duties), plus the moral imperative to further utilize the randomization so that society may indeed learn true value of the supposed boon. This is the ideology that makes possible "true experiments" in a large class of social reforms.

But if randomization is not politically feasible or morally justifiable in a given setting, there is a powerful quasi-experimental design available that allows the scarce good to be given to the most needy or the most deserving. This is the regression discontinuity design. All it requires is strict and orderly attention to the priority dimension. The design originated through an advocacy of a tie-breaking experiment to measure the effects of receiving a fellowship (Thistlethwaite & Campbell, 1960), and it seems easiest to explain it in that light. Consider as in Figure 12, pre-award ability-and-merit dimension, which would have some relation to later success in life (finishing college, earnings 10 years later, etc.). Those higher on the pre-measure are most deserving and receive the award. They do better in later life, but does the award have an effect? It is normally impossible to say because they would have done better in later life anyway. Full randomization of the award was impossible given the stated intention to reward merit and ability. But it might be possible to take a narrow band of ability at the cutting point, to regard all of these persons as tied, and to assign half of them to awards, half to no awards, by means of a tie-breaking randomization.

The tie-breaking rationale is still worth doing, but in considering that design it became obvious that, if the regression of premeasure on later effects were reasonably orderly, one should be able to extrapolate to the results of the tie-breaking experiment by plotting the regression of posttest on pretest separately for those in the award and nonaward regions. If there is no significant difference for these at the decision-point intercept, then the tie-breaking experiment should show no difference. In cases where the tie breakers would show an effect, there should be an ab-

FIGURE 12.   Tie-breaking Experiment and Regression Discontinuity Analysis.

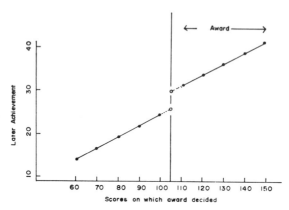

rupt discontinuity in the regression line. Such a discontinuity cannot be explained away by the normal regression of the posttest on pretest, for this normal regression, as extensively sampled within the nonaward area and within the award area, provides no such expectation.

Figure 12 presents, in terms of column means, an instance in which higher pretest scores would have led to higher posttest scores even without the treatment, and in which there is in addition a substantial treatment effect. Figure 13 shows a series of paired outcomes, those on the left to be interpreted as no effect, those in the center and on the right as effect. Note some particular cases. In instances of granting opportunity on the basis of merit, like 13a and b (and Figure 12), neglect of the background regression of pretest on posttest leads to optimistic pseudo-effects: in Figure 13a, those receiving the award do do better in later life, though not really because of the award. But in social ameliorative efforts, the setting is more apt to be like Figure 13d and e, where neglect of the background regression is apt to make the program look deleterious if no effect, or ineffective if there is a real effect.

The design will of course work just as well or better if the award dimension and the decision base, the pretest measure, are unrelated to the posttest dimension, if it is irrelevant or unfair, as instanced in Figure 13g, h, and i. In such cases the decision base is the functional equivalent of randomization. Negative background relationships are obviously possible, as in Figure 13j, k, and l. In Figure 13, m, n, and o are included to emphasize that it is a jump in intercept at the cutting point that shows effect, and that differences in slope without differences at the cutting point are not acceptable as evidences of effect. This becomes more obvious if we remember that in cases like m, a tie-breaking randomization experiment would have shown no difference. Curvilinear background relationships, as in Figure 13p, q, and r, will provide added obstacles to clear inference in many instances, where sampling error could make Figure 13p look like 13b.

As further illustration, Figure 14 provides computer-simulated data, showing individual observations and fitted regression lines, in a fuller version of the no-effect outcome of Figure 13a. Figure 15 shows an outcome with effect. These have been generated[5] by assigning to each individual a weighted normal random number as a

FIGURE 13.   *Illustrative Outcomes of Regression Discontinuity Analyses.*

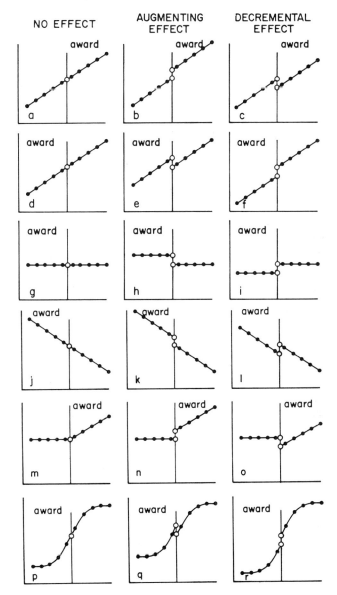

FIGURE 14.   Regression Discontinuity Design: No Effect.

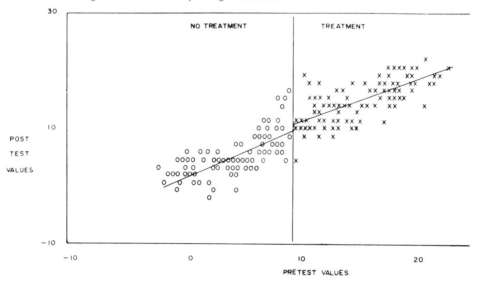

"true score," to which is added a weighted independent "error" to generate the "pretest." The "true score" plus another independent "error" produces the "post-test" in no-effect cases such as Figure 14. In treatment-effect simulations, as in Figure 15, there are added into the posttest "effects points" for all "treated" cases, that is, those above the cutting point on the pretest score.

This design could be used in a number of settings. Consider Job Training Corps applicants, in larger number than the program can accommodate, with eligibility determined by need. The setting would be as in Figure 13d and e. The base-line decision dimension could be per capita family income, with those at below the cutoff getting training. The outcome dimension could be the amount of withholding tax withheld two years later, or the percentage drawing unemployment insurance, these follow-up figures being provided from the National Data Bank in response to categorized social security numbers fed in, without individual anonymity being breached, without any real invasion of privacy—by the technique of Mutually Insulated Data Banks. While the plotted points could be named, there is no need that they be named. In a classic field experiment on tax compliance, Richard Schwartz and the Bureau of Internal Revenue have managed to put together sets of personally identified interviews and tax-return data so that statistical analyses such as these can be done, without the separate custodians of either interview or tax returns learning the corresponding data for specific persons (Schwartz & Orleans, 1967; see also Schwartz & Skolnick, 1963).

Applied to the Job Training Corps illustration, it would work as follows: Separate lists of job-corps applicants (with social security numbers) would be prepared for every class interval on per capita family income. To each of these lists an alphabetical designation would be assigned at random. (Thus the $10.00 per week list might be labeled M: $11.00, C, $12.00, Z, $13.00, Q, $14.00, N, etc.) These lists would be sent to Internal Revenue, without the Internal Revenue personnel being able to learn

FIGURE 15.   Regression Discontinuity Design: Genuine Effect.

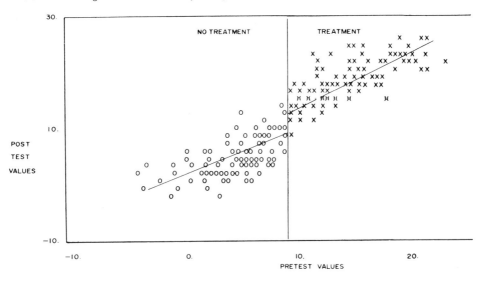

anything interpretable about their traineeship status or family income. The Internal Revenue statisticians would locate the withholding tax collected for each person on each list, but would not return the data in that form. Instead, for each list, only the withholding tax amounts would be listed, and these in a newly randomized order. These would be returned to Job Corps research, who could use them to plot a graph like Figures 10 or 11, and do the appropriate statistical analyses by retranslating the alphabetical symbols into meaningful base-line values. But, within any list, they would be unable to learn which value belonged to which person. (To insure this effective anonymity, it could be specified that no lists shorter than 100 persons be used, the base-line intervals being expanded if necessary to achieve this.)

Manniche and Hayes (1957) have spelled out how a broker can be used in a two-staged matching of doubly coded data. Kaysen (1967) and Sawyer and Schechter (1968) have wise discussions of the more general problem.

What is required of the administrator of a scarce ameliorative commodity to use this design? Most essential is a sharp cutoff point on a decision-criterion dimension, on which several other qualitatively similar analytic cutoffs can be made both above and below the award cut. Let me explain this better by explaining why National Merit scholarships were unable to use the design for their actual fellowship decision (although it has been used for their Certificate of Merit). In their operation, diverse committees make small numbers of award decisions by considering a group of candidates and then picking them from the N best to which to award the N fellowships allocated them. This provides one cutting point on an unspecified pooled decision base, but fails to provide analogous potential cutting points above and below. What could be done is for each committee to collectively rank its group of 20 or so candidates. The top N would then receive the award. Pooling cases across committees, cases could be classified according to number of ranks above and below the cutting point, these other ranks being analogous to the award-nonaward cutting point as far as regression onto posttreatment measures was concerned. Such group ranking would be costly of committee time. An equally good procedure, if committees agreed, would be to have each member, after full discussion and freedom to revise, give each candidate a grade, A+, A, A−, B+, B, etc., and to award the fellowships to the N candidates averaging best on these ratings, with no revisions allowed after the averaging process. These ranking or rating units, even if not comparable from committee to committee in range of talent, in number of persons ranked, or in cutting point, could be pooled without bias as far as a regression discontinuity is concerned, for that range of units above and below the cutting point in which all committees were represented.

It is the dimensionality and sharpness of the decision criterion that is at issue, not its components or validity. The ratings could be based upon nepotism, whimsey, and superstition and still serve. As has been stated, if the decision criterion is utterly invalid we approach the pure randomness of a true experiment. Thus the weakness of subjective committee decisions is not their subjectivity, but the fact that they provide only the one cutting point on their net subjective dimension. Even in the form of average ratings the recommended procedures probably represent some slight increase in committee work load. But this could be justified to the decision committees by the fact that through refusals, etc., it cannot be known at the time of the committee meeting the exact number to whom the fellowship can be offered. Other costs at the planning time are likewise minimal. The primary additional burden is in keeping as good records on the nonawardees as on the awardees. Thus at a low cost, an experimental administrator can lay the groundwork for later scientific follow-ups, the budgets for which need not yet be in sight.

Our present situation is more apt to be one where our pretreatment measures, aptitude measures, reference ratings, etc., can be combined via multiple correlation into an index that correlates highly but not perfectly with the award decision. For this dimension there is a fuzzy cutoff point. Can the design be used in this case? Probably not. Figure 16 shows the pseudo-effect possible if the award decision contributes any valid variance to the quantified pretest evidence, as it usually will. The award regression rides above the nonaward regression just because of that valid variance in this simulated case, there being no true award effect at all. (In simulating this case, the award decision has been based upon a composite of true score plus an independent award error.) Figure 17 shows a fuzzy cutting point plus a genuine award effect.[6] The recommendation to the administrator is clear: aim for a sharp cutting point on a quantified decision criterion. If there are complex rules for eligibility, only one of which is quantified, seek out for followup that subset of persons for whom the quantitative dimension was determinate. If political patronage necessitates some decisions inconsistent with a sharp cutoff, record these cases under the heading "qualitative decision rule" and keep them out of your experimental analysis.

Almost all of our ameliorative programs designed for the disadvantaged could be studied via this design, and so too some major governmental actions affecting the lives of citizens in ways we do not think of as experimental. For example, for a considerable period, quantitative test scores have been used to call up for military service or reject as unfit at the lower ability range. If these cutting points, test scores, names, and social security numbers have been recorded for a number of steps both

FIGURE 16. Regression Discontinuity Design: Fuzzy Cutting Point, Pseudo Treatment Effect Only.

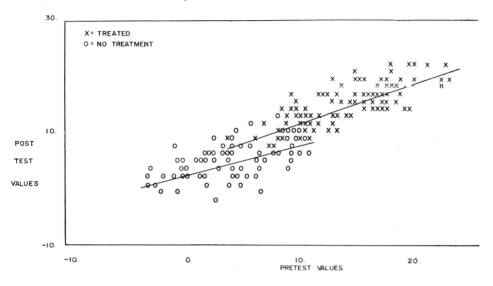

Figure 17. Regression Discontinuity Design: Fuzzy Cutting Point, with Real Treatment plus Pseudo Treatment Effects.

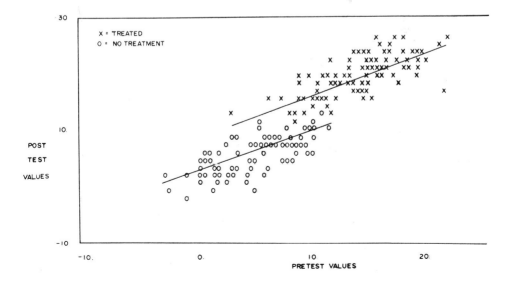

above and below the cutting point, we could make elegant studies of the effect of military service on later withholding taxes, mortality, number of dependents, etc.

This illustration points to one of the threats to external validity of this design, or of the tie-breaking experiment. The effect of the treatment has only been studied for that narrow range of talent near the cutting point, and generalization of the effects of military service, for example, from this low ability level to the careers of the most able would be hazardous in the extreme. But in the draft laws and the requirements of the military services there may be other sharp cutting points on a quantitative criterion that could also be used. For example, those over 6 feet 6 inches are excluded from service. Imagine a five-year-later follow-up of draftees grouped by inch in the 6 feet 1 inch to 6 feet 5 inches range, and a group of their counterparts who would have been drafted except for their heights, 6 feet 6 inches to 6 feet 10 inches. (The fact that the other grounds of deferment might not have been examined by the draft board would be a problem here, but probably not insurmountable.) That we should not expect height in this range to have any relation to later-life variables is not at all a weakness of this design, and if we have indeed a subpopulation for which there is a sharp numerical cutting point, an internally valid measure of effects would result. Deferment under the present system is an unquantified committee decision. But just as the sense of justice of United States soldiers was quantified through paired comparisons of cases into an acceptable Demobilization Points system at the end of World War II (Guttman, 1946; Stouffer, 1949), so a quantified composite index of deferment priority could be achieved and applied as uniform justice across the nation, providing another numerical cutting point.

In addition to the National Data Bank type of indicators, there will be occasions in which new data collections as by interview or questionnaire are needed. For these there is the special problem of uneven cooperation that would be classified as instrumentation error. In our traditional mode of thinking, completeness of description is valued more highly than comparability. Thus if, in a fellowship study, a follow-up mailed out from the fellowship office would bring a higher return from past winners, this might seem desirable even if the nonawardees' rate of response was much lower. From the point of view of quasi-experimentation, however, it would be better to use an independent survey agency and a disguised purpose achieving equally low response rates from both awardees and nonawardees, and avoiding a regression discontinuity in cooperation rate that might be misinterpreted as a discontinuity in more important effects.

RANDOMIZED CONTROL GROUP EXPERIMENTS

Experiments with randomization tend to be limited to the laboratory and agricultural experiment station. But this certainly need not be so. The randomization unit may be persons, families, precincts, or larger administrative units. For statistical purposes the randomization units should be numerous, and hence ideally small. But for reasons of external validity, including reactive arrangements, the randomization units should be selected on the basis of the units of administrative access. Where policies are administered through individual client contacts, randomization at the person level may be often inconspicuously achieved, with the clients unaware that different ones of them are getting different treatments. But for most social reforms, larger administrative units will be involved, such as classrooms, schools, cities, counties, or states. We need to develop the political postures and ideologies that make random-ization at these levels possible.

"Pilot project" is a useful term already in our political vocabulary. It designates a trial program that, if it works, will be spread to other areas. By modifying actual practice in this regard, without going outside of the popular understanding of the term, a valuable experimental ideology could be developed. How are areas selected for pilot projects? If the public worries about this, it probably assumes a lobbying process in which the greater needs of some areas are only one consideration, politi-cal power and expediency being others. Without violating the public tolerance or in-tent, one could probably devise a system in which the usual lobbying decided upon the areas eligible for a formal public lottery that would make final choices between matched pairs. Such decision procedures as the drawing of lots have had a justly esteemed position since time immemorial (e.g., Aubert, 1959). At the present time, record keeping for pilot projects tends to be limited to the experimental group only. In the experimental ideology, comparable data would be collected on designated controls. (There are of course exceptions, as in the heroic Public Health Service fluor-idation experiments, in which the teeth of Oak Park children were examined year after year as controls for the Evanston experimentals [Blayney & Hill, 1967].)

Another general political stance making possible experimental social amelioration is that of *staged innovation.* Even though by intent a new reform is to be put into effect in all units, the logistics of the situation usually dictate that simultaneous in-troduction is not possible. What results is a haphazard sequence of convenience. Under the program of staged innovation, the introduction of the program would be deliberately spread out, and those units selected to be first and last would be ran-domly assigned (perhaps randomization from matched pairs), so that during the transition period the first recipients could be analyzed as experimental units, the last recipients as controls. A third ideology making possible true experiments has al-ready been discussed: randomization as the democratic means of allocating scarce resources.

This article will not give true experimentation equal space with quasi-experimen-tation only because excellent discussions of, and statistical consultation on, true ex-perimentation are readily available. True experiments should almost always be pre-ferred to quasi-experiments where both are available. Only occasionally are the threats to external validity so much greater for the true experiment that one would prefer a quasi-experiment. The uneven allocation of space here should not be read as indicating otherwise.

MORE ADVICE FOR TRAPPED ADMINISTRATORS

But the competition is not really between the fairly interpretable quasi-experiments here reviewed and "true" experiments. Both stand together as rare excellencies in contrast with a morass of obfuscation and self-deception. Both to emphasize this contrast, and again as guidelines for the benefit of those trapped administrators whose political predicament will not allow the risk of failure, some of these alterna-tives should be mentioned.

Grateful testimonials. Human courtesy and gratitude being what it is, the most de-pendable means of assuring a favorable evaluation is to use voluntary testimonials from those who have had the treatment. If the spontaneously produced testimonials are in short supply, these should be solicited from the recipients with whom the program is still in contact. The rosy glow resulting is analogous to the professor's impression of his teaching success when it is based solely upon the comments of those students who come up and talk with him after class. In many programs, as in psychotherapy, the recipient, as well as the agency, has devoted much time and effort to the program and it is dissonance reducing for himself, as well as common courtesy to his therapist, to report improvement. These grateful testimonials can come in the language of letters and conversation, or be framed as answers to multiple-item "tests" in which a recurrent theme of "I am sick," "I am well," "I am happy," "I am sad" recurs. Probably the testimonials will be more favorable as: (a) the more the evaluative meaning of the response measure is clear to the recipient—it is complete clear in most personality, adjustment, morale, and attitude tests; (b) the more directly the recipient is identified by name with his answer; (c) the more the recipient gives the answer directly to the therapist or agent of reform; (d) the more the agent will continue to be influential in the recipient's life in the future; (e) the more the answers deal with feelings and evaluations rather than with verifiable facts; and (f) the more the recipients participating in the evaluation are a small and self-selected or agent-selected subset of all recipients. Properly designed the grateful testimonial method can involve pretests as well as posttests, and randomized control groups as well as experimentals, for there are usually no placebo treatments, and the recipients know when they have had the boon.

Confounding selection and treatment. Another dependable tactic bound to give favorable outcomes is to confound selection and treatment, so that in the published comparison those receiving the treatment are also the more able and well placed. The often-cited evidence of the dollar value of a college education is of this nature—all careful studies show that most of the effect, and of the superior effect of superior colleges, is explainable in terms of superior talents and family connections, rather than in terms of what is learned or even the prestige of the degree. Matching techniques and statistical partialings generally undermatch and do not fully control for the selection differences—they introduce regression artifacts confusable as treatment effects.

There are two types of situations that must be distinguished. First, there are those treatments that are given to the most promising, treatments like a college education which are regularly given to those who need it least. For these, the later concomitants of the grounds of selection operate in the same direction as the treatment: those most likely to achieve anyway get into the college most likely to produce later achievement. For these settings, the trapped administrator should use the pooled mean of all those treated, comparing it with the mean of all untreated, although in this setting almost any comparison an administrator might hit upon would be biased in his favor.

At the other end of the talent continuum are those remedial treatments given to those who need it most. Here the later concomitants of the grounds of selection are poorer success. In the Job Training Corps example, casual comparisons of the later unemployment rate of those who received the training with those who did not are in general biased against showing an advantage to the training. Here the trapped administrator must be careful to seek out those few special comparisons biasing selection in his favor. For training programs such as Operation Head Start and tutoring programs, a useful solution is to compare the later success of those who completed the training program with those who were invited but never showed plus those who came a few times and dropped out. By regarding only those who complete the program as "trained" and using the others as controls, one is selecting for conscientiousness, stable and supporting family backgrounds, enjoyment of the training activity, ability, determination to get ahead in the world—all factors promising well for future achievement even if the remedial program is valueless. To apply this tactic effectively in the Job Training Corps, one might have to eliminate from the so-called control group all those who quit the training program because they had found a job—but this would seem a reasonable practice and would not blemish the reception of a glowing progress report.

These are but two more samples of well-tried modes of analysis for the trapped administrator who cannot afford an honest evaluation of the social reform he directs. They remind us again that we must help create a political climate that demands more rigorous and less self-deceptive reality testing. We must provide political stances that permit true experiments, or good quasi-experiments. Of the several suggestions toward this end that are contained in this article, the most important is probably the initial theme: Administrators and parties must advocate the importance of the problem rather than the importance of the answer. They must advocate experimental sequences of reforms, rather than one certain cure-all, advocating Reform A with Alternative B available to try next should an honest evaluation of A prove it worthless or harmful.

MULTIPLE REPLICATION IN ENACTMENT

Too many social scientists expect single experiments to settle issues once and for all. This may be a mistaken generalization from the history of great crucial experiments in physics and chemistry. In actuality the significant experiments in the physical sciences are replicated thousands of times, not only in deliberate replication efforts, but also as inevitable incidentals in successive experimentation and in utilizations of those many measurement devices (such as the galvanometer) that in their own operation embody the principles of classic experiments. Because we social scientists have less ability to achieve "experimental isolation," because we have good reason to expect our treatment effects to interact significantly with a wide variety of social factors many of which we have not yet mapped, we have much greater needs for replication experiments than do the physical sciences.

The implications are clear. We should not only do hard-headed reality testing in the initial pilot testing and choosing of which reform to make general law; but once it has been decided that the reform is to be adopted as standard practice in all administrative units, we should experimentally evaluate it in each of its implementations (Campbell, 1967).

CONCLUSIONS

Trapped administrators have so committed themselves in advance to the efficacy of the reform that they cannot afford honest evaluation. For them, favorably biased analyses are recommended, including capitalizing on regression, grateful testimonials, and confounding selection and treatment. *Experimental administrators* have justified the reform on the basis of the importance of the problem, not the certainty of their answer, and are committed to going on to other potential solutions if the one first tried fails. They are therefore not threatened by a hard-headed analysis of the reform. For such, proper adminstrative decisions can lay the base for useful experimental or quasi-experimental analyses. Through the ideology of allocating scarce resources by lottery, through the use of staged innovation, and through the pilot project, true experiments with randomly assigned control groups can be achieved. If the reform must be introduced across the board, the interrupted time-series design is available. If there are similar units under independent administration, a control series design adds strength. If a scarce boon must be given to the most needy or to the most deserving, quantifying this need or merit makes possible the regression discontinuity analysis.

ENDNOTES

1. This list has been expanded from the major previous presentations by the addition of *Instability* (but see Campbell, 1968; Campbell & Ross, 1968). This has been done in reaction to the sociological discussion of the use of tests of significance in nonexperimental or quasi-experimental research (e.g., Selvin, 1957; and as reviewed by Galtung, 1967, pp. 358–389). On the one hand, I join with the critics in criticizing the exaggerated status of "statistically significant differences" in establishing convictions of validity. Statistical tests are relevant to at best 1 out of 15 or so threats to validity. On the other hand, I join with those who defend their use in situations where randomization has not been employed. Even in those situations, it is relevant to say or to deny, "This is a trivial difference. It is of the order that would have occurred frequently *had* these measures been assigned to these classes solely by chance." Tests of significance making use of random reassignments of the actual scores are particularly useful in communicating this point.

2. This list has been lengthened from previous presentations to make more salient Threats 5 and 6 which are particularly relevant to social experimentation. Discussion in previous presentations (Campbell, 1957, pp. 309–310; Campbell & Stanley, 1963, pp. 203–204) had covered these points, but they had not been included in the checklist.

3. No doubt the public and press shared the Governor's special alarm over the 1955 death toll. This differential reaction could be seen as a negative feedback servosystem in which the dampening effect was proportional to the degree of upward deviation from the prior trend. Insofar as such alarm reduces traffic fatalities, it adds a negative component to the autocorrelation, increasing the regression effect. This component should probably be regarded as a rival cause or treatment rather than as artifact. (The regression effect is less as the positive autocorrelation is higher, and will be present to some degree insofar as this correlation is less than positive unity. Negative correlation in a time series would represent regression beyond the mean, in a way not quite analogous to negative correlation across persons. For an autocorrelation of Lag 1, high negative correlation would be represented by a series that oscillated maximally from one extreme to the other.)

4. Wilson's inconsistency in utilization of records and the political problem of relevant records are ably documented in Kamisar (1964). Etzioni (1968) reports that in New York City in 1965 a crime wave was proclaimed that turned out to be due to an unpublicized improvement in record keeping.

5. Sween & D. T. Campbell, Computer programs for simulating and analyzing sharp and fuzzy regression discontinuity experiments. In preparation.

6. There are some subtle statistical clues that might distinguish these two instances if one had enough cases. There should be increased pooled column variance in the mixed columns for a true effects case. If the data are arbitrarily treated as though there had been a sharp cutting point located in the middle of the overlap area, then there should be no discontinuity in the no-effect case, and some discontinuity in the case of a real effect, albeit an underestimated discontinuity, since there are untreated cases above the cutting point and treated ones below, dampening the apparent effect. The degree of such dampening should be estimable, and correctable, perhaps by iterative procedures. But these are hopes for the future.

REFERENCES

Aubert, V. Chance in social affairs. *Inquiry,* 1959, 2, 1–24.

Bauer, R. M. *Social indicators.* Cambridge, Mass.: M.I.T. Press, 1966.

Blayney, J. R., & Hill, I. N. Fluorine and dental caries. *The Journal of the American Dental Association* (Special Issue), 1967, 74, 233–302.

Box, G. E. P., & Tiao, G. C. A change in level of a nonstationary time series. *Biometrika,* 1965, 52, 181–192.

Campbell, D. T. Factors relevant to the validity of experiments in social settings. *Psychological Bulletin,* 1952, 54, 297–312.

Campbell, D. T. From description to experimentation: Interpreting trends as quasi-experiments. In C. W. Harris (Ed.), *Problems in measuring change.* Madison: University of Wisconsin Press, 1963.

Campbell, D. T. Administrative experimentation, institutional records, and nonreactive measures. In J. C. Stanley (Ed.), *Improving experimental design and statistical analysis.* Chicago: Rand McNally, 1967.

Campbell, D. T. Quasi-experimental design. In D. L. Sills (Ed.), *International Encyclopedia of the Social Sciences.* New York: Macmillan and Free Press, 1968, Vol. 5, 259–263.

Campbell, D. T., & Fiske, D. W. Convergent and discriminant validation by the multitrait-multimethod matrix. *Psychological Bulletin,* 1959, 56, 81–105.

Campbell, D. T., & Ross, H. L. The Connecticut crackdown on speeding: Time-series data in quasi-experimental analysis. *Law and Society Review,* 1968, 3 (1), 33–53.

Campbell, D. T., & Stanley, J. C. Experimental and quasi-experimental designs for research on teaching. In N. I. Gage (Ed.), *Handbook of research on teaching.* Chicago: Rand McNally, 1963. (Reprinted as *Experimental and quasi-experimental design for research.* Chicago: Rand McNally, 1966.)

Chapin, F. S. *Experimental design in sociological research.* New York: Harper, 1947.

Etzioni, A. "Shortcuts" to social change? *The Public Interest,* 1968, 12, 40–51.

Etzioni, A., & Lehman, E. W. Some dangers in "valid" social measurement. *Annals of the American Academy of Political and Social Science,* 1967, 373, 1–15.

Galtung, J. *Theory and methods of social research.* Oslo: Universitetsforloget; London: Allen & Unwin; New York: Columbia University Press, 1967.

Glass, G. V. Analysis of data on the Connecticut speeding crackdown as a time-series quasi-experiment. *Law and Society Review,* 1968, 3 (1), 55–76.

Glass, G. V., Tiao, G. C., & Maguire, T. O. Analysis of data on the 1900 revision of the German divorce laws as a quasi-experiment. *Law and Society Review*, 1971, 6, 539–562.

Greenwood, E. *Experimental sociology: A study in method.* New York: King's Crown Press, 1945.

Gross, B. M. *The state of the nation: Social system accounting.* London: Tavistock Publications, 1966. (Also in R. M. Bauer, *Social indicators.* Cambridge, Mass.: M.I.T. Press, 1966.)

Gross, B. M. (Ed.) Social goals and indicators. *Annals of the American Academy of Political and Social Science*, 1967, 371, Part 1, May, pp. i–iii and 1–177; Part 2, September, pp. i–iii and 1–218.

Guttman, L. An approach for quantifying paired comparisons and rank order. *Annals of Mathematical Statistics*, 1946, 17, 144–163.

Hyman, H. H., & Wright, C. R. Evaluating social action programs. In P. F. Lazarsfeld, W. H. Sewell, & H. L. Wilensky (Eds.), *The uses of sociology.* New York: Basic Books, 1967.

Kamisar, Y. The tactics of police-persecution oriented critics of the courts. *Cornell Law Quarterly*, 1964, 49, 458–471.

Kaysen, C. Data banks and dossiers. *The Public Interest*, 1967, 7, 52–60.

Manniche, E., & Hayes, D. P. Respondent anonymity and data matching. *Public Opinion Quarterly*, 1957, 21 (3), 384–388.

Polanyi, M. A society of explorers. In, *The tacit dimension.* (Ch. 3) New York: Doubleday, 1966.

Polanyi, M. The growth of science in society. *Minerva*, 1967, 5, 533–545.

Popper, K. R. *Conjectures and refutations.* London: Routledge and Kegan Paul; New York: Basic Books, 1963.

Rheinstein, M. Divorce and the law in Germany: A review. *American Journal of Sociology*, 1959, 65, 489–498.

Rose, A. M. Needed research on the mediation of labor disputes. *Personnel Psychology*, 1952, 5, 187–200.

Ross, H. L., & Campbell, D. T. The Connecticut speed crackdown: A study of the effects of legal change. In H. L. Ross (Ed.), *Perspectives on the social order: Readings in sociology.* New York: McGraw-Hill, 1968.

Ross, H. L., Campbell, D. T., and Glass, G. V. Determining the social effects of a legal reform: The British "Breathalyser" crackdown of 1967. *American Behavioral Scientist*, 1970, 13, 493–509.

Sawyer, J., & Schechter, H. Computers, privacy, and the National Data Center: The responsibility of social scientists. *American Psychologist*, 1968, 23, 810–818.

Schanck, R. L., & Goodman, C. Reactions to propaganda on both sides of a controversial issue. *Public Opinion Quarterly*, 1939, 3, 107–112.

Schwartz, R. D. Field experimentation in sociolegal research. *Journal of Legal Education*, 1961, 13, 401–410

Schwartz, R. D., & Orleans, S. On legal sanctions. *University of Chicago Law Review*, 1967, 34, 274–300.

Schwartz, R. D., & Skolnick, J. H. Televised communication and income tax compliance. In L. Arons & M. May (Eds.), *Television and human behavior.* New York: Appleton-Century-Crofts, 1963.

Selvin, H. A critique of tests of significance in survey research. *American Sociological Review*, 1957, 22, 519–527.

Simon, J. L. The price elasticity of liquor in the U.S. and a simple method of determination. *Econometrica,* 1966, 34, 193–205.

Solomon, R. W. An extension of control group design. *Psychological Bulletin,* 1949, 46, 137–150.

Stieber, J. W. *Ten years of the Minnesota Labor Relations Act.* Minneapolis: Industrial Relations Center, University of Minnesota, 1949.

Stouffer, S. A. The point system for redeployment and discharge. In S. A. Stouffer et al., *The American soldier. Vol. 2, Combat and its aftermath.* Princeton: Princeton University Press, 1949.

Suchman, E. A. *Evaluative research: Principles and practice in public service and social action programs.* New York: Russell Sage, 1967.

Sween, J., & Campbell, D. T. A study of the effect of proximally auto-correlated error on tests of significance for the interrupted time-series quasi-experimental design. Available from author, 1965. (Multilith)

Thistlethwaite, D. L., & Campbell, D. T. Regression-discontinuity analysis: An alternative to the ex post facto experiment. *Journal of Educational Psychology,* 1960, 51, 309–317.

Walker, H. M., & Lev, J. *Statistical inference.* New York: Holt, 1953.

Webb, E. J., Campbell, D. T., Schwartz, R. D., & Sechrest, L. B. *Unobtrusive measures: Nonreactive research in the social sciences.* Chicago: Rand McNally, 1966.

Wolf, E., Lüke, G., & Hax, H. *Scheidung und Scheidungsrecht: Grundfrägen der Ehescheidung in Deutschland.* Tubigen: J. C. B. Mohr, 1959.

Questions for Study and Discussion

1. The advantage of designing social reforms as experiments is that the resulting measurements take on predictive rather than simply suggestive import (Churchman's terms). Would you agree with this proposition? Why or why not?

2. Find an example of a social reform comparable to the Connecticut crackdown on speeding reported by Campbell. The example should be one in which the administrator responsible might have made a statement such as that of the Connecticut governor: "With the saving of 40 lives in 1956, a reduction of 12.3% from the 1955 motor vehicle death toll, we can say that the program is definitely worthwhile." In your example, what alternative rival hypotheses might explain that which occurred subsequent to the reform?

CHAPTER **SEVENTEEN**

President Lyndon B. Johnson once proclaimed, "Doing what is right is not hard. Finding out what is right is the problem." Finding out what is right is indeed the major challenge facing any executive or policy maker at the societal level of decision making, especially the president of the United States.

Social information systems are those information systems designed to serve decision makers at the societal level. Modern computer-based techniques permit extensive societal data to be gathered, organized, processed, retrieved, and displayed for users by these systems. If the contemporary policy maker has difficulty in determining what is right, it is not for a general lack of data.

Social information systems are also typically based on *social indicators,* i.e., high-level measures taken to indicate the social condition in some respect. Measures of economic activity, discussed earlier, are examples. So are measures of criminal activity such as the FBI Crime Index, also discussed earlier. Still another example is the measurement of a community's air quality, illustrated by the Pollutant Standards Index (PSI) recently adopted by the four-county South Coast Air Quality Management District for the Los Angeles Basin.

THE POLLUTANT STANDARDS INDEX

In 1977 Los Angeles instituted a new method for reporting smog and issuing health warnings. The new index, called the Pollutant Standards Index (PSI), replaced an older method based on parts per million of pollutants. On the new scale, 100 represents the maximum daily concentration of oxidants, carbon monoxide, and sulfur dioxide a person can tolerate before the air becomes potentially injurious to health. A PSI reading of 0 to 100 is "good," 101 to 199 is "unhealthful," 200 to 299 is "very unhealthful," and 300 and above is "hazardous." An example of a day's smog forecast based on the new index is shown in Fig. 17.1.

An important feature of the PSI is its explicit tie to requirements for social action. The scale is constructed so that 100 is equivalent to the level at which a violation of Federal Environmental Protection Agency (EPA) standards occurs. At the "good" level no ill health effects are said to exist, and no cautionary warnings are issued. At other levels various actions are taken.

The "unhealthful" level represents a mild aggravation of symptoms for susceptible persons. Warnings are issued for those with heart or respiratory ailments. A PSI reading of 200 or over, "very unhealthful," triggers another level of action.

FIGURE 17.1

Source: Los Angeles Times, December 13, 1977.

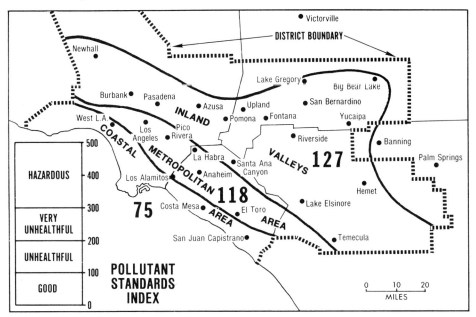

SIMPLIFIED SCALE—New index forecasts to-day's smog for three geographical areas— coastal, metropolitan, inland—at 75, 118, 127, respectively. Inset, what the numbers mean.

Times map by Don Clement

Health warnings are issued to schools and industry. Some industries are required to shut down. Schools are requested to discontinue outside exercise or play periods. Commuters are requested to car pool and to drive less. The "hazardous" reading, 300 to 500 PSI, leads to still more stringent action. Stronger warnings are issued requesting people to remain indoors and to avoid physical activity of all sorts.

Forecasts are issued every day at 10:00 A.M. for the following day's smog conditions. Action taken is based on these forecasts.

Plans to refine the pollutant basis of the index, to include particulates, nitrogen dioxide, and sulphates are being considered.

Concern for the public's reaction to the new index, and to new EPA standards on which it was based, were evident on the day of its implementation. Joseph A. (Jeb) Stuart, executive officer of the air quality district, declared, "There is no cause for any alarm in the early implementation of the new EPA standards." (Los Angeles Times, December 13, 1977.)

In the summer of 1979 Los Angeles suffered one of its worst attacks of smog in years, and readings approaching "hazardous" were recorded.

The Pollutant Standards Index (PSI) described above provides an excellent illustration of measurement and information systems for support of managerial decision making at the societal level. From the managerial point of view the index has decisive as well as predictive and suggestive attributes, as described by Churchman

(Reading 5). Thus the information system incorporates social values as a basis for choice, as described by Mason (Reading 6).

The two readings in the present section provide additional perspectives on the design of social information systems. In the first John C. Deshaies and David R. Seidman present a broad design for a health information system to support policy makers in the public health field. The exciting promise of such information systems is perhaps tempered, however, by the cautions offered by Eleanor B. Sheldon and Howard E. Freeman in the second article, in which deficiencies in both conceptualization and method which limit the potential of social indicators for policy making are identified.

HEALTH INFORMATION SYSTEMS

John C. Deshaies • David R. Seidman *READING 29*

INTRODUCTION

Definition

A health information system is specified here to be a collection of data useful for the planning and operation of the personal and environmental health delivery system of defined geographic areas, ranging from a nation or state to a city or neighborhood within a city. The World Health Organization defines health as "a state of complete physical, mental and social well-being and not merely the absence of disease or infirmity" [1]. While this is a philosophically pleasing definition, it creates grave measurement problems: what is complete well-being? is it a state of euphoria, or a state free of overt stress? which is preferable? To avoid philosophical debate on the ideal state of human existence we have chosen a related but less ambiguous definition: health has "a number of interrelated subcomponents which ideally reflect not only an absence of physical disorder or illness but also the absence of social, psychological and environmental stress which interferes with the maintenance of normal activities" [2]. Therefore a system of information concerning health would include not only health data, but other data reflecting social and environmental stress—for example: demographic and socio-economic data summarized from a census, behavioral data abstracted from other sources such as a special purpose survey (including attitudinal data), vital records and admission and diagnostic data from hospitals, mental institutions and the like.

A health information system should not be confused with a data bank made up of personal records. The information compiled from various sources in such a system does not relate to individuals; rather it concerns population groups living in small geographic areas. The information is summarized and stripped of individual identification, precluding any invasion of privacy.

A health information system is designed to be a base for planning, implementing and evaluating programs. The need for a systematized information base arises from the large quantities of uncoordinated data available, and requirements that these data be brought to bear in a quantitative manner to measure health problems, the

From *Socio-Economic Planning Science*, Vol. 5, 1971, pp. 515–533. Reprinted by permission.

utilization of health services, the quality of the environment, and social pathology, all of which contribute to stress (or lack thereof) of the population. The demand for statistical analysis has been accompanied by new and more efficient methods for assembling, organizing and utilizing data.

Purpose of This Article

This article has three main concerns: (1) the identification of sources of data input to a health information system and the derivation of meaningful health indicators, (2) discussion of techniques for organizing and analysing health information systems data and (3) recommendations on the uses of health information system data for health planning.

In deriving health indicators, which is the first concern of this article, we recognized that the data base should be program oriented, although the orientation should not be toward a specific program. Rather an information base should be sufficiently broad in its conceptual framework to have applicability to a number of health programs operating in a geographic area. The emphasis needs to be placed on delineating data items of common concern to all health programs. Given this emphasis, it is of course also desirable to define narrower categories which would be more relevant to specific programs. This article seeks to identify both types of data. While indicators of health status, demographic characteristics and socio-economic status are more general in their applicability, the data on the utilization of health services, available health facilities and the quality of the environment may be applicable to more limited program concerns. Another reason for identifying both the general and specific data items is to encourage program planners to interrelate the two. For example, it would be useful to correlate morbidity (generalized category) to concentrations of air pollutants (specific category).

A second concern of this article is to describe some proven techniques for organizing, structuring and analysing an information system constructed from multiple data files. Included here are statistical techniques for summarizing a large number of variables. The basic approach is to perform these analyses on small defineable geographic areas (neighborhoods). The small area approach is deemed desirable because many of the health problems to which an information system is addressed need to be specifically located, characterized and dealt with in an area small enough to permit the effective delivery of health services. In structuring a health information system one must recognize that the kinds of data required for planning at the neighborhood level will be different from that needed at the city level, and substantially different from that for the national level. To the extent that this article is geographically specialized, it is aimed at the city or sub-city level.

A third concern of this article is to describe some of the uses of the health information system. These uses fall into three broad categories: (1) program planning and development, (2) program analysis and evaluation, (3) defining interrelationships between variables as a contribution to the scientific fund of knowledge. These will be covered later in the article.

The primary impetus for the development of health information systems has been the intensification of health planning efforts in recent years, accompanied by great advances in computer technology. On the Federal level, the major forces for this trend have emanated from the Health Services and Mental Health Administration (HSMHA), of HEW. The agencies primarily involved within HSMHA include the Community Health Service (Comprehensive Health Planning), Regional Medical Program Service, Maternal and Child Health Service, National Institute of Mental Health, National Center for Health Statistics and National Center for Health Services Research and Development. In general, the programs are intended to have their related State and local planning agencies identify health goals and objectives, and existing health needs and health resources.

Significant Health Information System Efforts

The Federal thrust in health planning has helped create or encourage the development of information systems at the regional, state and local levels. There are numerous operational health information system programs which reflect the substance contained in this present article. We will briefly describe four such programs to exemplify the systems approach to organizing and analyzing health data.

1. Evidence for Community Health Organization (ECHO)—also known as the Michigan Health Survey. This program is operational in various communities in the State of Michigan [3]. The program constitutes a collaborative effort between Michigan communities and the Michigan Department of Public Health in conducting a health surveillance sample survey on a continuing basis. The program also utilizes other sources of data such as the vital record system, crime statistics, and the like.

2. Neighborhood Environmental Evaluation and Decision System (NEEDS), developed by the Bureau of Community Environmental Management, Public Health Service, U.S. Department of Health, Education and Welfare [4]. The NEEDS program is operational in several cities in the U.S. Its focus is on characterizing the environmental quality of localities and determining priority or target areas within each locality. In priority areas an intensive windshield survey is conducted to measure the conditions of housing and of the physical environment, and a household interview is conducted to obtain data on demographic, health status, health utilization and attitudinal characteristics. The surveys are conducted by the communities themselves with technical support from the Federal level. The information provided from the survey, when augmented with data available in the local area (e.g. census, vital records, etc.), will constitute a rich planning base.

3. Mental Health Demographic Profiles—National Institute of Mental Health [5]. A number of social indicators reflecting population characteristics, socio-economic status, family life cycles and life styles are being derived from 100 per cent and sample census summary tapes and vital records. The plan is to provide a printout tape to State Mental Health Authorities, provided that the State furnishes a current census tract delineation of catchment areas, and makes the profile data available to Federally funded mental health centers in the states. These data profiles can serve as a basis for an information system. However, state mental health authorities will have a great deal to gain by augmenting this base with available data files.

4. New Haven Health Information System [6]. This program constitutes a joint enterprise of the Census Use Study and the Connecticut State Department of Health supported by a research grant from the Children's Bureau, Department

of Health, Education and Welfare. The project compiled indicators from 5 sources of data including a dress rehearsal census conducted in New Haven in 1967 (head count and sample data), special purpose health survey, vital records and obstetrical records. Methods for structuring and distilling data files were developed, neighborhood profiles were constructed, and multi-variate statistical analyses were performed. A data base is being created with 1970 data, and a time analysis will be performed using multi-variate methods.

CATEGORIES OF HEALTH INDICATORS

The diversity of data desired and obtained is illustrated by a recent report of the Kansas State Board of Health [6]. Table 1, taken from this report, delineates the kind of information considered to be useful for health planning by the more than 125 organizations which the Board surveyed. The "number" and "per cent of total" show how frequently particular kinds of information were desired. The "outputs" column signifies data which are provided by a given agency as an output of its data collection activities. "Current inputs" refers to data obtained from organizations other than the specific data user, i.e. externally obtained data.

TABLE 1

	Information Items		% of Information Types for Each Kind of Information Item		
Kind of Information	No.	% of Total	Outputs	Current Inputs	Unavailable and Future Inputs
Total	1344	100.0	24.7	54.5	20.8
Epidemiological information	190	14.1	20.5	55.3	24.2
Health facilities	146	10.9	26.0	53.4	20.6
Maternal and child health	121	9.0	38.1	48.3	17.3
Vital statistics	119	8.9	14.3	78.2	7.5
Environmental health	111	8.3	32.4	48.7	18.9
Health manpower	110	8.2	27.3	41.8	30.9
Population data	103	7.7	8.7	56.7	34.6
Patients	58	4.3	29.3	62.1	8.6
Medical care	57	4.2	31.6	43.9	24.5
Accident information	51	3.8	19.6	68.6	11.8
Welfare	45	3.3	37.8	57.8	4.4
Mental health	41	3.1	29.3	58.5	12.2
Health education	39	2.9	35.9	38.5	25.6
Crime	29	2.2	13.8	48.3	37.9
Occupational and industrial health	12	0.9	25.0	33.3	41.7
Health costs	9	0.7	33.3	55.6	11.1
Rehabilitation	6	0.4	33.3	50.0	16.7
Other and miscellaneous	97	7.2	18.2	55.9	24.7

The kinds of information indicated in the above table have been recast into five broad divisions of health information system indicators. These are indicators pertaining to (1) status of community health, (2) utilization of health services, (3) general population and housing characteristics, (4) inventory of health facilities and health service manpower, and (5) status of community environment.

While these five divisions are designed to encompass a wide range of health indicators, they are by no means exhaustive. Consideration was given, for example, to designing separate divisions for mental health, crime statistics and welfare (rehabilitation). With regard to mental health, it was concluded that the categories designed for health *per se,* with a slightly different slant could be applied to mental health. For example, the social pathology and life cycle indicators derived from a census can and have been related to behavioral or psychological factors [5]. In addition, indicators of mental health status, utilization of mental health services and inventories of mental health facilities and manpower could be derived by using the same techniques, from similarly constructed sources, as described later in this article. Crime statistics, including statistics on violent crime, drug abuse and the like are very important inputs to an information system dealing with the health of a community. The classification of crime statistics, however, was deemed to be beyond the scope of the present article. Similarly, welfare statistics are an essential component to a health information system. These statistics were also considered outside the scope of this article. However, there are several indicators relating to welfare contained in the five broad divisions delineated for this article.

Status of Community Health

The purpose of this section is to recommend indicators that depict incidence and prevalence of mortality, morbidity or states of disability which interfere with the pursuit of normal activities. In attempting to define health status four subcategories can be set forth. These are: (a) mortality statistics; (b) health status of mothers and infants; (c) incidence and prevalence rate of specific diseases; and (d) disability rates.

(a) Mortality Statistics

Health measures derived from vital statistics are taken mostly from birth and death records, although the census or updated census estimates are used for denominators of mortality rates. In addition to providing health status indicators, vital records can be tapped for fertility and demographic indicators. In terms of health status vital records provide data for mortality rates and the health status of mothers and infants.

Mortality statistics are derived almost entirely from death certificates, using estimates of population by age cohorts (e.g. number of persons aged 50–55 at a given point in time) to supply the proper denominators for various rates. Most of the rates for persons over one year of age are provided separately by sex and race. Among the kinds of mortality indicators that are obtained from death records are the following:

1. *Infant mortality rate*—Number of live-born babies who died within 1 yr, per 1000 live born babies.

2. *Perinatal mortality rate*—Number of total stillborn and infants who died within 28 days of birth, per 1000 stillborn and live births.

3. *Fetal mortality rate*—Number of fetal deaths, per 1000 stillborn and live births.

4. *Crude death rate*—Number of deaths per 1000 population.

5. *Age-specific death rates*—Number of deaths of persons ages x to x plus 4 (e.g. 1–5, 6–10, 11–15, etc.) per 1000 persons ages x to $x + 4$.

6. *Death rates—age and cause of death specific*—Number of deaths of persons ages x to $x + 4$ due to a specific cause of death per 1000 persons ages x to $x + 4$. Causes of death are usually coded from the International Classification of Diseases. One broad category is cardiovascular diseases; others are neoplasms and renal. Accidents are also a cause of death classification.

7. *Death rates*—Specified by other characteristics or combination of characteristics, including race, ethnicity (nationality), sex, etc.

(b) Health Status of Mothers and Infants

In addition to fertility data (to be discussed in a later section), birth records contain some important information pertaining to the health and life chances of the mother and infant. Listed and briefly described below are some of the indicators of health status derived from birth records.

1. *Prematurity*—Defined usually in one of two ways: per cent of babies with (a) birth weight of 5½ lb or less; or (b) gestation period of less than 35 weeks. Of the two measures, weight is more accurate, since the length of the gestation period cannot always be accurately determined. Prematurity has numerous implications regarding the life chances of the child and its physical and mental development. Prematurely delivered babies are more likely to experience infant distress and disease, infant mortality and mental retardation.

2. *High risk pregnancy ages*—Per cent of live and stillborn births occurring to mothers under 20 and over 34 yr of age. This is an indirect measure of infant health status, since younger and older mothers are known to experience greater pregnancy complications and disorders. Pregnancy complications and disorders in turn affect the normal delivery of the baby.

3. *Other measures of health status from vital records*—In addition to the measures listed previously in this section and the prior one, medical and health sections on the standard certificate of live and still births are classified in many states (e.g. Kansas). Among the kinds of information available are: complications of pregnancy, Rh factors, whether or not labor was induced, method of delivery, condition of baby at birth and post-partum complications [7].

Incidence and Prevalence Rates of Specific Diseases

Measuring morbidity phenomena requires a move from the relatively accurate and uniformly collected vital record system into statistics which are questionable in terms of quality, standardization of data and extent of coverage. These statistics can be derived from basic sources (e.g. hospital records, doctor's records), secondary sources (e.g. registries of notifiable communicable diseases such as venereal diseases, mental retardation registries, cancer registries, etc.) or from special purpose health interview surveys. There are a number of problems associated with obtaining this information from all the sources mentioned. Basic sources such as hospital and doctor records, which are usually incomplete and unclassified, pertain only to users of services. Registries such as communicable diseases suffer from under-reporting even though identification of persons with some diseases is required by law.

Special purpose health interview surveys have several limitations. First, due to the exorbitant cost of surveying, they are seldom applied to small areas. The National Health Interview Survey, conducted by the Census Bureau for the HEW National Center for Health Statistics, provides reasonable mobidity statistics for the nation and for regions of the country. The sample size is, however, insufficient to produce reliable statistics for small, neighborhood-sized areas within a city.

Second, there is no universally accepted definition of morbidity. Although an operational definition is tied to the impairment of normal activity, respondents are not always able to make this differentiation. For example, congenital diseases, physical deformities, missing limbs and arrested chronic conditions may constitute states of morbidity in the sense that persons having these problems cannot pursue so-called normal activities to the same degree as persons not having these problems. However, affected persons may not consider themselves as being in a state of sickness or morbidity. An interview survey would more than likely result in the under-reporting of these kinds of morbidity. Under-reporting or other kinds of response error can be controlled or at least explained by evaluational procedures which might involve interviewing pre-selected respondents with a set of intensive questions designed to uncover hidden morbidity. Even with evaluational procedures, response error continues to exist.

Third, a special purpose health interview survey usually involves a probability sample, which indicates that the results are subject to sampling error. Sampling error refers to the difference that would be expected between interviewing a sample of respondents and conducting a complete canvass of the population.

Keeping in mind the limitations briefly indicated above, basic source records, disease registries and special purpose survey data could be tapped to derive the following indicators of incidence and prevalence of diseases:

1. *General mobility indices*—Per cent of population with identifiable communicable diseases, or with chronic (e.g. lasting more than three months) or acute health problems. If coverage is adequate, these indices may be derived by age, race and sex.

2. *Disease incidence*—Per cent of population (or subclass of population) that either reported or was identified as having a specific disease in the previous x period of time (e.g. 1 month, 3 months, 12 months, etc.).

3. *Disease prevalence rate*—Per cent of the population reporting (or otherwise identified as) suffering from a specific disease as of a particular point in time.

(d) Disability Rates

The last sub-category covered within the health status classification is the occurrence and extent of disability. For the purpose of our classification, disability is defined as a physical, mental or psychological condition which prevents a person from leading a normal existence. A state of disability can include not only confinement to a hospital or bed but also various degrees of impairment of normal activities—such as inability to work full time or the necessity of only being able to do certain kinds of work, or in the case of a handicapped child the necessity of attending certain kinds of schools. Data on disability are at best difficult, and at worst not possible, to obtain from existing record files pertaining to the users of hospitals and extended care facilities such as VA hospitals, nursing homes and the like. Even if such data were available and could be classified, they would only pertain to the users of the service. This suggests that the most adequate method for obtaining disability data is through a special purpose health interview survey. Some indicators of disability are listed below:

1. *Activity restrictions*—Percentage of population reporting frequent or complete limitation of normal activity because of a health problem.

2. *Days bedridden*—Mean number of days spent in bed all or most of the day within a specified period of time.[1]

3. *Days of work lost*—Mean number of work days missed because of illness by household head within a specified period of time.

4. *Days of school missed*—Mean number of days missed in school because of illness by children 6–16 within a specified time period.[2]

5. *Hospitalization*—Per cent of population confined in a hospital overnight or longer.

6. *Mean hospitalization period*—Mean number of nights confined in hospital by population confined in hospital overnight or longer.

Utilization of Health Services

Health service utilization statistics can be collected at the various health facilities at which patients receive services or through a special purpose sample survey in which respondents are asked what health services they sought and received within some specified period of time. Health service utilization data are therefore subject to limitations similar to that noted in the previous section with regard to morbidity data (e.g. non-systematically collected, no coverage of non-users, sampling variability and response errors).

In addition, developing a comprehensive set of indicators for the utilization of health services requires venturing into the difficult area of attitudes to get at such factors as predispositions not to use the service, and likes and dislikes of the services provided. Other important aspects of utilization statistics include eligibility requirements to use the service (e.g. residency requirements, income ceiling, etc.), travel time to the facility, queuing time to see a doctor and be provided the health service and other factors which interfere with or slow the delivery of the service to the client.

The following list of indices is by no means exhaustive of the essential dimensions of health service utilization:

1. *Routine physical examination*—Per cent of population receiving a routine physical examination from a physician within the last 12 months.

2. *Dental examination population*—Per cent of population over 7 yr of age visiting a dentist for routine dental care.

3. *Medical examination*—Per cent of population seeing a physician for any reason within past 12 months.

4. *Hospital visits*—Per cent of population visiting the hospital emergency rooms and clinics as a result of an immediate health problem.

5. *Hospital admittance*—Per cent of population being admitted to a hospital within the previous year upon the request of a physician.

6. *Physician visits*—Per cent of population having visited a physician within the previous x months (e.g. 6 months, 12 months).

7. *Mean physician visits*—Average number of visits to a physician per person within the previous 12 months.

8. *Medical care sought*—Per cent seeking each of various types of medical care for last illness or accident (e.g. hospital, clinic, private doctors, neighborhood health center).

9. *Hospital admissions by disease*—Per cent of hospital admissions by specific disease categories.

10. *Existence of private physician*—Per cent of population which considers itself to have a private physician to which it can go in case of illness.

11. *Multiple utilization*—Per cent of families which are enrolled in more than one clinic (e.g. public health clinic, OEO Neighborhood Health Center, Children and Youth Center).

12. *Lack of health insurance coverage*—Per cent of population not covered by health insurance (can specify insurance covering either or both hospitalization and doctor bills).

13. *Average health insurance coverage*—Per cent of total medical expenditures that were covered by patients health insurance (estimated from number of enrollees in major insurance plans and coverage of each plan).

14. *Satisfaction*—Per cent of clients utilizing the service (doctor, dentist, clinic, etc.) who expressed partial or complete satisfaction with the service.

15. *Need for service but not eligible*—Per cent of total poor or near poor families (using Office of Economic Opportunity criteria) who fail to meet eligibility requirements for obtaining service (e.g. residency, income level slightly above ceiling, man in the house rule, etc.).

16. *Average waiting time*—Mean number of minutes clients wait before health service is administered.

17. *Access to clinics*—Per cent of low income families with a neighborhood health center or free outpatient department within x distance (measured by miles, blocks).

18. *Access to pediatric clinics*—Per cent of low income population with a neighborhood

health center, free outpatient department or well baby clinic within x distance (miles, blocks).

General Population and Housing Characteristics

This category includes indicators derived from the decennial census, and fertility rates derived from census and birth records. Both describing the various dimensions of census data in terms of health planning, one must consider an important limitation: complete census data are collected only once in a decade. This places a temporal limitation on such data. Population estimates can be obtained between censuses, but because of the difficulty of measuring in- and out-migration, these estimates are not particularly reliable for small areas, especially as a basis for deriving social indicators. An adequate substitute for a census is yet to be found. However, one possibility again is to conduct small-area sample surveys. Some of the data items in a census may, with a great deal of difficulty, be obtained from independent data sources. For example, limited housing data are available from building permits and housing code violations; data on size of establishment (i.e. number of employees) can be provided by the Social Security Administration; migration data from school censuses; etc.

General population characteristics derived from census, birth records and other sources of data do not directly measure health status or health service utilization.[3] The characteristics of the population can be summarized into indicators which correlate highly with health variables. Measures of social pathology or social stress, such as disorganized families, dependency ratios, fertility and illegitimacy rates, low socio-economic status and migration are associated with physical and mental health status, and with availability of health services.

Below are provided a selective list of indicators of general population characteristics. These are organized into appropriate subcategories:

(a) Demographic and Life Cycles.

1. *Child rearing index*—Per cent of household heads with own children under 14 yr of age.

2. *Preschool children*—Per cent of household heads with own children under 6 yr of age.

3. *Child rearing completed (or no child rearing)*—Per cent of married couples with husband over 45 yr of age and no own children under 18 yr of age.

4. *Minor population*—Per cent of population under 21 (or 18) yr of age.

5. *High fecundity*—Per cent of women with three or more children.

6. *Childless women*—Per cent of women married more than 2 yr who have no own children.

7. *Dependency rate*—The number of persons under 18 yr of age or over 64 yr of age per 1000 persons.

8. *Elderly population*—Per cent of population 65 yr or older.

9. *Median age of household head.*

10. *Average household size*—Mean number of persons in household.

(b) Housing

1. *Overcrowding index*—Per cent of occupied housing units having 1.01 or more persons per room.

2. *Substandard housing*—Per cent of housing units that either lack a complete bathroom for exclusive use, or that have a combination of two of the following: low value or rent, inadequate heating, no complete kitchen for exclusive use.

3. *Low rent index*—Per cent of renter-occupied housing units with a contract monthly rent of less than a specified amount (determined by local rent standards).

4. *Low owner-occupied housing value*—Per cent of owner-occupied housing units in one family structures with a value of less than a specified value (determined by local property valuation).

5. *Older housing*—Per cent of population residing in houses built before 1950.

6. *Vacancy status*—Per cent of housing units that are vacant or unoccupied.

7. *Housing code violations*—Per cent of housing units which had one or more housing code violations within the past year.

(c) Migration

1. *Non-migrant index*—Per cent of population over 5 yr of age living in the same house for 5 yr or more.

2. *Interstate migrants*—Per cent of population born in another state.

(d) Ethnicity

1. *Negro population*—Per cent of population that is Negro.

2. *Indian population*—Per cent of population that is American Indian.

3. *Spanish-speaking*—Per cent of population in which Spanish is the primary language of the household.

4. *Ethnicity*—Per cent of population with one or both parents foreign born.

(c) Education

1. *Median educational attainment of household head*—Educational level at which 50 per cent of household heads are above or below.

2. *Grammar school education or less*—Per cent of population over 18 yr of age with eighth grade or less education.[4]

3. *Less than high school education*—Per cent of population over 21 yr of age with less than a high school education.[4]

4. *College education*—Per cent of population over 25 yr of age with a baccalaureate and/or advanced degrees.[4]

5. *Professional education*—Per cent of population over 29 yr of age with a master's, doctorate or other advanced degree.[4]

(f) Income and Occupation

1. *Median family income*—That income level at which 50 per cent of the families are above or below.

2. *Relief income*—Per cent of families receiving some relief income.

3. *Income ranges*—Per cent of families with income between x and $x + y$ (can be in increments of $1000–3000 up to a maximum of $15,000 or more).

4. *High-status occupation*—Per cent of employed males with professional or managerial occupations.

5. *Low status occupation*—Per cent of employed males in unskilled, semiskilled, or service occupations.

(g) Employment

1. *Under-employment, male*—Per cent of employed males working less than 30 hr per week.

2. *Unemployment, male*—Per cent of unemployed males of total males in the labor force.

3. *Married female employment*—Per cent of married women employed and working more than 30 hr per week.

4. *Working mothers with preschool children*—Per cent of mothers with children less than 6 yr of age and who are working more than 30 hr per week.

5. *Working mothers with school children*—Per cent of working mothers who have own children between ages 6 (but not below 6) and 17 and who are working.

(h) Other Economic Characteristics

1. *Automobile non-ownership*—Per cent of households who do not own an automobile.

2. *Multiple automobile ownership*—Per cent of households with more than two people, having two or more automobiles.

3. *T.V. non-ownership*—Per cent of households not owning a television.

(i) Family Organization

1. *Normal family life index*—Per cent of children under 18 yr of age living with both parents.

2. *Marital unrest index*—Ratio of divorced and separated persons to now married persons.

3. *Matriarchy index*—Per cent of household heads that are female heads with own children.

(j) Fertility

1. *General fertility rate* Births per 1000 females in age intervals 15–44.[5]

2. *Illegitimacy rate*—Illegitimate births per 1000 unmarried females in age interval 15–44.

3. *High birth order*—Per cent of births representing a birth order of 4 or more children.

(k) Urban Travel

1. *Mass transit*—Per cent of employed population not working at home using public transportation to get from home to work.

2. *Intercounty travel*—Per cent of employed population working in a different county than the county of residence.

3. *Long work trip*—Per cent of population with a distance to work greater than 10 miles.

Inventory of Health Facilities and Health Manpower

The fourth set of health indicators pertains to the inventory of health service facilities and health manpower. The organizations and persons included in this inventory are primarily in the business of providing health services directly, such as hospitals, private practitioners, nurses, health departments, various Federal health service grantees (e.g. Maternity and Infant Care Programs, OEO-supported Neigborhood Health Centers, Comprehensive Mental Health Centers) and organizations which are not primarily health service oriented, but finance or provide health services as a by-product of their operation (e.g. welfare departments administer Medicaid, school systems provide physical examinations, immunizations, psychological counseling, etc.).

Data on health facilities and manpower are available from many sources. One major source of data on inpatient institutions is the *Master Facility Inventory* prepared by the National Center for Health Statistics. The *American Hospital Association* has both survey data on facilities, and data on hospital manpower. More specific data on health manpower are collected by various health professional organizations such as the *American Medical Association, American Nurses Association, American Osteopathic Association,* etc. The Community Profile Data Center, DHEW-HSMHA has a large number of data files aggregated to various geographic units on such subjects as extended care institutions, Medicare, physicians, dentists, and the like. Survey data on medical schools can be obtained from the *Association of American Medical Colleges.*

Data on federally supported V.A. hospitals are available through the *U.S. Veter-*

ans Administration. Other inventories or directories of potential data sources include: *Hospital Guide Issue* published by the American Hospital Association; *Catalogue of Federal Domestic Assistance* published by the Office of Economic Opportunity—inventories federally supported programs; *Patients in Mental Institutions* published by the National Institutes of Mental Health; U.S. Bureau of the Census, *Directory of Federal Statistics for Local Areas* and *Directory for Non-Federal Statistics for State and Local Areas.* Finally, the *Consumer Price Index* published by the Bureau of Labor Statistics, provides estimates of the cost of physician services and hospital rooms.

There is no scarcity of materials pertaining to health facilities and manpower. However, there are a number of problems associated with compiling and analyzing these data by small areas. Most of the available data are classified by gross geographic units, such as region of the country, State, SMSA, county, etc. In many situations the data available neither afford complete coverage of the universe (e.g. not all nurses are covered in the American Nursing Association Directories) nor do they necessarily contain detailed characteristics of the facility or manpower.

Listed below are general types of organizations which provide health related facilities or health manpower.

(a) Types of Facilities and Services

1. *Hospitals*—Private, government, religious, voluntary; extended care (including ambulatory and convalescent homes); regular short term care (inpatient); mental hospitals, etc.

2. *Outpatient clinical facilities*—Attached to hospitals, Office of Economic Opportunity Neighborhood Health Care Centers, facilities provided by Health and Welfare councils, etc.

3. *Private offices*—Physicians in individual or group practices.

4. *Other health facilities*—Pre-natal care clinics, well baby conferences, family planning clinics, immunization centers, and mobile health facilities (immunization, blood mobiles, TB X-ray, etc.).

5. *Research facilities.*

(b) Types of Manpower

1. *Physicians (private practice, hospital, government, etc.)*—types of specialties; e.g. general practice, psychiatrist, pediatrician, obstetrician, gynecologist, neurologist, pathologist, surgeon, etc.

2. *Nurses*—Registered or practical—including visiting nurses.

3. *Osteopaths.*

4. *Dentists.*

5. *Public health workers*—Health statisticians, health planners, medical technicians and researchers, health services and facilities administrators, etc.

6. *Other health-related manpower*—Hospital personnel, social workers providing health services, health insurance companies and the like.

(c) Types of Organizations Maintaining Facilities or Providing Health Manpower

1. *State and municipal health departments and/or hospital departments.*

2. *State and muncipal welfare, sanitation, mental health, licenses and inspection departments and the public school system.*

3. *Federal health project grantees*—Examples: Office of Economic Opportunity Health Centers, Model Cities, Maternal and Child health services, Comprehensive Health Planning agencies, Comprehensive Mental Health Centers, Regional Medical Program.

4. *Professional organizations*—American Medical Association, American Hospital Association, American Nurses Association, American Osteopathic Association.

5. *Voluntary health agencies*—American Cancer Society, American Heart Association, National Society for Crippled Children and Adults, and numerous other voluntary health agencies.

6. *Voluntary social agencies*—United Fund and Community Chest, and health and welfare councils.

7. *Private insurance companies*—e.g. Blue Cross.

8. *Social organizations*—Kiwanis, Rotary, Lions, Masons, etc.

9. *Religious organizations*—Catholic and Jewish charities, Council of Churches, Salvation Army, etc.

Data on health facilities and health manpower are used as a basis for generating a multiplicity of indicators. Listed below are some of the more important indicators:

(a) Hospital and Facility Use

1. Number of admissions in hospital per day.

2. Number of patient days.

3. Average daily census of hospital population.

4. Number of beds available.

5. Average cost of hospital room.

6. Ratio of surgery admissions to admissions which do not result in surgery.

7. Size of establishment (measured by manpower, physical plant, capacity).

8. *Occupancy index*—Per cent of beds occupied to total beds available (calculated over some specified time period).

9. *Training capacity (nurses)*—Per cent of student nurses to total nurses.

10. *Training capacity (physicians)*—Per cent of interns and residents of total hospital base physician staff.

11. Ratio of nurses per patients.

12. Average cost of total services and use facilities (subclassified by type of patients).

(b) Manpower

1. Ratio of physicians per unit of population (e.g. 100,000).

2. Ratio of dentists per unit of population (e.g. 100,000).

3. Persons in health-related occupations per unit of population.

4. Ratio of osteopaths per unit of population.

5. Ratio of specialists (e.g. pediatricians, gynecologists, dermatologists, neurosurgeons, etc.) per unit of population.

6. Ratio of registered nurses per unit of population.

7. Number of medical school graduates per unit of population.

8. Ratio of pharmacists per unit of population.

9. Median income of profession personnel (by occupational classification).

10. Average total office hours per week.

11. Ratio of hours spent performing institutional services to hours spent in private practice.

Status of Community Environment

Unlike the other sections in this part, this section deals hardly at all with measurements on individuals or groups. It concerns instead a census and measurement of the environment. For this reason the sources of information are very different from those of the preceding sections; data can generally only be collected by some sort of monitoring process on the environment. Only a few environmental aspects are dealt with here; there are many others which an individual planner or analyst might wish to consider that have been left out, such as drugs, pesticides, etc.

Systems of monitoring tend to be very different from one type of pollution to another. For example, in some metropolitan areas air quality monitoring of some pollutants is done in a few expensive fixed installations. A major city may have fewer than a half dozen of these stations. Street cleanliness, on the other hand, is done by roving inspectors, who may look at a different section of streets each day. Many environmental conditions vary markedly in time—either by season, day, week or time of day, and in space—by block, census tract, or municipality. It should, therefore, be understood that in addition to annual averages, many of the measures described below must be portrayed for different time periods and small geographic areas to be meaningful. Besides the cyclical aspect, there can also be brief, randomly occurring intervals of much higher pollution values, for example when a prolonged air inversion occurs. For this reason some measures of extreme values are needed in addition to the average values taken for specific time periods—for example maximum 24 hr concentration, maximum 1 hr concentration or some intermediate time interval.

(a) Air Quality [8]

1. Number of days per year in which alert, serious and emergency level sounded.

2. Hydrocarbons, ppm (max. 3 hr concentration)

3. Carbon monoxide, ppm (max. 1 hr and 8 hr concentration).

4. Nitrogen oxides, ppm (max. 24 hr concentration).

5. Sulphur oxides, ppm (max. 24 hr concentration).

6. Particulate matter, ppm (max. 24 hr concentration).

7. Ozone, ppm (max. 1 hr concentration).

8. Hydrogen sulfide, ppm.

9. Lead, $\mu g/m^3$.

(b) Water Quality (At Upstream, Downstream Boundaries) [9]

1. Biological oxygen demand, mg/l.

2. Chemical oxygen demand, mg/l.

3. Dissolved oxygen, mg/l.

4. Total nitrogen, mg/l.

5. Total phosphorus, mg/l.

6. Total sulphates, mg/l.

7. Temperature.

8. pH level.

9. Total dissolved solids, mg/l.

10. Turbidity.

11. Threshold odor.

12. Color.

13. Suspended solids, mg/l.

(c) Water Supply [10]

1. Average demand as per cent of capacity.

2. Average main pressure.

3. Residual chloride at point of use, mg/l.

4. Per cent of samples with presence of coliform bacteria in 10 ml of water.

5. All items in (b) except oxygen demand and dissolved oxygen.

(d) Solid Waste Control [11]

1. Street appearance index, with ratings based on pictorial standards.

2. Index of solid waste health hazard.

3. Index of solid waste fire hazard.

4. Number of abandoned automobiles per population unit.

(e) Rat Control

1. Rat bites per 1000 population.

2. Estimated rat population per 1000 population.

(f) Noise

1. Average and maximum noise levels on streets and within office buildings and residences.

(g) Food

1. Number of reported cases of salmonella and other food-borne diseases.

2. Average sanitation rating of food establishments.

(h) Radiation

1. Per cent of radiation producing equipment meeting standards upon inspection.

(i) Industrial Hygiene and Safety

1. Per cent compliance with standards.

GUIDELINES TO DEVELOPMENT OF AN INFORMATION SYSTEM

The guidelines in this section concern: (a) the geographic level at which the data files are organized; (b) the methods for distilling and structuring the mass data file which results from this organization; and (c) the procedures employed for analyzing the information system in a manner that is meaningful to the health planners who will ultimately utilize the data.

Geocoding of Data Files

Organization of data files as inputs to an information system should be done at the lowest area level that can be obtained, for two reasons: first, small area classifications can always be aggregated into larger areas; the reverse is not true. Second, the smaller the area, the more homogeneous is the population residing in that area [2]. Files initially classified by some small homogeneous geographic areas, of course, would need to be aggregated into larger service size areas, since health planners would find it difficult to plan services for a city block or a small grouping of blocks.

Since a health information system ideally contains several separate sources of data involving numerous individual records, the geocoding of input records should be performed by computer rather than manually. Computer geocoding usually requires at least two components: (1) an address coding guide (ACG), and (2) an address matching program. Both of these components are available from the Bureau of the Census.

The ADMATCH system developed for the Census Use Study automates the processes of address matching and geocoding [12]. After the necessary information on the various types of areal units is inputed to the computer, the ADMATCH program is capable of taking an unformatted address record such as 6 South Main Street, New Haven, Connecticut, and determining which address within its files the address in question corresponds to. This match can be successfully done with a complete and updated Address Coding Guide generally in more than 90 per cent of the cases. The last few per cent would need some correction or additional information. Once a successful match has been made, any geographic code in the Address Coding Guide (e.g. block, census tract or special purpose areas such as school districts and police precincts) can be appended to the input record. The result of this process could be, for example, all the birth records of a city broken down into city blocks.

Distilling and Structuring the Data Files

Derivation of data summarizes from numerous data files coded to a common geographic level is likely to create an unwieldly mass of data if these are not somehow structured. For example, the New Haven Health Information System which contained some but not all of the variables specified in earlier sections, yielded some 300 indicators. If these were displayed in a matrix, the result would be some 90,000 cells. Clearly a method is needed for distilling such a mass data file into a smaller number of composite variables.

One of the most commonly used approaches is factor analysis. In general, a factor analysis simplifies a mass data file by finding hypothetical variables, or factors, which correlate well with a number of observed variables. These hypothetical factors are derived as variously weighted sums of the observed variables, and are assumed to represent underlying variables which in some way account for the high correlation with the variables they replace.

In many cases, the composition of the factors is such that they appear to represent some underlying qualities or aspects of everyday life which cannot be directly measured. An example is socio-economic status. There are numerous one-dimensional indicators that relate to socio-economic status, such as income level, occupational status, property ownership, educational attainment, housing quality and family organization. Through a factor analysis, a composite measure can be developed which includes all these facets of socio-economic status. This measure would then constitute a single statistic rather than an unwieldly collection of numerous statistics. The same principle can be applied to derive other composite indicators. Obviously, because of the general nature, such composite measures would only be used as background information when specific program areas are being considered.

Interpretation of the factors developed by factor analyses is a fine—and occasionally occult—art, generally drawing on sociological or psychological theory for its basis. One needs to make *a priori* judgements of the kinds of relationships that the factor analysis can reasonably yield. Various guidelines in interpreting a factor analysis of health information system data are discussed in Census Use Study Report No. 7 [13].

Procedures for Analyzing and Displaying Data

Data organized in an information system may be displayed and analyzed in a variety of ways, ranging from very simple tabular and graphic presentations to the more complex correlational and multi-variate analyses.

For tabular and graphic presentations, it is generally more efficient and less costly to utilize existing computer programs. There are a number of readily available computer mapping programs. Two of the most adaptable computer mapping programs are: (1) SYMAP, maintained by the Laboratory for Computer Graphics, Harvard University, and (2) GRIDS (Grid Related Information System) developed by the Census Use Study of the Bureau of the Census.

SYMAP has several mapping options which basically show density patterns of data on maps. In general darker symbols represent greater densities, and lighter shaded symbols represent lesser densities. The New Haven Health Information System project experimented with SYMAP, using ADMATCHED birth records as an input. The result was several maps locating concentrations in New Haven of high fertility, illegitimacy, high birth order and birth weights of 5½ lb or less.

The GRIDS mapping program is also an efficient method for presenting density patterns on a grid, again using small shaped symbols of varying darkness. In addition to representing density, the GRIDS program will also print numerical value on maps.

With regard to tabulation and statistical support programs, there are a variety of such programs available from commercial sources or public agencies. An evaluation of four "rapid programming systems for computerized data retrieval and manipulation" has been provided in a recent paper by Brounstein [14]. Brounstein points out that some tabulation programs are strongest on statistical analysis, while others are best for manipulation of large amounts of data on several different magnetic tapes. Two other data-manipulation programs which deserve consideration include: DATATEXT [15], developed by the Department of Social Relations, Harvard University, Cambridge, Massachusetts; and BioMedical Computer Programs (BMD) [16], developed at the University of California at Los Angeles for medical research.

USES OF HEALTH INFORMATION SYSTEMS

As indicated earlier in this paper, the uses of a health information system fall into three broad categories: (1) program planning and development; (2) program analysis and evaluation; and (3) defining interrelationships between variables. These categories of use are briefly discussed below.

A health information system provides a body of statistics which is an essential component for the efficient planning and developing of programs. Statistics are needed to locate the target population at risk, and define their needs. An information system could locate areas of a community which have both poor health status, and which lack adequate health services. The measures used in determining programmatic needs would depend on the particular program being considered. If it were a broad-gauged program such as the establishment of neighborhood health centers, measures of morbidity and socio-economic status (i.e. indicating population with health problems and financial problems) would be most appropriate. If a program were directed to a more specific concern, such as the establishment of a pre-natal clinic, then measures concerning pregnancy outcome, infant mortality, illegitimacy, parity, a number of women in high risk fertility ages, and indicators of poor health status of mothers would be most appropriate. These indicators, either individually or as composites, can be plotted geographically so that high incidence areas can be located. By relating the number of persons or families residing in a high incidence area who are below a certain socio-economic level, or have manifestations of social attributes associated with poor maternal health status (e.g. family disorganization), some estimates can be made of the maximum population that will require the services of the pre-natal clinic. In both the planning of a broad health facility (neighborhood health center) and a more categorical facility (pre-natal clinic), indicators from the sections on utilization and inventory of health facilities, services and manpower are useful in determining within target areas what other facilities need to be taken into account in planning the capacity and services of a new facility. Also, planners need to know the health manpower resources in the target area or in the community that can be brought to bear in support in new facilities.

The second use of an information system, analyzing and evaluating existing programs, is primarily directed toward monitoring changes in health status occurring over time. The establishment of a casual relationship between the institution of a service and changes in health status cannot, of course, be entirely achieved. For example, it would be difficult to determine how much of a long term decrease in fertility rates can be ascribed to an extensive ongoing family planning program, because there are numerous other factors that can act upon fertility rates, such as changes in attitudes, socio-economic status (periods of boom or bust), late marriages, postponement of child bearing and the like. However, in the evaluation and analysis of such a program, a health information system would provide a means of measuring changes in the configuration attending the decrease in fertility rates, since it draws data from a number of sources. For example, by statistically controlling for other intervening factors, one can estimate the extent to which the services provided have an effect on the fertility rate. However, definitive establishment of causality between a specific program and a social change would require extensive examination of control and experimental populations over time. Ideal experimental conditions seldom, if ever, exist in such a social situation [17].

The third use of a health information system has already been described to some extent in the above discussion of causality. That is, a health information system is a useful mechanism for defining causal relationships between various aspects of the health system. For example, demographic and socio-economic variables such as income levels, family organization and public assistance are related to health variables such as high illegitimacy rates, poor health status of mother and newborn infants, the failure to obtain pre-natal services, and post partum anemia [2]. Correlations can also be examined between such factors as air pollution levels and respiratory diseases, morbidity rates (specified by kinds of disease) and housing characteristics, and mental health and social stress. These are but a few simple examples of the manner in which data drawn from various sources can be meaningfully related.

ENDNOTES

1. Due to recall lapses, the reference period for obtaining these kinds of data should be relatively short.

2. Measures of school missed can be obtained from the Board of Education.

3. The 1970 census does have one item on the 5 per cent sample relating to disability.

4. These indicators attempt to identify various strata of educational attainment. These are structured to eliminate age as an intervening factor.

5. Should be standardized—age specific—to control for disproportionate child-bearing activity of female 20–29.

REFERENCES

1. World Health Organization Basic Documents, Edition 12, p. 1, Geneva, Switzerland (1961).

2. John C. Deshaies, Samuel Korper and Estelle Siker, U.S. Bureau of the Census, Census Use Study Report No. 12, Health Information System No. 11 (1971).

3. Michigan Department of Public Health, Lansing, Michigan, Michigan Health Survey, Reference and Procedures Manual (1970).

4. See pamphlet distributed by the Department of Health, Education and Welfare, Environmental Health Services, Neighborhood Environmental Evaluation and Decision System (NEEDS) (1970).

5. Harold F. Goldsmith and Elizabeth L. Unger, National Institute of Mental Health, Differentiation of Urban Subareas—A Re-examination of Social Area Dimensions, Laboratory Paper No. 35 (1970). Specific information may be obtained from State Mental Health Authorities.

6. Kansas State Board of Health and Kansas Regional Medical Program, Requirements Definition Study for a Health Information System in Kansas, p. 19 (1969).

7. Kansas State Department of Health, Perinatal Casualty Report, Kansas (1964–1965).

8. American Chemical Society, Cleaning our Environment: The Chemical Basis for Action, pp. 21–92, Washington, D.C. (1969).

9. American Chemical Society, Cleaning our Environment: The Basis for Action, pp. 93–162, Washington, D.C. (1969).

10. For additional measures, see Public Health Service Printing Water Standards (1962), Environmental Control Administration, Consumer Protection and Environmental Health Service, Department of Health, Education and Welfare, PHS Publication No. 965.

11. Louis H. Blair, Harry P. Hatry and Pasqual A. DonVito, Urban Institute, Washington D.C., Measuring the Effectiveness of Local Government Services: Solid Waste Collection (1970). The first three measures listed are drawn from this ongoing research. Operational tests of these measures are now being made by the Urban Institute in cooperation with the District of Columbia Government.

12. U.S. Bureau of the Census, Census Use Study, ADMATCH Manual (1970).

13. John C. Deshaies, U.S. Bureau of the Census, Census Use Study Report No. 7, Health Information System (1969).

14. Sidney H. Brounstein, Census Tract Papers, Series GE-40, No. 6, pp. 60–61 (1970).

15. Harvard University, Data-Text System, Department of Social Relations, Cambridge, Massachusetts (1967).

16. University of California at Los Angeles, Health Sciences Computing Facility, Department of Preventive Medicine and Public Health, School of Medicine, BMD—Bio Medical Computer Programs, revised edition (1968).

17. Joseph S. Wholly, Urban Institute, Washington, D.C. *et al.*, Federal Evaluation Policy: Analyzing the Effects of Public Programs (1970).

Questions for Study and Discussion

1. How do the measurement issues associated with the design of an information system of the type described by Deshaies and Seidman differ from the measurement issues associated with the design of a management information system for a business firm?

2. Does a health information system of the type described here provide a realistic alternative to the design of social reforms as experiments (as advocated by Campbell), in terms of providing essential information?

3. What would be the sources of error in a data base such as that described by Deshaies and Seidman? How might the validity of conclusions draw from the health information system be affected?

4. Is there a "dark figure" of health with which policy makers must be concerned? (See Biderman and Reiss, Reading 26)

5. How is the design of the health information system described by Deshaies and Seidman related to the model of measurement and information systems presented by Mason and Swanson (Reading 1)?

6. President Carter seemed to have a voracious appetite for information and encouraged the development of decision support systems to keep himself informed. One such DSS is the Domestic Information Display System (DIDS) developed jointly by the Bureau of Census and NASA's Goddard Space Flight Center. DIDS converts census and other social statistics to easy-to-read graphics, such as maps depicting national trends.

DIDS has interactive capabilities and permits the hierarchical structuring of data so that the user can "zoom in" on a problem area on request. Response times of about four seconds are said to be common. A typical sequence might be paraphrased as follows:

Policy maker: What is the extent of unemployment in the United States?

DIDS: Displays a map of unemployment by state.

Policy maker: How extensive is unemployment in Illinois?

DIDS: Displays a map of Illinois showing bands of equal levels of unemployment.

Policy maker: How does Chicago look?

DIDS: Displays a map of the Chicago Standard Metropolitan Statistical Area (SMSA) showing unemployment.

Policy maker: The inner city?

DIDS: Displays a map of unemployment in Chicago inner city.

Policy maker: How does unemployment correlate with poverty levels in the inner city?

DIDS: Overlays unemployment in Chicago inner city with poverty data showing class interval changes. Color is added for emphasis.

How might the decision support concepts of DIDS be applied in the design of a health information system? (For a futher discussion of DIDS, see the *Bulletin of the American Society for Information Science,* 5; 13–26.)

NOTES ON SOCIAL INDICATORS: PROMISES AND POTENTIAL

Eleanor Bernert Sheldon • Howard E. Freeman   *READING 30*

There is a new social movement afoot today, one advanced by a peculiar consortium of social scientists, social commentators, political activists, and legislators. It most commonly goes by the name of "social indicators," although occasionally it is referred to as "social accounts" or "social bookkeeping" or "monitoring social change." The central referent, however, is the concept of social indicators.

Usually one thinks of quantitative measures when referring to social indicators, although there is no reason why qualitative ones cannot also be included under the rubric (Gross, 1966; Gross and Springer, 1967a, 1967b). Even if the term is reserved for quantitative measures, however, it should be pointed out that not all statistics are social indicators. There probably is general agreement among those who banter the term about that only measures which are employed repeatedly and at regular intervals are to be properly considered indicators; in other words, social indicators are time-series that allow comparisons over an extended period and which permit one to grasp long-term trends as well as unusually sharp fluctuations in rates.

There also may be considerable agreement that social indicators are statistics that can be disaggregated by relevant attributes of either the persons or the conditions measured (such as skin color or year of construction) and by the contextual characteristics that surround the measure (such as region or city size). Even if one agrees to consider only statistics that can be disaggregated as social indicators, the meaning of the term "relevant" is most blurred. There is no agreement on the set of characteristics most relevant for purposes of disaggression.

But beyond the notions of time-series and disaggregation, the multitude of additional restrictions placed upon the concept by some, but not by others, is staggering. Some maintain indicators must be of direct normative interest (U.S. Department of Health, Education, and Welfare, 1969). The inclusion of the term *direct* raises an interesting question. Probably an acceptable synonym for "indicator" is "reflector." Persons who use the dictionary as an authority might challenge whether or not an indicator can be a direct measure: they probably could properly hold if you have a direct measure of a phenomenon it is no longer aptly described by the term indicator.

Perhaps more restrictive and confusing is the position that indicators must be

From *Policy Sciences I*, (1970) pp. 97–111. Copyright © 1970 by American Elsevier Publishing Company, Inc.

"normative." Obviously what is salient today may not be so next year and vice versa: if only statistics of a direct normative interest are maintained, currently invisible but subsequently critical social problems will not be encompassed by extant time-series it also is held that indicators need to be measures of welfare: the number of doctors or policemen in these terms are not regarded as indicators, only figures of health status, acts of crime, and so on. Yet, if one is going to make assessments of present and future welfare services, do not we need to know how rapidly or slowly resources pools are being developed?

Moreover, it is claimed that indicators need to have "direction," one pole being regarded as "good" and the other as "bad." But what is good in the minds of some may be bad in the views of others, let alone that the direction may be evaluated in opposite ways by some persons at different times—like days lost from work for illness and disability. It could be argued, for example, that an increase in this indicator may reflect either a decline in the health status of the employed population or liberalization of employment policies on sick leave.

The term social indicator must be regarded as an elusive concept. Moreover, the boundaries of the indicator movement are amoebic, and partisans to the cause come and go, often deserters to it quietly returning only to slip away again. But the existence of the movement is real: social indicators have been the subject of editorials in our most prestigious newspapers: the deliberations of a citizen-government group have been transmitted by the Secretary of Health, Education, and Welfare to the President (U.S. Department of Health, Education, and Welfare, 1969): Senator Mondale and his associates introduced Bill S-5 in 1969 to establish a council of social advisors and to promote indicator development and use: and the outpouring of papers and monographs on indicators will undoubtedly soon occasion the continual publication of review articles and bibliographies.

The elusiveness of the concept of social indicators stems from the multitude of views on the relevance and purpose of developing and organizing statistics about the state of affairs in the country and its constituent parts. At the same time, however, the vagueness of the concept encourages persons to advocate their own particular perspectives, further increasing the confusion about the utility of social statistics for planning, program development, and scholarly endeavors. Perhaps the time has come to provide a reasonably extended scrutiny of some impossible uses of social indicators and to specify in a programmatic sense the possible, if only potentially so, uses of indicators.

SOME IMPOSSIBLE USES OF INDICATORS

At least three claims of social indicators need to be regarded with extreme skepticism, for we are not only technically deficient at present, but the conceptual development required to fulfill to espoused promises has not taken place—and if the effort is not redirected may never take place. Each of the claims of indicator use, while overlapping, merits separate scrutiny:

1. The setting of goals and priorities

2. The evaluation of programs

3. The development of a balance sheet.

The Setting of Goals and Priorities

Among the partisans of social indicators are a relatively vocal group who regard the benefits of the movement to be primarily political, i.e., as to a key to social policy development. It may be of value to point out that government and business, as well as influential community groups, use statistics in order to support their ideas for action programs, and their own priority systems regarding what needs to be done. Further, it may be obvious that the more respectable the figures and the more prestigeful their source, the more potent a tool of political influence is available.

A robust social indicator movement permits well-intentioned politicians and program advocates access to statistics that can be presented with unusual persuasiveness. Dignifying a statistic by referring to it as an indicator may help, even though it may be no better conceptualized or measured before it is given status as an indicator. In the abstract it could be argued that, if one had a comprehensive and exhaustive set of social indicators available, it would be possible to identify those that show the most marked changes and to scrutinize the social problem phenomenon they reflect in order to locate areas that press for attention. As Henriot (1970) observes, however, the very process of developing indicators is value-laden; their very definition reflects sociopolitical values. Consequently, those indicators that may show startling changes if lodged in one system of measures might be regarded as of modest interest if placed in a different system.

It would be foolish to argue against the use of indicators in program planning and development, or to expect their employment to disappear as a means of influencing politicians and their electorates. But it is naive to hold that social indicators in themselves permit decisions on which programs to implement, especially that they allow the setting of priorities. The use of data to make a case either already decided on other grounds or one that inevitably is going to be determined by political rather than "objective" considerations—whether or not it is in good cause—is a weak basis for the indicator effort. Priorities do not depend on assembled data. Rather, they stem from national objectives and values and their hierarchical ordering.

In short, when used for purposes of setting goals and priorities, indicators must be regarded as inputs into a complex political mosaic. That they are potentially powerful tools in the development of social policy is not to be denied. But they do not make social policy development any more objective. Advocates of policy can strengthen their position by citing hard data and so can critics of those policies. In a situation where all sides have equity of resources to gather, interpret, and communicate indicator information, it could be argued that social indicators can serve to develop a more rational decisionmaking process in social policy development. But this is unlikely to be the case very often and in instances of unfair competition indicators are essentially a lobbying device (Henriot, 1970).

The Evaluation of Programs

Concurrent with the movement to promote social indicators, there has developed a strenuous effort on the part of key individuals in and outside of government to estimate the gains that are derived from the initiation and expansion of different types of preventive and rehabilitative action programs. The terms "evaluation research" and "cost benefits analysis" now are common jargon among a vast number of such practitioners, planners, and politicians. The rationality of being able to estimate the benefits of expenditures of money, time, and manpower is virtually incontestable, and the utility of knowing whether existing and innovative programs work clearly is desirable.

The empirical situation however is that there have been but a handful of respectable evaluation studies of social action programs: There simply are not very many craftsmanlike evaluations of national programs, and there is increasing dissatisfaction with the failure to document by careful research the current massive programs now underway to improve the occupational, educational, mental and physical health status of community members. As a consequence, there is the temptation to argue for social indicators as a substitute for experimental evaluations. The fact of the matter is, however, that social indicator analyses cannot approximate the necessary requirements of sound design in order to provide for program evaluation.

Investigators who have thought about the problems of evaluation generally agree that there is no substitute for experimental research that differentiates between the effects of treatments and programs on the one hand and of extraneous contaminating factors on the other. Experimentally designed evaluations often are not possible because of resistance to the requisite random assignment of persons to different treatment groups. Thus, there is a turning to efforts of evaluation through statistical controls or "systems analyses."

The use of indicators to evaluate programs would require one to be able to demonstrate, via statistical manipulations, that programs determine the outcomes measured by the indicators rather than other factors "causing" the results. The old example of a relationship between the number of storks in a community and its birth rate should suffice to make the point. There is no possibility at the present time of meeting the requirements of controlling for contaminating variables with available statistics that may be regarded as indicators, at least ones that cover large groups of individuals. In order to locate and identify factors that may be contaminating, knowledge of the determinants and interrelationships between determinants is required. Information is not available in many fields of social concern to do such analyses well, either on an empirical basis or a theoretical one.

Admittedly there are persons who are much more optimistic about the potential use of a feedback system for determining the full range of consequences of the society's actions and which thus would provide guidelines for future courses (Bauer, 1966). But the strongest proponents of the feedback system approach, who tell us that our knowledge can permit the development of a social system model and the derivation of measures from it to assess programmatic efforts, find it hard or impossible to supply guidance on how this is to be done. Even if it were possible in the abstract (and certainly most people in the evaluation research game would argue against the idea of evaluating programs by means of social indicators), realistically there is no basis or advice available on what to do and how to do it.

Modifications of trends and shifts in the behavioral conditions of populations either over time or for different groups do not provide enough opportunities for controlled analyses to muster any persuasive argument about the efficacy or efficiency of programmatic efforts. The development and refinement of social indicators and the activities of persons within the movement simply neither will satisfy the need nor serve as a substitute for evaluation studies of an experimental character. Arguing that the development of social indicators provides a means to decide on the cost-benefits and the efficiency of programs is a way of inhibiting the development of adequate means of evaluations and exaggerated claim of the potential of social indicators.

The Development of a Balance Sheet

The most publicly appealing notion of social indicators is their use in a system of social accounts. The claim is that it is possible to develop a system of national social accounting that brings together in an integrated fashion the relative concepts developed by economists, political scientists, sociologists, anthropologists, psychologists, and social psychologists (Gross, 1966). It is maintained that "The great advances in the social sciences during recent decades make it possible to establish such a system. The needs of administrators, government leaders, and international agencies make it imperative" (Gross, 1966, p. 155). Though such proponents do describe the major outlines of "a social system at a national level," such notions scarcely provide a social system model or conceptual framework amenable to a national accounting system.

The materials collected and the opinions obtained as part of the hearing on Senate Bill #S843, the Full Opportunity and Social Accounting Act of 1967, commonly referred to as the Mondale Bill, generally also support the social accounting idea. On reading the Bill we find that it is introduced

> to promote the general welfare . . . to encourage such conditions as will give every American the opportunity to live in decency and dignity, and *to provide a clear and concise picture* of whether such conditions are promoted and encouraged in such areas as health, education, and training, rehabilitation, housing, vocational opportunities, the arts and humanities, and special assistance for the mentally ill and retarded, the deprived, the abandoned, and the criminal, and *by measuring progress in meeting such needs.* (pp. 1–2) [Italics ours.]

The Bill then calls for an annual *Social Report of the President* setting forth (1) the overall progress and effectiveness of federal efforts designed to carry out the stated policy; (2) a review of state, local, and private efforts designed to create conditions of decency and dignity; etc. To accomplish this and related reports the Bill provides for the creation of a Council of Social Advisers to the President which is to prepare the Social Report; to gather information and data concerning developments and programs designed to carry out the policy of the Bill, to appraise federal programs and activities related to the achievement of such policy; to develop priorities for programs and recommend efficient allocation of federal funds, and so on.

Council activities are to be accomplished by compiling and analyzing social statistics and the development of a "system of social indicators" (*Congressional Record*, 1967). What is meant by "social accounting" and "social indicators" is not clarified. Presumably the legislators have in mind that social accounting and indicators parallel economic accounting and indicators—which provide data useful for the implementation of the Employment Act of 1946 (Senate Bill S843).

Another major thrust in the social indicators movement—at about the same time—came from the extension of some earlier thoughts expressed in the report of the National Commission on Technology, Automation, and Economic Progress, *Technology and the American Economy* (1966). Again a "system of social accounts" is proposed—this time to "indicate the social benefits and social costs of investment and services and thus reflect the true costs of a product" (National Commission on Technology, Automation, and Economic Progress, 1966, p. 95). The guidelines of the report argue for the measurement of social costs and the net gains of economic investments, the creation of performance budgets in areas that define social need, and the development of indicators of economic opportunity and mobility.

Evoking the economic analogy and proposing the development of social indicators that parallel economic indicators is confusing and in part fallacious. Despite its weaknesses and limited rigor, economic theory provides a definition and the specifications of an economic system, and the linkages are at least hypothesized, if not empirically demonstrated, between many variables in the system. From such a point of departure, an administrator or a set of administrators can design policies that make possible the manipulation of one or more of the variables in the system, thereby causing the prior hypothesized changes of other variables in that system. Because the changes are of a relatively short-term nature, feedback is rather prompt, say six months to a year, and policies and programs are vulnerable to further modification, alteration, and manipulation. At least to some extent, this model has worked and economic indicators and accounts are useful policy tools.

Although some social scientists have promised similar usefulness for social indicators and social accounts, this is not even a reasonable anticipation. There is no social theory, even of a tentative nature, which defines the variables of a social system and the relationships between them. It is even difficult to locate partial theories or so-called middle-range ones covering any single aspect of society which have convincing explanatory potential. Yet, without the guidance of theoretical formulations concerning significant variables and their linkages, one can hardly suggest that there exists, even potentially, a set of measures that parallel the economic variables.

There is also a problem of scale construction that is not often faced in the call for social indicators. A balance sheet not only requires a set of categories—ones conceptually based and integrated—but some common interval measure, such as money, for adding and subtracting apples and oranges or cancers and rapes simply is not possible. Money has meaning and allows one to sum values across a large number of different domains. Neither the state of conceptualization nor technique in the social sciences other than economics has produced necessary measures.

THE POTENTIAL OF THE INDICATOR MOVEMENT

The oversell of social indicators, which we have tried to confront in the preceding section, may suggest to some that the appropriate strategy of responsible persons should be an intensive and direct effort to render the movement ineffective. This need not be so: a viable alternative is to redirect and rechannel existing efforts, to reformulate the goals of the indicator movement, to modulate the promises on the utility of indicators in ways that make them realistic, and to exploit the momentum gained from the movement to improve the quantity and quality of data on the structural outlines and social processes of society. There are extensive needs and attractive possibilities of three types that can be promoted. The social indicator movement can contribute (1) to improved descriptive reporting; (2) to the analysis of social change; and (3) to the prediction of future social events and social life. The three tasks of course are interdependent. Adequate descriptive reporting is essential for the development of improved investigations of social change and correspondingly increased understanding of past social changes is required for the better prediction of future events.

Descriptive Reporting

While it may seem that we are virtually swamped with statistical data, there are not only many gaps in information about the structural and processional character of the American society, but severe technical weakness in what is available. Many different reasons account for the gaps and limitations: most of the data stem initially from particular program concerns and data series, then they become traditionalized and used for a variety of purposes besides those for which they were intended. Moreover, the complex relationships between the federal establishment, state and local political units, the overlapping responsibilities within the federal, state, and local governments, and the interdependence of voluntary and public groups, result in severe problems of completeness and reliability in data reporting. The changing purposes of interests in data collection and analysis limit the opportunities for long-range planning and development of adequate time-series data.

While technical problems should not be brushed aside and the craft in the field needs improvement, it should be emphasized that the conceptual needs are the greatest—what to measure and what are valid operational measures of critical phenomena. With more knowledge on what to measure and better operational measures, work on understanding the past and predicting the future would be made more effective. There are no simple solutions, for no agreement exists either on the outlines of the major institutions and social systems in the society or on what constitutes the major social problems, deviant behaviors, and conditions of social disorganization. We have yet to determine what degrees of regularity exist so that appropriate time intervals between measures can be determined in order to establish critical changes in rates and direction. There must not be an abandoning of efforts because of such problems—rather the energy of the social indicators movement should be exploited to accelerate interest in better social reporting, including the training of a much larger cadre of sophisticated investigators.

Both quite immediate and long-term work are required. In the various substantive institutional areas, the mere pulling together of the available statistics, careful examination of their inadequacies, and efforts to develop more comparable information by reworking data would reveal present limitations and possibly stimulate additional conceptual and technical developments (for example, Ferriss, 1969; Sheldon and Moore, 1968). At the same time, considerable thought should be given to the problems of aggregation and disaggregation and of appropriate measures for which aggregation and disaggregation are required. Another task to undertake is the examination of varying definitions of measures of some or similar variables. Such efforts may reduce the number of redundant measures and also lead to the development of new, better conceptualized ones.

On a more long-term basis, efforts are required to identify and understand the interrelationships between various social statistics, particularly those at the boundaries of various institutional sectors; for example, the relationship between rates of mental illness and of crime and delinquency. Such efforts require some ideas on the systematic character of different social phenomena, ideas that can be developed by inductive and deductive approaches, that is increased efforts to develop both empirical and logical models of the social system or aspects of it. In the long run, knowing better what to measure will depend upon how one social indicator fits with others, or at least blends into a complex mosaic.

Alongside these efforts, there needs to be strenuous organizational and political activities to improve reporting procedures, and the reduction of archaic divisions of responsibility and activity between various levels and organizations of government. There is a need to study how descriptive statistics are currently used and to estimate the potential impact of modifications in what is reported when the information is communicated and who receives and understands it. It might even be feasible to "market research," on a continuing basis the needs for statistical trend data of academics, politicians, and persons in planning and program development, and the difficulties they have in locating and having access to presumably available information.

Analytical Studies of Social Change

While there is no sharp distinction between the work outlined under descriptive reporting and that to be discussed in this section, there is some reasonable separation. By analytical studies, we refer to not only efforts to describe a particular trend but also efforts to identify predictors of it and sometimes to suggest the causal importance and sequence of relevant variables.

There are two studies that illustrate well the opportunities and utilities of such efforts. One, now regarded as a classic by many, is Goldhammer and Marshall's (1953) study of whether or not mental illness has increased. By taking into account the available institutional treatment resources over time, they adjusted hospitalization rates and consequently reversed or at least severely questioned the popular notion of the increasing rate of mental disorders. The second study is more recent. Blau and Duncan's (1967) work on the occupational structure and the view they advance that education is a key determinant of occupational mobility, a study noteworthy for its statistical sophistication and compulsive carefulness.

Analytical studies depend naturally on the descriptive data that are available; the conceptual difficulties and technical defects in available data limit the rigor and sophistication of analyses. Thus, there is an interplay between the work of an analytical nature that is done and the likelihood of effective developments in the availability of trend data. Analytical studies not only can make important contributions to macrosociology and the analysis of social change but have programmatic potential as well. To the extent that they allow hypotheses about the key causal variables and *suggest* causal sequences, they may be an important input and stimulus to the planners and policymakers in the design of various preventive and rehabilitative programs and in large-scale efforts to affect social change. While analytical studies cannot replace experimental ones, certainly in the face of the limited opportunities for undertaking the latter, they need to be encouraged. In many fields of social intervention and rehabilitation they undoubtedly would be far superior to the clinical insights that today are likely to determine programmatic efforts.

Prediction of the Future

The most dramatic view of the potential of social indicators is reflected in the interests of persons who wish to use scientific techniques in order to anticipate social and technical developments in future years. Such studies represent an extension in many ways, of course, of attempts to understand past processes of social change. There exist long-term interests among some sociologists and other social scientists in estimating the extent and rapidity of social change between groups and communities and in different social and technological areas.

Interest in predicting the future has been stimulated, among other things, by the novelty and presumed power of such tools as systems analysis, simulation techniques, automated central data banks, and information and game theories. Both "traditional" students of social change and the new breeds of futurists are strongly aware that the understanding of what is happening today and what has happened in the past depends now on too few reliable and valid facts. It is this data-poor condition that has spurred their participation in the social indicator movement. There also is an enormous conceptual gap that limits valid interpretation of what is happening in our society. The matter of inadequate and nonexisting theory about the nature of complex social processes explains at least in part why we know so little about what to measure and observe in order to predict the future well.

Obviously, the development of more reliable, valid, and conceptually related social indicators is important to students of social change and of the future. As for other needs, there is an urgent requirement that more reliable measures be developed and that data be available in forms that permit aggregation and disaggregation for relevant subgroups and communities. But what is probably most critically needed for the futurists are new and innovative concepts. The development of them depends, it bears emphasis, upon theoretical work which is being undertaken only minimally by social scientists, whether they be inside or outside the social indicator movement. Moreover, there needs to be an increased capability in collecting and making available data on existing and refined measures.

TOWARD A SOCIAL REPORT 1969

In discussing the possible uses of social indicators, we noted the work undertaken by the Department of Health, Education, and Welfare. In 1966, Secretary John Gardner appointed a panel of social scientists, chaired jointly by Daniel Bell and William Gorham, the latter replaced by Alice Rivlin when Gorham left HEW. *Toward a Social Report* is a document based in part on the working papers of the appointed panel members. It was released by the Secretary of HEW to promote the further participation of the federal government in the social indicator movement and to justify the time and expenditures, though quite small, of the panel's activities.

The Report itself is not an elaborate, scholarly, or particularly impressive document. The working papers on which it was based, in large part, are the work of a few weekend scholars and a pitifully small staff with only one senior, full-time person who often was given other responsibilities by HEW. The panel itself was most diverse, not only in terms of technical competence, but also with respect to the members conceptions of social indicators, their views on the limitations of them, and the very purposes for which they were called together and asked to reflect and write. Furthermore, with perhaps one exception, panel members were unable to do more than work with existing information—measures varying not only in reliability but in their capacity to be aggregated and disaggregated and developed into time-series. In the end, the public document that came out of this effort is the personal report of the few people who extracted materials from the panel's working papers and then added ideas of their own and data that they themselves selected.

The stated purposes of the Report are set forth in the letter of transmittal to the President (on the last day of the Johnson Administration) and in the introductory chapter. The letter of transmittal informs us that we must continue the allocation of resources to prepare a comprehensive social report and to develop social indicators "which will measure social change and be *useful in establishing social goals.*" The introduction also states that, in addition to satisfying curiosity, we need "a social report or set of social indicators" (and are they the same?) to improve public policy-making. Improve public policymaking, it is suggested, can be accomplished by *giving social problems more visibility; by making possible more informed judgments about priorities;* and *by providing insight into how different measures of national well-being are changing,* which it is stated "may ultimately *make possible a better evaluation* of what public programs are accomplishing."

It would be instructive to undertake careful assessment of *Toward a Social Report* in order to systematically identify which social problems are made more *visible* by the contents of the volume, and how the types of measures recommended or alluded to in it will aid in the *evaluation* of programs and in *establishing* national *goals* or *priorities.* This is not the forum for that assessment, but we would like to discuss briefly some of these promises.

Visibility

We are informed, among other things, of the following concerns:

- That we are not as healthy as we could be, as shown in calculations on expectation of life and of a "healthy life." The same point is made with data on infant mortality and on age-specific mortality for different population groups and nations as well as by a discussion of medical care costs and the maldistribution of medical services.

- That social mobility, though not declining in the United States, leaves room for improvement, particularly for Negroes.

- That while personal income levels have increased, some groups remain disadvantaged with respect to its distribution.

- That public disorders, crimes, have increased and that Negroes are more apt to be victimized than whites.

- That children are learning more in school than previously, though barriers persist among the poor and disadvantaged.

- That the performing arts are not doing very well.

- And about something called alienation.

With respect to visibility, it is possible at least to entertain the notion that the press and TV have done a pretty good job of making these very same problems highly visible—excepting perhaps the economics of the performing arts—and certainly most of the public policymakers attend to and cite many of these same data with or without invoking a concept of indicators.

Priorities and Evaluation

A perusal of the Report yields no "laundry list" of current social problems, let alone a hierarchical ranking of them. If the reader tries to count or weigh the number of pages devoted to a particular social problem as indicative of a hierarchical ranking system, then the Report provides very strange notions concerning national priorities: Drug use and addiction, welfare loads, suicide, alienation, venereal diseases, and so on all have a lesser priority than adding a fraction of a healthy year of life to the aged population. The authors of the report do in some ways both address and skirt the issue. Is homicide to be equated with 10 petty thefts, 100, 1000? Shall we conclude that 8500 murders represent about one-fifth as great a social problem as the approximately 45,000 deaths from vehicle accidents in the same year? How are these problems to be compared with five million unemployed, 50,000 drug addicts, and so on? Several years ago Merton commented on this problem:

> In short, there are no agreed-upon bases for rigorously appraising the comparative magnitude of different social problems. In the end, it is the values held by people occupying different positions in society that provide the rough bases for the relative importance assigned to social problems and. . . . this sometimes leads to badly distorted impressions of the social significance of various problems, even when they are judged in light of reigning values. (Merton 1966, p. 782)

We have already commented, at length, on the use of time-series data for the evaluation of programs. This *Report* (1969) illustrates the limited depths of such an "evaluation" in the following comment and little more need be said:

> Recent reductions in infant mortality offer some hope. Though the infant mortality rate was practically unchanged from 1950 to 1965, it decreased by more than 5 percent in 1966 and by another 5 percent in 1967. We cannot be certain about the causes of this possible trend, but the sudden reduction in infant mortality may well be related to the new Federal programs for maternal and infant care and family planning. (p. 4)

The Utility of the Report

Perhaps indicative of the disperse character of the materials from which this document was drawn, and perhaps also of the haste with which it was put together are the different levels of audiences to which the *Report* is addressed. At times the *Report* reads as a political tract aimed at persuading the moderately educated person in our society, invoking such words as "miserable," "poor," "too much," "too little," "some evidence that," and "no evidence that." At other times it resembles armchair social philosophy or common-sense theorizing (see the discussion on alienation and community and on motivations for criminal behavior). At still other times the reader is expected to be rather sophisticated, understanding covariation, correlation coefficients, multiple regression analysis, and knowing how to read complex tables.

It is also interesting to note that the authors have left their readers rather confused about what is a social indicator, though a definition, as we noted before, is elaborated in the report: "a statistic of direct normative interest which facilitates concise, comprehensive, and balanced judgments about the condition of major aspects of society" (U.S. Department of Health, Education and Welfare, 1969, p. 97). According to the *Report*, a social indicator in all cases is a direct measure of welfare and is subject to the interpretation that, if it changes in the "right direction," while other things remain equal, things have gotten better, or people are "better off." It takes very little effort in flipping the pages of the *Report* to find that there are scarcely two or three such relevant measures scattered among its pages.

The most highly touted "indicator" emerging from the *Report* is that called the "expectation of a healthy life." This measure is an index combining the expectation of death at different ages and the expectation of years of life free of bed disability. Without becoming technical about the basic concepts and data involved in the construction of such an index, it is worth pointing out that, although it was developed by specialists at the National Center for Health Statistics, the Center itself has been and continues to be hesitant about its use, interpretation, and even its very release. It is unfortunate that years of effort to develop a sound and useful measure of health status have been prematurely scooped and preempted by the release of this particular index—often times referred to as a "single dimension with a two-way stretch."

Perhaps most instructive about the character of the *Report* is the evidence it provides that the elusive boundaries of the social indicator movement prevent, at this time, any reasonably definitive effort to develop a social Report to the nation. It is necessary to develop a frame of reference on social indicators before launching into additional work and to understand something about the feasible and the impossible uses of social indicators. Certainly, the work in the *Report* points to the many problems in conceptualization and measurement that must be faced up to if one is going to be in a position to respond to the charge of providing a normative set of social statistics helpful in policy development and program planning, as well as in the academic enterprise. In part, this paper is a response to the HEW document which says too little too poorly and promises too much.

CONCLUDING COMMENT

The critical tone of this paper is by intention. Far too many promises and claims have been made for social indicators, and not enough delivered. The risks are too great that a continual oversell could indeed transform the indicator movement into a passing fad, and this probably is undesirable. Social indicators cannot do many of the things claimed for them. But from the standpoint of social policy and social action, as well as from that of social science development, there is critical need for providing a continuing body of data on the state of affairs of the nation and its constituent parts. This step is essential before any promises of utilization for policy and action purposes can be fulfilled. Rather than invent new claims for social indicators or keep on pushing forward the impossible ones advanced, what needs to be done is to look realistically at the great amount of work that must be accomplished.

At the outset of this paper, we described the field of social indicators as a social movement. But it is not an isolated movement. Rather it has occurred in the context of strong efforts to relate the work of social scientists to matters of policy and the contemporary affairs of the community and the nation. Witness, for example, the promises and optimistic assessments in two recently published expert documents (National Academy of Sciences, 1969; National Science Foundation, 1969).

Naturally, opinions differ on how far and how much the social sciences have contributed to the development of social policies and the selection and implementation of programs of social action. Certainly, however, we have fallen at least somewhat short of the projections of several decades ago, that the policy sciences offer techniques for making assumptions explicit, for testing their validity and operational viability, and for resolving the problems of conducting programs of rehabilitation and social improvement (see for example, Rothwell, 1951). Thus, it is not surprising that both the providers and the consumers of social research have been attracted to the indicator movement.

But the issue is simple, or at least it seems so to us. The current climate is so advantageous for persons with an investment in putting social science to work in relevant ways that uncritical acceptance of current efforts and developments is most likely; our cautionary remarks about the status of social indicators including *Toward a Social Report* were made to balance the exaggerated and overoptimistic evaluations by those in and out of the indicator movement. It is important that it be recognized, particularly by the policymaker, that the social indicator movement, neither in conceptualization nor in state of the art, is ready to deal effectively with the problems—the "fuzzy problems" as the late Max Millikin referred to them—that surround policy development and implementation (Millikin, 1959).

Improvement of the quality of social statistics and the reliability of social science information is both in the public and in the academic interest. But the enormity of the task needs to be underscored.

REFERENCES

Bauer, Raymond A., ed. (1966), *Social Indicators.* Cambridge: M.I.T. Press.

Blau, Peter M., and Otis Dudley Duncan (1967), *The American Occupational Structure,* New York: Wiley.

Congressional Record (1967), Vol. 113, No. 17, February 6, 1967.

Ferriss, Abbott (1969), *Indicators of Trends in American Education.* New York: Russell Sage Foundation.

Goldhammer, Herbert, and A. W. Marshall (1953), *Psychosis and Civilization: Studies in the Frequency of Mental Disease.* Glencoe: Free Press.

Gross, Bertram M. (1966), "The State of the Nation: Social Systems Accounting," in Raymond A. Bauer, ed., *Social Indicators,* pp. 154–271. Cambridge: M.I.T. Press.

Gross, Bertram M., and Michael Springer (1967a), "A New Orientation in American Government," *The Annals* of the American Academy of Political and Social Science, May 1967, pp. 1–19.

Gross, Bertram M., and Michael Springer (1967b), "New Goals for Social Information," *The Annals* of the American Academy of Political and Social Science, September 1967, pp. 208–218.

Henriot, Peter J., "Political Questions about Social Indicators," *Western Political Quarterly*, 23 (June 1970).

Merton, Robert K., and Robert A. Nisbet (1966), *Contemporary Social Problems*, p. 782. New York: Harcourt, Brace & World.

Millikin, Max F. (1959), "Inquiry and Policy: The Relation of Knowledge to Act," in Daniel Lerner, ed., *The Human Meaning of the Social Sciences*, pp. 158–182. New York: World Books.

National Academy of Sciences, National Research Council (1969), *Behavioral and Social Sciences: Outlook and Needs*, Washington, D.C.

National Commission on Technology, Automation, and Economic Progress (1966). *Technology and the American Economy*, Vol. 1, February 1966. Washington, D.C.: U.S. Government Printing Office.

National Science Foundation (1969), "Knowledge Into Action: Improving the Nation's Use of the Social Sciences." Washington, D.C.: U.S. Government Printing Office.

Rothwell, Charles Eastern (1951), "Forward," in Daniel Lerner and Harold D. Laswell, eds., pp. vii–xi. *The Policy Sciences*. Stanford Univ. Press.

Senate Bill #S843 (1967), The Full Opportunity and Social Accounting Act of 1967, *American Psychologist*, 22, (November 1967), 974–976. See also pp. 977–983.

Sheldon, Eleanor Bernert, and Wilbert E. Moore, eds. (1968). *Indicators of Social Change: Concepts and Measurements*. New York: Russell Sage Foundation.

U.S. Department of Health, Education, and Welfare (1969), *Toward a Social Report*. Washington, D.C.: U.S. Government Printing Office, January 1969.

Questions for Study and Discussion

1. From the viewpoint of Sheldon and Freeman, what would be the potential associated with the health information system proposed by Deshaies and Seidman (Reading 29)? What would be the pitfalls?

2. Should the concept of social accounting be abandoned? What is the reasonable potential contribution of accounting to social measurement in your view? (For background reading, see the book *Social Measurement*, published by the American Institute of Certified Public Accountants (AICPA), 1972.)

3. As argued by H. Brogden and E. Taylor in "The Dollar Criterion" (Reading 21), money is one unit of measure common to many different problem areas. Is money the best metric to use for measuring social problems? What are the alternatives?

4. Sheldon and Freeman state that, "There is a temptation to argue for social indicators as a substitute for experimental evaluation." How does their view relate to the position taken by Donald Campbell in "Reforms as Experiments" (Reading 28)?

5. Social indicators, The Domestic Information Display System (DIDS) and many other statistical reporting systems rely heavily on the ability to aggregate and disaggregate data according to the system's hierarchical structure. What problems are posed by this requirement?

6. Are social indicators psycho-technical measures in the sense intended by Flamholtz (Reading 18)?

CHAPTER **EIGHTEEN**

"Can Uncle Sam take away your livelihood to save your life?" So questions reporter James C. Hyatt in a *Wall Street Journal* article (March 16, 1977) describing a proposal by the Labor Department's Occupational Safety and Health Administration (OSHA) for a new standard for workers exposed to lead.

Excessive exposure to lead can cause lead poisoning, anemia, kidney disease, brain damage, and death. American industry uses more than a million tons a year, exposing more than a million workers in 100 occupations ranging from primary lead smelting to electronics assembly.

To increase protection for workers, OSHA proposes to have the current standard, which limits lead exposures to 200 micrograms of lead per cubic meter of air over eight hours, lowered to 100 micrograms. Further, OSHA proposes the adoption of a new "action level" concept requiring preventive action when exposure exceeds fifty micrograms. To meet these lower exposure levels the use of engineering controls will be required by OSHA where feasible, rather than simply requiring workers to use respirators, which OSHA has judged to be unreliable.

The government's Council on Wage and Price Stability, expressing concern for the economic impact of the new standard, estimates the cost to industry at over $300 million per year. The Labor Department's own analysis puts the cost at $548 million to 1.3 billion over several years, and acknowledges that many small, independent battery producers "aren't likely to survive" the new standard.

What is the true "social cost" of the OSHA proposal? What are the true "social benefits?" These are the fundamental issues of value so characteristic of modern societal decision making. Also characteristically, the answer to the question involves even more than first meets the "cost-benefit" eye. Among the issues involved, and scheduled for discussion of upcoming public hearings, as reported by Hyatt:

—Reproduction. Because lead in a mother's blood can damage a human fetus, as well as affect sperm in males, some experts will argue those hazards should be taken into account in setting exposure levels. Fearful of lawsuits, employers insist that fertile women shouldn't be permitted to work with lead; women say such exclusionary treatment would be discriminatory.

—Compensation. Workers with heavy exposure to lead often must be taken off their jobs to reduce lead levels in their blood. Although the Labor Department's proposal calls for employees to be removed from lead exposure when their health is threatened, the proposal doesn't require transfer to another job and doesn't guarantee earnings or seniority status won't be lost. Several unions will be demanding that workers taken off their jobs not suffer any loss in pay.

—Treatment. Some workers exposed to lead on the job are routinely given special drugs to purge the lead from their blood systems. But a number of medical authorities at the hearing will attack that approach as medically and morally unsound. They want it banned except in cases of extreme lead poisoning.

More than sixty groups have requested to be heard in the scheduled discussions.

In the readings that follow basic questions on the measurement of social value are addressed. In the first article Stafford Beer recommends a generalized unit of measure based on the concept of "eudemony," as well as a control systems approach to societal decision making. In the second article C. West Churchman implores us to focus first on the decision being made or the actions being taken, and only then to consider what measurements are necessary to facilitate appropriate choice and action.

QUESTIONS OF METRIC

Stafford Beer

Mr. and Mrs. David Stubbs wrote to the *Times* this February about the Norman church of St. Michael at Stewkley. The church stands in the middle of a possible runway of a possible Third London Airport. The complaint was that the Roskill Commission, studying alternative sites for the airport, and applying cost-benefit analysis, had adopted a wrong criterion for valuing the church. It seems that an irreplaceable twelfth-century work of art was being valued at the sum for which the church is insured against fire.

This led to considerable discussion. Can we indeed place a monetary value on a priceless heritage? If it really is price*less*, presumably not. Then why not have the cake and eat it—by moving the church, some said. The proper cost would then be the price paid for the move. But the Norman church at Stewkley is not the same church if it is somewhere else, replied others. The correspondence was effectively closed by Mr. R. J. Osborn. He said that £100 spent on building a church in 1182, when discounted at ten percent to 1982, represented roughly £1,300,000, 000,000,000,000,000,000,000,000. He did not add: 'stuff that in your cost-benefit and compute it'.

There is, to put it mildly, considerable divergence between these two estimates of value. The first noteworthy point is that cheerfully to adopt either extreme immediately solves the problem posed by this church. At fire-insurance value, the existence of the church is virtually irrelevant to the measure of social benefit; at the DCF evaluation, nothing conceivably matters *except* the preservation of the church. Then if we look at the problem through game-theoretic spectacles (with respect to the church), we are in either case confronted by a dominant strategy.

There could be a compromise value, of course, defined precisely as one which *would* affect the outcome of the decision when balanced against other factors. Now that is a point worth considering. Once we start, for reasons of good sense, to devise methods of evaluation deliberately intended to produce an effect on quantified judgment, so that we do not appear absurd, then it is very difficult indeed to ignore the actual effect those chosen methods will exert. And so I very much fear (since we are

Address to the joint plenary meeting of the Annual Conference of the Operational Research Society and the XVII International Conference of the Institute of Management Science, held at Imperial College, London, 1 July 1970. Published in *Platform for Change* by John Wiley & Sons Limited.

all human), that the arbitrary selection of the technique will not remain arbitrary for long, but become something tendentious.

The second point to note about that story is this. *We measure what it is convenient to measure.* That is natural enough; unobjectionable, too, so long as it makes sense. But I have lived for twenty-five years with the sneaking suspicion that as often as not there is something terribly wrong about taking the convenient option. Operational Research grew to a recognizable activity during the Second World War. Following the famous dictum of Lord Kelvin, we set out to measure what we observed. But enemies do not like being observed; and they will wriggle very fast, if they are observed, to avoid being measured. Thus it came about that questions of metric were an early pre-occupation of OR.

Today, I venture to suggest, we confront civil problems by uncritically accepting the measures that are readily to hand. There is no motivated enemy, anxious to evade and deceive us, true. But nature is an enemy of another sort, and a very old enemy indeed.

It may well be in the nature of aesthetic problems, such as the Stewkley parish church problem, that they are insusceptible to economic measures. Surely that should not surprise us, because the problem is in no valid sense an economic problem. People are persuaded that it is so, only because econometrics is the only tool available to use.

Those of us, most of us, who have worked in industry ought to be alive to this issue for another reason. Not only may the convenient metric not be particularly relevant, it may also be misconstrued. Again that would be because we, as professionals, have taken too little trouble to study not only the metric itself, but also its manner of application. I learned an unforgettable lesson about this, late in the Forties, soon after moving from the Army into the steel industry.

Studying the movement of steel ingots through a battery of preheating furnaces, I used the convenient records already available from the shop-floor. There was a clearly specified printed heading on the record form saying: *Number.* That was excellent: the number of ingots in a stack on a bogie was exactly what interested me, since bogies were rarely full—a fact which represented an opportunity cost. I discovered with amazement that the statistical distribution of this *Number* was exactly rectangular. It was only the gross improbability of this finding that led me to the empirical study I ought to have made in the first place. The heading 'Number' referred to the identify of the furnace, and not to the ingots-per-bogie; it was not surprising then that each furnace figured with exactly the same frequency as the others in the records.

So it seems we may uncritically adopt an inappropriate metric, because it is the accepted currency in which to discuss a topic, and even then we may misconstrue it. There is a third source of disaster. It arises from seizing upon a convenient but idiotic metric, in circumstances where none is already established. There has been a sensational public display of this error, also this year, to which I draw your attention. It occurred in attempting to answer the vital social question, pinpointed by the Home Secretary himself: whether violence and an over-permissive morality in real life were causally connected with displays of violence and sexuality on television.

For the whole of the week ending April 5th 1970, three newspaper reporters respectively watched the three TV channels we operate in this country for the whole of their broadcasting time. They measured what was convenient to measure:

namely, frequencies of objectionable words or incidents. That is not because this is an accepted metric; presumably it was because there was nothing else to do. As a result, we now know that there were seventy-one deaths on television during that week, while the word 'bloody' was broadcast forty-seven times. As to teaching youth that its ends may be achieved by threats of violence, this possibility was inculcated into our young by a truly appalling example, which solemnly appears in the record. We know that character is formed early on; well, the example occurred in a programme called 'Watch With Mother'. 'Come in', cried a mother duck to her ducklings, *'or you will have a special reason for not sitting down tomorrow'*.

It turned out that only one percent, at the most, of the whole week's broadcasting contained objectionable material—even by that ludicrous standard. Now just how useful is that particular statistic, and how useful would be any other statistics collected according to that metric? Surely the whole approach is totally worthless. The commentary I saw which accurately demolished it was not written by a management scientist, I am sad to report, but by that thoughtful critic Mr. Milton Shulman. He pointed out, that objectionable incidents as such matter only if they are imitated, and that the imitative urge applies only to a small, psychotic, unstable group. What does matter very much, in a world of adolescence in which television may have more influence than the 'classical' environmental factors such as home, school and church, is the set of values it propagates. And that propagation could easily be done without showing objectionable incidents, or uttering bad language, at all. What price the metric, then?

Here, in brief, is Mr. Shulman's excellent catalogue of five points which do bear significantly on the problem of violence, and which cannot be measured at all on the chosen metric. (i) Violence is done by good men for good reasons, and the best man is he who is best at violence. (ii) Violence does not hurt very much: its consequences are 'hidden, diminished, anaesthetized'. (iii) There is no pity for the victims of violence. (iv) Society demands no explanation for violence; instead of standing trial, the hero is 'rewarded with a smiling blonde and approving fade-out music'. (v) Since life is, as television appears to make it, 'trivial, frivolous, greedy, silly' is not violence the moral way to change it?

I want to congratulate Milton Shulman on that powerful indictment, and I wish he had included a similar catalogue of inducements to sexual permissiveness. But we are not here to indict television. The indictment we face concerns our own inability to come forward with a sensible way of measuring those things. If the Home Secretary really wants evidence about the social effects of television (as well he should), then our profession ought to have a valid approach to the appropriate mensuration—and it seems to me we have not.

Indeed we are in worse case. It was (hopefully) not an OR man who devised the experiment I have just criticized; but we are prone to the same error, which is clearly labelled *reductionism*. Aristotle taught us analysis, and the Schoolmen taught us about the reduction of the syllogism. All of that is fine in its place; but if our only scientific tool is the analytic reduction of a system to its components, so that the very nature of the system itself as a viable entity is lost, so that its synergies are denatured, so that it is nothing but a bag of bits, then we do not deserve the name of scientist in a world of complex systems and complicated syntax.

In the Operational Research Society we have recently instituted a new attack on the problems of collaboration between manager and scientist, a symbiosis to which the Institute of Management Science has I think already, and laudably, given more attention than we. May I remark at this point then, in parenthesis, that most of the criticism our own Council has received about our efforts has been of the reductionist kind. There is *no item* in our proposals, says this criticism, that is either novel or convincing; and I am prepared to believe that is true. But the total plan, in the opinion of many of our members, commends itself as both novel and convincing. Of such integrative stuff are system and synergy made.

I spoke also, just now, of a complicated syntax—as well as of complex systems. And I do reckon that language itself is a major element in the questions of metric that I raise today. For if we are prone to embrace a reductionist fallacy, we can most readily do so through picking the fabric of words apart . . .

> To-morrow, and to-morrow, and to-morrow,
> Creeps in this petty pace from day to day,
> To the last syllable of recorded time;

What is all this rubbish then? There is nothing novel about this: we have heard every one of those words before. It is not very convincing, either. Scientifically speaking, the records of time are not all written yet; they do not consist of syllables; there is no proof offered that the pace is petty—we have after all achieved 28,000 miles per hour on the way to the speed of light; and, speaking as someone who cares about efficiency, I might add that nothing is achieved by the reiteration of the word 'to-morrow'—which is logically redundant.'

That is how the reductionist operates: within the last ten days I have heard an argument almost as stupid as this. And so I say: beware of reductionism of both systems and syntax; as of the irrelevant metric; as of the established metric; as of error in interpretation itself. And I ask too: how shall we measure for our masters the novel situations—which matter to them because they must needs cope with them, and to us because it is our job?

I realize that I am talking about the need for measures of utility, and that the whole history of economics could probably be written in terms of its treatment of this concept. Therefore I shall try to illuminate a number of issues by reference to some discoveries made by economics in the last hundred years. The first of these issues was settled (one might not think so, looking around today) nearly that long ago.

Should we assert an additive axiom for sets of utilities, or are general utilities non-additive functions of contributory utilities? The switch between those two alternative views seems to have come in about 1880: an early date indeed, in any field of human enquiry, for the recognition of what is essentially a systems viewpoint.

So Gossen and Jevons were out, and before the turn of the century Edgeworth and Marshall were in—and clashing merrily. 'We cannot trust the marginal utility of a commodity to indicate its total utility', wrote Alfred Marshall. Because he thought in terms of consumables, he used the example of the commodity: salt. We cannot survive without salt; but when we have enough salt, there really is no point in buying any more—whatever the marginal price.

Now, should one take that attitude to Norman churches? There are other Norman churches than the threatened one at Stewkley, and perhaps (as Dr. Johnson said of green fields) when you have seen one you have seen them all. Let us carry forward from that the obvious point: whether Stewkley has a significant marginal utility for you, the consumer of Norman churches, depends on *who* you are, and *where* you are.

The second issue emerged, not many years later, from the work of Pareto. If we abandon the calculation of absolute differences between alternative pay-offs and simply order our preferences for them, we arrive at the idea of indifferent curves. When the pay-off between a group of alternatives is judged equal or indifferently good, we have a stationary point in a judgmental n-space from which to assess what is better or worse. This holds even when the sets of things compared are wholly dissimilar. If we now turn this static indifference map into the dynamic systems model which we need in order to offer any really useful account of society for any particular purpose, we confront a very cybernetic notion indeed, and another point to be carried forward.

It is that we should regard the various identifiable sub-systems of society, the social institutions which I have elsewhere defined under the term 'esoteric boxes', as opaque. They have inputs; they have outputs. Then we shall set up comparators across the outputs of separate boxes, and provide feedbacks to their respective inputs, with a view to detecting levels of activity for the boxes themselves which yield indifferently good results for them all. Thus we are no longer faced with a requirement to find analytic measures for the micro-systems we have failed to analyse, and seek useful answers instead at the macro-level where the social preferences actually emerge.

For example: it is a very long time since Sir Charles Goodeve noted that a population drift would be hard to measure in terms of the metrics on which individual decisions to move home were in fact taken—better pay, better concerts, snobbery, and so on almost indefinitely. We should have to devise a very complicated decision model, and then interview a sample of those moving, assessing each of them in terms of each of the model's parameters. He proposed instead that we measure the rate of drift itself, and also its rate of change (which is not difficult)—and then simply interpret the results in terms of potential difference.

Then what is the metric? I suspect we do not use these handy ways of measuring because we do not know *what* it is that a change of potential actually measures. In this case Sir Charles explained that it must be some complicated image of well-being; and he chose to call that by the entirely suitable Greek word 'eudemony'. This is one of the Greek words for happiness, though it comes nearer to meaning prosperity than ecstasy. You will find 'eudemony' and its adjective 'eudemonic' in the Shorter Oxford—with an attribution to Jeremy Bentham, which is appropriate. I ask you to bear with me in my attempt to regain currency for this moribund term, since I shall need it today very much. Meanwhile, the immediate point is that we may well be using unsatisfactory metrics, simply for want of recognition that others, though unnamed or unfamiliar, are to hand.

It appears to me that despite the modern work on indifference of such mathematically ingenious people as Herman Wold, this type of thinking has received too little attention—and that the reason is clear. The whole training of scientists and other numerate scholars emphasizes the potency of cardinality over ordinality: it is indisputable that cardinal metrics contain more information than do ranking schemata. It is sad to have to say, however, that they do so only if they exist. Have we faced up to the fact that even crude ordinal metrics may be more useful than the cardinal metrics we cannot actually devise?

The tool that might yet serve this cause to advantage is the theory of games, in which apparently ordinal measures become cardinal in a very specific sense (identified by William Baumol). This is that game-theoretic models are meant to be predictive of preferred action *by numerical calculation*, which is to say without asking anyone what they would rather do, once pay-off preferences have been subjectively decided. (Pollsters might note that methodological suggestion.)

This argument suggests that the number of murders, rapes and four-letter words published by television per week is a computable function of choices made about the sort of society one wants, on some set of scales dealing with permissiveness—or as we used to call it: freedom. That seems to me very likely; and it does not conflict with the earlier conclusion that the metric criticized would not measure the effect of television on society. What it does emphasize, and this is the next point to carry forward, is this. The embodiment of the choice between television strategies revealed in the broadcasting of actual programmes, closes a definable loop with a very short cycle time.

There is the citizen with a set of social values; there is the producer seeking (he says) to interpret these; there is the interpretation itself—called the programme; and there is the citizen again: the citizen *qua* viewer, *qua* comparator. Here is the dynamic system of which we spoke, with its unanalyzed components, its absence of an established metric. Then what is the commodity that moves around this network? Shall we say it is information? Then perhaps we are already entrapped. It soon appears that we shall need a model of the sorts of programme being broadcast, complete with measures of their informational content; a model which by its very existence and nature establishes norms for the number of murders and rapes. And the feedback from the citizen will indeed seem to consist of an irate phone call to the duty officer at Television Centre saying: 'I have just heard my eleventh four letter word this week, whereas ten is all I can tolerate'.

Let us rather call the commodity that flows round the network eudemony. Then it is the *frequency* of negative eudemonic response that affects the producers, rather than the content of the message—which inference again seems to reflect the facts very well. Please note also that we measure the intensity of sensation in our own bodies not by the content of neural messages, not by variations in amplitude of the signal or any kind of modulation, but exactly by the *rate* at which uniform and discrete spikes of potential arrive in the sensory cortex.

So protesting TV viewers, according to this model and this metric, are simply registering negeudemony at some level of intensity, and their protests may be offset by some other approving viewers who channel positive feedback into the system. The system's reaction, having measured the eudemonic balance, would be to insert either a low-pass filter into the broadcasting part of the loop, or for that matter a high-pass filter in the second case. This inference too seems to be borne out by the facts. Then if the whole system is operating correctly, why is there so much concern about the social effects of TV?

The emerging model can help us there too. We have so far supposed that society sets a standard, and that we are considering a straightforward servomechanism which adjusts output to that standard. But society is a learning machine, and the control we are modelling is really an *adaptive* controller. If the comparator, conceived now as being part of an evolutionary system (which society surely is), discovers that departures from its standard *increase* societary eudemony, what then? 'Errors' are supposed to be inimical to the system, and in this case to decrease eudemony; that is why we employ error-actuated negative feedback. But the notion of adaptation entails a metasystem, speaking a metalanguage in which the system's standards themselves are set. This means that a metamessage feeds back from the comparator to say this: 'The metasystem I serve approves of your 'error'; I am adjusting my standard to your signal. Just keep the increments of change as small as you can, otherwise we shall go into a state of mutually uncontrollable oscillation'.

This inference from the model in turn appears to me to fit the observed facts; and the oscillations we have observed have indeed been undamped from time to time. If we now add a further construction to the system, in the cause of good modelling, to the effect that many television producers are themselves high-pass filters anyway, we begin to see just how unstable the total system might well be. Therefore I conclude that the problems of television as a possibly bad social influence are not about four letter words at the micro-level of programmes, but about instabilities at the macro-level of social adaptation; and that point carries forward too.

From this vantage point, moreover, we can well understand why the call is often heard (particularly from the parliamentary back-benches) for some kind of consumers' association intended to monitor the BBC. The real demand according to our model is for feedback from the adaptive social metasystem; but it is always misrepresented by both the BBC and its own proponents as a demand for the kind of systemic feedback that already exists. The BBC operates a highly sophisticated and sustained type of audience research; it has a very elaborate edifice of advisory bodies; it listens to all those telephone calls *and* to Mrs. Mary Whitehouse. These are all mechanisms for supplying systemic feedback. No wonder the Corporation feels it is doing enough. But our model has already shown that these controls are not directed to the instabilities that matter. And, just for the record, it is obvious that a consumers' association would not help either: because it would inevitably operate on the systemic—not the meta-systemic—circuit.

The circuit that matters in this example can only be that connecting parliament with the corporation through the Minister and the Board of Governors, and it is this tenuous linkage which would have to be strengthened in order to attain metastability. It is obvious, then, why nothing is done. The existence of powerful societary servos at this level would offer no ready way of distinguishing between wise government of the medium and political interference in the content of broadcasting. Neither parliament nor the BBC, and still less the public, would be sure that freedom of speech was preserved. That is why the linkage remains tenuous, and must be seen as such, given existing methods of organization. Naturally, I am calling for the redesign of organizational structure at the metasystemic level—I always do. And here is one audience, hopefully, that will not demand to know precisely what structure is recommended before the OR has been done.

Now this same model applied, as I see it, to every public service; and the argument about government intervention and non-intervention is all about this missing servo at the metasystemic level. Government cannot have a health service, for example, costing two thousand million pounds in taxpayers' money, and either leave it alone to be what it likes to be, or try to run it as if government understood medicine better than doctors and nurses. This is a terrible dilemma, and we try to solve it at the wrong level by directly controlling the pay of the medical profession. That leads to a national scandal, and to the unexampled situation whereby a profession whose self-image is all about idealism, about a very real dedication to the plight of the sick, can hardly believe that it hovers on the brink of taking industrial action— as striking is euphemistically called. We are trying to control the system itself, which is quite stable on its existing servos, instead of the metasystem—which is unstable as hell. And again I attribute this mainly to the use of the wrong metric, which is money—which is obsessional in our society. A health service, more than any other public service, deals not in money but in eudemony.

So this brings me directly to the last lesson I shall draw from the history of social utility as an economic concept. You must have wondered when I should get round to John Maynard Keynes and the year 1936—when the *General Theory* was published. It is thirty-four years since Keynes tore apart the notion that the wage must be equal to the marginal product of labour. He noted that if labour supply really were a function of real wages alone, 'the supply curve for labour would shift bodily with every movement of prices'. It does not; and clearly Keynes was right to question whether 'the existing level of real wages accurately measures the marginal disutility of labour'. I want to add, in the light of all we have learned since those days about the socialization of welfare, that the level of real wages does not seem to measure marginal disutility in the social services at all. Otherwise we should today have no doctors or nurses, no teachers, and no policemen. They would all be members of SOGAT.

Money is terribly important, both to those paying and to those paid. But money is nonetheless an epiphenomenon of a system which actually runs on eudemony. It is for this reason that I have come to see money as a constraint on the behaviour of eudemonic systems, rather than to see eudemony as a by-product of monetary systems.

My own life is certainly about eudemony: is not yours?

Η ευδαιμογικ των χυταρκων εστι

said Aristotle—eudemony is for the self-sufficient. One cannot exert any measure of self containment without enough money to cope with one's perceived needs—whatever they happen to be. The same is true for the firm. Its plans have to be financed, its cash flows have to be positive; otherwise the firm cannot realize its own potential. But don't tell me that the firm is about maximizing profit: I have not encountered this economic fiction in real life yet. As to government, it is precisely to do with eudemony, and its budgets aim simply and solely to create eudemonic conditions.

If you and I, and the firm, and the government are to finance our needs, we are all calling for a steady metabolism of funds. Thus our control systems are designed to hold money flows steady. Taxation operates to stop me from adopting an income-maximizing policy. Taxation, the Prices and Incomes Board, and organized labour operate to stop the firm from adopting a profit-maximization policy: instead, it seeks to maintain its rate of return on capital. The main role of a post-Keynesian government is to offset local instabilities in the economic system, not to run at a surplus overall. All three of us, for our various reasons, are actually seeking to maximize eudemony within monetary constraints.

Then we are using the wrong metric. Cost-benefit analysis converts eudemony into money, which is fine for so long as the money-metric obeys the rules of mensuration: to be additive, to be linear, to be so formulated as to make sense of a maximizing objective function. For all the reasons I have given, money fails to be the metric we need. So if we want a decision about the Norman church at Stewkley, we must take it in terms of eudemony and no other. We can tart-up the decision afterwards, and rationalize what we have done in the established metric of money. But the decision is eudemonically pre-empted before we get to that stage of the cost-benefit game—a game which is therefore, and in essence, meretricious.

This discourse becomes emphatic at its most tentative point, and didactic now that there is nothing left to teach. Because eudemony is a behavioural artefact, I cannot tell you what it 'really' is; because it is measurable only as a potential difference. I can discuss it only in terms of equilibria, and not in terms of absolute values. And yet that fits with the story of man, for whom the search for happiness is held by many to be illusory, and it fits with a Buddhist enlightenment, which is about closing the gap between attainment and desire. Social utility seems to me to be concerned with the design and operation of systems that will keep the gap small. If those systems fail, then the whole population marches to the South East; television becomes a massively disruptive force; the government could fall because of Stewkley; and there is no more health, education or security.

Thus I am calling for the design of eudemonic metasystems, working in new metrics, which do not exist just because they have not been needed before. Issues of social utility have been with mankind for ever, it is true. They were not hitherto obtrusive, however, because our energies were consumed in the effort to survive. It is the rise of an expensive technology competent to guarantee survival that poses these problems of choice, and at the same time constitutes in itself the biggest threat to survival that man has ever faced. Let us look at the points carried forward in this talk, and at the conceptual model we have built, and see how much we seem to know about utility and those very questions of metric.

First of all, utility is not a number—and certainly not a number of pounds or dollars. Utility is a continuous function of system. Such a system cannot be static, as are so many systems described in economic theory: it must be dynamic in its very essence. I mean that it is not just a question of making our picture of the world move, but that the movement of the world is the subject matter of the picture. Next, such a system is not a closed micro-system, like the 'Robinson Crusoe' economy; nor is it an open macro-system—because at the macro-level it is so rich in feedback. It is a system concerned more with its own structure than with its internal transfer functions, a system whose behaviour is better understood through its lagged feedbacks than its input-output schemata. It deals in indifferent choices of pay-off rather than optimal courses of action, and these choices have to do it with equilibria, rather than the nature of 'the good'.

In saying all of that we reject most of the models of social utility that have ever been constructed, and we question the metric in which those models are couched. For they deal in the accepted measurements by which social institutions are already stably governed. But the choices we have to make lie only ostensibly within those systems, and are determined only ostensibly on the scales of their accustomed metrics. The choices are really made at the metasystemic level, in terms of eudemony; and here our institutions are wildly unstable because the required servo-controls do not exist, and no-one knows what the metric may be. Instead of measurement, we have a value system; and it is just this value system which the electorate judges.

It is inevitably on this question of subjective judgment that I must end. It is the judgment about eudemony that builds the value system that sets the standards we make numerical for a particular institution, so that its modus operandi may be computable. But how are we to agree on these eudemonic judgments? It was the first point we carried forward in this talk: *who* are you, *where* are you, when you judge— and is 'society' simply the consensus of 'you' and 'you' and 'you', or something more?

If you and I diametrically disagree about some issue of social utility, it does not mean that a right answer lies somewhere on the line between us. In the first place we may both have misconceived the problem altogether. But more importantly, each one of us is always right—because judgments always depend on who and where is the judge. There is a real and independent world out there in which change happens, and affairs are well or ill conducted. Each of us reacts to this from a special condition of partial knowledge and prior disposition, and our metric works outward from a base of eudemonic indifference. I put this earlier by saying that 'we have a stationary point in a judgmental n-space from which to assess what is better or worse'. But for each one of us that point is, theoretically, personal and unique.

I have sought illumination about this in a model from Relativity Theory, where there exists an obvious parallel. There is a unique turning-point in any system of time-reckoning for which a rate of change du, involving a rate of change proportional to du, is in fact proportional to du^2. Eddington says: 'In adopting a time-reckoning such that this stationary point corresponds to his own motion, the observer is imposing a symmetry on space and time with respect to himself'. It seems to me that each of us stands in a similarly unique situation with respect to social utility, and that we do indeed impose an egocentric symmetry on the society we presume to observe and to judge.

The well-known consequence of all this in Relativity is that the notion of simultaneity breaks down. If the model holds, then, the notion of an objective social utility has no meaning; utility does not exist apart from the observer who tries to assess it. I expect this to be right, but I am not sure whether it matters. Perhaps a democ-

FIGURE 1   *Any social service is based on the reading of societary need which the service's producer begins by interpreting. He provides the service, at a 'service standard' (ss), which standard is submitted to society to evaluate.*

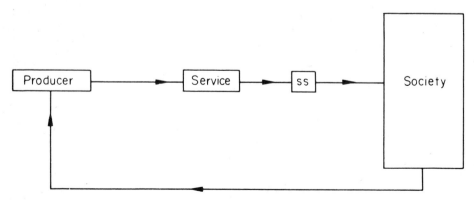

FIGURE 2 *Society for its part promulgates a formal standard (fs) that it intends to accept. This standard is set in many ways, by advisory bodies and any other mechanism which gives shape to social judgment. A comparator (x) can then be imagined as continuously comparing fs and ss, and feeding back an error-correction signal (ε) intending to modify the service so that fs is attained by ss.*

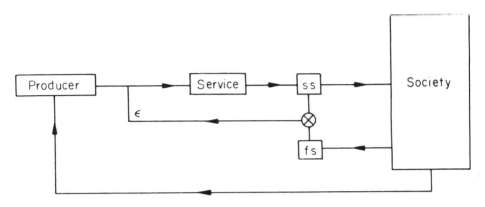

FIGURE 3 *But society itself is a learning system. It continuously compares (x) the eudemony (E: defined in text) experienced from the service now, at time t, with its stored knowledge of eudemony at an earlier time, t-1. This causes it to adjust its hidden standards (hs) which in turn modify the formal standards (fs). This adaptive controller may operate (as perhaps in broadcasting) to bring fs nearer to ss—even though the error (ε) feedback signal is supposedly operating to bring ss nearer to fs.*

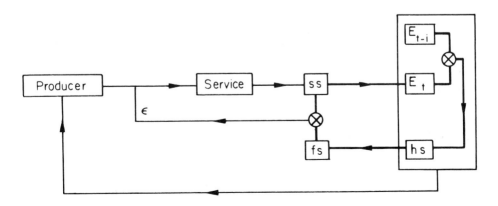

*FIGURE 4 This social metasystem (the thick black loop) ex-
ercises some kind of effect on the service's producer through
tenuous feedback mechanisms at the government level—for
government 'expresses the will of the people', or (more realistically) is sensitive to changes in social eudemony. Yet government finds it difficult in a democracy to exert control over the
service's producer and management, except through its ap-
pointments to the Board governing the service. There is a short-
age of structure and mechanism on this plane, which currently
transmits too attenuated a feedback signal.*

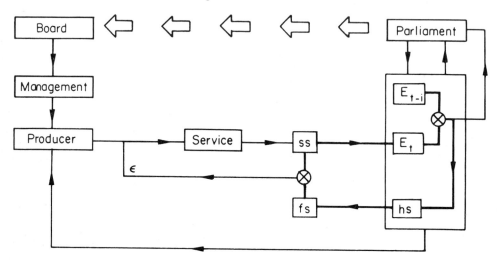

racy finds a broad consensus for which these divergencies of individual subjective
judgment are irrelevant. Or perhaps it is just those miniscule divergencies which become amplified into a force sufficient to blow society apart.

Of this much I am sure: some such force exists; it is very much at work. It must
be a product of eudemonic change, and it threatens to extinguish us all. I would like
to identify and measure this force before it gets me.

REFERENCES

Alfred Marshall, *Principles of Economics* (1890), Text and Notes edited by C. W.
Guillebaud, Macmillan, London, 1920.

Herman Wold, *Demand Analysis*, Wiley, New York, 1953.

William J. Baumol, *Economic Theory and Operation Analysis*, Prentice Hall, London,
1961.

John Maynard Keynes, *The General Theory of Employment, Interest and Money*
(1936), Macmillan, London, 1951.

R. H. Macmillan, *Non-Linear Control Systems Analysis*, Pergamon, Oxford, 1961.

A. S. Eddington, *The Mathematical Theory of Relativity* (1923), Cambridge, 1963.

Charles Goodeve, 'Science and Social Organization', *Proceedings of the Second In-*

ternational Conference on Operational Research, (Aix-en-Provence, 1960), EUP, London, 1961.

Questions for Study and Discussion

1. Are cost-benefit analyses in support of social decision making necessarily exercises in meretricious measurement? What would have been a reasonable approach to take in the analysis of the proposed Third London Airport?

2. How is the construction of a decisive measure at the societal level a more difficult problem that the construction of a decisive measure at the organizational level?

3. Does the concept of "eudemony" as discussed by Beer satisfy the requirement for a common unit of measure for social problems as identified by Sheldon and Freeman?

4. Some people argue that many social programs raise aspirations faster than they deliver satisfaction of needs. If this is true, what problems does it create for the measurement and evaluation concepts proposed by Campbell, Beer, and others in this book?

5. Should Federal Revenue Sharing funds be allocated on the basis of eudemony rather than population? Comment.

6. In what ways is the Los Angeles Pollutant Standards Index (PSI) a cybernetic system as defined by Beer?

ON THE FACILITY, FELICITY, AND MORALITY OF MEASURING SOCIAL CHANGE

C. West Churchman

READING 32

In a recent unpublished paper entitled "Questions of Metric," Stafford Beer cites some letters to the *London Times* addressed to a question of social change. The issue concerned the seven hundred years old Norman Church of St. Michael of Stewkley, which stands square in the middle of a possible runway of a possible Third London Airport—not by design surely. A cost benefit analysis had been made by a commission for each alternative site of the proposed airport. In the instance of St. Michael's Church, the commission had used the extant fire insurance policy on the church as the base. This method of analysis caused considerable anger among antiquarians throughout the United Kingdom. A Mr. Osborn suggested instead that one should take the initial investment, say 100 pounds in 1182, and discount it at 10 per cent per annum to 1982; the approximate result is a one followed by 33 zeros—a mere decillion pounds. As Beer points out, if you adopt either cost-benefit strategy, you automatically decide the issue. If you use the fire insurance approach, the church is virtually an irrelevant consideration in the decision of where to build the airport; whereas if you use the discount approach, the church is all that matters: it is inconceivable that one should build the runway there.

What I found most significant about this story of measuring proposed social change was the ease with which both the commission and Mr. Osborn were able to assign numbers. The facility is clearly a product of the history of enterprising accountants and economists, people who have spent their lives assigning numbers to social changes. So facile has the process become that so long as there is a hint of reasonableness, the numbers themselves carry the conviction of their accuracy. And both the commission and Mr. Osborn seem to have a plausible viewpoint. The commission might argue as follows: evidently, people do value St. Michael of Stewkley, in the sense that they are willing to pay a price for its value in the event that it is destroyed. This value is clearly represented by the amount of fire insurance they are willing to subscribe to, because the only reward for paying the premium is the expectation of a return provided the church is destroyed. Mr. Osborn, on the other hand, might argue that an investment was made in the year 1182, which could instead have been deposited in the yet-to-be Bank of England. Cashing in on the investment in 1982 would be like "cashing in" on the church to build a runway in

From *Accounting Review*, Vol. 46, No. 1, January 1971, pp. 30–35. Reprinted by permission.

1982; assuming rational decision making, the total imputed value of the investment cannot be greater than the current value of the church.

My main point is that the facility of assigning numbers means that only a modicum of plausibility is needed to convince people that the numbers represent reality. In both of the cases cited, just a little more thinking would have ruined the case. All one has to do is apply Immanuel Kant's moral law, which, paraphrased, says that if a particular principle is used to measure social change for policy making, then this principle should be universally applied. The principle, of course, may contain reasoned exceptions and stipulations, but once it is enunciated, it ought to be applicable to all instances, or else it is basically unfair, i.e., immoral. Now the commission's principle seems to read as follows: whenever there is a positive value (benefit) to destroying an object X, then the cost of destruction is to be computed by using the extant fire or life insurance as a base. The commission's policy, if universalized, would neatly solve the population problem. There is surely a value in not having all the people which the demographers predict will be here in the year 2000 if nothing is done to prevent it. So—merely calculate the benefit of eliminating X and compare it with X's life insurance! The result is that only the best will survive—the Kennedys and Onassises. Mr. Osborn's principle, on the other hand, is very nice for old criminals and professors: the investment in their birth for hospitals, nurses and doctors discounted to age 70 would make the decision to execute or retire unthinkable.

The two examples, then, are silly. So why mention them? Why, just to challenge any number assigners to come up with a better method, based on a principle which will pass Kant's test. More to the point, the examples clearly show how number assignment is based on very strong value and reality assumptions.

Suppose for the moment that we look at the reality aspect of measuring social change. We'd surely like to say that a measurement should reflect what really occurs. But what does this stipulation mean? We could make its meaning clear if somehow or other we could get outside the measuring system and what it is trying to measure. If we could do this, then we'd say to ourselves, "There's reality R in its box, and when R changes it sends a message or impulse to the measuring system M in its box. Since we're outside all this, and can observe it accurately, let's see if the numbers generated by M accurately correspond to the changes in R." We'd certainly have to fuss over the criteria of accurate correspondence, but that would be a technical matter we could hand over to some of the brilliant minds who like to fuss with these matters.

But of course this way of describing reality doesn't work at all, as an auditor knows. It isn't sufficient to stipulate that a good audit has occurred if a second party testifies that the auditor's numbers correspond to reality, because the second party may belong to the auditor's firm, or a competitor's firm, or the broad class of the inexperienced. To make any sense at all of this way of defining reality, we have to set down the stipulations of the competent, disinterested observer,[1] which as experienced auditors know, is no easy task. To accomplish the task we need a fairly elaborate theory of competence and honesty. So here is the same theme again: to know that we are measuring real change we need to have a strong theoretical base.

But suppose now that we do succeed in finding a satisfactory basis for assessing competence and honesty. Would we then want to say that M is measuring real social change if a sufficiently large class of competent, disinterested observes agree that it is? *Why* should agreement imply that reality is being measured? Here I'd like to introduce a pragmatic principle at least as old as William James. If I tell you that the last book on the top shelf of my study's bookshelf is red, and I present affidavits of color competent observers which certify my account, have I described reality to you? No, said James, because the description makes no difference whatsoever in your behavior relative to your practical goals. To be real for you is to make a difference for you. If I'd said that the red book is that set of dull platitudes of Chairman Mao, then some of you might report me, or admire me more, or whatever, and then reality comes into being.

Suppose we go back to Stewkley where the British Division of the Cleveland Wrecking Company is about to smash a priceless glass window of St. Michael's. We want to measure this social change. "There goes 3,000 pounds," says the commission and could hardly care less. "There goes a decillion pounds," says Mr. Osborn, and could hardly care more. But what has really happened? If we employed the method suggested earlier, we would bring in our disinterested observer to decide which number accurately maps reality. He would say things like "20 windows were broken, each 700 years old," or, "it took two weeks to haul St. Michael's away at an expense of 1,472 pounds and a sixpence."

Such a disinterested observer, in fact, would be very like many experts who today are measuring social change. Consider, for example, the issue of population. Here beyond a doubt is social change. In Paul and Ann Ehrlich's *Population Resources Environment*,[2] we are told that the doubling rate of the world's population around 1970 is about 30 to 35 years, in 1930 was 45 years, in 1850, 200 years. The book contains a number of other numbers: food production, pollution production, and so on. All of these numbers say something about social change, but you will note that they are all very much like the disinterested observer of the smashing of St. Michael's. No doubt in both cases the reports may be a bit shocking, and in this sense, they "make a difference." But the difference may have no pragmatic import whatsoever. The Ehrlichs have much to say about the number of people who will starve if things go on as at present. This is much like telling us that the round ball will break St. Michael's window unless its basic policy of motion is changed. Another disinterested observer, also using numbers, could tell us how many people felt sad and for how long when they learned about St. Michael's or the starving children of Biafra.

It is really astonishing how many crisis-numbers are being thrown at the public these days. They all describe what programmers call the rate of activity in a certain sector of society. Since often the rate of activity-pollution or poverty or information-spread yields uneasy or horrible feelings, people and politicians are apt to conclude that something must be done to lessen the rate, or even to make it negative. But even if the disinterested observer is telling us about real impending disaster provided an activity continues to increase, it by no means follows that he is telling us about real social change in a pragmatic sense. The reality question is, "So what?" Only when we can measure in such a way that we know what to do about the result, only then will we measure social change.

The point I am trying to make is that the amount of change in some property of society or its environment by itself does not "measure" social change. What is needed besides is the basis of decision making which shows how the amount of change makes a difference. A good illustration is the so-called "protein gap," which very much interests the nutritionists these days. We are told,[3] for example, that a pregnant woman who lacks a sufficient amount of protein in her diet may well give birth to a deformed baby. We are also told that the amount of protein (note, again, the amount theme) in certain areas of the world is seriously deficient. What can be called the Fallacy of Filling the Gap immediately infers that we should produce and distribute more protein. Perhaps we should, but the protein gap by itself does not imply any such action. Besides a knowledge of the gap, we need to assume that the crisis warrants certain expenditures, that policies of making more protein will not introduce concomitant gaps and inequities in other areas, e g , by changing the ecology of fish life. It so happens that protein is used as calories in calorie deficient diets, so that filling the protein gap by no means solves the nutritional problem. And so on.

Of course a profession may adopt a separatist philosophy to avoid the tremendous responsibility of measuring real social change in a pragmatic sense. The profession of accounting may say the same thing that many demographers say: "Look, we can't tell you what to do about the activity rate, but we can tell you what the rate is. We're like the speedometers on automobiles which measure changes in the car's velocity. The driver must decide what to do about a reading of eighty miles per hour." But the analogy doesn't work, for a very obvious reason: it's perfectly clear to both driver and auto designer that velocity is a critical aspect of the driving experience, and the method of correcting for too much or too little is also obvious. Given that we ought to drive automobiles if we want to, the speedometer is a great help and accurately measures social change. But the critical question is still there: ought we to drive automobiles? The speedometer is silent on this point. Given that we ought to reduce population by forcing every lady to take the pill, then the expert can or soon will tell us how to do the job. But the demographer is silent on the question whether we should so force pill taking.

The fallacy of the separatist philosophy is the one I mentioned earlier: once you begin to emphasize some aspect of real change by putting numbers on it, you may divert attention from the real issue. Consequently, I can't help but feel that the professions which try to place numbers on social change have the responsibility to go the entire way—to understand why the numbers make a difference and why the difference they make is the right difference.

For example, I believe the accounting profession should become deeply involved in helping society to measure the most critical aspects of social change—of pollution, population, information, whatever. But to do so, I think the profession will have to change some important traditional attitudes. It is to these social changes of the profession that I'd like to address the concluding remarks.[4]

In recent years, we have heard a great deal about how accounting and economics need to be enlarged to include "social indicators" or "social accounting." But I don't think the need is for more numbers, at all. The need is for the basis of justifying the numbers—the model or world view which tells us what difference the numbers make.

Decision-oriented accounting is quite different from accounting's traditional role in the private sector. Often the service which accounting has given is essentially comparisons: the accounts tell us how this period's costs, inventories, turn-over, profit, etc., compare with last period's. Comparative accounting is much like the rate-of-change of an activity mentioned earlier. It is useful if we know that the comparison makes a real difference in decision making, useless otherwise. Hence one basic change of attitude is towards finding a model for decision making. Of course, what I am saying is that the professions of operations research and accounting need to form a long-overdue alliance. But I think both professions will have to give up one cherished attitude—namely, the assurance of the expert. The "model" to which I referred is by no means easy to create, nor can any of us feel assured that a candidate model represents social reality. No longer can we call upon the disinterested, competent observer to settle our issues. There is no "outside" which can observe the "inside" trying to depict reality.

Returning to Stewkley once more, both the commission and Mr. Osborn had a model; there is no competent, disinterested observer to tell us which is right, if either. But is this so? Why not say as before that if a sufficiently large group of sufficiently competent experts agree, or—via the Delphi technique[5]—converge on agreement, then the model can be taken as representing reality? The answer, of course, is that to assume that a convergence of agreement of experts represents reality is to presuppose a fairly elaborate theory of the relationship between reality and expert knowledge, as well as a theory about how expert opinion is to be ascertained. Also assumed is our old friend the value judgment. Experts may tell us that in so-and-so many years we can expect brain-to-computer linkages and genetic engineering. This is like telling us that the population will double, the protein source will shrink, the air will be dangerously polluted. To repeat, what is left out of the expert's opinions is all we really need to know: what to do about it if they accurately portray a real trend.

No, if we are to serve society by measuring social change, I think we'll have to do so in an entirely different mode from the traditional one of being the separate, disinterested, and objective observers. These stipulations seem clear (to me):

1. We are not the only or even the basic methodology of assessing social change. There are other equally forceful methods: aesthetic, religious and political are three good examples.

2. We are not objective in the old-fashioned sense of "being apart," and "non-biased." Our bias is based on our conception (world view) of how social reality works and what "makes a difference."

3. (My own bias.) In Beer's paper mentioned earlier, which has a very similar theme to this one but a radically different approach, Beer argues for a "meta" measuring system, one that measures the "eudomonia," or "prosperity," which is flowing through the social system. Beer approaches the problem in this manner because he likes to see the world as a flow, with feedbacks and other cybernetic devices. My bias is to look for the fiber of the system, the structure that ought to hold it together. This approach amounts to saying that we require an explicit moral base for measuring social change. Far more important than "agreement of experts" is the moral prescription which says that our measure should be based on a policy of moral universality—everyone to count as an end—and not a means only—a deep analysis of how people are affected by the difference the measure will make.

For example, Mr. Osborn was nearer to being right than the commission, but for the wrong reasoning. The point is not whether to discount from the past—but whether to discount into the future. I can see no moral justification in our saying that the numerical reward (joy, aesthetic pleasure, inspiration) of some future viewer of St. Michael's must be discounted back to present value, much as a future insurance premium would be—though I have some feeling-deficient friends who say just this: "The hell with the values of a generation as yet unborn," or at least 10% the hell per annum." So if we paint our world view with the Third London Airport as a temporary value for, say, thirty years of use and then no value thereafter, but St. Michael's will always bring joy to some thousands or so, then the cost number to be assigned to smashing the church is very large, because no future joy is to be discounted to present value on moral grounds.

Now there is no authority for my moral law, and many may disagree with it. Indeed, many should disagree with it, because the essence of moral discourse should be debate, not agreement. Anyone like myself who takes part in measuring social change must on the one hand declare and argue for his moral position, but should never on pain of displaying hubris, assume that he is the authority. So I declare and argue for the position that every social policy needs not only a cost-benefit number, but that the basic theory of assigning such a number should be revealed and assessed for its moral implications—i.e., whether if generalized it would imply a world where people are treated as ends rather than means only.

4. As number assigners we must be stubborn but not necessarily humorless. We will insist the the value of a life can be numbered and compared, no matter what our enemies say. So the population scarers may horrify us, but let us number the cost of a human starved to death. Of course, we can't be all that deadly serious about it, either. We should take on a lesson from Kenneth Boulding, who suggests that each citizen be assigned 22 deciles of a child, which he can sell on the open market place. This way the population will remain stable, assuming no bootlegging operations occur. You see, once we give up the silly notion that numberers have the final answers, we can really enjoy ourselves now and then.

5. I hope the accounting profession will join other professional associations in looking at today's problems of society and suggesting some ways of assigning numbers to social change that make a difference—with all the humility, humor and purposefulness possible.

ENDNOTES

1. "Independent" in CPA language.
2. W. H. Freeman and Co., San Francisco, 1970.
3. See *International Action to Avert the Protein Crisis* (United Nations, New York, 1968).
4. To be sure, some changes have already been suggested.
5. Olaf Helmer, *Social Technology* (New York, Basic Books, 1966).

Questions for Study and Discussion

1. How does Churchman's position on the issue of social measurement differ from that of Beer?

2. What are some current examples of what Churchman terms "the Fallacy of Filling the Gap?" What is the specific nature of the fallacy in each instance?

3. What are some typical examples of measures for management decision making at each of the three levels:

    (i)   organizational
    (ii)   individual
    (iii) societal

Which would fail Churchman's moral test, in your judgment?

4. How do Churchman's five stipulations for measuring social change apply to the United States census? Los Angeles smog? Poverty? Hunger?

CHAPTER **NINETEEN**

How do I love thee? Let me count the ways.
I love thee to the depth and breadth and height
My soul can reach, when feeling out of sight
For the ends of Being and ideal Grace.

Elizabeth Barrett Browning
Sonnets from the Portuguese

Embodied in this famous passage is a classic measurement dilemma—quality versus quantity. The question is "Can quality ever be quantified?"

The humanist may argue that it cannot be. Love is a unique event. It is the quality of the experience that matters. It is irrelevant if not irreverent to talk about the number of times it occurs, or even the number of approaches that might be employed. Love in this sense can never be measured.

This is one side of the quantity versus quality controversy which is fundamental to all measurement. The quantification side, on the other hand, argues that in principle at least, all phenomena can be defined, distinguished, and counted. Love is no exception. In this view one can, in principle, measure the extent and intensity of love. Difficulties in accomplishing this are methodological only. Quantification conquers quality. Or does it?

One way out of this dilemma is found in Churchman's article "Why Measure" which appeared at the beginning of this book. Measurement is always purposeful in Churchman's view. Thus, measurement is a means to some end, not an end it itself. In this teleological theory of measurement quantity and quality are intertwined. Both are inherently a part of measurement.

In an ateleological theory of measurement, however, purpose plays no direct role. Measurement becomes an end in itself. It results in "true" numbers. Treating these numbers as ends in themselves leads to their deification. This results in what Abraham Kaplan (1964) refers to as the "mystique of quantity." The mystique of quantity is "an exaggerated regard for the significance of measurement, just because it is quantitative, without regard either to what has been measured or to what can subsequently be done with the measure" (p. 172). This mystique may account in large part for "The Vitality of Mythical Numbers" described in Max Singer's article (Reading 27).

The continual tension between quality and quantity in measurement is the theme of this closing section of the book. The fundamental questions are, "What are the limits of measurement? What are the basic premises from which all measurement flows?"

Mason addresses this issue in the first reading by suggesting that a dialogue on quality must precede the specification of the quantitative measurement process. Quality and quantity are integrated through a dialectical process.

Ackoff, in the second reading, focuses on aesthetics as the essence of the quality of life. He argues that measurement of this quality is very difficult, though not in principle impossible. He then offers a creative alternative to measurement in this domain.

An important aspect of quality for Churchman is the "mood" or feeling tone of a social group. In the final paper of this collection he presents an interesting paradox: In order to measure the mood of a social group one must first understand the mood of the group performing the measurement. He argues that in scientific measurement the mood of the measurers is repressed. However, in measurement for management decision as the concept is developed in this book, the mood of the measurers and of the measurement cannot be ignored. Feelings are the lifeblood of purposeful measurement.

THE ROLE OF DIALOGUE IN THE MEASUREMENT PROCESS

Richard O. Mason   *READING 33*

THE PROBLEM

There is a fundamental problem in "data analysis" that is essentially inherent in the term itself. That is, there is a tendency to take data as *given* and then proceed to analyze it. The question explored in this paper concerns just how "given" any set of data are and what might we do to help guarantee the truthfulness of data.

The discussion will be in part philosophical but it has some very strong practical implications. Data is collected in order to engage in a reasoning process. The purpose is to search for items of information that can be used to yield new items of information. These new items, in turn, will be used to make predictions and decisions and ultimately to serve as the basis for taking action. Action taking, of course, is a very practical activity. So, it will behoove us to look a little more closely at the concept of "data", and especially measured data since there seems to be something about quantification which blinds us to questions of underlying assumptions. A brief illustration will help.

According to the Bureau of Census there were 25,522,000 people living in poverty in March 1971. This datum derives from a series of observations in accordance with some very specific definitions and rules. For example, a person is either unrelated or in a family, families being defined as "a group of two or more persons related by blood, marriage or adoption and residing together". Any person or family earning less than $1,576 per annum (the threshold level for a 65-year-old female living alone on a farm) is automatically considered to be impoverished and there are additional threshold scales above this depending on the number of people in the family, their age, whether they are farm or nonfarm and whether the head of the household is male or female. However, any person or family earning more than $6,486 per annum (a nonfarm family of 7 or more with a male head of household) is not considered to be in poverty.

Now, many of us in the inflation ridden economy of today would question that these procedures capture the real poverty level today. We might argue, for example, that various cost of living factors are not included in the measure.

Beginning such a line of questioning would involve us in a dialogue or debate about the measurement process. We will not engage in a full-blown debate about

From *Communication and Control in Society*, K. Krippendorff, ed. 1979, pp. 89–98. Reprinted with permission of Gordon and Breach, Science Publishers, Inc.

measures of poverty nor criticize the existing poverty measures here. Rather, the measures will be used as an illustration of the role of dialogue in the measurement process and to serve as a backdrop from which to make some general observations. The discussion will follow from principles of measurement.

STEPS IN MEASUREMENT

There are at least three steps in any measurement process:

a) The conception of an underlying dimension. (The dimension is relevant to some current or future problematic situation.)

b) The definition of units and scales of the dimension.

c) Execution of operations to determine numerosity of units in a given object or collection of objects.

All three steps are difficult and subject to differing points of view. However, the first step, the conception of an underlying dimension, is the most critical and, hence, the source and object of most debate. The conception of a dimension (a construct or a measure space) requires the judgmental act of *distinction*. Among the vast and chaotic set of possibilities the measure must be able to identify those things to be included within the measure and those things which should not. That is, one must be able to set boundaries about the phenomena to be measured. Exactly how these conceptual boundaries or dimensions are set is not an idle matter. It impinges critically on the vital interests of those concerned with the measure's use, be it for scientific, policy and decision making, or for general public information purposes. Consequently, in a very real way debate, active or silent, is an integral component in any measurement process.

AN ILLUSTRATION

For example, in the creation of poverty measures we might imagine that the following hypothetical debate occurred:

QUESTION (Q):   What is poverty?
MEASURER (M):   Poverty is a deficiency in the necessary or desirable qualities of life in our culture.
Q: How do we measure it?
M: Well, in a capitalist exchange economy one's annual income in dollars is the best indicator of one's ability to have necessities and luxuries. Clearly, anyone who earns less than $1,576 a year simply could not purchase enough calories of food nor clothing and shelter to live comfortably.
Q: Perhaps, but ours is a culture in which the family is a central institution. People live together. Doesn't that affect their comparative poverty level? You know the old saw "Two can live cheaper than one".
M: Yes, we can incorporate a graduated scale which adjusts for the fact that two people living together do not need to earn twice as much as they would singly in order to achieve the same standard of living. Indeed the scale accommodates family sizes from 1 to 7 members.

Q: OK. But then some families are headed by a man, others by a woman. Does that make a difference?

M: Yes, a female headed household generally requires less income to live. There's an adjustment for that also.

Q: How about age?

M: Oh yes, elderly people receive aid, care and other benefits in our society. Consequently, a provision is made to reduce the poverty threshold level slightly if the head of house is 65 years or older.

Q: One last question. Many people are able to secure resources and benefits directly without going through the exchange economy and therefore their real standard of living is not reflected in their income figures. I'm thinking particularly of farmers who grow their own food. How do you account for this?

M: Of course it is very difficult to capture all of these possibilities and we really do not attempt to do so. However, we separate farm from non-farm families and the upper limit of the official poverty standard for farm families is somewhat lower. This accounts for the fact that they require less dollar income to live.

We could extend this debate considerably. Many readers, I'm sure, might add questions and responses that are perhaps more provocative than those already posed. However, by now the main point of the illustration should be clear. The process of setting dimensions and units for measurement is fundamentally judgmental. It is based on the values, beliefs and concerns of those involved in defining the measure. As William James [2] put it, measurement is a "teleological instrument". "This whole function of conceiving, of fixing, and molding facts to meanings, has no significance apart from the fact that the conceiver is a creature with partial purposes and private ends". Measures vary with the end the measures have in view. And the fact that some one goes to the effort to measure suggests that the phenomenon is important to him and that some use will be made of the measure.

Since the process is judgmental no truly analytical ways exist for completing the process. Yet measurements are the basis for many important decisions, decisions which affect many different lives in many different ways. Poverty figures, for example, are used to guide welfare and other social policy decision making. So, the question becomes: How can we aid the judgmental processes which underlie measurement? Much has been done on the mathematics of measurement, what can be done to improve the judgments on dimensions and units?

My response is that we must learn to design and structure the debate underlying a measure so that the richest set of possibilities is generated and best synthesis is achieved. An approach for designing such a debate is developed later in the paper. First, however, let us review a few short cases to clarify some of the issues involved.

Case 1

About two years ago a research team began a survey of the "state of the art" and current research in progress in the field of computer aided design and manufacturing (CAD/CAM). In order to complete their task they created a hierarchical taxonomy which subdivided the manufacturing enterprise into a series of elemental goal or process oriented tasks. Each item or current research was then classified as to its contribution to each task. An elaborate cross-indexing scheme was employed. One of the results of the effort was to show that rather heavy research efforts were underway to apply CAD/CAM to some selected manufacturing tasks and there were virtually none in other areas.

The team was aware of the difficulties involved in subsuming the research under its categories and undertook the process with great care. However, they were astonished at the line of criticism that was directed at their final report. Most people criticized the "differentia" employed in the classification scheme. The team believed its taxonomy was rooted in the logic of the manufacturing process and not subject to emotional debate. Not so, said the critics. Some researchers whose work was classified argued that their research was *different* from other's work subsumed under the same category, regardless of what classification scheme was used. Some researchers suggested a different, and for them more realistic logical model of manufacturing, which would result in somewhat different categories. Since most researchers like to be at the leading edge of their field a few criticized the taxonomy because it made those researchers "look good" who were working or had announced plans to work in categories with minimal or no activity. Those who were working in the "same old" areas did not look so good.

The team had not adequately confronted these issues earlier and the credibility of its results suffered accordingly.

Case 2

Several years ago a colleague and I were working with a large timber, lumber, pulp and paper company. The company was decentralized into a lumber division and a timber division both of which had strong profit incentive programs. Top management made a good part of its salary in incentive bonuses.

The management science group at corporate headquarters had just completed a large-scale linear programming model of the entire corporate production system starting with the source timber lands and ending in the final product markets such as lumber, furniture, paper, books, packaging, etc. In order to run the model they had to estimate its coefficients including one crucial cost coefficient that occurs at the point in the production process where logs are peeled. The peeled logs go to make lumber (lumber division) and the chips and bark are used to make paper (paper division). Joint costs had to be assigned to both peeled logs and chips. The measurement problem was, "By what principle do we assign costs to lumber and to chips?"

Historically, chips had been substantially a free good. Prior to the development of their use to make paper they were simply burned as surplus. But once the measurement question was posed it could not be ignored. Initially, the management science team set a price based on the production capacity used to process the chips. As it turned out this was a modest cost figure. However, the paper division's management complained vigorously because this cost figure adversely affected their profit rating. The paper division management's position was that they had created utility where no utility existed before by using these chips. Consequently, they should not now have to pay a premium for the "privilege" of providing this contribution. The MS group countered that they could sell all the chips they could get to the Japanese at a rate over 3 times that which they suggested charging the paper division. The division replied that it was company policy not to sell to the Japanese or to favor the company's competitors. Also, they claimed that since the Japanese government in effect subsidized much of the paper industry, it wasn't proper to charge the division the market price set by the Japanese. The MS group retaliated that company policy *does,* however, permit going out of the lumber business altogether. In this case the logs could be totally converted to chips and the division would have to pay the full cost, a cost which proved to be higher than the original estimate but less than the Japanese offer.

About this time the debate became so heated that corporate management, recognizing that if it were carried further it would destroy the company, scuttled the model. The implications of the alternative measures were simply too threatening to the organization, and the company management had no way short of a revolution for dealing with them.

Case 3

As part of a research program to evaluate the use of NASA's Earth Resource Technological Satellite, I surveyed some applications of satellite and aircraft remote sensing in the field of agriculture. One project involving forecasting the grape crop was especially interesting in terms of the debate it created.

Crop forecasts are a very important aspect of agriculture information systems. They are used by bankers, farm implement companies, canners, government officials, etc., to plan their activities. The forecasts are refined as the cycle from growing through to consumption progresses. It is well known that all of these forecasts and updating refinements are difficult to make and subject to considerable error. However, in the California grape market there was an additional complication contributing to the error. Grape growers have two basic options. They can elect to sell grapes on the open market or they can set them in the sun to dry and thereby produce raisins. Consequently, not only must natural events be forecasted, but also the grower's decisions must be forecasted in order to estimate the supply of grapes that will reach the market.

To solve this problem some researchers working with the Department of Agriculture came up with a rather creative solution. They commissioned airplanes to fly over the fields and to photograph them at periodic intervals. By means of an analyses of the aerial photography the researchers could determine how many raisin drying pans the growers were using and when they put them out. Since the pans were of generally standard sizes it was possible to estimate the amount of grapes dried per pan, multiply by the total number of pans and obtain an estimate of the raisin output. The total grape forecast minus the raisin estimate yields the new grape market supply forecast.

It would seem that a more accurate figure of this nature would have greater utility and that the researchers efforts would be applauded. Such was not the case. Grape growers, wholesalers and wineries alike complained when the first experiment was run.

The grape growers resented the invasion of privacy. They knew and trusted the field methods used to make forecasts previously. These served as the basis for bank loans, government activity and other business decisions and consequently were important to them. This new information potentially upset an information balance in a critical element of their business and they were very uncomfortable with it.

The wineries were even more incensed. They mounted heavy lobbying efforts

with the legislature to have the program stopped. The wineries were basically mo-
nopsonists in their supply markets. The lack of accurate information improved their
power to set prices. The new measurements threatened to change the way market
prices were determined. Consequently, they felt they would lose out, or at least not
gain, in the process. The measurement program became so politically hot that it was
eventually dropped.

These three cases illustrate several of the levels at which debate can occur in the
measurement process. Debate can occur when the basic distinctions are made which
define the dimensions that will be measured (Case 1 and the Poverty illustration).
Debate can occur when the alternative units and concepts used to measure within
the dimensions are determined and decided upon (Case 2). And, finally, debate can
occur when the measurement data itself is published and employed in the decision
process (Case 2 and Case 3). Thus, debate can occur at all stages in the measurement
process. This points to the need for a procedure for handling this debate and making
it more efficient. This requirement, as we shall see, calls for a new kind of reasoning.

DEDUCTION, INDUCTION AND DIALECTIC

In the history of reasoning two paradigms have dominated. One is deduction; the
other induction. Deductive arguments generally proceed from major premises and
minor premises to conclusions. The archetype for a deductive argument is:

	Form	*Example*
	A (assumption)	All men are mortal
and	D (data)	Socrates is a man
Therefore	C (conclusion)	Socrates is a mortal.

In the pure form of the argument the data are taken as *given*. The conclusion is true
if and only if the assumptions and data are true. Induction, on the other hand, is a
process by which data about some members of a class is used to arrive at conclusions
or explanations concerning more or all members of a class. Accordingly, the following archetype typifies induction:

$$
\begin{array}{ll}
 & D_1 \\
\text{and} & D_2 \\
 & \cdot \\
 & \cdot \\
 & \cdot \\
\text{and} & D_n \\
\text{Therefore} & \overline{C}
\end{array}
$$

Inductive arguments, of course, are very important in practical affairs. Most of
our current knowledge (and all of our forecast knowledge) is essentially based on
induction. Induction, however, is not a complete reasoning form. As with deduction, in an inductive argument the data are also taken as *given*.

Both induction and deduction are very useful. They are frequently employed together in most complex scientific and practical situations. Indeed, they often mutually support each other. Collectively, however they are incomplete as forms of rea-

soning. Both induction and deduction seek valid or probable conclusions *given* the data. They do not provide a guarantee for the data which they employ. In order to complete the reasoning process, an additional mode is required. For historical reasons I will call this additional mode of reasoning dialectic.

A SCHEME FOR DIALECTICS

In what follows, an outline for another form of reasoning will be sketched out. The method can serve as a checking process on data and as a means of structuring debate in the measurement process. The method is different from and a companion to deduction and induction.

The approach is dialectical. An argument can be said to be dialectical whenever a situation is examined systematically and logically from two or more points of view. Dialectical arguments seek an answer to the question, "What does it mean to say that . . . ?" A dialectic argument applied to data might proceed as follows:

1. Select the data item D_1 (e.g., the number of people in poverty, the level of CAD/CAM research pertaining to a manufacturing task, the cost of wood chips, or the number of grapes being converted to raisins). D_1 is considered to be a proposition.

2. D_1, in turn, is implied by an underlying set of assumptions of a system S_1. S_1 includes the formal definition of terms and units used in the measurement process and the rules used to employ them. S_1 should be specified as completely as possible.

3. The act of distinction which resulted in the formation of S_1 essentially selected a specific set of definitions and rejected or ignored all others. A relation of opposition or otherness was formed in the process. Since selections of this nature are based on purposes, values and beliefs, the third step is to identify the basic value and belief system W_1 which underlies S_1. In social systems the cultural, social and psychological history surrounding the measurement will serve as clues to W_1. W_1 represents the worldview, or root metaphor, behind the system and its data.

4. The fourth step is to create an opposing point of view. This can be done in one (or any combinations) of three ways:
   a) Select an alternative data item D_2 of the same form as D_1 (e.g. another estimate of the people in poverty). Repeat steps 2 and 3 to discover S_2 and W_2.
   b) Select an alternative system S_2. This can often be done by negating or redefining some of the premises in S_1. The relevant D_2 and W_2 are then found.
   c) Select an alternative worldview W_2 based on another set of metaphysical values and beliefs and derive its S_2 and D_2.

Criteria for choosing W_2, S_2 and D_2 are that they must be plausible, credible and in social-political as well as logical opposition. That is, they should have some force behind them in the real world.

5. Place (W_1, S_1, D_1) and W_2, S_2 and $D_2)$ in opposition to one another and systematically explore their respective implications and differences. This can take the

form of a programmed debate in which each element of each system is interpreted and the strongest possible case is made for including it instead of its counterpart in the system. The strongest case is also made for the counterpart.

6. The sixth step is based on a theory of systems. S_1 and S_2 are systems in opposition are at the same level in the hierarchy of world systems. This relationship suggests that there must exist a supra system S^1 that implies both S_1 and S_2. It will be based on its own, expanded worldview W^1. Step six is to discover or create S^1 and W^1. This will be the result of synthetic thinking and requires imagination and insight. The implications of S^1 are then derived.

7. The seventh step involves judgment. The measurer must now choose the "best" system S^* based on the insight and discoveries obtained in the dialectic process. This is, of course, the most hazardous step in the process. However, there is a substantial history of opinion which holds that good judgments are made in the context of opposition. In designing the dialectic we have tried to insure that the best context of opposition possible would be developed.

8. Finally, S^* is used to obtain a new measure D^*. D^* may now be employed in deductive and inductive arguments.

SUMMARY

In this paper some of the problems of using and understanding data have been discussed. All measurements, it was asserted, have a system of purposes, values and beliefs underlying them and therefore are fundamentally based on judgment. Some illustrations and cases were given. We found that deduction and induction were inadequate to the task of guaranteeing data. Both methods take data as given. A dialectical mode of reasoning, based on the thesis, antithesis, synthesis triad of Hegel, was developed and proposed as a companion mode of reasoning to be used with deduction and induction.

Dialectic is a structured way of improving dialogue in the measurement process. Churchman [1: 149–205] has developed an underlying rationale for this approach. Mason [3] has interpreted it and applied it in a decision-making context.

REFERENCES

1. Churchman, C. W., *The Design of Inquiring Systems*, New York: Basic Books, 1971.

2. James, William, *The Principles of Psychology*, Vol. 53, *Great Books of the Western World*, Chicago: Encyclopaedia Britannica, Inc.: 1952.

3. Mason, R. O., "A dialectical approach to strategic planning", *Management Science* 15, No. 8: B–403—B–414, 1969.

Questions for Study and Discussion

1. Describe the dialogue which might take place among the various interest groups concerned with obtaining a measurement of the population of the United States; or levels of smog; or the extent of hunger.

2. In accounting for the drilling of oil wells two points of view have emerged—the successful efforts position and the full-cost position. Successful efforts contends that the only drilling costs which should be capitalized as assets are the costs incurred in an effort which directly resulted in a gusher or "wet hole." Dry holes are expensed. The full-cost position maintains that the cost of the dry holes should be capitalized as part of the cost of finding one or more wet holes. How does this dialogue relate to the measurement problem of defining the appropriate underlying empirical relational system? How would you resolve the controversy?

DOES QUALITY OF LIFE HAVE TO BE QUANTIFIED?

Russell L. Ackoff

READING 34

PROLOGUE

After reading a draft of this paper, my most valued critic, Professor Thomas A. Cowan, wrote: ". . . there is just too much here." He was right, as usual. Much of the thought of a lifetime was condensed within that draft. This necessarily made for hard reading. I have since agonized over the earlier version of this paper, trying to take material out of it and to simplify what remained, but I have not succeeded in doing either well. This final version is as difficult to read as the draft. I apologize for this. My only excuse is the maturity and sophistication of the audience to which it is addressed.

PART 1. THE NATURE OF QUALITY OF LIFE

1. Quality of Life is a Matter of Aesthetics and Aesthetics is neither Sufficiently Understood nor Adequately Integrated with other Aspects of Life

The growing preoccupation with quality of life is evidence of the maturation of society along a very important and previously slighted dimension of progress. It indicates a growing awareness of the fact that we have been trying to sing a cultural quartet with only three voices: one voice that of science and technology, another that of political economy, and the third that of ethics and morality. The voice that has been missing is that of *aesthetics*. Quality of life is primarily a matter of aesthetics, and aesthetics is an aspect of life that has been seriously ignored in the process we call "development."

Let me expand and defend these stark assertions.

My principal witnesses are the philosophers of ancient Greece who never forgot the fourth voice. They divided the pursuits of man into four categories:

1. the *scientific*—the pursuit of *truth;*

2. the *political-economic*—the pursuit of *plenty;*

From *Operational Research Quarterly,* Vol. 27. Reprinted by permission.

3. the *ethical-moral*—the pursuit of *goodness*, virtue; and

4. the *aesthetic*—the pursuit of *beauty*.

These categories were refined out of the philosophical thought of centuries; they were not the product of a deliberate effort to divide man's activities into exclusive and exhaustive categories. Obviously, they are not mutually exclusive, since man clearly can conduct two or more of them simultaneously. Nevertheless, I believe that it is valuable to regard these categories as exhaustive, for reasons that will become evident in the course of this paper.

None of us wants merely to exist; we also want to *live*. The difference between existence and living is a matter of many things, not the least of which is self-control, hence of choice. To live is to be able to fashion one's own fate, to create one's self. In our studies of decision making and control—and these have increased exponentially in the last 25 years—we have made extensive use of science and have fashioned what are now called the *decision sciences* and *cybernetics*, the science of control. For a much longer time we have been concerned with the political, economic, ethical, and moral aspects of decision making and control. But what of the *aesthetics of decision making and control?*

The notion of the aesthetics of decision making does not yet convey much meaning to most who think about this process. To be sure, one refers to the *art* of decision making, of problem solving, of management, or of control, but the term "art" does not surely alert one to the aesthetic aspects of these activities; rather it points to our inability to understand them completely in scientific terms. Art in this sense seems to be the instinctive ability to decide without completely understanding what one is about. This is not the sense in which I will use the concept. I wish to direct attention to art *in*, not the art *of*, decision making and control, particularly self-control.

It is not surprising that we fail to reflect sufficiently upon or understand fully the meaning of aesthetics of self-control. Over the last 25 centuries, very few philosophers have been able to incorporate aesthetics into a comprehensive philosophical system. There has been little systematic development of aesthetics since the Greeks. On the other hand, "aestheticians" tend to give the other three categories of man's activities short shrift. As a result, we understand aesthetics much less than science-technology, political economy, or ethics-morality. It is safe to say that most of us have some idea as to how each of these three activities relates to the others, but somehow or other the idea that aesthetics is antithetic if not downright hostile to the other three has gained widespread, almost instinctive acceptance.

Thoughtful men would agree that considerable progress has been made in science and technology. Some would agree that progress has also been made in the domain of political economy and in ethics and morality. But one would be surprised to hear it argued that mankind has made aesthetic progress. Indeed, and regretfully, we must admit that little evidence exists on which to base a claim that contemporary man has a greater ability to produce or enjoy beauty than his predecessors.

In the last two decades, the quality of life has become a major preoccupation of certain sectors of our population. This concern is a concern with aesthetics, whether it is recognized as such or not. It is necessary, therefore, to recognize it as such and reestablish the harmony of the *four* voices if we are to deal effectively with the quality-of-life problem.

It has become traditional for affluent people to separate work from play, hence from pleasure. They have been conscious of aesthetics—or at least they know of the interrelation of beauty, play, and pleasure—in their homes and in their recreational and social activities. But their attitudes toward business and work have been dominated by the Protestant, or perhaps one should say more properly, the Puritan ethic. This ethic contrasts work with play. It conceptualizes work as an *ascetic*, not an *aesthetic*, activity. Work is widely thought of as both necessary and necessarily unpleasant. The dissatisfaction it has produced is justified or rationalized by many apologists of the Industrial Revolution who argue that it should be accepted, if not embraced, as a kind of earthly purgatory in which sin is expiated and virtue is gradually accumulated.

Post-Renaissance man came to conceptualize the universe as a machine created by God to do His work, to serve His purposes. Man already believed he had been created in the image of God. Therefore, it was natural for him to attempt to develop machines that would do his work, serve his purposes. This effort gave rise to the Industrial Revolution.

Let us look at this revolution more closely. It was carried out by analyzing work into its simplest elements; mechanizing those that could be mechanized; and inserting human beings into those elements which were impossible or uneconomical to mechanize. The men and machines thus assigned were organized into the production line that became the spine of the modern factory. The ironic consequence of mechanization is this. It imposes its machine-like character on man. Industrializing societies sought to fit men to jobs that had been designed for machines. Mechanization dehumanized man's work.

Industrial societies succeeded in this program of dehumanization so long as workers were economically and educationally deprived. But the Industrial Revolution also brought affluence with it, and with affluence came greater economic security and more and better education. Secure and educated workers are increasingly dissatisfied with and alienated from machine-like work [1]. Discontent with the quality of work, now widespread in developed countries, is reaching crisis proportions. It is hardly necessary to point out that this discontent is a part of a more general dissatisfaction with the quality of life.

The Industrial Revolution also accelerated urbanization and produced a fundamental qualitative change in the nature of man's environment. Most of the environment in which "developed" men spend their time is now man-made. Initially, man-made environments brought great comfort and convenience, but in recent years they have been deteriorating rapidly. This deterioration is exacerbated by inaccessibility to untouched Nature and has further sharpened dissatisfaction with the quality of life.

2. Style Is One Important Aspect of Aesthetics, Hence of Quality of Life

It is time now to look more closely at the meaning of "quality of life." The term is far from clear, but it is evident that it has less to do with what and how much we have in the way of material goods than with the conditions under which we acquire and use them. Quality of life—ordinary life, corporate life, work life, academic life, all kinds of life—is not a matter of products but of processes. It has to do with the satisfaction or dissatisfaction we derive from what we do with our possessions, material and spiritual, and not from what these possessions in fact are.

Even to specialists in decision making, it is apparent that consideration other than those of a scientific, technological, political, economic, ethical, or moral nature dominate our activity. Ordinary folk are never in doubt about it. I cite only a few examples drawn from my own corporate and governmental research experiences. A small company owned by its three executives wanted to diversify so that they could be challenged more and become more involved in running their business which, inconveniently, ran itself rather successfully. In their words, they wanted "to get more fun out of it." Fun is a matter of aesthetics, not science, technology, politics, economics, ethics, or morality.

Another example. A major corporation's profits had been suffering recently because of its commitment to producing only the highest quality products in its field. Its cost of materials is now inflating more rapidly than are its competitors', but it refuses to abort its products or abbreviate the processes by which they are produced, as its competitors do. To degrade its products would significantly reduce the satisfaction its managers derive from their work. This too is a matter of aesthetics.

Finally, there are two districts of the Federal Reserve banking system in my country [U.S.A.], both of which have exactly the same functions but which differ significantly in the way they are organized and carry out their functions. The "atmospheres" in these two banks are completely different. The difference cannot be explained in scientific, technological, political, economic, ethical, or moral terms; it is a matter of aesthetics, a matter of *style*.

The moral of these short stories is clear. *Style* is an important aspect of an individual's or organization's aesthetics. Because style is, in turn, an important aspect of decision making, let me focus on this process for a moment.

Decision making in the presence of doubt is problem solving. Through science we have developed rich and useful models of decision making and problem solving. It is necessary to consider these models at this point; to do so, I must become more technical. Decision models usually have four components: (1) the decision maker, (2) alternative possible courses of action defined by controllable variables, (3) alternative possible outcomes, and (4) the environment defined by those uncontrolled variables that, together with the controlled variables, can affect the outcome. The components are interrelated by three types of parameter: (1) the probability of choice, that is, the probability that the decision maker will select a particular course of action, (2) efficiency of choice, the probability that a course of action if selected will produce a particular outcome in the decision environment, and (3) the relative values of the outcomes to the decision maker in the decision environment. The sum of the products of these measures over all the possible courses of action and outcomes is the *expected relative value* of the choice situation.

Choosing the course of action which maximizes expected relative value is what many economists mean by "rationality." This, I believe, is an irrational concept of rationality because it omits a major type of value. Consider the following type of choice situation: only one of a set of exhaustive and exclusive courses of action can be chosen, each of which is certain to produce the same desired outcome. If maximization of expected relative value were the only appropriate criterion of choice, the rational decision maker would be completely indifferent to the alternatives in this situation. But this seldom happens, and for a good reason. We have preferences for means as well as ends, for we know that ends and means are relative concepts. We buy a book in order to read; we read in order to learn; we learn in order to earn; and so on. Every end is a means to a further end and every means is an *end-in-itself;* hence means as well as ends have value to us. Means have two kinds of value: *extrinsic* or instrumental, and *intrinsic* or stylistic. The extrinsic value of a means has to do with its efficiency relative to an end; intrinsic value of a means has to do with the satisfaction its use produces independently of its outcome.

Allow me a few examples. Brown shoes may be just as efficient for walking or for dress as black ones. We may, nevertheless, prefer one to the other because it pleases us more. My preference for black ink over blue, blue over green, and green over purple exists even though I am aware that each works as well as the others for the purpose for which I use them. The set of preferences which each of us has that are independent of considerations of efficiency constitute our *style.* Our individuality, our uniqueness, lies as much in our style as it does in our desired objectives and the efficiency with which we pursue them. Style has to do with the satisfaction we derive from what we do rather than what we do it for.

Desired outcomes are performance objectives that impart extrinsic value to the means we employ to pursue them. Uses of preferred means are stylistic objectives that have intrinsic value, value that is independent of the outcomes they bring about. If and when our theories of decision making, problem solving, management, and control do not take stylistic objectives, intrinsic values, into account, they are seriously deficient.

3. The Pursuit of Ideals Is the Other Important Aspect of Aesthetics, Hence of Quality of Life

I turn for a moment to the history of ethics and to the philosophers' search for the one universal desire that might define an ultimate *Good.* Their motive was the belief that only through such a desire might all men and women, past, present, and future, be unified into what we call "mankind." They hoped to demonstrate that mankind is a system whose parts are integrated by pursuit of a common ideal. How ironical that the search for such an ideal failed because those who engaged in it were too sophisticated. Let me explain.

Once upon a time a young man was granted three wishes. We all know that with the first two of them he managed to get himself into such difficulties that he had to use up his third wish to get back to the condition in which he started. On hearing any one of the many versions of this story, most bright children tell us they can do better than the hapless hero with only one wish; they would wish that all their wishes would come true. My teacher, the much-too-little recognized American philosopher Edgar Arthur Singer, Jr. [2], systematized this childlike wisdom by identifying a desire so universal that it unifies all men at all times. It is the desire to be able to satisfy our desires whatever they might be, even if we should desire nothing, Nirvana. It is the nature of purposeful systems—and human beings are purposeful systems—to desire; and there can be no desire not accompanied by the desire to be able to satisfy it. Therefore, an ideal that can be shared by all men at all times is *omnipotence,* the ability to satisfy any desire. The ideal character of omnipotence is reflected in the fact that virtually every religion of Western culture ascribes it to deity.

Omnipotence is an ideal which, if attained, would assure fulfillment of all desires, hence the attainment of all other ideals. Therefore, it is what might be called a "meta ideal" for mankind. Like any ideal, however, it must not be attainable, though it can be continuously approached.

I ask you now to consider the four conditions that are necessary and sufficient for continuous progress of *every* person toward omnipotence. This exercise will return us to the four-fold nature of human activity as conceived by the Greeks.

First, such progress requires a continuous increase in the efficiency of the means by which we can pursue our ends and, therefore, a continuous increase of our knowledge and understanding—an increase in our grasp of *truth*, the function of *science*, and our ability to use it effectively, the function of *technology*.

Second, it requires a continuous increase in the availability and accessibility of those resources needed to employ the most efficient means available and, therefore, increasingly efficient production, distribution, and preservation of wealth: the pursuit of *plenty*, the function of the *political economy*.

Third, it requires continuous reduction of the conflict within and between individuals, because conflict means that the satisfaction of one (or one's) desire precludes the satisfaction of another (or an other's) desire. Therefore, we pursue both peace of mind and peace on earth: the state of *virtue*—the function of *ethics* and *morality*.

Fourth, it requires continuous attention to the aesthetic life. To demonstrate this will be the burden of the rest of this part of my paper.

If man is continuously to pursue the ideal of omnipotence he must *never* be willing to settle for anything less. He must never be either permanently discouraged or completely satisfied. Therefore, whenever he attains one objective, he must seek another that he wants more than the previous one and the attainment of which requires a further increase in his power. Thus he must always be able to find new possibilities for improvement and satisfaction. He must always be able to generate visions of something more desirable than what he has.

Singer showed that it is the function of the aesthetic life to *inspire* us: to create the creator of visions of the better and to give this creature the *courage* to pursue his vision no matter what short-run sacrifices are demanded. Inspiration and aspiration go together. Inspired art consists of the works of man that are capable of stimulating new aspirations and a commitment to their pursuit.

In the *Republic*, Plato conceived of art as a stimulant that was potentially dangerous to society because it could threaten its stability. His perception of its function was the same as that put forward here, but his conception of utopia as a *stable* state is not consistent with the four conditions of omnipotence set forth above. These imply a dynamic idealized polity, one that is a *process* rather than a stasis.

I do not mean to imply that even in the ideal state, as I have presented it, man would have solved all his problems or attained all his objectives. There is at least as much satisfaction to be derived from the pursuit of ends as in attaining them. Therefore, the ideal society, as I conceived it, is not problem-free but problem-ful, though power-full.

In contrast to Plato, Aristotle viewed art as cathartic, a palliative for dissatisfaction, a producer of stability and contentment. While Plato saw art as producing the dissatisfaction with the present that leads to efforts to create the future, Aristotle saw it as producing satisfaction with what has already been accomplished, not as creative, but as *recreative*. Plato and Aristotle were concerned with two aspects of the same thing. Art is both creative and recreative. These aspects of it can be viewed and discussed separately, but they cannot be separated. Recreation is the effort to extract pleasure from the here and now, a reward for past effort. It provides "the pause that refreshes" and thus recreates the creator. Art is also inspiration; it drives us to further efforts. Art both pulls us from the past and pushes us into the future. Without art, we falter on the way in our continuous pursuit of ideals.

Note that the only end that can have purely intrinsic value is an end which cannot be a means to a more ultimate end. Hence only ultimate ends, ideals, can have purely intrinsic value. On the other hand, I have argued that the ultimate ideal of mankind must be omnipotence, the ability to attain any desired outcome. The value of this ideal is therefore purely extrinsic. Thus, in dialectical fashion, we find the complete synthesis of intrinsic and extrinsic value in this ideal.

4. The Quality-of-Life Problem Consists of Failure to Obtain Stylistic Objectives and Loss of a Sense of Progress toward an Ideal

I have tried to show that decision making has two important aesthetic aspects: (1) the *style* of decision makers, which has to do with immediate sources of satisfaction derived from doing rather than from the consequences of doing, and (2) the ideals of decision makers, the outcomes which, if attained, would be completely satisfying to them. Unless we understand the role of style and ideals in decision making, we cannot deal effectively with the quality-of-life problem.

Style involves the satisfactions one receives at the present moment from doing whatever one does, and ideal-pursuit involves the satisfactions one receives from a sense of progress. If one accepts this interpretation, it is easy to see the source of the current concern with quality of life. Less and less satisfaction is being derived from the ordinary things one does, such as taking a walk or a Sunday drive, riding to work on a bus or subway, going to school, or working. This, I feel, is a consequence of a deterioration in our aesthetic environment. Reduction of the quality of work-life is a special case of the dissatisfaction produced by activity that has little or no intrinsic value to the actor.

The second aspect of reduced quality of life derives from the growing belief that much of the increasingly rapid cultural and technological change is "getting us nowhere." This means that we have no sense of progress toward an ideal such as peace of mind, peace on earth, equality of opportunity, and the elimination of poverty. A sense of progress toward an ideal gives life meaning, makes choice significant. Today there is a growing belief that we are no longer in control of our futures [3]. This in turn tends to make us view our choices as illusory rather than real. Fatalism and resignation to a future that is determined by our past, rather than by what we will do between "now and then," degrade the quality of life.

Some of us are not fatalistic and are unwilling to abdicate our responsibility for the future. But can we meet this responsibility effectively without being able to measure the quality of life?

PART 2. MEASUREMENT OF QUALITY OF LIFE

5. Neither Good Measures nor Indices of Quality of Life Are Available

The "quality" in "quality of life" is a property of an individual's life. Quality of life in an organization, community, or society is derived from the quality of lives of the individuals within it. Needless to say, measurement of an individual's quality of life is very difficult but, I believe, not impossible. In another place, Fred E. Emery and I constructed measures of both satisfaction with one's current situation and of progress toward an ideal [4]. But these measures are sufficiently difficult to apply to make it infeasible to apply them to a large enough sample of individuals over a large enough sample of their states to produce useful statistics representative of a society. In time, these difficulties may be overcome.

Because of the difficulty of measuring quality of life, considerable effort has been made to develop *social indicators* of it: indices which are easier to obtain and which appear to serve as surrogates of appropriate measures. But here we come upon a fundamental methodological difficulty. The usefulness and appropriateness of an index depends on how well it correlates with the measure for which it is a substitute. Since we do not have such a measure, we cannot evaluate any of the proposed indices adequately. When this is recognized, attempts are made to develop indices which correlate with qualitative judgments of the quality of life. This in turn raises a number of methodological problems: whose judgment made when and where, should be used? What confidence can be placed in these judgments? Finally, and most crushingly, if we justify the use of indices by their correlation with qualitative judgments, why not use the judgments themselves?

To be sure, there is a certain attractiveness in the argument that qualitative judgments of the quality of life are good enough for our purposes. The quality of life is so desperately poor in some segments of our societies that qualitative judgments are said to be good enough to identify it. We appear not to need measures to identify the worst of the problem.

This might be so if sufficient resources were available to society to enable it to handle all of its deficiencies in the best known way. But this is not so even in an affluent nation. Many critical social problems compete for the limited resources that are or can be made available to a society. Therefore, there is a need for some type of *cost-benefit analysis* of what is proposed for each problem area to enable society to do the most good with what resources it has available, and to determine how much of its resources should be allocated to each of its problem areas. Such analyses of projects relevant to quality of life require measurement of that quality. Qualitative judgments are not good enough for such analyses.

In sum, qualitative judgments of the quality of life or the indices based on judgments of it may be good enough to enable us to identify the problems to be solved, but they are not good enough to enable us to determine effectively how much of our resources should be allocated to dealing with these problems, or how these resources can be used so as to maximize the benefits produced. We simply do not now have the capability of producing the kind and number of measurements of quality of life that are needed for a rational design of an effort to improve it.

Must we wait until an ability to measure quality of life is developed, before social system designers, planners, and managers can make effective efforts to improve it? Since this is intolerable, must we go ahead without the precision and accuracy that are required to use our resources effectively? Or is there an alternative approach to the problem of quality of life which does not require measurement but which will yield efficient and effective attacks on it? I believe there is such an alternative. It involves a radically new approach to the art and science of planning.

6. An Alternative to Measuring the Quality of Life Is Participative Planning

I have said that the quality of life is a property of an individual's life. But, since individuals who suffer from problems associated with quality of life can do little to improve it, social planners or philosophers of social planning try to do something for them and to them. To serve individuals effectively in this way does require measures of quality of life. However, if the victims had the opportunity to make choices which could effectively modify their quality of life, planners would not have to be concerned with the measurement problem.

This can be understood by returning to the more specialized problem of the quality of work. A number of the socio-technical systems planners concerned with improving the quality of work life have come to realize that they need not measure this quality. Once they give up the idea of redesigning the work of others and involve the workers in redesigning their own work, there are no difficulties in bringing about changes that lead to improvement. Workers are more likely to know what dissatisfies them, what causes these dissatisfactions, and what to do about them, than planners or managers are. To be sure, workers can make mistakes in judgment, but, even if they do, they can correct them since they are in control.

We know that participative planning in industry has led to significant improvements in the quality of work life. According to Paul Blumberg, a leading authority on this subject:

> There is hardly a study in the entire literature which fails to demonstrate that satisfaction in work is enhanced or that other generally acknowledged beneficial consequences accrue, from a general increase in workers' decision making power. Such consistency of findings, I submit, is rare in social research [5, p. 123].

Although such planning does not require measurement of the relevant quality, it would be foolish to say it could not benefit from it. But experience with participative planning has shown that it produces greater increases in satisfaction with work than planning by others, regardless of the measure with which the others are equipped. The reason is clear: participation, which is a form of self-control, is itself a major source of satisfaction and hence of improved quality of life. It is an end of intrinsic value as well as a means of extrinsic value.

For these reasons the planning problem of social planners should be, not how to improve the quality of life of others, but *how to enable them to improve their own quality of life*. Solution of this reformulated problem does not require measures of quality of life for its solution. It does require a different concept of social planning. Let me develop this concept by examining in more detail the relevance of individual style to social planning.

Style is at least as important in decision making as is efficiency and effectiveness. It has often been observed, for example, that individuals enjoy power—which is the ability to control—for its own sake. This means that controlling oneself or others can bring its own satisfactions. Control becomes an end-in-itself as well as a means to other ends. A control system, even a self-control system, that does not match the style of the controller will either not be accepted or, if accepted, will lead rapidly to dissatisfaction. Thus the designer or planner of social systems must understand the style and ideals of not only those who are to exercise control but also those who are to be controlled, if he is to design or plan a system that will work effectively.

The quality of an individual's life depends in part on the extent to which his stylistic objectives are satisfied; that is to say, to the extent to which he derives intrinsic value from his activities. But an individual's style is multidimensional. Every personality trait is an aspect of style. G. W. Allport and H. S. Odbert identified 17,953 trait names in English [6]. These include ascendant-submissive; introverted-extroverted; aggressive, sociable, charitable, courageous, apathetic, and so on and on. An introvert, for example, seeks to get along with as little information about his environment as possible; an extrovert, with as much as possible. The introvert prefers to have others do things to the environment that are required; the extrovert prefers to do them himself. The introvert prefers to work alone; the extrovert, with as many others as possible. No one set of circumstances will satisfy both equally. Determination of the traits possessed by the members of a social system which are relevant in designing that system is not easy.

There are not enough relevantly knowledgeable behavioral scientists to engage in all the social system design that is required. Another way out is called for, at least for the time being, and, as I have said, there is such a way: involvement of those who make up a social system in the redesign of that system. A system designer who is aware of the relevance of style can learn about the stylistic preferences of stakeholders in the system by making its design as participative as possible. Participants in the design process cannot help but put their stylistic preferences into their designs. Not can they refrain from incorporating their ideals into these designs.

7. The Kind of Participative Planning that Best Reveals Relevant Styles and Ideals Is Based on the Idealized Redesign of a System

Let me explain the nature of such a design. It is a design (or redesign) of a system "from scratch," with all but two constraints removed. First, the design must not be technologically infeasible, though it need not be practical. For example, one could not assume the availability of a direct transfer of the content of one mind to another by telepathy. This technological constraint does not preclude consideration of the technological innovations (for example, the picture phone or facsimile transmission), but it restricts them to what is currently believed to be possible. On the other hand, all considerations of financial or political feasibility are removed.

The second constraint is that the system design must be viable; that is, capable of working and surviving if it were implemented.

In brief, then, an idealized design is an explicit formulation of the designers' conception of the system they would create now if they could create any system they wanted.

Since any such design is unintentionally constrained by the designers' lack of information, knowledge, understanding, wisdom, and imagination, the designed system should be capable of learning from its own experience and adapting to internal and external changes. It should be flexible and capable of rapidly improving its own performance.

Such an idealized design is *not* utopian, precisely because it is capable of being improved and of improving itself. It is the best we can think of *now*, but its design, unlike that of a utopia, is based on recognition of the fact that no ideal state can remain ideal for long.

An idealized system differs from a utopia in another important and related respect. Its designers need not pretend to have the final answer to every question. Where they do not have answers, they can incorporate into their design experiments that are directed toward finding them. Thus not every issue needs to be resolved in an idealized design. Such a design is not absolute, fixed, or final. It is subject to continuous change in light of information, knowledge, understanding, and motivation acquired after the design is completed.

At my research home, the Busch Center, we have been and are currently involved in the idealized design and redesign of a number of social systems. Under the leadership of Professional Hasan Ozbekhan, we recently collaborated with a number of intellectual and political leaders in France in such a redesign of Paris. Currently, we are involved with a number of executives, managers, staff personnel, and users of the Federal Reserve (banking) system of the United States in an idealized redesign. A short while ago we prepared such a redesign of our nation's juvenile justice system, working together with a wide variety of participants in that system. We have been and are involved in such redesigns of several foreign and domestic corporations. At the moment we are engaged in a similar effort applied to the national scientific communication and technology transfer system. My own personal idealizations of a number of social institutions appear in my book, *Redesigning the Future* [7].

The redesign of Paris was directed at producing the kind of Paris that the French want, such desire being interpreted in the broadest aesthetic sense. It yielded a conception of Paris that not only incorporated many of the intrinsic values the French have, but it also is a *work of art* in itself that has inspired many Frenchmen with a determination to try to bring it about.

The idealization process provides an effective way of obtaining meaningful participation of those who will use or be affected by the system. It tends to generate consensus among those engaged in the process. Since most disagreements arise from considerations of efficiency, not value, and since idealized redesign is preoccupied with value—intrinsic value, not efficiency—it tends to breed agreement among participants in the process. It facilitates participation because *it is fun* and requires no special skills to be able to engage in and contribute to it.

Twenty-four of my students and I have been engaged in preparing a detailed idealized design of an urban area with a population of about two million, the size of Philadelphia. You may be interested in some of the properties of this yet-to-be-completed design because of their relevance to quality of life.

Every neighborhood contains a stratified proportional sample of the socioeconomic categories into which the total population falls. Hence each neighborhood is completely heterogeneous. This is intended to minimize discrimination in every form and maximize equality of opportunity.

There is a guaranteed minimal annual income which precludes anyone living in poverty. Funds required to support such a system are raised by a tax on consumption. Income taxes are eliminated. The consumption tax is made feasible by a fundamental redesign of the banking system, using electronic fund transfers and a bank account for every member of the society.

We estimate that approximately 80% of the trips which need to be taken—to work, play, school, recreation, shopping, and so on—can be taken without mechanized modes of transportation. This is accomplished by a decentralization of as many facilities as can be dispersed without economic penalty. An underground public transportation system is within walking distance of everyone.

Open green space exceeds occupied built-on space, and everyone is within walking distance of outdoor privacy in a natural setting.

Government is built from the bottom up, with the basic unit being small enough to permit direct participation of the governed. Power and resources are dispensed by the lower units up, not from the top down. Hence, government is completely participative.

These, of course, are only a few of the characteristics of the urban design that is emerging. Because they are part of an integrated design of a whole, they cannot be completely appreciated when presented as I have: as free-standing properties of a community. Nevertheless, their relevance to quality of life should be apparent.

Such an exercise in idealized redesign forces those involved to rethink each aspect of life and to become conscious of the interrelationships between them. They cannot get diverted into correcting an existing city in piecemeal fashion. Furthermore, it makes those involved realize that most of their ideal can be implemented *now*.

I have cited this student exercise for a particular reason. If a significant part of the educational process were devoted to such exercises, we would produce a generation that would do something significant about quality of life. The principal obstacle to creation of such a generation is ourselves, its teachers. Engaging our students in such a continuing exercise, it seems to me, is the least we can do to assure an improving quality of life. I think it is apparent that it would considerably increase the learning that takes place in the educational process.

The preparation of an idealized design of a community is by no means all there is to planning for it, but it is a critical first step. It makes it possible to turn planning from a retrospective point of view, that of correcting current deficiencies piecemeal, to a prospective and holistic point of view: planning to get what is wanted, rather than to get rid of what is not. Retrospective planners walk into the future facing the past: hence, though they know where they are coming from, they have no idea where they are going.

In sum, all phases of planning, not only idealized design, should be participative. It is only in a society in which most individuals take responsibility for their quality of life, rather than passively receive it, that continuous improvement of it can be realized.

CONCLUSION

I have argued that quality of life is a matter of aesthetics; that it involves satisfactions to be derived from everything we do, no matter how trivial. These are satisfactions derived from intrinsic values immediately experienced. Quality of life also arises from a sense of progress toward ideals, ultimate intrinsic values never to be experienced. Measurement of these two types of satisfaction may be possible in principle but not in practice, nor can we develop demonstrably appropriate indices of these measures without the measures themselves. Such measures are necessary only for those whose objective is to design, plan for, and develop a society in which the quality of life *of others* is to be improved. But, I have argued, an alternative strategy is available, one that does not require such measurement (even though it might benefit therefrom): to design, plan, and develop social systems in which each member of the system can participate effectively and thus bring more of his own future under his own control. Involvement in such a future-creating process is itself a source of satisfaction, hence an improvement in the quality of life, and its outcome can yield even further improvements. Therefore, the key to improved quality of life is not planning for or measurement of others, but enabling them to plan and measure for themselves.

There is a deep wisdom in the motto of an indigenous self-development group in Mantua, one of Philadelphia's black ghettos: *Plan or Be Planned for.* Our task is to make participative planning possible. To do this is to enable others and ourselves to make an art of living.

REFERENCES

1. Work in America: *Report of a Special Task Force to the Secretary of Health, Education and Welfare.* Cambridge, Mass. and London: MIT Press, 1973.

2. Singer, Edgar Arthur, Jr. *In Search of a Way of Life.* New York: Columbia Univ. Press, 1948.

3. Ellul, Jacques. *The Technological Society.* New York: Vintage Books, 1967.

4. Ackoff, Russell L., and Fred E. Emery. *On Purposeful Systems,* Chicago: Aldine-Atherton, 1972.

5. Blumberg, Paul. *Industrial Democracy.* New York: Schocken, 1969.

6. Allport, G. W. and H. S. Odbert. "Trait-Names: a Psycholexical Study." *Psychological Monographs,* # 211, 1936.

7. Ackoff, Russell L. *Redesigning the Future.* New York: Wiley, 1974.

Questions for Study and Discussion

1. Is the necessity for social measurement based fundamentally on an elitist bias? That is, is it based on the assumption that, in Ackoff's words, "since individuals who suffer from problems associated with quality of life can do little to improve it, social planners or philosophers of social planning (must) try to do something for them and to them."

2. Is participation really an alternative to the measurement of the quality of life?

3. Kaplan (1964) argues that a "mystique of quality" exists in our society, as well as a mystique of quantity:

> This mystique, like its counterpart, also subscribes to the magic of numbers, only it views their occult powers as a kind of black magic, effective only for evil ends, and seducing us to into giving up our souls for what, after all, is nothing but dross. In this perspective,

knowledge—and particularly, knowledge of human beings—consists in the apprehension of qualities, which by their very nature elude the net of numbers, however fine its mesh. As my friends . . . have sometimes formulated this view, "If you can measure it, that ain't it!" (p. 206)

Can the mystiques of quality and quantity be reconciled? Is there a "magic of numbers" worth believing in?

THE MEASUREMENT OF MOOD
AND THE MOOD OF
MEASUREMENT

C. West Churchman

READING 35

The purpose of this paper is to pose a question for discussion, not to arrive at a conclusion. However, to pose a question it is essential to state the assumptions on which the question is based since, as we all know, every intelligent question we pose to nature presupposes what Kant called an *a priori*.

The question in today's terms is, "Can we measure the feeling tone or mood of an organization (community, company, union, church, etc.)?" Now in a more traditional exposition we would attempt to define what is meant by the feeling tone; but to do this might very well answer a part of the question at the outset, since definition is a prelude to measurement.

But we can "walk around" the concept of feeling tone by presenting some suggestive levels and illustrations.

Some of the labels that have been or are being used: exciting place to be, uptight, dull, not the way it used to be (used repeatedly these days by old-time San Franciscans), dullsville, neighborly, inspiring or elevating (as, for example, in a church), ridiculous, threatening. A very important label doesn't seem to have a corresponding word in the English language. It describes the community where morality is a very active element, i.e., where moral issues are not only being discussed but also acted out in an intense manner. I'll call it "moral-ful," and also note that this label is totally different from "high morale."

Examples: in the city of Berkeley during the Cambodian affair, a group of neighbors organized a "block festival" in which each family had a booth in front of its house; it was well attended, well organized, without illegal incident. Yet the city council (even the new, so-called radical one) has consistently refused to grant permission for another block festival. The mood of Berkeley today is fright and anger.

Other examples: UAW in the 1930's: exciting, dedicated, right-is-on-our-side (moral-ful), heroic.

UC, Berkeley during the first (FSM) student dissent: exciting, dangerous, weird, angry, despairing, moral-ful.

A town in a deprived rural area: quiet (or sleepy), depressed, restful, moral-less.

Here are the assumptions of the question:

Paper presented at the 1971 Annual Meeting of the American Political Science Association, Chicago, Illinois, September 7–11. Used by permission.

542

FIRST ASSUMPTION:

The feeling tone or mood *of the social group* does exist and is readily apparent to anyone who is a member of the group or who tries to conduct research on the group. This assumption is quite important for discussion purposes because it's easy to predict that many academics will deny it, on the grounds that the mood applies to the individual and not to the community. I am asking them to be polite for the sake of discussion, and assume that there is a community mood.

SECOND ASSUMPTION:

The feeling tone or mood of the group can range from the very negative through the dull into the spirited, inspiring, joyful, etc. In other words there are qualitative differences in the feeling tone, but not necessarily a ranking.

THIRD ASSUMPTION:

A large part of the feeling tone is unconscious in the sense that many members of the group cannot express its properties even though they may "feel" the mood. It follows from this assumption that it is probably foolish to try to measure the feeling tone by means of questionnaires, interviews, and the like. Even though someone may respond to the question, "how do you feel about your community?" the response by no means indicates their true feeling, or the mood of the community.

FOURTH ASSUMPTION:

The feeling tone of the community is related to what Jung calls feeling in his *Psychological Types* or what E. A. Singer called "mood" in his *On the Contented Life* (Singer's "mood" is complex of emotions). It is noteworthy that in both the case of Jung and Singer there are no explicit attempts to measure feeling or mood. There are many other references one could cite as well.

FIFTH ASSUMPTION:

Concepts of utility, satisfaction, satisficing (aspiration level) and the like are either totally irrelevant as far as feeling tone of the community is concerned or else contribute only slightly to its meaning. The feeling tone is evidently a mixture of opposites. For example, where the feeling tone is running strong as in many religious movements, revolutions, new federal programs, etc., satisfaction and frustration are both present very strongly as are excitement and boredom, cooperation and conflict, etc.

SIXTH ASSUMPTION:

The measurement of the feeling tone (like all measurement) entails the construction of a causal model which explains the mood.

SEVENTH ASSUMPTION:

The feeling tone of the community is probably the most important aspect of community life in terms of the real human values: health, welfare, meaning of life, etc.

With these assumptions in hand, we have the question: "Can we measure the feeling tone which is so easily recognizable?"

I suspect that we would make a wrong start if we assumed that the critical problem was to transform the qualitative differences in feeling tone into a rank order or to try to assign numbers to each quality. As the title of this paper suggests, we are really engaged in examining how one social system called "measurement" can look at another social system called, e.g., the "community." I'd argue that, in this case at least, it is very essential that the social system called measurement, attempt to understand its own feeling tone. In *Challenge to Reason* I was trying my hand in doing this kind of thing in a chapter called "The Humor of Science," where I argued that the mood of science turns out in the main to appear phlegmatic to the layman because the scientist so often hides the real feeling tone of the research effort in his rather logical straightforward articles and books. In order to bring about a measurement of the mood of a community, I think it will be essential that we become a great deal more conscious about the mood of the observer (the social scientist) and his community.

Questions for Study and Discussion

1. Is a measurement-oriented management consistent with a spirited, inspiring, joyful organizational mood?

2. What feeling tone is reflected in the readings of this book?

BIBLIOGRAPHY

Ackoff, R.L., 1962. *Scientific Method: Optimizing Applied Research Decisions*. New York: Wiley.

Ackoff, R.L., 1971. Towards a system of systems concepts. *Management Science,* **17** (11): 661–671.

Alter, S.L. 1980. *Decision Support Systems: Current Practice and Continuing Challenges.* Reading, Massachusetts: Addison-Wesley.

Anthony, R.N. and J. Dearden, 1976. *Management Control Systems*. Third Edition. Homewood, Illinois: Irwin.

Arrow, K.J., 1959. Mathematical models in the social sciences. Chapter VIII in Lerner, Daniel and Harold D. Lasswell (eds.), The Policy Sciences, Stanford: Stanford University Press, pp. 129–154.

Bariff, M.L., and E.J. Lusk, 1977. Cognitive and personality tests for the design of management information systems. *Management Science,* **23** (8): 820–829.

Barnes, R.M., 1968. *Motion and Time Study: Design and Measure of Work*. Sixth Edition. New York: Wiley.

Bauer, R.A., 1966. Social indicators and sample surveys. *Public Opinion Quarterly.* Vol. **30** (3): 339–352.

Behan, F.L., and R.A. Behan. Football numbers (continued). *American Psychologist.* **9** (1954): 262–263.

Bell, D., 1969. The idea of a social report. *The Public Interest.* (15): 72–84.

Benbasat, I. and R.N. Taylor, 1978. The impact of cognitive styles on information design. *MIS Quarterly,* **2** (2), pp. 43–54.

Biderman, A.D., 1966. Social indicators and goals, in Bauer, R.A. (ed.). *Social Indicators.* Cambridge: MIT Press, pp. 68–153.

Biderman, A.D., 1970. Information, intelligence, enlightened public policy: functions and organization of societal feedback. *Policy Sciences,* **1**: 217–230.

Birn, S.A., R.M. Crossan and R.W. Eastwood, 1961. *Measurement and Control of Office Costs: Master Clerical Data*. New York: McGraw-Hill.

Blau, P.M., 1955. *The Dynamics of Bureaucracy.* Chicago.

Boring, E.G., 1961. The Beginning and Growth of Measurement in Psychology. *Isis,* **52**: 238–257.

Campbell, J.P., M.D. Dunnette, E.E. Lawler, and K.E. Weick, 1970. *Managerial Behavior, Performance, and Effectiveness.* New York: McGraw-Hill.

Campbell, N.R., Measurement, in Newman, James R., *The World of Mathematics,* 1956, Vol. 3, Simon and Schuster, 1797–1813.

Campbell, N.R., 1957. *Foundations of Science.* New York: Dover Publications.

Chambers, R.J., 1965 Measurement in accounting. *Journal of Accounting Research,* **3** (1): 32–60.

Churchman, C.W., 1961. *Prediction and Optimal Decision.* Englewood Cliffs, N.J.: Prentice-Hall.

Churchman, C.W., 1971. *The Design of Inquiring Systems.* New York: Basic Books.

Churchman, C.W., and Philburn Ratoosh (eds.), 1959. *Measurement: Definition and Theories.* New York: John Wiley.

Coombs, C.H., 1950. Psychological scaling without a unit of measurement. *Psychological Review,* 57, pp. 145–158.

Coombs, C.H., 1953. Theory and methods of social measurement, in Festinger, L. and D. Katz (eds.), *Research Methods in the Behavioral Sciences,* New York: Dryden Press, pp. 471–535.

Coombs, C.H., 1964. *A Theory of Data.* New York: John Wiley, 1964.

Coombs, C.H., H. Raiffa, and R.M. Thrall, 1954. Some views on mathematical models and measurement theory," in Thrall, R.M., C.H. Coombs, and R.L. Davis (eds.), *Decision Processes,* New York: John Wiley, pp. 19–37.

Cronbach, L.J., 1970. *Essentials of Psychological Testing.* 3rd Edition, New York: Harper.

Crossman, T.D., 1979. Taking the measure of programmer productivity, *Datamation,* **25** (5): 144–147.

Deming, W.E., 1944. "On Errors in Surveys." *American Sociological Review,* **IX:** 359–369.

Dermer, J., and J.P. Siegel, 1974. The role of behavioral measures in accounting for human resources. *The Accounting Review,* pp. 88–97.

Driver, M., and T. Mock, 1975. Human Information Processing, Decision Style Theory, and Accounting Information Systems." *The Accounting Review,* **1** (3): 490–508.

Drucker, P., 1973. *Management.* New York: Harper & Row.

Dyer, J.S., 1973. An empirical investigation of a man-machine interactive approach to the solution of a multiple criteria problem in Cochrans, J.L. and M. Zeleny (eds.). *Multicriteria Decision Making,* University of South Carolina Press, pp. 202–216.

Flamholtz, E.G., 1974. *Human Resource Accounting.* Encino, CA: Dickenson.

Flanagan, J.C. and R.K. Burns, 1955. "The Employee Performance Record: A New Appraisal and Development Tool." *Harvard Business Review,* **33:** 95–102.

Gerrity, T.P., Jr., 1971. The design of man-machine decision systems: An application to portfolio management. *Sloan Management Review,* **12,** (2): 59–75.

Gold, B., 1955. *Foundations of Productivity Analysis.* Pittsburgh: University of Pittsburgh Press.

Gray, D.H., 1971. Methodology: One approach to the corporate social audit in Sethi, S. Prakash (ed.), *The Unstable Ground: Corporate Social Policy in a Dynamic Society*, Los Angeles: Melville.

Green, P.E., and D.S. Tull, 1970. *Research for Marketing Decisions*. Second Edition. Englewood Cliffs, N.J.: Prentice-Hall.

Greene, V., E. Ostrom, R. Parks, and R. Rich (undated). *The Measures Project—A Theoretical and Methodological Overview*. Department of Political Science, Indiana University.

Grove, H.D., T.J. Mock, and K.B. Ehrenreich, 1977. "A Review of HRA Measurements from a Measurement Theory Perspective." *Accounting, Organizations, and Society*, **2** (3): 219–236.

Guion, R.M. 1961 Criterion measurement and personal judgments. *Personnel Psychology*, **14:** 141–149.

Guion, R.M., 1965. *Personnel Testing*. New York: McGraw-Hill.

Guion, R.M., and R. Gottier, 1965. Validity of personality measures in personnel selection. *Personnel Psychology*, **18:** 135–164.

Hurst, G. Choosing performance measures. Paper presented at the Joint National ORSA/TIMS Meeting, November 7–9, 1977, Atlanta, Georgia.

Ijiri, Y., 1967. *The Foundations of Accounting Measurement*. Englewood Cliffs, N.J.: Prentice-Hall.

Jaedicke, R.K., Y. Ijiri, and O. Nielsen (eds.), 1966. *Research in Accounting Measurement*. American Accounting Association.

James, L.R., 1973. Criterion models and construct validity for criteria. *Psychological Bulletin*, **80** (1): 75–83.

Kaplan, A., 1964. *The Conduct of Inquiry*. San Francisco: Chandler.

Keen, P.G.W., and Michael S. Scott Morton, 1978. *Decision Support Systems: An Organizational Perspective*. Reading, Mass: Addison-Wesley.

Keeney, R.L., 1972 An illustrated procedure for assessing multiattributed utility functions. *Sloan Management Review*, **14** (1): 37–50.

Keeney, R.L., and H. Raiffa, 1976. *Decision with Multiple Objectives: Preferences and Value Tradeoffs*. New York: Wiley.

Kendrick, J., and D. Creamer, 1965. *Measuring Company Productivity*. New York: The Conference Board.

Kerlinger, F., 1964. *Foundation of Behavioral Research*. New York: Holt, Rinehard and Winston.

Keyfitz, N., 1979. Income and allocation: Two uses of the 1980 census. *The American Statistician*, **33** (2): 45–56.

Kircher, P., 1955. Fundamentals of measurement. *Advanced Management*, **20,** (10): 5–8.

Kleijnen, J.P.C., 1980. *Computers and Profits*. Reading, Massachusetts: Addison-Wesley.

Krantz, D.H., R.D. Luce, P. Suppes and A. Tversky, 1971. *Foundations of Measurement*. New York: Academic Press.

Lawler, E., and J.G. Rhode, 1976. *Information and Control in Organizations.* Pacific Palisades, CA: Goodyear.

Lazarsfeld, P.F., and A.H. Barton, 1959. Qualitative measurement in the social sciences: Classification, typologies, and indices. Chapter IX in Lerner, Daniel and Harold D. Lassell (eds.), *The Policy Sciences,* Stanford: Stanford University Press, pp. 155–192.

MacKinney, A.C., 1960. "What Should Ratings Rate?" *Personnel,* **37:** 75–78.

Mason, R.O., 1973. "Measuring Information Output: A Communication Systems Approach." *Information and Management,* **1** (5): 219–234.

Mason, R.O., and I.I. Mitroff, 1973. A program for research on management information systems." *Management Science,* **19** (5): 475–487.

McGregor, D., 1957. An uneasy look at performance apraisal. *Harvard Business Review,* **35** (3): 89–94

McLean, E.R., and T.F. Riesing, 1977. The MAPP system: A decision support system for financial planning and budgeting. *Data Base,* **8** (3): 9–14.

Maynard, H.B., G.J. Stegemerten and J.L. Schwab, 1948. *Methods-Time Measurement.* McGraw-Hill.

Meador, C.L. and D.N. Ness, 1979. Decision support systems: An application to corporate planning. *Sloan Management Review,* **15** (2): 51–68.

Mirvis, P. and E. Lawler, 1977. Measuring the financial impact of employee attitudes. *Journal of Applied Psychology,* **62** (1): 1–8.

Mock, T.J., 1976. *Measurement and Accounting Information Criteria.* Studies in Accounting Research, No. 13. American Accounting Association.

Mock, T.J., and H.D. Grove, 1979. *Measurement, Accounting and Organizational Information.* New York: John Wiley & Sons.

Moonitz, M., 1961. *The Basic Postulates of Accounting.* Accounting Research Study No. 1. American Accounting Association.

Myers-Briggs, I., 1962. *Manual for the Myers-Briggs type indicator.* Princeton, N.J.: Educational Testing Service.

Nance, H.W., and R.E. Nolan, 1971. Office Work Measurement. McGraw-Hill.

Nunnally, J.C., Jr., 1969. *Tests and Measurements: Assessment and Prediction.* New York: McGraw-Hill.

Oppenheim, A.N., 1966. *Questionnaire Design and Attitude Measurement.* New York: Basic Books.

Ostrom, E. Multi-mode approaches to measurement of government productivity. Paper presented at the Fourth Colorado Regional Urban Conference on "Exploring Productivity vs. Effectiveness in Government Systems," Denver, April 24, 1975.

Patton, A., 1960. "How to Appraise Executive Performance." *Harvard Business Review,* Vol. 38, No. 1 (January-February, 1960), pp. 63–70.

Pratt, J.W., H. Raiffa and R. Schlaifer. "The Foundations of Decision Under Uncertainty." *American Statistical Association Journal,* June 1964, pp. 353–375.

Raiffa, H., 1968. *Decision Analysis: Introductory Lectures on Choice Under Uncertainty.* Reading, Mass: Addison-Wesley.

Rockart, J.F., 1979. Chief executives define their own data needs. *Harvard Business Review,* **57** (2): 81–93.

Rosenblatt, D., E. Glaser, and M.K. Wood., 1970. Principles of design and appraisal of statistical information systems. *The American Statistician,* **24** (4) 10–19.

Schocker, A.D., and S.P. Sethi, 1974. An approach to incorporating social preferences in developing corporate action strategies, in Sethi, S. Prakash (ed.). *The Unstable Ground: Corporate Social Policy in a Dynamic Society.* Los Angeles: Melville.

Schoeffler, S., R.D. Buzzell and D.F. Heany, 1974. Impact of strategic planning on profit performance. *Harvard Business Review,* **52** (2): 137–145.

Shoup, C.S. Risk as a dimension in measuring level of service, in Carter, C.F. and J.L. Ford (eds.). *Uncertainty and Expectations in Economics.* Oxford: Basil Blackwell, pp. 266–275.

Sirota, D. and A.D. Wolfson, August 1972. Work measurement and worker morale. *Business Horizons.* pp. 43–48.

Stevens, S.S., 1945. On the theory of scales of measurement, *Science,* **103:** 677–680.

Stevens, S.S., 1959. Measurement, psychophysics, and utility, in Churchman, C. West and Philburn Ratoosh (eds.). *Measurement: Definitions and Theories.* New York: John Wiley, pp. 18–63.

Suppes, P., and J.L. Zinnes, 1963. Basic measurement theory, in Luce, R.D., R.R. Bush, and E. Galanter (eds.), *Handbook of Mathematical Psychology,* Vol. 1, New York: John Wiley, pp. 1–76.

Swalm, R.O., 1966. Utility theory—Insights into risk taking. *Harvard Business Review,* **44** (6): 123–136.

Swanson, E.B., 1974. An MIS story, *IEEE Transactions on Engineering Management,* **EM-21,** (3): 90–95.

Taylor, F.W., 1911. *The Principles of Scientific Management.* New York: Harper & Brothers.

Teague, J., and S. Eilon, 1973. Productivity measurement: A brief survey. *Applied Economics,* **5:** 133–145.

Theil, H., 1969. On the use of information theory concepts in the analysis of financial statements. *Management Science,* **15** (9): 459–480.

Thompson, M.M., and G. Shapiro. 1973. "The Current Population Survey: An Overview." *Annals of Economic and Social Measurement,* **2** No. (2): 105–129.

Thornthwaite, C.W., 1953. Operations research in agriculture. *Journal of the Operations Research Society of America,* **1** (2), pp. 33–38.

Thurstone, L.L., 1928. Attitudes can be measured. *American Journal of Sociology,* **33:** 529–554.

Torgerson, W.S., 1958. *Theory and Methods of Scaling.* New York: John Wiley.

Vatter, W., 1958. Contributions of accounting to measurement in Management. *Management Science,* pp. 27–37.

Wehrung, D.A., D.S.P. Hopkins and W.F. Massy, 1976. Interactive preference optimization at Stanford University. Report 76-1. Academic Planning Office, Office of the Vice President and Provost, Stanford University.

Weinberg, G., 1971. *The Psychology of Computer Programming*. New York: Van Nostrand Reinhold.

Wildavsky, A., 1976. Economy and environment/rationality and ritual: A review essay. *Accounting, Organizations and Society,* **1** (1): 117–129.

Wilensky, Harold. Organizational Intelligence. New York: Basic Books, 1967.

Wolfe, J.M., 1969. Testing for programming aptitude. *Datamation,* **15** (4): 67–72.

Zionts, S., and J. Wallenius, 1976. An Interactive programming method for solving the multiple criteria problem. *Management Science,* **22** (6): 652–663.